D0301395

Land and Forest Economics

Land and Forest Economics

G. Cornelis van Kooten

Professor of Economics and Canada Research Chair in Environmental Studies, University of Victoria, Canada and Adjunct Professor of Agricultural Economics, Wageningen University, The Netherlands

Henk Folmer

Professor of General Economics, Wageningen University and Professor of Environmental Economics, Tilburg University, The Netherlands

Edward Elgar
Cheltenham, UK • Northampton, MA, USA

Published by
Edward Elgar Publishing Limited
Glensanda House
Montpellier Parade
Cheltenham
Glos GL50 1UA
UK

Edward Elgar Publishing, Inc.
136 West Street
Suite 202
Northampton
Massachusetts 01060
USA

A catalogue record for this book
is available from the British Library

Library of Congress Cataloguing in Publication Data
Van Kooten, G. C. (Gerrit Cornelis)
    Land and forest economics / G. Cornelis van Kooten, Henk Folmer.
      p. cm.
    Includes bibliographical references and index.
      1. Land use—Economic aspects. 2. Forests and forestry—Economic
aspects. 3. Environmental economics. I. Folmer, Henk, 1945– II. Title.

    HD156.V358 2004
    333.73—dc22

                                      2004047965
ISBN 1 84376 881 X (cased)

Printed and bound in Great Britain by MPG Books Ltd, Bodmin, Cornwall

Contents

Figures

Tables

Preface

It is difficult to find a textbook that covers land and forest economics at a mid to upper undergraduate level and that is not primarily a text on development economics. Land and forest economics are important in developed countries because there is a demand for the services from land and forests, whether these consist of commercial timber production, production of agricultural outputs, a source of fuelwood, forage for livestock, watershed protection, opportunities for outdoor recreation, and/or provision of habitat for wildlife species. The theoretical notions and tools that are used to manage land use at the urban–rural and rural–nature interfaces, and protect environmental amenities, are applicable in industrial/developed countries just as well as they are in developing countries, although the policies that should and can be implemented might differ. Thus, although this book should also appeal to those working in developing countries, it is not a book on development economics.

Many of the topics in this book are covered in various ways by texts in environmental, agricultural, forest and natural resource economics, but few focus on land use to the extent of this text. Yet, in addition to how society views land, public policy affects land use in profound ways, even though this is not always their intent. This book seeks to provide the reader with greater insights into the role of (particularly rural) land in the economy.

We owe a debt of gratitude to a number of individuals who have, in one way or another, contributed to this text. In particular, a debt of gratitude is owed to Erwin Bulte for his insights into many of the issues addressed in the text. Louis Slangen, Arie Oskam, Pavel Suchnek, Mark Eiswerth, and colleagues at the Forest Economics and Policy Analysis (FEPA) Research Unit at UBC – Emina Krcmar, Ilan Vertinsky and Harry Nelson – have provided inputs in uncountable ways. We are also indebted to Alison Eagle, Annelies Coppelmans, Margaret van Wissen, and Rachel Jantzen for assistance in the preparation of the manuscript.

The senior author acknowledges funding support from the Canada Research Chairs program and from a BIOCAP research grant, and support of various kinds from the Agricultural Economics and Rural Policy Group at Wageningen University and the Department of Economics at the University of Victoria.

1.   Introduction

Economics is often defined as the science of allocating scarce or limited resources in a way that leads to the greatest wellbeing of society or best contributes to economic development so that individual members of society are better off in the future. While economists have developed sophisticated tools for deciding how this can be done, economics remains a hybrid science, one that deals as much with politics and ethics as with mathematics. The purpose of this book is to present economic thinking as it pertains to the allocation of (natural) resources, more specifically land and forest resources as well as climate. The presentation is at a relatively low level of sophistication, mainly to appeal to a greater audience but also because many of the ideas of economics can be laid out in rather simple terms. The wish is that readers will come away with a better sense of the role that economic thinking can play in protecting natural resource systems for their commercial benefits (farming and wood harvesting) and environmental amenities, which include ecosystem services such as watershed protection, fish and wildlife habitat, scenic amenities, and recreational opportunities.

While this book is confined to what might be considered a small arena within the larger subject of economics, the discussion is nonetheless limited in its scope. In particular, we focus mainly on economic explanations and rationale for policy concerning land use, forestry and climate change. We also pay attention to the role of institutional factors, which have become increasingly important as an explanation of economic development (North 1990, 1994; Olson 1996; Landes 1998; Shleifer and Vishny 1998; Fukuyama 1995, 1999). Particular focus in that research has been on the institutional environment and social capital as drivers of economic development. The institutional environment consists of formal rules (constitutions, laws and property rights) and informal rules (sanctions, taboos, customs, traditions, and norms or codes of conduct) that structure political, economic and social interactions. Informal constraints are commonly referred to as "social capital", which is "the shared knowledge, understandings, norms, rules, and expectations about patterns of interactions that groups of individuals bring to a recurrent activity" (Ostrom 2000, p.176). Trust is perhaps the most important element of social capital, and it

1

affects the costs of transacting: If one's confidence in an enforcement agency falters, one does not trust people to fulfill their agreements and agreements are not entered into. There is an element of trust in any transaction where one has to decide (make a choice) before being able to observe the action of the other party to the transaction. One has to assume that the other person is not acting with guile, keeping hidden information about themselves that can be used to their advantage at the expense of the other party to the transaction. Trust is the catalyst that makes an economy function efficiently.

As illustrated in this book, transaction costs, which are related to the organization of a transaction (e.g., time and effort searching for a solution, brokerage fees, advertising costs), increase the costs of policies that address environmental spillovers – the (good or bad) effects associated with land use, forestry activities or use of the environment – even to the point of preventing policies from achieving their objective. In this book, however, we assume that a society already has in place the institutions and social capital that would minimize transaction costs, that protect private property, and so forth. The focus is, rather, on policies that are most likely to succeed in societies where the needed institutional framework is in place and where social capital is not deficient, which is usually industrialized countries.

Yet, the framework of analysis used in this book, and in most economic analyses for that matter, assumes something "warm and fuzzy" about government: it assumes that governments act only in the best interests of society. This model of government has been referred to as the "helping hand" paradigm (Shleifer and Vishny 1998): The main purpose of government is to produce public goods, such as safety and defense, and to correct market failure, such as air pollution and environmental degradation. Because private suppliers (firms) cannot capture the full benefits of producing public goods and correcting market failure, the function of the state is to do so on behalf of all citizens. Where a good or service is not provided privately, but "ought" to be provided, the state needs to step into the breach. However, "policy failure" is an all too frequent outcome. Policy or government failure occurs when state intervention to produce a public good, or correct market failure, causes an even greater misallocation of resources.

Policy failure is also a central theme of a second model of government, the "grabbing hand" model (Shleifer and Vishny 1998). Governments consist of individuals who are not always interested in the wellbeing of society but, rather, act in their own self interests, pursuing their own agendas rather than the common good. Governments consist of bureaucracies that take on a life of their own, with individuals inside these state agencies working to protect their own turf as much or more so than seeking the welfare of the citizens who pay their wages. A special case of the grabbing hand is corruption. Corruption is said to occur when government officials (elected or otherwise) do a favor in exchange for votes, and/or sell a government service or commodity (e.g., passport, work permit, building permit, variance to a zoning ordinance, etc.) in return for a "bribe". A bribe consists not only of an "under-the-table" payment of money, but might take various subtle forms, including gifts, dinner, implicit acceptance of abuse, and so on. The flip side of corruption is the lobbying of government to get it to do something that creates rents (see Chapter 3) and/or distributes rents in the direction of the lobbyist. Rent seeking occurs, for example, when the "Coalition for Fair Lumber Imports" in the United States lobbies to put a duty on imports of softwood lumber from Canada (see Chapter 12). Other examples include lobbying to circumvent zoning regulations by obtaining a variance (Chapter 8) or farmers holding rallies to highlight the farm crisis (Chapter 9).

An alternative to the helping hand model of government is the "invisible hand" model. The approach here is to reduce the role of the state. Market failures are considered to be small, and certainly much less of a problem than that of policy failure. By minimizing the role of the state many problems will resolve themselves, or so it is thought. Whether or not this is true is a moot point. It is simply unrealistic to think that the role of government in modern societies can be rolled back. State intervention in the economy is here to stay, although its limits have increasingly been recognized (LaPorta et al. 1999; Landes 1998; Hart et al. 1997; Fukuyama 1992).

Despite differing models of government, we take the helping hand model as a starting point for the analysis in this book. The "tools" developed here can be instrumental to policymaking and serve as a check on state intervention.

1.1 LAND AND FOREST ECONOMICS

This text seeks to provide an introduction to issues of land-use and forest economics. In particular, tools of economic analysis are used to address allocation of land among alternative uses in such a way that the welfare of society is enhanced. Thus, the focus is on what is best for society and not what is best for an individual, a particular group of individuals, or a particular constituency (e.g., loggers or environmentalists). What this text seeks to provide is a balanced and just approach to decision-making concerning allocation of land resources.

1.2 PLAN OF THE BOOK

Although the emphasis of the book is on land and forest economics, a degree of familiarity with general economic theory is required. Part I serves this purpose. The essentials of welfare economics – how economists measure gains and losses in monetary terms – are provided in Chapter 2. We discuss how changes in the wellbeing of consumers and producers are measured, and how such monetary measures might be aggregated. Concepts of consumer and producer surpluses are introduced. Overall wellbeing is measured as an aggregate of surpluses, although aggregation itself is an issue (also discussed in Chapter 2). While consumer and producer surpluses are straightforward to use in cost–benefit analysis, say, measurement problems arise for amenities for which markets are not available (such as biodiversity, scenic amenities); hence, the term nonmarket values. To address surpluses related to nonmarket values, additional concepts that relate mainly to consumer welfare, such as compensating and equivalent variations, are also provided. Actual methods for estimating nonmarket values are described in Part II, Chapter 4. In Chapter 3, we focus on the concept of rent, because rent is a form of surplus relevant to natural resources. We discuss rent as it relates to land and forestry, and discuss how the state as owner of the resource might collect these surpluses. Examples of rent collection in the forest sectors of Canada and Indonesia are provided. Since property rights are important, particularly as they pertain to land and forestry, different concepts of such rights are also discussed in Chapter 3.

A synopsis of environmental economics is provided in Part II. In Chapter 5, we introduce in a formal analysis what we mean by market failure and environmental spillovers (or externalities). The particular focus is on environmental spillovers that harm others and how these might be mitigated in practice. Also important as a form of market failure is the provision of so-called public goods. Public goods are provided by the state because no individual or firm has the incentive to supply wildlife habitat, clean air, open space, etc, because the private supplier cannot capture the benefits of providing such goods. Social cost–benefit analysis, or project evaluation, is needed to determine whether or not it would benefit society for the state to provide a public good. Indeed, social cost–benefit analysis can be used to evaluate many government policies or projects. Cost–benefit analysis is discussed in Chapter 6. While we examine some of the issues surrounding cost–benefit analysis, particularly pertaining to discounting, a major component of the discussion is devoted to applications of the technique.

The final chapter of Part II (Chapter 7) deals with the concept of sustainable development. There is much confusion in the literature about what sustainable development is and how it can (should) be measured. An economic perspective on this topic is provided. Indeed, we suggest that economists have long brought their tools to bear on issues of sustainable development, but then under the banner of "conservation". Economic conservation and depletion are defined, and the idea of a safe minimum standard is contrasted with that of the precautionary principle. Finally, we examine critically the concept of the ecological footprint, and consider other measures of sustainable development that have been suggested.

We begin our investigation of land and forest economics in earnest in Part III. In Chapter 8, we present economic insights into urban land-use planning. While land-use planning should contribute to economic efficiency (enhance social wellbeing), we find that the most common tool of land-use planning, zoning, leads to issues of income equity and political acceptability. These can be addressed using various economic instruments, thereby enhancing the efficiency of land-use planning. We also consider transportation because, while it gobbles up land, it affects and, in turn, is influenced by land uses in the urban region.

Degradation and conservation of agricultural land is the topic of Chapter 9. In this chapter, we investigate the role of agricultural support programs, including their perverse effects on land degradation, as well as programs designed to conserve agricultural land and protect environmental amenities and ecosystem services that land provides. Many of the economic instruments that can be used to protect agricultural land, or forestlands and natural areas from being converted to agriculture or urban uses, are similar to those that are available to the urban planner. As illustrations of the public goods nature of agricultural land, we examine wetlands protection on private agricultural land, while water use in irrigation is provided as an example of potential policy failure.

In Chapter 10, we examine the management of public lands, focusing in particular on rangeland. As a result of land development in the western United States and Canada, arid rangelands came under public ownership because, in the absence of property rights, cattlemen and sheep herders tended to degrade the range. However, the tool of management used by government was blunt – public control was and is mainly exercised by "limiting" the number of livestock that can be grazed in any given period. However, the public land agencies were unprepared for the inevitable conflicts between those possessing "rights" to graze livestock and environmentalists interested in protecting lands for wildlife. This conflict continues to the present and it provides an interesting area of research for applied economists. Many of the theoretical tools that have been applied are useful in analyzing other land-use conflicts as well.

Part IV of the book consists of Chapters 11 through 13, and these deal with forest economics. Various forest rotation ages are examined in Chapter

11, including how these might be modified to take into account nontimber values. Forestland tenures are also discussed. Forest certification and trade in forest products are the topic of Chapter 12. Interestingly, forest certification is a nonmarket, nongovernment governance structure that emerged to deal with environmental spillovers from forestry activities at about the same time that governments began to impose forest practices codes. As a result, some of the government regulations may have become redundant.

A particularly vexing issue in Canada–United States relations has been the softwood lumber dispute. In Chapter 12, we examine the dispute using a partial equilibrium trade model that can also be used to investigate other trade issues related to forestry and natural resources. One conclusion is that nations exporting natural resource products can potentially increase their economic wealth by restricting exports via a quota device and, at the same time, conserve those resources.

Tropical deforestation is the subject of Chapter 13. Not only do we consider the causes of deforestation, but we ask whether some countries might not have too much land in forests. We also investigate whether countries will deforest less as their per capita incomes rise.

Finally, Chapter 14 (Part V) is devoted to climate change, but from a rather narrow perspective. In this chapter, we briefly discuss international efforts to address climate change and focus on the role of terrestrial carbon sinks, or biological sinks, in mitigating projected climate change. The effect on land use is also considered.

Part I: General Economic Concepts

2. The Theory of Welfare Measurement

In this chapter, welfare theory is examined from the viewpoint of developing usable measures of changes in consumer and producer welfares resulting from government decisions with respect to public and private land use and from public investments in forestry and other natural resource sectors. The measures considered here are important for social cost–benefit analysis, which is the tool used to analyze the economic efficiency aspects of such decisions. Cost–benefit analysis is the subject of Chapter 6. It is important to recognize that cost–benefit analysis does not deal solely with financial measures of viability, which is why it is frequently referred to as *social* cost–benefit analysis. Social cost–benefit analysis takes into consideration such things as preservation and biodiversity values, scenic amenities, hunting and hiking benefits, costs of water and air pollution, and so on. Measurement of such values is difficult because markets are not always available for commodities such as clean air or wildlife habitat, which is why they are referred to as nonmarket values. While measurement of nonmarket values is the subject of Chapter 4, the theoretical measures developed in this chapter are the foundation for measuring them in practice. This chapter begins by considering welfare measures for consumers, followed by those for producers. The final section brings the measures together.

2.1 ORDINARY VERSUS COMPENSATED DEMANDS

Before proceeding to how economists measure consumer wellbeing, or welfare, it is important to examine the difference between ordinary (Marshallian) and compensated (Hicksian) demand functions. We do this with the aid of Figure 2.1, where we graphically derive the two demand functions. In the figure, it is assumed that the consumer allocates her budget between two goods, q and q_n. Good q is the one of interest, while q_n simply represents all other goods and services available to the consumer, so it is the numeraire good whose price equals 1.0. That is, if q constitutes only a small portion of one's budget, then q_n can be thought of as income, a measuring stick.

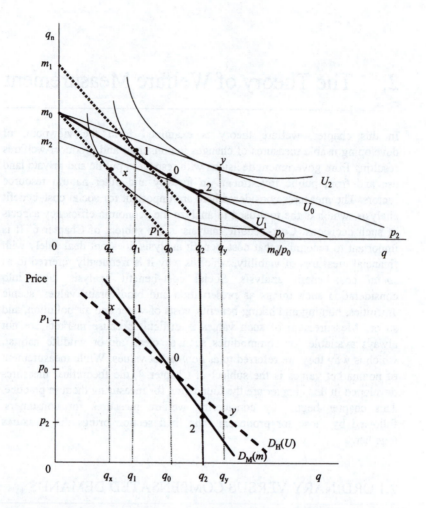

Figure 2.1: Derivation of ordinary (Marshallian) and compensated (Hicksian) demand functions

The upper portion of Figure 2.1 illustrates the case where a consumer maximizes utility subject to a budget constraint. It is assumed that the consumer initially faces a price of p_0 for q (recall that the price of q_n is 1) and that she has a fixed budget of m_0. The size of the budget and the price of q determine the location of the budget constraint and its slope, respectively. If the entire budget is spent on commodity q_n, then q_n equals m_0; if the entire budget is spent on q, then m_0/p_0 units of q can be purchased. The slope of the budget line equals the negative of the price ratio or $-p_0$. (The price ratio is determined by dividing the "rise" by the "run": $-m_0 \div m_0/p_0 = -p_0$.) In equilibrium, the consumer attains the indifference curve (utility level) U_0 at point 0 in the upper portion of the diagram; she consumes q_0 units of q. The combination (q_0, p_0) constitutes a common point on *both* the ordinary and compensated demand curves in the lower portion of the diagram.

To derive the ordinary demand function for q, we hold the budget m_0 fixed and change the price of q. At the higher price $p1$ $(p_1 > p_0)$, the budget line is steeper and the consumer adjusts purchases of q_n and q to achieve a new equilibrium at the lower utility level U_1 (point x). She now consumes q_x units of q. The combination (q_x, p_1) constitutes a second point on the ordinary demand function. A third point on the demand function is found by reducing the price of q from p_0 to p_2 $(p_2 < p_0)$. The budget constraint pivots out, as is shown in the upper portion of the diagram (the slope of the budget line is less steep), and the consumer adjusts purchases of qn and q according to her personal preferences. A new equilibrium is established at point y, with utility level U_2 and purchase of q_y. The combination (q_y, p_2) constitutes a point on the ordinary demand function, as shown in the lower portion of the diagram. By connecting the points x, 0 and y in the lower half of the diagram, the ordinary (Marshallian) demand function is drawn. It is labeled $D_M(m)$ to indicate that it is the Marshallian demand function and that it depends upon the level of income or budget m.

The ordinary demand function is correctly written as $D_M(p_q; m, P)$, where P refers to the prices of all other goods but q. That is, changes in the price of q constitute movements along the ordinary demand function, while the curve will shift whenever the budget level (m) changes. It will also shift whenever the price of q_n (other goods and services) is altered.

In Figure 2.1, we also demonstrate how to derive the compensated demand function graphically. We hold utility at the constant level U_0, say, but continue to alter the price of q. In order to compensate the individual so that she is able to maintain the original utility level U_0, we must either give the individual additional income or take some away. In this case, rather than allowing utility to change (as in the derivation of the ordinary demand function), we allow income to change as needed to maintain the original level of welfare or utility. That is why we use the term "compensated" – individuals are compensated to keep utility at a given level (whether U_0 or some other level). The fact that individuals are compensated to remain at U_0 says something about property rights – it assumes that the individual has a right to U_0 and nothing else.

At the higher price p_1 $(p_1 > p_0)$, the budget line is steeper. The budget line is shifted to the right (compensation is provided), so that the individual can attain the original level of utility (U_0). (In the figure, lines of the same type are parallel.) The consumer faces a new price regime, is compensated amount m_1-m_o, and adjusts purchases of qn and q to achieve a new equilibrium at point 1 on U_0. She now consumes q_1 units of q. The combination (q_1, p_1) constitutes an additional point on the compensated demand function – in addition to point (q_0, p_0). A third point on the compensated demand function is found by reducing the price to p_2 ($p_2 < p_0$). The slope of the budget line in the upper portion of the diagram is less steep, and income must now be taken away from the consumer in order to get her back to the original indifference curve. The amount that needs to be taken away is given by m_0-m_2 on the vertical axis (since income is measured in units of q_n). Again the individual adjusts purchases of qn and q, because the price ratio she faces has changed. A new equilibrium is established at point 2, with the original utility level U_0, but q_2 units of q are purchased. The combination (q_2, p_2) constitutes another point on the compensated demand function, as shown in the lower portion of the diagram. By connecting points 1, 0 and 2 in the lower half of the diagram, the compensated (Hicksian) demand function is drawn. It is labeled $D_H(U)$ to indicate that it is the Hicksian demand function, and that it depends upon the level of utility.

The correct form of the compensated demand function is $D_H(p_q;U,P)$. Again, changes in p_q will cause one to move along the demand curve, but changes in P will cause the compensated demand function to shift. Finally, the compensated demand function will shift whenever the *target* utility level (U) is adjusted.

Notice that the slope of the compensated demand function is steeper than that of the ordinary demand function. Also, the functions always intersect at the point that they have in common, namely, the original or some target situation. This is important in the analysis that follows, because whether the original or target situation is used says something about the property rights to which an individual is entitled. Further, the ordinary demand function for a market commodity can be estimated directly from actual data, because it is a function of own price, prices of substitutes and complements (other goods), and income, all of which are observable. Compensated demands are a function of, among other things, utility levels that are unobservable. Hence, they cannot be estimated directly from observed market data, but can be derived from information about ordinary demand functions (see Boadway and Bruce 1984).

From a mathematical point of view, the ordinary and compensating demands are analogous. The ordinary demand function is found by *maximizing* an individual's utility subject to the budget constraint. Diagrammatically, this requires finding the highest indifference curve that has at least one point in common with the budget line that represents the budget constraint. Upon doing the mathematics, one derives the ordinary demands as a function of prices and income. This is called the *primal* problem. The *dual* problem is then to *minimize* the budget subject to maintaining a certain level of utility (finding the budget line closest to the origin that has at least one point in common with the specified indifference curve). In this way, one derives the compensated demands as a function of prices and utility.

2.2 MEASURING CHANGES IN THE WELLBEING OF CONSUMERS

In this section, the theory of welfare measurement is examined from the viewpoint of developing usable measures of changes in consumer welfare resulting from government policies or other factors that affect prices of goods traded in markets or that affect the availability of environmental amenities. There exist a number of theoretical measures of consumer welfare. The most important of these are consumer surplus (S), compensating variation (CV), equivalent variation (EV), compensating surplus (CS) and equivalent surplus (ES). The latter two measures are used principally in nonmarket measurement.

Consumer Surplus

The French engineer Dupuit first introduced the concept of consumer surplus in 1833. Consumer surplus, *S*, is used to measure the welfare that consumers get when they purchase goods and services. The general concept is well known to economists and is simply the difference between an individual's marginal willingness-to-pay and the market price. The marginal willingness-to-pay curve is the individual's *ordinary* demand curve (denoted D in Figure 2.2). If the price of a commodity is given by p_0 in Figure 2.2, then consumer surplus is given by the area denoted by a. The consumer surplus is determined as follows. The consumer will purchase q_0 units of the commodity at a price p_0. The value that the consumer attaches to an amount q_0 of the commodity is given by area $(a+b+c)$ – the area under the demand curve. The demand function is simply a marginal benefit function, since the consumer must sacrifice an amount equal to area $(b+c)$ to purchase the commodity, the consumer gains area a, known as the consumer surplus.

In applied welfare economics, we are generally not interested in total consumer surplus but, rather, in the change in S that an action or policy may bring about. Suppose, for example, a program increases timber harvests and thus reduces price from p_0 to p_1 (Figure 2.2). Initially, the consumer purchased q_0 units of wood products but, given price p_1, q_1 units are purchased. Prior to the reduction in price, the consumer surplus was given by area a. After price is reduced, the consumers can purchase the same quantity (q_0) as previously, but they pay less for it. Therefore, they gain area b, which is the difference between the amount they paid for quantity q_0 when price was p_0 and the amount they pay for the same quantity at the lower price p_1. However, by increasing purchases of wood products from q_0 to q_1, consumers only pay an amount given by area e, but they place a greater *value* on the additional purchases, a value given by area $d+e$. Therefore, by increasing purchases from q_0 to q_1, the consumer gains a surplus given by area d. Thus, the *change* in S due to a reduction in the price of the commodity is given by area $b+d$. *Total S* from purchasing q_1 units of the commodity at a price of p_1 is given by area $a+b+d$.

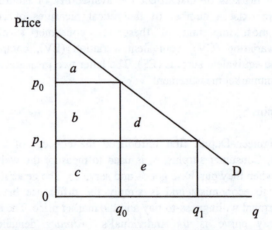

Figure 2.2: Consumer surplus in the wood products market

Now consider what happens when a government policy results in a change in the income received by consumers. A fall in income m causes the demand function to shift inwards, but in this case the fall in consumers' wellbeing should not be measured by the loss in consumer surplus (i.e., as the area above price and between the original and income-changed demand functions). Rather, it is measured by the change in income itself.

Now consider what happens to consumer welfare when both income and price change simultaneously. Suppose income increases from m_0 to m_1, while price rises from p_0 to p_1. The situation is illustrated in Figure 2.3 where consumers initially purchase q_0 at price p_0. We consider two cases:

1. ***Price increases, then income increases*** The loss in consumer surplus due to a price increase is given by the area under $D(m_0)$; that is, the loss in S is given by ΔS = area c. Since the increase in income is given by $m_1 - m_0$, the net welfare change for consumers is given by $m_1 - m_0$ minus area c.

2. ***Income increases, then price rises*** Once again the change in income is given by $m_1 - m_0$. However, now S is measured under $D(m_1)$ rather than $D(m_0)$. The loss in consumer surplus due to the price increase is, therefore, given by ΔS = area $(c+d+e)$, and the net welfare gain to consumers is $m_1 - m_0$ minus area $(c+d+e)$.

The difference between the two measures given by paths (1) and (2) is area $d+e$. It is important to note that measurement of consumer surplus is dependent on whether income changes before or after price changes. That is, consumer surplus measures are path dependent and, hence, are not unique.

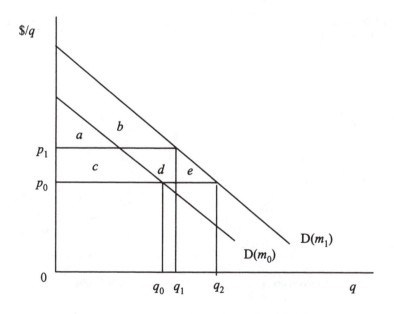

Figure 2.3: Change in consumer surplus due to change in income and prices

Another type of path dependency occurs when more than one price changes at any given time, keeping income constant. Suppose the prices of two goods q_1 and q_2 fall from p_1^0 to p'_1 and p_2^0 to p'_2, respectively. We need to consider whether the goods are complements or substitutes, and whether, for measurement purposes, the price of q_1 is considered to change before or after the price of q_2 changes, although in practice they change at the same time. Note, however, that if these are the only goods in the economy they must be substitutes.

Complements. Consider Figure 2.4 where panel (a) represents the q_1 (doors) market and panel (b) the q_2 (door frames) market. A reduction in the price of one commodity will shift the demand curve of the other commodity to the right when the goods are complements. Consider two cases:

1. ***First p_1 falls, then p_2 falls*** The initial fall in p_1 increases consumer surplus by area b and shifts the demand for q_2 to $D_2(p'_1)$. When p_2 falls, the gain in S is area $\beta+\delta$ and the total change in S is given by ΔS = area $b+\beta+\delta$.
2. ***First p_2 falls, then p_1 falls*** In this case, the change in consumer surplus is given by ΔS = area $\beta+b+d$.

The difference between the measures derived from paths (1) and (2) is given by the difference between areas d and δ.

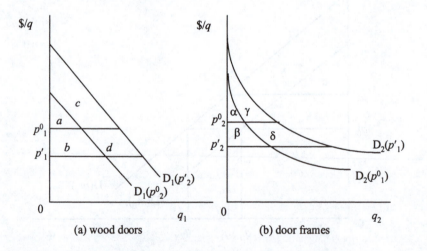

Figure 2.4: Consumer surplus when prices of complements change

Substitutes. The appropriate measures for calculating the change in S when q_1 and q_2 are substitutes (say, wood doors versus metal ones) can be derived via Figure 2.5. Reductions (increases) in the price of wood doors shift the demand for metal doors to the left (right). Once again, it is necessary to consider two possible paths:

1. ***First p_1 falls, then p_2 falls*** The change in consumer surplus is $\Delta S =$ area $(s+w+t)$.
2. ***First p_2 falls, then p_1 falls*** In this case, the appropriate measure is given by $\Delta S =$ area $(w+s+x)$.

The difference between the measures derived from paths (1) and (2) is given by the difference between areas t and x. Recall that, for complements, the difference was given by the difference between areas d and δ. In each case, the two areas need not be "close" or approximately equal to each other in magnitude.

Consumer surplus is an approximate measure of welfare. The compensating variation and equivalent variation measures of consumer welfare may be better; in any event, they do not suffer from the path dependency problem.

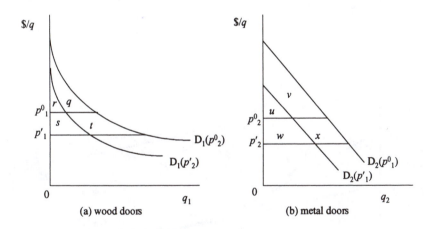

Figure 2.5: Consumer surplus when prices of two substitute goods change

Compensating Variation and Equivalent Variation

The compensating and equivalent variations enable economists to measure the difference between two levels of utility using a money metric. The CV of a move from situation 0 to situation 1 is the amount of compensation that needs to be provided, or the amount of income that needs to be taken away, to leave the individual as well off in the new situation as she is in the old one. Suppose again that there are two commodities q_n and q_1, where q_n is the numeraire (hence the subscript n). In Figure 2.6, the consumer is initially at point 0 on the indifference curve U_0 (in the figure, parallel lines are indicated using solid lines or identical dashed lines). A reduction in the price of q_1 from P^0 to P^1 and an increase in income from m_0 to m_1 due to some public policy enables the consumer to move to point 1 on the higher indifference curve U_1.[1] The CV of the public policy is given by $m_1 - e_K$, where e_K represents the minimum expenditure required to attain the utility level U_0 at the new set of prices (point K in Figure 2.6). CV uses the new prices and asks what income change would be necessary to compensate the consumer (either by adding money or taking it away) to accept (put up with) the proposed change.

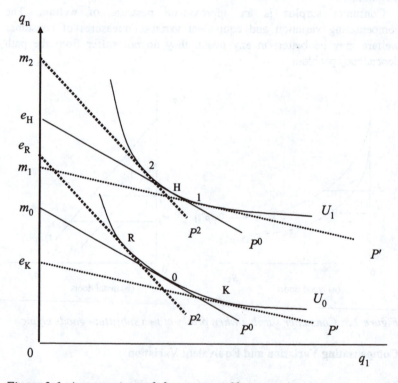

Figure 2.6: A comparison of alternative welfare measures

Equivalent variation uses current prices as the base and asks the question: What income change is needed to make a person as well off without the change as they would be if the change did indeed take place?

The EV of a move from situation 0 to situation 1 is the minimum amount of compensation an individual is willing to receive, or the maximum amount she is willing to pay, to forgo a move from the initial to the final situation. In this case, the reference level of utility is that which would occur in situation 1, the final situation. In Figure 2.6, e_H-m_0 is a measure of EV in terms of q_n (essentially income) and e_H represents the minimum expenditure required to achieve U_1 *at the old set of prices* (point H in Figure 2.6). Since the CV and EV measures are in terms of the compensated demand functions, these welfare measures do not depend on the "path" taken to calculate them (as was true in the calculation of consumer surplus) – the order in which the price changes are taken does not affect the value of CV or EV.

CV and EV differ only with respect to the reference set of prices: EV relies on base prices while CV relies on the prices that exist in the new situation. However, in the case of CV, any set of prices could, in principle, be used to construct a measure of welfare change.

Comparing Welfare Measures

McKenzie (1983) argues that only EV constitutes a true measure of welfare change since CV and S are inconsistent measures. This can be seen for the CV measure by considering Figure 2.6. The CV of a move from 0 to 1 is m_1-e_K. Suppose instead that prices rise to P^2, but that income is also raised to enable the consumer to still move to U_1. The CV in this case is measured by the move from 0 to 2, and is m_2-e_R, which is not the same as m_1-e_K. One would expect the two CV measures to be identical as they are monetary measures of the same change in utility. However, this is not the case (see also Boadway and Bruce 1984, pp.201–2). The EV of a change from situation 0 to situation 1 is given by e_H-m_0; similarly, the EV of a change from situation 0 to situation 2 (with a different set of prices and income than situation 1) is also given by e_H-m_0. Thus, EV provides the only truly consistent welfare measure. Further, EV relies on current prices that are empirically observable, while final prices cannot be known in the current period or can only be forecasted if *ex ante* evaluation is required.

Three additional points need to be raised. First, we can reverse the situation in Figure 2.6 so that point 1 with m_1 and P^1 constitutes our starting point, and we consider an increase in price to P^0 and a reduction in income to m_0, or a move to point 0. This reverses all of our results: what we previously identified as compensating variation is now equivalent variation and *vice versa*, except that one is the negative of the other. Thus, the compensating variation of a move from 1 to 0 is equal to the negative of the equivalent variation of a move from 0 to 1. Likewise, the EV(1→0) = – CV(0→1).

Second, in the case of a positive effect (e.g., a price decrease), if the indifference curves are asymptotic to the vertical axis, then the EV of a price reduction could be unbounded, while the CV is limited by the amount of income available to the individual. The reason is that EV is the compensation to be paid, while CV is what the person must pay to bring about the change. In the case of an adverse effect (e.g., a price increase), the CV may be unbounded (i.e., the amount of compensation required may be infinite), while the EV is bounded by the amount of income available.

Finally, consider Figure 2.7. There we show that the compensating demand is a function of the prices of q_i and q_n and utility – or, for good i in the diagram, $q_i^c(p_i, p_n, U_0)$. We denote the Hicksian (compensated) demand curves with a superscript "c" to distinguish them from ordinary demand curves (dropping our earlier "H" and "M" designations). Therefore, the CV of a price reduction from p_i^0 to p_i^1 is given by the area under $q_i^c(P, U_0)$ and between the price lines, or area a. The EV of the price change, on the other hand, is given by the area under $q_i^c(P, U_1)$ bounded by the price lines, or area $(a+b+c)$.

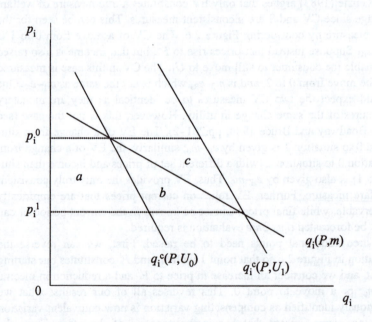

Figure 2.7: Relationship between S, CV and EV for a single price change

Consumer surplus is measured as the area under the ordinary demand curve, which is a function of prices and income, denoted $q_i(P,m)$, and bounded by the price lines. In Figure 2.7, the change in consumer surplus of a reduction in the price of q_i is then given by area $(a+b)$. Ignoring the signs on the welfare measures (i.e., considering only absolute values), EV serves as an upper bound on the measure of consumer surplus, while CV serves as a lower bound in the case of a reduction in price: CV $\leq$ S $\leq$ EV. The inequality signs are reversed for a price increase from p_i^1 to p_i^0: CV $\geq$ S $\geq$ EV. Willig (1976) has shown mathematically that one can expect areas b and c to be small compared to area a, or that EV $\approx$ S $\approx$ CV. This conclusion has been challenged, however, by mounting empirical evidence to the contrary (see below).

2.3 PUBLIC GOODS AND WELFARE CHANGE

In addition to CV and EV, Hicks introduced the concepts of compensating and equivalent surplus, mainly to address situations where the quantity consumed of a good or amenity does not respond to prices, either because the good in question is unpriced (e.g., environmental amenities are not priced in markets) or the government regulates quantity (e.g., restrictions exist in many countries that limit milk production). Environmental amenities such as clean air, wildlife and biodiversity more broadly are examples of public goods. A public good has the characteristic that, once it is provided, no one can be excluded from "consuming" it. What then is an appropriate monetary measure of change in wellbeing when a policy changes the availability of a public good? The compensating surplus (CS) is defined as the compensating payment or offsetting income change that will make the individual indifferent between the original availability of the public good and the opportunity to "consume" the new quantity of the good. Equivalent surplus (ES) is the income change required to keep the person consuming the old quantity of the public good, so that the consumer is indifferent to the new situation. Instead of permitting individuals to move along their indifference curves (perhaps adjusting to new prices in the case of market goods), CS and ES require that an individual consume the new bundle or the old bundle, respectively. CS and ES assume the individual is restricted to consume whatever amount of the good is available; in the case of public goods, each person has the same amount of the amenity. For example, each person in a society has available to them the same level of biodiversity or clean water.

Compensating and equivalent surplus can be considered with the aid of

Figure 2.8. Let Q be a composite commodity such that $\overline{Q} = \Sigma_i p_i q_i = m$. The budget line is horizontal since consumers do not pay for the public good (G) directly – there is no price associated with the public good G and the consumer cannot vary the amount she consumes. We measure the welfare change due to a change in the quantity of the public good from G_0 to G_1 in terms of good Q, or money. Since m is fixed, we do not change the level of expenditures on Q. In the diagram, E_0 represents the original consumption level and E_1 the final (or proposed) level with the public good having increased. The compensating surplus for an increase in the availability of the public good is determined from the original utility level U_0, and, just as compensating variation was measured using new prices, CS is measured using the new level of the public good, G_1. CS is the distance between U_1 and U_0 measured at G_1, that is, the vertical distance BE_1 in Figure 2.8. Likewise, the equivalent surplus is measured with respect to the new utility level U_1, and, just as equivalent variation was measured using current prices, ES is measured using the current level of the public good, G_0. ES is the distance between U_1 and U_0 measured at G_0 and equals the vertical distance E_0A. If the indifference curves happen to be vertically parallel, then the ES is equal to EV and the CS is equal to CV.

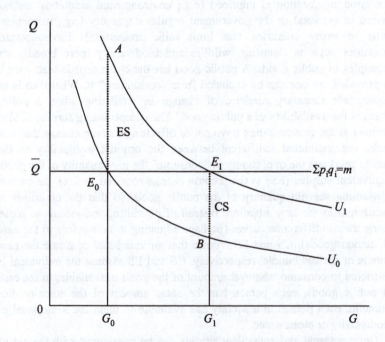

Figure 2.8: A comparison of compensating and equivalent surplus

Although the public good G is not traded in markets, its shadow price (w) is equal to the compensated *inverse* demand function, or marginal willingness-to-pay for changes in G:

$$w = G^{-1}(p_1, p_2, ..., p_n, G, U).$$

It is an inverse demand function because price (shadow price in this case) rather than quantity is being determined by the function. The area under the inverse demand curve between G_0 and G_1 measures the benefit to the individual of an increase in the supply of the public good, as indicated by the shaded area in Figure 2.9. This benefit is either the CS or ES measure of the welfare change depending on the reference level of utility (or reference level of the public good) at which it is evaluated.

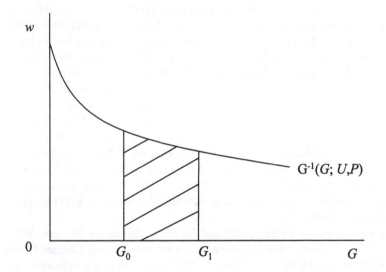

Figure 2.9: Compensating surplus benefit measure of change in a public good

Suppose a policy proposes to increase the availability of the public good, say numbers of grizzly bears in a national park, from G_0 to G_1. Then U_0 is the reference level of utility and CS is given by BE_1 in Figure 2.8, as noted above. Now, if the inverse compensated demand curve in Figure 2.9 is drawn for the reference utility level U_0, then the shaded area in Figure 2.9 equals the vertical distance BE_1 in Figure 2.8. If the level of the public good were to be reduced from G_1 to G_0, the CS measure now asks how much would be required as compensation for the individual to put up with less of the public good (i.e., CS = –ES); the CS measure is now vertical distance AE_0. The ES measure indicates how much to take away in order for the individual to be as well off with the original quantity of the public good as with the new (lesser) quantity. This is vertical distance E_1B and, thus, the ES in this case would equal the negative CS from moving in the opposite direction.

Compensating and equivalent surplus are important concepts when it comes to measuring the value to consumers of unpriced amenities (ones *not* traded in markets). Markets do not exist for such goods as recreational experiences, scenic amenities, old-growth forests, wildlife species and biodiversity in general. Whether CS or ES is employed depends on the reference level of the public good, or on property rights. If individuals have a right only to the original level of the public good – G_0 on the indifference curve U_0 in Figure 2.8 – then CS is the appropriate measure. On the other hand, if individuals have the right to G_1, then ES is the appropriate measure to employ. As shown in Chapter 4, determining CS requires one to know what individuals would be willing to pay (WTP) to have more of the amenity (i.e., level G_1). Alternatively, if individuals have the right to the higher level of the amenity (G_1), say number of bears in a wilderness area, the reference utility level is U_1 and ES is the appropriate welfare measure. To determine ES in this case, it is necessary to ask what individuals would be willing to accept (WTA) as compensation (also referred to as compensation demanded) to forgo the higher level of the public good – to forgo the number of grizzly bears. Again, using Willig's (1976) results, economists expected WTA and WTP to be relatively close, but empirical evidence indicates that there is a substantial difference between these welfare measures.

Two reasons have been postulated for large differences between WTA and WTP. Evidence from contingent valuation surveys (see Chapter 4) and experimental markets (see Knetsch 2000 for a review) indicates that individuals become attached to a particular endowment, requiring a higher level of compensation to part with something than they would be willing to pay to obtain it. For example, in one experiment, Kahneman et al. (1990) find that individuals with a mug must be paid on average $7 to give it up, while those without one are only willing to pay an average of $2 to purchase the same mug. Almost all studies that ask people to value changes in the availability of a public good (e.g., environmental quality, nature preserves) find that WTA exceeds WTP by a substantial amount (Knetsch 1989, 1995). As noted above, gains from a reference state are valued less than losses, implying that the utility function is not continuous at the endowment (Kahneman and Tversky 1979). This has sometimes been referred to as the endowment effect – the empirical evidence indicates that indifference curves are "kinked" at the endowment bundle of goods and services (Knetsch 1995).

The alternative explanation is due to Randall and Stoll (1980), Hanemann (1991) and Shogren et al. (1994). Randall and Stoll (1980) initially argued that WTP (CS) and WTA (ES) are identical if there is perfect substitutability between two goods, so they can be treated as equivalent to money. This is the same as arguing that the two indifference curves in Figure 2.8 are straight (parallel) lines that angle downwards from left to right, in which case $AE_0 = E_1B$. However, their case applies to goods traded in competitive markets with no transaction costs. Hanemann (1991) argues that health, species diversity and nature preserves are lumpy or indivisible "commodities" and that markets for them are incomplete. Then the indifference lines are curved (as in Figure 2.8), resulting in a divergence between WTA and WTP. Indeed, an increase in income elasticity or a decrease in the degree of substitutability between the good in question and all other goods increases the divergence between WTA and WTP. Since there are few substitutes for many environmental amenities and biological assets, one would expect a divergence between WTA and WTP. Thus, the divergence falls within traditional theory. But this is not an explanation for the observed difference between WTP and WTA for goods where there are adequate substitutes, such as mugs and candy bars. This discrepancy still needs to be resolved.

2.4 PRODUCER WELLBEING

Consider first the case of the single competitive firm producing wood products, say. The firm is assumed to be maximizing profit. The firm's input supply curve is assumed to be perfectly elastic as is the demand function for its products, implying that the firm is a price taker in both input and output markets. We are concerned with the welfare impacts on producers whenever some policy causes changes in output (or input) prices.

In the short run, the firm earns profit (π) given by the difference between total revenue (TR) and total costs (TC), where TC is the sum of total variable cost (TVC) and total fixed cost (TFC): $\pi = TR - TC = TR - TVC - TFC$. Since fixed costs are sunk, the firm will produce wood products as long as revenues exceed variable costs. As we note in Chapter 3, *rent* is equal to profit (rent $= TR - TC = \pi$) and *quasi-rent* equals the excess of total revenue over total variable costs: quasi-rent $= TR - TVC = \pi + TFC$. We then ask: To what extent are profit, rent and/or quasi-rent good measures of producer welfare? The answer depends on the notions of compensating and equivalent variation developed above.

Consider what is meant by compensating and equivalent variation in the case of producer welfare. Suppose, as in Figure 2.10, that the price of the firm's output increases from p_0 to p_1 as a result of some public policy. Then the:

> *compensating variation* associated with the price increase is the sum of money that, when taken away from the producing firm, leaves it just as well off as if the price did not change, given that it is free to adjust production (to profit-maximizing quantities) in either case. ... The *equivalent variation* associated with the price increase is the sum of money which, when given to the firm, leaves it just as well off without the price change as if the change occurred, again assuming freedom of adjustment. (Just et al. 1982, pp.52–3)

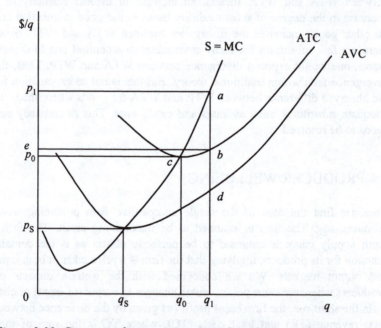

Figure 2.10: Concepts of rent, quasi-rent and producer surplus

In Figure 2.10, profit is higher at p_1 than at p_0 by area p_1abe. This area is also equal to the area above the marginal cost (MC) curve between p_0 and p_1, or area p_0cap_1. Area p_1abe is the producer's compensating variation (PCV) of the price increase. Similarly, profit is lower at p_0 than at p_1 by the same area p_0cap_1, which measures the producer's equivalent variation

(PEV) of the price reduction. Therefore, the change in profit associated with a price change is an exact measure of both the PCV and PEV as long as price is not below the shutdown price (p_S in Figure 2.10). Following Marshall, the area above the firm's short-run supply curve and below price measures producer surplus, as long as the firm is operating at or above its shutdown point. The change in producer surplus of either a price increase or a price decrease is given by area p_0cap_1. The producer surplus is identical to quasi-rent, and is given by area p_0cap_1.

Measuring Producer Surplus via the Input and Output Markets

Suppose that output can be produced using one input, so $q = f(x)$. Let r denote the input price (cost of input to the firm) and $f'(x)$ the marginal physical product of input x in production of output q. In this case, it is quite easy to measure the change in producer surplus due to price changes in the input and/or output markets. We first consider a change in output price. In Figure 2.11, the demand curve for input x – the value of marginal product curve (VMP $= f'(x) \times p$, where p is output price) – will shift to the right when output price increases. Then area Ψ in Figure 2.11 is a measure of producer welfare that is identical to area p_0cap_1 in Figure 2.10.[2]

Changes in input prices

Suppose input price falls from r_0 to r_1. In this case, the *compensating variation* is the "sum of money the producer would be willing to pay to obtain the privilege of buying at the lower price (that is, which would leave the firm just as well off at the lower price)". The *equivalent variation*, on the other hand, is the "sum of money the producer would accept to forego the privilege of buying at the lower price (that is, which would leave the firm just as well off at the original price)" (Just et al. 1982, p.58).

Now consider Figure 2.12 and suppose input price falls from r_0 to r_1. In the input market depicted in panel (a), this is represented by the downward shift of the price line (from r_0 to r_1). However, in the output market, panel (b), the supply curve shifts to the right, from $S(r_0)$ to $S(r_1)$. Given that the input price is r_0 and the associated quantity is x_0, then total cost is $r_0x_0 =$ area $b+c$, while total revenue is given by area $a+b+c$. The difference, area a, is producer surplus and is equivalent to area α in panel (b), ignoring the possibility of shutdown. Now, when the price of the input falls to r_1, the new total cost is area $c+e = r_1x_1$, while the total revenue is area $a+b+c+d+e$. The difference, area $a+b+d$, is the producer surplus. Therefore, area $b+d$ measures the increase in producer welfare that results from the reduction in input price. This area is identical to area β in the output market (panel (b)).

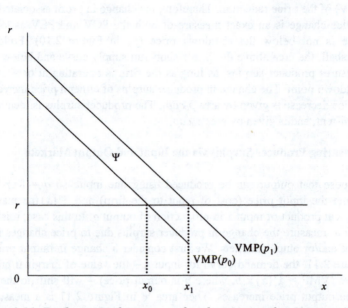

Figure 2.11: Producer surplus measured in the input market: increase in output price

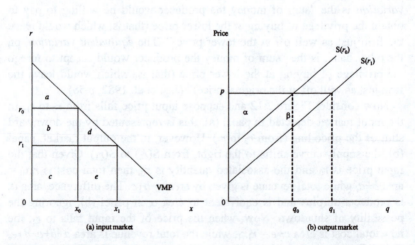

(a) input market   (b) output market

Figure 2.12: Welfare measures in input and output markets: reduction in input price

Simultaneous changes in input and output prices

Suppose that input price rises from r_0 to r_1 while, at the same time, the output price rises from p_0 to p_1. How do we measure the welfare change? The net welfare change can be measured in either the input market or the output market as illustrated in panels (a) and (b), respectively, in Figure 2.13. Before any change occurs, producer surplus is area $b+c$, which is equal to area $\beta+\mu$. When the input price rises, producer welfare *decreases* by area c in the input market. This is equal to area μ in the output market. Now output price increases and producers gain area a = area α. Therefore, the net gain (or loss) in producer welfare is area $a-c$ = area $\alpha-\mu$. It is easy to verify that we obtain the same result if we begin with an output price increase followed by an increase in input price. That is, unlike consumer surplus, measures of producer surplus are path independent.

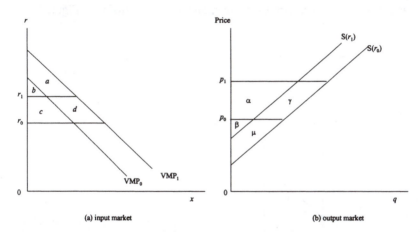

(a) input market (b) output market

Figure 2.13: Producer welfare measures when both input and output prices change

Quantity Restrictions

Quantity restrictions are common in natural resource systems. In the fishery, quotas are used to restrict harvests, while in forestry lumber import quotas have been used by the United States to keep out lumber from Canada, thereby maintaining high domestic prices and making available rents to US producers (van Kooten 2002). The former is an example of an output restriction (fish is sold to final consumers), while the latter is an example of an input restriction (lumber is used to build homes).

Consider first the case of an input restriction. With a quantity restriction

on an input, less of other inputs will be employed, if *all* inputs are to be
used efficiently and profits are maximized subject to the input constraint.
Technically speaking, restricting the availability of one input implies that its
marginal physical product rises (because marginal product falls as more of
an input is employed), so that the marginal physical product of all other
inputs must be increased. Marginal product is increased for any given input
by reducing its use. The result is a decline in output – say, from q_0 to q_R in
Figure 2.14. For example, if timber harvest is reduced by public fiat (say to
protect old-growth forests), one would expect a decline in wood product
output and a fall in the number of forest sector workers. Assuming that
output price is unaffected (perhaps because of imports of wood products
from abroad), the welfare impact of the restriction on input x_1 can be
measured in the output market as the loss in producer surplus, which is
given by area α in Figure 2.14. It can also be measured in the input market
as a loss in consumer surplus, as illustrated in the discussion of Figure 2.13.

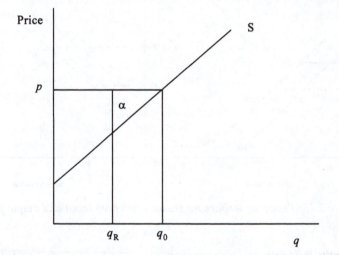

Figure 2.14: Welfare loss due to an input or output restriction

A quantity restriction on output is similar, and can also be analyzed using
Figure 2.14. Again assuming that demand elasticity is infinite, if quantity is
restricted to q_R, where previously it was q_0, the loss in producer surplus is
given by area α. Thus, a fish quota will result in a loss of producer surplus.
However, this is true only in the static case shown in Figure 2.14; it is quite
possible that, if the dynamics of fish stocks are appropriately taken into
account, the quota could make producers better off in the long run. To

determine whether this is true requires tools beyond the scope of this text.

2.5 AGGREGATION OF ECONOMIC WELFARE

Previously, discussion of welfare measures concerned only the individual consumer or producer. Now we need to find some method for aggregating over all producers and consumers. In this section, we consider aggregation of both consumers and producers. We also consider aggregation of welfare more generally, and the issue of how one might compare projects using social welfare functions and compensation tests.

Aggregation of Consumer and Producer Welfare

The concepts of welfare defined in the previous sections can be used to evaluate the economic efficacy of government programs and policies. By assuming that all individuals are to be treated equally, whether they are producers or consumers or whether they are rich or poor, it is possible to determine the gains and losses of various public policies simply by summing all of the welfare measures. Gains and losses accruing at different points in time are weighted depending upon when they accrue. This is called discounting and is considered further in Chapter 6. Here we assume that all the welfare gains and losses occur in the same time period.

To illustrate the usefulness of the welfare measurement concept, consider the case where the government invests funds in research and development (R&D) aimed at improving tree growth. At the same time, government policy results in a restriction on timber harvest. This restriction may be due to endangered species legislation that affects private forestland owners or it may be the result of a decision to reduce timber harvests on publicly owned lands. The situation can be analyzed with the aid of Figure 2.15, where the demand and supply functions D* and S* are assumed to take into account full adjustments in other, related markets.[3] Thus, there is no need to measure changes in input markets or other output markets. Market equilibrium before any government intervention occurs at price p_C and quantity q_C; p_S is the supply-restricted price and p_L the supply price.

Suppose the harvest restriction implies that no more than q_R can be harvested in any given period. Based on the original supply S* and ignoring income transfers between consumers and producers, the welfare loss due to a restriction in harvests is given by the reduction in consumer surplus plus the loss of producer surplus (area $c+d$). (The area below the demand function and above price measures the consumer surplus, area c, while the area below price and above the supply function gives the producer surplus, *d*.) Now suppose government-sponsored R&D investment shifts the timber supply from S* to S**. In the absence of a harvest restriction, there is a gain in welfare equal to area *e+f* (made up of producer and consumer surpluses). The harvest restriction compounds the loss identified by area *c+d*. The total dead-weight loss (resulting because resources are not employed in their most optimal or best uses) is given by area *c+d+f* if the supply function S** is used as the basis for the analysis. However, the welfare loss from the two public policies – harvest restriction and increase in R&D expenditure – is given by area *c+d+f–e* (since area *e* represents a gain in producer surplus) plus the added cost to the government of implementing the policy package. If the gain in welfare area *e* exceeds the loss, then the overall effect of this policy package will be to enhance social wellbeing.

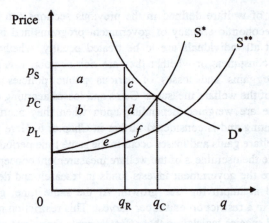

Figure 2.15: Aggregate welfare effects of quota and R&D: summing producer and consumer surpluses

Why is the government likely to impose restrictions on timber harvest? One reason is to achieve environmental objectives, such as preservation of wildlife habitat and protection of watershed or scenic amenity values. Such nonmarket benefits have been ignored in the foregoing analysis. Methods for estimating the benefits of protecting and preserving natural amenities are examined in Chapter 4, while an example of their use in cost–benefit analysis is provided in Chapter 6.

Social Welfare Functions

A complete and consistent ranking of social states ("projects") is called a social welfare ordering. If this ordering is continuous, it can be translated into a social welfare function (SWF), which is a function of the utility levels of all households such that a higher value of the function is preferred to a lower one. The SWF is defined as: $SWF = w[u_1(q_1), u_2(q_2), \ldots, u_n(q_n)]$, where u_k is the utility of person k as a function of the bundle of goods and services available to that person for consumption or trade, q_k. *A priori* there is little one can say about the specification of the SWF. Arrow (1951) has shown the impossibility of constructing a SWF that satisfies certain fundamental requirements that are associated with democratic, capitalist economic systems. Hence, the SWF is based on normative judgments. Utilitarianism requires that the SWF be maximized, but constrained by the production possibilities.

Using contract theory, Rawls (1971) proposed a lexicographical SWF (Figure 2.16). He argued that, under a veil of ignorance and in an initial position where one did not know one's lot in society (whether poor or rich, or of the current or some future or past generation), people would first agree upon a fundamental principle of liberty (individual freedom and how society protects it). Once it is satisfied, Rawls argues that the contractarian approach leads one to choose, as a social welfare rule, the objective of enhancing the wellbeing of the worst off group in society. Rawls permits gains to those who are better off as long as these enhance the prospects of the worst off, all subject to the fundamental principle of liberty.

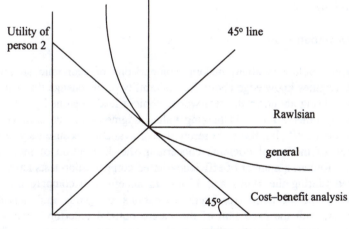

Figure 2.16: Three specifications of the social welfare function

A more extreme position prescribes that people are to be treated equally. In particular, a person with few goods (one in poverty) is treated the same as one who has more than enough (a rich person). Both are treated equally in deciding among projects – the distribution of income does not matter, only the sum of the utilities of the members of society, with a poor person's utility treated on par with that of a rich person. This is represented in Figure 2.16 by the downward sloping 45° line.

Finally, the more general utilitarian approach is to permit trade-offs among individuals, which is the objective behind the various compensation tests. The SWF in this case is represented by a curved line, with curvature a function of the marginal rates of substitution between the utility of one person and that of another.

It follows that the shape of the utility function depends on the value judgments one makes about how the wellbeing of one person is to be compared to that of another.

Other social welfare functions are possible, including choices based on intuition. However, other rules for evaluating projects lack the rigor associated with the utilitarian approach, particularly as used in cost–benefit analysis (Chapter 6).

To address issues of equity, avoiding more complex approaches to cost–benefit analysis, economists often employ the notion of compensation tests. Thus, if a proposed policy meets the standard requirement of cost–benefit analysis, namely that the policy leads to an increase in economic surplus (is efficient), compensation tests can be used to determine if the policy satisfies our notions of fairness.

Compensation Tests

Economic policy is about making comparisons of economic situations, which requires knowledge about the desirability of the change that a policy seeks to bring about. In the real world, choices lead to gains by some and losses by others. To avoid making value judgments in this context, one could use a SWF, but these are rarely if ever available because they require solution of the social dilemma concerning the distribution of income in society. Rather, a number of efficiency-based compensation tests have been devised (during the 1940s and 1950s) in an effort to compare different states of the economy (different allocations of goods and services). However, with the exception of the Pareto optimal criterion, attempts to devise a criterion based solely on efficiency, without resort to ethical judgments about the distribution of income, are incomplete. These attempts are referred to as compensation tests. We provide a brief discussion of compensation tests (for excellent overviews see Nath 1969; Chipman and

Moore 1978).

Pareto criterion
The Pareto criterion is the most unambiguous as it provides an unequivocal method of comparing two situations. According to this criterion, a public program is considered desirable only if at least one person gains by the program while no one loses.

Kaldor–Hicks compensation criterion
The Kaldor–Hicks compensation test (Kaldor 1939; Hicks 1939) states that there is an unambiguous increase in society's welfare in moving from one state to another if the gainers of a public program can hypothetically compensate the losers and still be better off than in the absence of the project. Hence, the Kaldor–Hicks principle is compatible with making the poor still poorer, as long as the rich gain enough theoretically to compensate the poor. If compensation is actually paid, the principle is nothing more than the Pareto criterion.

Scitovsky reversal paradox
Scitovsky (1941) recognized that, just as some state of the economy Q_2 can be considered better than state Q_1 on the basis of the Kaldor–Hicks compensation test, state Q_1 can be demonstrated to be better than state Q_2 on the basis of the same test. Just as, in moving from Q_1 to Q_2, the gainers could compensate the losers and still be better off, the gainers in an opposite move from Q_2 to Q_1 could compensate the losers and be better off. (The reason is that the distribution of income differs between Q_1 and Q_2.) Hence, Q_1 is better than Q_2 at the same time that Q_2 is shown to be better than Q_1. As a result, Scitovsky proposed the reversal (double) criterion: A project which moves the economy from state Q_1 to state Q_2 is deemed to increase social welfare (i.e., is efficient) if the gainers from the project can compensate the losers, but the losers cannot bribe the gainers to oppose the project.

Unfortunately, Scitovsky's criterion breaks down if the choice is to be made from more than two possible situations. Thus, it is possible for Q_2 to be superior to Q_1, Q_3 to be superior to Q_2, and Q_4 to be superior to Q_3. However, in comparing Q_1 and Q_4, Q_1 could be superior to Q_4. This implies that transitivity of choices does not hold, because Q_4 is shown superior to Q_1 along the path through Q_2 and Q_3 but in a direct comparison Q_1 is superior to Q_4, which violates rational choice (Nath 1969, pp.100–1).

Little's criterion

Little (1957) felt that the income distribution must be admitted as an explicit ethical variable so that "every reader of the economist's conclusions can decide this issue (equity) for himself" (p.11). He proposed that, if the Kaldor–Hicks criterion is satisfied and/or the Scitovsky criterion is satisfied, and the distribution of income is somehow considered to be "good", then the policy is deemed to be desirable. Others have demonstrated that there is a flaw in this criterion (e.g., Nath 1969, pp.107–9). To avoid problems, however, it is best simply to judge between states on distributional grounds only.

One is forced to conclude that there is no satisfactory, scientific method for choosing between different states of the economy and, therefore, among a variety of public programs. As a result, public decisions are made in the political arena rather than by appeal to scientific authority. In the political arena, the economist has an important role to play because she provides estimates of the efficiency and income distributional impacts of a proposed policy.

Society is often willing to trade-off a reduction in overall welfare for a better distribution of income – equity versus efficiency. Economists argue that income transfers should be done as efficiently as possible and, further, that the cost of increased income equality (measured in terms of lost allocative efficiency) be made explicit (see also Chapter 6). Likewise, society might want to protect biological assets at the cost of reduced allocative efficiency. Economists argue that the trade-off should be made explicit.

NOTES

1. Note that we drop subscripts on price of q_1 and use upper case P for notational ease since price of q_n equals 1.0.
2. In some cases, areas identified in diagrams are bounded by solid lines; in others, areas are identified by their corner points.
3. Rather than estimate demand as a function of other prices, only own price is used, with remaining prices included in the estimated intercept term (see Just et al. 1982).

3.   Resource Rents and Rent Capture

In the preceding chapter, we examined theoretically correct measures of consumer and producer welfare, respectively. Producer welfare measures do not take into explicit account natural resource inputs. However, because of their unique character compared to human-created capital resources, there is a welfare component associated with natural resources that needs to be treated separately. Rent is a surplus accruing to natural resources.

The concept of rent is closely associated with land and originally was not used in conjunction with any other resource. A review of the economics literature reveals that rent has a different meaning to different authors, with differences in meaning often being very subtle. The classical notion that rent accrues only to land has been broadened to include all types of natural capital, which may be defined as the "nonproduced means of producing a flow of natural resources and services" (Daly and Cobb 1994, p.72). The problem is that rent is an unearned windfall that can, and perhaps should, be taxed away. At the very least, the windfall should accrue to the resource owner and not to the agent granted the right to exploit the resource. However, the means used to collect rents may distort behavior, leading to inefficiency. As we illustrate in this chapter, the instrument used to capture rents will determine whether behavior is affected or not.

A consistent definition of economic rent and quasi-rent is helpful in identifying available rents and the effect that various instruments for rent capture have on output decisions. Defining rents and quasi-rents at least clarifies what rents accrue, in theory, to what factors of production. The definitions of rents are applied in this chapter to forestry (both in temperate and tropical regions) and to the fishery, where the resource owner's objective is to collect as much of the economic rent as possible. In this chapter, we examine theoretical aspects of natural resource rents and mechanisms that resource owners, generally governments, can use to capture those rents. The issue of property rights is of paramount importance here, and will be addressed in the context of the fishery.

3.1 WHAT IS RENT?

David Ricardo (1817) along with Adam Smith (1776) deserve credit for the classical notion of rent, which is often referred to as *Ricardian rent*, and just as often *differential rent*. In Ricardo's classic example, increasingly greater rent accrues to land of successively greater productivity, with least productive land receiving no rent (but still earning a return comparable to that available elsewhere in the economy). Recall from Chapter 2 that profit is zero for least productive land.

The concept of differential (land) rent is illustrated with the aid of Figure 3.1, where AC represents average cost and MC marginal cost of producing grain. Field A represents a more productive fixed factor (land) than does field B, and likewise B more productive land than C. In Figure 3.1, the rent on all fields is determined by costs and output price, *p*, which is determined by the intersection of demand and supply in the final goods market. Supply in turn is determined from the sum of the marginal costs of each of the fields producing the crop. Thus, fields A and B earn rents, but the marginal field C does not. Field C is defined to be located at the extensive margin of cultivation, where total costs just equal total revenue.

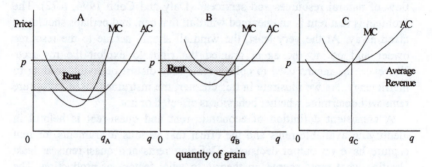

Figure 3.1: Concept of land rent: three different fields

It was Ricardo's contention that, as the price of grain rises (due to increases in population say), less and less fertile land would be brought into production. As agricultural product prices rise, an economy will expand its agricultural production onto marginal land, land that could not be profitably cultivated at a lower price. With an increase in price, however, farming can earn enough to cover all expenses, including an adequate return on capital used in crop production. When marginal land is brought into production, this implies that the owner of better land (more fertile land, land experiencing better weather or land situated nearer markets) will earn a differential rent.

The Ricardian concept of rent was extended and clarified as a result of Johann von Thuenen's 1840 critique. Von Thuenen (1966) considers rent as a function solely of location, and not fertility or climate, since land quality in the "isolated state" is uniform, with rent differentials arising from transportation costs. Because it is focused on location, the von Thuenen model has been used to study spatially separated markets and to estimate outdoor recreation benefits of parks or nature areas, where visitors travel from different locations (see Chapter 4). It has also been used, for example, to explain urban development and location decisions by pulp and paper mills.

Consider Figure 3.2 where a single city-state is surrounded by land of uniform quality. Different land uses form concentric rings about the city (located at the origin) as suggested by the rings below the horizontal axis. Land nearest the city is used for growing vegetables, dairying and grains (use *A*). Next is a ring of forestland (*B*) followed, respectively, by pastureland (*C*) and hunting (*D*) areas that are the farthest from the center. The reason for this pattern lies with rent differentials that are the result of transportation costs.

The rent–distance functions differ among land uses because revenues and costs of production vary; they decline at different rates because transportation costs are not the same. At the point labeled 1, the rent–distance function for land use *A* intersects that of *B* from above. Thus, beyond distance d_A the return to land use *B* is greater than the return to land use *A*, once production and transport costs are taken into account. Therefore, for distances from market up to $0d_A$, land use *A* will dominate; for distances from market between $0d_A$ and $0d_B$, land use *B* will dominate; and so forth for land uses *C*, *D* and any others.

If vegetables are grown next to the city, there is essentially no transportation cost associated with marketing them. Thus, the farmer located nearest the city can earn a rent given by $0R_A$ on the vertical axis. For farmers located at a greater distance from market, a transportation cost is incurred and this reduces the rent that they earn, but they continue to earn a normal profit in addition to any rent they may obtain. As the distance to market increases, the rent accruing to land use *A* declines as indicated by the rent–distance-to-market function for land use *A*. The same is true for the other land uses.

The changes in land use occur at the intensive margins – the margins of land-use transfer – where the rent for one use is driven to zero *if* the cost of the next land use is included as an opportunity cost. The extensive margins occur where the rent–distance functions intersect the horizontal axis – all differential rent associated with the activity is dissipated.[1] The result of landowners pursuing land uses that result in rent maximization is concentric rings of similar land use about the city (assuming land of equal quality throughout the region).

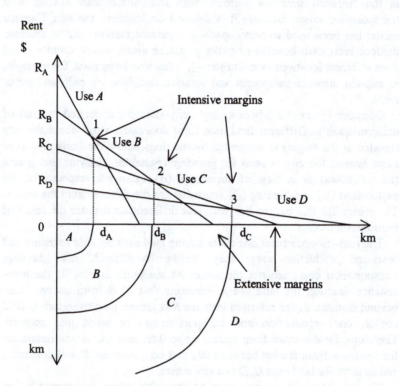

Figure 3.2: The von Thuenen rent model

Notice that farmers located near the city earn the highest rents and those living farther away earn lesser rents, even where land is employed in the same uses. In this case, it is location and not land quality that determines the rent; transportation cost is the key to rent differentials. In principle, it would be possible for the authority to tax away the rent without changing the land-use pattern, although the rent would have already been captured when land was sold as land price includes the capitalized value of the rent.

In determining the economic rent for forestland, for example, all costs must be subtracted from the estimated revenues including, where applicable, the opportunity cost (the net returns to land in its best alternative use), depletion or user charges (see below), a premium for risk, conservation costs, depreciation, and a normal rate of return for capital. The difficulty in measuring each of these cost components is what makes the determination of rent and its capture difficult and controversial. For example, two forest sites that are identical in terms of productivity may differ in terms of distance to market and transportation costs. The site with the lower transport costs would, *ceteris paribus*, have a higher differential rent. Alternatively, two sites may have equal access costs but differ in their productivity, so that, given the same inputs, one stand will yield more timber than the other at any instant in time, again generating a greater differential rent. Sorting out these differences can be a difficult task in practice.

Resource and Scarcity Rents

Scarcity rent results from scarcity and scarcity rent from natural resources is the result of their scarcity.[2] Given perfect competition, it is equal on a per unit basis to the difference between the marginal revenue and the marginal cost of production (see Figure 3.3). As its name implies, a scarcity rent can only exist when there are (natural or legal) restrictions placed on the supply of a factor from natural capital and a corresponding limitation on the produce obtained. A scarcity rent, unlike a differential rent, can occur even if the units of the factor of production from the natural capital stock are identical (i.e., having all the fields in Figure 3.1 of identical quality, with the same average and marginal cost curves). For example, irrespective of demand, a given area of forestland exploited on a sustained yield basis can only provide a certain level of wood volume; it may be impossible to increase marginal cost to the point where it equals price. The resource rent arises from the natural scarcity of the resource that restricts the supply of the output, causing output price to exceed the marginal cost of production. For resources where the marginal cost of exploitation equals the output price, the scarcity rent will be zero.

Even where the scarcity rent is zero, there may still exist a differential rent. This is illustrated in Figure 3.3, where the flow of services from land is restricted to an amount Q^0 by physical limits to the availability of land, or by government decree. Here MC represents the marginal costs of extracting the services from land, such as logging and transportation costs in the case of forestry.

The differential rent is not quasi-rent since all returns accruing to the human investment are already taken into account; the differential rent properly accrues to the remaining factor, the land itself. *Resource rent* is equal to the differential rent plus the scarcity rent, if any, as indicated in

Figure 3.3. It is the area below price and above the marginal cost curve.

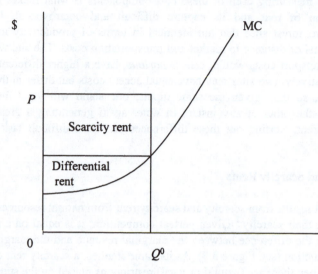

Figure 3.3: Differential and scarcity rents

Quasi-rent

Quasi-rent was defined in the previous chapter, and we want to expand on the discussion there to clarify its meaning. The term quasi-rent refers to any payment made to a (human-created) capital asset that is fixed in supply for the time being; any return to the "sunk" component of capital represents quasi-rent (Ruzicka 1979, p.47). It is commonly defined as the difference between total revenue and total variable cost, but this is not correct if there exist scarcity and differential rents. The usual definition of quasi-rent – earnings over and above those required to keep a firm in business in the short run – only considers the pecuniary returns to (human-created) factors of production and assumes this determines their allocation. But Mishan (1959) has shown that to be inadequate. A quasi-rent need not only accrue to a fixed asset but can also accrue to labor services and other factors of production whose employment is fixed over the short run. These quasi-rents are returns that accrue to firms from past investments and innovative practices and are not attributable to the natural capital stock. In contrast to resource rent, attempts to capture quasi-rents can change the efficient behavior of firms, often causing them to reduce investment and thereby the socially optimal level of output of the good or service in question.

Quasi-rents are not to be confused with differential rents, which accrue only to natural resources. Quasi-rent constitutes the return required to keep *human* factors of production employed. In forestry, for example, several types of quasi-rents exist. Investments in processing facilities or capital improvements required as a condition of receiving a forest license may generate quasi-rents, as may investments in the trees themselves (silvicultural investments). Improvements can take the form of direct investments in the growing stock, such as replanting, fertilization or thinning. This has been termed preserving the conservable flow, or the inherent productivity of a site (see below). The return from direct investments in the stock itself should accrue to the persons responsible for the expenditures. They should accrue to the owner of the site or trees only insofar as the owner has invested in the improvements. No problem arises with restrictions in harvesting that increase costs so long as such costs are fully deductible. Finally, some quasi-rents may accrue to firms from entrepreneurial innovation. To the extent rents vary across firms due to innovations and are not attributable to variations in the resource itself, such rents should accrue to the firm. These rents provide the necessary incentives for firms to engage in entrepreneurial activity.

A summary of the foregoing types of rents and implications for taxation are provided in Table 3.1.

Other Types of Rent

It is informative to discuss stock rents and land productivity rents, two terms that have appeared in the forestry literature (Luckert and Haley 1993; Luckert and Bernard 1993). They do not represent new types of rent but special sets of circumstances that generate one of the previously discussed types of rent. Stock rent has been used to describe the rent accruing to the harvest of old-growth timber, which far exceeds the present value of future returns in continuous rotations. These "stock" rents represent no previous investments so that all of the rent is a resource rent, with scarcity rent likely associated with high-grade lumber products that can come only from old-growth, temperate rain forests.

Land productivity rents are a combination of resource rents and quasi-rents (if silvicultural improvements have taken place). For land dedicated to timber management, timber rotations are chosen to maximize the present value of all future harvests. Where returns from harvesting exceed costs, this creates a stream of rents over time. The capitalized value of these rents is usually vested in the owner of the trees, who is usually the owner of the land as well. Consequently, land productivity rents for a site reflect those future rents. In a competitive market, the price of timberland would be a measure of the land productivity rent.

Table 3.1: Definitions of Various Types of Rent and Implications for Taxation

Type of rent	Definition	Implication for taxation
Resource	Sum of scarcity and differential rents	Taxation of rents does not affect behavior of firms or resource suppliers, assuming the rent capture mechanism itself does not distort behavior.
Scarcity	Difference between marginal revenue and marginal production cost that can only come about as a result of the natural or policy-induced scarcity of a resource.	
Ricardian/ differential	The excess of the market value of nonmarginal units of *in situ* resources over current scarcity rents.	
Quasi	Returns that accrue to resources supplied out of human and human-created capital, and which are not attributable to natural capital. Only for human factors of production do they equal the difference between total revenue and total variable cost.	Taxation of rents affects long-run efficient behavior of firms and resource suppliers.

3.2 AGRICULTURAL LAND AND RENT CAPTURE

Public-sector capture of economic rents has long been an important policy issue among economists. Rents can be an important source of government revenue and their appropriation, in theory, can take place without destroying economic incentives. For example, if one assumes absolute fixity of some resource, say agricultural land, then rents on land could be expected to rise over time as agricultural output prices increase. This led Walras to argue for the nationalization of land and, in its absence, for a tax on rents (Larmour 1979). Likewise, in 1879, Henry George (1929) put forward the following argument:

1. Private ownership of land is inherently monopolistic.
2. Rent is economic surplus not generated by entrepreneurship.
3. Therefore, the public should own the land or, if privately held, the surplus should be taxed away.

George advocated a single tax of land rent, believing that rising prices for agricultural outputs would drive up rents so that, by capturing those rents, all future agricultural and nonagricultural government programs could be funded from this tax.

Here we examine a particular aspect of that problem, namely, rent and taxation in the context of soil depletion. Particularly: What components of land income can be taxed away taking into account effects on soil erosion? It is possible to define land rent net of soil depletion. Depletion constitutes the loss ("sale") of the nonrenewable substance of the resource over time. The earnings from this component cannot be considered income, but rather a transfer comparable to the sale of title to land itself. Therefore, to analyze properly land rent and to identify that part of income that can be taxed away without affecting output decisions, one must examine four economic aspects or characteristics of land (Gaffney 1965).

Perdurable component (pure flow). The perdurable component of soil rent is determined by location, climate, subsoil, natural drainage, inexhaustible nutrients, macro-relief, and so on. It is a pure flow resource with no critical zone. Under ordinary circumstances, the pure flow is enduring, permanent or nonperishable; but it can be affected by human actions such as strip mining, flooding due to construction of reservoirs, paving, and so on. It is indestructible due to neglect or abuse incident to farm operations – the act of farming does not affect location, for example. If farming affects natural drainage, say, then it is no longer a part of the perdurable component. The question is: What contribution does this component make to land rent? What is the implication for taxation?

To understand this characteristic and its relationship to rent, consider two examples pertaining to location and fertility, respectively. (These examples can easily be related to Figure 3.1.) Two farmers have identical costs, yields, crops, macro-relief, and so on, but are located at different distances from the grain elevator. Jones trucks grain 5 miles to the elevator, while Smith trucks it 50 miles. Suppose each gets $4 per bushel (bu) at the elevator. Subtracting transportation costs, the farm gate prices for Jones and Smith are $3.97/bu and $3.78/bu, respectively. Smith receives $0.19/bu less than Jones. Since Smith stays in business (i.e., earns a normal profit), Jones must earn an economic rent of at least $0.19/bu. The $0.19/bu can be taxed away without affecting Jones' decision regarding what to produce and how to produce it – the tax does not affect resource allocation.[3]

Next, consider the case where Smith and Jones have identical farms next to each other, but Smith's soil is more saline than that of Jones. Say, Jones' yield is greater by some 5 bu per hectare (ha). Since Smith stays in business, the economic rent per hectare that can be taken from Jones by taxation is 5 multiplied by the farm gate price; if that price is $3.90/bu, the annual rent accruing to Jones is $19.50/ha. If land markets function perfectly and all of the rent is not taxed away, then Jones' land is also worth more than that of Smith by $19.50÷$i$ per hectare, where i is the real interest rate.[4]

Subject to the *ceteris paribus* assumption, other factors such as macro-relief have a similar impact. The pure flow (perdurable component of land) constitutes differential rent. The implication for taxation is that differential rent can all be taxed away without changing the farmer's input–output decisions. This conclusion only holds if the rent has not already been capitalized in land values that the current landowner has paid. An attempt to tax it away would result in substantial loss to the current owner, who might have to sell the land at a loss as a result. Nonetheless, the land remains in agricultural production. This illustrates the income redistributional nature of rents and their collection.

Conservable flow (flow with critical zone). The conservable flow element of virgin soil fertility is that which takes some pain to keep in the original state, but is worth those pains because they are less than the cost of replacement and less than the present value of future income from those investments ("pains"). An example of the conservable flow element of the soil is organic matter (humus). Conservation in this case is effort devoted to reducing the loss of the virgin flow resources that may, but need not, be deteriorated by annual cropping (depending on cultivation practices and crop rotations – the "pains"). Liquidation of a conservable flow component of the soil is considered to be inefficient because soil can never be rebuilt so cheaply as the cost of conserving the original condition.

Now consider the rent attributable to this characteristic of the soil. The net rent is equal to the net income (including as a cost the normal rate of return) due to conservable flow elements of the soil minus conservation costs. This is the value that can be taxed away without affecting production decisions. The difficulty lies in measuring the components of net income.

Revolving fund (stock resource). That element of original soil fertility that is not economical to conserve but is economical to replace or renew with materials imported from off-site is referred to as the revolving fund. It is a stock resource much like inventory. Examples of the revolving fund component are nutrients such as nitrogen and phosphorus that can be replaced by fertilizers, and, in some cases, moisture that can be replaced by irrigation water. Soil nitrogen can be conserved through crop rotations that include green manuring (growing a legume and simply plowing it under), but it is "cheaper" to replace lost soil nitrogen with fertilizers from off-site. Revolving fund components leave the soil and become embodied in crops and livestock.

The income imputed to the revolving fund is not a part of rent. Rather, it is a return to an improvement to the site, analogous to the return on capital tied up in storing grain – it is quasi-rent as defined in the previous section. After initial depletion of the original component, each decision to reinvest is an independent one that requires its own incentives. It represents a sacrifice of human alternatives – an opportunity cost. Taxation of quasi-rent would lead to reduced investment, so this component of rent should not be taxed.

Expendable surplus (finite fund). The expendable surplus is similar to the perdurable component except that the perdurable component is infinite, while the expendable surplus is a finite stock. The expendable surplus is often very large and, hence, its emplaced (non-use) value is very low at the margin. Elements of the expendable surplus are not economical to replace when they are expended. In the case of the perdurable matrix, the resource fund is infinite and all income accruing to it is rent. However, when the fund is finite, a depletion charge that takes into account the loss of part of a natural asset (much like a depreciation charge takes into account the wearing out of machinery) is to be subtracted from the imputed income. Rent is equal to the imputed income minus the depletion charge.

Consider, as an example, excess topsoil of 250 centimeters (cm) and its exploitation by sod farming. Assume the technology of sod farming is such that the growing and sale of grass sod removes 5 cm of topsoil every year. Then it is not until after 50 years that all of the excess topsoil becomes depleted. It is at that time that the topsoil must be considered to be like conservable flow, and steps must be taken to ensure that further soil loss either does not occur or occurs at a rate that does not affect the future availability of the resource. This might mean that soil is depleted (eroded) at the same rate as it is replaced, or that soil is rebuilt by intermixing of the layers below the humus and green manuring (adding humus).

When sod farming begins, the amount of surplus used this year has no effect on the amount available next year. Removing sod this year strips 5 cm of what amounts to surplus topsoil from the 250-cm base, but it is still possible to strip away 5 cm next year. After 50 years, the land can no longer be used for sod farming but, under our assumptions, is still available for crop production. The appropriate depletion charge today is the contribution of 5 cm of topsoil to the stream of net returns from sod farming discounted to the present. Suppose the contribution of 5 cm of topsoil is $1,000 (the return in a given year over what could be earned in normal cropping activities) and that soil cannot be "mined" at a faster rate. Then the current year depletion charge is equal to $1,000 $\div (1 + i)^{50}$, where i is the interest rate. The depletion charge next year is $1,000 $\div (1 + i)^{49}$, and so on for following years. The depletion charge is very small early on but increases each year as the expendable surplus becomes fully depleted.

The depletion charge is equal to the user cost (Howe 1979, p.75). User cost is defined as the opportunity cost associated with mining or harvesting a unit of resource today. This opportunity cost is what the marginal unit of the resource would be worth, in present value terms, had it been left *in situ* and mined or harvested at its most opportune time in the future. The amount of income that can be taxed away is equal to the income from the expendable surplus minus the depletion charge.

A summary of the foregoing discussion is provided in Table 3.2. In the analysis, we attributed land values to soil characteristics. However, the characteristics found in the perdurable matrix include elements that have nothing to do with the soil *per se*. They include location, climate, macro-relief, and so on. The one thing that prevents us from valuing land according to physical attributes or things such as agricultural productivity is the other uses of land and associated externalities (e.g., blowing dust). Land values cannot be related to soil characteristics except in very rare circumstances.

Table 3.2: Resource Rent from Various Components of Soil

Perdurable Matrix	Net income from this source is *all* rent
Conservable Flow	Rent = Net Income – Conservation Costs
Revolving Fund	Income is a return similar to any return on capital investment. This is quasi-rent, so no rent is available to be collected
Expendable Surplus	$Rent_t = Income_t - Depletion\ Charge_t$

3.3 TAXATION, CHARGES AND RENT CAPTURE IN FORESTRY

Timber-producing jurisdictions usually have a number of goals with respect to forest management, including maintaining employment, meeting environmental objectives, maximizing tax revenue, and so on (van Kooten 1995a). Here we only consider the goal of rent capture, which should occur with as little distortion as possible to economic efficiency. The objective is to transfer resource rents from private logging companies (or concessionaires) to the public land or resource owner. In this section, we review some methods of rent capture in forestry and describe the possible distortions they may impose on rotation, harvesting and management decisions. The resource owner is interested in capturing resource rents, but not quasi-rents that are attributable to factors of production other than the land itself. We also describe how rents may be dissipated and the implications for rent capture. As examples, we examine rent capture in British Columbia (Canada) and Indonesia.

Rent Capture and Efficiency

One way to determine whether a method of rent capture distorts decisions is to assess its effect on the extensive and intensive margins. The extensive margin for forestry is explained with reference to heterogeneity *across* sites or stands of timber and is illustrated in Figure 3.4(a). Suppose that there are N forest stands that can be harvested, arranged from left to right on the horizontal axis in terms of decreasing financial profitability. Financial profitability is determined by harvest costs (which are higher in steep terrain), transportation costs to mills (distance increases costs), and so on. The line ab represents the rent function, with the vertical distance between the rent function and the horizontal line at zero representing the resource rent, or simply the price of logs (p) minus marginal cost of harvesting the logs (c). Firms will harvest stands up to K, leaving KN stands unharvested because harvesting those would cost more than they yield in benefits at the margin ($c > p$). Forest stands $0K$ constitute the working forest. Imposition of a uniform stumpage fee (to collect rents) will shift ab to the left, reducing the number of stands that firms can profitably harvest. If stumpage fees are already in place (i.e., assume ab includes existing stumpage fees), a reduction in fees will shift ab to the right, increasing the number of stands that yield rent, encouraging firms to harvest a greater number of sites. An increase in log prices will also shift ab to the right. Tenure arrangements and administratively set harvest levels can prevent expansion of the working forest into marginal areas, however. In that case, the greatest impact of changes in output prices and stumpage fees occurs at the *intensive margin*.[5]

Figure 3.4(b) is similar to Figure 3.4(a), but illustrates the intensive margin. It refers to what happens at the stand rather than the forest level. Here, rather than arranging stands in decreasing order of financial profitability along the horizontal axis, trees (logs) are arranged in order of financial profitability, according to species and diameter. Large logs of the most valuable species are the most profitable, and generate the most rent.

For illustration, marginal cost (c) is assumed not to vary by log size and quality in Figure 3.4(b) (but see below). Yet, there comes a point where the marginal cost of harvesting an additional tree or log is less than the revenue it provides once all costs of bringing it to the mill gate or export point are taken into account. Marginal revenue is the value of the marginal product (VMP) of a log, which is equal to the price (p) of logs times the marginal physical product of the log. Marginal physical product falls as log size (measured by its diameter) declines. The difference between VMP and marginal cost equals the resource rent at the stand level; the intensive margin is found where VMP and c intersect. The effect of (an increase in) stumpage fees on the intensive margin can be shown either by shifting VMP inwards or marginal cost upwards.

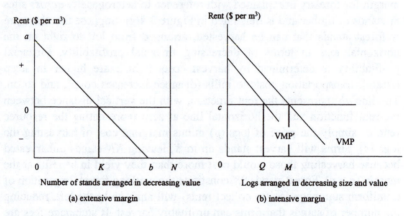

Number of stands arranged in decreasing value

(a) extensive margin

Logs arranged in decreasing size and value

(b) intensive margin

Figure 3.4: Extensive and intensive margins for timber harvesting

Suppose that the government increases stumpage fees. This is represented by an inward shift of VMP to VMP′, and a leftward shift of the intensive margin from M to Q. Loggers want to harvest trees of a larger size, leaving logs of sizes in the range MQ and smaller on the ground, or standing as trees, a practice known as "high grading". To prevent high grading, governments often implement utilization standards. For example, forest companies may be required to harvest trees with a diameter greater than 10 cm, even though they lose money on any trees that they harvest and haul to the mill that are less than 15 cm in diameter.[6] In British Columbia, if companies are found to be leaving logs that meet the utilization standard for a site, the Forest Ministry will harvest the stand, charging the company both harvesting costs and associated stumpage fees. Whether this occurs in other jurisdictions frequently depends on the ability of governments to enforce regulations, with corruption at the local level reported as one obstacle leading to the high grading of sites.

A common supply restriction in timber management is the sustained yield requirement or, alternatively, a requirement that harvests be nondeclining or greater than some minimal level over a specified time period. In British Columbia, where some 95% of all of the forestland is publicly held, the Ministry of Forests determines a sustained yield harvest level, or Allowable Annual Cut (AAC). The Province sets the AAC based on the Ministry's calculation of the amount of forestland that can economically and biologically support harvesting. By definition, the limit to timber production is determined by those timber stands whose returns will just cover the cost of harvesting. Those stands constitute the extensive margin and by definition would earn no rent. If the Province errs in determining the extent of the land base, two possibilities arise. The first is that the AAC has been set too low – more timber could be harvested profitably. In this case, the resource rent is scarcity rent and is the margin between the revenues and costs for that stand at the artificially created margin. The other possibility is that the AAC has been set too high, and firms incur a loss by harvesting at the margin. Because of the uncertain nature of administrative calculations, the Ministry does allow limited flexibility for firms to shift their cutting patterns within a five-year period. To the extent that the Province's AAC is a binding constraint on total production, a scarcity rent may be created reflecting the difference between marginal revenue and marginal cost of timber production.

A simple diagram can be used to illustrate concepts related to rent capture on public forestland. In Figure 3.5, individual trees (logs) on a concession are arranged in terms of quality from highest to lowest, where quality is determined by a tree's standing or stumpage value. This is reflected by the downward sloping derived demand curve, which is now equal to marginal revenue (MR) rather than VMP since log prices are not fixed (as was the case in Figure 3.4). In practice, MR is likely a stepwise function (Ruzicka 1979; Vincent 1990). MC_{SR} refers to the short-run, private marginal cost of logging trees and transporting them to the mill. Marginal costs rise for the usual reasons, but also because costs per m^3 are smaller for large logs of high quality than for logs of lower quality and size. These costs are short term because, in most cases, forest companies only have short-term rights to forestland – 25 years in BC and 20 years in Indonesia. Forest companies (or logging concessionaires) with short-term tenures do not protect (currently unprofitable) trees that are left to regenerate, providing a future return. The cost of protecting future returns is not incurred since those returns do not accrue to the current concessionaire.

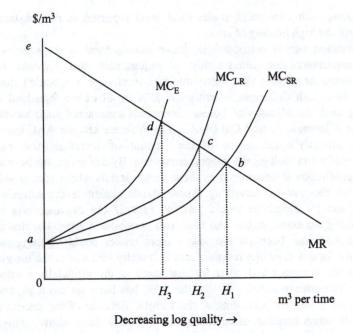

Figure 3.5: Rents in forestry, private and social

The curve MC_{LR} represents the marginal costs of extraction when long-run impacts are taken into account (the sum of short-run marginal costs and the marginal costs of protecting future expected returns, or user cost). Finally, MC_E represents the (short- plus long-run) private marginal costs of logging operations, plus the environmental or externality costs of logging. When tenure rights or concessions are short term, volume H_1 will be harvested and rent equals area *abe*. If loggers have rights to future harvests, so they take into account the user cost, they will reduce harvests to H_2 by leaving more trees standing on a site (intensive margin) and harvesting fewer sites at the extensive margin. The associated level of current rent from logging (and transportation to the mill) is area *ace*. (There will be greater future rents as a result, but we ignore these in this discussion.) Finally, if the externality effects of logging are taken into account, only the volume H_3 should be harvested in the current period. The social rent given by area *ade* is, therefore, less than the market rent.

The government should permit the logging firm or concessionaire to harvest only the amount H_3, discourage high grading and capture as much of the rent as possible (as it is the resource owner). Economic efficiency deals with the optimal harvest quantity (where MC = MR), while rent capture deals with the distribution of the surplus (total area between MC and MR). Efficiency and rent capture are separate (but related) issues, because efficiency in production determines how much rent is available.

Vincent (1993) argues that, based on empirical evidence from tropical countries, the differences between MC_{SR} and MC_{LR} are insignificant. This is due to the fact that investments in natural forestry (e.g., leaving certain trees standing so they can be harvested some 20 years later rather than waiting 80 years for new trees to regenerate a site) do not pay off due to the long rotation ages and, in developing countries, high rates of discount (see also Rice et al. 2001). In practice, we need only determine MC_{SR}, for which information may be available, and not worry about having to estimate user costs. Vincent (1993) also suggests that logging could result in environmental benefits, as well as costs. For example, logging leads to access for recreationists, open areas for some forms of wildlife (herbivores), and so on. It is not clear, therefore, whether MC_E lies to the left of MC_{SR} (as drawn in Figure 3.5) or to the right.

Methods of Rent Capture

Several methods may be employed to collect economic rents (Hyde and Sedjo 1992; Vincent 1993). We illustrate four such methods using Figure 3.6 and next discuss a fifth method. The concessionaire is assumed to harvest H_1 and the available rent to be captured is given by area *abe* minus the fixed cost, otherwise quasi-rent would be captured. We ignore quasi-rent and assume that economic efficiency occurs at H_1 (although H_3 in Figure 3.5 may actually be socially optimal).

(1) First, a fully differentiated royalty or tax would enable the authority to capture the entire area *abe*. Royalties would vary by tree species, size of tree, land quality, harvest costs by site, delivery costs, and so on. Such royalty discrimination is impractical, however, particularly in tropical countries where there are many tree species and the monitoring ability of Forest Ministries is limited, but also in developed countries. Informational requirements are simply too great.

(2) A second method of rent capture is a uniform fixed royalty (r_U), which is also referred to as the uniform specific royalty (Vincent 1993). This is shown in Figure 3.6 by an increase in MC to MC + r_U, where the vertical distance between the two curves is held constant at the fixed rate (r_U = *ad* = *cf*). The concessionaire reduces harvest levels from H_1 to H^0. The rent collected by the government amounts to area *afcd*, while the concessionaires receive a windfall of *dce*. Area *cbf* is the rent lost to high grading because concessionaires leave felled and/or standing trees on the site to avoid excessive timber charges. Therefore, it is recommended that the uniform and fixed stumpage fee be levied on standing timber as opposed to logs when they have been removed from the site, say at a government check point or weigh scale (Vincent 1990).

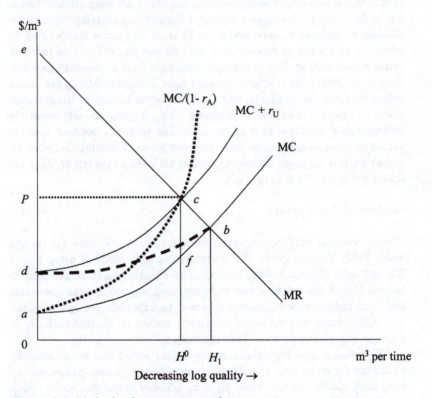

Figure 3.6: Methods of rent capture in forestry

That the uniform fixed royalty distorts harvest levels and leads to high grading is easily demonstrated. In the absence of fees and future considerations, the concessionaire will maximize the following profit function:

(3.1) $\pi = p(H)H - C(H)$,

where $p(H)$ is price as a function of the harvest and $C(H)$ is the total cost of harvesting and delivering logs to the mill gate or export point. To maximize profit requires that $p'(H)H + p(H) = C'(H)$, or MR = MC. Solving gives H_1

in Figure 3.6. With the uniform royalty, the profit function (3.1) becomes

$$(3.2) \quad \pi = p(H)H - C(H) - r_U H.$$

The optimization condition now requires that MR = MC + r_U. Solving for H gives $H^0 < H_1$ for some value of r_U. If r_U is set high enough, harvest volume could potentially be reduced to below H_3 (the point identified in Figure 3.5), which could imply that not enough trees are harvested even from society's point of view.

As noted by Hyde and Sedjo (1992), the incentive to "trespass, high-grade, and ignore off-site environmental values" (p.346) is greatest for the best sites and best trees. This is clear from Figure 3.6. Better quality sites and trees are found near the origin where the difference between the marginal revenue and marginal cost is greatest.

(3) A third method of rent capture is an *ad valorem* royalty ($0 \leq r_A < 1$) set as a proportion of the selling price or revenue. The profit function (3.1) can now be written as:

$$(3.3) \quad \pi = (1 - r_A)p(H)H - C(H).$$

The necessary condition for a solution is now MR = MC/$(1 - r_A)$. The royalty on revenue shifts the MC curve upwards to MC/$(1 - r_A)$ as indicated in Figure 3.6 (dotted curve). For convenience, we show a royalty that shifts MC so it intersects MR at c (so that $H^0 < H_1$ maximizes the concessionaire's profit).

The effect of the royalty on harvest level (efficiency) is the same as for the fixed rate royalty (efficiency declines as high grading occurs), but the distribution of the rent is different. The government gets *acf*, while the logging company gets *ace*. Again *cbf* is the rent lost due to high grading. For the same harvest level (degree of high grading), the government collects less rent under the *ad valorem* royalty on revenue (or price) than under the uniform fixed royalty. Further, the fixed royalty is easier to administer, thereby reducing administrative costs relative to the royalty on revenue.

Finally, from a theoretical perspective, it does not matter whether one assumes that prices vary according to log quality (MR is downward sloping) or price is horizontal (demand is infinite) as in Vincent (1990) and Hyde and Sedjo (1992). The essential difference is that H^0 will lie to the left of its current position in the case of the flat demand (= price P in Figure 3.6).

(4) A fourth method is to levy an *ad valorem* royalty ($0 \leq r_P < 1$) on the difference between price and marginal cost for each log. In essence, this is a profit tax. The effect of this levy is illustrated with the aid of Figure 3.6. In this case, the profit function is

(3.4) $\pi = (1-r_P)\,[p(H)H - C(H)]$.

The optimality condition requires that MR = MC, as in the case where there are no fees. The royalty-adjusted MC curve in Figure 3.6 shifts up (the dashed curve), but intersects MR at the original level of harvest H_1. For example, if the royalty-adjusted MC is given by segment *db*, the government collects an amount *abd* of the rent, leaving *dbe* to the concessionaire. The important point is that such a tax on rent does not distort economic efficiency. The only problem is that the Ministry must know not only selling prices but also something about marginal costs of harvesting and delivering timber to a mill or exporter. In that case, a fully differentiated royalty can also be used, but then to capture the entire rent. Unlike with a fully differentiated royalty, however, an *ad valorem* tax on net revenue only might work in practice if one does not attempt to calculate the net revenue on each and every log, but only on the company's net return from the site in each year.

(5) Hyde and Sedjo (1992) recommend a fifth method for collecting rents, namely, to charge a competitively bid lump sum fee for the right to harvest a particular site. In theory, this will capture the entire area *abe* in Figures 3.5 and 3.6. This method is used in the USA, where the federal government auctions off the harvest rights to tracts of public forestland. This approach is also employed in BC under the Small Business Enterprise Program through competitive bidding for Minor Timber Sale Licenses. In theory, competitive bidding for harvesting rights should extract the *expected* economic rents from forest companies. It does not, however, ensure that the resource owner collects all the economic rents as it is an *ex ante* rather than an *ex post* method of rent capture. Thus, if firms' expectations are incorrect due to unexpected changes in demand or technological advances (or because they use a different discount rate than the government), the appropriate amount of rent will not be collected. An example of this was the disequilibrium in timber prices caused by speculative bidding in the US Pacific Northwest (Mattey 1990; Perez-Garcia and Lippke 1991). Operators were willing to pay more for the wood than it was worth as they anticipated higher lumber values that never materialized.

Another problem with competitive bidding may arise when the timber rights represent a small proportion of the total timber requirements of the successful bidder. In this case, competitive bidding may reflect a firm's ability to slide down the variable cost curve, using cost savings on all units to bid a lower price on wood. Using these bids as a measure of the rent available for the entire resource will result in the collection of quasi-rents

(Schwindt 1992). Furthermore, in times of excess capacity, firms may be willing to bid prices in excess of the actual timber value since they attach a premium to remaining in business (and expect to recoup their losses at a later date). Again, quasi-rents could be collected if these bids are employed as the basis for setting royalties.

A third problem may arise where there are a limited number of bidders. In his classic work, Mead (1967) showed that the gap between the appraised upset price (minimum price acceptable to the seller) and the actual bid received for federal timber in the US Pacific Northwest varied directly with the number of bidders. Further studies have suggested that concentration on either the buyer or seller side may not lead to competitive outcomes. For example, Brännlund et al. (1985) looked at buyer concentration in Scandinavian pulpwood markets, arguing that pulp companies exercised their market power in setting prices along a transportation corridor (paying less for fiber to wood producers located near the mill than to those further away) and through systematic importation of foreign wood. Binkley (1991) has made similar assertions about market power in pulpwood markets in the American South.

The principal advantage of competitive bidding is that it should not change the optimal behavior of firms or the extensive or intensive margins. This is because the firm has every incentive to maximize the net return from the forestland. However, in the case where there are other distortions, such as insecure tenure, firms may not have the incentive to preserve the conservable flow from the site in the absence of regulations, and economic efficiency may not be assured.

Other methods of rent capture that may be employed include land rentals and land productivity taxes. Land rentals are an arbitrary annual payment that does not distort resource use provided the charge does not exceed the forestland's economic rent. Land productivity taxes are based on an estimate of forestland productivity or the annual growth rate of the trees at a site multiplied by an expected price for the timber. The charge, therefore, is based on a site's "best use" value and not on the value of the actual inventory or harvesting costs. Provided that the charge is set so that an amount equal to or less than the economic rent is collected, the behavior of firms is unaffected. The optimal area-based charges suggested by Nautiyal and Love (1971) are an example. The problem with the land rental and productivity taxes is setting the appropriate rate of rent capture.

Finally, the efficiency-distorting effects of the most common rent collection methods, uniform fixed royalties and *ad valorem* royalties on revenue or price, can be mitigated to some extent by regulations that prevent high grading. The regulations themselves can be a source of inefficiency and can lead to higher social costs (e.g., firms are required to haul small diameter logs that cost more to haul than they fetch in revenue).

Rent Capture in Practice

In the United States, most forestland is privately owned, but the US Forest Service employs competitive bidding on timber sales from National Forests (see above discussion). Competitive bidding generally works because there are an adequate number of companies engaged in the bidding process, but not always. Since bids are based on *ex ante* expectations about wood product prices, and these may not be realized, companies have on occasion defaulted on the purchase agreement, and no rent is collected. Sometimes forest companies are able to get lower prices because, when there are few bidders, they wield monopsonistic power, which prevents the public owner from collecting all of the rents. Indeed, the US Forest Service often fails to collect any rents, unable even to recover the costs of providing the timber (e.g., in the Rocky Mountain region) – a practice known as "below-cost timber sales". This practice is justified on the grounds that harvesting yields off-site (externality) benefits, such as enhanced stream flow or access for recreation purposes.[7]

In contrast to the USA, public forestlands account for the vast majority of timber harvests in Canada. As in other regions of Canada, two types of forest tenures are found on public forestlands in British Columbia. Tree Farm Licenses (also known as Forest Management units in other parts of Canada) guarantee forest companies access to timber in the license area for a period of 25 years, with the possibility of renewal. In exchange, firms must provide secondary manufacturing facilities (sawmills, pulp mills) and draw up management plans that are subsequently approved by the Ministry of Forests. The government sets five-year harvest targets, with firms having some flexibility to shift harvest levels within that time frame: harvests can vary by upwards of 50% from the target in a given year, but must be within 10% of the five-year target to avoid loss of future access to public timber. While forest companies had previously not been responsible for reforestation (it was a public responsibility), recent policy changes shifted responsibility to the companies, first enabling the companies to charge such expenses against stumpage fees but later imposing all of the cost on the companies (as a cost of harvesting) (see Wang and van Kooten 2001). Since rotation ages exceed 50 years, the length of tenure is inadequate to get firms to take into account the effects of current decisions on future timber availability. Further, vagaries in government policies concerning the Tree Farm Licenses led the private forest companies to view the tenures as ephemeral.

The second form of tenure is a harvest permit that only grants the logging company the right to a certain volume of timber. The permits require the concessionaires to submit harvest plans, but forest management responsibility resides solely with the government. Tenures are granted via competitive bids, although the process takes into account local employment impacts, the use to which logs are put, and similar nonprice factors that dissipate the total rent collected. The Ministry of Forests is responsible for the management of these lands (Wang and van Kooten 1999).

The earlier stumpage system for capturing forest rents was based upon the Rothery formula: $S = P - C - R$, where S is the stumpage fee or the assessed potential charge paid by the harvester of a site to the resource owner, P is the timber price, C is operating costs, and R is an allowance for risk and a normal rate of profit, all measured on a per cubic meter basis. Rent is determined by simply deducting total costs from total revenues, but S can be smaller or larger than actual rent so that, if larger, quasi-rents are captured. This approach is also used to calculate reserve prices, or the upset price, for timber sales on federal lands in the United States. Luckert and Bernard (1993) refer to these as Residual Conversion Return (RCR) methods of appraisal.

Appraised values for P, C and R and not actual values are employed, mainly because competitive markets for determining these values are generally unavailable as a result of widespread public ownership and associated tenure arrangements. A distinction is made between Coast and Interior; trees on the Coast tend to be larger and used primarily for high-quality grades of lumber, with residual wood "sold" as wood chips for pulp, while those in the Interior are used for lower grade lumber, studs and wood chips. On the Coast, P was given as the price of logs in the Vancouver log market, which is a residual market where companies trade excess logs. In the Interior, the value of logs is based upon "random length lumber" (average of prices of lumber of varying lengths), stud and chip prices, and estimated conversion factors. The appraised operating costs are estimated from surveys for an operator of "average efficiency". There was a minimum stumpage charge of 3% of the Average Product Value (APV) in the Interior, and 6% of the APV on the Coast, even if the above formula indicated a negative stumpage value, and charges were levied on the timber removed using uniform but species-specific rates.

This system caused a number of distortions predicted by economic theory (see above) and discussed in the BC context by Pearse (1976) and Percy (1986). It resulted in high grading as firms had an incentive only to harvest those trees that provided a net return equal to or in excess of average stumpage fees, with remaining trees generally left on the ground. Thus, the stumpage system shifted the intensive margin to the left and distorted firm behavior. This incentive for firms to harvest fewer trees from a stand with a per unit stumpage charge explains why the Province specified minimum utilization rates for timber stands. In addition, the USA argued that the system did not collect enough rent within the Province, and, by failing to do so, the Provincial government was subsidizing the forest industry. In response, the BC government adopted a new stumpage system in 1987 (modified in 1994) called Comparative Value Pricing (CVP). The new system was meant to meet the government's requirements for increased revenues and to eliminate the need for an export tax as required by the Memorandum of Understanding between the respective national governments (Grafton et al. 1998).

The CVP system changed many of the features of the stumpage system. In 1987, minimum stumpage rates were set at 25 cents per cubic meter, with all species in the same stand averaged together to determine the stumpage rate. Most importantly, the stumpage system changed from a Rothery or residual value approach to an *ad valorem* approach, with stumpage charges ultimately determined as a percentage of the selling price of timber products. Specifically, the government establishes target rates and uses relative values to allocate stumpage fees across the Province. This leads to a "waterbed effect", since a decrease in one operator's stumpage paid in one area means a concomitant increase in that of another operator and/or area. The actual formula is: $VI = P - C$, where VI is the value index for the cutting authority (logging operator), P is the selling price of logs on the Coast and lumber and chips in the Interior, and C is operating costs. The resulting VIs are aggregated to calculate a Mean Value Index (MVI), with negative rates (because in some cases operating costs exceed selling price) reset at the minimum stumpage rate of 25 cents/m^3. The MVI is then used to determine the average stumpage or base rate, given that the physical harvest changes from quarter to quarter. The base rate is then compared to the government's required revenue target, which is approximately known once the base rate is established because the government also controls log harvests on public lands. The MVI is adjusted upwards or downwards in an iterative process (because harvests fluctuate) until the expected stumpage billed equals the base rate. The resulting base rate is then used to determine the individual stumpage for each cutting authority as: Base Rate + (VI – MVI).

At the same time, the deductibility of costs changed dramatically, as major licensees assumed responsibility for management costs, road-building and reforestation – the latter two previously treated as dollar for dollar credits against stumpage (Wang et al. 1998). Under the new system, silvicultural and development costs are incorporated in determining stumpage values, but are no longer fully deductible. Since recent changes in the BC Forest Practices Code have increased operating costs and contributed to a 65% increase in average logging costs per cubic meter from 1992 to 1995, this potentially has an adverse impact on the viability of the industry.[8] Obviously, transferring funds in excess of the rent implies that firms earn less than normal profits, which may give rise to disinvestment.

It should be noted that, although stumpage payments make up the bulk of direct forest revenues, the government also collects several other (indirect) taxes. These include the sales tax, the corporate capital tax, logging taxes and property taxes. In addition, there are general methods of taxation that allow the Province to collect a share of the rents. To the extent that uncollected economic rents increase the profits of forest companies, any applicable corporate profit taxes should appropriate a share of the rent.

The proportion of available rent captured by the BC government over the period 1970 to 1994 was calculated by Grafton et al. (1998) as the ratio of stumpage revenue to the difference between total timber revenues and total harvest costs (as determined from Statistics Canada data). The proportions are provided in Figure 3.7. No rent data are available beyond 1994 due to confidentiality restrictions imposed by Statistics Canada on cost data after that period. Rent capture varied between a high of 174% (in 1981) and a low of 22% (in 1977). Rent capture averaged 71% over the 25-year period. As the following discussion of Indonesia illustrates, the BC government has on occasion performed no better than developing countries in capturing forestry rents, although rent capture has generally been higher overall.

In contrast to BC where rent capture has been relatively high at times and may even have resulted in hardships for forest companies on occasion, the situation in many developing countries is just the opposite – countries have generally been unsuccessful at capturing forest rents. Failure to capture economic rents contributes to excessive short-run exploitation, and inevitable waste of valuable resources.

The failure to capture rents has resulted in greater than normal profits for timber contractors. According to Repetto and Gillis (1988), excess profits resulted in a rush on concession contracts by private contractors (the so-called timber boom) and stimulated logging activity. Sub-optimally large areas of forestland were selectively logged and, as a consequence of roads constructed to transport the logs, opened up for shifting cultivators and settlers (see Chapter 12).

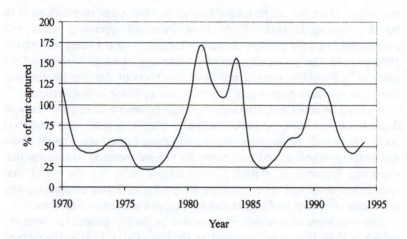

Figure 3.7: Rent capture in BC, percent of available rent captured

Excess profits also stimulate short-run deforestation because concessionaires are not sure whether the favorable terms of the concession contracts will persist. Concession rights are typically not acquired by competitive bidding, but by negotiation. This process clearly opens the door for "side payments" and favoritism, which may provide the concessionaire with little formal rights. To forestall risk of renegotiating or revision of contract terms, a rational concessionaire should enter the property immediately, harvesting the trees as quickly as possible. The opening up of closed forests is also promoted by a timber revenue system that promotes high grading. This suggests that rent capture and economic efficiency may be linked; it appears to depend on the institutional framework.

Why might rent capture be so low? Consider the example of Indonesia, which accounts for about 10% of the earth's remaining tropical rainforests, ranking third behind Brazil and Zaire. Indonesia has a long history of log export trade restrictions. In 1985, an outright ban was introduced, replaced in 1993 with high levies of $500–$1,500/m³ in order to comply with international trade rules (Rice et al. 2001). The purpose of trade restrictions was to industrialize the forest sector, creating employment in secondary manufacturing. These policies reduced the domestic price of fiber, thereby encouraging waste, as cheap fiber was substituted for technologies that would use less fiber to produce the same amount of output. By reducing the value of standing timber, trade restrictions made forestland more valuable in alternative uses, primarily agriculture. Thus, two forces have operated against each other – lower fiber prices have reduced supply of fiber as it reduced incentives to cut trees (but wood wastage has offset this effect to a large extent), while the opportunity cost of converting land to agriculture has increased the incentive to cut trees (see Chapter 12). Finally, Indonesia also imposed substantial taxes on sawnwood exports in 1989 in order to shift activities toward plywood, although the tax was also meant to improve overall competitiveness and efficiency in sawmills by, amongst others, forcing small companies to merge (Barbier et al. 1995). Further, illegal harvests have depressed domestic prices, thereby reducing royalties. (Although official records in the late 1990s put log production at some 26 million m^3, estimates based on wood product outputs suggest that actual log production is closer to 40 million m^3.)

The evidence suggests that the Indonesian government has not succeeded in capturing a great deal of the forest rent, although it has done better on some occasions. Estimates of rent capture differ depending on whether potential or actual rent is used as the benchmark. Potential rent is based on logging companies operating in open markets, so prices of freely traded logs from Sabah and Sarawak in Malaysia have been used to calculate the resource rent. Actual rent focuses on private profitability under existing trade regulations; it is the basis for the calculations used in the case of BC, for example. To estimate actual rents, it is necessary at least to determine domestic log prices, but this may be difficult if log prices reflect transfer prices (prices used by firms to exchange surpluses of various tree species directly circumventing the market) rather than competitive market prices. Obtaining information about transfer prices and logging costs from forest companies in Indonesia is also difficult. Further, government levies vary by species and location, as do production costs.

Using data on log exports from Sumatra and Kalimantan between 1979 and 1982 (prior to the log export ban), Repetto and Gillis (1988) estimate potential forest rents in Indonesia of approximately $62/m^3$. However, total identifiable government revenues (timber royalties, land taxes, reforestation fees and other charges) averaged no more than $28/m^3$, implying that, over this period, the government captured only 45% of the rents available from log exports. Timber that was domestically processed received even more favorable treatment: tax rates were lowered and investment incentives were provided to stimulate processing. An inefficient domestic industry was erected that, at least initially, generated economic losses and required more than average input of wood per unit of output. Repetto and Gillis (1988) have estimated that between 1979 and 1982 the potential economic rents generated by log production, whether for further processing or direct export, exceeded US$3.95 billion. Of this, the government's share, collected through official taxes and fees, was $1.64 billion. Five hundred million dollars of potential profits were lost because relatively high-cost domestic processing generated negative economic returns. The remainder, $2.8 billion, was left to private parties.

Marchak (1995) estimates that 8% and 17% of potential rents (of $3.1 billion and $2.5 billion) were captured by the Indonesian government in 1989 and 1990, respectively. The World Bank (1993) estimates that actual rent amounted to $40–$45/m^3, and that the government collected 19–33% of this rent. Whiteman (1996) estimates that actual rent equaled $44/m^3, with the government collecting 61% of the rent. Other studies suggest that the government captured somewhere between 25% and 57% of the available (actual) rents (Teter 1997).

Rent Dissipation in Forestry

The discussion on rents has so far assumed that a forest site will naturally yield (maximum) economic rent. In reality, there are a number of ways that economic rent and even quasi-rents can be dissipated, transferred or simply not realized. The most damaging type of rent dissipation from an economic point of view arises from market and policy failures that prevent the most efficient use of resources and benefit no one. Market distortions dissipate rent through the misallocation of resources, such as capital and labor, and through inappropriate rotations and harvest practices. Such distortions can arise from inappropriate forestry regulations, or policy failure. For example, uncertainty over tenure of forestland and harvesting rights may reduce investments and reduce the quasi-rents from the site that would otherwise have occurred under more appropriate tenure arrangements (see next section). In both the cases of BC and Indonesia, forest companies have tenure rights that are shorter in duration than the time required for the next round of harvest on a site.

In the standard theory of forestry, the owner of the resource balances the costs of silviculture today against future benefits, appropriately discounted. Luckert and Haley (1993) and Pearse (1985) have pointed out that most stumpage systems deduct current silvicultural costs from current harvests. Both companies and the government treat reforestation as a mandatory expenditure associated with timber harvest (see Wang and van Kooten 2001). Since these expenditures could have been collected as a rent, the government is transferring rent from one period to the next. If such investments are not profitable, the rent may be partially or totally dissipated (Benson 1988). Rules requiring the planting of trees on sites where natural reforestation is more profitable, or employing more intensive silviculture where returns do not warrant doing so, result in the dissipation of rent.

In some cases, rent may be dissipated to achieve other social objectives, such as maximizing employment in economically depressed regions. For example, a pulp mill on BC's northern Coast was provided hundreds of millions of dollars in subsidy payments (beginning in 1998) to continue production and prevent loss of employment. Yet, the mill is unlikely to survive in the longer run because fiber needs to be obtained from areas that are too distant from the mill to make logging profitable, a situation exacerbated by environmental regulations. Pursuing regional development or employment objectives is likely to be inefficient. Rarely is an attempt made to measure directly the costs and benefits of such actions, and rent is likely to be dissipated through forgone opportunities.

Transfer of the economic rent from the owner of forestland to other economic agents is a related consideration. Copithorne (1979) attributes higher wages in the BC forestry sector compared to that of Ontario as a rent transfer (or dissipation), but Percy (1986) concludes that much of the difference can be explained by the higher productivity of BC workers. Thus, it is not clear if union bargaining results in rent dissipation.

Yet another way economic rents can be lost to the public landowner is through capture and retention by forest companies. It has been suggested that economic rents left uncollected may be transferred outside of the forestry sector through transfer pricing by vertically integrated companies. This may take the form of overpricing inputs or underpricing outputs. Such appropriation of economic rents should be evidenced by companies with higher than normal profits taking into account risk premiums, but BC forest companies compare unfavorably with manufacturing industries in Canada based upon measures of financial performance (Pearse 1980; Zhang and Binkley 1995). It appears, therefore, that large integrated forest companies have not been successful in capturing forest rents.

The imposition of utilization rates at harvest sites may also dissipate rents, as does the method of allocating harvesting rights. In BC, firms holding long-term cutting rights (Tree Farm Licenses or Forest Licenses) are required to build and operate processing facilities. Logs harvested under a company's permit may be more valuable to another company, or as an export, rather than being used in the local mill. Where logs are not utilized in their highest value use, the economic rent is reduced or dissipated. This has been the case in Indonesia, for example.

Governments restrict log exports for industry development, employment and wellbeing reasons. It is argued that, by preventing log exports, processing is encouraged, thereby leading to greater employment and economic development. Economic development is confused with economic wellbeing in this case. Indeed, Margolick and Uhler (1986) show that social wellbeing might even be enhanced if log export bans are relaxed, while

Pearse (1993a) argues further that log exports could lead to higher and not lower employment. From economic theory, log export restrictions reduce the value of standing timber and lead to inefficiencies in the use of fiber. Thus, log export bans dissipate the available rent. Nondeclining timber harvests, even-flow and requirements to harvest close to AAC are all meant to stabilize employment in the forest sector. However, such restrictions force companies to harvest too much timber and sell too many wood products when prices are low and not enough when prices are high. Again, what is done in the name of economic development and community stability – although such policies do no such thing – leads to a dissipation of forest rents.

There is a further danger that, once firms commit capital or other investments, governments can take opportunistic advantage of these sunk costs. To the extent firms realize this, they will minimize their investments, thereby decreasing timber harvests and available rents.

Changes in environmental standards require significant pollution control expenditures by forest–resource companies, and such expenditures can lead to rent transfer or dissipation. Although increasing the welfare of some in society by requiring pulp mills to reduce drastically certain effluents and eliminate others (an example of rent transfer to beneficiaries of reduced pollution), such restrictions can be economically inefficient in some cases (see Chapter 5), thereby dissipating rent. Less well-known regulations include restrictions that, for a short time in BC, prevented sawmills from burning wastes to generate electricity that could then be sold into the provincial power grid (to prevent electricity prices from falling). The question here is whether the government should permit the increased costs of disposing wastes to be included in the estimation of operating costs (for sawmills). If these costs are not included, this is a rent transfer in the short run from sawmills to the beneficiaries of such a policy. In the long run, if quasi-rent is being captured (appropriating some profits that need to cover the costs of properly disposing of this waste) then capital would exit the sawmill industry. Flight of capital is not so obvious for pulp mills, since the price they pay for their input is largely determined by negotiations with sawmills. Offsetting some of the impact on pulp mills is a fairly generous federal tax code that permits water and air pollution control expenditures to be written off quickly.

Similar issues arise with codes of forest practice that many countries have adopted. To the extent costs are imposed and cannot be recovered fully either through the stumpage or income tax system, rent will be transferred from the forestry sector to others in society.

Finally, timber harvests are usually reduced, and with that the amount of rent captured, when forestland is managed for multiple use. One cost of providing outdoor recreational and preservation benefits is the foregone rents that a government could have captured. This is generally the case in industrial countries, but may be so in developing countries as well. For the latter, however, available rents are often dissipated as a result of unrestricted (perhaps illegal) fuel wood collection, grazing, and fruit and nut gathering by peasants – an example of open access exploitation (see next section).

3.4 PROPERTY RIGHTS AND RESOURCE RENT

Property rights, or their absence, play a central role in natural resource economics and the management of biological assets. The atmosphere is used as a carbon dioxide (CO_2) receptor by every country, and it is difficult to assign property rights to this resource to private individuals or even nations. As a consequence, more CO_2 is released to the atmosphere than is optimal, resulting in over-exploitation. Because property rights to forestlands are unclear, peasants harvest too much fuel wood, and nontimber forest products, resulting in forest degradation. In this section, we present different property regimes and their implications for resource rent. Ill-defined and enforced property rights have played an important role in the demise of African elephant populations, and the degradation of tropical forests in developing countries.

Property rights can be understood as characteristics that define the rights and duties associated with the use of a particular asset or resource. According to Bromley (1999), natural resources are exploited under one of four property regimes.

1. *State property.* The state owns the property but individuals may be allowed to use (exploit) the resource, but only according to the rules imposed by the state or its managing agency.
2. *Private property.* In this case, the private owner has the right to utilize and benefit from the exploitation, conservation or sale of the resource, as long as no (socially unacceptable) externalities are imposed on others. Private ownership does not imply absence of state regulation (control), as private property cannot exist without state sanction and protection.
3. *Common property.* In this case, a group owns and manages the resource, and the group excludes those who are not members. Members of the group have specified rights and duties, while nonmembers must accept exclusion.
4. *No property rights* (*res nullius*). When a property right is not assigned,

open or free access is the result. Under open access, each potential user of the resource has complete autonomy to utilize the resource since none has the legal right to keep another potential user out.

Classification and characteristics of property rights are provided in Table 3.3. In practice, resources are often held in overlapping combinations of these regimes (Feeney et al. 1996), and it is possible to shift from one (dominant) regime to another when conditions change. Failure to enforce or manage properly a state or common property resource (which is frequent) leads to open access (e.g., tropical deforestation, many endangered large-game species). The switch from common and state regimes to open access as a result of population growth is well documented (Murty 1994; Bromley 1999).

Table 3.3: Classification and Characteristics of Property Rights

Type	Characteristics	Implications for economic incentives
Private property	Exclusive rights assigned to individuals	Strong incentives for conservation of resources and for investment as well
State ownership	Rights held in collectivity with control exercised by authority or designated agency	Creating opportunities for attenuation of rights; managers have incentives for personal gains
Communal ownership	Exclusive rights assigned to all members of a community; approaching private property	Creating free-riders problem and low incentives for conservation
Open access	Rights unassigned; lack of exclusivity	Lack of incentives to conserve; often resulting in resource degradation

The absence of property rights (open access) has resulted in excessive depletion of resources and biological assets for the following reason. The cost of exploiting a resource consists of two distinct components: the private extraction costs and the unobserved opportunity cost, or the value of the resource *in situ* – the user cost. The intuition behind user cost in the context of a renewable resource is as follows: harvesting a unit of the resource today means that this unit and the growth (including any offspring) it causes are not available for future consumption. The (future) value of uncaught game or unharvested trees, for example, depends on many different factors, including the discount rate, future markets for the resource, technological developments, reproductive features, and so on. A sole private owner aiming to maximize profits will maximize the discounted value of this rent, and treat the resource as an asset. Hence, the value of unharvested trees prevents a rational logger from "over-logging" a site, but only as long as she expects to be the one to benefit from this "investment". Private property may result in a conservative harvesting policy. In the absence of externalities and given similar discount rates, the same applies for state ownership (Fisher 1981).

An open access resource exists if there is no possibility to exclude firms attracted by excess profits, although their entry will compete away those profits. If there is unrestricted access to the resource, no person can be sure of who will benefit from the value of uncaught game or unharvested trees. In an open access situation, no individual harvester has an economic incentive to conserve the resource, and none can conserve efficiently the resource by delaying harvest. Doing so will only enhance the harvest opportunities of competitors, which is the tragedy of open access. One might say that the individual does not care about escaped game or trees left standing, and discounts future harvests at an infinite rate (Neher 1990). New harvesters will be attracted to the activity, or existing ones will expand their efforts so long as they earn more than the opportunity cost of their effort, cE, where c is the cost of effort E. In *bionomic equilibrium*, all rent is dissipated, and total cost equals total revenue, rather than marginal cost being equal to marginal benefit.[9] The situation where marginal cost exceeds marginal benefit is usually referred to as *economic overexploitation*.

Consider the exploitation of sage grouse (*Centrocercus uropha-sianus*), a threatened species of bird found in dryland regions of western North America (see van Kooten and Eiswerth 2003). In some areas of its range it continues to be hunted. A simple static model of rent dissipation based on constant prices and the conventional yield–effort function reads: $y = qEx$, where y is yield, q is a catchability constant, E is effort (a choice or control variable) and x is *in situ* stock of grouse. This standard model for the economics of nonrenewable resources is illustrated with the aid of Figure 3.8. TR_1 represents total revenues for the base case; its shape is determined directly from the shape of the underlying growth function for the biological asset (sage grouse). TC_1 describes total cost; $TC = cE$, where c is assumed constant. Ignore TC_2 and TR_2 for now.

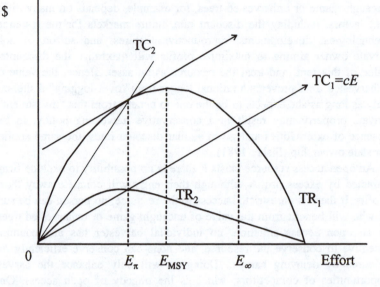

Figure 3.8: Rent dissipation (E_1) and optimal effort (E^*) in a static model of sage grouse exploitation

Rent dissipation occurs at an effort level of E_1 where total revenue equals total cost, i.e.: $\pi(x,E) = (pqx - c)E = 0$, where π is profit. Solving this equation for x to find the stock of grouse associated with overexploitation yields $x_1 = c/pq$. Clearly, effort is excessive and the resource stock is small compared to the two well-known benchmarks: (1) x_{MSY} (or E_{MSY}) corresponding with maximum sustained yield stock and effort, and (2) efficient harvesting where marginal benefit equals marginal cost (E_π) and rent (= π) is maximized – the economic optimum. E_π represents the effort level that maximizes rent if the discount rate is zero. E_π lies to the left of E_{MSY}, so economically efficient effort is less than maximum sustained yield effort. However, whether the stock associated with maximum economic yield (x_{MEY}) is higher or lower than the stock associated with maximum economic yield (x_{MSY}) depends on a number of economic and biological factors, although in general we expect $x_{MSY} > x_{MEY}$ (see Conrad 1999; Tahvonen and Kuuluvainen 2000). Finally, as the discount rate (r) increases, E_π moves to the right (passing E_{MSY} for some value of r) and eventually approaches E_∞ as r goes to infinity. Economic overexploitation occurs to the right of E_π, while E_∞ is the bionomic equilibrium.

When effort is socially excessive, the stock is smaller than is socially optimal; for the current model specification and assuming steady state harvest, effort E is readily translated into stock size x (see Neher 1990). Effort beyond E_{MSY} is referred to as *biological overexploitation*. Depending on the growth function and the specification of the production function, the stock may be driven to extinction under open access. Extinction will occur for positive stock levels as long as x_1 is smaller than the minimum viable population level. For the production function $y = qEx$, the catch per unit of effort, y/E, goes to zero as x approaches zero. With constant prices, rent dissipation will occur before the stock is totally depleted, although depletion of the stock may occur during the approach to equilibrium. If prices rise as the stock is depleted, it may be optimal to drive the stock to extinction.

Common Property

We might well ask whether public resources should be privatized. Because private owners take the value of *in situ* resources into account, the adverse effects of open access can be avoided. If property rights are completely defined and costlessly enforced, privatization of natural resources enhances efficiency; but, in the real world, problems arise (Baland and Platteau 1996). While generally promoting economic efficiency, the actual process of privatization may raise equity concerns. The newly established owner of the resource collects the rents (if any) that had previously been shared among those who exploited the resource under open access.

In addition to the distributional consequences, transaction costs are likely to increase when the property regime is altered. When privatization "hurts" former resource users and the legitimacy of the new property rights regime is questioned, enforcement costs may be considerable. Costs of monitoring and enforcing the new property regime can rise dramatically if former users protest the reallocation of resources. Unless former rights' holders are compensated (which is rare due to budget constraints), any gains in efficiency could be lost due to increased transaction costs.

In addition to transaction costs, privatization may not enhance efficiency if privatization leads to imperfect competition (so that harvests are below the social optimum) or externalities are prevalent. Further, some biological resources, such as migratory waterfowl, cross regional and national boundaries, so owners will have an incentive to take the animals on their territory before they migrate elsewhere, a characteristic associated with open access. In some cases, denying former users access to a resource (because of privatization) increases pressure on resources in other areas that are not privatized. Privatization might also increase uncertainty about conflicting resource claims, because privatization is usually incomplete with many of the conditions for private ownership not clearly defined. This then leads to a breakdown of traditional codes or norms of behavior and aggravating rather than improving management outcomes (Baland and Platteau 1996). For example, the Masai in Kenya have lost access to traditional grazing areas because lands have been confiscated for parks. This has resulted in a breakdown in traditional means of range use, resulting in overgrazing and range depletion of remaining rangelands.

These and other considerations suggest that privatization is not a panacea, but that governments will likely have some role to play in resource management. Some analysts favor management by a group of individuals (common property) over both state and private ownership. For example, in the preface to Baland and Platteau (1996), Mancur Olson argues that, "in view of the absolutely appalling record of most of the national governments of the poorest countries, the potential of the smaller rural communities in these societies cannot be ignored" (p.x). However, while common property can be efficiently managed (so-called regulated common property), it could also exhibit features of open access (unregulated common property) if everyone does not follow common property norms and rules.

Management of unregulated common property can be modeled as a game in which everyone's welfare can be improved by practicing constraint, but it is in no one's interest to do so. Ostrom (1998) refers to this as the social dilemma. The social dilemma paints a pessimistic picture about the potential of (small) groups to manage jointly a resource as individuals fail to do what is in their overall best interests. The result is that common resource stocks are overexploited and public goods are underprovided.

The case for common property is likely strongest in small communities in developing countries. In developed countries, private ownership or state ownership with usufruct rights (e.g., forest tenures) may be better options for allocating natural resources in an efficient manner. In choosing between these two types of ownership, it is likely that each case would have to be decided on its own merits.

State Intervention

The problem of open access, or overexploitation of natural resources, can be addressed via state intervention. A revenue tax will shift the total revenue function in Figure 3.8 from TR_1 to TR_2. In that case, the bionomic or open access equilibrium occurs at E_π, the desired profit-maximizing equilibrium level of effort. Alternatively, a tax can be levied on effort, thereby increasing total costs. In Figure 3.8, an input tax shifts total cost from TC_1 to TC_2 so that marginal cost again equals marginal revenue (based on TR_1) at E_π.

The problems of state intervention in natural resource sectors are well known. In the former Soviet Union, for example, natural resources and the environment were unpriced, leading to severe environmental degradation and overexploitation. In Indonesia, where relatives of an earlier President were given ownership of plywood mills and concessions to state forests, corruption resulted in the overexploitation of forests and inefficient use of fiber. In Brazil, the desire of government to generate foreign exchange, along with policies to reduce population pressures in the Rio de Janeiro and Sao Paulo regions, resulted in the deforestation of large areas of the Amazon (see Chapter 12).

State ownership and state intervention are no guarantee that efficient outcomes with respect to exploitation of natural resources will be realized. In theory, one can demonstrate that state intervention can lead to desirable social outcomes, but in practice the state has not always managed natural resources efficiently and effectively. However, this is not to suggest that private property is a panacea or that the state has no role to play as either a resource owner or regulator. Only that as an owner or regulator, the state needs to be cognizant of, or somehow held accountable for, potential policy failure.

NOTES

1. As indicated below, the intensive margin is important in determining rents in agriculture and forestry, as well as in other resource sectors.
2. Scarcity rent is defined similarly by Howe (1979) in reference to nonrenewable resources: It is the difference between "the user costs of the marginal unit being extracted at any point in time and, under appropriate market conditions, the market value of these marginal *in situ* resources" (p.78).
3. This ignores the fact that Smith might also be earning rent (in terms of Figure 3.1, Jones might represent field A and Smith field B). Hence, this estimate of rent is possibly incomplete.
4. This is an application of the bond formula: $V = \lim_{n \to \infty} \dfrac{A}{(1+i)^n} = \dfrac{A}{i}$, where V is the value of the bond, A is the annual payment that the bond provides, n is the number of periods that this payment is made, and i is the interest rate. Bond value is inversely related to the interest rate. A form of the bond formula is used to determine optimal rotation ages in forestry (see Chapter 11).

5. This definition of the intensive margin is different from that in Figure 3.2, but this is a matter of semantics only. In the forestry case, the intensive margin occurs where further log harvests on a particular site are no longer profitable; in the land-use case, further expansion of the particular land-use activity is no longer profitable if the opportunity cost of a "better" use is taken into account. However, the extensive margins have a similar explanation – it is not profitable to expand the land base further in this activity.

6. One forest company reported that utilization standards reduce the average value of logs by some $17/m^3 in the BC interior.

7. Enhanced stream flow is a benefit in the arid Western US but not in Europe or Nepal where it could lead to flooding.

8. Not including operating costs in calculations of stumpage has supposedly contributed to two high-profile bankruptcies (Grafton et al. 1998). In spring 1998, the government reduced stumpage fees by some $8/m^3 to help forest companies stem losses due to a US countervail duty on lumber and weak Asian markets, followed by further reductions in early 1999.

9. If fixed costs are considered, there exists a "gap" between entry and exit, as harvesters only enter when both variable and fixed costs can be covered, but will not leave the activity until revenues fall short of variable costs.

Part II: A Synopsis of Environmental Economics

4.   Valuing Nonmarket Benefits

Given the inevitability of ongoing environmental and social change, humans need to evaluate decisions regarding environmental development and interactions with natural ecosystems. Several difficult questions are raised. How do we quantify environmental change? How do we assess what proportion of the changes in the environment are caused by human activities as opposed to being the result of inherent natural variability (e.g., as in the case of climate change)? How do we value environmental changes, or changes in the availability of a public good (e.g., changes in species diversity)? How can we value ecosystem resilience, say, when we have an imperfect understanding of how ecosystems function and where thresholds exist? In response to these and many similar questions, the US National Research Council (1996) identified the development of improved social science and risk assessment tools as the top priority in environmental research and development. Specifically, research programs to improve analytical tools for nonmarket valuation and cost–benefit analysis (CBA) were identified as needing immediate attention.

Inclusion of the costs and benefits of changes in the availability of commodities not normally traded in the market place, such as recreational services and clean water, is an important component of CBA. It is also important in land-use planning where multiple uses of land exist and trade-offs need to be made. Such trade-offs can only be properly evaluated if the value of land in each of its uses is considered, and that includes taking into account the values of goods and services not traded in the market place. Nonmarket values are explicitly recognized in social CBA, which is the topic of Chapter 6. In this chapter, methods for estimating nonmarket costs and benefits are examined. The discussion is cursory due to the nature of the topic – there are many methods available and research in this area is prolific.

It is possible to distinguish indirect and direct approaches to obtaining information about nonmarket goods and services, or public goods. The *indirect approach* uses information on goods and services traded in markets to value the public good in question. In some cases (such as the household production function approach to health issues related to environmental quality) it may be possible to derive an *expenditure function* (as in Chapter

2) between market-traded goods and the public good, and from it draw inferences about the demand for the public good or environmental amenity. The indirect approach relies on information derived from market observations to say something about the value of an amenity that is not traded in the market. Alternatively, *choice-based models* employ information about a related activity (as opposed to the environmental good itself) to provide estimates about the values of public goods. Examples of this method include the *travel cost method* for valuing recreational sites and voter behavior (the activity), especially where citizens vote on government budgets that deal directly with expenditures on public goods (referred to as *voter referendum*). This information can be used to say something about the value of the public good in question.

The *direct approach* uses questionnaires or surveys to elicit directly an individual's *willingness-to-pay* (WTP) for more of a public good or her *willingness-to-accept* (WTA) compensation, or compensation demanded, to forgo or have less of the public good. Therefore, it is also referred to as the *income compensation approach*. WTP is often used to measure compensating surplus, while WTA is often used to measure equivalent surplus. Since this approach requires individuals to respond to hypothetical questions in a survey setting, it is also referred to as the *contingent valuation method* (CVM) if actual values are requested, or the contingent behavior method if a behavioral response is desired. Alternative approaches in this genre include contingent ranking, choice experiments (or *stated preferences*), which require respondents to state their preference between situations (much like in marketing surveys), conjoint analysis and other techniques that are briefly discussed in this chapter; see also Smith (1997) and Kriström and Laitila (2003). Our purpose is to introduce the reader to various approaches to measuring nonmarket or extra-market benefits.

4.1 MARKET VALUATION OF PUBLIC GOODS VIA PHYSICAL LINKAGES

There are two ways to observe data about unpriced or nonmarket values – through physical linkages or through behavioral linkages. Estimates of the values of nonmarket commodities can be obtained by determining a physical relationship between the nonmarket commodity and something that can be measured in the market place. One means is to estimate a *damage function*, which provides a physical relation between damage from, say, pollution and emission levels, and relates damages to monetary values. Alternatively, and depending on the situation, one can determine replacement costs for the resources that are lost (Pearce and Warford 1993, pp.125–6). Behavioral linkages, on the other hand, are traced through individual utility functions. These then appear as demands for market goods. By considering the effect upon the demands for related private goods, it may be possible to say something about the value of public goods. Behavioral linkages are considered in section 4.2.

A public good, G, can be an input into production. An example is ozone, with an increase in tropospheric ozone resulting in lower crop yields. An estimate of the benefits of cleaner air is then given by the loss in net returns to farmland, or the loss in value due to reduced crop yields. In the case where a public good is a factor input, the production function becomes $q = f(x_1, ..., x_n, G)$, where $x_1, ..., x_n$ refer to the n factor inputs (e.g., capital, labor and fertilizer) purchased in markets and G is the public good, perhaps clean air or water (Freeman 1979, pp.63–8).

What effect will a change in G have on the production of the good in question? This will depend, in part, on the effect that a change in G has on the output price of q. Suppose that there are constant returns to scale and G does not affect returns to scale. (Constant returns to scale implies a horizontal supply function.) Also assume for the moment that the changes in the output of q are sufficiently large to affect output price, i.e., that the demand for q is downward sloping. An increase in the availability of G only decreases the cost of producing every level of output. An example is water quality; due to government regulations affecting upstream use, the salinity of water available to downstream users may be reduced. Although the costs of producing crops are unaffected, yields will increase because water is less saline.

The supply or marginal cost function is a horizontal line as shown in Figure 4.1. An increase in G reduces marginal cost causing a shift in supply, say from S to S', and reduction in price from p_0 to p_1. All of the gain from the reduction in the price of q accrues to consumers in the form of consumer surplus, given by area A in Figure 4.1. Thus, the demand for the market commodity q provides information about the benefit of an increase in the availability of G.

A second situation is one where an increase in G does *not* affect the price of the final output q and we no longer have constant returns to scale production. For example, a reduction in the salinity of irrigation water in a local region is unlikely to have an impact on crop prices since these are determined in a much larger market. Thus, the demand function for q is a horizontal line as shown in Figure 4.2.

A reduction in the marginal costs of producing q (from MC to MC') resulting from an increase in G will provide no benefits to consumers. All

the benefits, given by area *B* in Figure 4.2, accrue to producers or, rather, to
the owners of the fixed factors of production. Then how does one measure
area *B*?

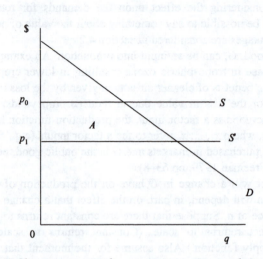

**Figure 4.1: Welfare measure with constant returns to scale in private
market**

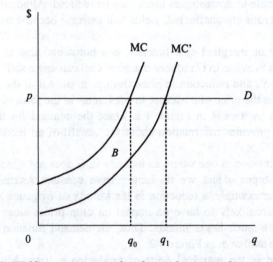

Figure 4.2: Welfare measure with infinite elasticity of output demand

If producers are price takers in output markets, they are likely price takers in input markets as well. Then the benefits of an increase in G accrue to the producers as owners of the fixed factor, land, since the owner of the fixed factor is the residual income claimant. The benefits of an increase in G are simply equal to the change in profits – the increase in rent (see Chapter 3). Since increases in rent are capitalized in land values, changes in the land values of those farmers now using less saline water can be used to measure the benefits of improved water quality. If the production unit is small relative to both input and output markets, then changes in land values are a good indicator of the change in producer benefits. If land values are not a good indicator, because speculation affects land value or firm supply is upward sloping (see next paragraph), then the researcher needs to determine the costs of each factor of production (i.e., rely on farm budget studies) to determine the benefits of improved water quality.

Finally, consider the case where an increase in the availability of G significantly increases the availability of q (local fresh vegetables), thereby shifting supply from S to S' and causing the price of q to fall (in the local market). Then there is both a change in consumer surplus and producer surplus due to the change in G (purer irrigation water). How does one estimate this area in practice? To obtain an estimate of the change in consumer surplus, it is necessary to estimate the ordinary demand function and calculate the appropriate area under it. The producer surplus needs to be determined using farm budget studies. It is measured by the change in the net income of factor inputs.

If government agricultural policies support crop prices, then actual or market prices overstate social benefits. Again, farm budget studies are required to determine the extent of producer benefits. Assuming that other crop prices are competitively determined (likely a heroic assumption), consumer benefits can be calculated in the same manner as above, but it will be necessary to include in the calculations the government support payments themselves as a cost to taxpayers. In all cases, it is worthwhile recalling the concept of *opportunity cost* and using it as a guide in calculating the benefits and costs of changes in the availability of a public good.

The above approaches are difficult to apply in practice. One means of doing so is through the damage function. Several studies have estimated damage functions for soil erosion for the Palouse region of eastern Washington and western Idaho, and for Saskatchewan (Walker and Young 1986; van Kooten et al. 1989). The physical component of the damage function provides information about the estimated yield loss when topsoil is removed, with topsoil loss related to particular agronomic practices. Given a physical relationship, it is possible to assess the value of topsoil, a commodity not traded in the market place, using information about crop yields, production costs and crop prices. It turns out that estimated damage functions for Saskatchewan and the Palouse region have steep slopes (high marginal damages) when topsoil depth is low, but slopes near zero (low to zero marginal damage) at topsoil depths that characterize most farms in the two regions. Damage from soil erosion in these regions is correspondingly small.

In Mali, a similar approach to that used in the Canadian and US studies was used to estimate a relationship between yield and soil loss. In contrast to the North American studies, costs of soil erosion in Mali were estimated to be significant, as high as 1.5% of GDP (Pearce and Warford 1993, pp.23–4).

Damages from deforestation have also been valued in indirect fashion. Deforestation reduces the availability of wood for burning in some regions, with animal dung being used instead. The animal dung, in turn, is no longer available as a fertilizer in crop production, thereby reducing agricultural output. Since dung is bought and sold on markets, it can readily be valued. Using dung values, the costs of deforestation in Ethiopia are estimated to be some US$300 million annually (Pearce and Warford 1993, p.25).

4.2 MARKET VALUATION OF PUBLIC GOODS VIA BEHAVIORAL LINKAGES

Behavioral linkages are more common than physical linkages, but they require a behavioral response to changes in the nonmarket commodity, and this response must somehow be measured. If there is no response to marginal changes in water quality, for example, then it is not possible to determine its value, even if it has value on average. Market valuation of public goods via behavioral linkages assumes that an individual's utility function includes the public good (G) as an argument: $U = U(q_1, q_2, ..., q_n, G)$, where q_i ($i = 1, ..., n$) represents goods that are traded in the market place.[1] As indicated in section 2.3, the inverse compensated demand function can be used to determine the compensating surplus benefit measure of a change in a public good (Figure 2.9), the total benefit to an individual of an increase in the supply of the public good G. Particularly, the appropriate area under the inverse compensated demand function represents the compensating surplus benefit measure of a change in a public good (Figure 2.9). This benefit is either the compensating or equivalent surplus of the change in the supply of the public good depending on whether the person has the right to the original or final level of the public good, respectively.

The tasks we are engaged in amount to detective work – we are attempting to measure the value of a change in the availability of a public good that is not traded in the market place using market data for related or affected goods and services. Of course, there are problems associated with investigations of this kind. The problems that are encountered in this particular piece of detective work concern the method by which the public good G enters the utility function. Several cases are discussed.

Separability

It is possible to partition goods in the utility function according to their "closeness". Suppose that there are six goods in the utility function and they are partitioned as $U(q_1, q_2, q_3, q_4, q_5, q_6) = \phi[u^1(q_1, q_2), u^2(q_3, q_4), u^3(q_5, q_6)]$ where ϕ refers to the overall utility function. A good q_1 is weakly separable in the utility function if changes in its availability affect only purchases of q_2, but not of q_3, q_4, q_5 and q_6. That is, a utility function is weakly separable if the marginal rate of substitution (MRS) between any pair of goods in the same group is independent of the availability of goods outside of that group (Freeman 1993, p.101). The demand for q_1 (or q_2) is a function only of p_1 and p_2, and the expenditure share of that subset of goods. However, the MRS across two *subsets* of goods, say MRS(q_2, q_3), is not necessarily independent of the availability of goods in the third subset, say q_5. More generally, a utility function that is weakly separable in the public good G can be written as $U(q_i, q_j, G) = \phi[u^1(q_i, q_j), u^2(G)]$, for $i \neq j$, $i, j = 1,...,n$, where q_i and q_j refer to market goods (of which there are n). Weak separability implies that residual traces of changes in G might be found in the demands for the market goods.

Alternatively, for the case of six goods considered above, the utility function is strongly separable if it is written as $\phi[u^1(q_1, q_2) + u^2(q_3, q_4) + u^3(q_5, q_6)]$. In this case, the MRS across two subsets of goods, say MRS(q_2, q_3), is independent of the availability of goods in the third subset, say q_5. If G is strongly separable in the individual's utility function, so that utility is written as $\phi[u(q_i, q_j) + v(G)]$, $\forall i \neq j$, $i,j = 1,...,n$, then purchases of other goods are unaffected by changes in the availability of G. Thus, while changes in the provision of the public good affect the level of utility, it is impossible to find a record of this impact in the market place.

Complements

Perfect complementarity between a market good and an environmental good implies that they must be consumed in fixed proportions, say $q_1/G = k$, with consumption of q_1 equal to $\min(q_1/k, G)$. Then the amount of the market good consumed will be determined solely by the availability of the public good, but only as long as p_1 is below some critical value, say p_1^*. As G increases, purchases of q_1 will also increase because the individual will thereby increase her utility, and marginal WTP for G is positive. However, if the price of the market good is above p_1^*, the individual purchases less q_1 than required to utilize fully the available amount of the public good and the marginal WTP for it is zero. This happens, for example, when area available for recreation exceeds the ability of recreation users to utilize the area – there is always recreation area that is underutilized. However, examples of perfect complementarity between an environmental amenity and a market good are difficult to envision (Freeman 1993, pp.103–4).

Suppose, instead, that there is weak complementarity between the market commodity q and the public good G, so that the utility from consuming q increases with increases in the availability of G, *ceteris paribus*. For example, there is complementarity between water quality and demand for water recreation. If the demand for q (water recreation) is zero, the marginal utility of G (water quality) is zero (assuming that water recreation is the only private good that depends on water quality and water quality does not give utility by itself). For welfare measurement, an increase in the availability of the public good must cause an outward shift in the demand function of the complementary good q. Then, under some restrictive conditions, the area above market price and between the new and old demand curves for q_i serves as an estimate of the benefit of increasing G. Without weak complementarity, there would be nothing to measure.

Consider Figure 4.3, where p^0 is the price of angling (q) that is a weak complement of the public good water quality G. Also assume that there is associated with some threshold level of water quality G^*, a choke price for angling, p^*, above which there will be no demand for the fishing activity. In other words, the compensating demand for q (angling) has a vertical intercept at some price: $h(p^*, G, U) = 0$. It is assumed, therefore, that there is some level of expenditure on other goods and services that sustains utility at the level indicated when $q = 0$.

Suppose that there is an increase in water quality from G_0 to G_1. This shifts the compensated demand functions for angling from $h(G_0)$ to $h(G_1)$. Calculation of the benefit associated with this measure is divided into three stages (Freeman 1993, pp.106–8). First, the price of angling increases from p^0 to p^*, and demand falls from q^0 to zero and the individual loses all surplus *A*, but is compensated for this loss. Second, the improvement in water quality causes an outward shift in demand for angling, as indicated, but there is no gain in utility because q is priced at the choke price $p*$. Finally, the reduction in price from $p*$ to p^0 results in a gain given by area *A* + *B* as consumption increases from zero to q^1. The net gain is given by area *B*, since the fisher was compensated *A* in the first step. This is the compensating or equivalent variation measure of welfare depending on the reference level of utility for the compensated demand functions.

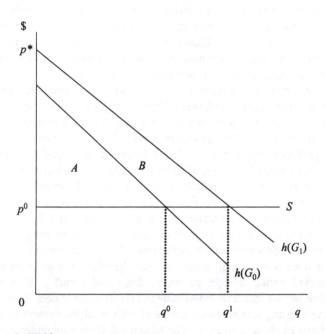

Figure 4.3: Welfare measurement in private market under weak complementarity

There remains a problem relating the compensated demand curves back to something that can be estimated. If the ordinary demand curves are used to determine the welfare estimate, Freeman (1993, pp.110–1) shows that the error of measurement can be positive, negative or zero – the errors are of unknown sign and magnitude. However, exact welfare measurements can be used that permit one to recover the compensating demands from market demands.

Substitutes

In the case of substitutes, welfare measurement often relies on knowledge of the underlying utility function. This is because the marginal WTP for the environmental amenity (w_G) can be expressed in terms of the price of a relevant market good multiplied by the MRS between it and the environmental amenity (Freeman 1993, p.113): $w_G = p_i \, \mathrm{MRS}(G, q_i)$. It is only in the case of perfect substitutes that it is possible to reduce w_G to something measurable. Expenditures on private goods that substitute for the environmental amenity (e.g., in-house water filtration systems, bottled water) are examples of *defense expenditures* or *averting expenditures*. The degree to which such expenditures are truly representative of the benefits of improving water quality depends, of course, on the degree of substitutability between, say, purchased goods and municipal water quality.

Averting measures related to drinking water, for example, are easily defined by consumers' purchases of bottled water or home water filtration systems. In effect the consumer is combining market purchases (in-house water filtration) with the available level of the environmental amenity (water quality) to produce the preferred degree of water quality. Essentially, they produce a good $z = f(G, q)$, where $f(\cdot)$ can be considered a household production function. Determination of the household expenditure function usually comprises two steps: first to see whether action is being taken to avoid contaminants in the water (e.g., bottled water, water filters, boiling), and second to measure the amount of money spent on averting action. The problem is an econometric or statistical one. In the first step, a binary ("yes" a person does take averting action, or "no" they do not) regression equation is estimated (using a logit or probit functional form) – it is used to determine factors that lead individuals to take averting action. A probability of taking averting action is estimated and used to adjust observed defensive expenditors by those who avert. The adjusted defense expenditures can then be employed as a measure of the potential benefits of public policies that change the availability or quality of the environmental amenity.

A marginal change in spending on the household good z is an appropriate measure of welfare change associated with marginal changes in G. This is not the case, however, if improvements in the environmental amenity are nonmarginal, or large enough to affect prices of goods and services in other markets. As environmental quality improves, people will reduce spending on q to produce z. If the change is large enough, there will be an income effect associated with reduced spending on q, thereby increasing purchases of q for other reasons. For example, in the case of bottled water, people may purchase bottled water because they acquire a preference for the convenience and fresher taste of bottled water, and not because they seek to avoid a real or perceived externality. In other words, first bottled water was bought for health reasons. When water quality improved, the income effect resulted in greater demand for bottled water for nonhealth reasons.

Finally, even if it is not possible to derive appropriate welfare measures based on averting behavior (especially in the case where substitutability is not perfect), defense expenditures do provide some guidance. As a check, if an individual's defense expenditures exceed their stated value for improvements in environmental quality, say, then the stated value is not reliable. We discuss elicitation of stated values below. But first we consider the use of property values as a means of valuing nonmarket amenities.

Property Values, Benefit Estimation and Hedonic Pricing

A particular example of nonmarket measurement using market transactions for other goods is the hedonic pricing method that studies property values. Hedonic pricing assumes that environmental characteristics and public goods affect the productivity of land in production or its desirability in consumption. The structure of land prices and rents reflects these environmentally determined productivity/desirability differences. The best example of individuals choosing the amount of public goods they want occurs with respect to the choices they make concerning house purchases. People choose to live in areas that have cleaner air or less crime, they choose to live near airports or along highways, and they choose to live on quiet or on busy streets. The choice is determined by what they are willing and able to pay for housing. Hedonic pricing exploits these choices by estimating implicit prices for house characteristics that differentiate closely related housing classes. In this way, it is possible to estimate demand curves for such characteristics or public goods as air quality and noise. Thus, the hedonic pricing technique requires that the following three methodological questions are answered in the affirmative:

1. Do environmental variables systematically affect land prices?
2. Is knowledge of this relationship sufficient to predict changes in land prices from changes in air pollution levels, say?
3. Do changes in land prices accurately measure the underlying welfare changes?

If any of these is not answered in the affirmative, the methodology cannot be applied.

Hedonic pricing is a two-stage procedure (Freeman 1979, 1995). Begin by letting Q be a composite consumption good (with price equal 1), C a vector of housing characteristics, N a vector of neighborhood characteristics, and G a vector of environmental amenities. For example, C includes such things as size of lot, number of rooms, age of house, number of bathrooms and livable floor space; N measures proximity to a fire station, nearness to shopping, distance to the city center, zoning characteristics of the neighborhood, and so on; and G constitutes such things as the crime rate, air quality and noise. The public goods must differ among neighborhoods (or houses) and must somehow be measurable; for example, air quality and the neighborhood crime rate can be measured, as can distance to the nearest fire hall and/or fire hydrant. It is assumed that the urban area as a whole can be treated as a single market for housing services and that people choose to purchase a housing bundle that best satisfies their utility over these characteristics, subject to their budget, m. Hence, they are assumed to have information on all the alternatives and are able to buy anywhere in the urban area (subject to their budget). The supply of housing and its characteristics is not modeled, so housing prices are assumed to be in equilibrium.

The price of the ith house, P_i, is a function of its various characteristics and amenities:

$$(4.1) \quad P_i = P(C_i, N_i, G_i).$$

Relation (4.1) is often referred to as the *hedonic or implicit price function* and is obtained by regression. The implicit price of a private characteristic of housing in the region of concern is found by partial differentiating the hedonic price function with respect to that characteristic. If c_1 is the number of rooms in a house, then $\partial P/\partial c_1$ is the implicit price of a room. This is the amount that an additional room will add to the value of a house, *ceteris paribus*. It is the additional amount that must be paid if an individual chooses a house with a higher level of c_1.

The utility of the household living in house i is given by $u(Q, G_i, C_i, N_i)$. It is assumed that preferences are weakly separable in housing and its characteristics so that the demands for housing characteristics are independent of the prices of other goods. The budget constraint for a household that occupies the ith house is $m - P_i - Q = 0$. Then it can be shown that:

$$(4.2) \quad b_j = \frac{\partial P_i}{\partial g_j},$$

where b_j is the WTP for an additional unit of the environmental amenity g_j.[2] Condition (4.2) says that a house buyer will purchase additional amounts of each amenity as long as the WTP for those amenities is greater than the cost of purchasing them. In equilibrium, the marginal WTP for an additional unit of the environmental amenity just equals the marginal implicit price of that amenity.

The above analysis results in a measure of the marginal WTP for (shadow price of) the environmental amenity g_j, but it does not directly reveal the marginal willingness-to-pay function. To find the marginal WTP or bid function, a second step is required.

In the second stage, it is assumed that the individual purchases only <u>one</u> housing bundle (or, if more, that they are equivalent). The individual stays at some level of utility with the utility function being weakly separable in housing so that prices of other goods can be omitted in the specification of the marginal willingness-to-pay or bid function. The bid function for environmental amenity g_j by the individual who chooses the ith house is:

$$(4.3) \qquad b_j = b_j(g_j, G^*, C, N, u^*),$$

where the i subscript is dropped for convenience, G^* is a vector of environmental amenities excluding g_j, and u^* is the reference level of utility. Equation (4.3) is also obtained by regression. Note that, if P_i in (4.1) is linear in g_j, then, from (4.2), the implicit price of an increase in the environmental amenity would be the same regardless of its current availability – the marginal value of air quality, say, does not change according to the level of air quality. When estimating equation (4.3), it is necessary (for estimation purposes) that the value on the LHS of (4.3) is variable, which is only true if (4.1) is nonlinear in g_j. Presumably, the value of an additional unit of clean air is worth more when air quality is poor than when it is good.

When there is a change in amenity g_j from g_j^0 to g_j^1, *ceteris paribus*, the change in the welfare of the individual who chooses the ith house is determined as the area under function (4.3) between g_j^0 and g_j^1. Aggregate welfare is the sum of all of these individual changes in wellbeing, which is found simply by multiplying the change in the wellbeing of the individual by the total number of people. A problem is that a change in one characteristic can change the quantities of the other characteristics a person desires and can even change the hedonic price function itself. This makes it difficult, in practice, to estimate (4.3) – it is difficult to separate the effects of demand shifters (such as income, air quality, individual tastes) from the price–quantity relationship itself. But this is a technical obstacle, not a theoretical one, and can often be overcome with sophisticated quantitative techniques (see Smith 1997 and the references therein).

Empirical studies that have used the hedonic pricing method to determine the effect of aircraft and traffic noise on housing prices find that there is a measurable effect. For aircraft noise, a one-unit change in the measure of noise (as related to human hearing and discomfort) resulted in housing prices that were 0.5–2.0% lower, while traffic noise reduced house prices by 0.1–0.7% per decibel (Lesser et al. 1997, p.281).

4.3 RECREATION DEMAND AND THE TRAVEL COST METHOD

To assess benefits from recreation, the travel cost method emerged as perhaps the first technique for valuing nonmarket benefits (Clawson 1959; Thrice and Wood 1958). The travel cost method is a type of revealed preference model where

1. individuals are observed to incur costs so as to consume commodities related to the environmental amenity of interest, and
2. the commodities consumed are not purchased in a market where prices are determined by supply and demand.

A number of different approaches are available for estimating welfare gains/losses in what is generally termed the "travel cost" framework, and some are examined in this section.[3] How does the approach work in principle? Consider the following example. Suppose one wished to value a park located at a particular site. One would approach the individuals using the park and ask them, among other things, where they came from. In this example, the park's users are divided into three zones according to distance traveled and comparable travel costs. The travel costs from each zone, the annual number of visitors, and the total population in each zone are determined in Table 4.1. The cost of travel from a zone is easy to determine – it is a function of distance and cost per unit distance traveled – and could include costs associated with traveling time.

Table 4.1: Travel Zones, Travel Costs, and Visitors to Hypothetical Park

(1)	(2)	(3)	(4)	(5)
	Travel	Number of		Visits per 1,000
Zone	cost/visit	visitors	Population	population
1	$1	1,800	3,000	600
2	$2	2,400	6,000	400
3	$3	2,000	10,000	200

A "demand" relationship is established by plotting column (2) in Table

4.1 against column (5), as is shown in Figure 4.4, but this is not a true demand function.[4] How do we derive the demand curve for the park? Assume that the travel cost serves as a surrogate for an admission charge. If the entry fee is $1, then people from zone 1 will incur costs of $2 rather than $1. From Figure 4.4, we find that only 400 individuals per 1,000 people in the population will visit the park if they incur travel plus entry costs of $2. Hence, only 1,200 individuals from zone 1 will visit the park if there is an admission charge of $1. The results for all zones and admission charges are provided in Table 4.2. Plotting the entry charge against the totals provided in the last row of Table 4.2 gives the demand relation for the hypothetical park, as is drawn in Figure 4.5. In the absence of an entry fee, the total area under this demand curve constitutes the benefit to that particular recreational site.

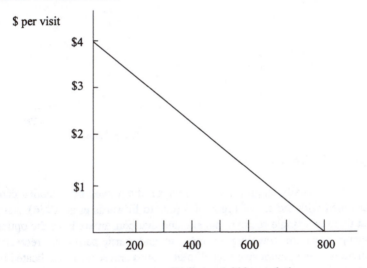

Figure 4.4: Visitor relationship for hypothetical park

Table 4.2: Impact of an Entry Charge on Visitation to Hypothetical Park

| Zone | Entrance charge | | | |
	$0	$1	$2	$3
1	1,800	1,200	600	0
2	2,400	1,200	0	0
3	2,000	0	0	0
Total	6,200	2,400	600	0

The criticism of the travel cost method as presented above is that the demand curve that is derived is not a true demand function after all; it is simply a statistical demand relationship and cannot be used to make welfare judgments. The reason is that it is not based on a well-developed and meaningful theory of consumer demand – utility maximization.

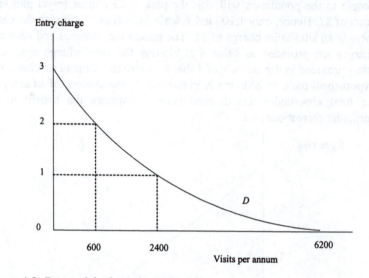

Figure 4.5: Demand for hypothetical park

A theoretically appropriate version of the travel cost model can be illustrated with the aid of Figure 4.6 (due to Edwards et al. 1976). Assume that there is a single recreational site and that consumers have the option of staying home or traveling to the site and participating in recreational activities. The amount spent on all other goods and services (indicated by $) is plotted on the vertical axis and the number of days spent at the site (d) is plotted on the horizontal axis. Since recreation is not a necessity, in the sense that individuals can live without it, the indifference curves do not intersect the horizontal axis; however, they do intersect the vertical axis since some amount of one's budget must be spent on "all-goods-other-than-recreation" to survive.

Now assume that the individual starts with some initial income m_0 (equal to an equivalent amount of goods whose price is 1). Further, suppose that the cost of getting to the site (the travel cost) is k_0, and the entry fee or price of q is initially P_0. If recreation is to take place, the budget line begins at the point labeled $m_0–k_0$ because this is the amount of budget available for recreation at the site once one takes into account the cost of getting to the site. Given that the indifference curve through m_0 (U_0) is tangent to the budget line with slope determined by P_0, the person is indifferent between staying home and going to the site and staying for d^* days. If the entrance fee to the park is greater than P_0, this person will stop visiting the site altogether. That is, for prices less than P_0, the individual will participate in recreation, but not for prices above this critical value. Thus, d^*, k_0 and P_0 are critical values for the given budget, travel cost and entry fee – the individual will either participate in recreation for d^* or more days, or not at all.

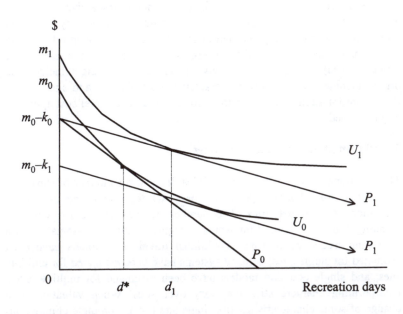

Figure 4.6: Constructing a theoretical recreation demand model

Now, if the entry price were reduced to P_1 ($< P_0$), the individual would take d_1 days of recreation at the site, enabling her to get on an indifference curve (U_1) that is higher than that going through m_0. The equivalent amount of income to this level of utility is given by m_1. From equation (2.19) in Chapter 2 and Figure 4.6, the compensating variation of a decrease in the entry price (from P_0 to P_1) is given by k_1-k_0.

Finally, the travel cost itself influences decisions. At a price of P_0, an increase in the travel cost to k_1 will prevent the person from going to the site for recreation. If the entry fee were subsequently reduced to P_1, then the individual can still attain U_0, but she remains indifferent to staying home or visiting the site.

It is clear that the graphical analysis in Figure 4.6 can be used to derive a demand curve such as $R = d(P, k, m)$, which differs from the demand curve $R = t(P', m)$, where P' refers to travel costs plus entry fee. In this case, not only does income shift the demand function, but so does the travel cost. The point is that the approach discussed with reference to Figure 4.6 can be used to formulate a demand function that can be empirically estimated: demand is a function of entrance fees, consumer income and travel cost. In principle, data can be collected on each of these variables. Furthermore, the model provides theoretically sound estimates of wellbeing.

In cases where it is not possible for the economic researcher to conduct her own travel cost survey, it may be possible to employ available information from parks, government agencies, and so on. Such information may consist simply of number of visitors to a site (or to a number of different sites), along with a variety of variables that might include the origin, income level and other characteristics of visitors, and site-specific data. If information on distance traveled is available, a travel cost approach might be used.

Travel Cost Model with Site Attributes

The traditional travel cost model explains demand for number of trips over a specified time horizon (a season or year) for either one or several recreation sites or activities. The number of trips is decided within a planning horizon where diminishing marginal utility is associated with increasing frequency of trips. Traditional travel cost models have been estimated for single sites; demand systems have been estimated for multiple sites; and single equation models have been estimated for multiple sites, incorporating characteristics that vary over sites. When valuation of a change of some characteristics at a single site (or its complete elimination) is required, a single-site demand curve can be used. However, behavioral models need to capture substitution among recreational sites if environmental quality changes are to be valued; variation in quality can often be found only by looking across sites with varying quality dimensions. Originally, recreation demand models were used to value sites and to predict how changes in travel costs and entry fees would affect demand. Now, however, they are used to assess the welfare effects (benefits or costs) of changes in environmental amenities or the quality characteristics of the recreational experience. Therefore, we wish to look at models that explicitly incorporate site attributes.

Hedonic Travel Cost

The hedonic pricing method can also be applied to recreation demand estimation, but the problems involved are complex. Simply, total household expenditures on recreation at a particular site take on the role of property value in the hedonic or implicit price function. Expenditures by a large number of households engaged in recreation at more than one site are regressed on a variety of private and public characteristics of the various sites. Again, by partial differentiating the hedonic price function with respect to any of the public attributes, an implicit price for that attribute is obtained. In the second stage, the implicit prices for the attribute are regressed on household characteristics, particularly income, and the amount of the attribute available, howsoever measured. The resulting equation is the demand function for the attribute. The area under the demand function can then be used to measure the benefit of a change in the amount of the public good. In practice, it is not easy to implement hedonic travel cost methods.

The hedonic travel cost method seeks to identify the demand for the various amenities associated with the physical attributes of recreational sites, and thereby the benefits of changes in site attributes. In this respect it is similar to the hedonic price method described in conjunction with the value of housing. However, the hedonic travel cost method is more closely aligned with the travel cost approach described above. Indeed, it is possible to derive the benefits of a change in attributes using the travel cost approach, but this requires that one estimate the demand for a site before and after the change in attributes occurs (Wilman 1988). Welfare measurement is illustrated with the aid of Figure 4.7.

In Figure 4.7, the curves labeled $V(P; z)$ represent the demand for recreation visits as a function of travel costs P (where P includes travel cost, time and entry fees) and site attributes z (e.g., number of wildlife species observed). Attributes shift the demand function; thus, the demand for visits when site attributes are z_2 lies outside the demand when attributes are z_1, and likewise for z_3. Suppose there are two sites that the recreationist might wish to visit. Site 1 has a travel cost of P_1, while site 2 has a travel cost of P_2. The demand functions for the two sites differ according to the level of physical attributes available at each site; suppose the demand functions are $V(P; z_1)$ and $V(P; z_2)$ at sites 1 and 2, respectively. Then the net benefits of recreation at site 1 are given by area ABP_1, while the net benefits of choosing site 2 are given by area XYP_2. If site 1 is chosen over site 2, then area ABP_1 must be greater than area XYP_2.

Now suppose that the attributes at site 1 change (e.g., some bird species are now observed at the site) so that the demand curve associated with site 1 is no longer $V(P; z_1)$ but $V(P; z_2)$, which for ease of presentation is assumed identical to that for site 2. Since site 1 was chosen previously, it will be chosen again. The net benefit of the improvement in attributes at site 1 is given by area $(XCP_1 - ABP_1)$ = area $AXCB$. If, on the other hand, attributes at site 2 were to change from z_2 to z_3, so that the new demand function is $V(P; z_3)$, then the benefit of such a change will depend upon whether the recreationist shifts away from site 1 or not. If site 1 continues to be the preferred site, the benefits of the improvements at site 2 are essentially zero. If site 2 is now chosen over site 1, the measure of benefits is given by area MNP_2 minus area ABP_1.

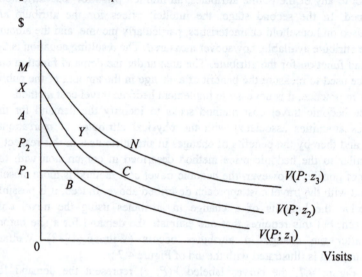

Figure 4.7: Valuing recreation site attributes

While the travel cost method is based on a marginal utility condition describing the number of visits to a site, the hedonic travel cost technique is based on a marginal utility condition describing the choice of site quality and, implicitly, the actual site itself. The travel cost method requires observations on a wide range of recreationists who have come various travel distances in order to be able to identify the demand curve for trips. With regard to the demand for attributes, the travel cost method works best if site choice remains fixed as the visit level changes.

The hedonic travel cost procedure works best when the visit level remains fixed as the site choice changes. The hedonic method seeks to measure the demand for site characteristics or attributes directly. It requires only that the sample of users be spread around at various sites within a recreational area (e.g., national park or forest area) so that they face various costs of using a particular site. These costs vary due not only to travel distances, but also to the physical attributes of the sites (e.g., number of camping sites, whether there is hot water, whether there are fire pits, etc.). In this way, a demand function for site attributes can be identified.

While the theoretical model upon which the travel cost method is based does not really permit visits to more than one site, it can easily be modified in practice to allow for the use of several sites (Johansson 1987, 1991). The same is not true of the hedonic price approach. It requires that individuals select only one site out of the ones that are available.

4.4 THE CONTINGENT VALUATION METHOD

It is generally thought that the methods described above, such as the travel cost and hedonic pricing methods, provide reasonable estimates of true values because they rely on market data. Yet, there remain basic difficulties with these methods (Sagoff 1994; Randall 1994; Knetsch 2000). Further, they can be used to estimate use values only. Use values refer to the values individuals place on the unpriced benefits that accrue to society as inputs into production or consumption. For instance, a forest provides ecosystem functions such as water storage, water cleansing and waste assimilation, as well as recreational and other "consumptive" use benefits. A further distinction is sometimes made between consumptive and nonconsumptive uses, where the former occurs when an environmental good is physically reduced, as with hunting or fishing (and restoration may, but need not, be possible), while the latter refers to the situation where the environmental good is not physically reduced, as with wildlife viewing. A special case of nonconsumptive use values relates to services indirectly provided through books, films, etc. However, this distinction can be confusing, so we only distinguish between use and non-use values.

Non-use (also referred to as passive-use) values include existence values independent of any behavior related to current use, as well as bequest, option, altruism and other inherent values. Existence value is the value of simply knowing that an environmental asset exists – people express a willingness to pay simply for the knowledge that the asset exists. Bequest value refers to people's WTP to endow the future generation with the asset, while altruism refers to the benefit that a person places on the benefit another person gets from the environmental asset. Option value, on the other hand, is a measure of people's risk aversion to factors that might affect future access to or use of environmental or biological assets (see

Carson et al. 1997).

In this section, we focus on the contingent valuation method (CVM) as a particular method for valuing non-use benefits – the benefits derived from individuals' demands to preserve forestlands and biodiversity, say. While non-use values are generally estimated using the traditional contingent valuation method, other methods have been proposed (e.g., conjoint analysis, choice experiments, fuzzy contingent valuation). Some of these are discussed in section 4.4. CVM attempts explicitly to elicit (via surveys) information concerning the minimum level of compensation required by an individual to forgo a public good (compensation demanded) or the maximum amount the individual would be willing to pay to obtain the nonmarket amenity. Because a survey is used, this approach is often referred to as the direct approach in contrast to the indirect approach of determining the value of nonmarket commodities from information about market transactions for other, related goods and services. It should be noted that, while used to determine non-use values, CVM can also be employed to value goods traded in markets, which is useful for testing how well responses to hypothetical purchasing questions correspond to actual ones (Harrison 1989; Kahneman and Knetsch 1992a; Knetsch 1995, 2000).

Contingent valuation devices involve asking individuals, in survey or experimental settings, to reveal their personal valuations of increments (or decrements) in unpriced goods by using contingent markets. These markets define the good or amenity of interest, the *status quo* level of provision and the offered increment or decrement therein, the institutional structure under which the good is to be provided, the method of payment, and (implicitly or explicitly) the decision rule which determines whether to implement the offered program. Contingent markets are highly structured to confront respondents with a well-defined situation and to elicit a circumstantial choice upon the occurrence of the posited situation. Contingent markets elicit contingent choices (Cummings et al. 1986, p.3).

The contingent valuation method is needed when amenities to be valued are assumed to leave no behavioral trail for economists to employ. This assumption has been questioned by Larson (1993), who argues that purchases of nature books, watching nature films, memberships in nature organizations, and so on constitute a behavioral trail that can be used for valuation. However, his interpretation requires untestable assumptions that restrict individual preferences (Bockstael and McConnell 1993).

An important use of contingent valuation surveys is to determine preservation values for such things as tropical rain forests (Kramer and Mercer 1997). Preservation value includes option value in addition to existence and bequest values. Preservation values can be substantial. For example, Kramer and Mercer found that US residents were willing to make a one-time payment of $1.9–$2.8 billion (assuming 91 million households) to protect an additional 5% of tropical forests. Preservation benefits for wildlife were estimated by Canadian economists to be in the neighborhood of $68 million per year for Alberta residents (Phillips et al. 1989), while preservation of old-growth forests is valued at perhaps $150 per household per year (van Kooten 1995b). This evidence suggests that ignoring preservation values in the management of natural resources could lead to substantial misallocation of these resources.

CVM has been approved by the US Department of the Interior for implementing regulations under the Comprehensive Environmental Response, Compensation, and Liability Act (CERCLA) of 1980 and its amendments of 1986. In 1990, the US Oil Pollution Act extended liability to oil spills (as oil was not considered a hazardous waste). A 1989 decision by the District of Columbia Court of Appeals involving CERCLA in the case of *Ohio v. Department of Interior* affirmed the use of CVM and permitted inclusion of non-use values in the assessment of total compensable damages (Castle et al. 1994). Thus, in the USA, CVM is used both for determining compensation when firms or individuals damage the environment and in cost–benefit analysis. Similar requirements for use of CVM in Canada and other countries do not exist, at least officially. Presumably this explains why economists in the USA have devoted more attention to CVM than economists in Europe and Canada (see Bateman and Willis 1999).

As noted, the contingent valuation method uses questionnaires or surveys to elicit directly how much individuals are willing to pay for an increase in the availability of a public good or how much they would demand in compensation to forgo the increase. The individual responses to the survey are then used to obtain a median or mean household value for the unpriced or nonmarket commodity. The contingent valuation method has been criticized because it requires an individual to respond to hypothetical situations. As a result, various types of bias may occur and these biases can only be removed through proper design of the contingent device and proper training of those responsible for gathering the required data. In the following subsections, we briefly discuss these issues (Bishop et al. 1995; Mitchell and Carson 1989; Cummings et al. 1986).

In the remainder of this section, we first consider the underlying theoretical and empirical foundations of the contingent valuation method. Then problems associated with contingent valuation surveys are presented. Since some argue that the contingent valuation method is fundamentally flawed, we consider some of the fundamental objections to the CVM approach. An alternative approach for obtaining benefit estimates using a survey device is discussed in section 4.4.

Welfare Measurement using CVM: Theory

The contingent valuation method uses surveys to elicit either WTP for a hypothetical change in the availability of an environmental amenity, such as improved water quality, or willingness-to-accept (WTA) compensation, or compensation demanded, to forgo the change. The maximum amount a consumer is willing to pay for improved water quality is a measure of compensating surplus (CS), while minimum WTA is a measure of equivalent surplus (ES) (see Chapter 2). Whether CS or ES is elicited depends on whether, in the contingency, the respondent has the right to the change (ES), or not (CS), and must pay for it. The two most widely used methods for eliciting WTP or WTA are the open-ended and dichotomous choice (DC) approaches. Kealy and Turner (1993) recognized that, if contingent values are sensitive to question format, the validity of either one or both of the methods is questionable. The two approaches assume different things about the respondent's knowledge of her utility function.

Open-ended model
Until the paper by Bishop and Heberlein (1979), the standard approach to eliciting information about non-use values in a CVM framework was to employ an open-ended format. Because no values are suggested to respondents (all values are possible), this is also called the continuous value approach. After providing the necessary information about the contingency to be valued (Mitchell and Carson 1989, 1995), the researcher would simply ask questions of the following types: "What is the maximum amount that you would be willing to pay in an increased water bill to improve water quality from 12mg nitrates per liter to 6mg nitrates per liter?" "What is the maximum amount you are willing to pay in increased income taxes for a program [described in detail in the survey] that will increase by 500 the number of grizzly bears in Alaska?" The target nitrate level or number of bears to be preserved can be varied across respondents, but often is not. The first question could be modified so that it asks about minimum compensation demanded to forgo an improvement in water quality. The second question could be modified in similar fashion. The answers to the open-ended question are then summed and divided by the number of respondents to obtain an average value of WTP or WTA for a household.[5] Assuming that the characteristics of households in the sample are similar to those in the population (which can be tested), an estimate of total WTP (value of the contingency) is obtained by multiplying average sample WTP by the total number of households in the target population.

Alternatively, one can estimate a bid curve,

(4.4) $W = f(g, m, s)$,

where W is the stated WTP or compensation demanded, g is the target nitrate level in water (for the first question above) or number of bears (second question), m is income, and s is a vector of respondent characteristics that might affect WTP (e.g., age, education, attitudes, household size). Differentiating (4.4) with respect to g results in an inverse compensated demand curve. There is no *a priori* assumption about the functional form of (4.4), except that it satisfies the theoretical requirements of an inverse demand function; Sellar et al. (1986) recommend the use of a function that is quadratic in g.

The open-ended format may lead to strategic behavior by respondents who know full well that it is unlikely they will have to pay the amount declared, although the survey instrument should identify clearly how the stated amount is to be paid (Mitchell and Carson 1995). Some researchers have found that the open-ended format leads to lower average WTP than do dichotomous choice formats, but this too might be evidence of strategic behavior by respondents (Boyle et al. 1996). However, with improvements in survey design (including better pre-testing procedures), more confidence has been placed in the open-ended format.

A variant of the open-ended approach is for the researcher to hone in on an individual's WTA compensation, or maximum WTP, using a bidding procedure. The interviewer suggests a particular value and then increments this value up or down (depending upon the respondent's answer) until the actual WTP or WTA is found for the contingency in question.

According to Hanemann and Kriström (1995), it is only if the respondent is thought to have a complete preference ordering, without any uncertainty, that it is appropriate to elicit WTP or WTA directly. If this is not the case, they argue, a dichotomous choice approach may be preferred.

Dichotomous choice model

A number of arguments have been raised in favor of dichotomous choice over the open-ended approach (Hanemann and Kriström 1995). First, the DC format best mimics an actual market choice. In actual markets, consumers are confronted with the choice of purchasing or not purchasing a commodity at a given price. A DC contingent question does the same thing. For example, in DC format the previous open-ended question about water quality would be: "Would you be willing to pay $\$A$ to improve water quality from 12mg nitrates per liter to 6mg nitrates per liter: yes or no?"

"Would you be willing to pay $A to increase by 500 the number of grizzly bears in Alaska?"[6] Answering yes or no simply makes more sense. Second, DC is less stressful for the respondent. Third, the DC approach is thought to provide greater incentive for respondents to answer truthfully, avoiding strategic behavior. This is only true, however, if respondents can be convinced that valuation is tied to a real payment. Fourth, the DC format provides the same set of guidelines for all respondents to use in determining their responses (Weisberg et al. 1989). Finally, the DC format addresses uncertainty respondents may have about the value of the resource and the observer may have about the respondent's utility function as we show in the next subsection).

Of these arguments, the first and last are probably the most powerful, although there may be some problems associated with the uncertainty argument. The major objection to DC is that it may result in higher values than the open-ended, or continuous, approach as a result of "yea-saying" – respondents are inclined to "vote" in favor of the bid amount by the nature of the question format (Ready et al. 1996; Boyle et al. 1996).

There are three sources of uncertainty. First, there is measurement uncertainty, which is the form of uncertainty addressed by the random utility maximization model discussed below. Second, preferences are uncertain. It may be possible to address this form of uncertainty by asking respondents how certain they are about their answer, and then use appropriate econometric methods (Li and Mattsson 1995; Li 1996). However, it is difficult to conceive of respondents identifying the extent of their uncertainty to a DC question, as preference uncertainty concerns the inability of the respondent to make a proper trade-off between the environmental good in question and income. The issue is not one of uncertainty about an assigned value, but lack of cognitive ability (see below). The third source of uncertainty originates with the commodity or contingency that is to be valued. Respondents may be uncertain about what it is that they are valuing, having no experience with it and perhaps never having seen it. For example, most people have never seen a spotted owl and may not even know what preservation of its habitat might entail; yet they are asked to value existence of the owl. Most people's notions about wilderness, wildlife species and biodiversity in general are simply wrong; they do not know what these things mean, what management or nonmanagement entails, and so on (Budiansky 1995).

Some uncertainty can be resolved by providing more information to the respondent, but there remain sources of uncertainty that cannot be addressed with more information. This is likely true for both the amenity that is to be valued (how can respondents know what biologists do not know?) and, given that the amenity is perfectly known, the trade-off between it and income in the preference function. Only in some cases can uncertainty be (partly) resolved by providing survey respondents with more information about what is to be valued. Respondents to contingent valuation surveys lack knowledge, or have only vague knowledge, about the amenity to be valued, and the appropriate approach may well be to use a linguistic approach to value what is essentially a concept or notion (Zadeh 1965; McNeill and Freiberger 1993, p.84).

Measurement of uncertainty: random utility maximization

Welfare measurement in the dichotomous choice model is based on the random utility maximization (RUM) model (Hanemann 1984). Let $u(j, m; s)$ be an individual's utility function, where j is an indicator variable (taking on 1 if the respondent accepts the opportunity to pay for the contingency and 0 if she rejects the opportunity), m is income, and s is a vector of respondent characteristics. The RUM model begins by assuming that the respondent knows her utility function, $u(j, m; s)$, with certainty, although some components are unobservable to the researcher and are treated as stochastic. Then, from the perspective of the investigator, the respondent's utility function is a random parametric function:

$$(4.5) \quad u(j, m; s) = v(j, m; s) + \varepsilon_j, \quad j = 0, 1,$$

where ε_0 and ε_1 are independent, identically distributed (iid) random variables.

The problem confronting the researcher is demonstrated with the aid of Figure 4.8. The individual originally has an amount g_0 of the amenity available to her, and is located at point K where the horizontal budget line m intersects the indifference curve, $u(X)$ or $u(Y)$. The question is whether a respondent to a survey would be willing to pay the (bid) amount $\$A$ for the opportunity to have g_1 ($> g_0$) of the amenity.

An individual Y with utility map represented by the indifference curve $u(Y)$ will choose to pay the amount indicated because the compensating surplus, or maximum WTP, for this person ($CS_Y = a - c$) exceeds the payment A. Thus, with budget constraint $m - A$, she is still able to move to a higher level of utility. Individual X, on the other hand, will choose not to accept the opportunity to pay A for the environmental improvement because compensating surplus ($CS_X = a - b$) is less than $\$A$. Thus, before an individual i will accept bid A, $CS_i > A$. Since the observer does not know which indifference map applies, utility is a random variable.

The individual, however, knows for sure which choice maximizes her utility. Then the probability that she will accept the opportunity to pay A for the amenity is given by:

(4.6) $P_1 = \text{Pr}\{\text{respondent will pay } A\}$

$$= \text{Pr}\{v(1, m-A; s) + \varepsilon_1 > v(0, m; s) + \varepsilon_0\},$$

and the probability that the respondent is unwilling to pay the stated amount is $P_0 = 1 - P_1$. The probability in (4.6) can be rewritten as:

(4.7) $P_1 = \text{Pr}\{\text{WTP} > A\} = F_{\text{wtp}}(\Delta v), = 1 - F(\Delta v)$

where $\Delta v = v(1, m-A; s) - v(0, m; s)$, and F is a cumulative distribution function, generally chosen to be the cumulative standard normal distribution or the cumulative logistic distribution function,

(4.8) $F(\Delta v) = \dfrac{1}{1+e^{-\Delta v}}.$

Other distributions, such as the Weibull, exponential (a special case of the Weibull), log-normal and log-logistic, are also used in empirical work.

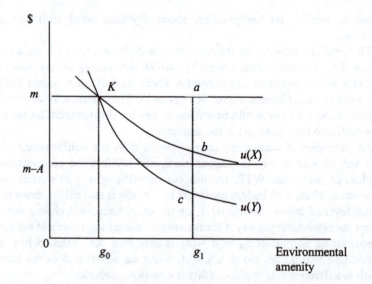

Figure 4.8: Interpretation of "yes" and "no" answers in RUM model

Assume that the utility function is linear: $v(j, m; s) = \alpha_j + \beta m$, with $\beta > 0$ and $j = 0, 1$. Then,

(4.9) $\Delta v = \alpha_1 + \beta(m - A) - \alpha_0 - \beta m = \alpha_1 - \alpha_0 - \beta A.$

For the utility function $v(j, m; s) = \alpha_j + \beta \ln m$, $\beta > 0, j = 0, 1$,

(4.10) $\Delta v = \alpha_1 + \beta \ln(m - A) - \alpha_0 - \beta \ln m$

$$= \alpha_1 - \alpha_0 + \beta \ln(1 - A/m) \approx \alpha_1 - \alpha_0 - \beta(A/m).$$

Denoting $\phi = P_1$ in the cumulative logistic distribution function (4.8), we can solve for the bid amount in each of the linear and semi-log functional forms of the utility function:

(4.11)   linear: $A = \dfrac{1}{\beta} [(\alpha_1 - \alpha_0) + \ln (\dfrac{1}{\phi} - 1)]$

(4.12)   semi-log: $A = \dfrac{m}{\beta} [(\alpha_1 - \alpha_0) + \ln (\dfrac{1}{\phi} - 1)].$

The binary response probabilities in (4.6) or (4.7) can also be written as:

(4.13) $P_1 = \Pr\{M > A\} = 1 - F_M(A),$

where M is the respondent's maximum WTP (their compensating surplus) for the environmental amenity, whether an improvement in water quality or protection of more spotted owl habitat, and $F_M(\cdot)$ is the cumulative distribution function of M (again taking on one of the functional forms discussed above). The compensating welfare measure can be either the median (M^*) or mean (M_μ) of the corresponding probability density function. As Hanemann (1984) points out, either is a valid measure to use, although they can give quite different welfare estimates. The median is simply that value of M where the estimated probability that a respondent answers yes to the contingent question is 0.5. If the goal of the analyst is to determine whether the policy to change the level or availability of an environmental amenity will pass a referendum vote, then the median is the appropriate measure to employ. If the payment vehicle used in the CVM survey is a tax increase, then any tax increase less than the median WTP estimate would presumably pass (Johansson 1993). Of course, a referendum would be preferred, except that in some jurisdictions such votes are not usual. The mean WTP, on the other hand, is considered the appropriate measure to employ for cost–benefit analysis (as it includes all people's WTP) and is given by:

$$(4.14) \quad M_\mu = \int_0^\infty \left(1 - F_M(A)\right) dA.$$

Both the mean and median are indicated in Figure 4.9, with the mean simply the area under the density function. The mean can be infinite due to nonconvergence of the tail of the cumulative distribution function, which is a particular problem in the case of WTA – as demonstrated by Hanemann (1984) in his recalculation of Bishop and Heberlein's (1979) original welfare values (see Table 4.3 below). One approach has been to truncate the distribution at the largest value of $A used in the CVM survey. The above integral would stop at the highest elicited value, thereby ignoring the tail of the distribution. However, the median measure would be unaffected.

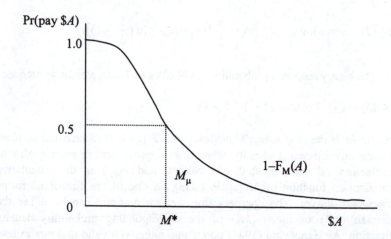

Figure 4.9: Welfare measures in DC models: median (M*) and mean (M$_\mu$)

The median and mean measures can, on occasion, provide substantially different passive use values for a resource. In the case of the March 24, 1989 *Exxon Valdez* oil spill in Alaska, estimates of WTP to prevent damages varied widely. For the Weibull, exponential, log-normal and log-logistic cumulative functional forms, median WTPs were found to be US$31, $46, $27 and $29, respectively, compared to respective estimates of mean WTPs of $94, $67, $220 and infinity (Harrison and Kriström 1995, p.37). Given an estimated 90 million US households, choice of functional form and whether the mean or median welfare measure is employed can lead to differences in damage estimates of 1,000% or more. The median appears to be a lower bound estimate, but there is no reason to prefer it over the mean in assessing damages or benefits simply because it yields lower estimates.

Other measurement issues are discussed by Adamowicz et al. (1989). Further, Hanemann (1984) derives all of the aforementioned properties for the case of compensation demanded.

Extending the basic dichotomous choice model

The dichotomous choice model has been extended in several directions. There has been an attempt to hone in on, or fine tune, the elicited WTP or compensation demanded. This is done by using a follow-up question to the original DC one; hence, the method is known as the double-bounded approach, where the use of a single question is referred to as the single-bounded approach (Kanninen 1993). Suppose the initial question asked a respondent to provide a yes–no answer to a willingness-to-pay "bid" of $\$A_0$. A probability distribution is assumed about $\$A_0$, such that the true bid lies to the left of $\$A_0$ if the respondent answers "no" and to the right of $\$A_0$ if the respondent answers "yes". The nature of the follow-up question is such that a value higher than $\$A_0$, say $\$A_U$, is asked in a second DC question if the response to $\$A_0$ was "yes", and a value below $\$A_0$, say $\$A_L$, if it was "no". This partitions the probability distribution about $\$A_0$ into four zones – moving from left to right there is a (no, no) zone for a "no" response to $\$A_L$; a (no, yes) zone for a "yes" response to $\$A_L$ and "no" to $\$A_0$; a (yes, no) zone for a "yes" response to $\$A_0$ but a "no" response to $\$A_U$; and a (yes, yes) zone for "yes" responses to both $\$A_0$ and $\$A_U$. This procedure improves the quality of the estimated welfare measures (Kanninen 1993; Harrison and Kriström 1995; Hanemann and Kriström 1995).[7]

A second extension of the model has been to address preference uncertainty. Li and Mattsson (1995) were the first to ask respondents how certain they were about their responses to the DC question. If someone responded "yes" to a bid of $\$A$, but subsequently indicated that they were less than 50% certain about their answer, they were interpreted to have responded "no" with a certainty equal to 100% minus the stated level of certainty (so that the certainty of the "no" response exceeded 50%). This is rather arbitrary (van Kooten et al. 2001).

Preference uncertainty can be illustrated via Figure 4.10 (which is similar to Figure 4.8). In this figure, three indifference curves are used – a linear indifference curve that exhibits perfect substitutability (u_0u_0), one that exhibits perfect complementarity or lexicographical preferences (u_1u_1), and an in-between case (u_2u_2) (Hanemann and Kriström 1995). The compensating surplus of an increase in the environmental amenity from g_0 to g_1 ranges from zero to total income m depending on the individual's preference map, which is unknown to the researcher. For perfect complements (u_1u_1), CS = 0; for perfect substitutes, CS = $a - c = m$; and for the in-between case, CS = $a - b$.

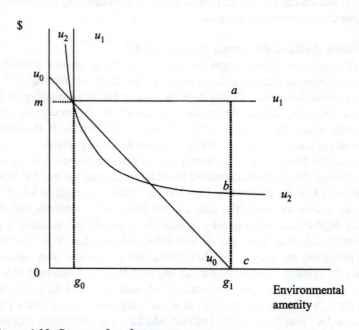

Figure 4.10: Source of preference uncertainty

Hanemann and Kriström (1995) (and Li and Mattsson 1995) talk about preference uncertainty related to the respondent, but they fail to make a clear distinction among the different types of uncertainty identified above. The RUM model addresses uncertainty in measurement and Li and Mattsson combine this with the uncertainty that respondents have about their yes–no response to the DC question (true preference uncertainty). Perhaps, true preference uncertainty pertains less to uncertainty about whether the respondent's compensating surplus is greater or less than the bid amount (and the trustworthiness of the response), than to cognitive uncertainty about what is valued or about how they in fact make trade-offs between the environmental good and income. It seems to us that true preference uncertainty cannot be addressed in the DC framework.

Finally, conventional methods that employ the log-logistics, log-normal, Weibull and other distributions implicitly rule out the possibility that respondents have nonzero probability for a zero WTP (in Figure 4.9 this is indicated by a 1.0 value for WTP = 0). To take into account a large number of zero responses, Kriström (1997) suggests using a spike model, with the spike occurring at zero WTP. This enables one to take into account the possibility that respondents have a negative bid price. He argues that there are three ways to view negative responses to the bid price. First, WTP is below the bid price. Second, there are some goods or amenity services over which the consumer has no preference; they do not enter into the utility function. Finally, the good or amenity does not contribute positively to utility, with the respondent not even willing to purchase it at zero price. That is, the respondents have negative WTP.

Castle et al. (1994), and others, have also noted that, while environmental and other programs are assumed to result in gains to citizens, there are likely to be losers as well. Consider a program to protect grizzly bears, or increase their numbers. While many would favor such a program, there are others who would prefer to see a reduction in bear numbers (*viz.*, hikers who are afraid of being attacked). The latter would attach negative value to such a program. Likewise, the literature has focused on positive WTP for protection of old-growth forests. However, some would prefer to see some development of such forests, as opposed to keeping them solely as wilderness. For example, Portney (1994, p.13) suggests that some will derive satisfaction from knowing that development (e.g., of wilderness) provides well-paying jobs, a benefit of development that could, in principle, be estimated using CVM. A case can also be made for assigning non-use value to development – logging roads that provide access, clearcuts that are planted to grass or other species of trees, and thinning of old-growth stands may provide non-use benefits to some. Non-use benefits can be attached to the development (loss) of wilderness as well as to its protection. Empirical support for the possibility that development has non-use value comes from Sweden, where Drake (1992) found that people attached positive non-use value to retaining landscapes in agriculture as opposed to letting them revert back to their natural state as forests.

Many respondents to CVM questions state that their WTP for the contingency is zero. The spike model takes this into account. Kriström (1997) employs a spike model to examine two Swedish studies – a proposal to re-route the Sweden to Finland ferry to prevent shoreline erosion in the Stockholm archipelago, and another to close Bromma airport in Stockholm (Arlanda airport 40 km outside Stockholm is the main airport). In the case of the ferry, 446 out of 575 respondents (or 77%) declined to pay anything to re-route the ferry. A traditional logistic distribution, which permits negative values (recall that log-normal, Weibull and other distributional functions do not permit negative values) resulted in estimated mean and median WTPs of US$ –340. From the spike model, on the other hand, the estimated mean WTP was US$ +200, while estimated median WTP was zero.

For the Bromma airport study, respondents were first asked their preferences regarding the future of the airport, with a slight majority favoring an expansion of air traffic as opposed to a reduction. Those who preferred a reduction in air traffic from Bromma over an increase were subsequently asked what they would be willing to pay for reducing activity at the airport. Only 7% of the sample provided a positive WTP to reduce activity at the airport. Some 18% of the sample indicated a negative WTP (i.e., would actually prefer an increase in activity at Bromma airport), while 75% indicated indifference or zero WTP. Thus, the spike is estimated to be 0.75. The median WTP is clearly zero, while mean WTP is also estimated to be zero if a symmetrical distribution is assumed. The traditional approach finds a positive mean WTP.

It is clear that it is necessary to address questions of a zero response to CVM questions using either a spike model or some other methodology.

Contingent Valuation Survey Techniques: Some Issues

Contingent valuation surveys enable economists to measure the value of commodities and services that do not leave a footprint in the market place, either because they are separable from privately traded goods and services in individuals' utility functions or they are separable in the production function. Surveys using questionnaires enable one to obtain information about such amenities in a direct fashion. A good contingent valuation survey (1) communicates the attributes to be valued, (2) communicates the terms of the bargain (see below), and (3) is consistent with economic theory. If the mechanism for obtaining responses is not consistent with economic theory, it is not clear what the resulting responses mean. Some problems with the survey approach (at least as identified by its practitioners) are as follows.

1. The survey approach places individuals in hypothetical situations with which they may be unfamiliar. They are unable to respond in a meaningful manner to the questions that are subsequently posed about these situations. To prevent this, the interviewer can use explanation, pictures or other props to identify clearly the hypothetical situation to

which the respondent is required to respond.

2. The relationship between the respondent and the interviewer may influence the values provided; the problem is that the observer is in the picture influencing outcomes. Questions pertaining to willingness-to-pay to have access to a resource or to have more of some public good, and questions pertaining to the compensation demanded for being denied access or having less of the public good, are subjective and the respondent may provide answers that she thinks the interviewer wants to hear. Thus, the respondent is not a *neutral* participant. This problem is likely the easiest to overcome by proper training of interviewers, or through mail surveys.

3. The respondent is not neutral to the hypothetical situations that are laid out. She may either *bias* the results up or down depending upon whether she thinks that the responses will, for example, prevent others from accessing a recreational site by making it either too expensive or less attractive. Responses may also be given in such a way that the value of the contingency is overstated because the respondent knows that she will not bear the cost of providing the public good (free-rider problem), or the respondent may purposely understate her WTP in order to escape charges. This form of bias or strategic behavior can be prevented by inclusion of a realistic payment device whereby the respondent recognizes that she will indeed be required to pay for the proposed change. For example, the payment device might constitute an increase in gasoline prices should further oil drilling in the Arctic be prevented.

4. *Starting point bias* is a problem in some instances. This refers to the value that is initially suggested by the researcher to the respondent. If the value is lower than that which the respondent had in mind, the respondent may revise values downward; likewise, they may be revised upward. Pre-testing can be used to overcome the problem of realistic starting values. Further, one can avoid starting point bias by using open questions (i.e., not suggesting starting values).

Different types of surveys are also available to researchers.

1. *Mail surveys* are the lowest cost and perhaps the easiest to administer. Sample selectivity may be a problem, because only educated people or only those interested in the topic will choose to reply. It can be addressed to some extent by using econometric tools that test and correct for sample selectivity bias. Other problems occur because those who are sent surveys may not be able to comprehend the material in the survey, due to high overall illiteracy rates.[8] This can account for low

response rates in some instances. It is also possible that those completing the surveys are those who have strong feelings one way or another about the issue, so mail-outs are likely beset by response bias. Further, it is difficult to get accurate lists of names for survey purposes and one does not have control over the survey itself. Follow-up is very important. It is often recommended that nonrespondents be contacted at least twice following the initial mail-out. Reminder cards can be used, followed, if necessary, by a telephone call and a second mail-out if the telephone contact leads to a positive response. To increase response rates, respondents can be offered token compensation for time completing the questionnaire, say $5 or $10, although this raises the costs of mail surveys.

2. *Telephone surveys* are perhaps twice as expensive as mail surveys. Nonetheless, the advantages of telephone interviews are that they are reasonably low cost, result in a high response rate, and enable the interviewer to answer respondents' questions when necessary. Although the surveyor can respond to questions regarding clarification, interviewer bias does enter in. One problem concerns choice of respondent: rather than choosing the person who answers the phone, the interviewer can ask for the person in the household who is over age 18, say, and whose birthday is next. Call back based on a household listing obtained at first contact is a more expensive method. Another problem with telephone surveys is information overload. Questions must be kept simple so individuals can easily keep track of items over the telephone. Yet, telephone interviews are often preferred to mail-out surveys (Portney 1994), although the preponderance of telemarketing has "poisoned the well" for telephone surveys to some extent.

3. *In-person surveys* are the most expensive means to elicit information, but they have the highest response and "success" rate. The major problem with this method is bias that arises due to personal contact, but again this source of bias can be overcome by training surveyors and through pre-testing.

It is important to pre-test any contingent valuation survey extensively. Using focus groups in one's pre-test helps the researcher to understand how and what people are valuing. Further, samples should be split so that the dimension of a particular item in the questionnaire can be asked in different ways. It is then possible to test if the phrasing of the question affects the answer or value provided, but this adds to the number of completed surveys needed for statistical significance. The current state of the art favors mail-out surveys, but only if all the conditions of proper survey design are satisfied.

The purpose of contingent valuation surveys is to get individuals to reveal values that correspond to the actual values that people put on commodities in real markets. Doing so is referred to as validity. If respondents do not answer honestly or meaningfully, validity is threatened. There are three kinds of validity tests.

1. *Content validity* focuses on the wording of questions in the actual survey. Questions need to identify clearly the items to be valued and the "terms of the bargain". The latter refers to the mechanism by which actual payment occurs, to whom the payment is made (from whom funds are received), in what form monies are paid or received, and how any funds raised are to be used in implementing the contingency.

2. *Construct validity* results when a survey's questions are consistent with economic theory; the responses can then be related to meaningful theoretical concepts. One measure of validity in these cases is to compare values from the contingent valuation survey with values obtained from market methods such as hedonic pricing.

3. *Criterion validity* relies upon comparisons with laboratory experiments. For example, one might wish to compare hypothetical responses to WTP and WTA for hunting permits with those obtained from a simulated market for permits, where *selected* hunters with permits are asked to sell them. Some comparisons of simulated market values and contingent values are provided in Table 4.3. It appears that contingent markets are able to provide estimates of value that correspond well with those provided by simulated markets. The greatest difference in values (in Table 4.3) is between WTP (lower panel) and WTA (upper panel) (see Chapter 2 and below).

Is the Contingent Valuation Method a Panacea?

There remains controversy over the use of CVM for valuing biodiversity and wilderness preservation. Some environmental economists (perhaps the majority) vigorously defend CVM as a valid theoretical and empirical means for estimating the benefits (costs) of changes in the availability of environmental goods; see, for example, Hanemann (1994) and Smith (1992). Their view is supported in CERCLA and other legislation. The CERCLA decision grants equal standing to expressed and revealed preference, accepts non-use values as a legitimate component of resource value, and favors restoration of a damaged natural environment over compensation (Gregory et al. 1993).

Defenders of contingent valuation methods have focused almost exclusively on its ability to provide monetary values in situations where none would otherwise exist (even as a starting point for negotiating damages), arguing that its shortcomings are best overcome by rigorous survey design and practice (Hanemann 1994; Arrow et al. 1993). However, CVM has also been criticized by economists, philosophers, psychologists and lawyers, resulting in questions about its use in litigation and in cost–benefit analysis (Knetsch 1995; Diamond and Hausman 1994; Hausman 1993; Kahneman and Knetsch 1992a, 1992b; Irwin et al. 1993; Kahneman et al. 1990; Sagoff 1988b, 1994; Niewijk 1992, 1994). The reasons for dissatisfaction or outright rejection of the method vary.

Table 4.3: Contingent Values and Simulated Market Values

		Dollar values	
Commodity	Valuation method	Contingent	Simulated market
For compensation demanded			
Goose permits	Dichotomous choice	$101($83.16)[a]	$63($31.02)[a]
Deer permits	Sealed-bid auction	$833	$1,184
Deer permits	Dichotomous choice	$420	$153
For willingness-to-pay			
Goose permits	Dichotomous choice	$21($5.30)[a]	—
Deer permits	Sealed-bid auction[b]	$32	$24
	Sealed-bid auction and bidding[b]	$43	$19
Deer permits	Dichotomous choice	$35	$31

Notes:
[a] Hanemann's (1984, p.340) corrections to B&H's original values are provided in parentheses. B&H calculate areas under the curve (means), but arbitrarily truncate the calculation of mean to avoid infinite numbers. Hanemann's median values are provided in parentheses. Mean values for WTA for goose permits are $∞ and $114.22 for contingent and simulated markets, respectively, and $15.54 for WTP.
[b] A sealed-bid auction asks participants to indicate the maximum amount they are willing to pay for the commodity, but then in a sealed envelope. Bidding is a variant of this as it allows participants to re-evaluate their WTP in an iterative (bidding) fashion.
Source: Bishop and Heberlein (1990, pp.97–8).

Ethical norms and valuation of environmental amenities
Rational values involve standards for truth; moral values involve standards

of conduct; aesthetic values involve standards for appreciation; spiritual values involve standards of meaning of life; and economic values involve standards for choosing among goods and services. Consider a social hierarchy, where personal consumption goods are lowest in the hierarchy, protection of global ecosystems and concern for the wellbeing of the least fortunate are ranked higher, and questions about who we are and how we relate to the world are highest. As a person deals with complex questions that are relatively high in the social hierarchy, many issues deal with intangibles or ill-defined "things". As More et al. (1996) argue, tangible goods have value because they allow us to fulfill certain functions, with market prices facilitating these choices. However, a person's willingness to pay, say, to preserve minke whales in the Atlantic Ocean – a much less tangible amenity – may relate more to helping provide a person with an identity (what kind of person am I?), rather than reflecting any intrinsic value of wildlife. While this view may justify the use of economic analyses for valuing nonmarket goods, because all non-use values are tied to the fulfillment of human goals and are really off-site values, it is important to be clear about what is really valued. Is it the resource, knowledge of the resource, the satisfaction people derive from the resource, or the satisfaction they derive from doing something to preserve nature, rather than preserving whales *per se*, that is being valued? While similar remarks can be made about market goods, environmental amenities are less tangible.

Do individuals make decisions based on market values or on a set of wider values based on social norms (or commonly accepted values)? The debate in the literature is intense about this point (Sagoff 1988a, 1988b; Kahneman and Ritov 1994; Common et al. 1997; Crowards 1997; Gowdy 1997). One view is that contingent valuation "actually captures a hodgepodge of market values and broader values and forces them into the indifference framework of market exchange" (Gowdy 1997, p.27). The other view is that values are derived from economic theory. "It is utility – whatever its source – that matters for total value. Motives are essentially irrelevant and acceptance of consumer sovereignty is one of the most enshrined principles of economics" (Carson et al. 1996).

Sagoff (1988b) proposes that people make choices according to "citizen values" or "consumer values", depending on the context in which the choice is placed. There are values other than economic ones that are important to individuals when they make choices as a citizen as opposed to a consumer; then ethical values matter (Sagoff 1994; More et al. 1996). Sen (1977) had previously pointed out that concepts of economic rationality are both too weak and too strong because humans have a capacity for maintaining multiple preference scales. Humans are cognizant of social duties that might conflict with personal welfare and may hold a land or environmental ethic that leads them to make decisions in a decidedly nonmarket fashion. Hence, individuals might reject offers to value an environmental resource or may provide answers that have no relationship to their true WTP.

Empirical research provides some support for the notion that individuals value environmental goods for reasons other than private benefits (Kahneman and Knetsch 1992a). One problem concerns "imbedding" of values within a questionnaire. Thus, an individual may respond that she is willing to pay $25 per year towards preserving the grizzly bear when asked only about this wildlife species. Summing over individuals leads to a large value for the grizzly bear. If the same individual were asked about her WTP to preserve all wildlife species, the answer may also be $25. Out of that amount, the person may only be willing to pay $15 towards the preservation of big game species; out of the $15, the individual may only be willing to contribute $5 per year for the preservation of grizzly bears. Likewise, studies have found that individuals are willing to pay the same amount to preserve one lake full of fish as they would to save all fish in the region (Knetsch 2000). One conclusion is that, while people are interested in the environment and protecting biodiversity (saving species), it is not well understood how they make decisions about their WTP to protect environmental and biological assets. It may also be the case that people may simply purchase the moral satisfaction of having made their contribution toward society by paying to save the environment or protect species (or contribute to cancer research, etc.). If it is moral satisfaction that individuals are actually purchasing, and not the contingent commodity, this raises questions about the validity of contingent valuation surveys.

Individuals might assign value to environmental goods out of an altruistic motive beyond that related to future generations (bequest value). People might value public goods, such as wildlife species, because these confer benefits upon others. It is useful to distinguish two types of altruism – nonpaternalistic, in which an altruist gains utility from increasing the wellbeing of others, and paternalistic, in which an altruist values the use of a particular resource by others. Paternalistic altruists believe that the availability of some environmental goods (wildlife species in tropical rain forests) is of benefit to others (forest dwellers) even if they gain no direct utility from their existence; the nonpaternalistic altruist derives utility only from knowing that the forest dweller has access to the wildlife species (regardless of whether the forest dweller desires them). Diamond and Hausman (1994) allege that altruistic externalities might result in double counting of benefits, but McConnell (1997) shows that altruism has no impact on benefit estimates if it is nonpaternalistic and that benefits for paternalistic altruists can legitimately be used in valuation without problems associated with double counting.

Property rights and endowments

As noted in Chapter 2, empirical studies find a large disparity between WTP and WTA for both environmental amenities and goods normally traded in markets, even though one would expect these to vary only by a small amount. Yet, recommended best practice is to elicit WTP in CVM surveys (see, e.g., Arrow et al. 1993). This assumes, in essence, that the respondent has to pay for the right to the environmental amenity, even where the amenity has deteriorated through carelessness or some other reason – the property right or endowment is assumed not to reside with the respondent. As a result, many survey respondents provide answers that can only be interpreted as protest against the contingent property right.

There are several reasons why WTP is considered best practice. Almost all CVM studies employ WTP with the values generated considered "reasonable" for whatever reason, although Arrow et al. (1993) consider such values to be on the high side. WTP makes people more cognizant of their budget constraints; WTP is bounded, while WTA could be unbounded. Yet, in many cases the appropriate measure is compensation demanded (Knetsch 1993). Finally, in the determination of punitive damages (damages over and above compensation for injuries to the plaintiff) in lawsuits, both sides have come to accept WTP as the appropriate measure of non-use value. The wrongdoer accepts WTP because it results in lower values than WTA, while the plaintiff accepts WTP because it addresses the punishment aspect ("the sense of community outrage") (Knetsch 2000).

In practice, the size of punitive damage awards is erratic and unpredictable. However, when those setting damage awards are able to use awards from other cases as a guide, unpredictability and variability are nearly eliminated. Therefore, as a practical matter, it may only be necessary to determine the perceived severity of environmental damage to decide the associated punitive damages (i.e., value the damage). That is, with input from stakeholders, governments can establish *ex ante* awards for different types of environmental damages. The courts would then use these values as a guide for situations not covered. Limits on damage payments would be used to ensure that businesses are not forced into bankruptcy (with significant job loss) due to litigation arising from accidental environmental damage, not caused by negligence on the part of the firm. This approach constitutes a way to get around the discrepancy between WTP and WTA, as both are considered valid welfare measures (Knetsch 2000).

Cognitive ability of survey respondents

One criticism of CVM is that it seeks to elicit values for natural resources from respondents who may lack the cognitive ability to make such assessments. Respondents to surveys often provide zero answers because of their inability to attribute value to something that they have a difficult time valuing, if they can ever ascribe a value to it (Sagoff 1994; Gregory et al. 1993; Stevens et al. 1991). Psychologists consider four possibilities:

1. Preferences exist and are stable, well-defined and easily measured.
2. Preferences exist and are stable, but are not easily measured because some of the resulting measures are biased.
3. Preferences exist and are stable, but all measurements are biased.
4. Preferences may not exist in many situations or, if they do exist, they are not stable or well-formed.

The main criticism is that CVM itself creates preferences and bias because context or familiarity matters.

It is possible to rank or value items with which one is familiar, but this ability declines as the degree of familiarity falls. For example, consider the following items listed from highest to lowest degree of familiarity (familiarity declines as one goes from category 1 to 7):

1. Groceries   5. Recreational activities
2. Appliances   6. Air and water quality
3. Automobiles   7. Nature (environment and
4. Homes   species preservation)

Valuing changes in the hypothetical availability of commodities in each of these categories becomes increasingly difficult as one moves from categories 1 through 7. Psychologists argue that it is likely impossible to place dollar values on hypothetical changes in the availability of commodities in categories 6 and 7.

This has led some to argue that, rather than employing CVM, it is necessary to help decision makers to "construct" their preferences for public goods. This approach would bring together all the stakeholders involved in a choice about some public good, help them construct their preferences about the good, and thereby lead to a policy choice. While discussed in more detail in the next section, we note that the major objection to this approach is that the stakeholder group may not be representative of the larger society.

Payment instrument

There are other issues of concern that are not addressed here, including protest responses related to the payment instrument. Although much research has gone into improving the payment device, many respondents indicate that they are against an increase in taxes because, while they may have a positive WTP for the contingency, they are against the current allocation of budgets. In this context, Sagoff (1994), for example, cites the large number of nonresponses in most contingent valuation surveys.

How valid are CVM measures of benefits?

The controversy surrounding CVM was sufficient that the US National Oceanic and Atmospheric Administration (NOAA) commissioned a panel led by two Nobel prize-winning economists (Kenneth Arrow and Robert Solow) to review the state of the art and make recommendations concerning the implementation of CVM (Arrow et al. 1993). The findings by the NOAA panel are summarized in the following points.

1. The CVM "technique is likely to overstate 'real' willingness to pay" (p.4604).
2. External validation of the CVM results is needed before one can reliably use the answers provided by survey respondents.
3. Relatively few CVM surveys "have reminded respondents convincingly of the very real economic constraints within which spending decisions must be made" (p.4605).
4. CVM frequently provides sketchy details about the project(s) to be valued and this calls into question the estimates of value that one thus derives from this information. However, if respondents were to be provided detailed information, it is unlikely that they would have the cognitive ability to proceed from the information given to answer the survey questions, often answering different questions from that elicited (p.4605). While some of this information overload might be identified and addressed in pre-testing, there is no way to eliminate the problem.
5. Related to 4, in asking individuals to place value on an environmental commodity (such as a biological species), surveys often fail to apprise respondents of the current level of availability and/or existence of the commodity elsewhere (say in another country). Thus, an average value is elicited rather than a marginal value, or the value of the next unit. Relying on average as opposed to marginal nonmarket values leads to the wrong conclusions about species preservation – it is marginal and not average values that count in designing appropriate natural resource policies (van Kooten and Eiswerth 2003).
6. Open-ended questions are unlikely to be reliable and, therefore, survey respondents should be asked to respond to a dichotomous choice (yes–no) question where WTP is provided.

7. Questions concerning potential sources of bias need to be included in questionnaires. In addition, dichotomous choice questions should be followed by an open-ended question asking why the respondent "voted" the way she did.

8. Outcomes should be compared with those provided by expert panels and, wherever possible, an actual referendum should be used.

9. Careful pre-testing of surveys is required and in-person surveys are preferred to mail-out surveys.

The NOAA panel provided support for the use of CVM, arguing that CVM "studies can produce estimates reliable enough to be *the starting point of a judicial process of damage assessment*, including lost passive-use values" (p.4610, emphasis added). Whether this constitutes an endorsement of CVM is not at all clear. Some of the NOAA recommendations have been adopted, including follow-up questions that seek to determine the reasons why respondents provide particular answers to some of the survey questions (e.g., reasons for zero WTP). Others have not been followed, including rejection of in-person surveys in favor of mail-outs. Despite the NOAA panel, controversy continues.

There have also been refinements to the methodology, mainly in terms of econometric approaches and development of alternative means of eliciting value information. At this stage, however, one can only state that contingent valuation methods are evolving and that, in the absence of a market-based approach to valuation of nonmarket (environmental) amenities, CVM or some other direct elicitation procedure will likely be around for some time to come. A major reason (noted above) is that CVM has come to be accepted in litigation.

4.5 OTHER DIRECT VALUATION METHODS

In this section, we consider some alternatives to the contingent valuation method. In some cases, the methods refine CVM, but in others they deviate substantially from the underlying notions of CVM.

Choice Experiments

Adamowicz and his colleagues (Adamowicz 1995; Adamowicz et al. 1998; Hanley et al. 1998) proposed an approach rooted in the marketing literature, and referred to as choice experiments (CE) or stated preferences. While the methodology has been used primarily to value recreational sites, Adamowicz et al. (1998) apply CE to the estimation of non-use values.

Unlike CVM, CE does not require survey respondents to place a direct monetary value on a contingency. Rather, individuals are asked to make pairwise comparisons among environmental alternatives, with the environmental commodity (alternatives) characterized by a variety of attributes. For example, a survey respondent is asked to make pairwise choices between alternative recreational sites or activities, with each distinguished by attributes such as the probability of catching a fish, the type of fish, the amenities for fishermen (e.g., availability of boat rentals), distance to the site, and so on. It is the attributes that are important, and it is these that are eventually assigned monetary value. In order to do so, one of the attributes must constitute a monetary touchstone (or proxy for price). Distance to a recreational site might constitute the proxy for price, but, more generally, one of the attributes will be an entry fee or an associated tax, etc. Once the values of all attributes are known (from the value of the one and the pairwise rankings), the overall value of the amenity is determined by assuming additivity of the attributes' values. Of course, it is possible that the total value of the amenity is greater than the sum of its components (or *vice versa*).

Design of the choice experiment is crucial. Suppose that there are five attributes that constitute the choice model design i (Hanley et al. 1998):

(4.16) $Z_i = f(A_i, B_i, C_i, D_i, E_i)$,

where A, B, C, D and E refer to attributes, and Z is the environmental amenity that these attributes produce. If A, B and C take on four possible levels, and D and E take on three possible levels, then the total number of combinations is $(4^3 \times 3^2)$. In CE, it is typical to offer respondents two alternative designs of the environmental good and the option to choose neither. An environmental design might consist of an access (entry) charge, a water quality level, availability of camping sites and washrooms, and tree cover – with at least one of the attributes constituting a monetary touchstone. Different designs consist of different combinations of these characteristics. Each triple is known as a choice occasion and implies a possible combination of $[(4^3 \times 3^2) \times (4^3 \times 3^2)]$ pairwise comparisons. Using design theory, it is possible to determine the subset of all possible pairwise comparisons needed to estimate the parameters in the model, because clearly one cannot elicit responses to every pairwise option.

Hanley et al. (1998) point out a number of advantages of the CE approach.

1. It enables one to value the attributes that comprise an environmental commodity, which is important as many policy decisions involve

changing attributes rather than the total gain or loss of an environmental commodity. For example, when a wilderness area is developed as a result of timber harvest, not all of its attributes are lost. Attribute valuation is also important because of its use in prediction.

2. Choice experiments avoid the "yea-saying" problem of dichotomous choice surveys as respondents are not faced with the same "all-or-nothing" choice.

3. It may offer advantages over CVM when it comes to the transfer of benefits (e.g., transfer of estimated benefits for water quality improvements in one jurisdiction to those in another).

4. Repeated questioning of the same respondent in CE enables consistency testing that is not possible in CVM where one valuation question is usually asked.

5. CE may be a means of getting around the embedding problem mentioned above. Finally, in the case of non-use benefits estimation, by allowing some attributes to take on levels both above and below the *status quo* level, it is possible to estimate both WTP and WTA compensation (Adamowicz et al. 1998).

CE differs from conjoint analysis because, with the latter, respondents are asked to rank all of the alternatives from highest (best) to lowest (worst). Such a ranking can then be used to infer the importance of the attributes that characterize each alternative within one's preference function. Conjoint measurement is a marketing technique that uses revealed choice among goods with different characteristics (as in hedonic pricing) with a survey that asks people to choose among or rank hypothetical alternatives (contingent ranking) to impute the values of the characteristics. It is used primarily to predict the potential for new products, but efforts to apply this technique to the valuation of nonmarket commodities in ways different from CE are underway (Smith 1997).

Constructed Preferences

Gregory et al. (1993) propose a multiattribute–utility-theory, contingent valuation, or MAUT–CV, approach to address the inability of respondents in a contingent valuation exercise to make holistic assessments about environmental resources. Individuals do not know the value of the resources they are asked to value, but "are constructing them, with whatever help or cues the circumstances provide" (p.181). Thus, rather than attempting to uncover environmental values, Gregory et al. (1993) argue that the analyst's task is to help individuals discover those values by helping them work towards "a defensible expression of value" (p.179). In essence, their approach is to work with stakeholder groups of less than 100 people, having them develop comprehensive, hierarchical attribute trees and then having them rank attributes on a 0 to 100 scale.

> Once all the pieces [of the tree and assigned utility values] are in place, [a] combination rule specifies how to calculate the total utility for any particular plan, program, or scenario. This total utility will be expressed using a single arbitrary *utile* unit of measurement. For contingent valuation, these units must be converted to dollars. In theory, this conversion need only be made at one place in the model. (Gregory et al. 1993, p.189)

The MAUT–CV method also has the advantage that it is able to address uncertainty as components with probabilities can be built into the model, so that the final calculation is an expected value. It is unlikely that it can address disparity between WTP and WTA (between the value placed on gains versus that on losses) as the results are path dependent, varying by the "path" used to help people discover their "values".

4.6 DISCUSSION

In this chapter, we have provided a brief review of the state of the art in the valuation of goods and services that are not traded in markets. It is our impression, however, that the field of nonmarket valuation is at a threshold. While damage functions are increasingly used to value loss in environmental goods such as soil and trees, their use in practice is limited. Likewise, the travel cost method and hedonic price technique are too limited in their applicability to current environmental concerns. This leaves the contingent valuation method as the most popular means for measuring nonmarket values. However, insights and critiques from the emerging field of behavioral economics (or economic psychology), and evidence from CVM itself, indicate that the values obtained from surveys may not reflect people's true worth. While the debate over CVM and the search for new techniques (some of which were identified here) continues, we feel that a significant challenge remains.

In the remaining chapters, we assume that the values obtained for environmental amenities using methods discussed in this chapter are a good indicator of their true value. Yet, as we demonstrate, this is not very helpful from a policy perspective. What is needed is information about how non-use values change as the availability of the amenity varies. Decisions are made at the margin and it is marginal and not total values that are important. We begin in Chapter 6 by considering cost–benefit analysis, providing examples of the use of nonmarket values in cost–benefit studies.

NOTES

1. The problem of aggregating over individuals is potentially serious, but usually ignored. This problem might be overcome by assuming a representative individual and multiplying the result by all persons in society. For more details see Just et al. (1982) and Boadway and Bruce (1984).

2. $\dfrac{\partial P_i}{\partial g_j}$ refers to the (partial) derivative of the function P_i keeping all other things constant. It is the slope of P_i with respect to g_j.

3. The original travel cost method was no more than an empirical means of deriving a demand schedule, without the theoretical background necessary for welfare measurement.

4. A true demand function is derived from economic theory – the result of a consumer maximizing utility subject to a budget constraint. Only then can one derive valid welfare measures such as consumer surplus. The demand relation in Table 4.1 is nothing more than a plot of two sets of numbers.

5. In CVM surveys, there is often no significant difference between the answers respondents provide as individuals and those they provide when asked to behave as a representative of a household (Hausman 1993).

6. In practice, $A varies from one survey to the next, but it may take as few as four to six, or many more, different values of A, with the highest value of A determined by pre-testing the survey.

7. A problem with the two-question, extended DC method is that a respondent's answer to the second question is not unrelated to the amount proposed in the first question – there is an anchoring problem.

8. Illiteracy is defined in the broad sense; while individuals who are considered illiterate may be able to read, comprehension is low and there is a general inability to do arithmetic calculations.

5. Environmental Economics

Market economies function because individuals are, in general, motivated to maximize their income (profit) or wellbeing (utility). They willingly enter into market transactions because these are to their mutual benefit. Prices are the barometer of the values that individuals place on the goods and services that are traded, but there are situations in which trades are not possible because *property rights* are not clearly specified. For example, a rational and well-informed individual would not be willing to purchase an automobile from another person without knowing whether or not that vehicle could be legally registered in the jurisdiction where it was purchased. Without a guarantee that this would indeed be possible, the current owner of the vehicle would have a difficult time selling the vehicle. Likewise, before purchasing a property, an individual would determine whether there exist environmental covenants or easements that restrict what can be done with the land. What, then, is meant by the term "property right"?

A property right establishes legal ownership to a resource and specifies limitations on the way one can use resources. It exists only if the following conditions are met (see also section 3.4):

- Property rights must be *completely specified*. This implies that ownership is clearly delineated, and that restrictions upon the rights of owners and penalties for violation of those rights are specified. Restrictions upon ownership must accompany property rights in order to avoid the confusion that would result if everyone used the things that they own in any way they pleased.
- A property right implies *exclusive ownership*. This is the right to determine who, if anyone, may use the property and under what conditions. However, all rewards and penalties in the exercise of the right accrue to the owner.
- Property owners have the right to *transfer* their property. In the above example, transfer was impeded by the vehicle registration process. Restrictions on the transfer of property lead to inefficiency – to market breakdown. It is important to recognize that it is *rights* that are transferred as opposed to just material property. When buying land, one

purchases the right to use that land, but the land is not physically moved. The same is true when you purchase an item at the store; even though the item is removed, it is the right to use the item that is purchased. Removal can be accomplished by shoplifting, but this does not constitute a transfer of the ownership rights; rather, ownership rights are violated.

• Property rights must be effectively *enforced*. Without enforcement, a system of property rights cannot be considered useful. If enforcement is imperfect, as it always will be in the real world, then the expected value of penalties must exceed any possible gains a violator can hope to make.

Finally, market transactions involve costs – information, contracting and policing costs. Indeed, avoiding transactions costs is one reason that firms integrate into forward or backward markets. Theory suggests that an internal organization will supersede a market if the market transaction costs are greater than the costs of making the same transactions within a single organization. It is important to recognize the existence of market transaction costs. Sometimes it is argued that, when something is not provided privately, public intervention is needed. However, transaction costs may be so high that provision of the good or service exceeds the value placed on it by demanders. Then, public intervention could be costlier than the benefit gained by correcting some perceived misallocation.

5.1 EXTERNALITY: THE RATIONALE FOR PUBLIC INTERVENTION

Externality is often considered to be at the "heart and guts" of resource economics – the reason for public intervention in private markets. Externality refers to some form of market imperfection or market failure. The existence of market failure, in and of itself, is not sufficient justification for government intervention, however (as alluded to in our discussion of transaction costs). Indeed, prior to action by the state, it needs to be demonstrated that intervention enhances social wellbeing. There are four types of externality, but only three of these have implications for how economists measure welfare.

Technical Externality

Technical externality results whenever the long-run average cost (LAC) curve falls over the relevant range of output – to the point where all demand is satisfied. A falling long-run average cost curve indicates that there are *economies of scale* in production. This is illustrated in Figure 5.1, where the demand function intersects the LAC curve before the LAC turns upward. In this case, as is shown in the diagram, the long-run marginal cost (LMC) function lies everywhere below LAC. Examples of industries or situations in which this phenomenon occurs are public utilities (telephone, water and sewage, cable TV, etc.) and bridges. Efficient allocation of resources occurs whenever marginal social valuation of a good or service is equal to the marginal social cost of providing that good or service. Marginal value is generally represented by the market price, except, for example, when there are subsidies. In the case of falling LAC, the situation where price is equal to marginal cost ($P = $ LMC) results in losses, because the average cost of production lies above the average return or market price. Thus, firms will lose the shaded area in Figure 5.1 if they set price equal to marginal cost.

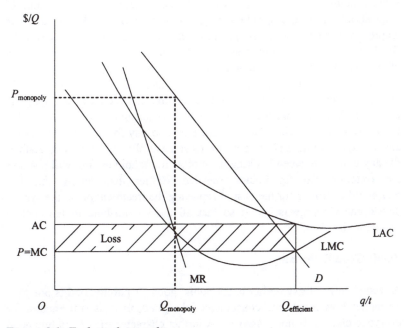

Figure 5.1: Technical eternality

The situation depicted in Figure 5.1 will lead to a natural monopoly if the good or service is provided privately. Since a monopolist determines the quantity to sell by setting marginal cost equal to marginal revenue and then determining price from the demand curve, the market price will lie above marginal cost and inefficient allocation results. Since monopoly leads to inefficiency, and competition results in losses, public intervention is required. This intervention can take several forms.

The most common form of intervention is regulation. Regulation of private or autonomous public utilities is a common method of preventing price from rising to the monopoly level. With regulation, some divergence between price and marginal cost is tolerated, but the regulatory authority attempts to keep this difference at a level that enables firms to recover their fixed costs and earn a rate of return comparable to that available in other sectors of the economy – the normal rate of return.

The second approach is public provision – the government provides the good or service in question. To maximize wellbeing, the state should set price equal to marginal cost and use a lump sum tax to pay for the fixed costs of providing the good or service. For example, taxes are used to build bridges, and, once a bridge has been built, the marginal cost of getting a vehicle across the bridge is essentially zero (at least to the point of congestion). The appropriate charge to levy is zero. A toll may be employed, but once again the primary purpose of the toll is to recover the fixed cost: the toll is not meant to allocate the bridge's services most efficiently by setting price equal to marginal cost.

For services such as sewage treatment, residents may be charged a hook-up fee to connect them to the main sewer line; it is equal to the marginal cost of making the connection. A *system development charge* may be added to the hook-up fee. This charge is not meant to pay for the existing sewers and sewage treatment plant, because these have already been built. Rather, the day will come when hooking up another household or firm will result in the system's capacity being exceeded. Rather than letting this last household or firm incur the cost of replacing the treatment plant, the system development charge is levied so that all users contribute to the cost of replacing the plant.

Public Good Externality

A second form of externality is the public good. A public good is one that, no matter how much one consumes of the good, there is still enough for everyone else – it is not *exhausted*. A further characteristic of a public good is that everyone has access to it and no one can be *excluded* from its consumption once it is provided. Examples of public goods are sunshine, clean air, national defense, biodiversity and scenic amenities. There are few pure public goods because most have a private element to them. There are also many private goods that are not purely private. For example, all residents benefit from a tastefully landscaped yard, but only one resident is responsible for the landscaping. On the other hand, some goods that are considered "public" have some degree of privateness to them: people living close to a fire hall have greater fire protection than those living further away. Goods and services with these characteristics are better referred to as *collective goods*.

Public goods are an important form of externality, because there is no incentive for individuals to provide them. The reason is obvious: once they are provided, no one can be excluded, so there is no way private individuals can benefit from their investment. No private property rights can be vested with respect to public goods. As a result, it falls upon the state to provide public goods. No private individual or firm would be willing to provide national defense services. Likewise, no private person would have an incentive to provide clean air or water, or protect biodiversity. In many cases, there are also no incentives to change one's behavior to prevent the befouling of air and water, or loss of species. In the absence of property rights, incurring costs to prevent pollution is the same as attempting to provide the public good privately. This then is one problem of environmental economics.

The public goods argument for government intervention also occurs in discussions concerning open spaces such as meadows and parks. Open space is a public good because others cannot be excluded from enjoying it. However, the same argument cannot be used to justify efforts to ensure the long-term sustainability of agricultural production, which is often invoked as an argument by those who are really interested in open space. The reason is that, if agricultural outputs are becoming scarce, prices will rise, land will become more valuable in agriculture, and markets will ensure that enough land is protected to maintain future agricultural capacity. Those who invoke this argument are generally more interested in protecting open space than they are concerned about maintaining national agricultural capacity (see also Chapter 8).

Technological Externality

The next type of externality is that which is usually meant when the term is discussed. A technological externality occurs whenever the actions of one economic agent are felt by a second (external) economic agent, but the impact on the second agent is not taken into account by the first agent in making decisions. The external agent incurs a cost, or receives a benefit, as a result of the actions of the first agent, but the first agent does not take the external cost or benefit into account. Thus, while economic processes are *physically* linked, the economic effects are separated. For example, pollution by a factory affects the success rate of downstream fishers, but this is not taken into account by the factory when it makes decisions regarding output and, hence, the amount of effluent it releases into the river. It is clear that, in this and similar situations, the factory would take into account its actions upon the downstream fishery if it also owned the fishery. The term "ownership externality" is sometimes used instead of "technological externality" because the externality is the result of a separation of ownership, but the term "environmental spillover" more aptly describes the problem. Hence, we will often use this term as a synonym for this form of externality.

While there are certain measures that can be taken to mitigate this type of externality, it is not possible to eliminate all technological externality. Rather, the objective is to find the optimal amount of externality to permit in order to ensure that the welfare of society is enhanced. In finding solutions, it will be shown that clear specification of property rights is particularly important.

Pecuniary Externality

Policy analysts and critics of land use and natural resource policy often confuse the pecuniary effects of externality with its real effects. Pecuniary effects concern income transfers. Pecuniary externality results whenever the actions of one agent affect another agent through the market. For example, suppose that a laundromat has trouble hiring labor because a pulp mill has recently moved into town. The pulp mill offers higher wages, and employees at the laundromat will remain in their current employ only if their wages are increased. The laundromat must either pay the higher wages or go out of business. Unless higher prices can be charged for laundry services, the laundromat may experience a reduction in net earnings. However, this is not a real loss to society; it is an income transfer that favors labor. A real externality occurs if the pulp mill affects the production function of the laundromat, requiring it to employ more soap and/or labor to obtain the same output as previously, or to purchase a dryer where laundry could earlier be hung out to dry. No government intervention is required in the case of pecuniary externality, but it may be required in the other three cases. Note the qualifier "may": government intervention benefits society only if the benefits of intervention exceed the costs (see Chapter 6).

5.2 ENVIRONMENTAL ECONOMICS

In recent years, concern over the environment has become more pronounced, especially as it relates to emissions of greenhouse gases and global warming (see Chapter 8). Environmental spillovers and public goods are of particular interest in environmental economics. In this section, we focus on policies to address spillovers and public goods.

Positive and Negative Spillovers

What does economic efficiency mean in an environmental context? We tend to know more about the *costs* of environmental improvements than we do about the *benefits* of environmental improvement. For example, biochemical oxygen demand (BOD) is a measure of the harmfulness of wastes. It is a measure of the amount of oxygen required by the wastes and, thus, unavailable for supporting aquatic life. It is easy to reduce BOD by 85%, but tertiary treatment to reduce it beyond 85% is expensive. Thus, the marginal cost curve is rather flat and then takes a sharp upward turn, as is indicated in Figure 5.2.

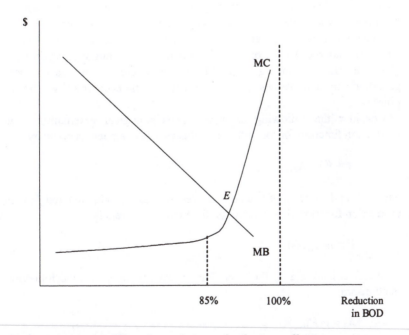

Figure 5.2: Marginal benefits and costs of reducing pollution

What, then, are the benefits of reducing BOD? There is little evidence regarding the marginal benefits of environmental improvement, although these benefits seem to be great when the environment is improved by a small amount. One role of the economist is to provide society with enough information concerning the marginal benefits (MB) and marginal costs (MC) to get us to some sort of equilibrium, such as E in Figure 5.2. In some sense the economist is a detective, seeking enough information to determine E, if not precisely, at least within some range of values. If we cannot attain E in this environmental market, then the market is economically inefficient.

The same thing is true of climate change. Compared to water pollution, climate change is a global rather than a local problem. It can be analyzed with the aid of Figure 5.2, except that the horizontal axis needs to be re-labeled as the "reduction in atmospheric concentration of CO_2". Again, more is known about the costs of reducing CO_2 emissions, or removing CO_2 from the atmosphere using terrestrial carbon sinks (see Chapter 8), than about the benefits of so doing. Also, the MC of reducing atmospheric CO_2 concentrations is probably flat over some range, after which it starts to rise dramatically. While the benefits from mitigating climate change are unknown (or only known with a high degree of uncertainty), a problem with climate change is that it impacts countries differently. Indeed, some countries are likely to benefit from global warming, while others might be devastated. Nonetheless, the objective of any international agreements to stabilize atmospheric concentrations of greenhouse gases (of which CO_2 is the most important) is to balance the global costs of doing so against the global benefits, of finding where MC and MB intersect as this is where global society achieves its greatest wellbeing – the economically efficient point.

Consider the following example of technological externality.[1] The production function for the output of industry A (say apples) is given by

$$A = f(X_1, X_2),$$

where X_1 and X_2 are inputs land and bees, say, into production and f is the production function. The production function for flowers is

$$F = h(X_1, X_3).$$

where X_1 is land and X_3 fertilizer. The externality enters via the following relationship:

$$X_2 = g(F).$$

That is, the quantity of bees (X_2) is positively affected by the production of flowers (F).

The "by-product" may be something "good" or it may be environmentally "bad". Whatever the case, it is clear that F has an impact on the level of A's production. A has no control over the output of F. Hence, producer F is the acting party and A is the affected party. Whether the production of F is good or bad for A depends on whether X_2 increases or decreases as F increases, and whether an increase in X_2 results in a decrease or increase in the output of A. In mathematical language, it depends upon the signs of the derivatives of the foregoing functions. Five cases can be distinguished (Buchanan and Stubblebine 1962).

1. $dX_2/dF > 0$ and $\partial A/\partial X_2 > 0$. An increase in output F will increase the amount of X_2 available for use in the production of A. An increase in X_2 will, in turn, cause an increase in the output of A. Since increases in F's output are beneficial to A, this is termed an *external economy* – a positive environmental spillover. The product X_2 is something considered "good". An increase in flower production leads to more bees that, in turn, will pollinate more of the apple blossoms, thereby increasing the yield of apples.

2. $dX_2/dF < 0$ and $\partial A/\partial X_2 < 0$. In this case, the second term indicates that X_2 is harmful to the production of A; that is, the more X_2 that enters into the production of A, the less A is produced. However, as a result of F's output, the availability of X_2 is actually reduced, as is indicated by the first term. The product or input X_2 adversely affects A, but B's output reduces it. Hence, we have an external economy once again.

3. $dX_2/dF < 0$ and $\partial A/\partial X_2 > 0$. Again, the availability of X_2 is reduced by an increase in output F, as is indicated by the sign on the first term. However, unlike the previous case, a decrease in X_2 will cause a decline in the output of A. Since the presence of output F is harmful to A, we refer to this as an *external diseconomy* – a negative environmental spillover.

4. $dX_2/dF > 0$ and $\partial A/\partial X_2 < 0$. The first expression indicates that availability of X_2 rises with increases in F; the second expression indicates that more X_2 results in a reduction in A. Thus, production by F is harmful to A, and we have an external diseconomy. An example is the case of a pulp mill polluting a river, thereby decreasing the number of fish caught by downstream fishers.

5. If either $dX_2/dF = 0$ or $\partial A/\partial X_2 = 0$, or both, there is no externality.

Now let us introduce some economic magnitudes into the foregoing analysis. This is done by introducing prices P_A, P_F, r_1, r_2 for outputs A and

F and inputs X_1 and X_2, respectively. Firms will employ an input (e.g., labor) as long as the marginal benefit of the hired input exceeds its marginal cost, with optimal employment occurring where the marginal benefit is exactly equal to marginal cost. In competitive markets, the marginal cost of an input is simply its price, say the wage rate. The marginal benefit is less straightforward but is also rather easy to find. It is equal to the additional product attributable to the employment of an extra unit of the input *multiplied* by the price of the product. Hence, the optimality condition is: $P \times MP = r$, where P is output price, MP is the marginal physical product attributable to the input and r is the price of input. The left-hand side of this relationship is also known as the value of the marginal product of the input.

Returning to our externality problem, private decisions about how much inputs to hire (output to produce) are determined from the following relations for industries A and F, respectively:

$$(5.1) \qquad P_A \times MP_{X_1 in A} = r_1,$$

$$(5.2) \qquad P_F \times MP_{X_1 in F} = r_1.$$

Now, A does not have any direct control over the amount of X_2 it uses; availability of X_2 is determined by F. In this sense, the technology can be considered *asymmetric*.

Society as a whole is concerned about efficiency in both industries. Thus, society would like industry F to take into account the effect production of F has on A's output. Social valuation of the amounts of input X_1 to be hired by A and F, respectively, would be as follows:

$$(5.3) \qquad P_A \times MP_{X_1 in A} = r_1,$$

$$(5.4) \qquad P_F \times MP_{X_1 in F} + (dX_2/dF)(\partial A/\partial X_2)P_A = r_1,$$

$$\Rightarrow P_F \times MP_{X_1 in F} + (dX_2/dF)(P_A \times MP_{X_2 in A}) = r_1.$$

Whereas a private producer would solve equilibrium conditions (5.1) and (5.2) to determine how much X_1 to hire, from society's perspective it is conditions (5.3) and (5.4) that must be solved simultaneously to take into account the externality and attain an efficient allocation of resources in each sector.

The signs on the terms dX_2/dF and $MP_{X_2 in A}$ (or $\partial A/\partial X_2$) will determine whether there is an external economy or an external diseconomy. In the case of an external economy more of the good resulting in the externality should be produced, while in the case of a diseconomy less than the private optimal should be produced.

In private accounting, F does not take into account the second term on the LHS of (5.4). In order to arrive at optimal resource use from society's perspective, it is necessary to get the producer of F to consider this term in the individual decision calculus. A number of alternative methods have been suggested.

1. If we have an external diseconomy, then we must tax F to get the firm to make decisions that are closer to the social optimum. If, on the other hand, we have an external economy, then we need to subsidize firm F in order to get it to make decisions that are optimal. This solution to the externality problem is referred to as the *Pigouvian tax or subsidy solution*.

2. The *Coase property rights solution* requires that property rights be correctly specified. Property rights could be specified so that A bribes F (i.e., F has been assigned the property rights) to take into account the damages (or benefits) accruing to A, or they could be arranged so that F would be required to pay compensation for damages inflicted upon A (i.e., A has the property rights). Specifying property rights involves legal wrangling and other transaction costs.

3. Another solution is *merger*. Take, for example, the case of pulp mill pollution that damages a downstream fishery. If the company that owns the pulp mill were also to own the fishery, then, in making its decisions, it would take into account the impact of the pollution generated by the pulp mill upon the landings of fish.

4. The final option is for the government to *nationalize* both industries A and F. In this case, the effect that firm F has on output A would be taken into account by the public manager. However, this may be the least desirable of all solutions, as is indicated by the environmental degradation that had taken place in the centrally planned economies of Eastern Europe and the ex-Soviet Union (Zylicz 1998).

Whatever policy is pursued, it is necessary to recognize that, if firm F does not take into account its impact upon the output of A, inefficiency exists in the economy; society's overall welfare is lower than it could be. Only when a proper social evaluation occurs – when F takes into account its actions upon A – will an efficient resolution to the externality problem result.

Finally, it is important to reiterate that not all externalities are relevant.

That is, simply because one discovers a pollution source, or some activity that impacts others, it does not mean that efforts should be taken to "correct" the externality. For example, suppose that a car runs inefficiently and spews out more noxious fumes than necessary. In a city such as Los Angeles, citizens may feel compelled to report the car's owner because, if everyone in the region were allowed to get away with such pollution, the effects on air quality would be onerous. However, in northern Canada where few people live, the cost of correcting the externality exceeds the benefits. Thus, vehicle pollution standards that apply to one region should not be imposed on other regions for efficiency reasons.

Environmental Spillovers and Economic Efficiency

It is possible to demonstrate a number of economic concepts concerning environmental pollution using the example of a pulp mill and a downstream fishery. The pulp mill pollutes a river, thereby affecting the catch of the fishers. We assume a two-actor world – fishers who want clean water that translates into more fish and an industrialist who dumps pollutants into the water, thereby killing the fish – and linear cost and benefit functions (for convenience of presentation). Benefits result from more fish as water becomes cleaner, while costs are related to the clean-up of industrial waste that pollutes the water.

In Figure 5.3, waste withheld is plotted along the abscissa, while dollars is plotted along the ordinate. The marginal benefit (MB) curve represents the marginal benefits to the fishers as wastes are withheld. The marginal cost (MC) curve represents the marginal costs to the industrialist of withholding wastes. The problem is an asymmetric one, since only the pulp mill can prevent or clean up the pollution. An economically efficient solution occurs at point C, where the costs to the industrialist are given by area $OACX$, and the costs to the fishers in terms of lost fish revenues are given by XCD. The solution at point C is termed Pareto optimal or Pareto efficient for reasons discussed below.

Consider reducing waste withheld to some amount less than X, say X_1. We strive to show that this is sub-optimal, with society better off at X than X_1. At X_1, the industrialist incurs total costs given by area $OAMX_1$, but the fishers lose X_1ND compared to what they would gain if the pulp mill was not there (equal to withholding OD waste). The total loss to society from the environmental externality in this case equals area $OAMX_1$ plus area X_1ND. This loss exceeds that associated with the higher level of waste withholding, X. At X, the total loss equals area $OACX$ plus area XCD. The social cost of withholding X_1 waste exceeds the total cost of withholding X waste by area NCM.

Similar reasoning is used to show that withholding waste beyond *X* is inefficient. Suppose *all* waste is withheld, as is often recommended. In moving from *X* to *D*, the added cost to the industrialist of withholding waste equals *XCKD* (while total cost is *OAKD*). The gain to the fishers from an additional amount *XD* of waste being withheld is given by area *XCD* (with total benefit given by *OBD*). The gains to the fishers are less than the costs incurred by the industrialist by area *CKD*. Since both the costs to the industrialist and the benefits (or losses) to fishers need to be taken into account by society, the optimal level of pollution from the standpoint of the social policymaker occurs when there is some amount of waste allowed to enter into the river, in this case an amount *XD*. Since society cannot improve upon equilibrium *C* (with waste *XD* permitted into the river), this point is considered Pareto optimal.

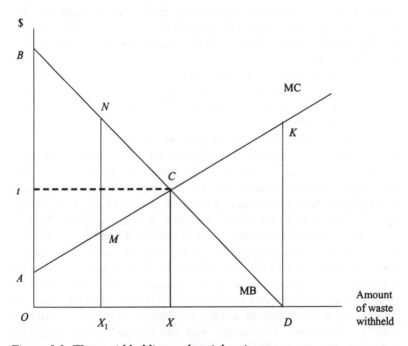

Figure 5.3: Waste withholding and social optimum

The foregoing example of externality, with the pulp mill affecting the profits of the fishery, illustrates that there still remain external effects, even at an economically efficient equilibrium. The reason is that complete elimination of emissions may be undesirable because it would also lead to the elimination of the desirable good whose production causes the environmental spillover. The optimal (Pareto efficient solution) is reached when the marginal benefits of producing the good equal the marginal production costs, which include the adverse costs of pollution. The problem from the point of view of the policymaker is: How does a society arrive at equilibrium point *C*, the economically efficient and hence socially desirable solution? A number of cases can be considered and these depend upon who has the property rights, the fishers or the industrialist.

5.3 INSTRUMENTS OF ENVIRONMENTAL POLICY

The problem of controlling pollution, preferably in an efficient way, is the subject of the theory of environmental policy. Below we review the main instruments that have been applied in industrialized countries. The discussion is primarily based on Baumol and Oates (1988), Barde (2000), and Romstad and Folmer (2000), and the reader is directed to these sources for further details.

There exist a number of different instruments that governments can use to protect the environment and encourage sustainable development. Although generally not promoted by economists, the traditional command and control mechanism, or regulation, is still a powerful tool in the policy arsenal. Economists generally emphasize instruments that promote efficiency and flexibility in achieving goals. For that purpose market-based incentives have been developed. Market incentives include tax (subsidy) and "cap-and-emission-trading" schemes. Whether regulations or incentives are employed, state involvement is required, if only to determine the cap level and enforce and monitor the subsequent trading mechanism. Reliance on private transactions to resolve environmental spillovers (as noted in the previous section) does not generally occur, usually because the transaction costs of getting together all those affected by the externality are onerous. While polluters can usually be identified quite easily, finding all those affected by the pollution may be difficult. This could explain why empirical evidence of market solutions without government intervention is lacking. Usually when firms voluntarily agree to "correct" an environmental externality, the explicit threat of state intervention is a prerequisite to such an agreement (Segerson and Miceli 1998).

It is remarkable, therefore, that there is now increasing evidence of the emergence of nonstate, market-driven governance structures for addressing environmental spillovers. These governance structures are appearing in a number of sectors, but certification of sustainable forest management practices is possibly the most comprehensive and advanced example of a nonstate, market-driven governance structure. Forest certification seeks to address environmental spillovers related to the "proper" and "sustainable" exploitation of forests – that forest operations do not endanger wildlife and watersheds, and that logging companies and landowners practice sustainable forest management. Forest certification is discussed in more detail in Chapter 12.

In this section, several methods of addressing environmental externalities are considered. Before doing so, we consider the characteristics that institutions should take in order that firms have an incentive to reduce spillovers.

1. Institutions must somehow reflect the parties that incur the external costs and benefits of the activity. For example, a surface mining reclamation board should not consist only of coal mining people. It should represent all individuals involved or affected by the decisions that are made.
2. The institutions should be able to influence behavior by either providing incentives or through direct control or regulation.
3. Government institutions should be set up in ways that enable society to take advantage of economies of size. For example, municipal waste disposal is characterized by economies of scale relative to individual treatment.
4. Institutions must be constructed so that economic actors take into account nonmarket benefits, such as recreational opportunities, protection of wildlife habitat (biodiversity), and scenic amenities.
5. Institutions must be concerned with a physically and economically relevant geographic area. A good example is the Rhine River in Europe. Germany wants a clean Rhine in Germany, but it cares less if the Rhine running through Holland is polluted. The same is true of the Colorado River, which crosses into Mexico as a stream of salt water. An institution developed to reduce pollution in these two rivers must have *effective* representation from Holland and Mexico, respectively, and not just from Germany and the United States.
6. Institutions should be capable of adapting to changes in technology. Unfortunately, institutions generally have an inertia of their own that may militate against finding optimal solutions to the problem of externality over time. The cost and benefit curves tend not to stay constant through time. Given that there are changes occurring over time, it is necessary that institutions be able to adapt to such changes.
7. Finally, institutions must operate by a set of rules that are considered to be fair by a majority of people. Otherwise, they will fail, because they are not politically feasible.

Regulations and Standards

At the early stages of environmental policy, regulators in most industrialized countries largely employed regulatory controls – denoted "command and control" (C&C) – and this still remains the principal instrument of choice (Stavins 2002). Command and control consists of the promulgation and enforcement of laws and regulations prescribing objectives, standards and technologies with which polluters must comply (Barde 2000). A distinction is usually made among:

- ambient standards that specify the characteristics of the receiving (ambient) environment (e.g., the maximum concentration of nitrates in drinking water);
- emission standards or effluent standards specifying the maximum allowable discharges of pollutants into the environment (e.g., the maximum SO_x emission by cars);
- process standards that specify the type of production process or emission reduction equipment that polluters must install (e.g., a specific type of scrubber); and
- product standards that specify the characteristics of polluting products (e.g., the composition of fuels or pesticides).

The most important feature of the C&C approach is its high likelihood of achieving a given environmental goal. Once a standard is fixed, the environmental goal will be achieved, provided there is enough effective enforcement. It is especially for this reason that C&C is used to prevent hazards and irreversible effects. Another feature of C&C is that there is a long-standing experience in other fields of public concern, such as health and safety.

For attaining an efficient solution (where marginal cost is equal to marginal benefit), regulation does not usually work. It is a satisficing method that works best over a particular range of waste withholding. In Figure 5.4, the standard is set at W. The policymaker will not usually be able to set the level of waste withholding at the point where society's welfare is maximized (point E) because the informational requirements of doing so are onerous. The loss to society from choosing W because the policymaker is unable to achieve E is given by area MNE. Even if the standard were set to attain E, efficiency is likely to disappear after some time. The reason is that standards and regulations tend to be rigid and difficult to change. If the marginal cost and marginal benefit curves change, then point E may also change. This implies that any regulation or standard has to be flexible.

Standards may not be sufficiently flexible to take regional differences into account. As discussed earlier, this is inefficient because what applies in one region may not apply in another. For example, a car pollution standard applicable in Los Angeles or Vancouver may be too stringent for cities located outside of these urban areas. Thus, buyers in cities located in low-population centers will pay too much for automobiles. Finally, regulation provides no revenues.

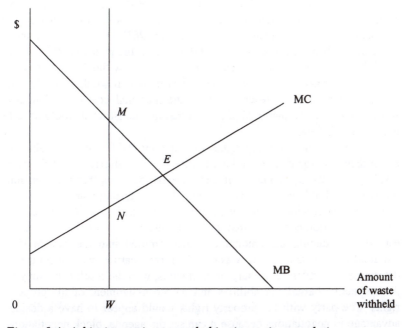

Figure 5.4: Achieving environmental objectives using regulation

To sum up, a major weakness of regulations is that they are inefficient in the sense that the same environmental objectives could be achieved at lower social cost using so-called economic instruments (see below). Another drawback is that regulations are static and lack incentives to technological innovation. Furthermore, enforcement of regulations may be difficult, weak or costly due to the great number of controls, administrative requirements, legal procedures in the case of noncompliance and so on. Finally, regulations tend to be subject to bargaining between the regulator and the private sector, which may lead to weakening of the regulations and consequently negative environmental impacts.

The Coase Theorem

The C&C approach depends heavily on state intervention to reduce pollution, and then the reduction achieved by regulations may not be efficient. Coase (1960) has shown that market transactions between polluters and victims can produce Pareto efficient outcomes without intervention by a regulator.

Consider again Figure 5.3 and assume that the fishers have the property right. If there is no waste withholding, then the pulp mill will have to compensate the fishers an amount equal to area *OBD* – the entire area under the marginal benefit curve. Given that the amount the industrialist must pay the fishers is initially much larger than the costs of withholding wastes, as given by the marginal cost curve, the industrialist will withhold waste until equilibrium point *C* is reached. There the marginal cost of withholding waste is equal to the marginal payments that the industrialist would have to make to the fishers.

Now reverse the property rights so that they reside with the pulp mill rather than with the fishers. In this case, the fishers will pay a "bribe" (make a side payment) to the pulp mill that exceeds the costs that the pulp mill incurs in withholding wastes. Once again, the equilibrium point is *C*.

Regardless of which actor has the property rights, in a world where there are no transaction costs, the area *ABC* in Figure 5.3 is a surplus that can be earned by reducing the amount of waste emitted into the system (i.e., withholding *OX* amount of wastes). The two parties will negotiate to determine how much of the surplus each gains, with the result depending on the respective bargaining abilities and on the assignment of the property rights. The party with the property rights would appear to have a decided advantage in negotiations because it can set the agenda, block negotiations, etc.

There are a number of factors that prevent actors from negotiating to achieve a Pareto optimal solution in the face of externality.

- Property rights may not be clearly defined. For example, who owns the rights to a river or, for that matter, who owns the rights to a lake, ocean or the atmosphere?
- Negotiation between the parties often leads to litigation, and court procedures are both costly and time consuming.
- The benefits of environmental improvement generally tend to be widely dispersed, and those who benefit from environmental improvement are unable to get together to discuss strategy, size of required bribes, and so on.
- Problems in technical information gathering often exist. Irreversibilities

may be present. Moreover, many effects are nonmarket in nature and, therefore, extremely difficult to measure. As mentioned, many effects are widely dispersed, and more than one geographic and/or political unit is affected.

- Finally, there may be threshold levels. The effects of pollution are often negligible over some range, but they become critical beyond a certain level. An airshed or watershed may be able to retain its integrity with (absorb the wastes of) five industrial firms, but the addition of a sixth results in loss of ecosystem integrity – a threshold is passed. Who is to blame and who pays? Is it just the sixth firm or all of them?

Merger

Another solution to the externality problem caused by the pulp mill without state intervention is merger of the two firms (see Löfgren 2000). Suppose that the profit function of firm 1 (the pulp mill) is:

(5.5) $\pi_1 = pq - C(q)$

where q is output, p is output price and C the total cost of production. Profit maximization gives

(5.6) $p = C'(q)$

That is, firm 1 would produce an amount q^* such that price equals marginal cost.

Now suppose that production of one unit of output by firm 1 inflicts a cost k upon firm 2, so production of q leads to kq costs for firm 2. If firm 1 owned firm 2 (the fishery), the former's profit function would be

(5.7) $\pi_1^A = pq - C(q) - kq,$

and the profit maximization condition is:

(5.8) $p = C'(q) + k.$

In this case, the merged firm would produce $\tilde{q} < q^*$. That is, the output level of the merged firm is lower than in the case where both firms are independent. For the merged firms, output of pulp is such that the social marginal valuation of fish, p, coincides with its social marginal cost, $C'(q) + k$. That is, the externality would disappear, since the divergence between private and social marginal costs would disappear.

A basic question is: Will the merger materialize? When firm 1 reduces its output, its profit will go down. However, the profit of firm 2 will go up such that the aggregate profit of the two firms increases. This is because the socially desirable combined output level increases compared to the situation before the merger when the pulp mill produced too much and the fishery too little from a social point of view. Given perfect asset markets, the arbitrage possibility of making a profit would lead to a merger. This implies that more markets and complete information could correct for an externality. Since the latter are strong assumptions that are unlikely to be met in practice, alternative policies are required to correct the externality.

Environmental Taxes/Charges

The upshot of the previous discussion was that the applicability of the Coase theorem and merger is limited, and it follows that state intervention is usually required to control pollution. However, rather than resorting to inefficient regulations, the authority can apply environmental (Pigouvian) taxes or charges that, under certain conditions, can be socially optimal and cost-effective. A tax or charge is also considered to be fair in some cases because they penalize an economic agent for the "damage" inflicted on others – the "polluter pays" principle.

Again consider Figure 5.3 where, as argued above, the optimal level of waste withholding is X. The pollution tax should be fixed to attain this optimal level, which can be done with a tax set equal to t. To see this consider pollution levels smaller than X. For these levels, the marginal abatement costs are smaller than the tax t. Hence, polluters will choose to abate rather than pay the tax. For abatement levels larger than X, the reverse holds. Thus, the optimal level of abatement is X.

It should be observed that the optimal tax level of an externality-generating activity is not equal to the marginal net damage it produces initially, but rather to the damage it would cause if the level of production had been adjusted to the optimal level. To give an example, suppose that initially (before any abatement) each additional unit of output causes $0.7 worth of damage. However, after installing optimal abatement measures, the marginal damage is only $0.3. The correct value of the Pigouvian tax is then $0.3 and not $0.7. The tax needs to be set equal to the marginal damage at the optimal output level.

There remains one problem: in practice the authority has little information about the benefits of pollution abatement. This is particularly true in the case of climatic change where little is known about the damages resulting from (additional) increases in atmospheric CO_2. In that case, the regulator can resort to the so-called *standards and charges approach*. This approach involves first of all the selection of a set of acceptable environmental standards, which amount to a set of constraints on production activities. Charges are then used to achieve the standards using an iterative "trial and error" procedure. Initially, the charge is determined on the basis of existing knowledge or a guesstimate. Next, the environmental effect is determined. If the initial tax did not reduce pollution sufficiently to satisfy the preset standard, the tax would be raised. If pollution reduction exceeds the standards, the tax will be lowered. In the second round the environmental effect is again estimated and, if necessary, the tax is re-adjusted. This continues until the desired trade-off between the tax and environmental quality is achieved.

The iterative procedure leads to inconsistencies in the tax base, however, because of the frequent changes in the tax rate. Such inconsistencies are strongly opposed by the business community, and are undesirable from a public finance point of view, because of the variation in the tax revenues they create. For these reasons the number of adjustments needs to be limited, which, in turn, is undesirable from the standpoint of environmental policy because one may be stuck with charges fixed at sub-optimal (inefficient and socially undesirable) levels.

Environmental taxes or pollution charges have several important features. First, if firms have different marginal abatement cost functions, which is usually the case in practice, then charges will minimize total abatement costs relative to a uniform (mandatory) percentage reduction in pollution that is the same for each polluter, independent of differences in marginal abatement costs. If the marginal abatement costs of one polluter are higher than those of another polluter, it is collectively more efficient to have the latter firm abate more than the former. With a uniform charge, each polluter will fix its abatement level where its marginal abatement cost curve (MAC) equals the charge. We demonstrate this with the aid of Figure 5.5.

Suppose that pulp mills *A* and *B* are both emitting effluent into a river. Each firm has a different marginal cost curve for waste withholding as indicated by MC_A and MC_B. Now assume that society wishes to have waste withheld to some point *E*, as is indicated on the horizontal axis in Figure 5.5.

If an equitable standard is used to achieve waste withholding of amount *E*, then each firm would withhold *K* amount of waste, such that two times *K* is equal to *E*. The cost to society of the regulation is then given by area *ONJK* + *OMGK*. If, instead of a standard, a uniform charge *C* was used, each polluter would fix its abatement level where its marginal abatement cost curve (MC$_i$, $i = A$, B) equals the charge. That is, firm A would withhold A amount of waste and firm B would withhold amount B. Notice that $A + B = E$. The cost to society of waste withholding in this case would be area *ONIB + OMLA*, which equals *OMTZE* by the way that the marginal abatement costs of the two firms are summed. This cost is lower than that incurred under regulation. The firm with the higher cost of withholding waste, firm B, would withhold less waste than would the more efficient firm A. Since charges result in lower *social* costs than does regulation, they are preferable from a social point of view.[2]

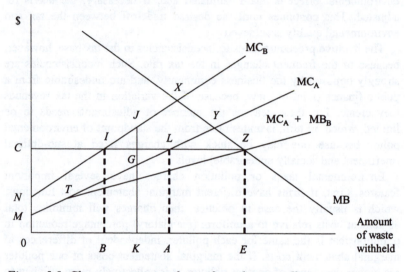

Figure 5.5: Charges versus regulation for reducing pollution

A second important characteristic of a pollution charge is that it provides a permanent incentive to abate. This follows from the fact that the polluter has to pay the charge as long as it produces pollution to which the charge applies. Hence, the polluter, as a cost minimizer, has an incentive to reduce pollution, say, by searching for and adopting cleaner technologies as they become available. The cost reduction from adopting a cleaner production technology can be illustrated using Figure 5.6. Suppose that under the current technology the marginal abatement cost function is MAC$_1$. In this case, the firm would reduce pollution up to P_1 and pay tP_1 as pollution taxes. By adopting the cleaner technology given by MAC$_2$, the firm will reduce pollution to P_2 and pay only tP_2 as pollution taxes. The reduction in pollution charges equals area P_1P_2AB. Moreover, the polluter saves *BCF* in abatement costs. However, overall abatement costs will have increased, from P_1BF to P_2AF, which is offset by the reduction in taxes, of course. Net savings to the firm equal area ABF.

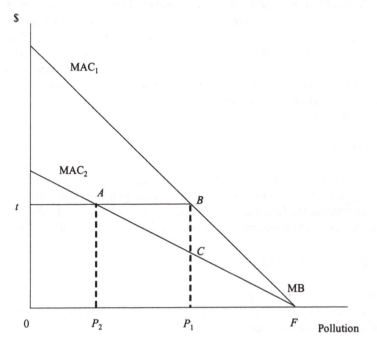

Figure 5.6: Advantages of adopting cleaner technologies

When will the polluter switch to the new technology? To answer this question we need to take into account the dynamics and investment costs of the new technology. Net savings will be realized over time, which means that they have to be discounted. Denote the net saving by S, the discount rate by r, the lifetime of the new technology by T and investment costs of the new technology minus the scrapvalue of the old technology by I. The polluter will switch to the new technology at time t if

$$(5.9) \quad \sum_{t=1}^{T}\left(\frac{1}{1+r}\right)^t S_t - I > 0.$$

Note that regulations provide no incentives to reduce pollution further. In contrast to emission charges that need to be paid for any unabated emissions, regulations do not require further reductions in emissions once the abatement measures have been implemented, nor are there economic incentives in the way of cost savings to the firm to reduce emissions beyond what is required.

A third characteristic of environmental taxes is that they provide revenues for the government, which can be added to the general budget or earmarked for specific purposes. For instance, the water pollution charges in Germany and France are earmarked for financing water treatment facilities. There may be an additional benefit to society from environmental revenues if these are recycled; by reducing distorting (income) taxes, environmental tax revenue can improve overall economic efficiency (see Bovenberg and Goulder 1996).

Subsidies

The regulator may also resort to subsidies rather than taxes to induce the individual firm to reduce production and hence pollution. This can be seen by comparing the firm's profit functions under both taxes and subsidies. In the case of an environmental tax levied on emissions, the profit function is:

$$(5.10) \quad \pi^t = pq - C(q,a) - t^e(q,a),$$

where q is output, p is price, costs C are a function of q and abatement expenditures a, and t^e is the tax rate per unit of emissions. In the case of subsidies, the profit function is:

$$(5.11) \quad \pi^s = pq - C(q,a) - s[e* - e(q,a)]$$

where s is the subsidy per unit of emissions abated, e is total emissions as a function of q and a, and $e*$ represents the environmental objective. The two profit functions only differ by a constant quantity $se*$. The first-order conditions for maximizing profits (5.10) and (5.11) indicate that the choice between a tax and a subsidy will not affect production decisions, except for the fact that a tax may induce a firm to cease operations and a subsidy to continue operations. (This result has to do with the so-called "shutdown" conditions.) In all other respects, the tax and the subsidy lead to the same outcome (Baumol and Oates 1988).

In spite of the identical outcome at the *individual* firm level, subsidies are regarded as inefficient. The main reason is that, in the case of a competitive industry, subsidies have a perverse effect in the sense that they may lead to an increase rather than a decrease in *total* emissions. The reason is that, in the long run, subsidies shift the supply curve in a competitive industry downwards and, with a negatively sloping demand curve, equilibrium output increases, thereby increasing pollution above what it would be with a tax. The intuition is that the subsidy induces the entry of firms, which results in a fall in price, an increase in industry output and industry emissions (Baumol and Oates 1988).

There are several other problems with subsidies. First of all, they are expensive, since there is no source of revenue. Further, government institutions may be open to extortion. For example, a firm may pretend to start producing some output implicitly, declaring its intention to pollute the river, but it is then paid not to produce. In a similar vein, subsidies may be claimed by polluters for abatement activities that they would have taken anyway, even without the subsidy. Finally, payments do not appeal to people's sense of equity and, as a result, may not be politically feasible. Particularly, they are incompatible with the polluter pays principle.

Marketable Emissions Permits

Another economic instrument of environmental policy is marketable or tradable emission permits. In this case, the regulator artificially creates markets to allocate a pre-set level of emissions among polluters in efficient fashion. The notion of marketable emissions permits was introduced by Crocker (1965).

Emissions trading is a broad concept that covers two types of schemes – credit trading or permit (allowance) trading. Credit trading occurs when the government mandates that firms (usually large industrial emitters) each reduce emissions of a pollutant by a certain amount, generally expressed as a proportion of baseline emissions. Firms that reduce pollution below the required level receive credits that can be sold to firms that, for whatever reason, cannot meet their target. There is nothing to prevent emissions from growing, however, because new firms can enter as the economy expands, or because the emission reduction target was based on the attainment of some standard of efficiency.

Allowance or permit trading first requires the establishment of an aggregate cap (or quota) on emissions, followed by the "issuance" of "rights to emit" (allowances/permits) that can then be traded. As a result, this scheme is referred to as a cap-and-trade system. Under a cap-and-trade scheme, the government simply sets a cap on the amount of a pollutant that can be emitted to the atmosphere, issuing permits or allowances in that amount. Tradable emission permits can be allocated to existing emitters at no cost to them (referred to as "grandfathering") or sold via an auction to the highest bidders, thereby generating revenue for the government. Emission rights (allowances) thus gravitate to firms with the lowest marginal emission-reduction costs.

In Figure 5.7 we consider permits in the context of reducing CO_2 emissions. Economic agents benefit from activities that release CO_2, with the benefits attributable to CO_2 emissions given by the area under the marginal benefit function in Figure 5.7. If release of CO_2 is costless, agents will continue releasing CO_2 to the point where the marginal benefit function intersects the horizontal axis. Restricting emissions to C^* (and issuing permits in that amount) results in a deadweight loss due to allocative inefficiency and a scarcity rent, as indicated in the figure. If permits are grandfathered, then firms (agents) that are provided allowances capture the rent; if allowances are auctioned (or a tax is employed), the authority captures the economic rent. The price or value of CO_2–emission permits is P, which is determined by the intersection of demand and supply, where supply is simply a vertical line at C^*.

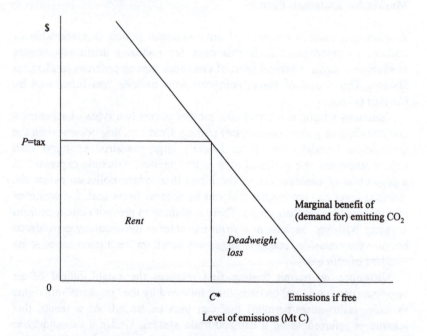

Figure 5.7: Controlling CO_2 emissions using economic incentives

The basic idea in the case of permit trading is that profitable firms with high abatement costs have a higher willingness to pay for emission permits than firms with low profitability or low abatement costs. Profitable firms with high abatement costs have an incentive to buy permits as long as the marginal benefit of buying a permit exceeds the permit price. Firms with low abatement costs will tend to sell the permits as long as the permit price exceeds their unit profits or marginal abatement costs. The market transactions of buying and selling permits leads to a socially desirable outcome since, in the case of profitable firms, society's opportunity costs of abating their emissions (the marginal profits) are high. Conversely, in the case of firms with low abatement costs or low marginal profits, society's opportunity costs are low. Therefore, the transfer of emissions permits from the latter firms to the former makes society better off. However, for a tradable permit system to function well, marginal abatement costs must vary sufficiently between polluters. Moreover, there must be a sufficient number of firms and gains from trade so that overall abatement costs are lowered before a permit scheme will function properly. As in the case of a tax/charge, a system of tradable permits will lead to substantial cost savings relative to regulations. The demonstration of this proposition is similar to that for the tax.

Economists generally like economic incentives because firms have an incentive to adopt technical changes that lower the costs of reducing emissions, because they can then sell permits or avoid buying them, or avoid paying the tax. Further, market instruments provide incentives to change products, processes, and so on, as marginal costs and benefits change over time. Because firms are always trying to avoid the tax or paying for emission rights, they tend to respond quickly to technological change.

Prices versus Quantities

Auctioned permits and pollution taxes are thought to be identical – opposite sides of the same coin in the sense that auctioned permits target quantity while taxes target price. Consider again Figure 5.7. The carbon tax determines the level of emissions; if the number of permits to be auctioned is the same as this level of emissions, the auction price should equal the tax. The state can choose the tax level (price) or the number of emission permits to auction (quantity), but if all is known the outcome will be the same – $0C^*$ emission permits trade at a price P (=tax). However, when abatement costs and/or benefits are uncertain (i.e., the demand function in Figure 5.7 is unknown), picking a carbon tax can lead to the "wrong" level of emissions reduction, while choosing a quantity can result in a mistake about the forecasted price that firms will have to pay for auctioned permits (Weitzman 1974). Such errors have social costs. If the demand curve for permits is relatively steep but damages accumulate only slowly, as is the case with climate change, the costs of relying on (auctioned) tradable emission permits is much higher than those associated with carbon taxes (Pizer 1997; Weitzman 1974, 2002).

If there is uncertainty about the marginal costs and benefits (damages avoided) of abating climate change, the choice of a price-based or quantity-based instrument will depend on which type of uncertainty is most prevalent. Since there appears little that can be done to halt climate change and since damages are likely to increase slowly over time, the choice of a price or quantity instrument will depend on the marginal abatement cost function. It is clear that, the steeper the marginal abatement cost function, the more beneficial it will be, *ceteris paribus*, to use a price (tax) rather than quantity instrument. More specifically, if the marginal benefit curve is relatively flat compared to the marginal cost curve, a tax is preferred to a quota. Contrariwise, the flatter the marginal abatement cost function, the better it is to employ a quantity instrument, such as a marketable allowance.

The success of the grandfathered SO_2 trading scheme in reducing pollution among (primarily) electrical power producers in the US northeast is often touted as the approach that CO_2 abatement needs to follow. However, one cannot expect the same results with a CO_2 trading system because the marginal benefit curve from controlling CO_2 emissions is relatively flat compared to the associated marginal cost curve, in which case a tax and not quota should be used.

> The prospects for welfare gains through quotas or non-auctioned permits are much dimmer in the CO_2 context. Quotas or non-auctioned permits have a greater chance at yielding welfare gains in the SO_2 case because the central estimates for marginal environmental benefits are relatively high (compared with marginal abatement costs) in this case. In contrast, central estimates for marginal environmental benefits from CO_2 reductions are fairly low relative to marginal abatement cost. (Parry et al. 1999, p.55)

Income Redistributional Effects

Regardless of how emissions are curtailed, doing so creates a wedge between the marginal costs of providing emission permits (which is effectively zero) and the price at which they sell in the market. As noted above, this wedge is a form of scarcity rent, with the total unearned rent equal to the restricted level of emissions multiplied by their price (Figure 5.7). The rent represents the capitalized value of the right to emit CO_2, which had previously been free. With a tax or auction scheme, the government captures the rent, but, in the case of grandfathered emission rights, it is captured by extant emitters. Those lucky enough to receive tradable emission permits experience a windfall. As a result, governments will be subject to tremendous lobbying pressure in their decision regarding the allocation of permits. Countries that have done the most to reduce emissions in the past may lose relative to ones that made no similar efforts; firms that are high-energy users may benefit relative to those firms that invested in energy savings technology.

Yet, emissions trading is often preferred by governments for two reasons (Snodden and Wigle 2003). First, total compliance cost for firms is generally lower than under a permit scheme, even though both a carbon tax and permit trading lead to the same result in terms of economic efficiency. Only the distribution of income differs: The cost to firms under a tax is given by area *OPZE* in Figure 5.5, while it is only *OMTZE* with emissions trading (although there will be income transfers among firms). The tax results in a transfer of income from firms to taxpayers that is absent under cap-and-trade unless permits are auctioned.

Second and perhaps more important for governments, a permit scheme has flexibility in the way it assigns the burden of climate change mitigation. If permits are not auctioned, older, less-efficient firms can be assigned a disproportionate share of the permits to enable them to better withstand the adverse impact of the measures. A greater share of the permits could also be assigned to the hardest hit regions of a country. The assignment of permits across firms and/or regions enables politicians to re-allocate income and thereby make pollution abatement more palatable, but it can also lead to further misallocation of resources as firms spend resources seeking a favorable assignment of permits.

Alternatively, governments can implement credit trading that focuses on particular sources, such as large industrial emitters, or projects (e.g., sink activities). However, as pointed out by Tietenberg et al. (1998) in their review of greenhouse gas emissions trading, credit trading schemes have generally performed poorly because of high transaction costs related to oversight and uncertainty. As argued in subsequent chapters, this is the problem with terrestrial carbon sinks.

If pollution taxes are used to capture the unearned rent, then the pertinent question is: What becomes of the tax revenue? If permits were auctioned, one would likewise want to know what happens to the revenue. First off, both a tax and a tradable permit scheme increase the costs of consumption goods, thereby reducing the supply of labor and increasing the marginal cost of abatement. This "tax-interaction" effect is the result of pre-existing taxes on labor.[3] The state can use tax revenue to offset the negative impact of restricting pollution (CO_2 emissions, say) – the economic inefficiencies resulting from a misallocation of resources (the deadweight loss in Figure

5.7) and the tax-interaction effect – by reducing distorting taxes (and associated economic inefficiencies or deadweight losses) elsewhere in the economy. So-called "revenue recycling" has the potential to reduce substantially the costs of pollution abatement policies. This is known as the "double-dividend" because the environmental improvement also leads to increased efficiency elsewhere in the economy. However, if the tax revenue is recycled in lump-sum fashion (e.g., every citizen is provided the same tax rebate) and not used to reduce distortionary taxes elsewhere in the economy, the pollution tax actually exacerbates inefficiencies, raising the marginal cost of pollution abatement (see Bovenberg and Goulder 1996). As a corollary, a cap-and-trade scheme with grandfathered permits is more costly than a carbon tax or a cap-and-trade auction scheme because the government collects no revenues.[4]

Damage Liability

Another internalization system of environmental damage costs is a damage liability system. It is based on the assumption that the polluter will continue abating as long as the marginal abatement costs are smaller than the expected marginal liability cost (expected because both the probability of being found liable and the compensation to be paid are uncertain). Barde (2000) enumerates several conditions that need to be met for the application of the present system, including that damage costs are correctly evaluated, polluters and victims can be identified, the causal relationship between pollution and damage is recognized, and the system can be enforced without excessive costs. These conditions are usually difficult to meet in practice so that the use of this instrument is limited primarily to accidental pollution, such as oil spills (see Segerson 2000).

Voluntary Agreements

Voluntary agreements are commitments from polluters to improve their environmental performance (Barde 2000). Voluntary agreements range from negotiated agreements, public voluntary schemes to unilateral commitments. Negotiated agreements are real contracts between the regulator and industry comprising objectives, a time schedule, compliance and control provisions, and possibly sanctions. A basic feature is that the regulator agrees not to introduce other instruments of environmental policy, such as taxes, if the objectives are achieved. On the other hand, in the case of noncompliance the regulator will intervene. In the case of public voluntary schemes, participating firms are invited to comply with objectives, rules or guidelines developed by the regulator but are not *a priori* obliged to comply. Unilateral commitments, finally, are private initiatives. The rationale is to prevent the emergence of new regulations, or to improve environmental performance or public image (see Lévêque and Nadai 1995).

Segerson and Li (1999) cite 3M Company's "Pollution Prevention Pays" and Dow Corporation's "Waste Reduction Always Pays" programs as having reduced production or operating costs. Likewise, programs that promote energy efficiency, thus reducing pollution, can reduce a firm's energy costs and, if packaged correctly, earn the company public relations' benefits. In the forest sector, forest certification might cause a change in management that lowers operating costs.

Markets might dictate whether firms enter environmental agreements (say, certify their forest operations) without state involvement. Threats of product boycotts (loss of market share) or lawsuits related to spillovers (e.g., that destroy critical wildlife habitat or result in emission of dangerous pollutants), which increase costs or threaten a firm's survival, can motivate companies to take action voluntarily. These might be considered negative factors as they do not increase earnings, but they are actions taken to protect earnings. For example, markets for wood products can be delineated according to whether consumers care that products come from sustainably managed forests. In contrast to the view that certification is a defensive tactic, the possibility of gaining market share at the expense of rivals or obtaining a price premium for one's products can induce companies to take noncoerced, unilateral action. However, if too many companies become certified, then the wedge between certified and noncertified wood product prices might be small, or even negligible, and certainly less than the costs of becoming certified and maintaining that status.

Finally, there is the view that firms will voluntarily enter environmental agreements without the threat of the state because it gives them the social license to operate in a manner that permits some environmental harm, since not all spillovers can be mitigated in any event. This can be considered an ethical argument related to "corporate responsibility" – managers of firms feel that they have to behave in a socially acceptable manner.

As Barde (2000) points out, the main advantage of voluntary agreements is the flexibility it offers both the private sector and the regulator. The former is in a position to influence the environmental targets; to apply the most appropriate means to achieve the targets and to adopt its own time schedule. For the regulator flexibility consists of avoidance of heavy control and sanction procedures. But there are pitfalls, including weak control because of lack of sanctions on the side of the private sector or the regulator; free-riding, particularly in the absence of monitoring and sanctions provisions; high transaction costs, especially if the number of stakeholders is large; and "regulatory capture" – the risk that powerful industry organizations "capture" the policy by obstructing the introduction of a policy or influencing the policy to their own benefit and to the detriment of society. Moreover, private enterprises have incentives to implement lax ojectives, rather than ambitious ones.

5.4 CONSUMERS, PRODUCERS AND EXTERNALITY

The pulp mill–fishery example is one of "producer–producer" externality. This case illustrates the effect of one firm's output decisions on the production function of another. There are also "consumer–consumer" and "producer–consumer" externalities.

Smoking is an example of a consumer–consumer externality. Scientific evidence indicates that smoking is a definite cause of lung cancer, that smoking is linked to cancer of internal organs and to heart disease, and that smoking is harmful to non-smokers. In one province of Canada (Saskatchewan) during the 1980s, the provincial government collected approximately $17 million per year from cigarette taxes but spent $21 million per year on lung cancer alone. Given the fact that smoking is linked to other types of cancer and heart disease, and is harmful to non-smokers, it may be that the smoker does not pay a fair share of the costs of medical expenses. These costs are borne by non-smokers, and this is both inefficient and unfair. The solution is to tax cigarettes so that smokers bear the true costs of smoking. Some governments have actively pursued taxes. For example, Canada implemented an onerous tobacco tax in the 1990s that led to cigarette smuggling on such a scale that the government was forced to lower the tax. One problem was that the government was motivated as much by its revenue needs as by a desire to reduce the externalities related to smoking. In the USA, as a consequence of lawsuits, cigarette companies have agreed to make "compensatory payments" to various states for the externality effects of smoking, but states have looked upon this tobacco money as a revenue source and have not used it to reduce levels of consumption. The externality could be addressed in other ways.

Smokers endanger the health of non-smokers. In many jurisdictions non-smokers must bribe smokers not to smoke. By changing the law so that smoking is prohibited in a public place, property rights are effectively changed. The situation can be illustrated with the aid of Figure 5.8. Amount smoked by an individual is plotted along the horizontal axis. The marginal benefit (MB) curve measures the benefits (pleasure) that the smoker derives. The curve labeled MC_{private} is the private marginal cost of smoking,

what the smoker pays. The cost to the smoker includes the price of
cigarettes, the costs of more frequent cleaning of draperies, the costs of
painting more often, and so on. The curve labeled MC_{social} is the marginal
cost to society of that person smoking. It includes both the private cost of
smoking and the cost to non-smokers. There is a divergence between the
private and social costs of smoking. The smoker will smoke an amount
given by Q_P, whereas society would prefer that amount Q_S is smoked.
Notice that, in order to attain a social optimum or economically (Pareto)
efficient solution, it is not necessary that consumption of tobacco be
reduced to zero (as the reader can verify using the analytical techniques
illustrated above). Yet, the intention of government appears to be to
eliminate all smoking; this is inefficient, unless the intersection of MB and
MC_{social} occurs at a nonpositive value for the amount smoked.

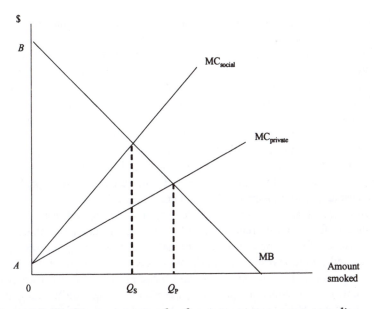

Figure 5.8: Smoking as an example of consumer–consumer externality

An example of a producer–consumer externality is coal unloading in a
port city. The coal unloading activity imposes an externality on nearby
residents who cannot hang out laundry to dry, have to wash their windows
more frequently, etc. The coal company could add to its costs payments to
residents in order to put up with the coal unloading facility, or the residents
could pay the coal company to choose an alternative site. Who pays

depends upon the assignment of the property rights. The only problem is that the transaction costs of bringing residents together could outweigh the benefits.

The diagram employed for the smoking example, Figure 5.8, could apply in this case as well. Rather than labeling the horizontal axis as the amount smoked, we simply re-label it as the amount of coal unloaded. Once again, there is a divergence between private and social costs, with the social costs being higher than the private costs. By getting the coal company to take into account the costs it imposes upon nearby residents, less coal will be unloaded at the facility. Alternatively, if the costs of compensating residents are large, it may pay to re-locate the unloading facility to another port.

5.5 DISCUSSION

We end this chapter with some remarks. First, environmental policy in a given area is usually implemented through several policy instruments, rather than only one. For instance, market instruments are not well suited to handle extreme, infrequent and unacceptable environmental conditions that require rapid temporary control. For example, a given level of air or water pollution may be acceptable under normal circumstances, but may become intolerable in extreme, infrequently occurring situations. In such situations the regulator could resort to a mixed system that relies on both taxes and regulations. The former would be used to achieve prescribed environmental standards during normal periods, whereas flexible regulations would be applied on a standby basis, to be put into effect when unpredictable circumstances call for them (see Baumol and Oates 1988).

Instruments of environmental policy can also be applied in a combined fashion to focus on different aspects of a given environmental problem. The Netherlands, for example, uses a combination of user charges, taxes, speed limits and public investment (subsidies) to get people to drive less and to rely more on public transportation and bicycles. The various instruments aim not only to reduce air pollution, but also to reduce traffic congestion and accidents. High taxes are levied on the purchase price of automobiles so that fewer are sold; these taxes increase the costs of an automobile by more than 40%. A road tax is levied, with the charge varying by the type of fuel used. Such taxes are designed not only to make driving more expensive, but also to reduce gasoline consumption. Taxes on automotive fuels are extremely high. There is a speed limit of 120 kilometers per hour (kph) on freeways, whereas in urban areas where there is a higher likelihood of congestion the limit on freeways is 100 kph. At the same time, the Dutch have improved the road system in an effort to reduce congestion; standing still in traffic is considered costly because of the opportunity cost of time and because idling engines lead to greater pollution. These efforts have undoubtedly made an impact, but the Dutch continue to rely heavily on automobiles as a personal means of transportation.

Finally, Coase argues that the correct course of action with respect to the design of environmental policies to start the analysis "with a situation approximating that which actually exists, to examine the effects of a proposed policy change and to attempt to decide whether the new situation would be, in total, better or worse than the original one" (Coase 1960). That is, the value of the total production of goods and services (widely defined to include nonmarket commodities) with the corrective policy in place must be compared with that in the absence of such a policy.

In this regard it is important not only to take into account environmental effectiveness, economic efficiency and dynamic efficiency (i.e., the continued incentive to reduce pollution and innovate), but also other criteria. In this regard, the following items should be considered in the implementation of any environmental policy:

- Polluters should have maximum flexibility in the ways and means to comply with environmental regulations.
- Any instruments should encourage full compliance, reduce fraud and avoid excessive administrative costs.
- Environmental policies should be harmonized with related or existing policies in other sectors so as to remove detrimental environmental effects.
- Environmental policies may have socially regressive impacts. Baumol and Oates (1988) argue that distributional impacts should be compensated for by social policy rather than modifying environmental policy.
- Environmental policies should be politically acceptable. In this regard, the polluter pays principle is often acceptable, while subsidies are not. Political acceptability may also be an obstacle to an emissions trading scheme because it implies that firms can pay to pollute.
- Environmental policies have wide-ranging impacts on prices, employment, growth (international) trade and competitiveness. These need to be carefully considered in the design of environmental policy.
- Environmental policies may be costly to implement, with some instruments costing the authority more than others. All costs of design, monitoring and enforcement must be taken into account, particularly the possibility that due to monitoring and administrative problems, for example, corrective action may result in higher rather than lower social costs. That is, the authority must not implement policies whose overall costs are greater than its benefits.

- Finally, a country cannot implement environmental policies that do not conform with international agreements that the country may have entered into.

NOTES

1. Here we consider producer–producer externality, but consumer–consumer and producer–consumer externalities are examined in section 5.3 below.
2. The private costs of charges need not be lower than those of regulation.
3. Other distortionary taxes, such as gasoline taxes (with no equivalent taxes on coal and other fuels), can also bring about a tax-interaction effect.
4. Even if firms are taxed on the *sale* of emission allowances (probably unlikely as quotas are freely provided to begin with), revenue will be lower than with a carbon tax.

6.   Social Cost–Benefit Analysis

Since planners and decision-makers are frequently required to choose among two or more alternative programs, or policies, project evaluation plays a key role in public investment planning. Project evaluation, or even impact assessment, is used to describe any consistent set of criteria – financial, environmental, economic or social – that can be used to judge whether potential public investment projects are likely to achieve stated policy objectives. Objectives might be to increase employment, diversify the economy of a particular region, increase the number of individuals living in a certain location (e.g., the far North of Canada), attain the largest net social economic benefit for the public expenditure, or protect wolves in Yellowstone National Park. Only the restricted objective of economic or allocative efficiency – to achieve the greatest net *economic* benefit for society – is addressed in this chapter. Social cost–benefit analysis (CBA) in a broader sense can also be used to address the income redistributional aspects of policy, although this is not done here.

There is a difference between a financial accounting of costs and benefits (one taken by the private sector, say) and economic or social CBA, which takes into account externalities, such as nonmarket values, as well as private costs and benefits. In this chapter, we describe the methodology of social cost–benefit analysis and consider its role in the evaluation of several natural resource policies. The examples we use are from actual cost–benefit studies. While the methodology described in the examples is applicable to *social* evaluation of land and resource projects in general, CBA is not the only evaluation technique (Smith 1986). Environmental impact assessment, cost-effectiveness analysis and stakeholder processes have all been used to evaluate government programs, regulations and projects. Alternatives to CBA are often put forward and used in practice to address nonmonetary aspects of project evaluation or because CBA is considered a "black box" beyond the reach of most citizens (see Hanley 2000). However, the alternative methods of project evaluation also have their limitations. Environmental impact analysis ignores nonenvironmental impacts of projects, while cost-effectiveness analysis only considers the economically efficient means of achieving a particular target, without questioning the target itself. Multiple decision-making criteria that rely on stakeholder processes take a number of different forms, but may fail to take into proper account the majority of citizens who may not be considered stakeholders. Nonetheless, multicriteria decision-making can be used to provide useful information about the costs of various trade-offs, but then the methodology itself could be quite technical (e.g., see Krcmar et al. 2001; Krcmar and van Kooten 2003).

We begin by examining the origins of cost–benefit analysis in section 6.1. Included in this section is a discussion of multiple accounts analysis and the role of value added in cost–benefit analysis. In section 6.2, we consider the role of government in the economy and the associated need for project evaluation. Since costs and benefits accrue at different points in time, and people prefer to delay pain but not pleasures, some means of weighting their occurrence is required. The weighting scheme that is employed is referred to as discounting. Given the controversies surrounding discounting, discount rates are examined in greater detail, although the discussion will inevitably be cursory since books have been written on the subject. The actual mechanics of CBA are considered in section 6.3, with three case studies provided in section 6.4. Our conclusions ensue in section 6.5.

6.1 BACKGROUND TO COST–BENEFIT ANALYSIS

As the government's role in the economy expanded, it was necessary for decision-makers to develop guidelines to determine whether public funds spent on various government activities were likely to achieve their aims. One guideline developed by US legislators in the Flood Control Act of 1936 required that the benefits of water development projects, "to whomsoever they may accrue", should exceed all the social costs related to the development of the project.[1] This requirement was subsequently expanded upon in the economics literature, culminating in what is now known as cost–benefit analysis.

As a result of the 1936 Flood Control Act, an Inter-Agency River Basin Committee, with representatives from the Department of Agriculture, the Army Corps of Engineers, the Bureau of Reclamation and the Federal Power Commission, was set up to develop procedures for testing whether benefits exceeded costs. The Sub-Committee on Costs and Budgets published criteria for the appraisal of water resource projects in the so-called "Green Book" of 1950. The US Inter-Agency Committee on Water Resources published a revised edition of the "Green Book" in 1958. In that same year, McKean (1958) and Eckstein (1958) published procedures for evaluating the economic efficiency of projects. Since then, Mishan (1971),

Harberger (1972), the Treasury Board Secretariat of Canada (1976), Sassone and Schaffer (1978), and many others have outlined procedures for conducting cost–benefit analyses.[2]

In 1961, the US Secretaries of the Interior, Agriculture, Army, and Health, Education and Welfare were requested to review evaluation standards for water and related land resources development projects. Their recommendation (US Inter-Agency Committee on Water Resources 1962) was that economic development, environmental preservation and individuals' wellbeing should be considered equal objectives. The suggested approach was to formulate plans on the basis of economic benefits and costs, but constrained by environmental preservation and wellbeing objectives. The effect was that preservation and wellbeing were not given equal status with development or economic efficiency. Subsequently, further effort was expended on the development of guidelines for conducting project evaluation.

The methodology for performing project evaluations, particularly social cost–benefit analyses, began to take concrete form with the US Water Resources Council's "Principles and Standards" (P&S) for water project evaluation, which appeared in the *US Federal Register* in 1973 and 1979 (US Water Resources Council 1973, 1979). In 1973, the US Water Resources Council (hereafter WRC) identified four objectives for project evaluation:

1. All the benefits and costs of a project had to be considered in the evaluation, regardless of who bore the costs and who received the benefits. This is the objective of national economic development (economic efficiency).
2. Impacts on the environment had to be calculated and included in the cost–benefit analysis. This implied that the nonmarket benefits of recreation, environmental degradation, etc., had to be taken into account.
3. The regional benefits of resource development projects were to be included explicitly in the analysis, making it possible to justify a project on the basis of its regional development benefits.
4. Finally, the impact of a project on social wellbeing had to be taken into account. For example, the analyst or planner was to take into account the impact of the project on certain groups in society (e.g., on blacks or on those with lower incomes). This objective, then, required explicit consideration of social issues in evaluating resource development projects.

The 1973 P&S for evaluating projects focused only on the first objective.

The 1979 P&S attempted to extend the evaluation methodology to the second objective. It is clear that, for water projects, the measured benefits from recreation were to be included, while, for environmental programs, the benefits of improving air and water quality were also to be determined. (Unlike 1973, the 1979 P&S included detailed instructions for evaluating projects.) The last two objectives were not addressed in the 1979 P&S, perhaps because the WRC did not feel these could be handled within the P&S framework then proposed.

In 1982, the 1979 P&S were repealed, only to be reinstated the following year (WRC 1983). Given the requirements of various pieces of US legislation relating to water (and other) resource developments, a method for including items 2, 3 and 4 into the evaluation process had to be found. Such a method was developed in the 1983 "Principles and Guidelines" (P&G); by recognizing noncommensurability among the various objectives, which was not explicitly done in the earlier P&S, the WRC adopted a *multiple accounts* approach to project evaluation. The 1983 P&G are currently in use in the USA, but have not been wholeheartedly adopted by other countries (although they do serve as a guideline).

Since the publication of the P&S and P&G, the basic techniques of evaluation have been extended to the appraisal of all US government projects and programs, particularly environmental regulatory programs.

In Canada, guidelines for project appraisal were established in 1976 by the Federal Treasury Board Secretariat, but these are vague and, in most instances, not very useful to the practitioner. One reason is that they appeared before the 1979 P&S were released in the USA. Project evaluation guidelines have also been developed by most provinces, but many of these are internal documents and unavailable to the general practitioner.

One of the most comprehensive cost–benefit studies ever undertaken concerned a third airport for London, England. The Roskill Commission, which reported in 1971, had been asked to recommend where a third London airport should be located, and when it should be built (Layard 1972, p.61). The first step that the Commission took was to provide a draft cost–benefit analysis. Flowerdew (1972) provides an overview of the study's CBA, which was criticized by Mishan (1972).

In practice, the cost–benefit methodology is often not strictly adhered to in making decisions about public investment projects. For example, there is no evidence that the US Bureau of Reclamation used cost–benefit guidelines in determining whether to construct many of the dams that were placed on rivers in the western USA during the decades of the 1940s, 1950s and 1960s (Reisner 1986). Perhaps this is because social CBA methodology was in its infancy, but it could also be the result of political factors or project evaluation criteria other than social cost–benefit analysis, and that

CBA was not mandatory at the time.

Multiple Accounts Analysis

Four accounts are identified in the P&G (WRC 1983), and these are similar to the four categories indicated in the P&S. The important difference between the approaches is the recognition that the various accounts deal with different issues and are not commensurable. Thus, the 1983 P&G include a description of methods for displaying the different accounts. The four accounts can be summarized as follows:

1. National Economic Development (NED) Account
2. Environmental Quality (EQ) Account
3. Regional Economic Development (RED) Account
4. Other Social Effects (OSE) Account

Cost–benefit analysis is used only to evaluate those items that can be measured in dollar terms, namely, those found in the NED account and quantifiable components of the EQ and RED accounts. The items that cannot be monetized are to be presented in each of the EQ, RED and OSE accounts and are briefly described in the following paragraphs.

According to the P&G, environmental items that are to be displayed in the EQ account are ecological attributes, cultural attributes and aesthetic attributes. Ecological attributes include functional aspects of the environment (e.g., assimilative capacity, erosion, nutrient cycling, succession) and structural aspects such as plant and animal species, chemical and physical properties of air, water and soil (e.g., pH of rainfall), and so on. Cultural attributes are evidence of past and present habitation that can help in understanding and propagating human life. Aesthetic attributes include sights, scents, sounds, tastes, impressions, etc., of the environment. It is clear that, while these attributes could be measured in monetary terms (Chapter 4), it may be too costly or difficult to do so (hence the term "intangibles"). However, they can be measured in other ways that include both quantity indicators that employ numeric and non-numeric scales and quality indicators such as "good" and "bad". It is obvious that the EQ attributes need to be presented in a clear and concise fashion if they are to be of use in the decision-making framework.

Several principles govern the planning process with respect to the environmental quality account. Both an interdisciplinary approach and public input are required in the planning process, although the means for involving the public is left to the discretion of the planning agency. The EQ account is designed to assist agencies in meeting the requirements of the US

National Environmental Policy Act (NEPA) of 1969 and the NEPA guidelines established by the US Council on Environmental Quality. As such, the procedures established by the WRC are meant to facilitate water resource planning to satisfy the aforementioned requirements, plus environmental requirements under the Endangered Species Act (1973), the National Historic Preservation Act (1966), the Fish and Wildlife Coordination Act (1972), and the Coastal Zone Management Act (1972), and their subsequent amendments. Finally, as discussed below with respect to costs and benefits (NED account), the EQ attributes need to be displayed in a way that highlights the comparison between the "with project" and "without project" scenarios.

The OSE account includes any items that are not included in the other three accounts but are important for planning. While the US WRC's Principles and Guidelines provide no procedures for evaluating other social effects, it does indicate that such effects include "urban and community impacts; life, health, and safety factors; displacement; long-term productivity; and energy requirements and energy conservation". They also include effects on income distribution, employment, population distribution, fiscal effects on state and local governments, quality of community life, and so on. While some of these effects can be measured in monetary terms and, to the extent they measure changes in surplus areas (as discussed in Chapter 2), are included in the economic efficiency (NED) account, others need to be displayed using guidelines similar to those of the EQ account. It appears that public agencies have substantial freedom within the planning process to include whatever items they wish in the OSE account and how they are to be displayed.

A problem occurs with the multiple accounts approach to cost–benefit analysis when all of the accounts are given equal status – when no account is given precedence over any other account. In that case, proponents of any one account are not required to seek compromise, conceding to trade off one benefit for another, but they tend to become entrenched in their position. In British Columbia, where the multiple accounts philosophy treats all accounts as equal, protection of wilderness areas may even be threatened by the failure to compromise (van Kooten 1995a). One way out of this dilemma is to employ the tool of multiple-criteria decision-making (e.g., Krcmar and van Kooten 2003). This tool provides decision-makers with the trade-offs among different objectives, so that the explicit "damages" to other accounts are identified when a choice is made. These "damages" are opportunity costs that are expressed in both monetary and nonmonetary terms.

Regional Economic Development and Employment

Increases in GDP cannot in and of themselves be considered a benefit measure because costs are neglected. Thus, input–output (social accounting) analysis is able to identify changes in value-added throughout the economy (change in GDP) as a result of a resource development project, but changes in value-added are a measure of changes in economic activity and not a measure of benefits (or costs) in the welfare economics sense. Rather, value-added represents an upper limit on the opportunity cost of the resources employed in the various activities that generate the value-added.

We briefly consider regional economic development and employment because of the emphasis that politicians place upon this aspect of project evaluation. Politicians often focus exclusively on the impact that projects or programs have on job creation, without paying adequate attention to opportunity costs and economic efficiency. Included in the economic efficiency, or national economic development, account are all the monetized measures of changes in surplus areas (see Chapter 2). Regional impacts are the purview of the RED account, and these have historically been addressed using input–output (social accounting) analysis. It is important not to confuse economic impacts obtained from such analyses with economic efficiency or welfare measures (e.g., see Stabler et al. 1988; Hamilton et al. 1991).

Input–output (I–O) analysis is able to identify changes in value-added activity (and thus gross domestic or regional product and jobs) resulting from an economic development project. Changes in value added measure changes in economic activity (or GDP), but do not measure project benefits (or costs) as defined in terms of surplus areas (see Chapter 2). Indeed, if the major benefit of a program or project is an increase in nonmarket values, which are not included in GDP measures, then GDP or value-added could even decline. Changes in value-added are merely the upper limit on the opportunity cost of the resources employed in the various activities that generate the value-added.

One possible approach to valuing the opportunity cost of a project is to compare the effects of the alternative use of the funds (as determined from an appropriate I–O model) with those generated by spending the available funds on the resource development project under consideration. The former might be thought of as project-specific opportunity costs and might be positive or negative, or inconsequential. If an alternative project gives rise to impacts greater than those generated by the project being evaluated, the inclusion as benefits of the proposed project's impacts minus the project-specific opportunity cost results in a reduction in the net benefits of the project. The economic efficiency of the resource development project is overstated if changes in value-added are included while ignoring the potential value-added generated by using the funds in a "better" fashion.

When labor resources are not fully employed, their shadow (true) value is not given by the observed wage rate. If there is persistent unemployment of resources, particularly labor, the opportunity cost of such resources (their shadow price) is nil and an argument can then be made to include the value-added benefits of a project in the CBA. But there are a number of arguments against this view:

1. It needs to be determined if unemployment is indeed persistent, and, if it is, whether the cause is structural (e.g., a poorly trained labor force) or not. If it is structural, a publicly funded regional development project aimed at job creation will not help local residents as it will attract workers from outside the region. From a national perspective job losses in other regions need to be counted as a negative impact of the project.

2. If unemployment is not structural, it is not clear that resource development projects are the best device for creating jobs. Macroeconomic policies may be more effective in reducing unemployment. Further, the time required between authorization and construction of the project may militate against the use of resource development projects as a method for reducing unemployment.

3. Finally, if the shadow price of labor is zero, then the opportunity cost of capital must also be higher than is evident from the observed rate of return to capital. The reason is that returns from capital must be diverted to support unemployed labor. Therefore, since the discount rate is determined by the opportunity cost of funds used in the project (see next section), the discount rate to be employed in the benefit–cost analysis must be higher than calculated. The higher discount rate militates against resource development projects, and it offsets the supposed benefits due to secondary or regional impacts.

If a public project is funded by an increase in local taxes, an interesting question that arises is whether or not the same multiplier is used to measure the contractionary impacts of those taxes as is used to measure the expansionary impacts due to the project itself. Use of the same multiplier leads to offsetting impacts, although the overall impact would likely be negative as a result of leakages – the revenue required to fund the project will be greater than the project costs because of transaction costs and inefficiencies inherent in tax collection and government bureaucracies. Likewise, spending public funds on projects to create jobs, while popular with politicians, ignores the jobs lost elsewhere due to the contractionary impact of higher taxes.

As an example, consider the decision by governments in some cities to provide subsidies to professional sports teams. The argument is that a professional sports team generates economic activity and jobs because people spend money to attend games, purchase concessions, etc, while the team hires a variety of locals and players spend their earnings in the regional economy. All this is true, but it ignores what happens to the money flows. In the absence of a professional sports team, people are still likely to spend their recreation budget locally, but in other ways (theatre, viewing nonprofessional sports, etc.). Leakages out of the regional economy may indeed be greater with professional sports than other recreational activities, especially if players (who receive the greatest proportion of revenues) spend their salaries outside the local economy. In that case, subsidies to the local professional team reduce economic activity and jobs. This is not to suggest that subsidies may not be worthwhile. If the presence of a professional sports team in a city leads to private investments that might not have occurred otherwise, they can contribute to economic growth. Further, they may provide utility to residents who are also fans but may not attend games on a regular basis; thus, a professional sports team may provide nonmarket benefits. Such a benefit enhances economic efficiency.

The RED account recognizes that, despite being valued in monetary terms, regional impacts (changes in economic activity) are not the same as economic efficiency (costs and benefits as surplus areas). Benefits to a region may be costs to the nation as a whole, indicating that the RED account focuses on income transfers. By separating the NED and RED accounts (and the other accounts as well), the incompatibility between economic efficiency and income distribution (or equity) is explicitly recognized.

6.2 POLICY EVALUATION AND DISCOUNTING

The Role of Government

Government intervention in the economy through direct investment has long been taken for granted. More recently, economists have applied insights from the New Institutional Economics (Furubotn and Richter 1997) to question whether public or private provision of goods and services is preferred. While the goods and services in question relate to health care, education and prisons, it can equally apply to provision of many environmental amenities (e.g., recreation, watershed protection and wildlife habitat). Shleifer (1998) and Hart et al. (1997) make the case for private provision of health care, schools and other services that are usually associated with government provision. The reasons for private provision are that it leads to incentives for innovation and cost minimization, but possibly at the expense of quality. Where cost of provision is important and quality is less important, the case for private provision is strongest. However, even where quality is important, the ability of government to use contracts to get what it wants could mitigate the need for public provision. While private firms providing a service have an incentive to innovate so as to reduce costs, contracts can be written in ways that prevent deterioration of quality as a result of cost-minimizing efforts or encourage innovation to improve quality (e.g., via performance incentives).

In addition to the quality-cost of provision trade-off, corruption and patronage are important in deciding whether public or private provision is preferred. Corruption and patronage are opposite sides of the same coin. Corruption occurs when private firms are effectively able to "bribe" government officials to extend them favors (e.g., providing contracts for provision of services with weak or vague performance clauses). Patronage occurs when government (elected) officials favor particular constituents in return for their political support (e.g., public service union workers are provided large pay raises, environmental groups are given freedom to protest even if they break the law). Where corruption is a severe problem, the case for in-house provision is enhanced; where patronage is a problem, the case favors privatization.

In the mainstream literature, one of the accepted reasons for government intervention in the economy is linked to market failure (as discussed in Chapter 5). Governments have a number of instruments (ranging from taxes to public ownership) at their disposal to correct the market failure. Governments might also intervene in the economy on the basis of actual or perceived inter-temporal inefficiency, and on income inequality or equity grounds.

It is now recognized in mainstream economics that government itself can be a source of failure in the economy. This source of failure is labeled policy failure (see, e.g., Panayotou 1993a). As noted, the new institutional economists point to possibilities of corruption and patronage as a source of policy failure. Even well-meaning policies, some of which are meant to correct market failure, can lead to a worsening environment or reduction rather than improvement in the overall wellbeing of society. An example is provided in section 6.5, where government regulations of forest practices are designed to protect environmental amenities (correct a market failure), but they result in a diminution of social welfare. Likewise, government agricultural policies in developed countries have led to environmental deterioration, although the original aim of such policies was to protect family farms. Government policies are also a contributing factor to tropical deforestation, as shown in Chapter 12. Policy failure may be a greater source of failure within the economy than market failure.

What can cost–benefit analysis contribute? CBA offers primarily a consistent criterion for evaluating the costs and benefits of government intervention through direct investment, regulations or other policies, leaving the final decision to the political process. Consider water resource development projects, which are often not provided without government intervention. Although water development projects enhance navigation, flood control and water supply, the major benefits are often electrical power generation, water for irrigation and water for recreation. Electric power generation and irrigation projects have elements of technical externality. Moreover, they require enormous investments, so marginal costs inevitably lie below price once the project is built, and benefits are disbursed to many individuals in society. Hence, such projects may not be provided privately or, if they are, they are smaller in capacity than desired from a social point of view. Provision of recreation, on the other hand, is a proper function of government because of its public good characteristics; in particular, it is unlikely to be provided privately since those who bear the direct costs of facilitating the recreational activity frequently can appropriate only some of the benefits. Finally, public investment in water projects may serve as a catalyst for economic development. For these reasons, a strong case can be made for public investment in the development of water resources.

Although public investment in the economy is justified in many situations, this does not imply that the government should pursue all investments that might be deemed worthwhile, however the term "worthwhile" is defined. Indeed, the government's ability to pursue certain investments is limited by the availability of funds. Therefore, given the limited amount of public funds, some method of determining the priority of investments is needed and the mechanism for doing this is known as "project evaluation". Smith (1986) discusses several approaches to project evaluation, but CBA is probably the most comprehensive. However, because cost–benefit analysis is a more restrictive concept than project evaluation *per se*, it often constitutes an input into the broader politics of policy evaluation.

Whenever project evaluation is undertaken, it is important for the practitioner to recognize, and to identify clearly, the viewpoint that is taken. If economic efficiency is important to the decision then CBA is an appropriate tool to employ, but its limitations must be recognized. CBA in the narrow sense has been criticized precisely because it focuses on economic efficiency only, while the objective of most public programs is not simply, or even principally, economic efficiency. CBA in the narrow sense also embodies an ethic that is not acceptable to everyone, namely, utilitarianism. For example, some cannot accept measuring everything in monetary terms or they argue that CBA may be largely irrelevant or relevant to only a small part of the problem of evaluating public projects and programs (e.g., Layard 1972, pp.61–2; Self 1972). (For counter arguments, see also Chapter 4.) Clearly, it needs to be understood that political feasibility and acceptability are important aspects of project evaluation.

There are three important points that should be made. First, economists trained in welfare economics frequently refuse to consider alternatives to economic efficiency as having any validity in policy analysis since these approaches have to do with social and political matters that are beyond the scope of economic science. In fact, some economists stress that CBA cannot embrace the wider considerations that the political system must deal with, but whether these criticisms relate to the economist's inability to quantify certain items is not clear. Yet, there is nothing wrong with a practice of quantifying the quantifiables and leaving the qualitative factors (sometimes referred to as "intangibles") as additional considerations. Additional considerations are addressed in the multiple accounts framework discussed above.

Second, and related to this, it is not possible to mix measurement tools since this results in confusion about, and possible misrepresentation of, the project analysis. Benefits and costs constitute surplus areas (as defined in Chapter 2) and should not be confused with changes in gross domestic (or regional) product, although projects that result in a net increase in social welfare should also increase GDP. (This issue was also discussed previously.)

Finally, benefits and costs of resource projects or government programs accrue at different points in time. Since individuals prefer to delay pain (costs), while they are eager not to delay pleasure (benefits), it is necessary to weight gains and losses as to when they occur, a procedure known as discounting.

Choice of Discount Rate

Associated with any natural resource development project, or any government program (such as a program to reduce CO_2 emissions) for that matter, is a stream of costs and benefits over time. In order to determine the economic feasibility (efficiency) of a program/project, it is necessary to determine if the stream of benefits exceeds that of costs. To make this comparison, however, it is necessary to measure and compare the stream of benefits and the stream of costs at a single point in time, whether that is at the beginning or at the end of the time horizon, or at some intermediate point. This requires that benefits and costs – the surplus or deficit areas of Chapter 2 – be weighted according to when they accrue. Since $1 or €1 today is worth more to an individual (or society) than that same dollar or euro received at some future date (say, next year), it is necessary to "discount" future dollars (euros) so that they are worth less today than if they were available today. This is the purpose of the discount rate. The problem is to choose an appropriate discount rate that reflects society's preferences for current consumption over future consumption. Whether a program/project is efficient from an economics perspective will depend to some extent on the discount rate that is employed – the outcome is sensitive to the rate of discount (interest rate) that is employed in CBA. What, then, is the appropriate rate of discount to use in weighting future costs and benefits?

Gains versus pains

The first problem of choosing a discount rate is that individuals have different rates of time preference, but even the same individual employs different discount rates. In determining a social rate of discount, not only is it difficult to reconcile the fact that different people use different rates to discount the future, although everyone will equate their individual rates to the private market rate at the margin, but evidence from behavioral economics indicates that people commonly discount future losses at a lower rate than future gains, and that they use higher rates to discount outcomes in the near future than those in the distant future (Knetsch 2000). In one survey, half of respondents were asked for the largest sum of money they would be willing to pay to receive $20 a year from now, while the other half was asked to provide the smallest sum of money they would accept today to give up receiving $20 a year from now. "The rate used to discount the future gain was, on average, about three times higher than the rate used to discount the future loss" (Knetsch 2000, p.283).[3]

There are other quirks associated with discounting, although these also relate to risk perceptions. People express greater willingness to discount environmental benefits from a government program at a lower rate than the benefits of a program that enhances future consumption of material goods. Individuals also express greater willingness to pay to avoid extremely small risks of death from an environmental disaster (e.g., related to construction and operation of a nuclear power plant) than they do to avoid much higher risks of death associated with something with which they are more familiar (e.g., riding on a motorcycle) (see Fischhoff et al. 1981). Individuals may also have different preferences with respect to the environment in their role as citizens than in their role as consumers (Sagoff 1988a), but such preferences are usually expressed politically.

Hyperbolic discounting

A particular controversy about the discount rate relates to the weighting of different generations. This is particularly important for climate change where it is future generations that benefit from investments in climate mitigation made by those currently alive. An individual may require a payment of $1.05 next year in order to forgo receiving $1 today, which implies a discount rate of 5%. However, the same individual may be willing to give up $1 in 20 years' time to obtain $1.01 in 21 years, implying a discount rate of 1%. In other words, the discount rate declines as costs and benefits accrue in the more distant future – the discount rate declines as a project's or program's time horizon increases. This is referred to as "hyperbolic discounting" in contrast to exponential discounting that uses a constant rate of discount (see Weitzman 1998, 1999; Dasgupta 2002). This notion has been used to argue that, when comparing investments that affect future generations, a very low rate of discount should be employed.

The problem with the idea of hyperbolic discounting is that, in the above example, when the individual in 20 years' time needs to make the choice between $1 today and $1.01 next year, she will choose $1 today, *ceteris paribus* (assuming her current-period discount rate continues to be 5%). The use of a declining discount rate leads to time-inconsistent decisions because the mere passage of time causes an individual to change their choice. However, if the discount rate itself is uncertain because the world is uncertain, then there is always the possibility that "*ex ante* good decisions turn out to be regrettable *ex post*, once nature has revealed herself" (Newell and Pizer 2003, p.10). The notion of uncertainty about the rate of discount is considered further in the next subsection, with Dasgupta (2002) providing an additional perspective on hyperbolic versus constant discounting.

What discount rate?

Consider, first, whether a nominal or real rate of discount is to be employed. While a nominal rate might be used in cases where one wishes to examine cash flows, it is generally preferable not to use a nominal rate of discount because it requires that inflation be taken into account. Since the allocation of investment and consumption over time is based on expectations, adjusting the nominal discount rate by *ex post* inflation is not quite correct. Further, it is not possible to predict inflation over the life of a project/program, which could quite well exceed 100 years. There is already enough uncertainty about the future, real rate of interest (and this is discussed further below). In any case, economists generally prefer to use the real discount rate.

It also makes sense as a principle for choosing a discount rate to focus on consumption. Then, the consequences of an investment or government program (regulation) "should be converted into effects on consumption (versus investment) and then these consumption effects should be discounted using a consumption rate of interest – the rate faced by consumers when they save, rather than businesses when they borrow" (Newell and Pizer 2003). In the United States, the real rate of return on investments by large companies over the period 1926–90 was about 7%, after taxes, while it was 8% over the period 1926–98. Given a corporate income tax rate of about 35%, the pre-tax rate of return is thus about 11–12%. Since individuals in the USA pay up to 50% in income taxes, the rate of return to individuals as owners of companies is closer to 4%, which can then be considered the consumption rate of interest – the rate at which people trade off spending over time. Interestingly, the US Office of Management and Budget requires the use of 7% for valuing costs and benefits external to the government and 4% for internal costs and benefits (Newell and Pizer 2003).

Despite this straightforward reasoning for deriving a (social) discount rate from market data, there are several problems that need to be considered. First, the use of 4% as the consumption rate of interest does not agree with actual behavior in many circumstances. People willingly invest their savings in Treasury bills and guaranteed investment certificates that yield perhaps as little as 2% after taxes (and perhaps even less). Of course, these are riskless investments.

Second, when a government invests in a natural resource project, for example, funds could come from income taxes (displacing an equal amount of consumption) or from increased public-sector borrowing. In the latter case, borrowed funds displace an equal amount of private investment, so it might be appropriate to use the higher rate of 7–8%. If borrowed funds originate with private savings or if income taxes are used, the lower interest rate is more appropriate. In practice, of course, public funds come from a mix of sources. Thus, it might be appropriate to calculate the discount rate as the opportunity cost of the funds. Suppose that a public investment project costs $100, and that $40 displaces private investment and $60 consumption. If the rate of return to private investments is 10% and the consumption discount rate is 4%, then the opportunity cost of the funds is 6.4% (= 0.40×10% + .0.60×4%). The main difficulty in deriving the opportunity cost rate is that it is not easy to determine where the *marginal* funds originate. Further, not all government revenues come from income taxes and/or domestic borrowing, as governments earn income through charges, tariffs on imported goods, and so on.

Finally, ethical issues arise when one discounts across generations – it is ethically indefensible to discount the utility (as opposed to consumption) of future generations. As future generations have always been richer, a zero discount rate on the utility of future people does not imply that their consumption cannot be discounted, because the marginal utility of an increase in their consumption is lower than that of current generations.

Further, society may choose to save more collectively than the sum of all individual savings decisions (Marglin 1963). The government is considered a trustee for unborn generations, whose wealth will (at least in part) depend on the state of the environment that they inherit, so real consumption (and rates of return on investments) may not grow, and may even decline, when we degrade the environment. Further, because of risk and uncertainty (giving rise to "risk premiums"), society's rate of time preference will be lower than that of individuals, as society as a whole is better able to pool risks; certain individual risks are mere transfers at the level of society. While individuals face real chances of death, society does not really face such a risk. All in all, these more or less ethical arguments suggest that society's rate of discount is lower than that of individuals making up the society. The social discount rate is likely lower than the opportunity cost of capital rate (real rate of return on investments) or the marginal rate of time preference, but it is not immediately clear how much lower.

Based on the above reasoning a case can be made for using a very low discount rate to discount consumption by future generations. Again, a 2% rate of discount might be appropriate. This is a somewhat arbitrary low rate and might be considered to be the social rate of time preference.

Since any rate between about 2% and 8% appears justifiable, what might constitute *the* appropriate social rate of discount for use in social cost–benefit analysis? Newell and Pizer (2003) make the case that rates in the lower end of this range should be employed. Their argument rests on an analysis of uncertainty about the future path of interest rates. Using Monte Carlo simulation and historical information on the pattern of inflation-adjusted interest rates, and assuming the stochastic process for interest rates is not mean reverting (does not trend towards a mean in the absence of exogenous shocks), they find that the value of $100 received 400 years in the future is worth many orders of magnitude more today if interest rate uncertainty is taken into account than if a constant discount rate is used (see Table 6.1). While a constant discount rate is to be used in CBA, the results indicate that, because actual discount rates vary in unpredictable fashion (i.e., follow a "random walk"), the discount rate to be employed should be lower than in the absence of this consideration. Thus, if a 4% consumption rate of discount is considered appropriate because it is market derived, the true (constant) rate might be 2–3% if uncertainty about future interest rates is taken into account. Indeed, "correctly handling uncertainty lowers the effective discount rate in the future in a way that all generations after a certain horizon are essentially treated the same" (ibid.).

Table 6.1: Value Today of $100 Received in 200 and 400 Years: Comparison of Constant vs. Random Walk Discounting, Selected Discount Rates

Discount rate	Constant discounting		Nonmean-reverting random walk	
	200 years	400 years	200 years	400 years
2%	$1.91	$0.04	$7.81	$3.83
4%	$0.04	$0.00	$1.54	$0.66
7%	$0.00	$0.00	$0.24	$0.09

Source: Derived from Newell and Pizer (2003).

Clearly, there is a strong case to be made for the use of a low discount rate in the evaluation of natural resource projects and government regulations. Given continued controversy about what might constitute an appropriate rate, one suggestion is to use a rate of 2% for evaluating programs/projects that affect more than one generation, and then use sensitivity analysis about this rate to determine how choices might be affected if the future is somehow weighted differently.

What about a zero discount rate?
Based on the above arguments, one might think that a zero (or very near zero) discount rate might be appropriate for any project that involves intergenerational transfers of resources. This argument is often used in the context of climate change to justify large current investments in mitigation because these provide high benefits, albeit far in the future. If rates of return in the private sector are high, then an optimal strategy might be for the government to take some proportion of the money earmarked for mitigation, invest it in the private sector, and use the returns to compensate those adversely impacted by climate change and/or to subsidize adaptation to climate change. This is true for other government programs or projects as well. Thus, the use of an arbitrarily low or even zero rate of discount is not the panacea for justifying expenditures, as a proper accounting of opportunity costs (what else can be done with the fund?) might lead to a different conclusion. This might explain why the Government of British Columbia, for example, used a rate of 10% for CBA during the 1990s,

although the CBA calculations were only one input into a broader multiple accounts analysis.

A second issue related to the use of a zero discount rate involves the weighting of physical things. For example, should physical carbon be discounted according to when it is released to or removed from the atmosphere? Interestingly, some economists object to discounting of physical carbon, although they accept discounting if the physical carbon is multiplied by an arbitrary constant that converts the carbon into monetary units. Discounting or weighting of physical units is clearly an acceptable practice in economics, as is evident from Ciriacy-Wantrup (1968) and subsequent literature on conservation (see Chapter 7). One cannot obtain a consistent estimate of the costs of carbon uptake unless both project costs and physical carbon are discounted, even if at different rates of discount. To illustrate why, consider the following example that is considered in greater depth in later chapters.

Suppose a tree-planting project results in the reduction of CO_2–equivalent emissions of 2 tons of carbon (tC) per year in perpetuity (e.g., biomass burning to produce energy previously produced using fossil fuels). In addition, assume the project has a permanent sink component that results in the storage of 5 tC per year for 10 years, after which time the sink component of the project reaches an equilibrium. How much carbon is stored? Suppose the present value of project costs has been calculated and that these are then allocated equally across the years of the project – so that the discounted stream of the equal annual costs is the same as the calculated present value of costs. (The methods for calculating present values and annualizing costs are discussed in the next section.) If costs and carbon uptake are compared on an annual basis, does one use 2 tC or 7 tC per year? Suppose the discounted project costs amount to $1,000, or annualized costs of $40 if a 4% rate of discount is used. The costs of carbon uptake are then estimated to be either $20/tC if 2 tC is used, or $5.71/tC for 7 tC.

Suppose instead that we divide the present value of project costs (or $1,000) by the sum of all the carbon that eventually gets removed from the atmosphere. Since 7 tC gets taken up annually for the first 10 years, and 2 tC per year thereafter, the total amount of carbon sequestered is infinite, so that the cost of carbon uptake is essentially $0.00/tC. Therefore, an arbitrary planning horizon needs to be chosen. If the planning horizon is 30 years, 110 tC are sequestered and the average cost is calculated to be $9.09/tC; if a 40-year planning horizon is chosen, 130 tC are removed from the atmosphere and the cost is $7.69/tC. Thus, cost estimates are sensitive to the length of the planning horizon, which is not usually made explicit in most studies.

Cost estimates that take into account all carbon sequestered plus the timing of uptake can only be achieved if physical carbon is discounted. Then, using the methods described in the next section, the total discounted carbon saved via our hypothetical project amounts to 147.81 tC if a discount rate of 2% is used, and the correct estimate of costs is $6.77/tC. If carbon is discounted at a rate of 4%, the project results in costs of $10.62/tC.

Finally, what discount rate should be applied to physical carbon? Richards (1997) demonstrates that, if physical carbon is not discounted, this is the same as assuming that damages from rising atmospheric concentrations of CO_2 are increasing at the same rate as the social rate of discount. If damages rise slower than atmospheric CO_2, a positive discount rate on physical carbon is appropriate. A zero discount rate on physical carbon implies that marginal damages of atmospheric CO_2 are increasing over time at exactly the rate of discount, but there is no reason to think that this might be the case. It also implies that there is no difference between removing a unit of carbon from the atmosphere today, tomorrow or at some future time; logically, then, it does not matter if the carbon is ever removed from the atmosphere.

6.3 MECHANICS OF COST–BENEFIT ANALYSIS

In the remainder of this chapter, we focus only on social CBA as a tool for evaluating projects.[4] We provide a discussion of the methodology of cost–benefit analysis and, in the section that follows, examples of how to apply CBA in practice. CBA is in many ways an art. It requires that one first identify a project and its scope (determining whether or not CBA is even warranted), establish a proper economic framework for identifying surplus areas, separate out items that can be monetized (and are worthwhile monetizing), and then determine the present value of costs and benefits in the manner described below (see also Hanley 2000). Any nonmonetary items (intangibles) and income distributional effects are likely best addressed in the multiple-accounts framework, although some argue that judgments about the way a project/program redistributes income can be included directly in the CBA (see Prest and Turvey 1974).

Cost–benefit analysis employs several important assumptions, some of which are ethical in nature and not necessarily acceptable to all in society. Many of the assumptions are needed to make the step from economic theory to application. The assumptions are:

1. Only marginal changes in the economy are to be evaluated. That is, the impact of projects to be evaluated is small compared to national output. If changes are large, prices will change elsewhere in the economy.

Then computable general equilibrium modeling is required.

2.   There are no significant distortions in other markets. Those that exist must be taken into account either by using shadow prices or by measuring indirect net benefits or costs in other related markets of substitutes and/or complements (see Chapter 2).

3.   The *status quo* or some other distribution of income is taken as given. Usually CBA is based on the existing income distribution.

4.   The tastes, income and wealth of the current generation are the starting point for the desires and ability to pay of future generations.

5.   All individuals are treated equally so that a marginal dollar accruing to a rich person is valued the same as a dollar going to a poor person.

6.   Either uncertainty is absent or the public's attitude toward risk can be represented by changes in the discount rate.

It is clear that these assumptions impose limits on the interpretation of the results of project evaluation using CBA. However, if these presuppositions are recognized, cost–benefit analysis becomes a useful tool for analyzing public policies.

Economic efficiency is simply defined. First, it is necessary to calculate the present value of all the social costs (PVC) of a proposed project as:

$$(6.1) \qquad PVC = \sum_{t=0}^{T} \frac{C_t}{(1+r)^t},$$

where C_t refers to *all* of the project-related costs incurred by society in year t, the life of the project is T years, and r is the rate of discount. The costs are calculated for each year; these are costs over and above those that would be encountered in the absence of the project. The *"with–without"* principle of CBA is important since it illustrates the economic concept of opportunity cost. The term C_0 is sometimes referred to as the capital or construction cost.

Likewise, it is necessary to calculate the present or discounted value of all the social benefits of the project (PVB):

$$(6.2) \qquad PVB = \sum_{t=0}^{T} \frac{B_t}{(1+r)^t},$$

where B_t refers to *all* of the benefits that result from the project in year t, regardless of who in society receives them. Again benefits are defined as the difference between benefits that accrue with the project in place as opposed to without it. As we demonstrate in the examples of the next section, it is important that T is identical in (6.1) and (6.2), even though benefits or costs may be zero for later years.

The next step in determining economic efficiency is to calculate the difference between PVC and PVB; the present value of net social benefits or simply net present value (NPV) is defined as NPV = PVB – PVC. If NPV > 0, then the project adds to the welfare of society and is deemed to be economically efficient. If NPV < 0, the present value of costs is greater than the present value of benefits and the project should not be pursued because society will be made worse off overall. Such a project should only be undertaken if the attainment of some other objective such as income redistribution warrants the overall loss to society.

The formula for making cost–benefit calculations is straightforward. Problems occur in the choice of discount rate and in measuring the actual costs and benefits. In particular, there is controversy about what is to be included in the measurements. The concept of economic surplus is important in this regard.

For a given project, one could identify three types of benefits or costs:

1. Benefits and costs for which market prices exist and for which these prices correctly reflect social values (see Chapters 2 and 3).
2. Benefits and costs for which market prices exist, but where such prices do not reflect social values (e.g., labor input that would otherwise be unemployed) (Sassone and Schaffer 1978, pp.63–95).
3. Benefits and costs for which no market prices exist because the commodities (e.g., recreation, water quality, historic sites) are not generally traded in the market place.

The first two types of benefits and costs are most easily included in a CBA, while the last category of benefits (or costs) is frequently presented as additional considerations because these values are costly to measure (see Chapter 4).

All projects with a positive NPV should, in principle, be undertaken because they add to the welfare of society, but budget constraints prevent this from happening. Therefore, a project with a positive NPV may not proceed because an alternative project has a higher NPV. When there are a large number of projects and programs available to decision-makers with a limited budget, it is necessary to rank projects. This can be done by comparing the social benefits on a per \$1 basis of social costs; a B–C ratio can be constructed for this purpose, namely, B/C = PVB ÷ PVC. As long as B/C > 1.0, the project is worthwhile undertaking since, for every \$1 society spends, it gains more than \$1. While all projects yielding a B–C ratio greater than 1.0 should be developed, if there are a number of different projects competing for limited funds, the B–C ratios can be used to rank the projects. Projects are then chosen from the highest to the lowest B/C, until either all of the available funds are expended or there are no more projects with B/C > 1.0.

A source of confusion arises when there exist other ways to construct B–C ratios. The following ratios are simply different ways of presenting the information, but they can be misleading in the sense that projects that do not have NPV > 0 may have an "alternative" benefit–cost ratio exceeding 1.0. Other types of B–C ratios include the following:

1. Governments may want to determine the benefits accruing to each \$1 they spend, as opposed to what society has to lay out. In this case, one subtracts from benefits the private costs and divides the result by public costs only; i.e., $(PVB - PVC_{private}) \div PVC_{public}$, where PVB is defined in (6.1), $PVC_{private}$ and PVC_{public} refer to the present values of private and public costs, respectively. Thus, a distinction is made between costs incurred by the private sector and those incurred by the government.

2. If it is necessary to distinguish between capital costs and the costs associated with the operation, maintenance and routine replacement (OM&R) of a facility, the B–C ratio might be written as $(PVB - PVC_{OM\&R}) \div C_0$, where $PVC_{OM\&R}$ is the present value of the OM&R costs, and C_0 represents the capital or construction costs of the project. (If construction of the facility requires a period in excess of one year, then C_0 can be thought of as the present value of capital costs.) For example, the authority might purchase a biological preserve but hand it over to a nongovernmental organization for operation.

3. Finally, one might wish to determine the impact of each \$1 of project costs only. The present value of associated costs (AC) is then subtracted from social benefits and divided by project costs. An example of associated costs is the increased on-farm costs that result when a water resources project is built for irrigation purposes. Then the B–C ratio can be written as $(PVB - AC) \div PVC_{project}$. This concept of the benefit–cost ratio can also be interpreted as the "direct costs" B–C ratio.

None of these representations of the B–C ratio should replace NPV and the social B–C ratio; they can be presented as additional considerations. This has occurred in cases where the government has constructed irrigation works but ignored the associated costs of agricultural improvements.

As indicated in the previous section in the discussion about discounting carbon, costs and benefits can be presented on an annual basis. Costs and benefits (or net benefits) can be "annualized" using information about the present value of costs and the present value of benefits. To annualize a current value is similar to asking: What equal annual payment y is required over some period T that, when discounted at rate r, gives the current value V? Alternatively, if a person pays $\$V$ for a bond, what annual payment y would be required if the bond expires after T years? The answer to these questions can be found by solving the following relationship for y:

$$(6.3) \qquad V = \sum_{t=0}^{T} \frac{y_t}{(1+r)^t}.$$

Suppose that the bond yields y in perpetuity. In that case,

$$(6.4) \qquad V = \sum_{t=0}^{\infty} \frac{y_t}{(1+r)^t} = \frac{y}{r},$$

which is known as the bond formula.[5] Equation (6.4) can be used to annualize the present value of a sequence of costs and/or benefits so that comparisons can be made on an annual basis. This is useful if, for example, one knows that a certain physical quantity (such as carbon or a timber harvest) is available each and every year, but the costs of providing it occur at irregular intervals. Costs can then be calculated in present value terms using relation (6.1) and then annualized via (6.4).

It is unimportant for economic efficiency whether the project is funded locally or by taxpayers outside the project region, unless the outside funds are tied to that particular project and would not be available under any other circumstances. In that case, regional value-added becomes important and might be considered a benefit to the project if the project is evaluated from a regional perspective. Otherwise, regional value-added constitutes an income transfer that should not be included in the CBA as a welfare area (as discussed in section 6.1).

Finally, the internal rate of return (IRR) criterion is an alternative to NPV and the B–C ratio in selecting the most efficient projects, but it is not widely used by natural resource economists although it is used in private industry. In principle, IRR yields the same ranking of projects as NPV and the B–C ratio, as long as care is taken in specifying reinvestment alternatives. The IRR is found by setting NPV equal to zero and solving for the discount rate or IRR:

$$(6.5) \quad \sum_{t=0}^{T} \frac{B_t - C_t}{(1 + \text{IRR})^t} = 0.$$

To find IRR requires solving a polynomial of degree T, which implies multiple solutions. Although solving for IRR is simple to accomplish numerically on a computer, this requirement and the possibility of multiple solutions (i.e., determining which is appropriate) are some of the reasons for the unpopularity of this criterion. The basis for project selection is to compare the internal rate of return with an appropriate discount rate; if IRR is greater than the selected discount rate, the project is a desirable one. This criterion can also be used to rank projects.

6.4 APPLICATIONS OF COST–BENEFIT ANALYSIS

In this section, we provide examples of how CBA can be used in evaluating public investment projects or policies relating to the environment. We begin with the example of a hypothetical flood control project. Then we examine a more complicated evaluation of environmental regulations relating to forest practices. This example is based on a real-world problem and illustrates the difficulty of using nonmarket benefits. Other examples of cost–benefit analysis are provided in Chapters 13 and 14 in relation to climate change issues.

Choosing a Dam Size for Flood Control

Suppose that a low-lying agricultural area is prone to periodic flooding, with the extent of damage dependent on the severity of the floods. Based on historical records and current yields and prices for commodities grown in the region, it is possible to construct a discrete probability distribution for damage (Table 6.1). Assuming that there is no change expected in the hydrological cycle, and ignoring possible future price and yield changes, it is possible to recommend various investment projects (dams) to reduce the losses due to flooding. The dam sizes vary from a weir, to prevent minor flooding, to a full-scale earthen dam that eliminates the possibility of flooding altogether (at least as experienced in the historical record). The investment alternatives correspond to the "dams" indicated in Table 6.2 – that is, seven dam sizes from small to large will prevent flooding damage to the extent indicated in Table 6.2.

Table 6.2: Hypothetical Probability Distribution for Flood Damage

Dam Size	Flooding damage prevented ($)	Probability (%)	Cumulative probability (%)
1	10,000	8	8
2	20,000	12	20
3	30,000	30	50
4	40,000	26	76
5	50,000	12	88
6	75,000	8	96
7	100,000	4	100

To keep the analysis simple, we assume that, whatever dam is built, its life is infinite, and that there are no OM&R costs. Under these assumptions, there is only a capital cost; discounted benefits are determined by finding the annual benefit and simply dividing the result by the discount factor. The annual benefit is an *expected* value determined by multiplying the loss times the probability of occurrence. The PVCs, PVBs, NPVs and B–C ratios for a discount rate of 10% are provided in Table 6.3.

Table 6.3: Crude Cost–Benefit Analysis of Alternative Flood Control Investment Projects

Alternative	Capital cost (PVC) ($'000s)	Present value of benefits (PVB) ($'000s)	Net present value (NPV) ($'000s)	Benefit–cost ratio (B/C)
1	15	8	–7	0.533
2	40	32	–8	0.800
3	100	122	22	1.220
4	150	226	76	1.507
5	250	286	36	1.144
6	340	346	6	1.018
7	500	386	–114	0.772

As an example of how to calculate the present value of benefits, consider investment alternative (dam size) 3. The annual benefit is $12,200 (= 0.08×$10,000 + 0.12×$20,000 + 0.30×$30,000); then PVB = $122,000 (= $12,200/0.10). While any of dam sizes 3, 4, 5 or 6 yields a positive NPV, the optimal size dam to build is the one that yields the greatest NPV and the highest B/C. This is dam size 4. It is important to notice that preventing all possibility of flooding is an option that is not economic and, indeed, yields substantial losses to society. For dam size 7, the investment yields a return of 77.2 cents for every dollar that is invested, or a loss of 22.8 cents for every dollar of construction costs! Thus, it is economic to suffer the more devastating floods that are likely to occur 4 years out of 100; it does not pay to spend money to prevent them.

While the foregoing analysis gave the correct answer (choose dam 4), there is something amiss. Suppose that alternative 4 was not available. In deciding between 3 and 5, the B–C ratio indicates that alternative 3 should be chosen, while the NPV criterion requires one to choose 5. (The same contradiction occurs if one is required to choose between alternatives 1 and 2.) The problem is that none of the investment opportunities in Table 6.3 uses the same investment funds. In the choice between alternatives 3 and 5, alternative 3 costs $100,000 while 5 costs $250,000.

What happens to the $150,000 difference between these investments? It is assumed that this money can be invested in its best alternative at a rate of return of 10%. Therefore, the correct approach to valuing the various alternatives presented in the previous two tables is to assume that $500,000 is available to be invested. Thus, alternative 3 consists of an investment of $100,000 in flood control and a $400,000 investment at a 10% rate of return; alternative 5 consists of $250,000 invested in flood control and a similar amount invested at 10%. The same is true for the other alternatives. Making this adjustment gives the results in Table 6.4. Alternative 4 remains the preferred choice, but there are no contradictions between the NPV and B/C criteria. Notice also that incorrect application of the B–C methodology can lead to mistaken impressions concerning the profitability of investment projects.

Table 6.4: Cost–Benefit Analysis of Alternative Flood Control Investment Projects: Equal Capital Investment Amount

Alter- native	Cost of dam ($'000s)	Capital cost (PVC) ($'000s)	Present value of benefits (PVB) ($'000s)	Net present value (NPV) ($'000s)	Benefit –cost ratio B/C
1	15	500	493	–7	0.986
2	40	500	492	–8	0.984
3	100	500	522	22	1.044
4	150	500	576	76	1.152
5	250	500	536	36	1.072
6	340	500	506	6	1.012
7	500	500	386	–114	0.772

Evaluation of British Columbia's Forest Practices Code

In response to growing pressure from the general public, the BC government has taken steps to protect forestlands, of which it owns more than 95% of the Province's total. Among these steps is the 1994 Forest Practices Code, which regulates harvesting to protect environmental amenities by, for example, reducing the size of clearcuts, implementing riparian corridors and leaving seed trees. In this subsection, which summarizes more detailed analysis in van Kooten (1999), we provide an economic evaluation of BC's Forest Practices Code to illustrate the difficulty of CBA in the context of evaluating policy related to nature preservation.

On the benefit side, what is important are nonmarket values – outdoor recreation, protection of biodiversity, scenic amenities provided by forest landscapes, wildlife habitat, watershed protection, and so on. Also important, but not calculated here, are the possibility that more timber might be available in the future, and the quasi-option value associated with preservation of old growth (logging old growth is a type of irreversibility; see Arrow and Fisher 1974).

Measuring nonmarket benefits can be a problem (Chapter 4). On the cost side, foregone benefits from timber harvest are most important. In principle, these are relatively easy to measure, but that is not always the case, as shown below. If the discounted benefits to society from the Forest Practices Code exceed the discounted costs, then the wellbeing of BC's citizens is improved by the policy. If not, then the Code results in the overall impoverishment of the Province's citizens, even though some individuals or groups might be made better off. In essence, it is necessary to demonstrate that the value citizens place on the environmental amenities that are protected by the Code exceeds the costs of the Code.

Costs of the Forest Practices Code

The major costs of the Forest Practices Code are measured by lost surplus in the markets for stumpage and wood products. Consider first the stumpage or forest-level market in Figure 6.1. The marginal costs (MC) of growing and harvesting timber for commercial purposes consist of silvicultural costs (if any), and road construction and logging costs. The value of stumpage is given by P_s, which exceeds MC because of resource scarcity.

Since the stumpage available for harvest in any given period is limited on average to S, which is equal to the allowable annual cut (AAC) that is determined by government fiat, the scarcity rent is given by area P_sbmc, while the differential rent is given by area cme, where c is the marginal cost of producing timber. As indicated in Chapter 4, scarcity rents are simply the result of existing stands of natural and mature trees that came into being without human intervention. Differential rents, on the other hand, relate to differences among stands, with some stands being more valuable than others because they are closer to the mill or the terrain is not as steep. The differential rent is related to logging and transportation investment. Together these constitute the producer surplus or total economic rent accruing to the trees.

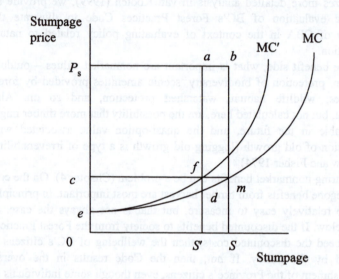

Figure 6.1: Lost rents in stumpage market

The Code does two things at the forest level. First, the amount that can be harvested is reduced from S to S' – there is a reduction in the AAC; the available economic rent is reduced by area *abmf*, consisting of lost scarcity rent *abmf* and quasi-rent *mdf*. Second, the marginal cost of forest operations increases from MC to MC'. This results in a reduction in producer surplus equal to area *def*. The cost associated with the Code, as measured in the timber market, is then given by area *abmef*.

The wood products market is also affected by a reduction in the availability of fiber. The producer surplus is measured in this market and not in the stumpage market because, given government regulation, it is not possible to determine a derived demand for stumpage. The welfare in the wood products market is illustrated in Figure 6.2. In the figure, it is assumed that BC producers face a horizontal demand for their products, whether pulp, lumber or other wood products. Reductions in the supply of BC wood products could raise world prices because of BC's market power. However, this response is likely to be short-lived as higher prices stimulate wood product supply from other producing regions, technical advances in the use of wood products and greater use of nonwood substitutes. In the longer term, therefore, BC firms likely face a horizontal demand for their products.

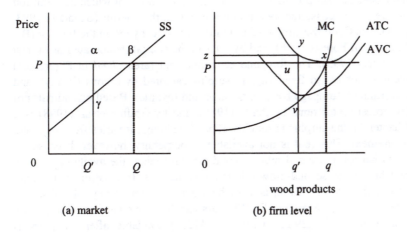

(a) market   (b) firm level

Figure 6.2: Producer surplus loss in wood products market

A reduction in fiber availability has the effect of restricting the output of wood products, as illustrated in Figure 6.2(a) by a shift in output from Q to Q'. Given the supply curve SS, and output price P, the loss in producer surplus is given by area $\alpha\beta\gamma$, which is a quasi-rent. The case of an individual mill or firm is indicated in panel (b). The reduction in fiber availability means a reduction in mill output from q to q', with the sum of the individual reductions in output totaling the output reduction by the industry as a whole. For the individual mill, the reduction in output results in excess capacity as production slides up the average total cost (ATC) curve from point x to y in Figure 6.2(b). However, only marginal costs and average variable costs (AVC) are relevant to the calculation of the true economic loss, which is given by the producer surplus or the area above MC and below price. This is area uvx in panel (b), which is also equal to the difference between total revenue and total variable cost. The sum of these firm-level areas over all producers or mills is equal to the area in panel (a). To obtain the total economic loss, we add over the stumpage and wood product markets.

Given that there is little or no information about the curves in Figures 6.1 and 6.2, measuring the costs indicated above is difficult. Nonetheless, it is possible to gain some insight into the magnitude of these costs. In addition, there are costs that have not been considered above, but are discussed after the results. The costs associated with the Forest Practices Code can be summarized as follows.

Foregone scarcity rent. The reduction in AAC is one important cost of the Code. Current provincial AAC is 72.1 million m^3, of which 22.3 million m^3 are on the coast and 49.8 million m^3 are in the interior (Saunders 1993, p.13). The Code was projected to reduce the AAC by 6% in the Interior (BC Ministry of Forests 1996), and by 10% in the coastal (temperate rain) forest (Saunders 1993). The foregone economic rent (area *abmd* in Figure 6.1) includes returns to fixed capital, surplus captured by unions (if any), and government stumpage fees, rents, taxes and royalties. Based on estimates of BC forest sector rents by Percy (1986), and by Grafton et al. (1998) (see Chapter 4), the surplus is roughly $25/$m^3$, although it varies from one year to the next. This rent is not available in perpetuity, however, because, as firms harvest more and more second-growth timber, the available scarcity rent falls since second-growth logs are worth less. It is assumed that only half of the $25/$m^3$ of rent is available after 30 years. Using a 4% discount rate, the $25/$m^3$ available for 30 years can be converted into a perpetuity equivalent of $17.29/$m^3$, while the $12.50 available after 30 years is converted into a perpetuity equivalent of $3.85/$m^3$ using the bond formula (6.4).[6] In that case, the net adjusted surplus is $21.15/$m^3$ (upon rounding up to the nearest cent). Multiplying this surplus by the reduction in AAC determines the economic value of the lost timber. Assuming the reduction is 10% on the coast (2.23 million m^3) and 6% in the interior (2.99 million m^3), the cost amounts to $110.4 million per year.

Increased delivered wood costs: lost differential rent. As a result of increased costs of road building (more roads need to be built as size of clearcuts is reduced by more than 50%), road maintenance, changed logging practices and so on, harvest costs will increase. An in-depth study of changes in delivered wood costs as a result of the Code was conducted by McIntosh et al. (1997). Delivered wood costs increased as a result of added costs of planning and administration, and forest practices. In the former category, the greatest cost increases were in the form of additional plans, amendments to approved plans, greater sawmill and pulp mill inventory requirements, administrative delays, and various costs associated with increased need for permits. Increased costs of forest practices are associated with reductions in cut-block size, road and landing requirements, greater soil conservation, protection of riparian areas and green-up requirements.

These Code-related costs have increased delivered wood costs by $19.68/m^3 on the coast and $8.41/m^3 in the interior. (The higher costs on the coast are due to steeper terrain, greater biodiversity and lack of a winter "deep freeze", when logging takes place in the interior.) The increase in this component of costs on the coast equals $395.6 million (=$19.68/m^3 × 20.1 million m^3 adjusted AAC) and $393.6 million in the Interior (=$8.41/m^3 × 46.8 million m^3). The total loss of differential rent then amounts to some $789.2 million per year, which is an estimate of area *def* in Figure 6.1.

Loss of producer surplus in the wood products market: quasi-rent. There is no readily available information to estimate the loss in producer surplus in the wood products market from a reduction in AAC. A reduction in AAC will mean that mills will either have to obtain logs or fiber elsewhere (e.g., from Alaska, Alberta, Saskatchewan), causing the AVC and MC curves in Figure 6.2(b) to rise (not shown). It could also lead to reduced output, which results in excess capacity and higher per unit costs as fixed costs are spread over a reduced output. For sawmills these are estimated by Saunders (1993, p.41) to cost $113.7–$229.0 million per annum for the first five years after the Code's implementation. Saunders converts this to an annual cost of $20.2–$40.8 million in perpetuity using a 4% rate of discount. COFI (1994, pp.2–5) estimates the increased costs of excess capacity in pulp mills to be $77–$156 million per annum for the first 10 years of the Code, or annualized cost of $25.0–$50.6 in perpetuity at 4%. Both Saunders and COFI use reductions in AAC of 10% and 20%, thus giving them a range of values. In terms of Figure 6.2, the excess capacity estimates by Saunders and by COFI are represented by area *Puyz*, but then summed over all mills. Notice that the costs associated with excess capacity (inability to adjust plant size in the short run) differ from those of lost producer surplus in going from *q* to *q'*.

Increases in excess capacity are the result of inappropriate plant investment, but such an investment now constitutes a fixed cost, or "water under the bridge". As noted in Chapter 3, if government policy continues to affect returns to such investments, companies will simply quit making them and sawmills and pulp mills will not be built. Recall that the relevant surplus area is given by the quasi-rent or producer surplus and not by area *Puyz* – the cost of excess capacity. The correct measure of loss is the surplus area above the marginal cost curve and below price over the range *q'q* in Figure 6.2(b), or area *uxv*. This is the loss in producer surplus. In order to determine the loss in producer surplus, some assumptions need to be made.

Assume that areas *xuy* and *xuv* are triangles (which amounts to a linearity assumption), and assume that area *xuv* is twice as large as area *xuy*. This is a strong assumption, but any other assumption will be just as foolhardy. For sawmills, the cost of excess capacity (area *Puyz*) is $22.0 million when AAC is reduced from 72.10 million m^3 to 64.89 million m^3 (a 10% reduction); the height of the rectangle (distance *uy*) is thus 0.339 (= $22.0 million ÷ 64.89 million). Similarly, for pulp mills, distance *uy* is 0.385 (= $25.0 million ÷ 64.89 million m^3). It is possible to calculate the loss in producer surplus for sawmills and pulp mills on the coast and in the interior by multiplying the height *uv* by *q–q'* (this is the assumption that area *xuv* is twice area *xuy*). The results are presented in Table 6.5. Total foregone producer surplus as a result of the Forest Practices Code is estimated to be $3.780 million annually.

Table 6.5: Annual Code-Related Producer Surplus Reductions in Sawmill and Pulp Mill Sectors ('000s)

	Coast	Interior	TOTAL
Sawmills	$756	$1,014	$1,770
Pulp mills	$859	$1,151	$2,010
TOTAL	$1,770	$2,010	$3,780

Increase in government administration costs. Saunders (1993, pp.16–19) estimates the increase in costs to government because of the Code to be $49.0–$71.0 million annually. These cost estimates may be low if overhead costs by the Forest Renewal BC (FRBC) are any indication. FRBC is a publicly-owned corporation created in 1994 and charged with investing forest resource rents of some $500 million per year back in the forest sector. Overhead amounts to some 40% of expenditures (Hamilton 1997). We assume that overhead expenses due to the Code amount to 20% of the expenditures of FRBC as it was at the time the main entity responsible for investment in forestry; this amounts to some $100 million annually.

Social adjustment costs. While job losses and consequent reductions in forest sector wages are important considerations in formulating policy, these do not comprise an economic cost in the true sense. Many displaced forest sector workers will find jobs at lower pay, but this constitutes an income transfer from them to the rest of the economy, not an economic cost. However, there are economic costs brought about by the displacement in forest sector workers. These are the costs of job search, retraining and moving, plus the psychological costs on workers and their families, and costs associated with, for example, increased alcohol abuse, crime, and so on. Similar costs are incurred by merchants and communities, while the federal and provincial governments incur added costs in administering unemployment insurance and welfare schemes. (The actual payments made under these programs are a form of income transfer and not an economic cost.) The social adjustment costs are difficult to measure. Assuming 1.57 direct jobs per 1,000 m³, some 8,200 (=5.22 mil m³ × 1.57 jobs per 1,000 m³) forest sector jobs will be lost as a result of the Code. Since forest sector workers have low education levels and experience difficulty finding alternative employment (even at lower wages), an adjustment cost of $40,000 per forest sector worker is *assumed*. The social adjustment cost amounts to about $328.0 million. Additional jobs will be lost elsewhere in the economy, but such workers are likely to experience lower adjustment costs. Assuming an employment multiplier of 2.5 and an adjustment cost for those workers of $10,000, the social adjustment cost outside the forest sector is $130 million. Thus, the total adjustment cost is $455 million, or using a 4% discount rate, some $18.2 million on an annualized basis.

Lost nonmarket amenities. While the benefits of the Forest Practices Code will be primarily nonmarket in nature, there will be lost amenity values because there will be "negative public reaction to coarse woody debris" (Saunders 1993, p.10) that is to be left on cut-over sites according to the Code's regulations. These and other such costs are not quantified here – they are assumed to be negligible.

Other costs. As noted above, reductions in the supply of BC wood fiber will raise world prices, at least in the short term. This increases the welfare of producers (including government) because rents will be higher for the AAC that remains available, but consumers are worse off. However, higher prices stimulate supply from elsewhere and substitute products that will reduce prices in the longer run. Some of the increase in supply may come from regions that are ecologically more sensitive than BC and, to the extent that such areas are valued by BC residents, this constitutes a cost. Substitute products may be less friendly for the environment than wood products, with the environmental damage that they cause also attributable to the Code. These costs (and benefits) are difficult to trace and value, and are assumed to be negligible or to cancel one another.

A summary of all the aforementioned costs of the Forest Practices Code is provided in Table 6.6. The economic costs of the Code, as estimated here, are $1,021.7 million per annum. Of course, there is substantial uncertainty associated with such a point estimate, perhaps as large as 50% of the value reported here. For comparison, the BC government collected an average $953.0 million in rent per year over the period 1990–94, compared to available annual rents of $1,609.6 million (Grafton et al. 1998). Thus, the Code's costs (irrespective of the large estimated variance) are large compared to rent collection. Compared to estimates of the Code's costs, however, estimates of the benefits of the Code are likely to be even more uncertain.

Table 6.6: Estimated Annual Costs of BC's Forest Practices Code ($ mil)

Cost of foregone economic rents	110.4
Increased harvest costs	789.2
Lost producer surplus in wood products	3.8
Increased government administration costs	100.0
Social adjustment costs	18.3
TOTAL	**1,021.7**

Benefits provided by the Forest Practices Code

If the Forest Practices Code is to benefit the citizens of the province of British Columbia, and increase their wellbeing as defined above, it is necessary that the benefits exceed these costs. The benefits of the Code need to be determined from nontimber uses and this requires the estimation of nonmarket values. Expenditures by tourists cannot be used as a measure of benefits, because they do not take into account the costs of providing services – they are a gross measure comparable to the value of timber exports, say (van Kooten 1995c). The benefits of the Forest Practices Code are primarily nonmarket in nature. They consist of use and non-use benefits. Recreation is the major use to be affected by the Code. Non-use benefits derive from forest attributes, such as biodiversity, because individuals derive utility from simply knowing that these amenities exist even if they are unlikely to ever visit the area where they are found (existence value) or from passing on such amenities to the next generation (bequest value). In the analysis that follows, it is assumed that the amenities that the Code seeks to protect are similar to those that the Province's Protected Areas Strategy seeks to preserve.

Recreation Benefits. The BC Ministry of Forests (1991) has estimated forest recreation use benefits, *plus* the value that recreationists attach to the future option of continuing to pursue these activities. These are provided by forest region in columns (4) and (5) of Table 6.7. Forest recreation use and wildlife viewing are valued at about $40 million per year, while preservation for purposes of future recreation and wildlife viewing (option demand) is valued at slightly more than $147 million per year. Thus, forest recreation is valued at $187.0 million annually. Forest recreation benefits on an annual per hectare basis and by forest region are provided in column (4) of Table 6.8. The average annual value per hectare is about $11.80, with the highest value ($34.00/ha) occurring in the Vancouver forest region and the lowest value ($1.49/ha) in the Prince Rupert forest region. Such an allocation assumes that all recreation value is attributed to mature forest area, which is clearly not the case. Thus, the values reported in Table 6.8 are high and any other means of allocating benefits over hectares would result in much lower per hectare values for recreation.

Table 6.7: Population of BC and Forest Recreation Use and Preservation Values by Region, $1992

Region	(1) Total popul'n (000s)	(2) Adults (000s)	(3) Regional % of adult popul'n	(4) Recr. use value ($mil/y)	(5) Recr. Pres. value[a] ($mil/y)	(6) Non-use benefit[b] ($mil/y)
Vancouver	2,102	1,583	74.5	4.54	111.13	339.22
Pr Rupert	83	54	2.5	4.97	4.49	11.49
Kamloops	328	240	11.3	10.03	11.23	51.34
Pr George	162	105	5.0	6.83	8.22	22.59
Nelson	148	105	4.9	8.15	9.40	22.47
Cariboo	59	39	1.8	5.11	2.87	8.44
TOTAL	**2,883**	**2,126**	**100.0**	**39.62**	**147.34**	**455.53**

Notes:
[a]Recreation preservation value includes preservation for purposes of future recreation and future wildlife viewing.
[b]Household WTP for non-use benefits is estimated at $300 per year. Divide adult population by 1.4 to get number of households and multiply by $300 (see text).
Source: BC Ministry of Forests (1991, pp.15, 48–9, 51).

There is very little information about the potential impact that the Forest Practices Code will have on recreational benefits. It could be argued that recreational values may, on balance, be unaffected by the Code if site characteristics are taken into account. The reason is that the Code will bring about better access because of an increase in road building. This will be a positive benefit. Further, there exists evidence that wilderness recreation is less highly valued than developed recreation (Edwards et al. 1976), suggesting that protection of wilderness attributes beyond some amount is unlikely to enhance benefits from recreation and may even reduce them. On the negative side, recreational values might be reduced because site attributes are adversely affected (e.g., coarse woody debris or too many roads) and there may be restrictions on access and/or the types of activities that can be pursued (e.g., hunting, motor homes, all-terrain vehicles and snowmobiles may be banned).

Table 6.8: Mature Forest Area, Recreation Expenditures by Area, by Forest Region, $1992

Region	Mature timber (000s ha)[a]	Recreation use value ($/ha/y)[b]	Recreation preservation option value ($/ha/y)[b,c]	Total recreation benefits ($/ha/y)[b]
	(1)	(2)	(3)	(4)
Vancouver	3402	1.34	32.67	34.00
Pr Rupert	6367	0.78	0.71	1.49
Kamloops	2373	4.23	4.73	8.96
Pr George	9596	0.71	0.86	1.57
Nelson	1390	5.86	6.76	12.62
Cariboo	3565	1.44	0.81	2.25
Total[d]	**26 693**	**(1.48)**	**(5.52)**	**(11.80)**
Interior	**23 291**	**(1.51)**	**(1.56)**	**(3.06)**

Notes:

[a] Source: BC Ministry of Forests (1992b).

[b] Source: Calculation.

[c] This is the value of retaining the option to pursue recreational activities at some future date.

[d] Averages in parentheses.

To determine the extent to which the Forest Practices Code increases recreational benefits, it is assumed that Code-induced reductions in AAC (10% on the coast, 6% in the interior) increase the area of mature forest that has wilderness-type attributes by a similar amount. This increase in wilderness attributes is then assumed to increase recreation benefits by similar percentages over what they are currently. Thus, recreation benefits increase by $11.6 million (= 0.10×$34/ha×340.2 million ha) on the coast (Vancouver forest region) and by $4.3 million in the interior (all other forest regions), for a total increase of $15.9 million per year. It is important to recognize that this is an arbitrary assumption.

Non-use Benefits. It is likely that the increase in non-use benefits is the most significant aspect of the Code. But it is not clear how the Code will affect such benefits. A significant future research effort will be needed to make the link between the forest attributes that the Code seeks to protect and their economic value. For example, we do not know (and do not attempt to measure) possible adverse economic effects of logging operations on fish habitat (see, e.g., Aylward 1992, p.52). At this stage, the data are unavailable and some detective work is required to provide even cursory estimates of potential benefits from contingent valuation data that do exist. Hence, we employ the method of benefit transfer. This is done below.

Given the paucity of information, a number of assumptions will need to be made to implement this example of the benefit transfer method. For BC, a government study (Vold et al. 1994) found that households were, on average, willing to pay $136 per year to double the amount of wilderness in the province from 5% of BC to 10% of BC; households were also willing to pay $168 per year to triple the amount of wilderness preserved from 5% of the province to 15%. A US study by Hagen et al. (1992) found the annual non-use or preservation value of spotted owl habitat, which they equated to old-growth ecosystems in their survey, to be as much as US$200/household (about C$300/household) – the largest value found in any CV studies on spotted owl or protected areas. In this study, therefore, some scenarios assume that households would be willing to pay as much as $300 annually for increasing wilderness protection from its current level to that under the Province's Protected Areas Strategy (BC Ministry of Forests 1992a); *this value is high compared to other studies.* If households consist of 1.4 adults on average, it is possible to calculate the total non-use benefits by forest region; total annual non-use benefits are $455.5 million (col. (6), Table 6.7).

Estimated non-use benefits of $455.5 million per annum cannot simply be added to annual estimated forest recreation benefits of $15.9 million to obtain the total benefits attributable to the Forest Practices Code. The reason is that the non-use benefits are a total value, while recreation benefits are the additional benefits associated solely with the Code. If the non-use values identified here are to be representative of true WTP, these values cannot all be attributed to changes in forest practices. Given that the Code protects wilderness attributes, much of the value needs to be attributed to the preservation of intact ecosystems, as occurs under the Protected Areas Strategy. Suppose that the value of $300 per household per year was determined at the time that 8% of the Province's land, or 7.6 million ha, was officially protected. In 1994, 8.9% of the Province's land base was protected, but the area in Provincial Parks (constituting by far the largest area set aside) had increased by 42.3% since 1987, to 7.6 million ha (BC Ministry of Environment, Lands and Parks 1996). Then, the $455.5 million represents total WTP (total non-use benefits) from increasing wilderness protection beyond 7.6 million ha.

Decisions are necessarily made at the margin. Hence, it is necessary to determine the marginal WTP function for setting aside further wilderness. Without additional information, it is simply assumed that the marginal WTP function is linear as shown in Figure 6.3, where $u'(W)$ represents marginal utility (marginal WTP) as a function of wilderness (W) and W^0 is the current amount of wilderness.

Let W^P represent the area that is protected under the Province's Protected Area Strategy (11.4 million ha) and $W^C - W^P$ the area equivalent (AAC converted to area) protected by the Code, and which has similar wilderness attributes to other protected area. Thus, the non-use benefits of the Code are determined as the area under the marginal utility function, $u'(W)$, between W^P and W^C.

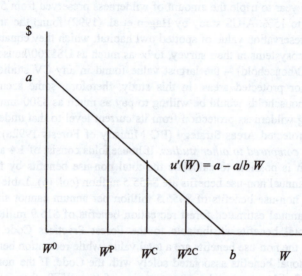

Figure 6.3: Marginal willingness-to-pay for protection of wilderness

The area "protected" by the Code remains protected next year as well, and the year thereafter, and so forth. The area "protected" the second year as a result of harvest restrictions relating to the Code is over and above W^C–W^P, and is equal to the area under the marginal utility function, $u'(W)$, between W^P and W^{2C} in Figure 6.3. The benefits of protecting this area are lower than those associated with W^P–W^C, but this benefit is also available in the second year and thereafter. To obtain the total non-use benefit, it is necessary to calculate the discounted value of this stream of increasing benefits, at least increasing to the point where the marginal benefit function cuts the abscissa. Negative benefits (or costs of too much protection) are ignored.

Neither a nor b is known; only the area under the curve is known and fixed (equal to $455.5 million). However, once a is known, b is also known because $b = 2A/a$, where A is the area under the curve. Parameter a is the amount households are willing to pay to protect the next hectare of wilderness, given that they already have W^0. As a starting point, begin with a value of $120 per ha, which is obtained by dividing $455.5 million by the difference $W^P - W^0$ (= 11.4 million ha – 7.6 million ha). Of course, the higher the value of a, the steeper the slope of the marginal preservation function.

To simplify the calculations and because the Province's target of protecting 12% of BC's land base applies equally to the coast and interior, the calculations are conducted for the Province as a whole (i.e., $W^0 = 7.6$ million ha). Assume standing inventories of approximately 400 m³/ha on the coast and 200 m³/ha in the interior. This is low for mature stands, especially on the coast, but serves our purpose since it increases the estimate of non-use benefits attributable to the Code. Using these values to convert AAC to area results in the protection of an additional 20,515 ha each year, which equals 10% of coastal AAC (of 22.3 million m³) divided by 400 plus 6% of interior AAC (49.8 million m³) divided by 200. Further, since nonforest lands constitute some 45% of the land area, the Code actually protects an additional 30,000 ha every year. Non-use benefits from the Code are provided in Table 6.9 for various values of a. Total discounted benefits are calculated using a discount rate of 4%, and are then annualized. A scenario with double total non-use benefits ($900 million rather than $455.5 million) is also presented; this scenario is meant to address potential unaccounted-for ecosystem benefits (e.g., protection of salmon habitat, weather regulation, carbon sink). From Table 6.9, maximum annual non-use benefits of the Code are between about $40.4 million and $79.8 million.

Table 6.9: Estimated Annual Non-use Benefits of BC's Forest Practices Code, 1992 ($ mil)

Assumed non-use value of marginal ha before Protected Areas Strategy and Code (a)	Value to BC household of protecting more wilderness attributes	
	$300 (max. stated WTP)	$600 (WTP plus nonmeasured benefits)
$ 40	25.9	29.1
$ 80	38.8	51.6
$100	40.4	60.4
$120	38.8	67.5
$160	25.9	77.0
$180	14.5	79.2
$200	–	79.8
$240	–	76.2

Summary

The costs of the Forest Practices Code are estimated to be approximately $1,021.7 million annually. Recreation benefits are estimated at $15.9 million per year, while non-use benefits are calculated to be $40.5–$80.0

million annually. Not included in the benefits of the Forest Practices Code are those primarily non-use benefits that accrue to people living outside BC. There are two issues. First, it is not clear that one should count benefits to those outside the Province unless they are prepared to compensate BC residents for their foregone timber rents and other costs associated with the provision of forest ecosystem amenities. Second, given that the calculations provided in the last column of Table 6.9 are based on an unrealistically high level of benefits over and above those provided by the (then) existing parks and other protected areas, the higher non-use benefit values might take into account benefits to nonresidents. Even with these caveats, it is clear that the costs of the Forest Practices Code exceed benefits by a significant amount, by almost $900 million annually.

One could well ask why the provincial government would want to impose such costly regulations on the forest sector. One reason is that there needed to be changes in BC forest practices, because existing practices simply were not sustainable; they consisted of large clearcuts in mountainous terrain, with significant soil erosion, wood fiber wastage and so on. Although fish and other critical wildlife habitat were threatened by these practices, as was the ability to grow trees on a sustainable basis, by the early 1990s these damages were already being addressed by other means before the Code was brought to bear (see, e.g., Chapter 11). Further, protection of many of the attributes associated with non-use benefits (including protection of critical habitat and preservation of biodiversity) was also being addressed by initiatives, such as the Protected Areas Strategy (which sought to protect 12% of each of the Province's biogeographical zones), timber supply reviews, and the Spotted Owl Recovery Team (which identified northern spotted owl nests and declared areas around them off limits to loggers).

Political factors were also present. The Forest Practices Code may have enabled the government to claim the moral high ground while appeasing their environmental constituency. At the same time, the regulatory legislation was designed to counter charges and boycotts of BC forest products by the international environmental movement (as were some of the other forestry initiatives). These factors are difficult to quantify as benefits, if indeed they can be considered as such.

The economist can only compare costs and benefits, and it is difficult to argue that the political benefits are large. Although they may well be large, it is necessary to make this case. Otherwise, one can only conclude from the analysis presented above that, even under the most optimistic estimates of non-use benefits, the Forest Practices Code will result in a significant reduction in the wellbeing of BC citizens.

NOTES

1. The first application of BCA occurred in 1902 "when the US River and Harbor Act directed the Corps of Engineers to assess the costs and benefits of all river and harbor projects" (Bentkover 1986).

2. The literature on project appraisal is profuse and it would be inappropriate to document all of it here. It should be noted that much of the early literature originated with the World Bank and other development agencies (e.g., Gittinger 1982; Squire and van der Tak 1975; Little and Mirrlees 1974; Dasgupta et al. 1972).

3. This result is indicative of an endowment effect: researchers found that individuals were willing to pay, on average, $5.60 for a 50% change *to win* $20, but the same individuals demanded an average of $10.87 *to give up* the identical chance to win the $20 (Knetsch 2000, p.271).

4. The theoretical foundations of CBA have been well documented by Harberger (1972), Boadway (1974), Just et al. (1982), and Boadway and Bruce (1984), among others. See also Chapter 2.

5. The bond formula is derived as follows: Let $V_n =$

   $$\frac{y}{1+r} + \frac{y}{(1+r)^2} + \ldots + \frac{y}{(1+r)^n}$$. Multiply both sides by $1/(1+r)$ so that

   $$V_n/(1+r) = \frac{y}{(1+r)^2} + \ldots + \frac{y}{(1+r)^n} + \frac{y}{(1+r)^{n+1}}$$. Now subtract the latter

   from the former: $V_n - V_n/(1+r) = \frac{r}{1+r} V_n = \frac{y}{1+r} - \frac{y}{(1+r)^{n+1}}$, which upon

   solving gives $V_n = y \left(\frac{1}{r} - \frac{1}{r(1+r)^n} \right)$. Then, $\lim_{n \to \infty} V_n = V = \frac{y}{r}$.

6. The bond formula is modified because the annual amount of $25 is only available for 30 years. Thus, the result in the text is determined as:

   $$\frac{\$25}{0.04} - \frac{\$25/0.04}{(1+0.04)^{30}} + \frac{\$12.50/0.04}{(1+0.04)^{30}}$$. Values are in Canadian dollars.

7.   Sustainable Development and Conservation

Sustainable development became a popular term in the (late) 1980s and 1990s for expressing the idea that economic growth must occur in harmony with the environment, and not at the expense of future generations. The term was coined by the World Commission on Environment and Development (or Brundtland Commission) as development that "... meets the needs of the present without compromising the ability of future generations to meet their own needs" (1987, p.8). This definition is not very helpful because it provides no guidance as to what it is that is to be sustained and how sustainable development is to be measured (e.g., what constitutes "needs"?) or put into practice. But it does highlight the political nature of the conflict (real or perceived) between economic growth and the environment: the definition is purposely vague so that it would receive unanimous political support, while many interpretations can be assigned to it (Daly and Cobb 1994, pp.75–6).

Sustainability and economic efficiency are different and possibly conflicting concepts. While economic efficiency is a relatively unambiguous concept ("maximize the net present value of society's wellbeing"), and cost–benefit analysis can be used to identify efficiency in the public realm, it can result in unequal distributions of welfare over time. Maximizing net present value (NPV) may be to the detriment of distant generations (mainly because of discounting), and sustainability may be worth pursuing for moral reasons (justice and fairness), even though economic efficiency may be pushed aside because of concern about intergenerational equity. In addition to concerns about future generations, the sustainability concept is sometimes used to acknowledge environmental integrity and rights in nature (van den Bergh and Hofkes 1998).

While there is consensus that sustainable development concerns intergenerational transfer of natural resources, if not wealth, there are differing views about what this really implies. Yet, most definitions appear to have one or more of the following essential ingredients:

1.   Concern with the long-term health of the environment.
2.   Apprehension about the welfare of future generations.

3. Condemnation of rapid population growth.
4. Worry over whether it is possible to maintain economic growth in the face of resource scarcity.
5. Guilt about the large gulf in incomes and standards of living between the developed and developing countries, between rich and poor.

Some components of the resource base are ultimately fixed – there are limits to the reserves of fossil fuels and to the ability of the atmosphere to absorb anthropogenic emissions of greenhouse gases – but others, such as solar and wind sources of energy, are limitless.

Judging by most literature, it appears that sustainable development is a relatively new concept, one that the scientific community has recently, and perhaps fortunately, stumbled across. Economists have been concerned with many of these issues, particularly resource scarcity, since at least the time of Robert Malthus, whose argument was alluded to above, namely, that food scarcity (due to a fixed land quantity, continued population growth and diminishing returns) would keep the majority of people in poverty. This same theme shows up in more recent times under various guises, including the Club of Rome's "Limits to Growth" research (Meadows et al. 1972), and now, in some forms, as sustainable development. It is in this respect that the debate is seen as one of neo-Malthusians versus the optimists.

The goal of this chapter is to investigate some of the topics surrounding sustainable development, with a particular focus on economics. Unfortunately, many topics are addressed only in cursory fashion, mainly because of their complexity and because our focus is on nature conservation and management. We address the issue of subsitutability between reproducible and natural capital (section 7.2) and indicators and evidence of sustainability (section 7.4). We also address related concepts found in the economics literature, some long before the term sustainable development was coined (section 7.3). Before doing so, however, we examine what it is that needs to be sustained (the object of sustainability), viewpoints, and what is meant by sustainable consumption.

7.1 BACKGROUND

Before considering what is meant by sustainable development, we address the question: What are we to sustain? We also consider the role of people'sviews on sustainability and what sustainable consumption (utility) implies.

What is to be Sustained?

Before answering this question, note that there are economic, social and ecological components of sustainability. This is sometimes referred to as "triple-P" sustainability, where the three Ps denote People, Profit and Planet. The essence of developing a policy of sustainability is to strike a balance between these three components.

One answer to the question about what is to be sustained is that we want to sustain current per capita income. But whose per capita income is to be sustained – the incomes of those living in rich countries or of those living in poor countries, or do we wish to sustain global per capita income (output)? If global output is to be sustained, then, unless global per capita output can be raised (by reducing population or increasing output, or both), it may be necessary to redistribute incomes from rich to poor (say, for ethical reasons). However, maintaining global output can result in lower per capita output simply because of population growth, while redistributing income could result in adverse incentives, which actually reduce output. For instance, large-scale redistribution of income in rich countries could lead to less investments in those countries which, in turn, would lead to lower or even negative growth. It would also be met with strong opposition. Clearly, without economic growth it is not possible to maintain high incomes in rich countries while it is wrong to somehow deny opportunities for raising standards of living to those in developing countries. It is for this reason that the World Commission on Environment and Development (WCED) adds the word "development". It would seem that sustainability must include opportunities for raising the living standards of the poor, while maintaining those of the rich at current (or higher) levels. While this is a value judgment, it is realistic because the richest countries (Western Europe, North America, Australia, Japan) and those in the process of raising their living standards to the levels of the richest countries (South Korea, Singapore) are unlikely to make significant sacrifice to their incomes. This is seen, for example, by the failure of the developed countries at Kyoto, Japan (in December 1997), to agree on CO_2–reduction targets. Moral suasion alone is likely inadequate to prevent climate change from occurring or to convince rich countries to accept declining living standards to help poor countries.

Rather than per capita income, perhaps it is the stock of total capital, or human plus natural capital, that is to be sustained. As discussed below, this object of sustainability creates its own set of problems. Perhaps, the object is to sustain growth, but then the same questions as those in the preceding paragraph arise: Whose growth is to be sustained? What rate of growth is to be sustained?

Some argue that it is the earth's ecosystems or life-support functions, varyingly referred to as the "environment", the "web of life" or the "stock of natural capital", that are to be sustained. For example, Common (1995) notes that "… ecological sustainability is, then, not a well-defined state to be attained by simple rules. We can say it is the requirement that the resilience of the system is maintained through time" (p.54). To some extent this implies a departure from the focus on human preferences and desires. A crucial issue is whether the structure and characteristics of the ecological system, as well as its dynamics, are maintained. The concepts of resilience and stability are of paramount importance (Holling 1973; Holling et al. 1995). Stability refers to the ability of populations to return to "equilibrium" after some disturbance, while resilience is a broader concept, measuring the propensity of ecosystems to retain their main features after some disturbance. It has been argued that system resilience is related to system diversity, complexity or interconnectedness (Common and Perrings 1992), suggesting that human impacts that reduce these properties should be avoided. However, recent ecological insights indicate that links between complexity and stability, for example, may be extremely complex (Budiansky 1995).

In general, proponents of the "ecosystem stability" view tend to favor curtailing of economic activity, so that interactions between the economy and the environment do not negatively impact system resilience. But there is disagreement about the resilience of ecosystems, about how human activities affect the earth's ecosystems, and about the degree to which human intervention (management?) interferes with life-support functions. These are important questions as the opportunity costs of maintaining natural capital are almost certainly considerable. Those concerned about possible ecosystem collapse often argue that we must maintain natural capital at its current level and, in some cases (as with greenhouse gases in the atmosphere), that steps should be taken to restore ecosystems to an earlier (better?) state, regardless of the costs involved. Yet, even among those who dissent with this view, there are few, if any, who would agree to economic development that would threaten the very continuance of human life. The debate, therefore, is reminiscent of, and has its parallels in, the aforementioned Malthusian debate about whether geometric population growth will be limited by arithmetic growth in agricultural output, thereby dooming everyone to live at a subsistence level (see Zebrowski 1997, pp.96–109).

When all is said and done, there is no consensus as to what is to be sustained. In order to investigate sustainability in a scientific fashion, bringing to bear scientific facts that are analyzed in one or more theoretical frameworks, it is important that a definition of sustainability be rigorous. But definitions of sustainability typically lack rigor, as exemplified by the definition provided by the WCED. One can only conclude that attempts to define sustainable development need to be purposely vague if they are to be politically acceptable (as noted above), but this is not helpful for scientists seeking to measure and debate sustainability.

Viewpoints and Sustainability

The role of investment is clearly important, and especially the form that such investment takes. Investment is to take place not only in natural capital (e.g., protecting biodiversity, planting trees), but also in reproducible capital (human-made and knowledge). Much of the controversy about sustainability concerns

1. the allocation of resources for investment between natural and reproducible capital, and
2. consumption versus investment, since investment implies a need to sacrifice consumption.

Perhaps current generations place too much emphasis on current consumption, and not enough on investment. Of an earlier generation, John Maynard Keynes wrote that the West experienced progress because "... owners [of capital] were free to consume profits but refrained from so doing, and workers to issue excessive demands but again did not do so" (Hall 1985, p.160). It would appear that previous generations reduced consumption in order to provide more for future generations, but that this ethic has abated. The earlier generation focused on investment in reproducible capital, which required inputs of natural capital to produce. Would the earlier generation also have been willing to protect (invest in) natural capital?

In an interesting twist, White (1967) turned the ethical position of the earlier generation on its head. He argued that, by refraining from consumption and investing in reproducible capital, previous generations created the high levels of prosperity that brought about levels of consumption that led to an environmental crisis. Leaving aside arguments about the relationship between high levels of prosperity and environmental quality (see section 7.5), it is not clear whether it is prosperity *per se* or a change in society's ethics that is responsible for White's conclusion that the environment has deteriorated to the point of crisis.

The concept of sustainable development clearly involves an ethical dimension. Implicitly (if not explicitly), it requires judgments about the right relationship between people and the environment. Further, definitions of sustainable development, and much of the discussion surrounding it, suggest purpose, and purpose can be judged only on ethical grounds.

But differences exist for other reasons as well. The notion of sustainability "... embodies deep conceptual ambiguities [that] ... cannot be easily resolved because they rest ... on serious theoretical disagreements that transcend disciplinary boundaries. In particular, economists and ecologists employ different conceptualizations for explaining the interactions of humans with their environment" (Norton and Toman 1997, p.553). The underlying philosophical viewpoints of disciplines vary, which becomes a source of disagreement that is not easily resolved. As discussed later in this chapter, many biologists and ecologists take a neo-Malthusian view of resources and resource scarcity, while mainline economists are more optimistic about the ability of humans to manage their way out of environmental crises. Many ecologists have adopted a position that state intervention is required to protect natural systems, while economists, for the most part, emphasize the individual and property rights (see, for example, Chant et al. 1990; Pearse 1993b; Panayotou 1993a). Whatever position one takes, politics and special interests may well determine how sustainable development policies are implemented. Our view (admittedly rooted in economics) is that this could potentially be a problem since, in the absence of a clear definition of sustainability, well-intentioned policies may be enacted that could endanger the economic health of resource-based industries to the detriment of society and potentially the resources themselves. In Chapter 12, for example, we show how important property rights and incentives are with respect to tropical forest conservation.

Sustainable Consumption

Define C_t^m as the maximum consumption level that can be held forever constant from time t onward, and $\bar{C}$ as the subsistence level of consumption. As alternative definitions of sustainability, Pezzey (1997) distinguishes three constraints on maximization of net present value – three constraints on maximizing the discounted value of consumption over time:

SD$_1$: Sustainable development	if $C_t \leq C_t^m$,	at every t
SD$_2$: Development is sustainable	if $C_{t+1} \geq C_t$,	at every t
SD$_3$: Development is survivable	if $C_t \geq \bar{C}$,	at every t

SD$_2$ (nondeclining consumption) seems to be too strong a requirement for sustainability, while SD$_3$ would seem to be too weak because it would permit a reduction in living standards to the subsistence level at some future date. Historically, SD$_2$ has been the most popular definition of sustainability, but it implies sustained development and not sustainable development, since there is no cap on consumption (as expressed by SD_1). Pezzey prefers SD_1 as a constraint on economic activities because it prevents consumption from growing without limit, and thereby reducing future consumption possibilities (although whether it does is an empirical issue).

In practice, conflicts about sustainability "… cannot be resolved without forming an ethical view of what intertemporal goal society should have" (Pezzey 1997, p.453). Sustainability is not about choosing the "correct" discount rate to ensure that future generations are sufficiently well off, but about choosing how much the current generation will pass on to the future one. The discount rate that allocates between generations is endogenous to the ethical choice of how much to pass along to the next generation (see Howarth and Norgaard 1995 for a review). The decision is ethical because the current generation must decide whether to ensure that the future has the opportunity (is able) to be, or actually is, as well off as the current generation (Pezzey 1997, p.451). Farmer and Randall (1998) go further, arguing that the current generation must even decide how many individuals there will be in the future (see below).

Inevitably, a sustainability constraint on economic activity must be politically acceptable. Pezzey (1997) argues that political developments in the late 1980s seemed to express support for sustainable development as an overriding constraint. But the realities (as opposed to the rhetoric) of developments since the WCED (1987) and the Earth Summit in Rio de Janeiro in 1992 indicate that people only have a preference for sustained development, and that it is not an overriding constraint – it does not take pre-eminent status.

7.2 SUSTAINABILITY PARADIGMS: MAINTAINING CAPITAL STOCKS

What form of capital should the current generation pass on to the next? Coal, petroleum, natural gas and minerals are examples of resources that are, by their nature, subject to exhaustion. If consumption continues at current rates, there will come a point in time when these resources are no longer available, although technical advances and new discoveries may delay their exhaustion. Obviously, sustainable development cannot imply that nonrenewable resources are prevented from being depleted, or even kept at the current or some other level. It will be necessary eventually to replace the flow of services from nonrenewable resources with services obtained from renewable ones. At the same time, it will be necessary to reduce input of natural resources and the environment per unit of standard of living, or output. This implies greater reliance on human capital (knowledge) and human-made capital, which are collectively referred to as *reproducible capital*. Reproducible capital is important, even though it is resource using, because it can substitute for natural capital to some extent; reproducible capital can reduce society's reliance on natural resources by increasing the usefulness of each unit of service provided by the nonrenewable and renewable resource stocks.

The degree of substitutability between natural capital (whether renewable or nonrenewable) and reproducible capital is the subject of considerable debate. Victor (1991) distinguishes two viewpoints regarding sustainability, which can be referred to as the ecological and the neoclassical paradigms – or strong and weak sustainability, respectively. Before examining each of these in turn, we must define weak and strong sustainability.

Daly and Cobb (1994) define weak and strong sustainability in terms of whether reproducible and natural capital are to be kept intact together (weak sustainability) or separately (strong sustainability). Weak sustainability requires a high degree of substitutability between reproducible and natural capital, while strong sustainability "… assumes that they are complements rather than substitutes in most production functions" (p.72). Barbier et al. (1994) also define weak and strong sustainability in terms of the substitutability between reproducible and natural capital. "As long as the natural capital that is being depleted is replaced with even more valuable human-made capital, then the value of the aggregate stock – comprising both human-made and the remaining natural capital – is increasing over time" (p.54). This is weak sustainability. Strong sustainability, on the other hand, stresses that there are limits to substitutability between natural and reproducible capital; it "… suggests that it is difficult to ensure that future economic opportunities are maintained without imposing some conditions on the depletion of natural capital" (pp.55–6).

Strong Sustainability: The Ecological Paradigm

Among others, Herman Daly and John Cobb (1994) favor strong sustainability for several reasons. First, some natural resources are essential for production, and their loss would constitute a catastrophic event. Second, even for production processes where natural capital is not yet an essential ingredient, substitutability declines as resource stocks are depleted. Finally, they argue that there are no substitutes whatsoever for many natural resources, especially wilderness – that the elasticity of substitution between natural and reproducible capital is zero, because of the unique character of some forms of natural capital. The implication is that certain stocks of so-called critical natural capital should be conserved, regardless of the opportunity cost of so doing.

The ecological position downplays the role of prices and technological change (Victor 1991). Prices are considered to be imperfect signals of resource scarcity because of market imperfections brought about by "... a preponderance of large companies or powerful resource-owning governments, or because the environmental effects of resource extraction are not reflected in resource prices" (p.201). Prices do not capture the interests of future generations, and, because they reflect conditions at the margin, cannot be used to value entire stocks of the resource. Prices cannot be relied upon to signal scarcity because resource owners likely have too optimistic a view of technological change; they will continue to supply scarce natural resources even as scarcity increases for fear of technical changes that will lower prices in the future. Further, private resource owners' time horizons are too short to bring about sustainable resource use. The short time horizon causes too many natural resources to be supplied, consequently depressing prices. The ecological view is pessimistic about the future contribution of technological change, which is considered too uncertain to rely on for solving environmental problems.

An implication for management is that it is not aggregate capital that should be maintained, but rather natural and reproducible capital separately. Even within the strong sustainability tradition, there are different views about whether natural capital is too broad a category. Some advocate maintaining each separate element of the natural capital stock, or even all components and the structural relationships among them (Wackernagel and Rees 1997). Another position is that only specific, critical elements of the natural stock should be protected, while permitting substitution among others (see, e.g., Barbier and Markandya 1990; Pearce and Atkinson 1995). When substitution between different subclasses of natural capital is allowed, however, one encounters an aggregation problem. Is it possible to compensate for SO_2 emissions in excess of critical loads by having a moratorium on herring harvesting? Is it meaningful to aggregate fish stocks, biodiversity and *in situ* exhaustible resources in physical units? Should monetary units be used instead? In section 7.4 we discuss an alternative approach – the ecological footprint – but it too employs a subjective aggregation measure (hectares).

The ecological view is clearly influenced by developments in biology and ecology. Concern about the demise of natural (biological, meteorological) systems is a common theme in the biology-ecology literature, and is at the heart of the strong sustainability perspective. The ecological view often supports some form of population control, regulations and/or incentives to prevent loss of species, agreements to limit trade in threatened and endangered species, international agreements to reduce CO_2 emissions, subsidies or sanctions to prevent further tropical deforestation, constraints on free trade (as these might lead firms to locate in countries with less concern about the environment), and other similar interventionist policies. While similar objectives of environmental policy are promoted by the neoclassical paradigm, the ecological view eschews economic instruments and relies more on the command and control approach. Moreover, the ecological view ascribes no role or, at best, a limited role to substitutability, technological change and prices in solving environmental problems.

Weak Sustainability: The Neoclassical Paradigm

The neoclassical paradigm is associated with Julian Simon (1996), Robert Solow (1974, 1986, 1993), Lomborg (2001) and John Hartwick (1977), among others. It is the antithesis of the ecological (dubbed neo-Malthusian) view that natural capital imposes severe constraints on growth – that economic collapse might be brought about by ecosystem collapse. The neoclassical view is that, as resources become scarce, their relative prices will rise, which leads to conservation and substitution toward alternative resources and the development and use of new technologies (Scott and Pearse 1992). Rising relative prices cause substitution away from those resources that are becoming scarce. Neoclassicals point to empirical evidence indicating that this is exactly what has happened in the past and continues today. For example, the technology to produce electric automobiles that are capable of traveling distances of 150 to 300 kilometers on a single charge is already available, but the adoption of such technology is prevented by the relatively low price of gasoline.

The neoclassical view is that the elasticity of substitution between natural capital and reproducible capital is high, with some even going so far as to suggest that it is infinite (Simon 1996). Neoclassicals point out that there are two possibilities for sustaining growth. First, there is likely sufficient substitutability between reproducible capital and the nonrenewable resource so that economic growth can be sustained while generating a continuous decline in the nonrenewable resource stock. In the case of petroleum resources, this will be true if economies become more reliant on public transportation and/or people purchase only the most fuel-efficient vehicles (e.g., abandoning the current penchant for gas-guzzling sport utility vehicles). Second, technological change will inevitably enable society to shift from reliance on one nonrenewable resource to another (e.g., trains converted from coal to oil), and finally to a renewable resource (e.g., solar energy). Although not denying that it is difficult to assess exactly how past technical change has affected the elasticity of substitution between natural and reproducible capital, economists point to the undeniable impact that technological advance has made (Lipsey 1996). As a result, they are optimistic about the potential for technological change in the future.

Indeed, it is the link between past evidence and future projections that is likely most contentious between the two positions, although interpretation of past evidence may well be a source of controversy in some cases. For example, based on current and historic trends, Simon (1996) does not consider population growth to be a problem, while Ehrlich and Ehrlich (1972, 1990, 1991), relying on the same data, maintain that population growth is *the* major threat to the environment and sustainable development. Biologists project that continued habitat destruction (*viz.*, tropical deforestation) and over-indulgent lifestyles (e.g., demand for ivory and tiger bones) will result in the loss of a million or more species in the next 10 years (Leakey and Lewin 1995). Yet, economists (and others) point to the fact that there have been few documented extinctions. Different viewpoints also exist with respect to natural resource scarcity (see below). Although interpreting the historical data differently in some cases, ecologists argue that the past is no guide to the future. However, Simon (1996, p.27) maintains that, in the absence of other information, the past is a reliable guide to the future. Different views with respect to the future are apparent, for example, in the environmental Kuznets curve (EKC) debate. The EKC describes the relation between income and environmental degradation, and has inspired some researchers to speculate that it may be possible to "grow out" of environmental problems (see section 7.5).

The neoclassical economics' view on sustainability of resource capital pertains to the flow of income from capital. The objective is to maximize the annual income that can be derived from the natural resource over all remaining time – forever. We illustrate this concept with the example of a mine. The concept of *user cost* is important here. The user cost of removing ore from a mine today is the benefit one obtains from removing that same ore at some future date, appropriately discounted. Since the mine will eventually be depleted, it is useful to consider the sustainability of the resource revenue from that mine. El Serafy (1989) argues that the net revenue R from a nonrenewable resource should be allocated into an income component (to be used for consumption: R_I) and a capital component (R_C). The capital component is to be set aside and invested at the real (inflation-adjusted) rate of discount, r. The amount of revenue allocated to the capital fund as opposed to the consumption component is determined as follows:

once the mine is depleted, the capital component will need to generate an annual income in perpetuity that is equal to the income made available during the period the mine is in operation.

The implicit assumption is that natural and reproducible forms of capital are infinitely substitutable, so that the economy does not collapse when the mine is exhausted.

Consider a mine that generates net revenues of $1,000 per year ($= R_t$) for a period of 10 years, which is the useful life of the mine. The general formula for determining the sustainable annual income available for consumption from the mine, R_{It}, is as follows:

$$(7.1) \quad R_{It} = rR_C = r \sum_{t=1}^{T} R_{Ct} (1+r)^t = r \left(\sum_{t=1}^{T} (R_t - R_{It}) (1+r)^t \right),$$

where T is the time required to deplete the mine (10 years, in this case), R_{It} is the sustainable annual income available for consumption (every year forever); R_t is net revenues in year t; R_0 is the income from the mine allocated to capital stock in year t; R_C is the total capital stock ("money in the bank") after the mine is depleted; R_{Ct} is the money put in the bank in year t. The second term on the right-hand side of the equation is the capital fund ("money in the bank", which could be a planted forest) available at the time the mine is closed. Numerically solving this equation for the mine using a discount rate of 4% gives $R_I = \$333.09$ and $R_{Ct} = \$666.91$. That is, the mine is able to provide a sustainable annual income of $333.09. The problem of determining the sustainable income (the equation to be solved) is complicated when R_t varies from one year to the next and when there is uncertainty, but these complications can be addressed and do not change the essential notion of sustainable income. Given certain assumptions with respect to the depletion path and substitutability between natural and reproducible capital, reinvesting resource rents implies that consumption can infinitely be maintained, even if the (exhaustible) resource stock is depleted.

Equation (7.1) is an example of the Hartwick rule for sustainability. It states that resource rents should be invested at a rate equal to what is extracted multiplied by the shadow price of the remaining or *in situ* stock. This will maintain the value of total national wealth (sum of natural plus reproducible capital) constant when appropriate shadow prices are used for valuation. Correct shadow prices are crucial to the argument. For example, Toman et al. (1995) argue that the optimal (efficient) depletion rate of many resources (both renewable and nonrenewable) may be too fast for sustainability, causing the current resource price and rent to be low relative to what is sustainable. In this case, even full investment of the resource rent will not ensure enough capital formation for sustainability.

The Paradigms in Contrast

A summary of the main positions of the neoclassicals and ecologists is provided in Table 7.1. It is the different viewpoints that lead one to be optimistic about the actual and potential for substitutability between natural and reproducible capital, and the other to be pessimistic. Reconciling these positions poses a tremendous challenge for the development and implementation of natural resource policy, and economic policy more generally. It cannot be done as long as "... the current strategy of asserting, defending, and applying opposed, monistic systems of value in exclusive disciplinary contexts is continued" (Norton and Toman 1997, p.565).

While an interdisciplinary approach might resolve some of the issues, it may not be able to resolve those related to world or ethical viewpoints as opposed to theoretical approaches.[1]

It is important to stress that substitution possibilities between different forms of capital are an *empirical* matter (and not an ideological issue, although this sometimes seems the case), and that nobody really knows what will be feasible in the future. Until recently, economic models generally treated technical change as a residual, embodied in the time trend of regression models, although more recent theoretical work attempts to endogenize growth (see, for example, Romer 1994). To what extent is it possible to substitute reproducible capital and knowledge (management) for (some) natural resources? The empirical evidence of substitution possibilities is still fragmented. For example, using a macroeconomic model, Manne (1979) estimates that the elasticity of substitution between energy and other inputs is 0.25. Dasgupta (1993), on the other hand, is fairly optimistic, at least about the possibility to replace natural resources in production processes. He describes a series of innovative mechanisms, of which substitution of capital for vanishing resources is but one example. Other mechanisms include the development of new materials, and new technologies that increase efficiency in the use of resources, or that enable substitution of low-grade reserves for high-grade deposits.

While depletion of (high-grade) deposits may force prices up, new technologies will drive them down. With the exception of hydrocarbons, Dasgupta does not foresee any problems for extended periods in the future. And even for fossil fuels, Dasgupta is optimistic that hydrocarbons will not constitute a binding constraint, as alternatives become available as prices rise.

Table 7.1: Differences Between the Neoclassical and Ecological Views of Sustainability

Neoclassical (economists)	Ecological
1. Focus is on what happens at the margin, because it is at the margin that decisions are made. The scale of the economy relative to the resource base is irrelevant.	1. Focus is on large-scale ecosystems and possibilities for irreversibility. There are scale effects – certain "triggers" could set in motion large-scale ecosystem processes that result in irreversible loss in ecosystem functioning.
2. Economists employ steady-state models that assume equilibrium (e.g., computable general equilibrium models, partial equilibrium trade models).	2. Models in ecology focus on resilience and nonequilibrium dynamics.
3. The value system employed is utilitarian.	3. A value system must come from outside ecology as ecology does not have its own.
4. Monetary values are used to measure and "value" changes in environmental quality.	4. Monetary valuation is generally opposed, especially as it is applied to decisions affecting threatened, large-scale ecosystem productivity.
5. Prices play an important role signaling scarcity and, as a result, encouraging substitution and technological innovation. While unpredictable and difficult to measure, technological change has been shown to be a powerful factor in the past and will continue in that role in the future.	5. The role of prices and technological change is downplayed. Prices do not reflect reality because of the existence of externalities. Technological change is unpredictable and unreliable for solving future problems.
6. Discounting and present values are used.	6. Discounting is generally opposed, and the emphasis is on future generations.
7. The current generation owes the future opportunities equal to its own, which means maintaining a nondeclining aggregate capital stock. Adequate investment needs to be maintained to compensate the future for the use (or degradation) of certain resources.	7. Safeguarding the functioning of large-scale ecosystems figures prominently in satisfying concerns about intergenerational fairness. Preservation of variety of ecosystem functions (with aesthetic services featuring prominently) is what matters for the future.
8. Attempts are made to measure the wellbeing of various generations and then compare them (referred to as teleology, implying the making of decisions for the future generation).[a]	8. The rights of future generations trump the mere enjoyments of current generations, enjoyments that come at the expense of future wellbeing. This is a rights-based theory, or deontology.[a]
9. The Safe Minimum Standard of Conservation allows trade-offs.[b]	9. The Precautionary Principle permits less scope for balancing costs and benefits.
10. Property rights of individuals feature prominently, with government's role specified as that of setting and enforcing the "rules of law", and, where justifiable, relying on the state to correct externalities.	10. Individualism is seen as a source of environmental degradation. State intervention is needed to protect ecosystems.

Notes:

[a] See Norton and Toman (1997).

[b] SMS is discussed in section 7.3.

Natural capital is not just used in production, however, as natural ecosystems are also essential as a waste receptor and may be essential for mental health. Perman et al. (1996) note that "... differences in (estimates of substitution possibilities) probably reflect, in large part, differences in the breadth of functions of the environmental resources being considered" (p.120). Wilderness is often used to make the case that no substitutes exist for some natural capital, but Budiansky (1995) argues that wilderness is a matter of degree. There are no areas that have been untouched by humans and, even in the distant past, humans managed "wilderness" to suit their needs, usually by fire. There is some evidence that recreation in "managed" areas (e.g., certain types of production forest) is preferred over recreation in wild areas, implying that some form of (forest) management may be desirable. Similarly, many of the life-support services of nature are not only provided by unmanaged ecosystems, but are provided by ecosystems that have been dramatically altered. Hence, substitution possibilities *within* the set of natural capital are also important.

It appears that there is ample confusion about substitution possibilities. Yet, some minimum standard likely exists below which (aggregate) natural capital should not be reduced. While certain managed forests may serve as a substitute for "nature", both for recreation and as a waste receptor, it is unlikely that a combination of "virtual reality devices" and mechanical air cleansing can ever be a true substitute for forests. Concerning production possibilities, the case favoring the neoclassical view is relatively strong, but this does not mean it is the right one. Ethical issues come into play as well, and these may include sentiments concerning other life forms that likely make large-scale depletion of natural capital intolerable.

7.3 RELATED CONCEPTS

In this section, we briefly address concepts related to the sustainability debate. Sustainable development includes ideas that economists have been considering for quite some time, particularly the notions of conservation and the safe minimum standard of conservation. In addition, we examine what is meant by coevolutionary development, a term that Norgaard (1984) adapted from biology. We consider coevolutionary development primarily for its insights. Finally, we turn to two central concepts of the neo-Malthusian tradition: population growth and resource scarcity.

Economics of Conservation

An early definition of conservation defines it as a redistribution of use rates into the future. Depletion is then a redistribution of use rates toward the present. This definition of conservation is due to Ciriacy-Wantrup (1968), who some regard as the father of resource conservation. It requires that there be some benchmark distribution of use rates to begin with. Consider a hypothetical coal mine. There are four planning periods as indicated in Table 7.2 and four alternative plans for removing coal. Alternative #1 is the benchmark, perhaps the current rate of extraction. Relative to the benchmark rate of extraction, the second alternative is resource conserving since it redistributes use rates into the future − more of the resource is available in the future. The third plan is resource depleting, however, as use rates are redistributed toward the present − less coal is available in the future. The third plan has greater current consumption than either the benchmark plan or the second alternative.

Table 7.2: Extraction or Use Rates for a Coal Mine

Alternative plan	Planning period				Weighted change in use rates (at 10%)
	1	2	3	4	
	(tonnes/year)				
#1 (Benchmark)	4	3	3	2	—
#2 (Conservation)	3	3	3	3	
Change in use rate	−1	0	0	+1	0.331
#3 (Depletion)	5	4	2	1	
Change in use rate	+1	+1	−1	−1	−0.401
#4 (Unclear)	5	1	3	3	
Change in use rate	+1	−2	0	+1	0.131

A problem arises in attempting to categorize plan #4. It is not clear whether plan #4 is conserving or depleting since the net change in use rates is zero and there is no clear indication that all changes are either into the future or toward the present. Whenever there are a large number of pluses and minuses in the row indicating how the plan's use rates have changed from those of the benchmark plan, it is necessary to employ a weighting scheme. The weighting scheme should be one that accounts for the need to discount the future. Thus, weights should increase as the distance from the present time period increases. If the weighted change in use rates is positive (indicating that weighted use is postponed to the future), then there is resource conservation; if it is negative (indicating that use is speeded up), depletion of the resource occurs.

Consider a system of weights that begins with 1.0 for the current period and increases 10% for each subsequent period. Then, the weighted change in use rates for alternative #4 is given by $+1 + (1.1)(-2) + (1.1)^2(0) + (1.1)^3(+1) = 0.131$. The weighted changes in use rates are provided for the alternative plans in the last column of the table; they show that alternatives #2 and #4 are resource conserving. Only the classification of plan #4 as conserving depends crucially upon the weights that are chosen, as it is clear that plan #3 is depleting.

Some argue that stewardship requires that resource availability in the future be weighted exactly the same as that in the present. In that case, the weighted change in the use rates for alternative #4 is simply zero, but this is not very helpful because it does not discriminate between the three cases. Likewise, a zero discount rate cannot be used by a society to abrogate its responsibility in determining ethical issues pertaining to how much natural and reproducible capital to leave future generations (see below); treating current and future dollars equally is simply unrealistic, it does not work.[2] One problem with discounting is that people are unlikely to ever agree upon an appropriate weighting scheme. Nonetheless, the point remains that conservation is a comparative concept and one cannot judge whether something is conserving or depleting without reference to some benchmark, and that may require employing a weighting scheme that values the future more than the present.

Anthony Scott expands on Ciriacy-Wantrup's definition of conservation by taking explicit account of political and other factors.

> Conservation is a public policy which seeks to increase the potential future rates of use of one or more natural resources above what they would be in the absence of such policy, by current investment of the social income. The word investment ... covers not only such policies as investing the social income in restoration, education, and research, but also policies of reservation and hoarding of stocks. (Scott 1973, p.30)

Scott's definition includes a method for achieving the objective of conservation, namely, by investing part of the social income. It is also based on six conditions including that, as a practical point, focus should generally be on a single resource within a defined geographical region, and that conservation should be measured in physical as opposed to monetary units. Further, Scott's definition is confined not to natural resources alone, as it recognizes the necessity of trade-offs between investments in natural capital (e.g., preservation of ecosystems) and investments in human-made capital and knowledge. Importantly, this definition recognizes that conservation is a political as well as a biophysical and economic concept.

In Table 7.2, the resource is to be completely exhausted at the end of the planning horizon. Does this fact of exhaustion violate the concept of sustainable development? It may well be that the activity of exhausting a nonrenewable resource does violate the concept of sustainable development, but only if the ability of future generations to meet their needs is compromised.

The Safe Minimum Standard (SMS)

Ciriacy-Wantrup (1968) first used the term "safe minimum standard" and urged its adoption to allow for uncertainty in resource development and to increase "flexibility in the continuing development of society". As demonstrated by Bishop (1978), the safe minimum standard can be thought of in terms of game theory – it expands upon the *minimax* principle of game theory, as illustrated in Table 7.3.

Table 7.3: Matrix of Losses

Strategies	States		Maximum losses[a]
	#1	#2	
E	0	y	Y
S	x	x	X

Notes:
[a] Assumes $x, y > 0$.
Source: Modified from Bishop (1978).

Two states of nature or outcomes, denoted by #1 and #2, are possible, but their occurrence is uncertain. Society has two strategies to cope with environmental uncertainty: extinction could possibly occur if the resource is exploited (E), while strategy S (for safety) leaves the resource in its current state. If the state of nature turns out to be #1, then there is no damage to the environment from "development". If the strategy had been to avoid development (strategy S), the benefits of development, given by x, are foregone. If development (strategy E) takes place, there is no loss. On the other hand, if the state of nature turns out to be #2, then development (strategy E) results in irreversible damage (i.e., extinction of one or more species) worth y. However, if strategy S is now adopted, there is no environmental loss, but society does lose x – the cost of implementing S.[3] The decision is determined in this "game" by choosing the strategy that minimizes the maximum possible loss, i.e., choosing E if $x > y$ and choosing S if $x < y$, with equality of x and y indicating indifference.

There are problems with this particular game-theoretic approach. (1) The minimax solution is conservative, with E chosen if the costs of preventing extinction (x) are only slightly higher than the losses (y) to society under the worst conceivable future outcome. (2) Payoffs (and costs) are assumed to be known with certainty, while the distribution of income is ignored – it does not matter who gains or loses. (3) The approach is static and the probabilities of each state of nature are assumed to remain unknown. Particularly, there is no learning effect as time passes. (4) More importantly, it fails to recognize that a decision not to develop a resource (e.g., construct a dam that floods a valley, harvest old-growth timber) constitutes a deferral – exploitation can still take place in a future period.

The safe minimum standard (SMS) of conservation modifies the minimax principle. The modified decision rule is: adopt S unless the social costs of doing so are unacceptably large. It is clear that this rule places development of natural resources beyond routine trade-offs, although the SMS does not permit deferral or nondevelopment at a cost that is intolerably high. Failure to recognize that there are intolerably high costs to not developing a resource in some cases inevitably leads to dangerous conflicts within society (e.g., between loggers and environmentalists). Decisions regarding what level of costs is considered "intolerably high" and what trade-offs are acceptable are political ones. Randall and Farmer (1995) argue that intolerable costs could be defined as extreme deprivation for society, at least based on moral principles. Berrens et al. (1998) employ a much lower standard for intolerable cost. Their recommended threshold for exclusion is a one percent deviation of economic activity from the baseline.

The Precautionary Principle is similar to SMS, but it permits less scope for balancing costs and benefits, often blocking trade-offs. It is "a general recommendation to expect an unfavorable course of events, and to choose policy measures accordingly" (Zylicz 2000, p.145). The Safe Minimum Standard, on the other hand, is all about trade-offs, with the purpose being to identify explicitly the trade-offs that are made (Norton and Toman 1997). As noted by Berrens et al. (1998) "… the SMS will be unpalatable to some strong sustainability advocates, … [but it] will be equally unpalatable to unfettered CBA advocates. As such the SMS approach may be identified as falling between weak and strong sustainability perspectives" (p.158). It is unpalatable to advocates of cost–benefit analysis because it is unclear why irreversibility mandates a change in the decision rule: one decision criteria (CBA) is jettisoned for another (SMS), but only as long as the costs of avoiding irreversibility are tolerable. As Farmer and Randall (1998) point out, "… an efficiency program cannot generate an SMS departure from the efficiency rule, just as strong sustainability clearly rejects the efficiency appeals to permit substitution in production and in consumption" (p.291). In this regard, the Precautionary Principle is at least a consistent decision rule.

Farmer and Randall (1998) make the case for SMS despite the seemingly unjustified switch in decision criteria when faced by irreversibility on the grounds that most stakeholders involved in the decision consensus "… do not possess well-defined, fully articulated ethical positions for sustainability" (p.292). They argue that a "… theory of sustainability must start with the question, What defines a moral agent to whom we have moral obligations?" (p.293). To answer this question, and to address the issue of intergenerational equity, it is necessary to determine the specific numbers of future agents current agents are to "create" and how well off to make them (see also Howarth and Norgaard 1993, 1995). Farmer and Randall defend SMS on the grounds that, until there is a consistent moral theory delineating duties of present agents to each other and to future agents, avoiding irreversibilities has value that is not adequately captured in cost–benefit analysis. This, then constitutes a defense of the authors' earlier position that, when it comes to resource management and possible irreversibility, cost–benefit analysis needs to be *constrained by the safe minimum standard* (Randall and Farmer 1995).

To illustrate the concept of a SMS, consider the northern cod fishery. In the late 1980s, it became apparent that stocks of cod were disappearing off the coasts of Newfoundland and Norway. Inshore fisheries in both regions experienced declines in catch and, more importantly, the cod tended to be smaller. The cod on the Grand Banks and the Barents Sea appeared to be in trouble, although the science permitted leeway for different interpretations (Harris 1998). The responses by Canada and Norway to the threat of a possible collapse in the cod fishery differed dramatically. While Norway imposed an immediate moratorium, which led to the recovery of stocks, Canada continued to permit fishing, even setting the total allowable catch on one occasion above what fishers were actually capable of catching with all their sophisticated gear. The northern cod stocks of Newfoundland collapsed and the fishery has yet to recover. It would appear that Norway implemented a SMS, while Canada did not.

One question remains. Suppose that a proper cost–benefit analysis, with the dynamics of the fishery included in the calculations, were conducted for both fisheries. Would the cost–benefit results have favored a moratorium for both fisheries? Quite likely it would have. That is, an appropriate economic efficiency analysis would have led to a policy similar to one that follows the SMS. It would appear, therefore, that the role of the SMS is to permit the inclusion of intuitive values as a means for addressing uncertainty in cases where CBA is incomplete or key elements are uncertain.

Population Pressure

There are two components to the neo-Malthusian argument – population growth and resource depletion (which subsumes degradation of the environment). Consider first population growth. Environmentalists often view population growth as the main cause of poverty and the greatest threat to "spaceship earth"; they consider humans to be a curse upon the planet (Ehrlich and Ehrlich 1972, 1991; Smith et al. 1995). The following statement is typical of this view:

> Everything has been visited, everything known, everything exploited. Now pleasant estates obliterate the famous wilderness areas of the past. Plowed fields have replaced forests, domesticated animals have dispersed wild life. Beaches are plowed, mountains smoothed and swamps drained. There are as many cities as, in former years, there were dwellings. Islands do not frighten, nor cliffs deter. Everywhere there are buildings, everywhere people, everywhere communities, everywhere life. ... Proof [of this crowding] is the density of human beings. We weigh upon the world; its resources hardly suffice to support us. As our needs grow larger, so do our protests, that already nature does not sustain us. In truth, plague, famine, wars and earthquakes must be regarded as a blessing to civilization, since they prune away the luxuriant growth of the human race. (Bratton 1992, p.76 as quoted by Beisner 1997, p.97)

What is interesting is that Tertullian wrote this in Carthage around 200 AD when the total population of the earth was probably less than 500 million.

People are consumers, but they are also a resource capable of producing wealth under the "right" circumstances (which include certain liberties and freedoms). People are the ultimate resource (Simon 1996). It is not surprising, therefore, to find ambiguous empirical evidence related to population density and income (see Table 7.4 and Figure 7.1). Further, there is no compelling evidence that links population growth to either poverty or environmental degradation (Simon 1996; Olson 1996; Eberstadt 1995). Population growth often goes hand-in-hand with poverty and (local) environmental degradation, but the causal links between population growth and size, and poverty and the environment, are complex (Dasgupta 1995). Simply showing that per capita income is positively correlated with population density, as suggested in Figure 7.1 and in Table 7.4 and statistically demonstrated by Olson (1996), says nothing about causality. Indeed, Olson (1996) demonstrates that it is differences in institutions that cause some countries to be rich and others poor, and that population is not that important. Further, while sheer population size multiplies per capita impacts on environmental degradation, population size and growth need not have exclusively negative implications for the environment. Rich countries generally have a cleaner environment than poor ones, regardless of population levels.

Table 7.4: Relationship between Population and Wealth

Country	Pop'n (10^6)	Area (10^6 km^2)	GPD (US$bil)	Persons per km^2	GDP per person ($US)
Bangladesh	127.7	0.143	46.0	981	360
Brazil	168.0	8.512	752.0	20	4,470
Chile	15.0	0.757	67.5	19	4,490
China	1,249.6	9.561	989.0	134	790
Czech Rep.	10.2	0.079	53.1	129	5,170
France	60.8	0.544	1,432.0	112	23,560
Germany	82.0	0.358	2,112.0	235	25,750
India	997.5	3.287	447.0	336	450
Iran	63.0	1.648	111.0	38	1,760
Japan	126.5	0.378	4,347.0	336	34,340
Malaysia	22.7	0.330	79.0	68	3,480
Netherlands	15.8	0.042	394.0	466	24,910
Poland	38.7	0.313	155.0	123	4,010
USA	272.9	9.373	9,152.0	29	33,540

Source: *The Economist Pocket World in Figures, 2002 Edition* (London: Economist Newspaper Inc., 2001).

Population growth is endogenous and the determinants of fertility are generally known. The theory of demographic transition indicates that the death rate initially falls, but birth rates decline only after a lag. Population growth is high during this transitional stage (Perman et al. 1996, p.288). According to the economic theory of fertility, households choose number of children by setting the perceived marginal costs of bearing and raising them to the perceived marginal benefits. Preoccupation with households as optimizing units and the historical evidence that richer countries are associated with lower fertility rates has led some analysts to opine that high population growth rates in developing countries are a temporary and relatively harmless phenomenon (Kelly 1988). It is often thought that economic growth can be relied upon to reduce population growth (e.g., Simon 1996), but there is some evidence that the drop in mortality rates in many developing countries is a result of knowledge (technology) transfer and not income growth. As a result, the drop in mortality rates is not soon matched by a decline in birth rates related to income growth, which might lead to rising populations that create the potential for a vicious circle of poverty and environmental degradation, at least in some countries (Perman et al. 1996).

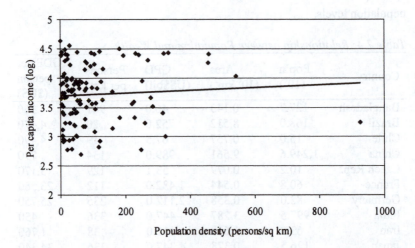

Figure 7.1: Per capita GNP and population density (with fitted trendline)

While fertility behavior may be rational from the perspective of the household, there may be collective failure due to external effects in reproduction. Dasgupta (1995) describes two main motives for procreation and indicates how reproductive externalities may arise.

1. Children can be considered as ends in themselves, as they are generally wanted and valued. If every household's desired family size is an increasing function of the average family size in the community (e.g., for reasons associated with status), the community as a whole may end up in a sub-optimal equilibrium. Imitative behavior encourages sub-optimally high fertility rates.
2. In some circumstances, children can be considered productive assets. Children can be both a source of security for old age, when public support for the elderly is absent or weak, and an income-earning asset when they are young. In developing countries where common property resources are frequent, children (extra hands) can contribute towards exploiting the commons for private gains, even though such behavior is socially sub-optimal. This provides households with an incentive to raise extra children. A potentially adverse feedback relation may now be triggered: as the resource base gets depleted, households need to invest more labor effort to collect the desired inputs, which is an incentive to enlarge and produce yet more children.

Children not only contribute towards common property exploitation, but they can also be used to invest in sustainable resource management under different institutional arrangements (Dasgupta 1995). Children are also minds that help solve problems, providing new solutions; in that sense, they are the ultimate resource. The neo-Malthusian notion should be contrasted with the equally powerful ideas of Boserup (1965), who has described how changing population pressure may translate into different institutions and production techniques. The net effect of such changes on the environment should be determined on a case-by-case basis. For Kenya, for example, Tiffen and Mortimore (1994) have determined that increased population is consistent with more trees and less erosion. They argue that "... increased population density has helped to make markets and information more accessible, thereby stimulating wise investments in new technologies, which have enabled output and incomes to rise faster than population growth, and which have restored and improved the resource base" (p.1007).

We conclude that the impact of population growth on the environment is ambiguous, depending on, among other things, the institutional setting (i.e., presence or absence of relevant markets, tenure arrangements, etc.), and government incentives. Also, the outcome will depend on the environmental issue concerned; while it is easy to think of a growing population as having a favorable impact on soil conservation, a similar impact on protection of biodiversity is harder to conceive. In some cases, the combination of poverty and population pressure will have detrimental effects on the environment, thus perhaps justifying intervention (see also Pearce and Warford 1993). Dasgupta's (1995) review of efforts to reduce population growth suggests that issues related to power and gender within the household are crucial: "high fertility, high rates of female illiteracy, low share of paid employment and a high percentage working at home for no pay – they all hang together" (p.1886). Education and employment of women may be especially important in efforts to reduce fertility. Education and employment of women raise the marginal costs of child bearing and raising, thereby reducing the total number of children a household desires. Further, increasing state-sponsored (or private) social security for the elderly reduces the need to rely on children, thereby lowering the marginal benefits of children and, hence, numbers borne.

Resource Scarcity

An important issue related to sustainability is scarcity of resources and environmental amenities. Economists have been concerned with resource scarcity since at least the time of Robert Malthus. Rather than monitoring physical quantities or measures (such as the reserve-to-consumption ratio, which is an unreliable indicator of scarcity), economists typically study resource scarcity by examining commodity prices (Hall and Hall 1984). (Prices are generally not a useful measure of scarcity for environmental services, such as waste receptor services, as these are not privately "owned".) When firms adopt efficient depletion paths, a much better but more difficult measure, because it is not observable, is the course of resource rents over time. If the real (inflation-adjusted) price of a resource increases, this is a sign of increasing scarcity. If real commodity prices fall, this is evidence that either the demand for the resource has fallen (e.g., because less of the resource is required to achieve the same or a greater level of final product than previously) or that there is more abundant supply (possibly from a substitute). For example, more efficient means of harvesting timber and processing logs into lumber, and greater use of a tree's mass (less waste), increase the supply of wood products available from the same forestland. Planting faster growing species also increases timber supply. New discoveries, secondary or enhanced recovery, more efficient ways of extracting oil from tar sands, and the ability to pump oil from deep sea wells increase the supply of oil and gas. Fuel efficiency and alternative fuels (e.g., electricity, solar and wind) have reduced the demand for oil and gas. In addition, there often exists a sustainable backstop technology that is based on sustainable resource use (e.g., solar or wind power). A relatively plentiful nonsustainable resource (say, oil) may be used in the beginning of the growth process, but, as it becomes increasingly scarce and more expensive, the sustainable resource (say, solar power) is used as the substitute technology.

For whatever reasons (whether the result of economies of scale in production, technical change, substitution, imports, government policies or new discoveries), the real prices of many nonrenewable resources have not increased over time. To determine whether exploitation of natural resources is somehow sustainable, two types of empirical tests can be used. First, the price path of the resource can be analyzed, as was done by Barnett and Morse (1963) in a seminal study of mineral prices over the period 1870–1957. They found that prices were nonincreasing over that interval and rejected the hypothesis of increasing scarcity. In contrast, Slade (1982) found that the prices of many resources over the period 1870–1979 followed a U-shaped path, which is consistent with increasing resource scarcity over time. More recent work does not confirm her empirical results, however. For example, Slade (1991) shows that resource prices have been volatile after the sample period used in the earlier study, which is at odds with steadily increasing scarcity. Berck (1995) argues that the parameters of Slade's U-shaped path are not constant for different subperiods, and that the price series may be more aptly modeled as a stationary series around a stochastic (rather than a deterministic) trend. According to Berck and Roberts (1996), there is no evidence of rising prices over time.

Second, some analysts have attempted to measure changes in resource *rents* (rather than prices) over time. As rents are not observed on markets, they have to be computed. For this purpose, an extraction cost curve can be postulated and estimated. Tests using this line of reasoning provide inconclusive support for the theory that extraction of nonrenewable resources occurs along an optimal (economically efficient) path, with some refuting the theory (Halvorsen and Smith 1991) and others providing evidence consistent with theory (Stollery 1983).

Some caveats should be mentioned. Rents (and under some conditions prices) are good indicators of scarcity if certain conditions are satisfied. For example, resource owners should have perfect foresight. If resource owners have only access to imperfect information about future prices (which is likely the case as futures markets for resources are generally absent and "thin"), price paths may measure ignorance of decision-makers rather than changing scarcity conditions (Norgaard 1990). Further, environmental costs associated with resource exploration and exploitation may curtail extraction before exhaustion occurs. In principle, environmental costs should be included as a component of (marginal) extraction costs, but we are not aware of any (net) price series that takes this cost component into account. A related point is that the resource base is actually infinite, but that extraction costs eventually become prohibitively high (Farzin 1992). Even though the resource will not be exhausted, resource rents are positive as extracting a unit of the resource today drives up future extraction costs. (The value of the *in situ* resource equals the discounted increment in future costs avoided.) Farzin demonstrates that the resource rent path is governed by the specification of the cost function, and rent can rise, fall or remain unchanged over time. This sheds new light on the theory of efficient extraction of exhaustible resources.

Interestingly and somewhat paradoxically, there is considerably more concern in the economics literature about depletion of stocks of renewable than of nonrenewable resources. This is due to the questions associated with proper management of renewable resources, particularly with reference to institutional arrangements and the possibility of catastrophe. Resource management has not been properly implemented in many parts of the world, and commercial exhaustion of certain renewable resources (especially fish) and pollution remain serious problems (World Resources Institute 1995).

Overall, however, the majority of the dismal predictions of the "limits to growth" tradition have simply been proven wrong and there is little or no evidence to expect an impending resource shortage (Beckerman 1992; Scott and Pearse 1992). Nonetheless, widespread poverty in the Third World, signs of environmental stress in large parts of the world, and overexploitation of some open access and even common property resources are taken by some as a sign of impending scarcity. Clearly, as discussed above, the view one takes depends on one's view of sustainability.

As far as we are aware, only one person has been willing to wager that their view is the correct one. The late Julian Simon (1996, pp.8–9) offered to bet anyone who cared to take him on that the future for ecosystems, environment and natural resources is not as bleak as suggested by "doomsayers", or even those in the ecological economics camp. We refer to this as Simon's bet. Simon argued that "... supplies of natural resources are not finite in any economic sense", the long-run future of energy supplies is bright, food scarcity is not imminent, and population growth is not going to overwhelm the earth's ecosystems (pp.5–7). He was optimistic concerning biodiversity and ecosystem health. Simon based his wager on historical evidence that indicates scarcity has not been a problem in the past, that humans have not been responsible for ecosystem collapse, that standards of living are rising, and that people's health (an indicator of ecosystem health) is better now than ever before. Biologists would dispute much of this, but, with the exception of Paul Ehrlich who lost some $1,000, none had taken Simon up on his wager.[4] None of this is a guarantee, however, that there will be no future resource scarcity or ecosystem collapse, but then we live in a world of uncertainty. More recently, Lomborg (2001) has taken up Simon's arguments.

Consider the role of the government in more detail. It is interesting to note that, in 1891, the US Geological Survey predicted that there was little or no chance of finding oil in Texas. In 1926, the US Federal Oil Conservation Board predicted that the USA had only a seven-year supply of oil left, leading some to argue that the price of a gallon of gasoline would soon rise to $1. Similar predictions were made in 1939 and 1949, but none ever materialized (Maurice and Smithson 1984). The so-called energy crisis of the 1970s occurred primarily because price controls on oil in the USA (implemented by the Nixon Administration) meant that there was no incentive to encourage conservation (reduce demand), exploration for new sources of oil (increase supply), or investment in alternatives to fossil fuels (reduce demand). The energy crisis abated rapidly once price controls began to come off in 1979. Deregulation of prices was complete in early 1981. As a result, energy consumption declined by 20% during that year and drilling activity increased by 50%. The resulting fall in energy prices led to the eventual collapse of the OPEC oil cartel. In 1995, the Paris-based International Energy Agency argued that energy supplies are not running out, but that deregulation, freer flow of products among countries and new technologies are making it possible to increase the supply of fossil fuels; indeed, it predicts that, by 2010, 90% of the world's energy consumption, which is forecast to rise by 34–45%, will be accounted for by fossil fuels (Moore 1995).

The 2000–01 energy crisis in California is the result more of government incompetence than a real crisis. While electricity markets were deregulated at the wholesale level, strict controls on consumer prices prevented utility companies from passing on higher costs of obtaining electricity. This price–cost squeeze led to huge losses so that the major distributors of power in California could no longer pay suppliers, causing power to be diverted to other markets where suppliers did get paid. California is dependent on power from the Pacific Northwest and Canada because it had failed to permit construction of new capacity (due to stringent environmental regulations and opposition by those who wanted no power generating facilities in their "backyard") even though demand rose at a rapid rate. Thus, this latest energy crisis is more the result of policy failure rather than market failure.

In Canada, the National Oil Policy of 1961 guaranteed western oil producers (mainly the Province of Alberta) a market for oil by preventing consumers west of the Ottawa River Valley from purchasing oil from sources other than western Canada. This resulted in Ontario prices for western crude that were 25 to 35 cents per barrel higher than what they would otherwise be. When world oil prices increased dramatically in 1973 as a result of OPEC, the federal government responded by freezing the price of all oil at $3.80/barrel. Taxes on exports and oil company profits were used to subsidize oil imports east of the Ottawa River Valley. Although the oil producing provinces (primarily Alberta) increased their royalty rates to capture a large portion of the resource rents, the low Ontario price and the export tax kept these rents well below their potential. In an attempt to offset the power of the western producing provinces and increase the available supply of oil, the federal government encouraged and subsidized exploration outside the producing provinces in northern and coastal areas.

Throughout Canada the low-price oil policy weakened concurrent policies to conserve energy, adopt energy-efficient technologies and alternative fuels, and reduce polluting activities in general. Later, when domestic and world prices converged, these policies inadvertently were to give Canada's industry a competitive disadvantage relative to its trading partners who had already adopted energy-saving technologies. Although the federal government was forced to back away from its price freeze when Alberta decided to reduce oil production in 1980, the National Energy Program that was introduced in 1980 did not go the full step. It slowly increased domestic prices to the world level via phased-in price increases. The producing provinces and the primarily foreign oil companies continued to object to this policy because the resource rents available to them remained lower than under a free market. This redistribution of resource rents was objected to as a matter of discriminatingly unfair income redistribution, but it was the rent dissipation among Canadian consumers in the form of lower than world prices that likely led to inefficiency and resource misallocation (van Kooten and Scott 1995).

In retrospect, it appears that attempts to control prices of resource commodities led to increases in prices, and that they were not the result of free market forces. An examination of oil, wood products, aluminum, copper, zinc, nickel and other resource commodities indicates that, while consumption has increased, real prices have either remained relatively constant or even declined. This indicates that there has been both an increase in the availability of the resource *in situ* and greater efficiency in mining and production. One is forced to conclude that, with few exceptions, there does not appear to be an impending shortage of natural resources. To reach the same conclusion about ecosystem resources that are not priced in the market place is not as straightforward. What the foregoing discussion does indicate is that by somehow pricing ecosystem services, the chances of maintaining these resources may well be greatly enhanced.

7.4 SUSTAINABILITY INDICATORS AND EVIDENCE

Ecologists and economists employ different indicators of sustainability. Depending on beliefs with respect to the degree of substitutability between natural and reproducible capital, analysts may prefer some "sustainability indicators" over others. Advocates of strong sustainability will probably prefer ecological indicators or direct biophysical measures (e.g., carrying capacity relative to exploitation, ecological footprints and measures of resilience), while advocates of weak sustainability will employ economic indicators, such as those associated with "green" national income accounting and "genuine savings" (Pearce et al. 1998). In terms of empirical progress, the indicators preferred by neoclassicals seem further advanced and less speculative. In this section, we briefly consider two opposing approaches. We present some empirical work related to weak and strong sustainability as defined above, and we discuss the so-called ecological footprint, a measure preferred by some ecologists.

Weak and Strong Sustainability: Evidence

A "weak sustainability index" developed by Pearce and Atkinson (1995) is complementary to environmentally adjusted national accounts, and addresses whether countries are on a sustainable path or not. As noted earlier, countries should seek to keep aggregate capital K (defined here as the sum of human-made K_M, human K_H and natural capital K_N) constant in order to satisfy the criterion of weak sustainability. The weak sustainability rule then boils down to the following condition:

$$(7.2) \quad S(t) - \delta_M K_M - \delta_H K_H - \delta_N K_N \geq 0,$$

where $S(t)$ represents aggregate gross savings at time t and δ_i ($i = K, H, N$) is the depreciation rate for the relevant capital stock. If δ_H is assumed to equal zero, there is no depreciation of knowledge and skills, which seems a reasonable assumption. Hence, an economy is assumed sustainable if it saves more than the depreciation on its reproducible and natural capital. Depreciation of natural capital takes the form of depletion (e.g., extraction of a nonrenewable resource) and degradation (e.g., air and water pollution). Dividing by income m yields the basic condition for weak sustainability:

$$(7.3) \quad Z = \frac{S}{m} - \frac{\delta_M K_M}{m} - \frac{\delta_N K_N}{m} \geq 0,$$

where Z is the weak sustainability index.

Similarly, a strong sustainability criterion requires that $\delta_N K_N / m \leq 0$. Monetary valuation is used for this specific strong sustainability indicator (but see below for an alternative approach). Where sufficient information with respect to natural capital is available, it would be possible to produce additional, more segregated sustainability indexes. Pearce and Atkinson advocate a combination of weak and strong sustainability rules to address the complex issue of sustainability. Evidence for both weak and strong sustainability is presented for selected years and countries in Table 7.5.

None of the countries in Table 7.5 passes the strong sustainability test. Pearce and Atkinson (1995) suggest that eight countries out of the 22 they investigate (not all of which are given in Table 7.5) have negative values for Z, with six of these found in Africa. Relatively high savings ratios contribute to but are no guarantee for weak sustainability, as can be observed from Indonesia and Mexico. The fourth column indicates that not a single country meets the strong sustainability standard, because all values for $\delta_N K_N / m$ are positive. However, it should be added that data on both depreciation and accumulation of natural capital are incomplete, so that the results are biased in an unknown direction. Again, we emphasize that Table 7.5 provides a static picture for addressing an inherently dynamic issue; the potentially offsetting, but highly relevant factors of population growth and technological change are ignored, so these empirical results should be interpreted with care.

Table 7.5: Testing Sustainable Development for Selected Countries: An Indicator[a]

Countries	S/m	$\delta_M K_M/m$	$\delta_N K_N/m$	Z
Sustainable economies				
Japan	33	14	2	+17
Poland	30	11	3	+14
Costa Rica	26	3	8	+15
Zimbabwe	24	10	5	+9
US	18	12	3	+3
Brazil	20	7	10	+3
Marginally sustainable economies				
Mexico	24	12	12	0
Philippines	15	11	4	0
UK	18	12	6	0
Unsustainable economies				
Indonesia	20	5	17	–2
Nigeria	15	3	17	–5
Madagascar	8	1	16	–9
Mali	–4	4	6	–14

Notes:
[a] Assumes $\delta_H = 0$.
Source: Selected from Pearce and Atkinson (1995).

Finally, as pointed out by Asheim (1986) and Pearce and Atkinson (1995), the Hartwick rule for investing resource rents should be adapted for open economies, implying that the results presented above should be corrected for international trade. Japan, for example, performs best according to Table 7.5, but this is partly due to the fact that Japan is a major importer of natural resources (e.g., wood and oil). Hence, while domestic natural capital is not subject to much depreciation, Japan may be drawing down natural capital stocks in its trading partners. Hartwick and Olewiler (1998) intuitively discuss why, in this case, the net investment figure Z should be adjusted downwards (i.e., why the importing country should save more than the sum of domestic depreciation of reproducible and natural capital to meet the criterion of weak sustainability). One interpretation is that the importing country will face rising prices in the future as stocks are depleted, and should save more today to counter this negative "terms of trade effect" tomorrow to keep consumption constant. Conversely, exporting countries such as Indonesia may be excused for not having positive Z-values; as resource prices rise in the future, it may be possible to maintain current consumption patterns without keeping aggregate capital constant. However, sustainability is an issue for the (very) long run, and whether "underinvesting" is truly sustainable for extended periods is an open question.

The Ecological Footprint

Strong sustainability indicators often focus on scale aspects of production and consumption, on whether or not the demands society places on the ecosystem exceed the carrying capacity of the environment. It is assumed that a "sustainable scale" exists, and this scale is measured in absolute physical limits. There are several indicators that employ biophysical measures (see, for example, Rennings and Wiggering 1997 for a discussion), but we focus on the ecological footprint (EF).

Wackernagel and Rees (1996, 1997) take a strong sustainability stance, arguing that each generation should inherit a stock of essential biophysical assets that is no less than the stock of such assets inherited by the previous generation. What is the best approach to measure constancy of natural capital? How can the various essential components of natural capital be aggregated in a meaningful way? Wackernagel and Rees reject monetary valuation as this is "blind to ... biophysical realities" (1996, p.6), and instead propose the ecological footprint. The EF represents the natural capital requirements of an economy. It is variously defined as "the 'load' imposed by a given population on nature" (p.5) or "an accounting tool that enables us to estimate the resource consumption and waste assimilation requirements of a defined human population or economy in terms of a corresponding productive land area" (p.9). It is measured by "the aggregate area of land and water in various ecological categories that is claimed by participants in that economy to produce all the resources they consume, and to absorb all the wastes they generate on a continuous basis, using prevailing technology" (p.7). The EF is the area of land required to "sustain" economic activities – the common denominator is hectares of ecologically productive land, rather than dollars.

The footprint measure can be illustrated with the aid of Table 7.6, where the EF for Canada is calculated as 4.27 ha per person. Annual energy consumed in the production of food requires 0.33 ha per person for sequestering the carbon released into the atmosphere from fossil fuel burning. For housing, 0.41 ha per person is required to offset the addition to atmospheric CO_2, while it is 0.79 ha annually for transportation. Food production also "consumes" 0.02 ha of land for growing fruits and vegetables, 0.60 ha of cropland and 0.33 ha of pasture per person. Housing construction requires 0.40 ha of forestland per person per year, while consumer goods requires 0.17 ha (presumably for paper and other wood products). Annually some 0.20 ha of "degraded land" are required per person for housing sites, transportation corridors, and production of goods and services. The EF for the USA is 5.1 ha, for Eastern Europe it is 0.3 ha, while it is 0.4 ha per person for India; the world's EF is 1.8 ha per person.

What does the EF say about sustainability? Land area is finite by definition, and thus constitutes a clear upper limit for extraction. When a region's EF exceeds its size, the difference can be covered either by imports or by (further) drawing down the stock of natural capital. Thus, Wackernagel and Rees (1997) argue that the ecological footprint is a useful yardstick for identifying and measuring sustainability. At the global level, the footprint must be smaller than the (essentially given) carrying capacity.

The carrying capacity EF is calculated to be 1.5 ha per person, below the current global EF of 1.8 ha; further, the average person in an industrialized economy currently has a significantly greater footprint (ranging from 2 ha per capita for Japan to 5 ha for the USA) than the global carrying capacity. Therefore, a "sustainability gap" exists. When incomes in developing countries increase and approach western standards, production and consumption patterns will inevitably mean that natural capital stocks need to be run down. Wackernagel and Rees argue that excessive depletion is already taking place: "our rough calculations suggest that the ecological footprint of all industrialized nations, representing less than 20% of the world population, is larger than the available ecologically productive land on earth" (1997, p.10). Hence, current economic activity is not sustainable, as determined by the EF.

How useful is the EF as a measure of sustainability? It is important to recognize that the EF is less a scientific measure than one designed to raise public awareness and influence politics. From that perspective, however, it must be regarded a success. Proponents of the EF oppose the aggregation and substitutability inherent in a monetary metric, they are against discounting, and they reject marginal in favor of absolute (average) valuation. However, in the construction of the EF metric, the very same measurement issues (aggregation, substitutability, discounting, valuation) have not been dealt with in a meaningful way. Due to this imperfection, the EF has limited use for policy analysis where trade-offs at each moment in time and over time are essential. Some of its shortcomings are highlighted in the next paragraphs.

Table 7.6: Ecological Footprint for Canada (ha per person per year)

Item	Food	Housing	Transpor-tation	Consumer goods	Services
Energy (land required to sequester carbon to offset fossil fuel emissions)	0.33	0.41	0.79	0.52	0.29
Degraded land (built up environment)	–	0.08	0.10	0.01	0.01
Garden (for vegetables & fruits)	0.02	0.002 (?)	–	–	–
Cropland	0.60	–	–	0.06	–
Pasture (for dairy, meat & wool production)	0.33	–	–	0.13	–
Forest (prime forest area assuming a MAI of 2.33 m^3)[a]	0.02	0.40	–	0.17	–
TOTAL	**1.30**	**0.89**	**0.89**	**0.89**	**0.30**

Notes:
[a] MAI refers to mean annual increment, which equals annual forest growth.
Source: Wackernagel and Rees (1996, pp.82–3).

First, about one-half of the footprint for developing countries is associated with the need to assimilate carbon from fossil fuel burning – land as a carbon sink (discussed further in Chapter 14). This implies that the EF is substantially overestimated if the greenhouse effect is not as damaging as currently perceived, adaptation is possible, or low-cost carbon abatement is available in the future. The costs of sequestering terrestrial carbon rise substantially as more land is used for that purpose. Indeed, a mix of carbon abatement options is more cost effective than simply using land as a "carbon sink", even if such land use is currently cost effective *at the margin*. As noted in Chapter 5, eliminating pollution entirely is economically inefficient. Further, terrestrial carbon uptake has a temporal dimension, but it is impossible not to discount physical carbon if the effectiveness of various land use options is to be compared. Further, the EF calculation assumes that all of the CO_2 emitted by fossil fuels needs to be offset by terrestrial activities, but this ignores the fact that not all CO_2 emissions from fossil fuels show up as increased atmospheric concentrations of CO_2 as oceans and other sinks absorb some of the CO_2 that enters the atmosphere. Therefore, to calculate this component of the EF is fraught with a degree of difficulty not addressed in the EF metric.

Second, the EF is chosen because of its apparent "ease" at aggregating sustainable development data (especially compared to monetary measures); resource and waste flows are easy to measure, it is claimed, as is the conversion of such flows to "productive" land area. However, with some exceptions, little is known about what happens to wastes when they enter ecosystems (e.g. how they are broken down, how long they reside in ecosystems, potential damages they cause), and even less is known about how to convert resource and waste flows into a productive land area – the aggregation problem.

Third, the EF depends on (implicit) assumptions about how one substitutes between various forms of nature and how they are aggregated. The differences are addressed in part by assuming different yield factors for different land uses in different countries, presumably based on some measure of actual output. For Italy, pasture is given a yield factor of 6.5 while arable land has a yield factor of 1.49 (Wackernagel et al. 1999). These indicate that output in Italy is that much higher than the global average – Italian land (nature?) is that much "better". Although yield factors address differences in land quality among regions, economic factors are not taken into account. In less developed countries, perverse economic incentives lead to low output levels, while subsidies in North America and Europe have resulted in higher agricultural output than would otherwise be the case. By using yield factors that are based on these distortions, the proponents of the EF are making judgments about the substitutability between various kinds of natural capital, and about the correctness of distorting economic incentives. As a result, solutions to environmental problems that depend on substitution cannot be studied using the EF tool. Further, in addition to the yield factors, various "weights" are used to convert human investment activities into land area. For example, in determining how much land is needed to cover a country's demand for wood products (say for construction), the footprint uses average annual growth rates of 2.0 m^3/ha for Italy (Wackernagel et al. 1999) and 2.3 m^3/ha for Canada (Table 7.6). The EF overestimates the land area required to provide human capital, in the form of housing say, because countries could use timber from forests in regions that yield 40 m^3/ha per year or more. This requires an increase in trade, but it will reduce the globe's EF. The alternative is for countries to rely on timber harvests from primary and other less productive forests or on wood substitutes, such as cement and aluminum, which are much less environmentally friendly.

The point is that other ways of aggregating the same data, and other assumptions about substitution possibilities, can lead to opposite conclusions about local, regional and global sustainability. The EF is a metric that depends on how aggregation occurs.

Fourth, van den Bergh and Verbruggen (1999) criticize the EF because, as it is currently measured, the footprint does not distinguish between sustainable and unsustainable land use, and thus abstracts from most real-world policy issues (see, for example, intensification of agriculture).

Fifth, it assumes that land use is associated with single functions only, whereas it is well known that land often provides multiple products and services.

Finally, van den Bergh and Verbruggen (1999) point out that the EF is autarkic, against all but a minimum level of international and inter-regional trade. The reason is that trade enables unsustainable economic activities to continue by imposing costs on others in a fashion reminiscent of imperialism – environmental imperialism in this case. As van den Bergh and Verbruggen (1999) argue, "the ecological footprint hides the favorable impact of specialization, not merely in terms of efficiency, i.e. the standard trade story ... but also in terms of environmental sustainability given the erratic clustering of people in space". Hence, while the EF may be an informative statistic at the global level, but certainly not the single dimensional yardstick for sustainability that many seek, it does not and cannot serve as a guide for policymaking in the real world. It ignores the real world and the real trade-offs that need to be made. Regional footprints are even more confusing. As the critics note, the economies of urban areas and small densely populated countries like the Netherlands will never be sustainable, by definition. But what lesson are we to draw from that?

In summary, the EF is an attempt to replace extant measures of sustainability, both monetary (see Pearce and Atkinson 1995; Hueting 1989) and biophysical (Rennings and Wiggering 1997), with a single one. This is much like replacing measures of humidity, temperature and air pressure as indicators of weather with a single measure, altitude, since each of the former are (perhaps imperfectly) correlated with the latter. Clearly, this would lead to a much less useful indicator, just as the EF is a much less useful indicator of sustainability than the indicators its proponents wish to discard. Further, claims that the EF avoids problems of aggregation and substitutability (and even discounting) are empty ones that simply do not hold up under careful methodological scrutiny. Nonetheless, the EF can be

used alongside other measures of sustainability to provide a symbolic
indication of direction, but it should not be relied upon as a sole measure or
even a reliable measure of how societies might "overshoot" their carrying
capacities.

7.5 THE ENVIRONMENTAL KUZNETS CURVE

A relatively recent phenomenon in environmental economics is the so-
called environmental Kuznets curve (EKC) hypothesis. According to this
hypothesis, environmental damage first increases with income, but after a
"turning point" declines. The hypothesis proposes an inverted U-shape
relation between damage and per capita income.[5] It would be a comforting
idea that environmental quality will, in the long run, improve as economies
grow, with strong implications for policymakers. The implications for
sustainable development run counter to the central hypothesis of the "limits
to growth" research (Meadows et al. 1972). Obviously, the EKC concept is
meaningless where there is a great potential for irreversibility of some
environmental good (e.g., extinction of species or, perhaps, depletion of
old-growth forests).

According to Grossman (1995), the effect of economic activity on the
natural environment can be decomposed into three components. First is the
"scale effect" that features prominently in the limits to growth tradition.
This effect captures the simple intuition that more output, *ceteris paribus*,
results in faster depletion of reserves and increases pollution. However,
EKC adherents, who believe that the second and third mechanisms offset
the scale effect, debate the *ceteris paribus* assumption. The second
mechanism is the "composition effect", which refers to the possibility of a
decline in environmental damage when the share of pollution-intensive
activities in GDP decreases over time. That is, the structure of the economy,
or the goods and services produced, changes over time (International Bank
for Reconstruction and Development, hereafter IBRD, 1992). The third
mechanism is the "technique effect", which refers to potential changes in
methods of production. The World Bank points out that enhanced
efficiency, substitution and the introduction of clean technologies and
management practices play an important role in determining the
environmental impact per unit of economic activity (IBRD 1992).

The extent to which the composition and technique effects offset the
scale effect is determined by incentives. As per capita income rises, the
demand for environmental quality may increase, resulting in an "induced
policy response" (Grossman and Krueger 1995; Selden and Song 1994).
Hence, environmental regulations are expected to tighten as wealth (and

education and awareness) increases. In addition to this effect, environmental quality may improve because fertility is assumed to be a declining function of income, or simply because there are more resources available for investment in clean production when income is higher (IBRD 1992; Beckerman 1992). Further, as pointed out by Perman et al. (1996), while many forms of regulation or control may benefit society, the initial resource cost could be prohibitively high for some economies.

The foregoing implies that economic growth is sometimes considered part of the solution rather than the source of environmental problems. Some researchers have been very optimistic about this finding. Beckerman (1992), for example, argues that "... in the end, the best and probably the only way to attain a decent environment in most countries is to become rich". On the other hand, Stern et al. (1996), Arrow et al. (1995) and the World Bank (IBRD 1992) have been more careful and emphasized the role of proper policies. The empirical work indeed suggests that "becoming rich" will not be a panacea for environmental quality. Shafik and Bandyopadhyay (1992) argue that, while it is possible to "grow out" of some environmental problems, there is nothing automatic about doing so.

Some support for the EKC hypothesis comes from work by Shafik and Bandyopadhyay (1992), Panayotou (1993b), Selden and Song (1994), Cropper and Griffiths (1994) and Grossman and Krueger (1995). The results of Grossman and Krueger (1995) indicate that, at high-income levels, further increases in income may be detrimental to the environment. Hence, instead of an inverted U, environmental damage may describe an N shape – a re-linking of damage and economic growth after a period of de-linking. Most empirical work typically consists of fitting a single regression equation between degree of air pollution and income (Grossman and Krueger 1995; Selden and Song 1994; Panayotou 1993b), but the hypothesis has also been tested in the case of deforestation (see Chapter 12) and urban sanitation-clean water (Shafik and Bandyopadhyay 1992). The results do not point in a single direction, but indicate that environmental improvement is more likely to occur when it concerns a local environmental problem (*viz.* sanitation), where there is a clear link between cause and effect (Beckerman 1992). Other problems, notably those with global effects that occur in a relatively distant future (e.g., global warming) are more difficult to put into an EKC framework.

One approach to improving EKCs is searching for important omitted variables. Boyce (1994) and Torras and Boyce (1998), for example, argue that in addition to income levels, the distribution of income and measures of civil rights may be important in explaining environmental degradation. Access to information about environmental pressure and valuing of environmental degradation are likely affected by the degree of inequality in an economy. Considering the "induced policy response", one can expect that the demand for environmental amenities and the political will to respond to this demand are affected by income distribution. A more equitable distribution of income may lead more people to demand a cleaner environment, thereby giving a larger effective voice favoring higher environmental quality. It may also bring about a social harmony that is more conducive to the long-term perspective necessary to make investments in environmental quality (Sandler 1997). Scruggs (1998) is cynical about this line of reasoning, arguing that the effects of distribution are ambiguous; depending on the distribution of preferences across groups in society and the institutional rules, a more equitable income distribution may both enhance and mitigate environmental pressures.

Most studies that examine the EKC hypothesis are fraught with problems. Regression analyses tend to be biased and inconsistent due to simultaneity problems. Feedbacks exist between the state of the environment and economic growth (e.g., because a low-quality environment results in higher costs associated with illness and lower productivity of workers), and many empirical regression models fail to capture this source of bias by using appropriate estimators such as two-stage least squares or simultaneous equations models. Another problem is related to international trade. While the data provide some evidence for a structural change in the economies of developed countries, this does not imply that a similar option exists for developing countries. Stern et al. (1996) cite evidence that the energy intensity of US imports has increased over time, with imports having, to a certain extent, taken the place of domestic production. As the structural change in the USA may have been "... partly accomplished through specialization towards activities with lower energy and resource intensities, it is not clear that the world as a whole can achieve a similar transformation" (p.1156).

Estimated EKCs are sometimes used to project environmental damage in the medium term. Since the so-called turning points of many statistical EKCs lie in the vicinity of current mean income levels (turning point estimates range from several hundred US dollars to $12,000, with many outcomes close to $5,000), further economic growth seems to contribute to higher incomes and a cleaner environment. But an implicit assumption underlying this claim is that incomes are normally distributed. Stern et al. (1996) argue that the global distribution of income is highly skewed, with much larger numbers of people below world mean income per capita than above it. To evaluate the effect of economic growth on the environment, *median* rather than *mean* income may be relevant, and median income is not close to estimated turning points. Taking estimated EKCs as given and simulating the impact of economic growth on the environment, these authors demonstrate that matters could become worse before they get better. They conclude that EKCs are no justification for policy inaction. For sensible courses of action concerning the trade-offs that arise when sustainable development is pursued, however, policymakers will find little guidance in EKC relationships. We return to the EKC in the context of deforestation in Chapter 13.

NOTES

1. Ecological economics is a recent field of study that attempts to bridge the gap between the two views, but the success of this endeavor is uncertain at this time.
2. The discounting issue is revisited in Chapter 11 where we consider whether physical carbon should be discounted in calculating costs of carbon uptake. It turns out that, by not discounting carbon, methodological problems arise.
3. Bishop (1978) erroneously suggests that the loss would be $x-y$, but y is not a gain if strategy S is adopted.
4. Simon bet Ehrlich that the price of commodities thought to be scarce would actually decline over a 10-year period. The comparison involved prices at the beginning and end of the period, with Ehrlich actually choosing the commodities.
5. The original Kuznets curve describes a relation between income inequality and per capita income (Kuznets 1955).

Part III: Land Economics

8. Efficiency and Equity in Land-Use Planning

Most citizens accept government intervention in private decisions regarding land use. However, it is important to determine both why public intervention is required and why intervention may be desirable. Economics is interested in determining efficiency and equity aspects of public policy related to land use and the efficacy of institutions that are developed to exercise society's control over land use. In this chapter and the next, these issues are addressed by examining the regulation of urban land use and social control over and preservation of rural land. In this chapter, the focus is on methods for analyzing land use in and around urban areas (including the rural–urban faultline); in particular, we examine land-use planning and social control over private land-use decisions. The effects that zoning has on land use and, more importantly, on economic efficiency and income equality are investigated from an economics perspective. Because of its income redistributional effects, zoning by itself is not a panacea for land-use planning, and instruments have been coupled onto the zoning approach to address income redistributional implications. Finally, because transportation systems gobble up land, especially in urban areas, different modes of transportation and their effect on land use are examined. Transportation policies have important implications for land use and social wellbeing. We delay to Chapter 9 conservation and preservation of agricultural land, while public lands are the subject of Chapter 10.

8.1 THE RATIONALE FOR LAND-USE PLANNING

Land-use planning and control are increasingly employed by governments in order to direct land development in ways that are considered socially desirable. For example, a land control and development commission controls all decisions regarding land use in the state of Oregon (Sorensen and Stoevener 1977). In British Columbia, land-use control is exercised through the Agricultural Land Reserve (ALR), which was established as an attempt to preserve agricultural lands by freezing development on lands in the reserve. Both these examples illustrate cases of social control over private land use. The question that one has to address is: What enables the state to exercise control over land that is considered to be private property?

British common law has never given anyone exclusive right to acquire, use and dispose of property. In feudal England, no person, except the king (and later the state), owned the absolute right to property. In biblical Israel, all land was held as a trust from God, and property could only be leased to others, returning to the original owners or stewards in the fiftieth year, the year of Jubilee. Further, in Israel, the poor had a right to some of the produce of the land; they had a right to "glean" the fields behind the harvesters. Early American settlements followed this biblical tradition in their own land-use planning (see Hecht 1965).

With the age of individualism, there arose the view that property rights were inviolable. Since the 1770s and up to the mid-1960s, the US courts considered property rights to be absolute. Since the mid-1960s, however, this attitude has changed, primarily because it has come into conflict with human rights. Externality in the acquisition, use and disposition of property are the major reasons for social control over the use of private property; the social costs and benefits of land use are not the same as are the private costs and benefits. Eminent domain or takings illustrates the social limitations upon the private rights of ownership: eminent domain permits the government to take private property for public use but only if just compensation is provided. Not only does eminent domain apply to land, it also applies to any takings from individuals (e.g., taxes to pay for public welfare programs). While there are many ingenious arguments for taking things from individuals, political philosophers question whether or not many government actions justified under the "takings" clause in the US Constitution are, indeed, constitutional (Epstein 1985). Nonetheless, today there are many public institutions that regulate and exercise control over the use of land. Control is exercised either by direct regulation or through an incentive structure, such as taxes and subsidies, or through some combination of these.

Zoning is the oldest and most easily recognized form of control over land use (Ervin et al. 1977; Sorensen and Stoevener 1977). It was used as a means of separating activities of adjacent but dissimilar firms and households that imposed externalities upon each other. In general, zoning is viewed as a means of implementing a land-use plan, while land-use planning is the process of developing the desired allocation of land uses across a landscape. In both legislation and administration zoning and land-use planning are frequently separate functions, but this is unfortunate because they are not truly separate functions, as how a plan is implemented will affect its outcome. Later in this chapter, the role of zoning as a method of land-use control and planning is examined.

Land markets have been profoundly influenced by the impacts of public programs and policies, such as those related to transportation, gasoline pricing, interest rates, foreign ownership of land and so on, and not just policies related to land use itself. Since these policies have a historic root, they have created land-use patterns that may not be desirable by today's standards. For example, urban sprawl caused by government policies in North America that favored low-priced energy, ownership of single detached homes, and the consumption of open space may no longer be desirable because of their impacts upon land use. Sometimes public land-use planning is required to counteract the effects of other public programs and policies and to rationalize land-use conflicts arising therefrom. For example, smaller lots and development of rapid public transportation can offset the adverse income effects (higher housing prices, greater commuting distances) from the creation of open space within urban regions. Unless government intervention in land use enhances economic efficiency – results in an improvement in the way land is used, perhaps by reducing external disceconomies (see Chapter 4) – the intervention cannot be justified. For example, an increase in land-use efficiency may be offset by increased transaction costs through land-use intervention.

A major problem with land-use planning is that there are always conflicts among various interest groups (Sorensen and Stoevener 1977). These groups include: (1) developers, speculators, builders and lenders, who wish to maintain their present control over land use; (2) the coalition of environmental groups; (3) groups interested simply in preserving the size and/or quality of their neighborhoods or towns; and (4) farmers who are located at the rural–urban fringe. Given such diverse groups, the goals of land-use planning agencies tend to be rather vague. For example, one could find the following goal statements for many public agencies that exercise control over private land uses:

- to manage and control urban growth and confine it to the most suitable lands;
- to control population distribution;
- to preserve open space and scenic landscapes;
- to lower pollution levels;
- to preserve agricultural land, especially prime agricultural land;
- to protect critical natural areas such as wetlands;
- to provide decent, safe housing at affordable prices;
- to provide more rational transportation systems; and
- to provide an adequate economic base and employment opportunities.

Goal statements are purposely vague, and very few would be opposed to any of the aforementioned goals. Indeed, the goals are much like "motherhood and apple pie". They are purposely vague in order to minimize conflict and, thereby, gain acceptance with interest groups.

It is important to distinguish between a *goal* and an *objective*. Everyone will agree with the goal of lowering pollution levels; but when one considers the objective of reducing pollution levels by one half, there will definitely be disagreement. The same is true when one considers the goal of providing more rational transportation systems. To one group this might mean providing a new freeway through a certain area. To another group it means providing greater and easier access to public transportation facilities, including, perhaps, the construction of light rapid rail systems. Obviously, the goal itself creates no conflict; but once the goal is stated as an objective, conflicts will arise.

Cost–benefit analysis is, increasingly, the main tool used to evaluate land-use developments. One of the problems with CBA is that of determining benefits. While the costs of land-use planning are generally easy to identify, the same is not true of the benefits. The costs of land-use planning are (1) the transaction costs of organizing, implementing and administering land-use controls and (2) the social costs associated with restricting land use. For example, if land is zoned open space, its market value will go down. This loss in value is a measure of the opportunity cost of using land for, say, housing. However, there remains one problem with this second cost: Does the market price of land exceed its social value or not? Land prices are generally higher than suggested by its productivity in agriculture. Perhaps this is because land serves other social functions, such as a hedge against inflation, collateral on loans, and/or an outlet for speculation. In addition, particularly in agriculture, government subsidies, tax incentives and so on frequently become capitalized in land values.

What, then, are some benefits of land-use planning?

- A number of goals of land-use planning are environmental in nature. There are many studies suggesting methods of measuring benefits of environmental improvement (see Chapter 4). Environmental impact coefficients have also been added to regional development models (e.g., input–output models) to assess environmental impacts associated with various economic activities.
- Outdoor recreational benefits are also tied to land-use issues. These include such things as hunting, hiking, camping, biodiversity and scenic amenities.
- Benefits are also associated with population distribution. Some studies have looked at economies of scale in the provision of public services,

while others have examined preferences regarding optimal town size. Economic efficiency generally increases with population density, so land-use policies that increase density reduce the costs of providing public services in perpetuity.

● Preserving agricultural land is a benefit of land-use control, but little work has been done with respect to measuring these kinds of benefits.

Land-use planning in many jurisdictions, particularly in North America, is in practice often fragmented. What criteria can then be used to evaluate alternative land-use controls? One can consider a set of criteria that includes the following: (1) effectiveness in achieving planned objectives, (2) the effects on the distribution of costs and benefits, (3) the organizational and administrative costs, (4) political and legal acceptability, (5) the effects on the provision of other public services (e.g., financing), and (6) how the controls affect stakeholders (e.g., are they direct or indirect). Information-gathering costs are also affected by the form of controls used in land-use planning, as will be examined in greater detail below. However, it is important to note that safe minimum standards are best achieved by direct controls such as zoning. Therefore, we examine zoning in greater detail.

Before turning to zoning, we consider how land-use planning proceeds. In this regard, it is useful to distinguish between two extreme forms of planning – the informational model and the blueprint model. The differences between the two models are illustrated in Figure 8.1. The informational model relies on a cybernetic or feedback approach to planning. As a result of uncertainty, the incremental approach to planning (as illustrated by the informational model) would be most appropriate for development planning. The incremental approach is often associated with Charles Lindblom's (1959) concept of "muddling through". Zoning is representative of the blueprint model as opposed to the informational model. However, whether or not land-use planning has achieved its objectives is still a matter of conjecture.

8.2 DIRECT LAND-USE CONTROL: ZONING

Land-use planning tends to rely on direct government controls (regulation), and zoning is the most common type of control available. Zoning comes in a variety of different forms. It might entail detailed specifications regarding the types, sizes and use of buildings and/or land, or broader forms such as an urban service boundary or agricultural land reserve. The urban service boundary is designed to control urban sprawl, because the costs of providing public services, such as sewage, gas, electricity and transportation services, escalate rapidly with urban sprawl. This method is designed to confine growth by increasing population density. The location of the urban service boundary can be modified through *appeals* and *variances* – political or legal means of circumventing land-use regulations – that tend to favor those who have better access to the political process.

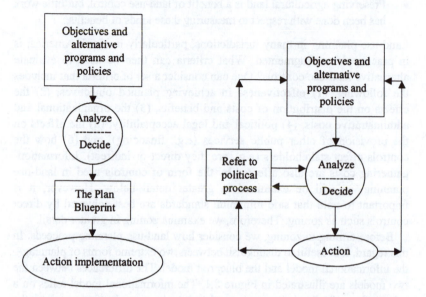

BLUEPRINT MODEL   INFORMATION MODEL

Figure 8.1: Land-use planning models

A number of criticisms have been raised with regards to zoning. First, zoning is considered to be ineffective. Critics point to Houston, which has no city-wide zoning ordinances, as a city that developed land-use patterns that are not much different from those found in zoned cities, particularly Dallas.

> When planning decisions are made [in Houston], they are made by developers on their own land. ... Lack of zoning laws hands power to developers who insist that new developments be large to capture economies of scale. ... Lack of zoning also makes neighbourhoods slightly more mixed – mixed in terms of usage (residential and commercial are more muddled up than elsewhere) and racially. (The Economist 2001, p.31).

Second, the costs of zoning are borne by certain groups (usually the poor), while zoning is most often aimed explicitly at protecting and promoting the value of private property – it has little to do with the social plan. In some instances, however, such as in Europe, zoning is often designed specifically to benefit the poor by restricting certain areas to subsidized housing for lower income persons, for example. Third, zoning is negative in that it only specifies what cannot be done. Finally, like the urban service boundary and agricultural land reserves, zoning is open to appeals and variances that favor larger and wealthier property owners.

When economists consider land-use planning and land-use issues, they look at (1) efficiency, which usually dominates their thinking, (2) equity and (3) political acceptability. The latter is a very important but often neglected component, although each of these issues has an influence on land-use decisions. Each is considered in turn as it relates to zoning.

Efficiency

Efficiency is associated with externality, and, as was seen in Chapter 5, there are three types of externality that are of concern here: technological externality, public goods externality and technical externality. The objective of land-use planning is to eliminate or at least reduce negative externalities, and/or address the need for public goods. The idea is to keep different land uses separate. Thus, some of the first zoning laws were passed in colonial Boston in order to keep polluting leather manufacturers out of residential areas (Hecht 1965). But zoning is not an efficient way of eliminating this type of externality. Why? First of all, it is not always necessary that commercial enterprises be separated from residential areas. For example, a portrait painter may not create a negative externality. Further, land-use controls provide no incentive for reducing externality. Zoning does not, in and of itself, provide the needed incentives to eliminate or reduce noise, smoke, flashing signs, and so on; zoning operates by forbidding certain land uses. If the objective is to reduce traffic, zoning may be used to prevent commercial activities that are considered to result in increased traffic, but there is no incentive to get one's neighbor to reduce her driving.

In this regard, performance standards are a better alternative than zoning. They are more flexible, provide an incentive to reduce the externality, and directly focus on the objectionable behavior. Thus, it may be desirable to zone an area in such a way that air or noise pollution is restricted to some maximum permissible level. Residential areas would then no longer be zoned according to criteria such as number of dwellings per lot but by the number of flashing signs, greatest permitted noise level, vehicle trips per day, and so on. Thus, a portrait painter may fit in, but a business requiring a large sign (whether it flashes or not) or generating a lot of traffic may be objectionable. There is no zoning according to heavy, light and so on, but there are incentives to increase efficiency. The major problem with performance standards is that monitoring and enforcement may be difficult.

In Europe, performance standards form part of the zoning regulation. This is done by restricting the types of activities that can be permitted according to, for example, how much noise they (are expected to) create, whether they are obtrusive relative to the rest of the neighborhood, and so on. Thus, a bicycle repair shop located behind one's house may be permitted, but not other, more disruptive, economic activities.

Public Goods Externality: Preservation of Farmland and Open Space

Two reasons are often cited for preventing the development of farmland. Each of these reasons has a public goods element to it. The first is the argument that prime agricultural land must be preserved for future food needs, while the second is open space. Each is considered in turn.

Preservation of prime agricultural land

The main argument for protecting prime farmland is to maintain agricultural production potential for reasons related to food security – to assure that citizens can be fed in the event that food cannot be obtained through imports. Since this is of interest to all citizens, protection of farmland can be considered a public good. However, protection of farmland is often used by those who are really advocating more open space, and who generally object to development and economic growth that inevitably involves expansion of commercial and residential uses onto agricultural land (or forests). Farmland preservation is driven by desires to protect environmental amenities, such as groundwater, wildlife habitat and scenery, rather than agricultural production potential (Kline and Wilchens 1996).

The real issue of preserving agricultural land pertains to uncertainty. To address uncertainty related to "prime agricultural land" economists employ two concepts. The first relates to uncertainty about the future supply of agricultural land. To capture this value, economists employ the concept of *option value*. Option value is the additional amount a person would pay to preserve agricultural land, over and above its current value, to maintain the option of having agricultural land available for the future, given that the future availability of farmland (its supply) is uncertain (see Graham-Tomasi 1995). Option value assumes uncertainty in supply, but it is caused by risk aversion on the part of demanders. If there is uncertainty about the future supply of agricultural land, people will demand farmland in anticipation, thereby causing its price to rise. This increases the opportunity cost of developing the land. Empirical evidence suggests that the value of land as determined by its marginal productivity is often less than its current market value. People buy land, suffer low returns initially, but feel that returns will increase when agricultural output is worth more. Society is probably already exercising the option of preserving agricultural land; this is reflected in its high price compared to low productivity.

The second concept relates to uncertainty about benefits and costs of farmland protection or development. It is clear that there is some value to delaying development in the current period if more becomes known about future benefits and costs in the next period. That is, the expansion of choice by delaying development of agricultural land represents a welfare gain to society, while a reduction in the options available to society represents a welfare loss. The value of this welfare gain (loss) is *quasi-option value*. Quasi-option value assumes uncertain benefits, but is derived under risk neutrality (Arrow and Fisher 1974). The basic idea is that, as the prospect of receiving better information in the future improves, the incentive to remain flexible and take advantage of this information also increases (Graham-Tomasi 1995, p.595). It is not really the prospect of better information about the costs and benefits of delaying development that is important, but, rather, having access to better information results in greater revision of one's initial beliefs. Thus, it is "greater variability of beliefs" rather than "improvement of information" that leads one to choose greater flexibility over irreversible development.

In cost–benefit analysis, expected values are used to represent uncertain future benefits or costs. If the current and future returns from the decision to develop prime agricultural land are uncertain, then, in general, it is not correct to replace the uncertain returns by their expected values in calculating the present value of the decision to protect farmland. By waiting until the uncertainty is resolved, the actual value of the benefits of preserving farmland will be known, and this value will be different from the expected value. By using expected value in calculating the next period's benefit from protecting agricultural land, the value of farmland protection is underestimated. The difference between the value obtained using expected values and the true value once the uncertainty is resolved – the shortfall – is quasi-option value. This is the loss of options that an irreversible decision entails. Thus, if there is any chance that some uncertainty is resolved by delaying development, the decision to develop or preserve farmland favors protection.

As time passes, the policymaker gets more and better information about costs and benefits of maintaining the land in its present, reversible state. Thus, if the decision-maker has to choose between developing and not developing land, she can obtain additional information about present and future returns by delaying the decision. It is important to recognize that the problem's decision and information structure evolve through time; the decision is not a timeless one.

The question is: How large is quasi-option value and what is the implication for preserving farmland as a public good? Economists have provided estimates of quasi-option value for irreversible decisions related to protection of prime agricultural land (Kennedy 1987; Hodge 1984) and tropical forests (Bulte et al. 2002). Compared to current values, quasi-option value tends to be small and, with some exceptions, unlikely to change significantly decisions to preserve or develop farmland based on cost–benefit analysis.

Consider protection of agricultural land in British Columbia as an example. The Province zoned all land outside urban areas and commercial forestland into the Agricultural Land Reserve (ALR) in 1973. Upon investigating whether or not land outside the city of Kamloops, located in the interior of the Province, should be moved out of the ALR so it could be developed into a recreational resort, Quayle (1998) argued that land in the ALR should be preserved regardless of what it costs in terms of foregone opportunities. The land in question is used primarily for grazing and would be converted into a golf course, with the land providing society greater benefits than had it continued as rangeland. Given a vast area of farmland producing grain in the Province's Peace River region in the northwest, and that grain production is generally subsidized, it is clear that development of the land posed no threat to food production. Indeed, given that the land would become a golf course, the decision to develop the land could not be considered truly irreversible. Clearly, the case for protecting the agricultural land was based on either an environmental ethic that opposes any such developments or an argument to preserve open space.

Open space

Open space is a public good because nonexclusion exists. One person's viewing does not exclude another person's viewing; one person's enjoyment does not exclude another's enjoyment. However, it also has an element of a private good. Residents located around or near the open space have a more pronounced interest in the meadow, as reflected by their property values, than do those traveling on the road through the meadow. The problem with public goods is that, if they are provided via zoning, the individuals who gain do not always bear the costs. The beneficiaries often overstate the value of such goods and often make no sacrifice, except through participation in the political process. Sometimes those who bear the cost and do not gain will fight back, but the tendency is otherwise. Zoning protects open spaces, but it is not clear that optimal levels of these goods are provided. The problem is that zoning does not get individuals to reveal their true willingness to pay or their true preference for open space.

As an example, suppose a hayfield can be turned into a shopping center. What yardstick is required to measure one alternative, open space, against the other, the shopping center? The alternatives available are: (1) we can let the government buy the hayfield and place an *ad valorem* tax on the property of nearby residences in order to get those who benefit the most to pay towards the purchase of the hayfield, or (2) perhaps nearby landowners can be made to pay some of the cost, with the government paying the remainder, since some of the benefits accrue to others. By getting individuals to pay some of the costs, it is hoped that they will better evaluate the true worth of open spaces.

To summarize, the amount of farmland preserved will be less than socially desirable if left to private markets. Regardless of whether preservation of prime agricultural land or simply need for open space is used as an argument, some form of public intervention is needed to provide public goods of this nature (see also Irwin 2002).

Protecting farmland along the urban–rural fault line

Preservation of farmland usually results in conflict at the urban–rural fringe. Farms located near urban centers are characterized by what is sometimes referred to as the *impermanence syndrome*. This refers to the loss in agricultural productivity that occurs because farm operators in the urban–rural fringe are unwilling to make needed investments (e.g., in buildings and equipment) in order to maintain or enhance productivity (Corbett 1990). The area affected by the "syndrome" depends upon distance from the urban center and government policies regarding agricultural land. Here, we focus on government policies to preserve agricultural land.

Governments usually employ one or more of four farmland preservation policies: (1) tax breaks when land is maintained as farmland, (2) right-to-farm legislation, (3) zoning and (4) purchase of property rights. It has been shown that various tax policies designed to preserve farmland actually have the opposite effect: they increase the area affected by the impermanence syndrome and provide incentives that encourage urban sprawl. One reason is that the tax policies raise housing prices, encouraging commuters to drive farther in their search for affordable housing, resulting in greater fragmentation of farmland and thereby increasing the area affected by the impermanence syndrome.

Right-to-farm legislation is designed to protect farmers against nuisance complaints from nearby residents. Many governments, including most US states and provinces in Canada, have implemented such legislation to "protect" farmers. However, right-to-farm laws fail to preserve farmland because (i) their purpose is not specifically designed to stop farmland conversion, (ii) they may not apply to succeeding owners of the land, and (iii) they do not protect farmers against nuisance suits brought about as a result of changes in agronomic practices, no matter how insignificant such changes may be (see Hardie et al. 2004).

Agricultural zoning is often considered an effective means of preserving farmland and is used in many countries, with BC's ALR providing one example. Zoning may fail because farmers are discouraged from making investments, due to the fact that the agricultural value of their land has fallen and/or they are affected by the impermanence syndrome. Since farming is less profitable as a result and because someone will eventually be willing to pay more for the land for residential use than it is worth in the now less profitable agricultural activity, farmers are encouraged to sell their land (in the smallest parcels permitted by the ordinance). Zoning also leads to public pressure for variances, especially where population growth continues and the authority has not taken steps to increase densities in residential areas. Zoning encourages rent seeking that results in the eventual demise of the regional plan.

One method for addressing concerns that zoning leads to its own demise and provide landowners with the resources to invest in agricultural "renewal" is to use a system of transferable development rights (TDRs). These are discussed in section 8.3, but their purpose is to provide landowners with income to develop agricultural land while protecting such land.

Finally, the state can purchase property rights to agricultural land surrounding the city, thereby preventing its development. One option is for the government to purchase land and subsequently sell it back to the original owner or another producer minus certain rights, although this may be economically inefficient as transaction costs might be high. Another possibility is to sell back only parts of the purchased land, retaining ecologically sensitive areas, areas that are most susceptible to land degradation, and/or areas that it wants to keep as open space or farmland. This option requires that the land be subdivided, which may not be permitted. In essence, society purchases development rights to the land that keeps the land in agriculture. Purchase of development rights was successfully used in King County (Seattle, Washington) to preserve agricultural land, although this turned out to be very expensive.

While public purchase of development rights provides farmers with money to make investments for increasing agricultural productivity (thereby avoiding the impermanence syndrome), there are several problems with this approach.

- The costs of purchasing development rights can be prohibitive.
- Conflicts along the urban–rural fringe will continue: farmers will be plagued by vandalism and urban residents will complain about farm noise and smell. Right-to-farm legislation will be required, but externalities such as vandalism, smell and farm noise remain and farmers will have no legal recourse.
- Preserving farmland will not alleviate population pressures. Again, urban residents will eventually purchase the farm as a principle residence, either leasing the land to a bona fide farmer or leaving it in an unused state. Creation of ranchettes or super-large housing lots simply contributes to urban sprawl.
- Population pressure may also result in the eventual sale of development rights by the government authority that initially purchased those rights.

Some researchers have argued that social purchase of development rights coupled with advanced planning (a blueprint development plan for a region) is the best means for preserving farmland, increasing farm productivity, and eliminating speculative values. Empirical evidence concerning the success of farmland preservation efforts is mixed. In the decade since 1983, residents of New Jersey twice voted decisively in favor of preserving farmland; yet, more than 100,000 acres (about 12% of total farmland) was lost during this period. In Maryland, farmland area declined from 4 million acres to 2.2 million acres between 1950 and 2000, with another half million acres projected to be developed in the next 25 years. In 1998, 72% of 240 ballot measures to protect farmland, parks and open space were passed in Maryland, but surveys indicated that people prefer open space rather than farmland preservation (Lynch and Musser 2001). A system of state and county-level land purchases, zoning with TDRs, and purchase of development rights now protects one-third of 342,000 acres of farmland in four counties, with zoning and TDRs accounting for about 17% of the total (see Lynch and Musser 2001).

A major reason why farmland preservation programs are less than successful is a failure to involve agricultural producers in the process. Environmental legislation and zoning ordinances created by local legislative bodies that are not representative of farming interests have had an adverse effect on farmland conversion. It appears, therefore, that preservation of agricultural land will require (i) a change in attitudes toward and a greater understanding of agricultural activities, (ii) greater incentives to expand onto the poorest or least productive agricultural lands, and (iii) a recognition that greater urban population densities are needed. In this regard, urban transportation policies are also important, as we discuss in section 8.5.

In British Columbia, no compensation was provided to those landowners who may have experienced a wipeout as a result of the ALR. In some regions, where urban pressure exists, farmers are having a difficult time as technology advances. Not only is it difficult to move equipment between fields, but also fields are often too small to achieve economies of scale. Conflicts along the urban–rural fault line exacerbate the problem of maintaining viable farming operations. Finally, there is pressure from both farmers and urban citizens to develop the land, either for urban uses or for golf courses. The farmers benefit financially, thereby receiving compensation for their earlier wipeout, and urbanites gain from retention of open space, reduction in farm smells, and recreational opportunities (low green fees).

Although the ALR appears to be preserving agricultural land, the process for obtaining variances (removing property from the ALR) is political. A property-owner can appeal to the Agricultural Land Commission to have land removed from the ALR, and failing that, can appeal directly to the Provincial cabinet's Environmental Land Use Committee. The latter operates without public hearings and can override any ruling made by the Agricultural Land Commission. Hence, there is the perception that, if one wields sufficient power, a variance can be obtained. Given urban pressures in the Okanagan and Lower Fraser Valley, it is very likely that intense future lobbying will occur to remove lands from the ALR. This is as it should be: given the rigidity of zoning ordinances, some mechanism is needed to address economic issues. The political process at least permits this to happen. One can only hope that the income distributional consequences of decisions are adequately addressed (see section 8.3).

Technical Externality and Costs of Providing Services

It is expensive to provide people with police and fire protection, transportation services, sewer, water, electricity, and so on. A denser settlement pattern will economize on the costs of providing public services. The question is: What kinds of economies of scale are present in the provision of public services? This question hinges on another question: What is the optimal size of a city? In some situations, it may be economically efficient to integrate functions (e.g., public transit and water services) and make cities larger, while in other cases they should be made smaller (e.g., creating sub-districts within a city that are responsible for recreation, social services, and so on).

In one of Canada's less-densely populated provinces, Saskatchewan, each rural municipality has its own government. Since the population of many rural municipalities is very small, it would be better to aggregate their functions, thereby reducing the costs of many services. (Of course, not all of the costs are borne by the residents themselves, but certainly they constitute costs to the rest of society.) While rural municipalities have formed larger units in order to construct such things as recreational and medical facilities, considerable inefficiency remains in the way most services are provided, both because *ad hoc* committees are not as workable as single, all-encompassing entities and because the remaining functions are handled at the rural municipality level (e.g., clearing roads of snow in winter).

Zoning is a tool that can be used to get people to "crowd" together and thus increase population density. Some people will, nonetheless, continue to want to live on acreages; but if we truly believe in consumer sovereignty, we should also make these people bear the full additional costs of providing public services such as school buses, fire protection, and construction and maintenance of roads. Marginal-cost pricing should apply to those who wish to live in the rural areas surrounding cities. They should be made to pay the added or marginal cost that society incurs in providing the services they require. Even so, some of the fixed costs will inevitably be borne by society as a whole.

8.3 EQUITY

One problem with zoning is that it results in its own demise because it sets up incentives that lead to changes in the overall or ultimate plan. The reason is that zoning results in changes in the value of land. Consider Figure 8.2. Prior to zoning, all of the acres in the diagram are assumed to be valued at $2,000/ac. After the zoning ordinance has passed, land values in the area zoned nondevelopmental are $500/ac, whereas those in the commercial zone are now $10,000/ac.

Now suppose that commercial interests are having trouble finding appropriate land in the area zoned commercial. They purchase 100 acres of land in the area that is zoned nondevelopmental, as is indicated by the shaded area. The purchase cost for the 100 acres is $50,000. Now the developer has a vested interest in getting the zoning regulation or ordinance changed in her favor. The developer will be willing to pay some amount in what is termed a *rent-seeking activity* in order to get a variance to the ordinance so as to permit commercial development on the 100 acres in question. If the zoning ordinance is changed, the land will be worth $1 million (100 ac × $10,000/ac). Given that the developer paid $50,000 for land, the difference of $950,000 is the amount that could be gained through the rent-seeking activity. The developer will gain, if it costs her some amount in lawyer's fees, bribes, etc., less than $950,000 to obtain a variance to the zoning ordinance. It is obvious, therefore, that zoning provides incentives to change zoning laws.

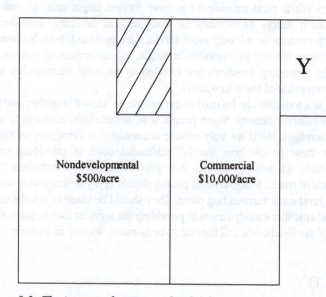

Figure 8.2: The impact of zoning on land values

The second problem with zoning can also be illustrated here. In most cities, the municipal government constitutes the zoning authority, and it is limited to its own jurisdiction. Zoning can be circumvented simply by moving outside the zoned area or outside the urban service boundary, say to the area marked with Y in Figure 8.2. This, then, provides a major argument for land-use control at the provincial, state or national level, depending on the size of the entity needed to take into account all of the spillovers from land use, including pecuniary spillovers as they are a source of unwelcome income redistribution.

The income distributional, or equity, issue of zoning can also be illustrated using Figure 8.2. Zoning results in windfalls for some and wipeouts for others. Consider what happens to the land that is zoned in the example of Figure 8.2. Those in the commercially zoned area experience a windfall of $8,000/ac. They did nothing to earn this windfall – they were simply fortunate in terms of the location of their land. However, those in the other zone experience a wipeout of $1,500/ac. Obviously issues of equity are involved. There are two means to address the equity issue caused by zoning – *zoning by eminent domain* (ZED) and *transferable development rights* (TDRs). We consider each of these in turn.

Zoning by Eminent Domain

The idea behind zoning by eminent domain is that windfalls should be taxed in such a way that wipeouts are covered. A capital gains tax attempts to do this by taxing gains and compensating losses, with tax revenues used to provide compensation (windfall-for-wipeout compensation). To some extent, taxing windfalls and compensating wipeouts lessens the incentives to change the ultimate plan. This can be seen with reference to our earlier example. If the zoning ordinance is changed (in this case zoning is brought to bear on previously unzoned land), a tax of $950,000 could be levied on the commercial developer who obtains a variance to the zoning ordinance (as described in relation to Figure 8.2). This will reduce the developer's incentive to change the zoning ordinance; indeed, developers should then base their appeals solely on site suitability. However, while the idea of windfall-for-wipeout compensation is appealing, the chance that actual windfalls will balance wipeouts is remote.

Under zoning, the responsible authority designates different areas for residential, commercial and industrial purposes. The zoning authority essentially transfers the development rights from one set of landowners to another and, to guard against windfalls and wipeouts, uses its power of eminent domain to "correct" the subsequent redistribution of income. The property that becomes more valuable as a result of the zoning ordinance is specifically assessed to recapture the incremental gain resulting from public action; those properties in essence must pay for the associated development rights. The collection of windfalls is then used to compensate those experiencing wipeouts. ZED effectively entails public purchase and sale of development rights. There are three problems associated with zoning by eminent domain.

Identification of Windfalls and Wipeouts

Only those changes in land values resulting from zoning are to be treated. All other changes in value due to individual or private market actions can be ignored. To separate the two types of changes is difficult in practice. A zoning ordinance produces both a direct effect and an indirect effect. A *direct effect* occurs when changes in the intensity of use on land results in changes in the value of that land. An *indirect effect* takes place when the value of land is affected by changes in zoning regulations that apply to some other property. For example, when preserving farmland as open space, it not only lowers the landowner's property value but also increases the values of adjacent residential properties. The direct effect is the actual lowering of the farmland value, while the indirect effect is the raising of adjacent residential property values. Direct effects are generally easier to identify than are indirect effects. Furthermore, losers will aid the authority in identifying their wipeouts, but gainers will not be as willing to assist in the identification of their windfalls.

Measurement of Changes in the Value of Affected Land

The problem of measuring changes in the value of land affected by a zoning ordinance can be illustrated with the aid of Figure 8.3. Suppose that land is rezoned from use B to more restrictive use A. Two time periods are indicated: T_1 refers to the time when the zoning ordinance was changed, while T_2 refers to the date at which (post-zoning) valuation occurs.

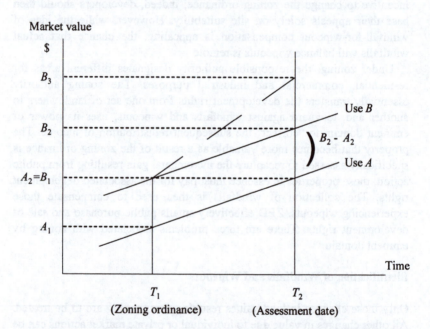

Figure 8.3: Measuring changes in land value due to a zoning ordinance

If the land value in use A at time T_2 ($=A_2$) is compared with the land value in use B at time T_1 ($=B_1$), then no compensation is indicated, which is obviously not true – comparing the pre-zoning value of land at T_1 with its post-zoning value at T_2 suggests that there has been no loss in value. The reason for this misleading conclusion is that there was a failure to account for the factors that cause the price of land to rise over time, such as the real rate of return on land in uses A and B as well as inflation.

Now assume that the land is rezoned from use A to less restrictive use B. How does the time lag in assessment affect the calculation of windfall recapture? Under full recapture, the owner would be assessed B_2-A_1, when the true windfall is B_1-A_1 at T_1 or B_2-A_2 at T_2 (with $A_2=B_1$ by the way the diagram is constructed). In cases where land values are rising for both uses, the time lag in assessment will understate wipeout compensation and overstate windfall recapture.

What about assessing both parties at time T_2? Suppose the zoning change from B to A is significant in terms of its impact on future land values. Without the rezoning ordinance, the time path of land values for B is given by the solid line. With the rezoning ordinance at T_1, it shifts to the dashed line, as less land is available for use B. Then land assessments for use B rise to B_3 rather than to B_2. It is obvious that B_3-A_2 may overstate the desired level of wipeout compensation for those zoned from use B to use A, since the correct compensation is B_2-A_2 if measured at T_2.

Financial Solvency

It may well be that windfalls exceed wipeouts as a result of zoning; indeed, if zoning is to increase economic efficiency, this should be the case. But measurement and transaction costs may prevent this. Hence, financial solvency of any windfall-for-wipeout plan may be in jeopardy, even if windfalls exceed wipeouts.

When to recapture windfalls is also related to the issue of financial solvency. Most ZED plans call for immediate recapture of windfalls and immediate compensation for wipeouts. However, owners of the land do not experience either until they sell their property. Setting up a tax and compensation scheme in such a way that the recapture or compensation occurs when the land is sold results in an incentive for the losers to sell their land as soon as possible and for the gainers to wait. This, then, places a financial burden on the system.

Transferable Development Rights

There are two basic property rights – the right to sell and the right to develop or improve a property. A system of transferable development rights attempts to separate the right to develop land from the right to sell it. Unlike ZED, this separation of rights does not subsequently vest the right to develop with the state; rather, it resides with private individuals. How can we take development rights away so as to ensure equity in zoning? How does a system of transferable development rights (TDRs) work?

Land and Forest Economics

Consider Figure 8.4. The previously unzoned area in the diagram has now been zoned into four areas. Those four zones are: I – pure agriculture, II – single-family dwellings, III – multiple-family housing, and IV – commercial use. Development increases from least developed to most developed in going from zones I to IV. Those in zone IV experience windfalls, while those in area I experience wipeouts. Now assume that, initially, each piece of property has the same price and development potential. Each landowner, regardless of what zone she falls in, is now assigned development rights based on the amount of land she owns. In order to develop a piece of property, an owner needs development rights. The TDR system is designed so that no one person in areas III and IV has enough development rights to develop property to the limit permitted by the zoning regulation. A person in area IV may own 100 acres but only have enough rights to develop 35 acres. If the person's property is of value once it is developed, she will seek more development rights in order to develop that property. Where will those development rights come from? Those in area I will have development rights but will be unable to use them because their property is zoned to prevent development. Thus, individuals in area I are willing to sell their development rights to those in area IV, because the development rights are useless to them. It is in this way that a system of TDRs reduces windfalls and wipeouts associated with public policies regarding land use.

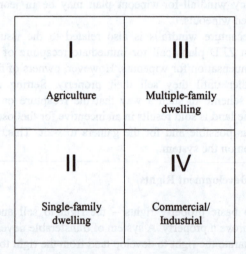

Figure 8.4: Zoning of previously unzoned land: the case for TDRs

Now consider Figure 8.5. In the region represented in the figure, land is either zoned for urban use (different types of urban land use are ignored) or as open space. The value of a unit of land in urban use is P_u (panel b), while land in open space is worth P_0 (panel a); obviously, $P_u > P_0$.

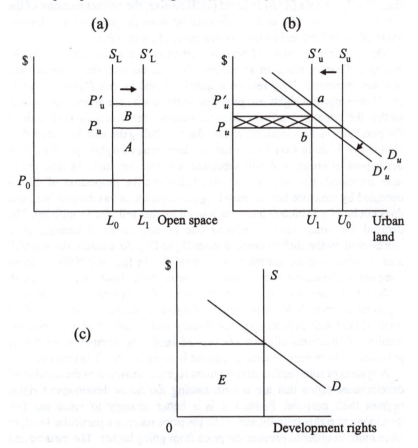

Figure 8.5: Rezoning and use of TDRs

Now the authority decides to rezone some of the land designated urban use to open space. This is shown by a reduction in the supply of urban land from U_0 to U_1 in panel (b) and an equivalent increase in the supply of land for open space from L_0 to L_1. The price of urban land increases from P_u to P'_u because the demand for urban land is downward sloping. For simplicity, it is assumed that the price of open space remains constant at P_0; this could be thought of as the agricultural value of the land. Landowners affected by the zoning ordinance – those whose land was zoned from potential urban use to open space – experience a reduction in the value of property (a wipeout). They will argue that the amount of the wipeout is equal to the difference between the current value of land and its value in open space (i.e., $P'_u - P_0$) or area $(A+B)$ in panel (a). However, the correct measure of the wipeout is area A only, or the difference between the pre-zoning ordinance value of urban land and its use in open space (P_u minus P_0).

The remaining owners of potential urban land are also affected by the zoning ordinance, albeit in an indirect fashion, because the value of their land has increased. They receive a windfall equal to area $P'_u abP_u$ in panel (b). If development rights are provided to those who are zoned open space, so that the remaining urban landowners cannot develop their land without the purchase of development rights, the windfall gain will be reduced or eliminated. If there exists a market for development rights (panel c), then developers of urban land will substitute structure for land. As land prices have increased, not only has lot size fallen but the proportion of the lot occupied by structure has increased – garden/yard area has decline (*viz.*, one does not build a \$100,000 house on a small lot that sells for \$1 million). The demand for urban land is reduced due to this structural change, as is represented by the shift in demand from D_u to D'_u. As a result, the windfall area is reduced to the shaded area in panel (b). In fact, windfalls could be completely eliminated if the demand for urban land should shift far enough to the left. Indeed, we can even have wipeout for wipeout compensation if D_u shifts far enough down as a result of higher residential density. The final price of land will depend upon the density that is permitted and upon the number of structures allowed per unit of land. The compensation that is provided to those experiencing a wipeout is given by area E in panel (c).

A system of transferable development rights is sensitive to the number of development rights that are issued. Issuing too many development rights negates their purpose. Perhaps it is a better strategy to issue too few development rights initially and, once the price reaches a particular level, to issue more in order to prevent the price from going higher. The method and allocation of development rights can have repercussions on the political acceptability of a TDR system.

Further, there is the issue of the conversion factor between TDRs and development. For example, one TDR might be worth X square feet of single-dwelling space, Y square feet of multiple-dwelling space and Z square feet of commercial space. The government can use the conversion factor to finetune the market; for example, the conversion factors can all be reduced if there are too many development rights in the market. The problem is that changes in the conversion factor result in uncertainty, which, in turn, reduces the political acceptability of a TDR scheme.

The final issue regarding transferable development rights concerns the basis for distributing them. We can examine this by considering the example in Table 8.1. There we have three different owners of one-acre plots of land, each with an agricultural value of $500. Their actual market values are assumed to be $600, $900 and $1,500, respectively. Assume that the authority issues 30 development rights, each valued at $50.[1] Consider four different mechanisms for distributing development rights to the owners.

1. *Distribute development rights according to the number of acres that are owned* (10 per acre in Table 8.1). The problem with this mechanism is that it does not reflect either the physical or the economic potential of the land. Thus, 100 acres of swamp would receive just as many development rights as would 100 acres of prime agricultural land located next to an already thriving commercial area, despite the fact that this land is now zoned open space. In terms of our example, each of the three owners would receive 10 development rights. Thus, each is compensated to the tune of $500. As is indicated in row 4 of Table 8.1, the compensated value of land is $1,000. This consists of the $500 value in agricultural land plus $500 in development rights. Obviously, this system is unfair to the third owner, as he/she is only compensated $1,000, whereas the market value of that land prior to zoning was $1,500. Both owners 1 and 2 are overcompensated.

2. *Development rights could be distributed according to the physical potential of the land.* Scientists can determine the development potential of land and distribute development rights accordingly. The problem is that this leaves out economic factors. Land suitable for development may be uneconomic for any other activity. For example, steep hills may be suitable for multiple-unit housing but certainly not for agriculture. Thus, this criterion for distributing development rights simply misses the mark.

3. *Development rights could be allocated according to land value.* This case is illustrated in rows 5 and 6 of Table 8.1. The distribution of development rights in this case is based on the current value of land. Owners 1, 2 and 3 would be given 6, 9 and 15 development rights, respectively. The value of the development rights that the individuals are given is determined by multiplying this number (row 5) by $50, the value of one development right. When that value is added to the agricultural value of the land ($500/ac, as is found in row 6), we notice that owners 1 and 2 are overcompensated, while owner 3 remains undercompensated by $250. As with the first mechanism, this system is unfair to individual 3, while individuals 1 and 2 would support it. Again, distributing development rights according to land values misses the mark, because changes in land values are of interest.

4. *Distribute development rights according to opportunity cost for loss of
    value.* This implies that development rights be distributed on the basis
    of the difference between current land (market) value and agricultural
    value. Owners 1, 2 and 3 would receive 2, 8 and 20 development rights,
    respectively. The value of those development rights is determined by
    multiplying the numbers in row 7 by $50. As can be seen from row 8,
    the owners are compensated in a way that is equitable, at least in terms
    of preserving the *status quo* distribution of income.

*Table 8.1: Wipeout Compensation under Alternative Mechanisms for
Allocating TDRs*

Item	Owner of 1-acre plot		
	1	2	3
(1) Current value ($/ac)	600	900	1,500
(2) Agricultural value ($/ac)	500	500	500
Compensation according to acres owned			
(3) Number of TDRs	10	10	10
(4) Compensation* ($)	1,000	1,000	1,000
Compensation according to land value			
(5) Number of TDRs	6	9	15
(6) Compensation* ($)	800	950	1,250
Compensation according to opportunity cost			
(7) Number of TDRs	2	8	20
(8) Compensation* ($)	600	900	1,500

Notes:
* Each TDR is worth $50. Compensation is determined by row 2 plus the value of
the TDRs.

Now notice that, in the above example, if the price of development rights
exceeded $50, everyone would be overcompensated, and eventual
homebuyers and those who lease or own commercial property would suffer.
They might suffer even more if there were no system of TDRs to militate
against the adverse distributive effects of zoning. If the price of
development rights was less than $50, landowners would be
undercompensated.

Let us return to this idea of windfall-for-wipeout compensation. The
system of transferable development rights emphasizes the importance of
windfall-for-wipeout compensation. However, this should, perhaps, be de-
emphasized for the following reasons. First, it is difficult to establish what
constitutes a windfall and what constitutes a wipeout – measurement is
difficult. Second, in most cases windfalls do not equal wipeouts, although
the converse is implied by the expression "windfall-for-wipeout
compensation". Third, payments for development rights are not a windfall

recapture, as often seems to be implied. Rather, such payments are exactly that – a payment for the right to develop one's property.

To make these concepts somewhat clearer, consider two examples: (1) Mr. Adams buys a piece of land. A year later, a highway is built nearby and the value of the land doubles. Mr. Brown thinks that Mr. Adams has received a windfall, but Adams argues that this is not the case. He has researched the growth potential in the area and expended effort in research to recognize that a highway was needed. It is clear that, in this case, trying to recover windfalls might be a misguided effort. (2) Mr. Jones owns land in an area that is recently zoned for agriculture only. He feels that the zoning ordinance has wiped him out. Several farms in his area were sold to speculators at high prices in recent years, and his farm has been assessed higher than its agricultural value. However, no one has ever made Jones an offer, since his farm does not have a view. Has he really experienced a wipeout? How is it to be measured if he did indeed experience a loss?

Finally, one might consider other cases where a system of tradable development rights could be used. We noted that TDRs could be used in the context of the rural–urban fringe. However, a system of transferable development rights will not work there if rights are allocated to farmers without taking into account distance from the urban center, because farmers least likely to be affected by development sell their rights, while those nearest urban areas reduce farm investment and hold onto development rights (the impermanence syndrome).

8.4 POLITICAL ACCEPTABILITY

Public intervention in the private use of land is justified when private land use imposes costs or confers benefits upon others. Such public intervention takes place through instruments such as zoning, regulation of permissible land uses, taxes, subsidies, and so on. The "takings" clause in the US Constitution requires that compensation be provided whenever the government uses its eminent domain power to restrict land use (see Epstein 1985); Canada does not have a takings clause in its constitution, but provincial laws prevent governments from expropriating property rights without compensation. Where private land-use activities impose real costs on others, common law provides that compensation be paid to those that are affected. If land-use control is accomplished by zoning, at least partial compensation for the loss of valuable property rights may be necessary in order to make land-use control politically acceptable and, perhaps, even to make it legal (although that would be a much more difficult case to make).

Even if zoning is a politically acceptable means of exercising social control over land use, problems regarding the distribution of the costs and benefits of land-use control may limit the usefulness of such methods of social control. Part of the problem concerns appeals and variances and the perception, whether based in fact or not, that the system or plan can be tampered with if one is sufficiently rich or well connected. Tradable development rights are one means of mitigating the adverse income distributional effects of zoning and of providing for some compensation. Unfortunately, development rights have never truly been implemented on a large scale, and education may be needed to make this mechanism more appealing. However, a system of tradable development rights might well become politically attractive for dealing with a number of issues related to public control over land use.

8.5 TRANSPORTATION AND URBAN LAND USE

Transportation is a major land use in urban areas; typically, cities in developed countries relinquish one-third or more of their land to motor vehicles for roads and parking lots. In the United States, about 0.6 ha (1.5 ac) of land per capita is paved; if China were to pave land at the same rate, about 64 million ha would be required, which is equivalent to more than 40% of the country's cropland. While automobiles have altered land use, there are costs associated with the private use of motor vehicles. In OECD countries, the transportation sector's share of pollution is significant, accounting for 89% of carbon monoxide (CO) emissions, 52% of nitrogen oxides (NO_X), 44% of volatile organic compounds (VOC) and 29% of CO_2 (Bohm and Hesselborn 1999, p.36). Passenger cars are responsible for much of the ozone and other pollution (including CO_2 emissions) in urban areas (Table 8.2). In addition to environmental pollution, automobile use results in large numbers of traffic injuries and fatalities, which imposes a large social cost on society; there are almost 50,000 fatalities per year in both the USA and Europe. Further, private automobiles are an inefficient means of moving people (Table 8.3).

Attempts to get individuals to take into account the externalities they impose on other drivers and society more broadly have met with varying degrees of success. Bohm and Hesselborn (1999) review a variety of economic incentives used in various part of the world to reduce the adverse impacts of private automobile use, and even truck transportation. These range from (differentiated) taxes on fuels to road-user fees and taxes on the purchase of vehicles. In addition, regulations and performance standards have sought to address externality in the transportation sector. These measures have had various degrees of success, but "drastic increases in petrol taxes are needed to internalize the external costs of motor vehicle travel and ... this might lead to significant changes of activity patterns and land use" (ibid., p.24). The demand function for private automobile use is highly inelastic.

Table 8.2: Pollution Emitted from Typical Work Commutes in the United States[a]

Mode	Hydrocarbons	CO	NO_X
	(grams per 100 passenger-kilometers)		
Rapid rail	0.2	1	30
Light rail	0.2	2	43
Transit bus	12	189	95
Van pool	22	150	24
Car pool	43	311	43
Auto[b]	130	934	128

Notes:
[a] Based on national average vehicle occupancy rates.
[b] Based on one occupant per vehicle.
Source: Lowe (1990, p.14).

Table 8.3: Operating Speeds and Number of Persons per Hour that One Meter-width of Land can Carry, Selected Travel Modes

Mode	Typical operating speeds (km per hr)	Persons (per m-width of land per hr)
Auto in mixed traffic	15–25	120–220
Auto on highway	60–70	750
Bicycle	10–14	1,500
Bus in mixed traffic	10–15	2,700
Pedestrian	4	3,600
Suburban railway	45	4,000
Bus in separate busway	35–45	5,200
Surface rapid rail	35	9,000

Source: Lowe (1989, p.22).

One of the challenges facing policymakers is that of encouraging individuals to adopt other forms of transportation, whether public transportation or alternatives such as bicycles. Attempts to get individuals in North America to choose alternative modes of transportation have been largely unsuccessful. The reason is that, compared to Europe and places like Singapore, externalities related to private automobile use – the congestion, traffic accidents, pollution and adverse impacts on land use – have never been seriously addressed in Canada and the USA. One reason is political: the political will to spend large sums of taxpayer money to construct rapid rail or light rail transit systems and to tax private automobile use in order to take into account its externality effects is lacking.

In the past, governments appeared to favor freeway construction, but it is now recognized that this only encourages urban sprawl and, eventually, exacerbates the problems of traffic congestion, pollution and lost hours due to commuting. Consequently, rapid transit lines have been constructed in the Portland and Los Angeles areas in the last decade. While this has resulted in urban renewal in some areas, such as Long Beach (a terminus of the LA light-rail line), such efforts are only a first start in efforts to address larger issues related to transportation and land use. As a result of conflict between vested interests (environmental groups, developers and local residents) and inappropriate institutional structures for dealing with transportation problems (*viz.*, a transportation board with no power over zoning as is the case in Vancouver, Canada), the political system in many urban areas is deadlocked – politicians are often unwilling to make difficult decisions pertaining to transportation. Nothing gets done about resolving transportation issues, even though these affect the living environment of an entire region; urban areas continue to grow in an *ad hoc* fashion.

Evidence from European countries, such as the Netherlands, indicates that a "carrot-and-stick" approach is needed. One cannot impose penalties on the private use of motor vehicles (e.g., gasoline taxes, high parking rates) without, at the same time, providing alternative modes of transportation that are competitive with private vehicles. In cities such as San Francisco and Vancouver, where house prices fall as one moves farther into the suburbs and commuting distances increase, the burden of penalties falls upon those in the relatively low-income categories, who cannot afford housing close to their jobs in the city. They must either take lower paying jobs in the outlying regions or incur high commuting costs. European experience indicates that, since time is a major factor in commuting and is highly valued, penalties must be very high indeed before a commuter chooses to take public transit that increases commuting time.[2] Therefore, it is necessary to employ the stick of high penalties with the carrot of a good public transportation system.

In the Netherlands, for example, policies for dealing with transportation continue to evolve. In 1988, the government announced a policy designed to reduce the number of automobiles from 5 million to just 3.5 million in 20 years, compared to the forecast number of 8 million. The policy would increase the costs of buying and operating an automobile by about 50%, but $5.7 billion per year would also be spent on improving public transportation. The policy has not been all that effective, partly because the public transportation system is at full capacity. The national railway has since been privatized, new freeways are being built and extra commuter lanes are being used to reduce the time spent commuting. At the same time, taxes on fuels and automobiles continue to be high, but attempts to implement road-user fees on some freeways to re-distribute use to other times and thereby reduce congestion have languished. In Norway and Hong Kong where road-user fees have been implemented, they have been successful in reducing traffic during peak hours. The Netherlands also promotes greater use of bicycles by giving cyclists greater rights and providing dedicated bicycle paths.

In many low-income countries, where there is greater reliance on bicycles because motor vehicles are too expensive for many citizens, high rates of traffic fatalities are the result of collisions between bicycles and motor vehicles. Data from cities in developed countries indicate that, unless bicycles can be physically separated from motor vehicles, only a small proportion of daily vehicle trips will be made by this environmentally preferred mode of transport. For example, 50% of daily passenger trips in the city of Groningen in the Netherlands are made with bicycles, compared to 20% for Copenhagen, Denmark. The main reason has to do with the adoption of a pro-bicycle policy designed to separate bicycles from motor vehicular traffic in the former city, as well as limiting automobile access to downtown areas.

The economic viability of public transportation systems and their being chosen by commuters depends upon a variety of factors that are related to land use. Urban densities and commuting choices are provided in Table 8.4. It is clear that the higher the urban density, the more likely that a commuter will choose public transport. However, public transport must also be available and its availability affects commuter choices. For example, rapid-rail transit is more developed in Stockholm than Amsterdam (although the system is expanding in the latter city). Consequently, more workers rely on private automobiles and walking/cycling in the latter city compared to the former. Rapid rail transit is unlikely to be a viable option in areas of low-density housing – urban sprawl. Then, in order to make transit viable in the long term, it is necessary to use zoning and other land-use incentives to increase the population density along rail transit corridors and to encourage a denser population that is more tightly bound to the urban center. It is also necessary to change land-use regulations in order to permit development of office towers and other places of employment close to rapid transit stations. Thus, by exercising its control over land use, the authority can make public transportation more feasible than it currently appears.

Table 8.4: Urban Densities and Commuting Choices, Selected Cities

City	Land-use intensity	Private car	Public transport	Walking & cycling
	(population + jobs per ha)	(% of workers using)		
Phoenix	13	93	3	3
Perth	15	84	12	4
Washington	21	81	14	5
Sydney	25	65	30	5
Toronto	59	63	31	6
Hamburg	66	44	41	15
Amsterdam	74	58	14	28
Stockholm	85	34	46	20
Munich	91	38	42	20
Vienna	111	40	45	15
Tokyo	171	16	59	25
Hong Kong	403	3	62	35

Source: Newman and Kenworthy (1989).

Likewise, tools of land-use planning, particularly changes in zoning regulations, can be used to compensate those who may be adversely impacted by the development of transportation corridors in their backyard. Landowners along a new rapid rail corridor will experience a loss in land values as a result of added noise and/or possible vandalism from "unwanted" commuters who have easier access to the neighborhood as a result of the commuter line. To compensate landowners who are adversely impacted by the rapid rail corridor, the authority could rezone the land to a higher-valued use, thereby providing compensation to current owners and opportunities to develop land along the corridor for commercial use, thereby creating employment and greater ridership. Purchase of transit rights of way can be facilitated by appropriate land-use policies, for example, that enable the owner of the right of way to construct developments that might straddle the future rail line. Thus, zoning could be used to provide compensation and make rapid rail transport more viable by increasing land-use intensity along the corridor.

It is clear that urban land-use policies have an important impact on the way people in urban areas live their lives. Public policies related to agricultural land use also have a similar impact on rural residents, plus they affect the utility of city dwellers in a variety of ways – dust from soil erosion can affect cities, soil erosion pollutes rivers and lakes, rural land use affects scenic amenities and biodiversity, and subsidies to farmers constitute a redistribution from those living in cities to those on the farm. In the next chapter, we examine government policies related to rural land use. Then, in Chapter 10, we examine public lands, lands owned by the state.

NOTES

1. It is implicitly assumed that there is a larger, over-arching market for development rights where the price is determined by the intersection of supply and demand, such that price is $50. Development rights allocated to the three owners in this example have no effect on this price.
2. During the 1980s, Sweden had a gasoline tax of 133% and automobile sales tax of 41%, compared to respective taxes of 41% and 5% in the USA. Yet average number of kilometers driven per person was higher in Sweden than in the USA (8,000 km versus 7,700 km). Other cross-country comparisons also indicate how little impact taxes appear to have on automobile use (see also Bohm and Hesselborn 1999).

9. Degradation and Conservation of Agricultural Land

Land degradation is a worldwide problem; it refers to soil erosion, loss of organic matter and natural fertility, and the destruction of the soil's structure due to compaction (caused by heavy equipment) and other abuse. Unless economic analysis is correctly applied to the study of soil and land degradation, it will be difficult to determine appropriate and efficient policy responses. Economic research focuses on human as opposed to only nonhuman factors that cause degradation of agricultural lands; it centers on farming practices and on economic institutions and incentives (signals), all of which affect land degradation. Soil erosion is the most readily identifiable form of land degradation, but land degradation also occurs as a result of the conversion of forestlands, wetlands and native rangelands to intensive crop production. In many cases, government agricultural programs are a primary driver of land degradation. Government agricultural programs consist of output and input subsidies that encourage an outward shift of the extensive and intensive margins. At the extensive margin, marginal lands that are currently in forests or wetlands are brought into production, while at the intensive margin more inputs are employed in crop production, including chemicals and use of irrigation. Greater use of chemicals (pesticides, nitrogen fertilizer) leads to water pollution, while irrigation frequently results in soil salinity. Policy failure can also occur when institutions are inappropriate (e.g., property rights are not clearly specified), thereby leading to land degradation.

We begin in this chapter by examining the negative environmental impacts of government agricultural programs on land use. Because agricultural programs increasingly have a conservation component, in section 9.2, we examine the effect of agriculture on wildlife habitat, particularly wetlands. Then, in section 9.3, we consider the economics of soil erosion. We end the chapter by looking at the economics of irrigation (section 9.4), because irrigation subsidies have resulted in degradation of land is various ways.

9.1 EFFECTS OF AGRICULTURAL PROGRAMS ON LAND USE AND THE ENVIRONMENT

Government agricultural programs have been in existence since the mid to late 1800s. Early programs consisted primarily of research and extension (providing advice to farmers), followed by farm credit policies, implicit irrigation subsidies (see section 9.4), voluntary soil conservation programs, and, at least in Canada, pooling of grain receipts via state trading in order to spread risks.[1] Stabilization programs also evolved to cushion farmers from the vagaries in agricultural prices. Since the Second World War, however, programs increasingly contained production subsidies. These subsidies reached unprecedented levels during the 1980s and 1990s. They remain quite high to the present day (Schmitz and Furtan 2000, pp.79–93). In Europe, Canada and the USA, the primary aim was to compensate farmers for declining returns and thereby "preserve a way of life". Unintended adverse effects on land use and the environment are a consequence of agricultural subsidies in all countries that provide them. The objective in this section is to demonstrate how agricultural programs result in adverse effects on land use and the environment.

In Canada's Census of Agriculture, farmland is classified as either improved or unimproved. Improved land is land that is, or has recently been, cultivated and is either growing crops or in (tillage) summer fallow. Unimproved land includes woodlands, areas of native pasture or hay land that had not been cultivated, brush pasture, grazing and waste land, sloughs, marshes, rocky land, etc. Unimproved land provides important breeding grounds for waterfowl, protection of biodiversity and habitat for wildlife, as well as forage and shelter for domestic livestock. A plot of the ratio of unimproved land to total farmland in western Canada over the period 1951–2000 is provided in Figure 9.1. Also provided in Figure 9.1 is a plot of agricultural subsidy payments over the same period. It is clear that farmers steadily brought unimproved land into production over the period 1951–81, mainly because farming became increasingly profitable. Agricultural programs influenced farmers' decisions to expand the extensive and intensive margins by bringing unimproved land into cultivation, depending on location. However, in the mid-1980s, conservation compliance provisions in farm programs (see below) and subsidies aimed directly at conserving unimproved lands began to shift the extensive margin back as indicated in the figure. Remaining unimproved lands were used for domestic grazing or simply left as wetlands, forests, etc. These lands act as a buffer for soil erosion, habitat for wildlife, and waste receptor for pollution from agronomic activities. After 1981 and into the 1990s (data are for census years only), the rate at which unimproved land was converted to improved land decreased as a result of agricultural subsidies and crop insurance programs that discouraged livestock rearing (not indicated in figure).

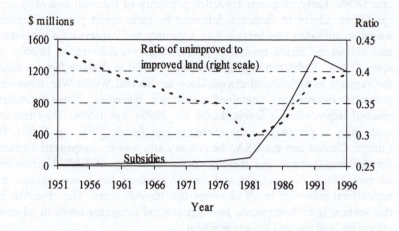

Figure 9.1: Ratio of unimproved to total farmland and subsidy payments, Canada, census years

One reason for increases in environmental degradation on agricultural lands in Canada (*viz.*, soil erosion, loss of wildlife habitat) was the rapid rise in grain prices during the 1970s, which encouraged farmers to sell off livestock herds and bring pasture land into grain production. Then, during the 1980s when agricultural prices collapsed, government agricultural programs provided subsidies that took the place of high grain prices. However, these agricultural policies further encouraged farmers to drain wetlands and bring unimproved land into production, mainly because they made eligibility dependent on output and area under cultivation. In the next paragraphs, government agricultural policies in three main grain trading areas are described – the United States, Canada and the European Union. We consider the USA first because it has a plethora of agricultural programs that affect land use. Many of these programs have been adopted in one fashion or another by Canada, although Canada likely has the lowest levels of agricultural support of the three jurisdictions. What sets Canada apart, however, is that it employs state trading to export grain. Much of the discussion on Canada relies on Schmitz and Furtan (2000, pp.48–50, 79–93); however, while Schmitz and Furtan's focus is on trade, the purpose here is to indicate the effect that farm programs have on land conversion and the environment. We end the section by considering (mainly US) programs that are intended to protect nature and the environment.

United States

Agricultural policies in the USA are often seen as a direct response to European agricultural policy, but they are driven by a desire to maintain or increase market share. US farm support programs have been designed with three broad, related objectives in mind: supplement (and protect) producer incomes, manage supplies and support farm prices. The effect of these programs has been to encourage the expansion of agricultural production to the detriment of the environment.

The main subsidy elements of the program operate under the mandate of the US Department of Agriculture (USDA), with the Commodity Credit Corporation (CCC) overseeing the financial management of farm support programs. Under the CCC, the Farm Service Agency (FSA) distributes program benefits through a network of county offices overseen by elected farmer committees. Supplements to producer income are typically provided via "production flexibility contract" payments (grains and cotton) and "marketing loans" and "loan deficiency" payments (grains, cotton and oilseeds). Production flexibility contract payments provide fixed, but declining, annual payments to farmers based on applicants' established acreage and per-acre output. "Non-Recourse Marketing Assistance Loans" provide loans to eligible producers at rates typically set at 85% of a moving average of past market prices. Loan rates are subject to caps, and must be repaid with interest within nine months (ten months for cotton). In order to secure a nonrecourse loan, producers must pledge their stored crop as collateral to the CCC. Failure to repay loans as negotiated results in forfeiture of the pledged crop, so the "loan rate" serves as a lower bound on price. To minimize crop forfeitures, the marketing loan repayment rate approximates market prices. Thus, if the repayment rate is less than the original USDA loan rate, the farmer is effectively subsidized at an amount equal to the difference of the two rates. Eligible producers who choose not to participate in the marketing loan program also receive marketing loan gains in the form of "loan deficiency payments". In recent years, producers have seen large increases in funding provided through the marketing loan program (Figure 9.2). Peanut and tobacco producers operate under supply management, with marketing quotas limiting the quantities of crop that can be produced, and thus land allocated to these crops. However, producers in these sectors remain eligible for nonrecourse loans and special supplemental direct payment programs.

To offset the negative impacts of subsidies on land use and the environment, proponents of US farm policy point to ever-increasing contributions to conservation programs. However, in reality, environmentally sensitive areas will remain at risk as long as the USDA continues to allocate the vast majority of its funds through programs that encourage over-production and thus the over-use of natural resources (compare agricultural program payments with conservation payments in Figure 9.2).

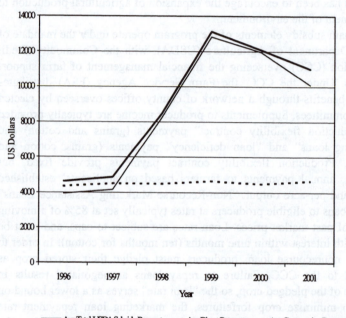

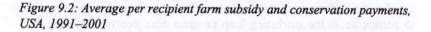

Figure 9.2: Average per recipient farm subsidy and conservation payments, USA, 1991–2001

Farm legislation characterized by large subsidies first appeared in the 1980s. The first major farm bill of this type was the Food Security Act (1985), which had the following main components:

- Target prices are set by the Congress as a price guarantee, with farmers receiving a deficiency payment equal to the difference between the market price (at which the farmer could sell grain) and the target price. (A limit was imposed upon the number of acres eligible for deficiency payments.) The effect was to increase prices, which provided incentives for farmers to increase their use of agro-chemicals (expand the intensive margin) and bring marginal land into crop production (expand the extensive margin). Increased use of agro-chemicals resulted in the pollution of ground and surface waters, while expansion of the extensive margin resulted in the loss of wetlands and forests, reducing wildlife habitat and increasing soil erosion. In response to the latter effect, the farm bill required farmers to set aside a certain amount of land. The area set aside was generally put into pasture to prevent soil erosion, and thus could easily be brought back into production.

- The CCC provided farmers with nonrecourse loans for eligible crops. Although the loan rate was set well below the target price, farmers were still, in effect, subsidized to produce grain, thereby encouraging environmental degradation.
- A Payment in Kind program paid farmers in commodity certificates instead of cash to take land out of production, and these were honored by the CCC.
- A Conservation Reserve Program (CRP) paid farmers to set aside land for conservation purposes. More than 30 million acres were put into the CRP using a bidding procedure to keep costs to a minimum.
- An Export Enhancement Program effectively moved surplus US grain to export position (using subsidies as needed). Its objective was to maintain US market share in international markets. This meant that US farmers needed to continue producing grain, thereby encouraging expansion of the intensive and extensive margins of production and, thus, negative environmental spillovers.

Despite its conservation focus, the overall environmental impact of the 1985 Farm Bill was negative, simply because it encouraged grain production above what it would otherwise be.

The 1990 Farm Bill continued the policies of the 1985 Bill, although it reduced the target price and the number of acres eligible for deficiency payments. However, money for export subsidies and marketing continued to be made available, although conservation aspects were enhanced. Swampbuster legislation prevented the loss of wetlands ("no net loss") and a Wetlands Reserve was added.

The Federal Agricultural and Improvement Reform (FAIR) Act of 1996 made sweeping changes to farm policy, and was to remain in effect until 2002. Acres eligible for subsidies would constitute 85% of base (contract) acres, which included base acreage plus lands coming out of the CRP. Land in hay, alfalfa and grazing remained eligible for determining payments, subject to conservation compliance (see below). Production flexibility contracts replaced the deficiency payment system, while the nonrecourse loan system remained in place (but with greater flexibility). An effort was made to decouple the effect of subsidies on production and thus reduce their adverse environmental impacts. The CRP was capped at 36.4 million acres, but the Wetlands Reserve Program was expanded, a farmland preservation program was implemented, and new environmental programs (such as the Environmental Quality Incentive Program) were introduced on a cost share basis. Further, while earlier farm legislation had made crop insurance mandatory, under FAIR it became voluntary.

Recent proposals for a new Farm Bill in 2002 suggest that existing programs will continue. Direct subsidies will be paid through a fixed decoupled program (with upper limit of $40,000 per farmer) and a counter-cyclical program (with limit of $75,000). The latter depends on the difference between the target price and the market price or loan rate (whichever is higher), eligible acres, and presumably some measure of (historic) yields. The CRP is increased to 40 million acres and other conservation programs remain. The draft of one proposal that circulated on the web indicated that the program would cost $73.5 billion over 10 years.

Many of the agricultural programs used in the USA have been adopted in one form or another in Canada, although Canada also has a number of unique programs.

Canada

Freight rate subsidies for grain were among the first form of agricultural subsidy provided to western Canadian farmers. These subsidies had two objectives – to reduce grain prices to domestic livestock producers located outside the grain belt and to subsidize movement of grain to export markets. In the late 1800s, Canadian railroads agreed to a ceiling on freight rates for hauling grains to export market in exchange for rail building subsidies. This "Crow Rate" was to apply in perpetuity and there was no provision to adjust it for inflation. For nearly 75 years, freight rates were generally below the Crow Rate, but with high rates of inflation in the 1970s and increased costs associated with operating a deteriorating rail system, the Crow Rate became a *de facto* subsidy that lowered transportation costs. In addition, as a result of the Feed Freight Assistance Act (1941), movement of feed grains to feed deficit regions in Ontario and British Columbia was subsidized. The Crow Rate and feed freight assistance programs effectively raised the farm-gate price of grain, because a lower transportation cost was deducted from the world price, thereby causing a shift in production from livestock towards grain in Canada's grain belt. This encouraged cultivation of marginal lands and land degradation.

The Western Grain Transportation Act (1983) replaced the fixed statutory Crow Rate Benefit with a grain transportation subsidy that went directly to the railways, but the subsidy continued to distort land use. It is only when a transportation subsidy is paid directly to farmers, and then as a lump sum payment not tied to improved acreage or output, that there is no distorting effect on land use (because a direct lump-sum payment does not affect price). In 1995, both Acts were repealed and grain and grain products were placed under the National Transportation Authority, which continued to set maximum freight rates for grain shipped to ports for export until 2000; then farmers were required to pay the full compensatory rate. Given that transportation subsidies discouraged livestock production, it is unlikely that lands will return to pasture in the near future. Other programs, such as crop insurance, and lifestyles militate against this.

Crop insurance began in 1959. It offers financial protection against crop loss caused by uncontrollable natural hazards but militates against the environment in several ways. First, it encourages crop specialization and discourages livestock (an activity more compatible with the environment as drylands are not plowed and trees are grown to provide shelter for livestock) by reducing the risks of relying on a single farming activity, such as grain growing. Further, since farmers do not pay the full premium or the costs of operating the program, crop insurance constitutes a subsidy that encourages greater production, shifting the intensive margin of production. Finally, payments are generally based on average yields in a region. Farmers are encouraged to bring marginal land into production because the yields on marginal lands may be significantly below the recent yield history for the eligible crops in the area, allowing the farmer to receive crop insurance benefits on this land. The effective coverage on marginal land may be significantly greater than its capability to produce a crop. Although this yield effect declines as more marginal land is brought into production in the region, it does not completely disappear.

The Canadian Wheat Board is a compulsory export-marketing agency for wheat, oats and barley grown on the Prairies. Quota is assigned to farmers on the basis of cultivated land area, thereby encouraging the cultivation of unimproved land and excessive tillage summer fallow. Aside from causing excessive soil erosion, tillage summer fallow increases soil salinity and reduces the availability of nesting cover for migrating waterfowl (see sections 9.3 and 9.4). Tillage summer fallow rather than chemical summer fallow is normally used because it is less expensive. As an alternative, chemical summer fallow reduces erosion and salinity problems but may harm populations of invertebrates and aquatic plants, and result in the poisoning of young mammals and birds.

The Western Grain Stabilization Act (WGSA) of 1976 was a program whose intent was to stabilize net income but the consequence of which was to provide income support. The WGSA discouraged farmers from maintaining lands in their natural state (or as pasture) in three important ways. First, WGSA effectively raised the price of grain received by producers, since the program was not actuarially sound; producers gained from WGSA over the length of time that the program was in existence (1976–90). Second, program payments were related to past output: the higher one's output, the greater the payment received from WGSA. Producers were encouraged to increase output over time, thereby causing them to use too many agro-chemicals, particularly nitrogen fertilizer – thereby shifting the intensive margin of cultivation. Finally, WGSA encouraged farmers to grow only those grain crops covered under the Program and not to raise cattle. The Special Canadian Grains Program of 1986–91 was also used to subsidize prairie grain producers for depressed world grain prices (as a response to European and American subsidies), and its environmental effects were similar to WGSA. The Special Grains Program paid out C$1 billion in 1986 and $1.1 billion in 1987.

In 1991, the Gross Revenue Insurance Plan (GRIP) and the Net Income Stabilization Account (NISA) replaced the Special Canadian Grains Program and WGSA.[2] The NISA acts as a safety net to prevent a farmer's income from falling below her five-year average returns after costs (or below $10,000 taxable income). This policy appears to be somewhat decoupled from the production decisions of farmers, because it is paid on a lump-sum basis as opposed to a production or acreage basis. Thus, NISA may not have a distorting effect on resource use.

GRIP is basically designed to provide subsidies to farmers. Under the GRIP program, farmers are assured a target revenue per acre based upon the individual producer's past production and defined target prices for the grains or oilseeds grown. The program and payment method may encourage crop choices, input decisions and land use in a manner that maximizes GRIP benefits, but is detrimental to the environment (i.e., planting of grains or oilseeds instead of forage or pasture on marginal land). While Agriculture Canada (1991) has argued that "the program promotes environmental sustainability because it does not encourage production of one commodity over another", the large subsidies to be provided under GRIP and the fact that forage and pasture are not eligible crops under the program may actually encourage the cultivation of marginal lands and land degradation.

Fuel rebates and tax incentives have encouraged the use of large machinery, thereby making field obstacles (*viz.*, potholes and brush cover) nuisances to be eliminated. Large machinery also results in soil compaction, encourages farming of ever-larger fields, and discourages development of shelterbelts. Fuel rebates are paid on the basis of amount used, thereby encouraging excessive use of energy resources (and release of CO_2) while discouraging research into alternative energy sources for agriculture.

Fertilizer rebates have contributed to greater fertilizer use. This economic incentive causes farmers to disregard the deterioration of the soil's natural fertility; the natural fertility of the soil may have declined 30 to 50%, with the natural nitrogen-supplying capacity of the soil likely affected. Excessive concentrations of nitrates now affect many ground and surface waters. Chemical rebates and government programs that provide subsidies on a production-level basis encourage the use of agro-chemicals. Agro-chemicals contribute to the problem of water pollution by leaching into groundwater and by contaminating the surface waters, thereby affecting both water availability and its quality.

Farm improvement grants have encouraged the draining of wetlands and the clearing of brush, both of which have been considered "improvements". Federal mortgage interest rebate programs, such as the Farm Purchase Program, were targeted towards the purchase of cropland, thus exacerbating the decline of livestock operations and the conversion of unimproved land to annual crop production.

European Union

The Common Agricultural Policy (CAP) protects European farmers against competitive market forces. The CAP is characterized by intervention support prices, export subsidies, variable import levels, and domestic support payments. The intervention support price is the floor price at which intervention agencies must buy all eligible grains offered to them. The EU then exports the grain at lower prices, with the difference amounting to a direct subsidy to European farmers. Import levies are used to ensure that imported grains are priced at or higher than those produced in Europe. Finally, producers receive direct payments based on the area in production and historic yields, although they are required to set aside 10% of their land (in 1998–99) for conservation purposes.

The effect of these subsidies has been felt most at the intensive margin, with EU productivity increasing more than threefold since 1975 while yields in Canada and the USA have remained fairly flat. As a consequence, the EU has become a major player in export markets while the USA more than Canada has had trouble maintaining its share of export markets. Thus, between the early 1980s and late 1990s, the USA's share of exports has declined from about 48% to nearly 30% (Schmitz and Furtan 2000, p.84). This loss has driven the USA to increase production efforts and, thus, agricultural subsidy levels.

Agricultural Programs to Protect Nature and the Environment

Financial incentives: taxes

Financial incentives can be an effective method for achieving environmental protection goals, even on agricultural land. Penalties or fines can be assessed for activities that cause harm to the environment. For example, fines could be levied on farmers who illegally drain sloughs and burn associated uplands or on producers who do not have sufficient trash cover on fields during certain times of the year, thereby increasing the potential for soil erosion. Charges or taxes can be imposed to reflect the external damages from erosion. The problems with fines and charges are that (1) they may not be politically acceptable, (2) enforcement may be lax (based on past experience), and (3) they imply a reassignment of property rights away from agricultural producers.

Alternatively, charges or taxes can be levied on fuel and agro-chemicals. Higher fuel prices cause farmers to reduce tillage operations (which increases carbon storage and reduces soil erosion) and discourage them from cultivating marginal fields. Taxes on chemical inputs reduce fertilizer use, thereby lowering pollution of surface and ground water, and mitigate the adverse effects that chemical use has on populations of invertebrates and aquatic plants as well as on waterfowl (especially young). However, taxes on chemicals also make chemical (in contrast to tillage) fallow and reduced tillage systems less attractive for reducing soil erosion or increasing carbon storage. Again, this approach may not be politically acceptable, as it increases costs to farmers.

Conservation programs: contracts to protect land

Governments have increasingly adopted direct "performance" contracts as a way to protect the environment. The state enters into long-term contracts with agricultural producers to idle specified parcels of land or to restrict land use in environmentally sensitive areas. The Conservation Reserve Program of the 1985 US Farm Bill and subsequent Farm Bills employs this approach for taking marginal, environmentally sensitive land out of production. Initially, lands in the lowest soil capability classes plus those with a soil-loss tolerance rate of 3 tons per acre or less were eligible,[3] but this was changed in 1987 to include all lands with a high potential for degradation. Eligible lands were identified in each region, and competitive bids were designed to keep program costs down. However, since the US

Department of Agriculture established an upper limit on accepted bids, bids in subsequent rounds converged on the cap, thereby undermining the cost-saving potential of the bid system. In addition, the CRP affected enrolment in other conservation programs.

Another example is the Province of Saskatchewan's 1984 Permanent Cover Program. It provided financial incentives to farmers to take cropland out of production, planting it to trees or forages. The purpose of this Program was to reduce soil deterioration on high-risk lands that were under cultivation. Producers entered into 10- or 20-year agreements to "seed" land to permanent cover and maintain it, receiving $20 per acre to offset the costs of establishing permanent cover in addition to an annual payment. Initially, the government used a bidding procedure to determine how much producers would be paid (and thus which lands and producers participated), but, subsequently, payments were fixed. Given low program payments, economists criticized the program for encouraging enrolment of land that might not have been cropped in any case. If that is the case, then this program is simply another mechanism for transferring income to farmers.

Cross compliance
Unlike the aforementioned policies, cross (conservation) compliance explicitly recognizes that government subsidies are needed to enable farmers to keep pace with the standard of living enjoyed by the rest of society. It also recognizes that, in many cases, environmental programs simply offset incentives provided under other farm programs. There are two alternative approaches to cross compliance (Batie and Sappington 1986): (1) program payments are provided only if certain conservation standards are attained (the "red ticket approach"), or (2) program benefits increase as farmers meet or exceed specified (and increasingly higher) conservation thresholds (the "green ticket approach"). In essence, farmers are required to implement certain conservation practices in order to be eligible for subsidies from applicable present or future government agricultural programs.

The USA is the only country that has implemented cross compliance using a number of different approaches (in addition to the CRP). Under the "Swampbuster" and "Sodbuster" provisions of the 1985 Farm Bill, farmers become ineligible for agricultural program subsidies if they destroy wetlands (including swamps) or cultivate land that has not previously been producing annual crops. It does not aim to prevent land degradation by producers not eligible for farm subsidies. The Acreage Reduction Program (ARP) requires that farmers retire or "set-aside" land (and seed it with grasses to prevent erosion) each year in order to remain eligible for price supports and deficiency payments. The amount prescribed by the regulator to be set aside each year depends upon the perceived over-supply of various crops. The main objectives of the ARP have been to reduce supplies and, thereby, program payments rather than to reduce land degradation. However, the ARP has had little impact on supply due to "slippage" – the potential supply effects are dampened by farmers idling their least-productive but not necessarily most-erosive lands. Thus, the main effect of the set-aside program has been net budget reduction for the United States government.

Finally, there is the conservation compliance provisions that require those farming highly erodible lands to implement acceptable farm conservation plans in order to remain eligible for agricultural subsidies. The emphasis of conservation compliance is enhanced management. Examples of conservation plans include retaining a certain level of trash on fields during the winter months to retard soil erosion, contour plowing, grassed waterways to reduce water erosion, planting trees to mitigate wind erosion, and flexcropping to reduce tillage fallow or to include conservation practices (*viz.*, green manure) in management strategies that maximize returns and minimize risk. Conservation plans differ among regions and crop types. However, many problems with conservation compliance have already been identified. Examples of problems include: enforcement of trash levels may give rise to conflicts because local committees of farmers determine whether or not other farmers (their neighbors) are complying with the conservation plan; and implementation of flexcropping requires knowledgeable management personnel.

Canada has no conservation compliance provisions in its farm subsidy programs, although there is information about erosion rates on some lands. However, this information is based on physical attributes only and is incomplete; clearly, economic factors play a role in determining what lands to target for conservation measures – unless economic information is incorporated, it will be difficult to identify and implement cross compliance strategies that are not doomed to fail. In particular, it is necessary to identify lands that are subject to the most serious degradation problems (provide information on erosion rates for each parcel of land), determine the on-farm costs of erosion (i.e., estimate damage functions), and calculate the off-farm costs of erosion. Otherwise, the benefits of cross compliance could turn out to be lower than the costs.

Education and moral suasion

Education and awareness programs can be used to make agricultural producers more sensitive to the environmental impacts of their operations. In some cases, it is then possible to persuade farmers to enter into programs to conserve soil or maintain wildlife habitat either voluntarily or at lower cost than before. For example, some Saskatchewan farmers were persuaded to employ continuous cropping or rely on chemical as opposed to tillage summer fallow, even though this has resulted in lower net returns and higher risks. However, Canadian economists have argued that education and moral suasion have limited usefulness unless accompanied by adequate economic incentives (van Kooten and Schmitz 1992). Nonetheless, Canadian agricultural policies emphasize education and voluntary compliance.

Discussion

Overall, government agricultural programs have encouraged the cultivation of marginal lands and intensive practices that have resulted in environmental spillovers. Programs have contributed to water and wind erosion, and to the pollution of surface and ground waters. Specifically, water erosion affects the users of drinking water, water recreation sites, navigation channels, water storage facilities, commercial fishing sites, water conveyance facilities (i.e., drainage ditches for flood control and irrigation canals), power plants and water treatment facilities. Costs from water erosion result from an increase in sediment concentrations in water, which must be treated through the building of larger sedimentation basins, the addition of chemical coagulants, and the more frequent cleaning of filters. Wind erosion can result in damage to buildings, clogging of equipment, increased maintenance of roads and drains, and increased domestic cleaning and maintenance costs. Chemicals attached to the soil particles can have an adverse effect on health and safety, as can greater amounts of particulates in the air.

In addition to their land degradation and other environmental costs, agricultural subsidies in the developed world are detrimental in their impact upon both the livelihoods and land use of farmers in low-income countries. By reducing the prices these farmers receive for their own products, rich-country subsidies encourage farmers to sacrifice their own environments (lands) simply to produce enough to survive. Low output prices do not encourage farmers to be stewards of their land as land improvements yield little in the way of financial benefits. Thus, agricultural subsidies are like a two-edged sword, causing land degradation in both the country providing subsidies and in developing countries as well.

In response to the adverse effect of government programs on land use and the environment, rich countries (most notably the USA) have moved to implement stricter control over agricultural operations, including instituting environmental compliance provisions that require farmers to meet certain environmental standards in exchange for subsidy payments. Programs have increasingly included provisions to encourage conversion of cultivated land back into its "natural" state. Unfortunately, as demonstrated in the next section, programs to conserve the land and protect environmental amenities would have been unnecessary except for the high rates of subsidy on agricultural commodities.

9.2 ECONOMICS OF WETLANDS PRESERVATION

Wetlands loss is attributable, at least in part, to government agricultural policies that have encouraged agricultural producers to cultivate such areas. In particular, tax laws have encouraged farmers to use larger machinery than needed, thus enabling them to cultivate closer to ponds and also making ponds a nuisance (and, thus, something to be eliminated). In addition, government agricultural policies have enabled farmers to focus on a single enterprise; farmers with livestock need wetlands and the shelter of trees and shrubs, but farmers producing only grains do not. (If cattle densities are high, however, fencing or other management may be required to prevent trampling of eggs.) Further, input subsidies often encourage excessive use of chemicals that are harmful to wildlife, particularly young birds and the insects they feed on. In this section, therefore, we examine preservation of wetlands on the northern Great Plains of America. Wetlands are important because they produce ducks, which have value to hunters, and provide scenic amenities and biological diversity. They also provide habitat for bird species that may become endangered. Wetlands are also important to the agricultural ecology of dryland cropping regions, with their disappearance possibly signaling a reduction in the potential level of sustainable development.

Background

Migratory waterfowl constitute an important recreational resource, having value both in consumptive use (hunting) and nonconsumptive use (bird watching, existence value). In a major study of migratory waterfowl and wetlands nearly 30 years ago, Judd Hammack and Gardner Brown (1974) concluded that duck numbers and ponds in North America are well below economically optimal levels. Increasing wetlands areas and waterfowl numbers could substantially enhance social welfare. Since their study, wetland areas have declined, as have waterfowl numbers.

Migratory waterfowl generally winter in the southern parts of the continental USA, but major breeding grounds are found in Canada. One of the most important breeding grounds for the Central and Mississippi flyways is the pothole country of southern Alberta, Saskatchewan and Manitoba. Although the prairie pothole region is also a breeding ground for the Pacific Flyway, California's Central Valley and the McKenzie River delta in northern Canada are more important in this respect. The prairie pothole region of Canada accounts for between 25 and 60% of North American breeding populations, but it also supports other waterfowl and migratory birds. The wetlands in the region function as breeding, staging and molting habitats for numerous species of waterfowl, wading birds, colonial nesting birds and shorebirds. Rare, threatened and endangered bird species, such as migrating Whooping Cranes, Piping Plovers, the White Pelican, the Caspian Tern and the Trumpeter Swan, utilize prairie wetland regions. Wetlands also provide habitat for Arctic-nesting geese and other shoreline birds (that migrate to the Arctic) when they stop in the prairie pothole region for extended periods to fatten during spring migration.

It is the temporary and seasonal wetlands that are most important from the point of view of migrating birds and most species of waterfowl (except diving ducks), because these wetlands supply marsh and aquatic birds with food in the early spring. The proportional use of these wetlands by breeding waterfowl is greatest, because rapid warming of shallow wetlands in the spring results in the early development of invertebrate populations. Although accounting for less than 60% of wetlands area, these types of wetlands likely account for more than 80% of broods. Further, although generally dry during mid- to late-summer, these regions may fill with fall rains, providing important temporary habitat for fall migrant dabbling ducks. It is clear, therefore, that temporary wetlands located in bands around more permanent ponds or in singular low-lying basins in the prairie pothole region are important for North American duck production.

Temporary and seasonal wetlands are most affected by agricultural operations. Agricultural damage occurs as a result of mechanical disturbance at the margin and cultivation or drainage of the entire basin. Marginal disturbance by clearing, burning and cultivation results in the disappearance of natural woody or meadow vegetation and leads to increased erosion and infilling of the wetland basin. Cultivation of the entire wetland area could destroy the organic seal, thereby causing the area to drain more rapidly when re-flooded. Drainage and consolidation of sloughs and larger wetland areas alter the ecology of the region, make it difficult for plant and animal species to reproduce, and ruin its biological diversity. It also results in a less diverse and less visually appealing landscape. Agricultural disturbance of temporary wetlands results in a deterioration of marsh-edge vegetation, which is an essential component of waterfowl habitat, while heavy machinery and use of herbicides and pesticides reduces the populations of invertebrates and aquatic plants, which are important to waterfowl and other bird and animal species.

Although damage to wetland areas does not need to be permanent, a substantial degree of agricultural activity in and around potholes results in the irreversible loss of wetlands. Just as conversion to agriculture is the main reason why tropical forests have disappeared (see Chapter 12), agricultural reclamation is the main cause of wetlands decline in the prairie pothole region. Loss of wetlands contributes to global warming because such loss increases emissions of greenhouse gases (Chapter 13). Estimates suggest that between 15 and 75% of wetlands in Canada's prairie pothole region have been lost since pre-settlement. It also appears that about one-quarter of the wetland areas that existed in the early 1960s were lost by the early 1980s.

A 1988 survey of landowners in southeastern Saskatchewan indicated that approximately 58% of all the land that respondents considered to be feasible for draining or clearing in 1986 was subsequently drained or cleared; this land was considered to be good waterfowl habitat by the farmers themselves (van Kooten and Schmitz 1992). Respondents also indicated that 5.9% of their cultivated land had been in potholes within the previous 10 years. It is not known whether these results are representative of the prairie pothole region as a whole, but it does appear that these trends are the direct result of government incentive programs (see Figure 9.1). These losses in wetlands do not translate directly into a corresponding reduction in waterfowl numbers, because waterfowl will breed in the less-productive boreal forest wetlands north of the prairie ecosystem. However, changes in wetland characteristics have resulted in a different mix of waterfowl species, with geese having increased in numbers relative to most species of ducks.

The North American Waterfowl Management Plan (NAWMP) was formally initiated in 1986, with the goal of restoring North American waterfowl numbers to their mid-1970s level. This joint venture between Canada and the USA called for an outlay of US$1 billion over 15 years, with the USA paying 75% of program costs. One objective of NAWMP is to encourage agricultural producers to set aside agricultural land in order to permit the establishment of potholes for waterfowl habitat – that is, to maintain potholes and native uplands for nesting cover as opposed to putting them into crop production. Pilot projects under NAWMP were established in each of Canada's Prairie Provinces; since 1989, these have come under the umbrella of the Prairie Habitat Joint Venture, which is a component of NAWMP, and whose members constitute the Canadian implementing agencies. The focus of the Prairie Pothole Project has been primarily biological (monitoring duck populations and broods and determining wetland cover), with economic factors largely overlooked.

The Saskatchewan project and the pilot projects in Alberta and Manitoba are considered by NAWMP to have been a huge success. The strategies tested in the pilot projects are used to design land-management programs for the preservation of wetlands. In this section, economic components of managing land for habitat conservation are examined. While the management techniques adopted by the Prairie Habitat Joint Venture are worthwhile from a narrow point of view, there are more efficient means for preserving waterfowl habitat on private agricultural lands.

Wetlands Preservation on Private Agricultural Land

Government agricultural programs affect variables that impact on farmers' decisions to develop wetland areas.[4] The stock of wetlands on a farm is influenced by government policies that affect (1) crop revenue (e.g., price supports), (2) the cost of converting wetlands to agricultural production (improvement subsidies and tax write-offs), and (3) factor input costs (e.g., quicker depreciation that encourages use of larger equipment, thus enabling cultivation closer to ponds, and input rebates). In many cases, wetlands provide positive benefits to farmers. For example, wetlands and their associated uplands and brush might provide water and shelter for livestock and reduce soil erosion. Wetlands could be useful during years of drought and might provide private benefits from hunting. All told, these private benefits might have a positive value to farmers, but, clearly, the private value, say K, takes into account only private benefits, since extra-market values or spillover benefits are ignored by the landowner. For some farmers, the value of wetlands could well be zero, in which case farmers will maintain some wetlands and associated uplands as long as land quality is sufficiently low or conversion costs sufficiently high.

The effect of government programs and extra-market benefits can be analyzed with the aid of Figure 9.3. All axes measure positive values. The abscissa in panel (a) represents cultivated land of decreasing quality. Marginal benefits of converting unimproved land fall as more marginal land is brought under cultivation. This is indicated by the declining marginal benefit of crop production curve labeled MB_C. Marginal benefit functions are translated into marginal cost curves in panel (d) via panels (b) and (c); this is done by projecting a line from MC_W through W_0, say, to the 45° line in panel (c), across to the 45° line in panel (d) and upwards through C_0 to MB_C. (By way of symmetry, the figure illustrates what is meant by opportunity cost, with subscripts C and W referring to cultivated and wetland, respectively.) Thus, the marginal benefits of reduced cultivation (MB_C) become the marginal costs of increasing wetland area (MC_W), where MB_C is comprised of the crop revenues minus production costs, minus an annualized cost of bringing unimproved land or wetlands into crop production. For convenience, the marginal private benefit of retaining land as wetlands is assumed to be constant and equal to K. It is equal to the marginal opportunity cost of cultivating or cropping the land (MC_C).

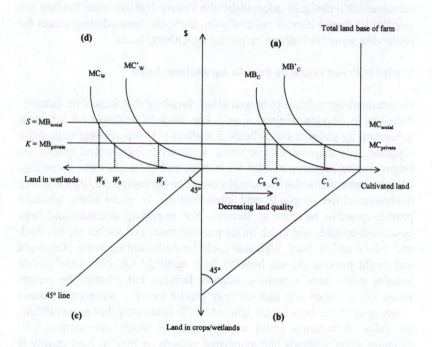

Figure 9.3: Effects of government programs on farm-level land use

With no government programs and assuming land in wetlands has a private value of K, C_0 amount of land is cultivated and W_0 is left unimproved or in wetlands and associated uplands. If there are private benefits to retaining wetlands ($MB_W=K=0$), the amount of land that is cultivated is determined by the intersection of MB_C and the horizontal axis; likewise, the amount in wetlands is determined by the intersection of MC_W and the abscissa.

Government programs affect revenues, production costs and conversion costs in ways discussed above. The effect of government programs that favor crop production, either through direct subsidies or through rebates or tax write-offs that lower factor costs, is to shift the marginal benefit curve for crop production to MB'_C in panel (a) or increase the marginal cost of wetlands to MC'_W in panel (d). The amount of land in crop production will be greater than it would be in the absence of government programs, C_1 rather than C_0, while wetlands area will be lower, W_1 compared to W_0.

What about the divergence between social and private costs in the maintenance of waterfowl habitat? It may well be the case that society values wetlands more highly than does the farmer. Suppose, in Figure 9.3, that S represents the value of wetlands to the farmer plus their value to hunters, environmentalists, neighboring farmers, and others in society (the off-farm benefits); the marginal benefits to others are given by S–K, which is assumed to be constant. In this case, society would wish to maintain an amount W_S of wetlands and only have C_S amount of the farmer's land in crop production. To encourage the farmer to take into account the off-farm benefits of retaining wetlands, it is necessary for the authority to provide her with a subsidy of amount S–K to get her to preserve the desired amount of wetlands. It is clear that, when farmers are subsidized to produce crops or bring uncultivated land into crop production, the amount of the subsidy will need to be greater. The reason is that the subsidy to preserve wetlands will also have to offset any payments that provide an opposing incentive.

Farmers could be encouraged to preserve wetlands even if government support payments continue to favor development of land for crop production through environmental compliance. Further, it might also be possible to get policymakers to take into account the off-farm benefits of wetlands preservation through institutional arrangements that permit farmers to collect revenues from nonagricultural users (e.g., duck hunters), although this still ignores many nonmarket values (Chapter 4).

Wetlands Preservation: A Case Study

As an example of a wetlands preservation project, the Prairie Pothole Project in southeastern Saskatchewan is briefly examined. The project was started in 1986. Baseline waterfowl population and wetland densities for 1987 were determined for a 432-square-mile study region, divided into a project area and a control area. The purpose of the baseline evaluation was to determine if a significant difference could be detected in waterfowl population responses between the project and the control areas – to determine if the cumulative effects of treatments during the five-year study were effective. Project treatments consisted of license agreements for wetlands (minimum 15 acres of water with an equal or greater area of uplands); lease agreements on good quality agricultural land on which an area was seeded to dense nesting cover and enclosed with a predator fence; and hayfield agreements.

By comparing duck populations on the control and project sites, it should have been possible to determine if the treatments (agreements with landowners) were effective. On the project area, there should have been an overall increase in duck populations due to raised recruitment rates and subsequent homing of surviving ducks, provided that adequate water was available to hold breeding pairs. However, the evidence was only suggestive of success or inconclusive at worse, and certainly not statistically significant. Obvious problems exist.

1. The duration of the study was deemed too short to permit evaluation of waterfowl trends. Since the years 1986 and 1987 were required to establish treatments, their effects were not operative until 1988, leaving only three years for evaluation.
2. A drought cycle that started in 1986–87 persisted for much of the study, leading to no increments in duck populations.
3. The project was unable to lease sufficient uplands for habitat preservation to counter the rate of loss due to clearing and draining of land.
4. Ducks may simply have migrated to more productive wetlands despite efforts at enhancement as the study region constituted only a very small part of duck breeding habitat.

Not taken into account in the analysis are scenic values (diverse landscape), environmental benefits (e.g., reduced wind erosion), benefits from viewing and photographing wildlife, and preservation values. That is, wetlands have value to nonhunters because they provide scenic amenities and ecological diversity, although these values may be difficult to measure (Chapter 4). Some studies suggest that preservation values for wild game may be four times as great as is their value for hunting. Thus, if the value of migratory waterfowl for hunting is assumed to be between $15 and $25 per bird (Prins et al. 1990), preservation plus nonconsumptive use values could range from $60 to $100 per bird, for a total value of between $85 and $125 per bird (see also Loomis and White 1996; Loomis and Giraud 1997). This implies that waterfowl habitat may be quite valuable (although it is still necessary to convert bird values into habitat or land values).

One policy to retain wetlands is to provide subsidies to farmers. There is evidence to suggest that payments to agricultural producers to maintain wetlands are an effective method for preserving them, but only if such payments are adequate and cover the farmers' opportunity costs for keeping land out of agricultural production. While agricultural production subsidies are an important contributing factor to the loss of wetlands, incentive payments provided under NAWMP simply substitute for these subsidies. The Canadian experience indicates that payments offered farmers have been inadequate; indeed, payments were sometimes provided for preserving wetlands and associated uplands (i.e., nesting areas) that would likely not have been brought into production in any event, because agricultural operations on these lands would have been difficult or impossible (van Kooten 1993b). Canada has no definitive wetlands policy, and it does not require landowners to obtain permits to dredge or fill in wetlands (as is required by the 404 Permit Program of the US Federal Clean Water Act). While Canadian law prevents farmers from draining sloughs, except for the purpose of consolidating sloughs on a single field, these regulations are not enforced.

Drought is a problem for wetlands preservation. An important policy consideration is that it may be possible to provide incentives for wetlands preservation during the drought cycle only. If that is the case, substantial sums of money can be saved by appropriate policy design.

While NAWMP-funded research in the pothole region of western Canada has focused primarily on biological aspects of habitat preservation (identifying suitable wetlands areas, monitoring populations, etc.) and communications (*viz.*, public relations and education), economics has been all but ignored. While economics may not be important to many biologists, it would seem that economics would be a major concern to those environmentalists and taxpayers who contribute to NAWMP. Given the scarcity of environmental dollars, it is necessary to ensure that the greatest potential increase in waterfowl populations be obtained at the least cost.

9.3 THE ECONOMICS OF SOIL CONSERVATION

Despite the problem of soil erosion having been well documented worldwide (Anderson and Thampapillai 1990), farmers have been slow to change their agronomic behavior in order to slow erosion. There are a number of reasons why this has been the case.

- Increased yields due to technical change have offset or masked reductions in yield resulting from soil erosion.
- Soils in the Great Plains region of North America are not susceptible to the rapid degradation that occurs in the shallower soils of the tropical rain forests. As a result, one might expect farmers in North America to be less sensitive to land degradation than those in tropical regions, *ceteris paribus*, but producers in the tropics may face institutional constraints and incentives that cause them to deplete the soil faster.

These include less secure land tenure, higher discount rates, lack of
access to credit, and so on.

- As argued in section 9.1, government agricultural programs often have the
  unwanted effect of encouraging farmers to cultivate marginal lands –
  lands that might be most susceptible to wind and water erosion.
- Finally, degradation of soils results in on-farm costs and off-farm costs.
  The former cost is measured in terms of the forgone future productivity
  due to erosion today, and is borne by the farmer. Economic research
  indicates that these on-farm costs are often incorrectly measured and may
  be small (Walker and Young 1986; Weisensel 1988). The spillover costs
  of erosion are difficult to quantify, but may be large, because, when soil
  erodes into water systems or the air, society bears the costs associated not
  only with soil particles but also with the chemicals that are attached to the
  soil. Together, the private plus spillover (on-farm plus off-farm) costs
  constitute the social costs of soil erosion. However, farmers lack the
  incentive to change their practices because they do not incur the off-site
  costs of erosion.

When assessing soil erosion damages, it is necessary to take the
following into account:

- The opportunity cost of changing agronomic practices requires that crop
  yields be compared using the "with–without" principle (recall Chapter 6).
- Yield penalties that result from using conservation practices should not be
  confused with the assessment of erosion damage. The former are the cost
  of investing in soil conservation, with return expected at a future date,
  while the latter are the damages of permitting soil erosion. If this
  distinction is ignored, the cost estimates have little economic meaning.
- It is necessary to distinguish between *reparable* and *residual* yield
  damages. Reparable yield damage refers to fertility lost due to mining
  of the soil that can be restored by an increase in fertilizer and other
  inputs (*revolving fund*). Residual yield damage refers to erosion that
  affects the *conservable flow*; residual yield damage results in reduced
  moisture infiltration, diminished rooting zone and weakened soil
  structure, all of which reduce yields.
- Finally, an economic assessment of soil erosion must separate the impacts
  of erosion from those of technology (see below).

Much of the controversy in soil conservation research is due to the
various definitions of conservation advocated by opposing groups. Some
argue that conservation is wise use of the soil resource, and others that
conservation is the maintenance of the resource for future generations. Both
of these views on conservation are based on value judgments regarding the

meaning of the words *wise* and *maintenance*. Furthermore, neither definition provides a clear method by which to quantify conservation: How does one measure "wise use of soil"? A more concrete and rigorous definition of conservation is required (see Chapter 7).

In this section, we examine the economics of soil conservation/erosion in greater detail. We begin, however, by briefly considering physical aspects of soil erosion.

Physical Aspects of Soil Erosion

Wind and water are the main agents of soil erosion. The amount of soil they can carry away is influenced by speed (the faster wind or water moves, the more soil it can erode) and plant cover, since plants protect the soil and, in their absence, wind and water can do much more damage. Plants provide protective cover on the land and prevent soil erosion by:

- slowing down water as it flows over the land (runoff), thereby allowing much of the rain to soak into the ground;
- binding the soil through the roots and preventing it from being washed away;
- breaking the impact of rain before it hits the soil, thus reducing its ability to erode;
- slowing down the flow of water in wetland areas, thus preventing erosion.

The loss of protective vegetation through deforestation, overgrazing, plowing and fire makes soil vulnerable to being swept away by wind and water. In addition, over-cultivation and compaction (from heavy equipment) cause the soil to lose its structure and cohesion, so that it is more susceptible to erosion. Erosion will remove the topsoil ("A horizon") first. Once this nutrient-rich layer of soil is gone, plants will still grow in the "B horizon" or even in the subsoil, but their productivity and ability to grow is much diminished. Without soil and plants the land becomes desert-like and unable to support life, a process referred to as desertification.

To understand the causes of soil erosion, we must be aware of the political and economic factors affecting land users. High rural population density has been cited as a reason for severe erosion. As land becomes increasingly degraded and less productive, subsistence farmers are often forced to further over-use land to meet their food requirements. The intensive agriculture and overgrazing that follow usually cause greater degradation. Soil erosion can be seen as both a symptom of underdevelopment, and as a cause of underdevelopment. A reduced ability to produce, invest one's profit and increase productivity contributes to increasing poverty, and can lead to desertification, drought, floods and famine.

On commercial farmlands, overstocking, mono-cropping and the plowing of marginal lands unsuitable for cultivation has led to soil erosion and desertification. Frequently these practices have been unwittingly encouraged by the state offering subsidies that made it profitable to exploit the land in the short term.

Remote sensing has been used to evaluate the magnitude of soil degradation globally (Oldeman et al. 1992). Land can be classified according to its land quality class (LQC), with lands in categories I, II and III having the highest potential and least constraints for sustainable agriculture, while those in the highest categories (VII, VIII and IX) are considered highly fragile and extremely vulnerable to degradation, and thus not fit for sustained agricultural production (Eswaran et al. 2001). Land in categories IV, V and VI is considered to be at risk from high rates of soil erosion, but such lands can be protected by implementing one or more of the practices indicated above (including in combination). An indication of the importance of the land quality classes is provided in Table 9.1, while estimates of land area that could be considered vulnerable are provided in Table 9.2. The latter estimates were determined by overlaying global maps of population density with soil vulnerability maps (Eswaran et al. 2001).

Preventing soil erosion requires political, economic and technical changes. While economic aspects are discussed below, technical changes include:

- using contour plowing and wind breaks;
- leaving unplowed grass strips between plowed land;
- making sure that there are always plants growing on the soil, and that the soil is rich in humus or organic matter (decaying plant and animal remains), which is the "glue" that binds the soil particles together and helps prevent erosion;
- employing minimum or even zero tillage in place of conventional tillage in crop production;
- avoiding overgrazing and the over-use of croplands;
- allowing indigenous plants to grow along the river banks instead of plowing and planting crops right up to the water's edge;
- encouraging biological diversity by planting several different types of plants together; and
- conserving wetlands.

Table 9.1: Land Quality Classes and Population, Latitudes 72°N to 57°S

Land quality class (LQC)	Land area mil. Km²	%	Population millions	%
I	4.1	3.2	337	5.9
II	6.5	5.0	789	13.7
III	5.9	4.5	266	4.6
IV	5.1	3.9	654	11.4
V	21.4	16.3	1,651	28.8
VI	17.2	13.2	675	11.8
VII	11.7	8.9	639	11.1
VIII	37.0	28.3	103	1.8
IX	21.8	16.7	625	10.9
Global	**130.6**	**100.0**	**5,759**	**100.0**

Source: Eswaran et al. (2001)

Table 9.2: Estimated Nonsustainable and Vulnerable Land Area and Affected Population, Latitudes 72°N to 57°S

Vulnerability class	Area of severe degradation million km²	% of global area	Population Affected Millions	% of global
Low	14.60	11.2	1,085	18.9
Moderate	13.61	10.5	915	15.9
High	7.12	5.5	393	6.8
Very high	7.91	6.1	255	4.4
TOTAL	**43.24**	**33.3**	**2,648**	**46.0**

Source: Eswaran et al. (2001)

It is often assumed that soil erosion of any kind cannot be maintained indefinitely, but soil does regenerate to some extent and soil erosion can take place as long as it remains below the rate of natural regeneration or soil formation. The rate of natural regeneration is referred to as the *T factor*. To determine a "tolerable" level of soil loss, one that equals the rate of natural regeneration, the Soil Conservation Service of the US Department of Agriculture has calculated the rate at which the subsoil in a soil profile becomes topsoil. For most deep soils this occurs at the rate of one-thirtieth of an inch (0.85 mm) or five tons per acre (11.2 tonnes/ha) per year. Soils that are shallow to bedrock or groundwater, or that have some other obstruction to the rooting zone, can tolerate much lower levels of soil loss, perhaps only one ton per acre (2.25 tonnes/ha) per year (six-thousandths of an inch or 0.17 mm per year). In tropical areas, for example, soil forms at lower rates of about 0.01 to 0.50 mm per year. Soils covered with natural vegetation lose less than 0.01 mm of topsoil per year on the North American Great Plains, but 0.02 to 1.00 mm of topsoil annually in the tropics. Converting grasslands to row crops increases erosion by a factor of 20 to 100 in the tropics and by as much as 300 times on the Great Plains, while tillage summer fallow increases erosion by an additional factor of 5 to 6 over row crops. Conversion of forests to row crops increases erosion by a factor of 20 to 1,000 times, with the higher rates occurring in the tropics. The problem with converting forests to crops is that the rate of soil formation is also reduced. Naturally, by exceeding the tolerable soil-loss rate the productivity and fertility of the soil is threatened, in some cases jeopardizing its ability to support vegetative cover.

User Cost and Opportunity Cost of Soil Erosion

The economist recognizes that it is technologically difficult, and seldom economical, to keep soils as productive as they were during the first few years after breaking the virgin sod. Thus, the cost of soil degradation is to be determined by comparing the offending cropping practices with the best soil-conserving alternative. This is the *opportunity cost* concept. What then is meant by the *user cost* of soil erosion? The user cost of any natural resource is simply the present value of future sacrifices implied by current resource use. The user cost of soil erosion is the impact of lost soil on future profits via the level of stock – it is the present value of future revenues that are lost when a unit of soil is used today. How, then, does user cost relate to the opportunity cost of soil erosion? This is illustrated with the aid of Figure 9.4.

Many researchers who have provided estimates of the on-farm (or private) costs of soil erosion have actually assessed the user cost of soil erosion. This is done by assuming that production can occur without soil erosion. Suppose that R_0 in Figure 9.4 represents the discounted value of the path of net returns from growing a crop on a field where topsoil depth is somehow continuously replenished so that topsoil depth is maintained at its existing level, which is admittedly unrealistic. Assume that R_1 represents the discounted returns of an alternative cropping strategy, say, continuous row cropping. (Further returns end at the dashed vertical line, indicating that identical planning horizons are used.) The on-farm cost of the cropping system represented by R_1 is then given as R_0-R_1, but this is *not* the on-farm cost of soil erosion: it is the total user cost of soil erosion (which is discussed below). Farmers do not, however, make decisions based on total user cost. Since producers are able to switch from more erosive to less erosive cropping systems at any point in their planning horizon, they consider the *marginal user cost*, a concept discussed in conjunction with Figure 9.5 below.

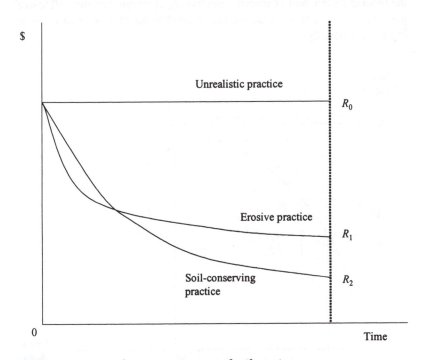

Figure 9.4: User and opportunity costs of soil erosion

Estimates of total user costs (R_0–R_1) have ranged between \$468 million per year for the Canadian Prairies to \$1 billion per year for Saskatchewan alone. Similar estimates for the United States are quite a bit lower, ranging from three-hundredths of one percent to one-tenth of one percent of total crop revenue per year. While it is not always clear as to how researchers obtain these estimates, they are estimates of user costs, and such estimates are sensitive to assumptions regarding rates of soil erosion, starting topsoil depths, the rate of discount used, and grain prices. Again, for Saskatchewan, empirical evidence suggests that total user costs range between \$0.87/ha and \$168.83/ha per year (Weisensel 1988).

The correct measure of the on-farm or opportunity cost of soil erosion is determined by comparing the "offensive" crop practice R_1 with the best available, soil-conserving practice, say R_2, where R_1 and R_2 refer to the respective discounted values of the paths of net returns for the two agronomic practices. The difference R_1–R_2 constitutes the on-farm or opportunity cost of soil erosion. If $R_1-R_2<0$, then there is an on-farm cost from using the erosive crop practice; if, on the other hand, $R_1-R_2>0$, then the recommended, soil-conserving practice R_2 is worse than the "offensive" practice R_1, and farmers who choose to employ the erosive techniques are behaving rationally.

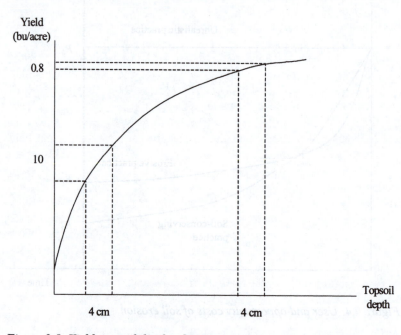

Figure 9.5: Yield–topsoil depth relation

A biological relationship between yield and topsoil depth is illustrated in Figure 9.5. The positive intercept on the yield axis indicates that it may be possible to achieve some crop growth even if topsoil depth is zero, because some plants are able to grow in subsoil, albeit not very well. This is an empirical issue, and the arguments presented here do not change if the yield–soil depth function passes through the origin. The degree of growth, if any, differs by soil types, location and plants. More important, as topsoil depth increases, the increase in yield from additional topsoil declines – the "law of diminishing returns". The reason is that, once the depth of topsoil exceeds the rooting zone, additional topsoil is not required for crop growth. The yield–topsoil depth relation drawn in Figure 9.5 also indicates that there is a physical/biological yield limit, and the functional form demonstrates this by the fact that yield reaches an asymptote.

At higher levels of topsoil depth, the curve is flat, indicating that a rather substantial decrease in topsoil (say 4 cm) will not have a large impact on yields (a 0.8 bushels per acre reduction, say) – the marginal product of topsoil depth is very small. When topsoil is relatively abundant, as it is on quality farmland, the value of the marginal product of soil is practically zero. At lower levels of topsoil depth, the yield–depth relationship is steep. In this case, a 4 cm reduction in available soil depth will result in a substantial yield loss (a 10 bu/ac reduction, say); the marginal product of soil depth is high.

Figure 9.5 can also be used to clarify what is meant by the marginal user cost of soil erosion. As a field is cultivated, the farmer notices that production slides down the yield–topsoil depth curve. Additional losses of soil entail greater yield losses – the marginal user cost of soil erosion rises. As production slides further down the curve to the left, and marginal user cost increases, the farmer's incentive to practice conservation on that field rises. The losses become sufficiently large to warrant expenditures to prevent them. As long as farmers are in the flat portion of the yield–topsoil depth function, they have little incentive to incur outlays to prevent soil loss; but, when production occurs in the lower ranges of the relationship, the benefits of soil conservation increase. This explains why economists, for example, have found that farmers are unwilling to employ chemical fallow when topsoil depths are adequate, but that they would adopt this soil-conserving method when topsoil depths decline to a much lower level. It appears that farmers in North America and Europe do behave rationally; the evidence indicates that, for these farmers, topsoil depths are currently at a level at which the marginal user costs of soil erosion are insufficient to warrant adoption of soil conservation practices (van Kooten et al. 1990).

Soil Erosion, Depletion of Soil Nutrients and Technical Change

Some argue that the cost of soil erosion can be measured by the increased cost of fertilizer required to replace lost soil fertility, but this is incorrect from an economic theory standpoint. The problem is complex. It is important, first off, to distinguish two factors related to soil: the depth of soil needed to accommodate the roots of plants, and the quality of soil, which refers to its natural fertility (*in situ* nitrogen and other nutrients) and its tilth (organic matter content). Depletion of replaceable soil nutrients concerns loss of organic matter and natural soil fertility, while soil erosion concerns soil depth. It is possible to destroy soil quality while maintaining adequate topsoil depth (e.g., through excessive tillage), but it would likely be difficult to maintain soil quality while losing soil.

We observe that farmers tend to use more fertilizer on fields that have greater rooting zone capability (depth). Agricultural producers will expend more inputs and effort on "better" quality fields. Economic theory suggests that, as the marginal product of topsoil depth rises due to a loss of soil, the amount of fertilizer (and other inputs) used by a rational agricultural producer declines, *ceteris paribus*. Here is why: Assume that all factor prices (r_i, where subscript i denotes the type of input) and output price (P) remain constant, and that marginal product falls as input use increases. Consider the following well-known equilibrium condition:

$$(9.1) \qquad \frac{P \times MP_{SoilDepth}}{r_{SoilDepth}} = \frac{P \times MP_{Fertilizer}}{r_{Fertilizer}}$$

where MP_i refers to the marginal physical product of input i. A loss of soil depth implies an increase in its marginal physical product. Assume that the marginal product of fertilizer is unaffected by the available soil depth, which is a reasonable assumption if there is sufficient topsoil but less realistic when soil depth falls to more critical levels. Then only a reduction in fertilizer use will increase its marginal product, thereby maintaining the equality in equation (9.1).

The situation is somewhat different if we consider soil quality, as represented by the amount of fertilizer available in the soil. In that case, the shadow price of soil fertility is given by $P \times MP_{Fertilizer}$ – the marginal value product of fertilizer. In equation (9.1), as natural soil fertility is depleted, the marginal product of fertilizer increases (because marginal product increases as input use falls). It is then necessary to increase the amount of applied fertilizer in order to get its marginal physical productivity back down and restore equilibrium in (9.1) (i.e., get back on the efficient production expansion path).

Only if the marginal product of fertilizer is affected by changes in topsoil depth can changes in fertilizer applications be used to provide information about the costs of soil erosion. However, in this situation, measurement is complex, and it is certainly not true that all of the increase in fertilizer costs can be attributed solely to the reduction in topsoil depth. Furthermore, if soil depth falls, thereby increasing the marginal productivity of soil, equality (9.1) suggests that, rather than fertilizer applications increasing, they should be reduced. This makes sense, since farmers are more likely to apply greater amounts of fertilizer on more productive (deeper) soils.

Residual versus Reparable Yield Damage and Welfare Effects

If the marginal physical product of fertilizer is unaffected by topsoil depth (fertilizer and soil depth are independent in production), farmers would not respond to changes in topsoil depth, except to reduce fertilizer use (as indicated above). However, for other aspects of the soil, farmers might well respond to reductions in soil quality by increasing their expenditures on inputs. This is illustrated in Figure 9.6, where soil quality rather than topsoil depth is represented on the abscissa. Y_0 represents the yield function, given constant input use (input use is unaffected by soil quality), and Y_R represents the restored yield curve (inputs such as fertilizer and manure from off-site replace *in situ* resources). Suppose that soil quality declines from Q_A to Q_B as a result of agronomic practices that degrade the soil, whether such practices are avoidable or not. Yields will decline from Y_A to Y_{B0}, which represents the total yield damage from soil degradation, given that farm practices and/or input use do not change in response to the decline in soil quality. An amount $Y_{B1}-Y_{B0}$ of the lost yield can be recovered by changing farming practices and/or input use. This is the *reparable* yield damage. For example, as long as there is adequate topsoil, even losses in organic matter can be overcome by one or two years of "green manure" – growing a crop that is then plowed under. This leaves the amount Y_A-Y_{B1} that represents the *residual* yield damage.

With regard to the welfare effects, these can be analyzed with the aid of Figure 9.7. Suppose that the component of soil quality of interest is nitrogen (N). Let VMP_A and VMP_B represent the values of the marginal products of N at soil qualities Q_A and Q_B, respectively. Let N^*_i and N'_i represent, respectively, the optimal nitrogen required in production and the pre-seeding nitrogen in soil for soil qualities i ($=A$ or B). The difference between the optimal and available N can be made up using artificial or inorganic fertilizers.

The net welfare effects of lost production due to a decline in soil quality from Q_A to Q_B are found by finding welfare at Q_A and subtracting that at Q_B:

$$W(Q_A) = \text{area}(OacN^*_A - N'_A ecN^*_A) \text{ and } W(Q_B) = \text{area}(ObdN^*_B - N'_B fdN^*_B)$$

Then, $\Delta W = W(Q_A) - W(Q_B) = \text{area}(N^*_B dcN^*_A - acdb - N'_B feN'_A)$.

This is the net residual yield damage caused by a decline in soil productivity; the damage is also equal to $P(Y_A-Y_{B0}) = VMP_A-VMP_{B0}$ (from Figure 9.6), where P is the price of output. It is difficult to show the welfare effect associated with the reparable damage via Figure 9.7, because this assumes that inorganic fertilizer use remains at $(N^*_A - N'_A)$, not that the optimal amount of fertilizer use is N^*_A. However, the marginal welfare cost is given by $P(Y_{B1}-Y_{B0}) = VMP_{B1}-VMP_{B0}$.

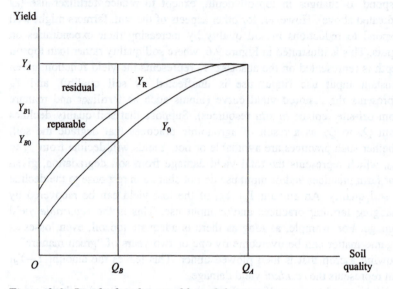

Figure 9.6: Residual and reparable soil damage

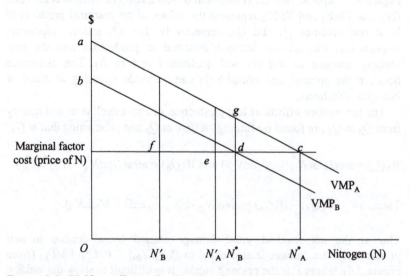

Figure 9.7: Welfare effects of reduced soil quality on fertilizer use

The change in welfare between the two situations depends upon how much nitrogen is in the soil under Q_A versus Q_B. Further, whether use of inorganic fertilizer from off-site will rise or fall depends on the size of $(N^*_A - N'_A)$ relative to $(N^*_B - N'B)$. If $(N^*_A - N'_A) = (N^*_B - N'B)$ or $(N^*_A - N^*_B) = (N'_A - N'B)$, then the welfare loss is given by area(*acdb*).

Economic Assessment of Erosion Damage with Technological Advance

Agricultural yields have increased in spite of soil erosion, and this persuades some farmers that erosion damage is insignificant and that there is little need to adopt soil-conserving agronomic practices (Walker and Young 1986). Technology has boosted absolute crop yields in spite of declines in topsoil depth. However, the yield loss due to soil erosion – the loss farmers should be using in their conservation decisions – is the difference between the potential yields they could have if they had used conservation techniques and actual yields. This argument is illustrated using Figure 9.8.

In the figure, farmers are initially assumed to be on production function Y_0, producing at A. The function Y_1 represents the production function at some time in the future. Technical change enables the farmer to produce more wheat, say, for every level of topsoil depth. The way in which the two functions are drawn indicates that technical change provides a greater yield benefit on fields with more topsoil ($AA'>BB'$). As a result of soil erosion, from topsoil depth D_0 to D_1, the farmer finds that yields have declined, say, from 58 bu/ac (point A) to 53 bu/ac (point B'), or by 5 bu/ac. The conclusion that one draws is that erosion damage has been partly offset by technical change. However, this conclusion is wrong unless all technical change is induced by concern over erosion – that technical change is endogenous. If this is not the case but technical change is exogenous, the correct comparison is between points A' (70 bu/ac) and B' (53 bu/ac), or 17 bu/ac in this illustration. This is the correct measure of the erosion yield damage. With exogenous technical change, it is inappropriate to conclude that technical progress partly offsets erosion damage.

Farmers and policymakers can be lulled into a false belief that technical progress will continue to offset erosion damage. In the early years, agricultural producers will move along a path from A to C (Figure 9.8) by continuing to use erosive agronomic methods. With conservation practices, they would move along a path from A to K instead. Technical progress will continue, shifting the production function to Y_2, but continued use of erosive practices at point C will cause a movement along path C to F. In this case, yields decline in spite of technological improvements. Conservation could, however, provide a yield increase, as is indicated by the movement from *C* to *E*.

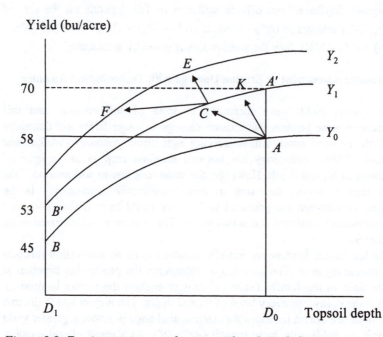

Figure 9.8: Erosion assessment damage with technical change

Technical change that relates to soil erosion can be divided into two categories. Technical change can be exogenous to erosion; in other words, enhancements in production take place independent of soil erosion. On the other hand, induced technical change can take place in order to remedy soil erosion. Exogenous technical change can be divided into land-neutral, land-complementary, and land-substituting technical change.

Let the crop production function be

(9.2) $Y = f(D)$

where Y is crop yield and D is topsoil depth. Then land-neutral or additive technical change results in the production function (9.2) shifting up by the same constant amount for all soil depths, so that it can now be represented by

(9.3) $Y = f(D) + A(t)$

where $A(t)$ represents technical change as a function of time. With land-neutral technical change, the true economic damage from soil erosion is no different than it would be if no technical change had occurred, but it is still possible for farmers to experience increased yields even though erosion has occurred. An example of land-neutral technical change is provided by the introduction of large farm equipment, which allowed producers to farm a larger area.

Land-complementary or multiplicative technical change is mathematically illustrated by modifying (9.2) as follows:

(9.4) $Y_t = B(t) \, f(D)$

where $B(t) > 1.0$ is the technical change factor. An example of land-complementary technical change is provided by improvements in crop cultivars. This type of technical progress tends to increase yields for greater topsoil depths. Land-complementary technical change results in potential costs of erosion that are greater than would have been the case if the technical change had not taken place.

Land-substituting technical change means that there are greater increases in yields at shallower soil depths. An example of this type of technical advance is provided by tillage improvements that conserve soil moisture. Land-substituting technical change actually decreases the potential costs of soil erosion.

The economic assessment of erosion damage, given the presence of erosion-induced technical change, is quite different from that encountered in any of the other categories. In this case, damage assessment should be based on yield with conservation and unchanged technology versus yield with erosion and induced technology. Therefore, the induced technology actually offsets some of the costs of soil erosion.

With this overview of technical change and its impacts upon the economic assessment of erosion, it is necessary to consider the following questions: What type of technical change has been most prevalent in agriculture? Is technical change different in its impact on crop yields and erosion damages in different regions of the world? The vast majority of technical change in North America, and likely elsewhere in the world, has been exogenous with respect to soil depth, since breeding to prevent lodging, improvements in inorganic fertilizers, and research into new cultivars have not been a reaction to eroding soils. Furthermore, it appears that the vast majority of the research in North America has been land complementary or multiplicative. Plant breeding research, among other objectives, strives to develop cultivars with greater genetic potential for converting available plant nutrients and moisture to harvestable grain. This, in itself, is not proof that technical change has been multiplicative, but empirical evidence does support this conclusion. A survey of 272 farmers in the Palouse region of southeastern Washington and northwestern Idaho indicated that they expected future yield increases on deeper soils to be three times those expected on shallower topsoils (Walker and Young 1986).

The previous discussion certainly indicates that the economic assessment of erosion damage is complex. Failure to heed the impact of technical change, confusion regarding the production function from which the yield costs are measured, and/or failure to take into proper account opportunity cost will undoubtedly lead to inaccurate estimates of the true costs of soil erosion.

Is Land Degradation a Problem?

Now consider the question: Is agricultural land degradation a problem sufficient enough to demand government intervention? To answer this question, we consider the on-farm and off-farm costs of soil degradation.

On-site costs

From an economic perspective, the on-farm costs of soil erosion (the main form of soil degradation) have been shown to be rather small. Other forms of soil degradation, such as loss of organic matter and salinity, are related to soil erosion, because the factors that contribute to the latter (*viz.*, monoculture and tillage summer fallow) also contribute to other forms of degradation. To some extent, each of these forms of degradation is reversible, with the degree of reversibility decreasing from organic matter loss to salinity to soil erosion. Loss of natural soil fertility is also related to organic matter, salinity and soil erosion, but artificial fertilizers can be brought from off-site in order to alleviate this problem and green manure can be used to restore lost organic matter.

The economics of soil degradation have been characterized by inadequate empirical evidence and/or improper economic reasoning. As Pierre Crosson and Nathan Rosenberg write in the September 1989 issue of *Scientific American*:

> The USA is the only country in the world that has *reasonably* accurate and comprehensive estimates of soil erosion and its effect on productivity. Those estimates suggest that if current rates of cropland erosion prevail *for 100 years*, crop yields will be from 3 to 10 percent lower than they would be otherwise. Yield increases (resulting from technology) that are modest by historical standards would much more than compensate for such a loss ...

Estimates of erosion have been made for other parts of the world ... [but] these evaluations have little scientific merit ... Apocalyptic scenarios ought to be evaluated sceptically. (p.128)

An example of empirical research is provided by Weisensel and van Kooten (1990), who used an optimal control approach to estimate soil erosion time paths. They used actual field-level data for a large sample of farmers in Saskatchewan. The research indicated that a wheat–tillage summer fallow rotation would completely erode about 40 cm of topsoil in 93–190 years, depending on whether a high or low rate of erosion is assumed. The length of time required to erode the soil is substantially reduced if, rather than the erosive two-year, wheat–fallow rotation, cropping decisions are based on a flexcrop strategy derived from a dynamic optimizing model (plant wheat, if available spring soil moisture is above some critical level, otherwise fallow). The results for various prices, discount rates and rates of soil erosion are provided in Table 9.3. They confirm the above observation that on-site costs of soil erosion are likely small (see also Lerohl and van Kooten 1995).

Table 9.3: Erosion Rates using Flexcropping in Southern Saskatchewan

Item	Scenario							
Price of wheat ($/bu)	2.50	2.50	2.50	2.50	4.50	4.50	4.50	4.50
Discount rate (%)	0	5.0	0	5.0	0	5.0	0	5.0
Erosion rate	low	low	high	high	low	low	high	high
Years to erode 36 cm of soil	285	269	157	135	373	362	195	185

Source: Lerohl and van Kooten (1995).

Off-site costs
Soil erosion from exposed land and dried lakebeds, and run-off from forest and agricultural land is a nonpoint source of pollution. In making agronomic decisions, farmers do not adequately take into account these spillovers, so inefficiency in resource use results. Measurement of the external costs or damages of water and wind erosion, and, thus, the benefits of policies to prevent it, is a difficult task. Research on off-farm costs gives some indication of their magnitude.

Hedonic pricing methods and questionnaires have been used to estimate off-site damages from soil erosion (see Chapter 4 for a discussion of measurement techniques). For example, the cost of *wind erosion* to residents of New Mexico was estimated to be about $1 per day (Huszar and Piper 1986). A Canadian study estimated the damages to society of wind-borne dust from the exposed lakebed caused by lowering the Upper Arrow Lake Reservoir in the interior of BC by more than 80 feet to be no more than $2 million per year. On a per resident basis, the damages may be as large as $200 per year (van Kooten and Thiessen 1995), nearly half those found in the New Mexico study. The differences in measures are due to differences in the severity of dust storms, among other things. The damages estimated in the BC study could not justify the capital construction required to prevent them.

Off-site costs from water erosion can also be considerable. Studies conducted in the 1980s indicate that the overall annual off-site costs of water erosion to the USA amounted to more that $6 billion, or about $250 per resident, with increased costs of clearing sedimentation from erosion amounting to nearly $5 per person (Froster et al. 1987; Clark et al. 1985).

Other sources of land degradation have already been alluded to. Soil salinity needs to be included in estimates of soil degradation, as does loss of organic matter, which causes atmospheric CO_2 to increase. A more significant source of degradation occurs as the result of land conversion, either from an unimproved to an improved state or from cropland to urban use. As alluded to in the previous sections of this chapter, loss of wetlands and associated uplands, native range, tree cover, and so on has an impact on ecosystems that is valued for its ability to assimilate farm pollution, provide scenic amenities, produce wildlife, and so on. These values are often external to the farm enterprise and constitute a real cost to society. Except for attempts to value ducks and other species that are hunted, few attempts have been made to measure these losses. However, they may well be considerable.

It appears that off-site as opposed to on-site damages constitute the more significant cost of soil erosion. Public intervention to prevent soil erosion, via direct subsidies, regulation, or other means, is best justified on the basis of its spillovers – the costs imposed on the nonagricultural sectors of the economy. It is probably true that off-site damages are correlated with on-site damages, so that reducing erosion on the most erosive lands will also yield on-farm benefits in the form of increased future production capability, although this need not be the case. The point is that government farm policies to ameliorate the adverse environmental consequences of agricultural activities can best be justified on the basis of a reduction in the externality costs or off-site damages caused by soil erosion.

To argue that government intervention is required in order to prevent farmers from injuring themselves is insufficient justification for such intervention. Political acceptability of this argument will be difficult to obtain, and programs that are designed on the basis of this presupposition will probably not achieve the desired results (in terms of reducing erosion and protecting the environment). On the other hand, if a public role is justified on the basis of the external costs of agricultural land degradation, political acceptability by the nonagricultural sector will be easier to achieve. Only then might it be possible to commit the funds and effort (in terms of institutions and personnel) to achieve environmental objectives.

9.4 IRRIGATION AND LAND USE

That irrigation projects affect land use is obvious to anyone who has flown over or driven through regions where irrigated agriculture is prevalent. Irrigation projects are popular in most countries because the benefits of such projects accrue to a small number of individuals, while costs are widely dispersed. The beneficiaries of water resource development projects are able to influence politicians, who not only cater to these special interests but also find the outcomes of irrigation projects to be attractive – the "make-the-desert-bloom" syndrome. Engineers are interested in large construction projects that require the building of dams for inter-basin transfers, hydropower generation and irrigation, and they often lobby on behalf of those that ultimately gain the most in terms of enhanced property values. However, irrigation projects are generally uneconomic, and, given current agricultural prices, there is likely no need for inter-basin transfers although they continue to be considered for hydropower generation in Canada. Often it is not that there are regional water shortages, but, rather, that water resources are inefficiently allocated (Reisner 1986). In this section, we focus on the economics of irrigation and the effects on land use. We also consider briefly the possibility of future inter-basin water transfers in order to alleviate real or perceived water shortages.

Irrigation and Water Development in the United States

The western half of North America – that area west of the hundredth meridian – is generally quite arid, with most of the region receiving less than 700 mm (about 28 inches) of precipitation annually and large areas receiving much less. Many settlers were enticed into the region by false promises: in the US, the belief that "rain follows the plow" was promulgated. The promises seemed real during the 20 years of settlement prior to 1886, but then came the harsh winter of 1886, followed by the drought of 1888–92. The number of farm families in the 17 western states fell from about a million to 400,000. Many of the survivors in the most arid regions farmed along river valleys and constructed irrigation works. By the early 1890s, there were some 3.5 million acres (1.4 million ha) of private irrigation in the west. However, the rugged terrain and deep valleys limited the economic feasibility of investments in irrigation by private groups and individuals, even where subsidies from state governments were made available. Only federal intervention could bring about the massive investment required to develop water resources on a large scale. Under President Theodore Roosevelt, the National Reclamation Act was passed in 1902. This initiated federal involvement (through the Bureau of Reclamation) in the building and management of irrigation projects in the arid west and the draining of water from swampy land in other areas (mainly in the southeast USA).

Initially, the Reclamation Act limited water subsidies to 160 ac, but in 1926 this was increased to 320 ac (for a husband and wife), although a farmer could also claim subsidies on leased land. In 1982, eligibility was increased to 960 ac, but this included owned plus leased land. Initially, the subsidy amounted to the interest on capital or construction costs with payback to occur over 10 years, but it soon became apparent that farmers would not be able to bear even that burden. Eventually, the payback period was increased to 50 years. However, while all costs (including operating, maintenance and replacement costs plus costs of installing irrigation works and underground drainage to prevent salinization) had to be covered in principle, it appears that even these costs were not all being borne by the agricultural producer.

Between 1902 and 1930, the US government constructed some 50 dams, while it constructed about 1,000 dams between 1930 and 1980, mainly in the western states. These were built for reasons related to hydropower and flood control, and not necessarily for irrigation. Since 1980, no additional dams have been built, primarily due to the need for environmental impact statements. The environmental costs of dam construction have never been fully taken into account and, when they are, it appears that dam building is not a socially profitable activity. Not only do dams adversely affect scenic landscapes (e.g., Grand Canyon), but they result in the loss of wildlife habitat. Dams on the Columbia River have reduced the historic salmon run by some 80% (from 10 to 16 million adult fish per year to about 2.5 million currently), with about half of the watershed's historic spawning grounds effectively and irreversibly blocked by the Grand Coulee Dam (which is too high to permit construction of fish ladders). The salmon run on the Sacramento River has been reduced to a mere trickle, while riparian habitat for many species has been irreversibly lost or significantly reduced throughout much of the west. A major factor causing a turn-about in attitude toward irrigation development was the result of publicity surrounding deformities and death among waterfowl at California's Kesterson National Wildlife Refuge during the early 1980s, which was caused by selenium from farmers' fields.

Total irrigated acreage in the 17 western states increased from 17.2 million ac in 1939 to 30.8 million ac in 1959 and reached a peak of 43.6 million ac in 1978. The proportion of total irrigated acreage accounted for by the Bureau of Reclamation increased from 18% in 1939 to about one-quarter today, with a peak area of 10.6 million ac in 1982. The Bureau accounts for 53% of irrigated area in Arizona, 40% in California, 17% in Montana, and 8% in Utah. Other public and private institutions account for the remainder. An indication of the importance of water use in irrigation, and thus an indicator of how land use is affected, is provided in Table 9.4. Irrigation constitutes well over 80% of all water use in the western states, where water shortages have become serious problems.

Table 9.4: Average Offstream Water Uses in Selected Western States (%)

State/Item	California	Nevada	Colorado	Washington
Irrigation	83	90	85	81
Public water supply	11	5	4	7
Industry	6	5	7	11
Rural water supply	<1	<1	2	1

Source: Reisner and Bates (1990, pp.28–9).

In addition to low prices, institutional and historical factors often resulted in inefficient water use in the western USA. In all 17 western states, two doctrines have characterized the allocation of water among users. First, the appropriation doctrine of "first in time, first in use" says that an appropriative water right becomes vested when a person intentionally diverts water and applies it to some "beneficial use". The term "beneficial use" is ambiguous and, in practice, means any productive use. The second doctrine is that of "use it or lose it" – water rights can be lost if they are not used for several years. These doctrines have resulted in inefficient use of water, leading to the practice of "water ranching" in order to prevent the loss of rights. Water ranching refers to irrigation for the purpose of maintaining water rights rather than crop production for profit, although crops are still sold.

Markets for water rights are slowly developing and water banking is increasingly used to get around institutional problems related to the "use it, or lose it" principle. The Colorado River Compact allocated water from the Colorado River to states and native people on the basis of the expropriation doctrine (where the federal government expropriated all rights), but the amount of water has been over-allocated (since measurement of water flow took place during the wet years noted above), and, until 1982, states had been able to prevent interstate transfers of water rights. The law is not clear as to whether or not water provided by the Bureau of Reclamation may be transferred from one user to another (even if the 960-acre provision is met). While native rights were not subject to the "use it or lose it" rule, because they fall under federal and not state jurisdiction, the federal government has in place obstacles that make it difficult, but not impossible, for tribes to transfer water rights. For the most part, creation of markets for water transfers is determined at the state level.

Development of water markets in California had been slow, likely due to the vast amounts of federal water (12 million acre feet[5]) tied up in delivery contracts that restrict or prohibit water transfer. Institutions have only recently developed to get around these obstacles. During periods of drought, the state of California's groundwater resources end up accounting for about one-half of water use, compared to a third previously. There is concern that fish habitat in the Sacramento River delta may be destroyed, requiring the allocation of water towards the environment; some 800,000 acre feet (acf) is now targeted for that purpose.

There is no set price for water. Farmers in Nevada, for example, pay around \$30/acf, while the water is worth some \$3,000/acf in residential uses. Water is also valuable for protecting wildlife, particularly certain species of fish. In the Klamath River basin of southern Oregon, the government prevented farmers from using water for irrigation during the dry spring and summer of 2001 to protect a species of fish that lived in the river. Given that farmers regard farming as a way of life and have a distrust of the cities and environmentalists, it will be difficult to get their cooperation in making more water available for wildlife. Farmers will employ all of their political clout to protect water for irrigation, but in the final analysis it appears to be a losing battle. As a result, more and more irrigated farmland will return to dryland cropping or rangeland.

Irrigation and Water Development in Other Countries

In Canada, the story is similar to that in the United States. In 1859, the explorer John Palliser identified a triangular area of about 260,000 square km, consisting mainly of southern Alberta and southern Saskatchewan, to be infertile and unfit for agricultural settlement because of its aridity (with precipitation less than 400 mm annually). Henry Hind had provided a similar report in 1857; he described the southern Prairies as too dry and infertile for farming. Lack of precipitation and organic matter in the soil are evidence of this. In 1872, a botanist, John Macoun, explored the region and reported that the region was well-suited for crop production; but 1872 was a wet year, as indicated above. Acting on Macoun's advice, the government actively recruited immigrants from Eastern Europe with exaggerated claims of the land's productivity. Under the Dominion Lands (Homestead) Act of 1872, settlers were provided with a quarter section of land for a $10 registration fee. The land was unsuited for crop production, and the size of a homestead was too small to permit ranching. Thus began government participation in prairie agriculture.

In 1886, the federal government set up the first in a series of Dominion Experimental Farms in Brandon, Manitoba. The practice of tillage summer fallow to conserve moisture (enabling farmers to use two years' of moisture to grow one crop) was developed several years later at the federal government's experimental farm at Indian Head, Saskatchewan. Tillage fallow contributed to soil erosion, which was a particular problem in dry years such as 1910, 1914 and 1917–19. The wet years of the 1920s produced bumper crops and temporarily solved the problem of soil erosion. However, droughts returned in 1929, and these continued, along with low prices and insect infestations (grasshoppers) through most of the 1930s. In response to the drought, the federal government passed the Prairie Farm Rehabilitation Act in 1935, thereby creating the Prairie Farm Rehabilitation Administration (PFRA). PFRA approached the task by encouraging research, development, the adoption of new farming methods and water conservation. Dams were also constructed for hydropower and irrigation purposes.

Between 1939 and 1979, 30 dams were built in the southern portions of Alberta, Saskatchewan and Manitoba, primarily for irrigation purposes and, to a lesser extent, for provision of water supply, flood control and hydropower. Unlike the USA, where dam construction was effectively halted, several major dam projects have been built since 1980 (e.g., Three Rivers Dam on the Oldman River in Alberta and the Rafferty–Alameda Project in Saskatchewan). However, it is likely that major dam construction may be difficult in the future because of federal environmental assessment reviews.

Agriculture constitutes the largest use of water on the Canadian Prairies, accounting for some two-thirds of consumptive use. Irrigation is particularly important in the drier, southwestern region of the Prairies – the "Palliser triangle". The South Saskatchewan River Basin is the most important basin in western Canada in terms of consumptive use, with irrigation accounting for three-quarters of its use; in dry years, when irrigation use is high and river flows are reduced, about 96% of water consumption in the basin is for agriculture. Agricultural use in the South Saskatchewan basin can be expected to increase as more land is brought under irrigation in Alberta and Saskatchewan. Irrigation acreage expanded by more than 20% in the early 1980s, particularly in Saskatchewan, where it expanded by approximately 50%, but Alberta has the greatest amount of acreage currently under irrigation (nearly 1 million acres).

Finally, elaborate and expensive means for diverting water from northern rivers (i.e., inter-basin transfers), many of which are in Canada, have been proposed. The seriousness of the proposals fluctuates according to whether there is drought, which also results in a shortage of electric energy. Such mega-projects have an adverse impact upon the environment, and this may prevent their adoption. However, water efficiency and a reduction in the high demands for water by agriculture at least can come about by implementing price schemes for water. This is the best means for solving the "water shortage" in the arid western part of the continent.

In Egypt, the construction of the Aswan Dam on the Nile River has been a source of controversy. While it was built to provide hydropower, the dam effectively stopped the annual flooding of the Nile in the lower basin, something that had been taking place since the beginning of agriculture in the region. This brought about declining yields as the soil lost its fertility, which had been annually renewed. As a result, Egypt was forced to rely increasingly on chemical fertilizers, with much of the power generated by the dam used in the production of fertilizer. A proper cost–benefit analysis may have concluded that construction of the dam was not worthwhile undertaking.

In developing countries some 30–60 million people have been forcibly moved from their homes as a result of dam construction. The largest hydroelectric dam in the world will be China's Three Gorges Dam on the Yangtze River, which is scheduled for completion in 2009. This dam is expected to cost more than US$24 billion and take 20 years to complete. The dam will displace between 1.2 and 1.9 million people and inundate some 30,000 ha of farmland, much of which is marginal at best. Nonetheless, the dam is considered an environmental disaster, partly because people are forced to leave their homes, but also because many natural and historic sites are to be lost. The most important benefit from the dam will be reduced downstream flooding, which has taken substantial numbers of lives in the past. Additional benefits include hydropower from a "clean" (non-CO_2) source and increased water for farmers. However, there have been charges of massive corruption, spiraling costs, technological problems, and major problems in accomplishing the resettlement of so many people. It is also clear that no cost–benefit analysis has ever been conducted.[6]

Economics of Irrigation Agriculture

With notable exceptions, irrigation does not occur unless subsidies are provided to agricultural producers and/or the state builds the dams and brings the water to the landowner's property. In both Canada and the United States, there are important misunderstandings about such subsidies. Foremost among these is the notion that the full amount of the subsidies is what the farmer actually receives as a subsidy. This is far from the case. In the San Joaquin Valley of California in the 1980s, farmers paid $20/acf for irrigation water that was worth $50/acf but cost the Bureau of Reclamation $300/acf to deliver in terms of transportation and other costs (Reisner 1986). Thus, the cost of providing a subsidy to farmers is about ten times greater than the actual amount of the subsidy – a very inefficient means of transferring income to agricultural producers. Studies are not available for Canada, but it would not be surprising to find a similar relationship between costs and benefits as reported for the San Joaquin Valley. Thus, for example, many farmers in southern Saskatchewan simply refused to adopt irrigation because it was unprofitable, despite having water brought right up to their property.

Economists have almost unanimously demonstrated that the economic benefits from irrigation are marginal or negative. In Canada, cost–benefit analyses often fail to take into account the opportunity cost of water, which is usually its value in producing electricity. Even when the opportunity cost of water is ignored, benefit–cost ratios tend to be less than 1.0. In eastern Washington, the cost–benefit analyses of irrigation projects indicate that the most optimistic benefit–cost ratio is 0.78 even when secondary benefits are taken into account. Too often, however, secondary benefits are not appropriately calculated and the increase in economic activity associated with an irrigation project is taken as a benefit that is included in the cost–benefit analysis. This is inappropriate, as discussed in Chapter 6. Nonetheless, many irrigation projects have been justified on the basis of the estimated change in economic activity, including it as if it were a true economic benefit.

In Canada, one argument along these lines that has been used in support of irrigation projects is that irrigated hay and grain stimulates a livestock sector. For example, Saskatchewan points to the livestock sector in southern Alberta to justify expansion of irrigation in that province, but expansion of the Alberta sector occurred as a result of subsidies to livestock producers and not as a result of irrigation. Why would higher hay and/or feed grain yields (as a result of irrigation) bring about a livestock industry that would not exist when yields are lower? After all, the feed requirements could simply be produced on a larger area. The answer is clear: development of a livestock sector is not dependent on irrigation. Economists have specifically identified "forward-linked" markets as an inappropriate justification for irrigation projects (Hamilton et al. 1991).

It is important that each project or program be considered on its own merits. Thus, if irrigation works are already in place, it may not make economic sense to place restrictions on subsidies if, by so doing, farms are prevented from achieving scale economies. Likewise, decisions to install irrigation works on a farm should be made solely on the basis of the on-farm costs and benefits, not on the basis of the costs of bringing the water to the farm, *if the irrigation canals that bring water to the farm are already in place*. Any costs that have already been incurred should be ignored – bygones are bygones.

This reasoning can be extended to larger development projects. Before considering a series of dams on a watershed, a cost–benefit analysis needs to be conducted for the entire project, but the worthiness of each dam within the project also needs to be determined prior to its construction. This prevents the use of "cash register" dams as part of the larger project. Cash register dams provide no irrigation benefits, only hydroelectricity, but are included within the larger irrigation project to make the overall project appear economically attractive. Without the hydropower benefits from such a "cash register" dam, the entire project to provide irrigation water would fail a cost–benefit test. To meet the evaluation criteria established by the Flood Control Act (1936), the Bureau of Reclamation evaluated irrigation projects as part of a parcel that relied upon revenues from the sale of electricity ("cash registers") to subsidize irrigation. The point is that the irrigation components of the project need to be evaluated on their own, without reliance on subsidies from other components in the project.

Another problem is that low-valued crops are often grown under irrigation. In western Canada, for example, over 70% of irrigated acres are sown to grains and hay, with a small proportion sown to specialty crops (sugar beets, potatoes, etc.). There are limits as to where specialty crops can be grown as heat units are adequate for growing sugar beets only in some parts of southern Alberta and Manitoba, but not in Saskatchewan. Further, sugar beet acreage is fixed by government programs, because Canadian sugar beet cannot compete with cheaper sugar from abroad. Further, an irrigation subsidy for subsidized agricultural products (such as sugar beets, wheat, cotton and rice) makes no economic sense; it implies that farmers are provided with a double subsidy – an irrigation subsidy and a crop production subsidy.

Problems such as those identified above are not unique to North America. In many parts of the world, large-scale irrigation projects (requiring large dam construction) are undertaken, despite questionable economic efficiency benefits. Where public investment in such projects is required, farmers are usually provided with subsidies to build irrigation works, and water is priced below market rates, if it is priced at all. This results in excessive water use, inappropriate irrigation works (e.g., sprinklers rather than drip), and watering at the hottest times of day when evaporation is greatest. Further, irrigated agriculture results in land degradation by increasing soil salinity. Historically, wherever irrigation was practiced, agriculture was eventually abandoned because the soil became saline. Salinity occurs because the water table rises during periods of watering, and salts are deposited when it recedes. Optimal timing of irrigation and flushing of soils might be used to reduce salinization. But water-pricing policies and management expertise in many countries do not provide much hope on this score.

Finally, while we have discussed the opportunity cost of irrigation water in terms of lost hydropower benefits, water is also needed for domestic and industrial consumption, and to protect wildlife and their habitat. Large-scale water development projects often result in the loss of biodiversity, and these costs are not usually taken into account in evaluating water development projects, such as the Three Gorges Dam in China or the Grand Coulee Dam in the USA. The California energy crisis of 2000–01 and the protests by irrigation farmers in southern Oregon over reduced water availability resulting from the need to protect fish habitat came as a result of lower precipitation in the US Pacific Northwest. Lower precipitation meant less water available for fish habitat, hydroelectric generation, domestic/industrial use and irrigation. The problem with the current system of allocating water is that institutions do not exist to enable water to be allocated to the highest valued uses in the most efficient manner. Indeed, existing institutions and pricing mechanisms often prevent water from being used in ways that maximize society's overall wellbeing.

In conclusion, the best hope for appropriate allocation of resources is to rely on sound economic principles and careful social cost–benefit analysis in the development of water resources. Subsidies to construct large irrigation works should be avoided, whether these subsidies are from the federal government to a region or from developed to low-income countries. Finally, given the scarcity of water in many regions of the world, the best hope for its conservation is to establish water markets and price the resource at its true economic value.

NOTES

1.   Grain producers in western Canada can only sell grain to the Canadian Wheat Board (CWB), which then markets the grain abroad. Producers are then paid the average price determined by CWB sales.

2. Farmers and governments working together designed GRIP from the ground up. The problem was that the committee that designed the program consisted of 19 farmers and 14 provincial and federal representatives, with such representation bound to favor farmers.
3. See section 9.3 for a discussion of soil-tolerance rates.
4. The discussion in the section borrows from van Kooten (1993a).
5. An acre-foot of water is the amount of water required to cover one acre to a depth of one foot and is equal to 1,233 cubic meters of water.
6. Taken from information found at websites: http://iso.hrichina.org:8151/old_site/reports/3gorges.html#C1 and http://www.irn.org/programs/threeg/.

10. Economics of Public Lands

A high degree of public ownership of forest and rangelands characterizes much of North America, especially the more arid western half of the continent and the far north. Public ownership resulted in the 1800s as governments enclosed forest and rangelands beyond the extensive margin to protect them against open-access exploitation.[1] This resulted in institutions and policies for managing public lands in Canada and the USA that are not found elsewhere, with the main difference between these countries pertaining to the role of the federal government. In the USA, the federal government controls much of the public land through the Bureau of Land Management (BLM) and the US Forest Service; in Canada, the constitution has vested ownership primarily with the provinces. However, there remain commonalities. Both countries require sustainable, multiple-use management of lands. Grazing fees on public lands in Canada are based on what they are in the USA, despite the controversy that has surrounded the setting of fees. The USA has pursued multiple-use management much earlier and more vigorously than has Canada. This is a result of differences in legislation, the political structure, the role of the courts and, more importantly, greater population pressure on the land resource in the USA than Canada.

In Europe, public lands constitute a much smaller proportion of total land area, but public provision of the services provided by public lands has increased. This has been accomplished both by the "creation" of public lands (purchase of private land, better management of extant lands in the public domain, "development" of coastal areas) and the purchase of public amenities through contracts with private landowners. The main reasons for interest in public lands in Europe have been the increasing demand for environmental (nature, waste services of ecosystems, etc.) and recreation services of land. In Europe, the main pressure on land and water is recreational, a direct result of higher population densities and higher incomes (see Table 7.4).

Public lands are important because they provide environmental services in addition to commercial products, and there is often conflict between the production of commercial outputs and management for environmental services. In addition to recreational use and watershed functions, public lands provide timber, minerals, fish and wildlife, and domestic grazing. Recreation may contribute as much as half of the total social values of public lands, but not by receipts. Likewise, watershed and wildlife values may be high, but again public agencies are not paid for producing such services. Thus, if the agency responsible for public land has the incentive to maximize or maintain revenues, it will neglect public goods in favor of those that provide it with income. Recalling Chapter 1, public land managers need to face appropriate incentives before they are likely to manage lands for the good of all.

Even if land managers are interested in maximizing society's overall wellbeing, they generally know more about the total and marginal contribution of commercial products to land value than they do about nonmarket or environmental services. Further, if land is to be allocated among uses in an optimal fashion, knowledge of total value is not very helpful because decisions are made at the margin (Bulte and van Kooten 1999). For example, the earth's ecosystems are infinitely valuable for supporting human life – their total value in providing environmental amenities is infinite. However, when making a decision about whether to harvest the next hectare of trees, or whether to destroy (create) an additional acre of riparian habitat, it is marginal value that is important (see section 10.4 for a discussion). At the margin, protecting an acre of old-growth forest, say, may yield only very small environmental benefits compared to large commercial values by harvesting that acre (van Kooten and Bulte 1999). Nonetheless, it is clear that multiple uses are an important consideration in managing public lands, but that valuation of uses can be a considerable problem (see Chapter 4).

Economic efficiency is only one of several criteria that can be used to evaluate multiple uses. Other criteria are income distribution, fairness, political acceptability and operational practicality. The income distribution criterion refers primarily to local economic impacts: management decisions pertaining to public land use have an impact on regional incomes that cannot be ignored. Fairness deals with a variety of issues that involve protection of property rights and dealings between citizens and government. For example, is it fair suddenly to prevent a rancher from accessing public forage when such access had been granted for more than 50 years? Can a state agency restrict hunter access to public lands if such access has been permitted historically and there is no threat to the species being hunted? If one purchases a property among other developed properties, can the state prevent you from developing your property by enacting legislation to protect a particular species? Political acceptability pertains to such issues as maintenance of land productivity, acceptability of land-use policies, and so on. Finally, operational practicality refers to the feasibility of making multiple-use decisions in the field. Regional managers often rely on rules of thumb and intuition when making decisions, often a practical thing to do in light of the constraints they face.

The focus in this chapter is on the economics of public lands. We begin by briefly examining how the management of public lands evolved in North America. Since public lands are an important resource, and because rangelands are important to many stakeholders (beef ranchers, commercial horse operators, sheep producers, hunters, guides and outfitters, consumptive and nonconsumptive wildlife enthusiasts, recreationists, timber companies, trappers, and Aboriginal peoples), so that land-use conflicts are inevitable, we provide a framework for economic efficiency and multiple use management of public land in section 10.2. In section 10.3, the setting of grazing fees is considered. Although we examine fees from the perspective of economic efficiency, issues of fairness, equity and political acceptability are also considered. Forest economics is addressed in Chapters 11 and 12.

10.1 BACKGROUND TO PUBLIC LAND MANAGEMENT IN NORTH AMERICA

It is useful to briefly consider the history of public land management because it provides useful insights for economists and a background to existing institutional structures. Management of public lands in North America began in the United States as a result of land acquisitions. In 1782, the original states gave their western lands (from the Ohio River to the Mississippi River) to the federal government. The Louisiana Purchase of 1803 for $15 million gave the US rights to the area drained by the Mississippi River, while Florida was acquired from Spain in 1819 for $7 million. The Texas rebellion against Mexico (1836) led to its annexation to the USA in 1848, with subsequent cession of lands outside its current boundaries to the federal government in 1850. The US government gained the territories of New Mexico, Colorado, Arizona, Nevada, Utah and California as a result of the 1848 war with Mexico and the Gadsen Purchase in 1853. A compromise with Britain over disputed western territory in 1846 established the 49th parallel as the international boundary between Canada and the USA, while Alaska was obtained from Russia in 1867 for about $7 million.

Britain controlled the remainder (northern part, except Alaska) of the continent. Canada was established by the British North American (BNA) Act in 1867, with British Columbia added to the Confederation in 1872.

(Alberta and Saskatchewan were carved out of Canadian territory in 1905, while Newfoundland joined the Confederation in 1949.) The BNA Act granted control over public land to the provinces, with federal control confined principally to the Yukon and Northwest Territories. However, the federal government maintained control over land use in a number of ways.

Since much of the land in both countries was not yet settled, governments were involved in the disposal of "public" lands, particularly agricultural land. (In Canada, where provincial governments were established, they took over this responsibility from the federal government.) Both countries employed the rectangular cadastral survey method that was used in the USA to survey public lands at the suggestion of President Thomas Jefferson (1801–09).[2] Each country granted lands to railway companies to get them to build railways (see section 9.1 with reference to the Crow Rate freight subsidy in Canada): the land could be sold or given to settlers so that rail traffic could be built up. In addition, homestead acts were used to encourage settlement by providing individuals with land for farms; settlers were sold a quarter section of land (160 ac) at a very low price, with the proviso that they must establish a homestead and farm the land. While 160 ac were adequate for those locating in moist climates, they were too little to encourage ranching or farming in the arid regions of the west.

United States

Reservation of land began in the United States in the latter part of the 1800s, because the eastern establishment was concerned about the potential loss of wildlands in the west. As a result, Yellowstone National Park was established in 1872. In 1891, the Forest Reserve Act or Creative Act was passed, and, with it, land management became a task for public foresters. The act gave the president authority to withdraw public domain lands and put them into a wildland reservation, even if these lands had commercially valuable timber growing on them. Although Congress never intended to create forest reserves, 40 million ac (16 million ha) were reserved by 1897. However, there was no provision in law for the management of this land. This was provided by the Organic Act of 1897, which superseded the Creative Act and was interpreted to provide authority for rehabilitating degraded forest and rangelands; it introduced active management of public lands. As a result, managers of public lands became somewhat schizophrenic, not quite knowing whether they were managing public wilderness or timber stands.

An important event in the evolution of institutional arrangements for managing public lands in the USA (which also had an effect upon Canada) occurred in 1898, when a disgruntled Gifford Pinchot went from the General Land Office (GLO), which was established in 1812 and managed all lands in the public domain, to head up the small Division of Forestry in the US Department of Agriculture. In 1905, his friend, President Theodore Roosevelt (1901–09), created the US National Forest System and made the Division of Forestry into the Forest Service, assigning it responsibility for managing the forest reserve lands. The GLO had managed the forests from 1891 to 1905. As a result of Roosevelt's friendship with Pinchot and the latter's unhappiness with the way his career at the GLO had been progressing, the USA ended up with two large and bureaucratic agencies to manage its public lands. Whether this has resulted in better management or not is a question open to debate.

During his presidency, Roosevelt reserved vast amounts of public lands, increasing the forest reserve almost to its current level. The Weeks Act of 1911 permitted the federal government to purchase private lands for reservation in the public domain under the guise of soil and water conservation. This enabled the federal government to establish forest reserves in the eastern states, where there were few National Forests.

The Taylor Grazing Act of 1934 was a watershed piece of legislation for two reasons. First, it marked an end to both acquisition and disposal of further federal lands. The US public land base was fixed and has remained about the same ever since. About half of the remaining unappropriated and unreserved public lands in the 48 contiguous states was placed in a grazing reserve under federal government ownership, with the rest being included two years later. Second, it put a stop to the grazing commons and its deleterious effects – that is, overgrazing on public lands (especially by sheep). A Division of Grazing (Grazing Service) was set up in the Department of the Interior, as opposed to in the GLO. By 1936, the Grazing Service looked after 142 million ac of public land, but political pressure on Congress by ranchers resulted in its becoming ineffectual. In 1946, the Grazing Service was amalgamated with the GLO to become the Bureau of Land Management (BLM). Currently, the federal government owns some 738 million acres of land, with 188 million acres under Forest Service management and 398 million acres under the BLM. The remainder is administered by a variety of federal agencies, including the National Parks Service, Bureau of Reclamation and the Department of Defense.

Ever since the 1940s, US foresters have debated their role: was forestry part of multiple-resource management or was it to be confined to trees? The appropriate role of foresters has profound implications for the type of training that a forester should receive. During the 1950s, outdoor recreation became an increasingly important use of public lands, and there was increasing concern about preservation of wildlands and roadless wilderness areas. The broader view of forestry was advanced with the Multiple Use and Sustained Yield (MUSY) Act of 1960, which explicitly recognized the importance of public wildland management. It gave the legislative foundation for multiple-use management, which had always been practiced by the Forest Service. The Classification and Multiple Use Act of 1964 did the same for the BLM.

Despite MUSY, the conflict intensified between those interested in the production of a larger volume of natural resource commodities from public lands and increasingly militant outdoor recreationists and preservationists. Knowledge of resource matters among the public also increased. As a result of rising public pressure, Congress passed a number of pieces of legislation to appease various interests, but this resulted in a greater role for the courts – something that was neither anticipated nor desired by Congress.

The Wilderness Act (1964) sought to set aside wilderness areas. In 1967, John Krutilla (an economist with Resources for the Future) argued that 10 million acres of land should be preserved as wilderness; when Congress passed the Wilderness Act, it implicitly agreed to a set-aside of about 15 million acres. However, by 1972, more than 105 million acres were under consideration for wilderness designation.

As a result of court cases and the fact that Congress was unhappy with the annual budget presentations of the Forest Service, it passed the Forest and Rangeland Resources Planning Act (RPA) in 1974. But it turned out that the Forest Service was ill-prepared for analyses and report writing. Additional manpower and budget for intensifying management became available, but, while an objective of RPA was to balance supply and demand, it consisted of little more than an inventory process. Resource availability was known, but there was no provision for such things as jointness in supply or provision of multiple outputs. The 1974 RPA was amended extensively in 1976, with a piece of legislation known as the National Forest Management Act (NFMA). This act replaced the Creative Act and sought to introduce more economic considerations into the 1974 act. A similar planning act was passed for the BLM in 1976, namely, the Federal Land Policy and Management Act (FLPMA).

During this period, other acts impacting on public land management were the National Environmental Policy Act (1970), which required environmental impact statements, and the Endangered Species Act (1973). As a result of court decisions, environmental impact statements are now required for almost all activities related to public land management and the environment. However, the environmental statements have become very complicated (e.g., filled with many meaningless figures), restricting their usefulness as a decision tool.

The National Forest Management Act (1976), the Federal Land Policy and Management Act (1976), and the Public Rangeland Improvement Act (1978) have mandated that management of public lands in the USA must satisfy both a sustained yield and a multiple-use mandate. (For example, US Forest Service planning regulation 36CFR219 pursuant to the National Forest Management Act requires that wildlife species in a national forest be maintained at viable population levels.) A number of court cases have reinforced the multiple-use mandate in the legislation. In the legislation, sustained yield implies that annual consumption by *all* users be no greater than annual growth, as determined by government fiat. In effect, multiple-use management of public lands has been interpreted as a trade-off that does not give timber interests, recreational activities, domestic livestock, or wildlife an exalted status over other uses.

There are problems with this legislation, however. The main one is that the courts have become so involved in interpretation of the legislation that rulings are sometimes against what the Congress originally intended. For example, the Congress never intended that, if a species is endangered, it should be protected regardless of the cost. A ruling by the courts to this effect has led to undue expenditures on one or two high-profile species – high profile in the sense of having made it to court – to the neglect of other endangered or threatened species that could be protected at lower cost. Further, considerable confusion, frustration and cynicism have been generated by conflicts between centralized planning and control (mandated by the Endangered Species Act and RPA) and decentralized land management planning (mandated by NFMA and FLPMA). These problems need to be resolved if the USA is to maximize the future wellbeing of its citizens from managing its public land resources.

Canada

Public land management in Canada has evolved differently than it has in the USA, although there are similarities. As noted, disposal of agricultural lands relied upon homestead acts, as it had in the USA. But differences arose for two reasons. First, Canadian settlement occurred much later than did settlement south of the border, and even now there is less population pressure on, or demand for, Canadian wilderness areas. There are large forest areas that remain unexploited and inaccessible, although that is likely to change in the future, as evidenced by the development of pulp mills in northern Saskatchewan and Alberta in the late 1980s and 1990s.

Second, and perhaps more important, political institutions in Canada differ from those in the USA. Ownership and administration of public or

Crown lands mostly falls under the jurisdiction of individual provinces. Each province is responsible for determining its own criteria for managing public lands. Resource development projects are often undertaken with the consent, and even urging, of a provincial government, and development subsidies are sometimes involved. As a result of the British North America Act (1867), natural resources are owned by the provinces, and they jealously guard their right to develop these resources, although with subsidies from, and without benefits to, the federal government. Even environmentalists are unwilling to recommend transfer of resource ownership to the federal government, although they do want to retain the ability to appeal to a higher authority than the province.

In Canada, the constitution plays a key role in the environment and public land use. The federal government exercises some authority over the environmental impacts of public land-use decisions through one of a number of mechanisms. Since land resource projects (e.g., reforestation, construction of dams) often rely on some federal funding, the federal government is able to require some standard with respect to their impact on the environment. As well, the federal government is responsible for (1) transboundary movement of resource products (control over exports of pulp, electricity, uranium, etc.), (2) fisheries, (3) migratory species, and (4) navigation and shipping. Finally, the federal government can invoke its *declaratory power* in matters dealing with the environment, although this power is rarely exercised and is used primarily in cases of emergencies. It would seem, therefore, that the federal government can have a large say in land-use decisions. While the federal government may lack a jurisdictional basis for intervention in agricultural and forest practices that are ecologically objectionable, its powers to offer and withdraw financing give it wide powers to exercise control over the environmental impacts of these practices as well as those of resource development and other land-use projects. For example, there is nothing to prevent the federal government from implementing cross-compliance provisions for agricultural subsidies (Chapter 9).

On the basis of the federal cabinet's Environmental Assessment Review Process Guidelines Order of 1973, an environmental review is required for all resource development projects. Although the review process was criticized because it lacked a statutory basis and appeared to represent the voice of the federal government's ecological conscience, it was given the force of law by the Federal Court of Canada (which was created in 1971 to adjudicate disputes involving federal law), a judgment that was confirmed in 1992 by the Supreme Court of Canada in the decision concerning the Oldman River in southern Alberta. In 1992, the Canadian Environmental Assessment Act replaced the "guidelines". This Act (as its predecessor) requires only that projects be delayed until an environmental review is completed, but there is no means to enforce compliance with the findings. However, a negative environmental statement results in adverse publicity that could halt a project.

In 1988, the Supreme Court invoked the Peace, Order, and Good Government (POGG) provision of the constitution in a case involving marine pollution by a forest company in provincial waters. There is no reason why the POGG provision cannot be used in the future in other cases dealing with the environment, resource development, and public or private land use. This introduces an added degree of uncertainty in decisions concerning resource use.

Federal intervention in resource development and land-use decisions can be justified on one or more of the grounds indicated above (see van Kooten and Scott 1995). In some cases, the federal government has assigned its jurisdictional powers to the provinces, but it is not clear that this would preclude federal intervention in provincial decisions concerning the environment and resources. In 1991, there was a proposal to change the Constitution to offer greater control over certain aspects of resource development to the provinces, including environmental impacts, in an effort to streamline federal government services. The areas for increased provincial responsibility would include wildlife conservation and protection, and soil and water conservation, while forestry, mining and recreation would fall exclusively under provincial responsibility. The federal government has not proposed to grant exclusive responsibility to provinces for agriculture, likely because no province would be willing to forgo federal aid to agriculture. With regard to the declaratory power and POGG provisions, the federal government has offered to transfer to the provinces authority for non-national matters not specifically assigned to the federal government under the Constitution or by virtue of Supreme Court decisions. Perhaps this is in recognition of the fact that external effects of provincial decisions on other parts of Canada may not be that great, and, therefore, that a provincial government may be at least as capable of achieving an optimal solution to environmental spillovers as is the federal government.

The guiding principle regarding the level of policymaking is the subsidiarity or federalism principle. It states that the primary responsibility and decision-making competence should rest with the lowest possible level of authority in the political hierarchy capable of handling a particular public policy problem. It implies that the lower-level authority (e.g., a province in Canada) should deal with any problem it can adequately handle, rather than deferring to the higher level (federal government). The rationale of the principle is that regional preferences and information can be more adequately taken into account and that the complex process of regulation at the federal level can be substantially reduced. The principle implies that regional problems, such as land use, should be handled at the regional level, except when federal interests are involved, such as protection of the national heritage. In the case of transboundary spillovers, the ability of the lower-level authority to deal with the problem may be limited, but, then, any responsibility or power should be allocated to the lowest level that is capable of encompassing the externality (see, e.g., van Kooten and Scott 1995). In principle, the state/province directly involved should resolve the problem. If that does not lead to a solution, say because of significant spillovers into other jurisdictions, federal involvement is required.

10.2 FRAMEWORK FOR ECONOMIC ANALYSIS OF PUBLIC LANDS

Public lands are important because they provide timber and nontimber products, forage for both domestic livestock and wildlife herbivores, and habitat for other wildlife such as waterfowl and predators. While the economic surpluses associated with timber and nontimber products and domestic forage consumption can readily be calculated, the same is not true of wildlife resources. Yet the latter need to be taken into account in making decisions about how public lands are to be utilized and managed for multiple resource use. In this section, we indicate how cost–benefit analysis can be applied to public lands and provide a framework for analyzing multiple use of land.

Social Cost–Benefit Analysis of Improvements to Public Lands

Consider a project to improve public rangeland through, say, investments in seeding, weeding and/or provision of water. We can conduct a simple social cost–benefit analysis that takes into account private ranch profits plus benefits from improved "environmental" amenities, which include recreation benefits (from hunting or wildlife viewing) as well as non-use benefits. For this purpose, we define total economic value (TEV) as the sum of direct use value, indirect use value, option value and existence value (Pearce and Warford 1993, pp.102–5). Then, denoting net environmental costs by E, the cost–benefit rule for stocking livestock on a particular range is:

(10.1)
$$\sum_{t=0}^{\infty} \frac{B_t - C_t - E_t}{(1+r)^t} > 0,$$

where B_t are the benefits from sale of domestic livestock (as measured by the value of the forage consumed) in each period t, C_t are the costs of grazing domestic animals plus any other costs related to ranch operations (e.g., provision of salt licks, damage to range caused by overgrazing), and r is the social rate of discount. Benefits, private costs and environmental spillovers are all a function of the stocking rate. The time horizon is taken to be infinite, thereby allowing for regeneration of depleted range.

The variable E is treated as a cost separate from C in order to emphasize that environmental costs are different from costs of commercial ranching, with the latter borne by the ranchers but not the former. An example of environmental costs is the damage caused by cattle to riparian areas (and wetlands more generally), damage that reduces habitat for waterfowl and aquatic life. In principle, this damage can be measured by the reduction in hunting or fishing (e.g., reduction in catch), reduction in the benefits from wildlife viewing, changes in water quality, and the loss of existence values associated with a reduction in wildlife and their habitat, if any. It is clear that many of the environmental damages need to be estimated using a nonmarket method such as contingent valuation (Chapter 4). E can be negative (constitute benefits from ranch activities) as well as positive. For example, range improvements benefit not only domestic livestock but also wildlife herbivores. Further, ranchers who graze cattle on public lands may serve to monitor recreational activities on public land, while logging results in clearings that provide range or other habitat for certain wildlife species (e.g., elk) in addition to cattle. In general, it is unclear whether E is positive (there is a reduction in environmental benefits) or negative (there is an overall gain in external benefits) as a result of range improvements. The type of range improvement will determine whether there are net environmental costs or benefits.

In a deterministic world with no uncertainty, total environmental costs or benefits of range improvements are given by:

(10.2)   TEV = TUV + TEXV,

where TUV is total (direct and indirect) use value and TEXV refers to total existence value. Use value includes nonconsumptive use benefits from recreational activities such as wildlife viewing and the consumptive use value of hunting.[3] Existence value, on the other hand, can only be estimated using a contingent valuation method (see Chapter 4). A particular investment in range improvement should proceed as long as:

$$(10.3) \qquad \sum_{t=0}^{\infty} \frac{B_t - C_t - TUV_t}{(1+r)^t} - TEXV > 0.$$

In addition, one needs to take into account *demand uncertainty* that results because future income and preferences are uncertain – individuals may value the environmental good more in the future. In this regard the following components are distinguished. First, the amount a person would be willing to pay for an environmental amenity, over and above its current value, to maintain the option of having that environmental asset available in the future – or option value (OV) (see also section 8.2). Second, the expected consumers' surplus where consumer surplus is the amount the individual is willing to pay to visit the site after having decided to become a demander. The expected CS is obtained by multiplying CS by the probability of wanting to visit the site. The option price (OP) is the maximum amount an individual is willing to pay to purchase an option to visit the threatened ecosystem, or view the threatened species, in the future. Option price is given by:

$$(10.4) \qquad\qquad OP = E(CS) + OV$$

OV is associated with risk aversion and is generally positive, although in rare situations it can be negative (Ready 1995, pp.575–8). Option value is thus a cost associated with range developments that are negative in their impact on wildlife habitat (food source, shelter and/or breeding area). It is generally measured in conjunction with existence value (see below).

Finally, one needs to take into account *supply uncertainty*. This is the uncertainty related to people's concern about the future availability of the environmental services (e.g., waterfowl and other species that may be locally threatened or endangered). Future availability may be threatened by disturbing (developing) the native range or enhanced by range improvements. As discussed in section 8.2, supply uncertainty is related to irreversibility and quasi-option value (QOV) measures the benefit of delaying development decisions in the face of irreversibility. The problem with QOV is that it is difficult to measure in practice. Hence, its use in cost–benefit analysis is limited.

The social cost–benefit model is extended to account for all of these costs and benefits. The decision rule to invest in a range improvement (or utilize native range) is now:

$$(10.5) \quad \sum_{t=0}^{\infty} \frac{B_t - C_t - \mathrm{TUV}_t}{(1+r)^t} - (\mathrm{TEXV} + \mathrm{OP} + \mathrm{QOV}) > 0.$$

This formulation takes into account all social costs and social benefits associated with the range improvement. Clearly, it is necessary to account for all of the (discounted) benefits and costs. The problem is one of determining costs and benefits in practice.

Several caveats remain. What is neglected in the foregoing framework is the impact that the existence of alternative sites and amenities has on nonmarket values. For example, the amount that someone is willing to pay for an option to view sage grouse at a particular site in the future is sensitive to the availability of similar species of upland birds at other (possibly nearby) locations. If there is an abundance of such sites, one expects OP to be small; if there are few sites, OP is much larger. Hence, it is not the total or average nonmarket value that is of importance, but the marginal value. Too often the focus is on total as opposed to marginal value.

Making decisions on the basis of average or total value leads to loss of economic wellbeing or welfare, as illustrated with the aid of Figure 10.1. In the figure, AB represents the average benefits of providing wetlands. Average benefits are the total area under the marginal benefit curve, labeled MB, divided by the wetland area (as a measure of the availability of the amenity). Average benefits are generally greater than marginal benefits.[4] The marginal cost (MC) of providing the environmental amenity, say the cost of changing agricultural or ranching practices to protect wetlands, increases as more of the amenity is provided. A decision based on average or total value would lead to the provision of W^* amount of wetlands (determined from α), while the correct amount to provide (as determined by economic efficiency considerations) is W^E. The social cost of providing the last unit of the amenity is given by c^*, but society assigns a value of zero to that unit. The total loss in economic wellbeing from providing too much of the amenity (the cost to society) is given by area $\alpha\beta\gamma$.[5]

This thinking cuts both ways. Suppose, rather than an environmental amenity, it is ranch output (number of long yearlings produced and sold) that is the object. If a decision is made on the basis of average and not marginal returns, the last yearlings produced would cost more to produce than they yield in revenue. This can occur, for example, if forage is valued too low by the rancher.

Ignored in the forgoing discussion of social cost–benefit analysis are the range dynamics and the interaction between biological and economic processes over time. One cannot talk about range economics without taking into account the dynamics of the herbivory, especially the interactions among various species of domestic and wildlife herbivores, and between the herbivores and the vegetation. Management has a profound impact on the dynamics through decisions about stocking rates, harvests of wildlife, and investments in range improvements. Dynamic models integrate the biological dynamics of range with the resulting economic behavioral response. Unfortunately, it is beyond the scope of the current text to address dynamic optimization problems.

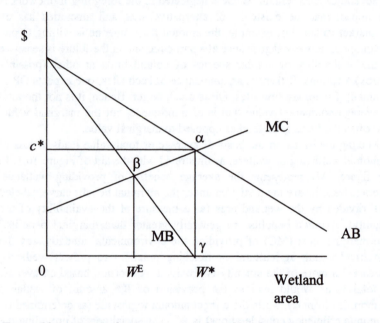

Figure 10.1: Marginal versus average benefits of ranch decision-making

Economics of Multiple Use

Prior to the 1920s, much of the southern Rocky Mountain Trench in Canada was covered with forests. As a result of intensive logging at lower elevations (to supply a growing prairie economy) and subsequent fires, large rangeland areas became available for domestic and wildlife grazing. As a result, populations of whitetail and mule deer, elk and bighorn sheep peaked in the East Kootenay region during the 1950s. Over the next 30 years, wildlife populations declined, partly as a result of overharvesting, but also because forage availability declined. Forest succession and ingrowth, combined with fire suppression, reduced the available range, thereby exacerbating conflicts for forage between domestic cattle and wildlife. In this region, conflicts remain between those who wish to increase cattle numbers and those who desire increased use of the range by wildlife; between those advocating the land be used for timber production and those favoring range; and between the aforementioned groups and those who would promote some form of residential or suburban development. To a greater or lesser degree, similar conflicts among commercial timber, wildlife, ranching and other interests characterize public land conflicts in all regions of the world. In this section, economic analysis of multiple use is described.

Various land uses can be considered outputs produced by the land resource. Alternative land uses are (1) competitive, (2) complementary, (3) supplementary and (4) antagonistic. Competitive and complementary land uses are discussed with the aid of Figure 10.2. Competitive products are those for which an increase in the utilization of land for one use results in a decrease in output from the other use. When products are complementary in their use of the land, this implies that an increase in utilization by one use actually increases the amount of product available from the other use.

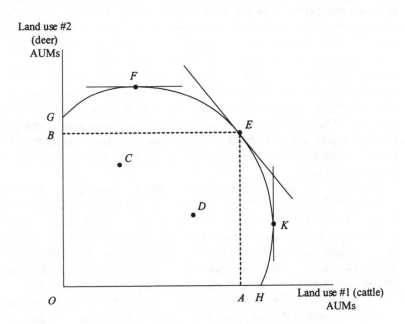

Figure 10.2: Complementary and competitive land uses

Before proceeding, we introduce the concept of an animal unit month

(AUM), the metric used here to compare different land uses. An AUM is the amount of feed or range services required to maintain a 1,000-lb. (450-kg) cow or its equivalent for a period of one month. Since it is based on metabolic weight, the AUM serves as a conversion factor of forage requirements across herbivorous species. Cattle equivalents are used to measure the forage requirements of other animals; for example, forage required by a sheep is equivalent to 0.2–0.25 AUMs, or the forage requirements of five sheep are the same as those of one cow. The general formula for converting the forage requirements of other animals is $(W/AU)^{3/4}$, where W is the weight of the animal in question and AU refers to the basic animal (cow) unit (Workman 1986).

In Figure 10.2, suppose that rangeland can be used by cattle or by deer. If range is utilized only by domestic livestock, the number of animal unit months (AUMs) of grazing that can be supported is given by *OH*. If the land is utilized only by deer, then the *carrying capacity* of the range is *OG*. When cattle are introduced onto a range that is currently used only by deer, there may be an increase in the number of deer that can be supported by the range. By grazing cattle, more winter range becomes available for deer, because cattle prefer grasses and forbs that compete with shrubs and other plants preferred by a browser. By grazing cattle, the shrubs grow better, providing more forage for deer. Likewise, if cattle currently use the range, introducing deer will increase the carrying capacity of the range for cattle. In both cases, there is complementarity in land uses that is illustrated by the segments *GF* and *HK* in Figure 10.2. At moderate stocking levels, and with proper management, the interaction between deer and cattle can be mutually beneficial. (As another example of complementary land uses, sheep are sometimes grazed in reforested areas in order to reduce competition for trees. The sheep will eat the plants that compete with trees in the early stages of growth.)

At higher stocking levels, complementarity often gives way to competition. Competitive use implies that there is substitution between the products available from the land, and this substitution can be either constant or increasing. Because the curvilinear segment *FK* in Figure 10.2 is concave to the origin, this indicates that the marginal rate of substitution is increasing. Thus, as more cattle graze on the land, the number of deer that are displaced increases – deer are supplanted at an ever-increasing rate.

A constant rate of substitution implies that the rate at which deer are dislodged by cattle is the same, regardless of the number of cattle that graze on the range, up to the carrying capacity of the range for cattle (see Figure 10.3). A constant rate of substitution is frequently postulated for the interaction between elk and cattle, which is the most common range conflict studied in western North America. Given the paucity of information about the actual shape of the biological trade-off function, researchers have found it convenient to express forage requirements of one species as a fixed proportion of those of another. For elk, the trade-off in BC, for example, has been between 0.33 and 0.625 AUM per elk; with the best estimates of the trade-off appearing to be 0.33 AUM per elk in the summer and 0.43 AUM per elk in the winter. (While somewhat suggestive of a nonlinear trade-off function, linearity remains the workable assumption.) Further, there is evidence to suggest that elk and cattle have similar foraging habitats, which permits a linear trade-off or transformation function, as is illustrated for deer and cattle in Figure 10.3.

The case of supplementary outputs is a special case of complementarity, in which the output from one use is unaffected by the other use. Rather than an upward slope on the production possibility function, the trade-off function is horizontal, as is indicated by the straight-line segments *GF* and *HK* in Figure 10.4. Suppose that range is utilized by sheep and cattle. The segment *GF* is horizontal (and *HK* is vertical), because the two types of livestock (cattle and sheep) prefer different plant species.

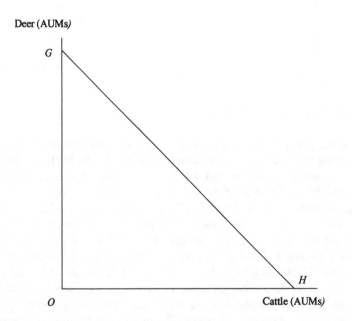

Figure 10.3: Constant rate of substitution between land uses

At sufficiently low numbers of cattle, there is no competition for forages between sheep and cattle; nor does grazing of plants preferred by sheep increase availability of plants preferred by cattle. However, as the number of cattle increases, they begin to compete with the sheep for the same plants. Once again, the shape of the curved segment *FK* indicates an increasing marginal rate of substitution between competing uses of the range.

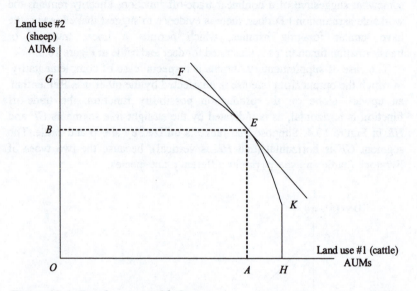

Figure 10.4: Supplementary land uses

Given positive values (prices) for the land uses discussed above, and assuming that multiple uses are indeed possible for the land, the optimal or best economic use of the land will be determined where a line with slope determined by the ratio of the prices of the alternative uses (= $-P_1/P_2$) is tangent to the trade-off function. (Prices are on a per AUM basis.) This is illustrated by point *E* in Figures 10.2 and 10.4. In Figure 10.2, optimal multiple use of the range implies that *OB* AUMs are allocated to domestic (cattle) grazing and *OA* AUMs are allocated to deer. Likewise, in Figure 10.4, *OA* AUMs are allocated to sheep and *OB* AUMs to cattle. Although it is difficult to determine the price of an AUM for domestic cattle (and sheep), because grazing fees on public land are set by government fiat (albeit using a formula), the major difficulty in this analysis is determining "prices" in wildlife production (Workman 1986; Martin and Jeffries 1966). It is in these instances that the valuation methods discussed in Chapter 4 need to be employed (see also below).

Wildlife-associated nonmarket values need to be appropriately included in the decision to allocate range resources, as illustrated with the aid of Figure 10.5. In general, finding a single price (nonmarket value) for an AUM in elk production and comparing that to the value of an AUM in cattle production will lead to the exclusion of one of the two uses of the range – to a corner solution. The exception occurs when the ratio of the AUM "prices" happens to equal the biological trade-off between elk and cattle use of the range; in that case, any point on the line *GH* in Figure 10.5 is economically optimal (Martin et al. 1978).

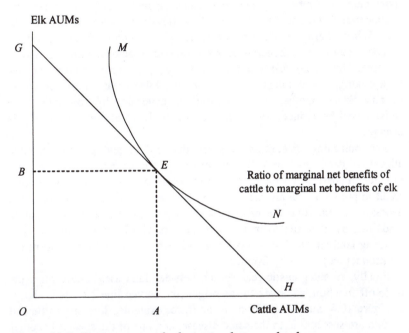

Figure 10.5: Constant rate of substitution between land uses

The use of a price ratio is an approximation, however. The correct method is to determine how the net benefit to cattle ranchers changes as an additional AUM is allocated to cattle versus the net benefit to hunters and nonconsumptive users if it is allocated to wildlife grazing instead (Cory and Martin 1985). As more and more of the resource becomes available for any of the uses, the value of that use declines relative to that of the other use at an increasing rate, thereby giving rise to a nonlinear marginal value function such as *MEN* in Figure 10.5. That is, the ratio of the fixed AUM prices is replaced by the ratio of the marginal net benefits, and this function will have the form indicated by the curve *MEN*.

The foregoing analysis can be extended either to cases of commercial timber production versus livestock, timber production versus wildlife grazing, snowmobiling versus cross-country skiing, heli-skiing versus snowmobiling, hunting versus hiking, and so on or to the case of three or more possible uses of the land. (In the case of more than two land uses, the dimensions of the diagrams simply need to be increased, which makes visual but not mathematical conceptualization of the problem more difficult.) For commercial timber production and cattle grazing, it is necessary to determine the shape of the biological transformation function (how much is timber production reduced as more cattle are grazed on commercial forestland) in addition to the (shadow) values of each of the uses. Where there are conflicts (or harmony) between recreational uses, it will be necessary to ask recreationists, professional guides, outfitters, and so on about how one use interferes with (e.g., hunting activity reduces backpacking) or complements (e.g., snowmobiles create trails for cross-country skiers) another. It is necessary to determine by how much one activity will be reduced (or increased) as the level of another activity is changed.

The preceding discussion assumes that public and private resource allocation decisions are efficient, enabling the economy to attain the production possibility frontier. However, resource allocation decisions often result in production at an interior point, such as C or D in Figure 10.2. It is necessary to improve the efficiency of public institutions so that public lands can be managed to make more outputs of all kinds available, thus allowing land-use decisions involving trade-offs to occur along, not inside, the production possibility frontier.

Finally, an antagonistic relationship between land uses results when the trade-off function is convex to the origin (the curved line YX), as is shown in Figure 10.6. Such a situation occurs if, for example, domestic cattle and buffalo are susceptible to the same disease, and one of the species becomes infected. In Figure 10.6, an economically optimal mix of land uses occurs at one of the corners (either point X or Y in the figure), depending on whether the ratio of prices for AUMs in cattle to bison is given by, respectively, $(P_1/P_2)_x$ or $(P_1/P_2)_y$. This implies incompatible land uses, with single use constituting the best outcome.

Determining Optimal Use of Range

The literature on range management has been slow in recognizing values other than those accruing to livestock and slower yet in modeling the economics of multiple use.[6] Those studies that do take account of nonmarket values have focused on the value of grazing by wildlife ungulates. Standiford and Howitt (1992) considered the optimal allocation of forage among domestic livestock and wildlife, where wildlife could be hunted. However, hunting benefits in their case accrued to the landowner, so there were no spillover or extra-market benefits. There have been only a few attempts to determine optimal multiple use of public lands. Some are described below.

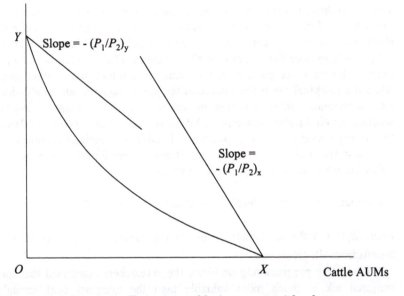

Figure 10.6: Economically incompatible (antagonistic) land uses

Martin et al. (1978) focused on trade-offs between hunting and domestic grazing of cattle in Arizona. In their model, the public range manager is interested in determining the allowable level of cattle grazing, the level at which game species should be encouraged, and the level of public access for hunting. However, the authors focus on the average, rather than marginal, trade-off between land uses, concluding that beef production has a social worth five times greater than hunting. In their view, hunters have been able to protect their rights only because they have greater economic potential for political activity.

Cory and Martin (1985) address the issue of average versus marginal valuation by postulating a biological trade-off between cattle and elk as follows: $C = \alpha - \beta E$, where C is the size of the cowherd, E is the size of the elk herd, and α and β are positive constants. The capacity of the range is given by α for cattle and α/β for elk, or points H and G, respectively, in Figures 10.3 and 10.5. In the central plateau of Arizona, 32 acres are required to support one animal unit, while 170 acres are required to support one AU in the deserts of the southwestern part of the state; thus, to support a 700-cattle operation in the central plateau requires about 22,400 acres (9,068 ha) of rangeland. The Arizona researchers set $\beta = 0.5$; the carrying capacity for the range is half as many animal units of cattle as of elk.

In order to determine optimal multiple use (single use occurs if the solution to the problem occurs on one of the axes in the above figures), it is necessary to derive marginal net benefit functions for both cattle and elk. However, to avoid a corner solution (such as at point H in Figure 10.3), it is not possible to have fixed prices for elk and cattle. The marginal net benefit function for public range in cattle production was found from market data, while the marginal net benefit function for public range in elk production was determined from information about hunters' willingness-to-pay function for elk hunting. Hunters' WTP for an elk hunting license is related to hunting success (or elk population). Finally, the optimal numbers of cattle and elk to allow on a given size of range were found by solving the following mathematical programming problem:

(10.7) maximize $\ B_C(C) + B_E(E)\ $ subject to $C = \alpha - \beta E$, with $C, E > 0$,

where $B_C(C)$ is the net benefit from grazing cattle, and $B_E(E)$ is the net benefit from elk production.[7]

Solving this programming problem, the researchers concluded that the marginal elk is much more valuable than the marginal beef animal, indicating that cattle and elk numbers are far from an economically efficient equilibrium (by point E in Figure 10.5, say). In particular, the evidence indicated that fewer cattle should be permitted on the range, thus encouraging greater elk numbers. This conclusion differs remarkably from that of Martin et al. (1978), thereby illustrating how analysis based on average rather than marginal value can result in misleading conclusions for range management. It is important to specify the correct model.

The main problem with the approach used by Cory and Martin is that it is static, with biological growth not taken into account. It is preferable, instead, to use a dynamic optimization, bioeconomic model (Keith and Lyon 1985). Although such models are beyond the scope of this book, we report the results of a study conducted by van Kooten et al. (2001) for management of public range in British Columbia. The range improvement considered in the study was to seed a clearcut so that more forage would be available for both wildlife and domestic livestock. Since the range improvement occurs on public forestland, the land manager takes into account the domestic grazing values, benefits to hunters of increased wildlife herbivores (elk, deer), nonconsumptive use values (from viewing wildlife), and existence values – wildlife are a public good. In the simple static analysis where wildlife is ignored, the range improvement results in the capacity to graze an additional 10,782 cattle (see Table 10.1). If nonmarket benefits of wildlife are taken into account, then, for the base dynamic case, 170 less cattle would be grazed, 165 wildlife units would be added to the stock of wildlife in the region, and hunters would be able to take 70 animals per year. Further, society would benefit to the tune of $86,730, although ranchers and/or the public agency responsible for the land would be worse off by $13,460 per year while hunters gain $99,690 per year in consumer surplus. The difference between these values constitutes the nonconsumptive use and non-use benefits amount to $500 per year.

Table 10.1: Effects of a Forest Range Improvement, British Columbia

Item	Static result		Dynamic analysis			
		Base case	Flatter marginal non-market benefits	Steeper marginal Non-market benefits	Greater hunting value	Lower value of forage in grazing
Increase in:			(animal numbers)			
Cattle	10,782	10,612	9,721	10,723	10,531	10,609
Wildlife	0	165	1,034	58	245	167
Wildlife harvest	0	70	204	32	75	71
Benefits to:			('000s $)			
Rancher/agency[a]	857.15	843.69	772.79	852.45	837.15	421.74
Hunters	0	99.69	85.03	71.21	217.97	100.72
Society (net gain)[a]	749.15	835.88	749.82	815.66	947.12	414.46

Notes:
[a] Grazing fee of $2.11 per AUM is included as a benefit to the agency overseeing public range; net social benefit includes $108,000 annual cost of range improvement.
Source: Adapted from van Kooten et al. (2001).

If the benefit from grazing domestic livestock is reduced by half, the optimal number of cattle to be grazed decreases only slightly (last column compared to second column, Table 10.1). In this case, hunting benefits increase only slightly, while benefits to the rancher and public agency decline (as does overall social value) due to the lower forage value. If hunting values are greater than in the base case, the optimal number of wildlife units increases (from 165 to 245), but wildlife harvests only increase by five units because they are constrained to be sustainable (second last column).[8] The most dramatic changes occur when different assumptions are made about the rate at which marginal benefits change (middle two columns of Table 10.1). If the marginal hunting, nonconsumptive use and non-use values of wildlife are relatively constant (flat marginal benefits), then much less cattle are grazed, permitting many more wildlife to graze on the seeded clearcut.

10.3 ECONOMICS OF PUBLIC FORAGE

It is clear that ranchers cannot be permitted to graze domestic livestock on public land without some mechanism for allocating forage. Historically, overgrazing by domestic animals (especially sheep) resulted in rangeland degradation in the western USA. The reason was that the range was an *open access* resource. Ranchers had no stake in conserving or improving the range, because they did not own the resource and would, therefore, not be the sole beneficiaries of any efforts on their part to preserve it. Rangeland degradation currently occurs in the Sahel, for example, because property arrangements permit individual farmers to obtain the benefits from planting annual crops but discourage investments, such as seeding forages or planting trees, which yield benefits over a longer period. Others would capture benefits of long-term investments. It is because individuals are unable to reap all the future benefits of investments that rangeland degradation often occurs, and that public intervention is required. As noted in the introduction to this chapter, this intervention often takes the form of public ownership of rangeland.

Open access and lack of investment in range resources do not, by themselves, warrant public ownership of the resource. Simply providing tenure rights to the range can solve the problem of open access, but tenure does not necessarily imply ownership. There are legitimate externality reasons for retaining public ownership of the land, principally that the range provides public goods that would not be provided by private owners. Rangelands have nontrivial nonmarket values. The private resource owner does not generally capture recreation, hunting and preservation values, and these range benefits are not taken into account in private investment decisions concerning public range. These factors have resulted in public ownership of rangelands in much of the western USA and in regions of Canada.

The rancher with a mix of private land and public grazing leases has to make decisions concerning the allocation of own lands subject to the availability of public range or community pastures. Tenure requirements may also make the rancher responsible for allocation decisions on public range, subject to any constraints imposed by the public agency. In Canada, tenure is such that ranchers are given grazing licenses, which provide some guarantee regarding long-term use of the range, or grazing permits, which are renewable but subject to periodic review. In the USA, grazing rights take the form of permits, which have been considered an inviolable property right, although US courts have ruled otherwise.

Grazing rights on public rangelands and the fees charged to ranchers are not determined in the market place; public grazing fees are an example of administered prices. In Canada and the United States, public agencies determine both the amount of domestic livestock that can be grazed and the amount that needs to be paid in order to graze them. The government agency responsible for rangeland management also makes decisions concerning range improvements, although ranchers themselves will sometimes make improvements on public lands.

Administered Prices

The effect of grazing on public rangelands and the impact of administered prices (grazing fees) is illustrated in Figure 10.7. In the figure, the derived demand for range and pasture services is assumed to have the usual negative slope. Although final output price (price of beef) is a parameter to the individual beef producer, it is likely that some of the inputs into production will have finite supply elasticities, thereby giving rise to the negative slope for derived demand.

The supply of private foraging services (S_{Pr}) is upward sloping, because sources of supply can be ordered according to their basic unit costs: unimproved land (with little alternative use) owned by the farmer, pasture land rented from other private owners, and improved land on the farmer's own property that can be used for hay or grain production. The supply of public rangeland (S_R) is determined by public agency fiat and, therefore, is assumed to be totally inelastic at the number of AUMs of public grazing made available by the government agency (amount OR).

Given that there is a public supply of rangeland services (measured in AUMs) of amount q_2q_1 ($= OR$), the supply of grazing services is given by $S_{Pr} + S_R$, and the net amount of grazing services resulting from public provision of rangeland is given by q_0q_1, with the actual amount depending on the elasticities of supply and demand. If N is the increase in total range and pasture consumption as a proportion of the amount of public range made available ($N = q_0q_1 \div q_1q_2$), then $N = E_d/(E_s + E_d)$, where E_s is the elasticity of supply and E_d is the elasticity of demand.

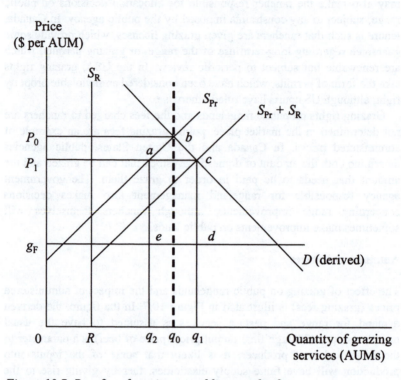

Figure 10.7: Benefits of grazing on public rangeland

The benefits of grazing on public rangeland are the results of two effects. (1) There is an increase in the benefits accruing to cattle producers, because the price of private range/pasture services has fallen from P_0 to P_1. This increase in benefits is measured by the area under the demand function, namely, q_0bcq_1. (2) An amount q_2q_0 of range/pasture services is released for use in its best alternative. In the current situation, there is a shift of grazing from own pastureland to public range. The freed pastureland can be used to produce hay or other crops (e.g., barley) that can be fed to the cattle during the winter months. This benefit is measured by the area q_2abq_0.

The private users of the public range (i.e., cattle ranchers) pay a grazing fee (g_F) that is administered and likely below the market price. There are several reasons why the grazing fee might be below the market price: (1) the agency does not know what impact provision of public range has on market prices (i.e., P_1 versus P_0); (2) the opportunity costs of providing public range are negligible – a result of normal forest harvesting and administrative activities (e.g., cattle graze on clearcuts until the next stand of trees is sufficiently mature to preclude grazing); and (3) the administered price structure is an institutional arrangement that has bestowed historic property rights upon cattle ranchers (politically it is difficult to change). These historic rights or benefits are capitalized in ranch values, and withdrawal of them, now or in the future, may require some form of compensation. Compensation is required because current owners paid for the grazing rights when they purchased the ranch.

In terms of Figure 10.7, ranchers pay a price of P_1 for Oq_2 AUMs of grazing services and g_F for the remaining q_2q_1 AUMs. Thus, the net benefits to cattle ranchers from public grazing are given by area *eabcd*, which consists of a subsidy equal to the rectangle *acde* plus an efficiency gain equal to triangle *abc*. The efficiency gain may be quite large if ranchers are able to increase herd size and, thereby, achieve economies of scale that are not possible without publicly provided range services.

Whenever cattle are shifted from private pasture to public range during the spring, summer and fall grazing periods, a constraint on cattle numbers is relaxed. Private pasture can now be used to produce hay, forages or other feed that can be used in the winter months. Thus, an increase in grazing on public range will make private lands more productive and ranchers better off. These benefits are capitalized in ranch values or grazing permits (generally attached to ranches). The capitalized value of these grazing permits is given by area (*abc* + *eacd*) divided by the private discount rate (with the discount rate including an allowance for risk). In a 1986 study, the US Departments of Agriculture and the Interior estimated that the value of public land grazing permits was between a low of $30/AUM in Idaho and a high of $140/AUM in Nebraska. These estimates represent the capitalized value of the two areas identified in Figure 10.7, as derived from the bond formula, $V = B/r$, where V is the value of the bond, B is the annual benefit and r is the discount rate (see section 6.3, equation 6.4). Assuming a discount rate of 5% ($r = 0.05$), the annual benefits (B) average between $1.50 and $7.00 per AUM. If a higher discount rate is employed (e.g., to account for the risk that grazing rights might be lost at some future date), then the value of grazing is greater (e.g., $3–$10 at a 10% rate).

There remains the question of whether or not ranchers receive a subsidy; this question concerns the size of rectangle *eacd* or, put another way, the nearness of the grazing fee g_F to the price P_1. The costs to taxpayers are equal to the amount spent by the public agency in providing grazing services minus revenues from grazing fees, where revenues equal g_F times *OR*. Suppose that public agency costs are covered by a grazing fee g_F that is strictly less than P_1. Is there still a subsidy to ranchers? Since the public grazing fee could be set at P_1 without changing the amount of forage services demanded by ranchers (i.e., the number of AUMs utilized), the public agency does not collect the rent to which it, as the owner of the range, is entitled. Hence, the low grazing fee g_F constitutes a subsidy to ranchers even if the fee covers all agency costs. This does not constitute an argument to raise grazing fees, however, because proprietary property rights and political factors also need to be taken into account in setting fees.

Often the public agency is faced with decisions regarding *marginal* changes in animal units of grazing on public rangeland. The decision is whether or not to make a particular range improvement or whether or not to reduce domestic grazing so that more is available for wildlife. Since changes are marginal, the total benefits of an increase (costs of a reduction) in public grazing can be approximated by the market price P_1 of an AUM of grazing times the number of AUMs made available by the program (decision). Again, the net private benefit of (loss due to) such a decision is given by the change in AUMs times the difference between the market price and g_F. However, if the changes in the availability of public range are *non-marginal*, then an analysis similar to that in Figure 10.7 is required. For example, *OR* might be considered the change (increase or decrease) in public range services rather than the total forage available from public rangelands.

The difficulty in the foregoing analysis is that of determining the costs of providing public range, since these are not incurred by the private operators but by the public agency that administers the range. These nonprivate costs are difficult to measure and may even be negligible in cases where excess capacity exists or where the public range was previously poorly managed. The costs of providing grazing services on public lands consist of two components. First, there are administration costs, transaction costs and outlays for range improvements. These costs are measurable. The second, and more difficult, component of costs involves alternative uses of the range, including wildlife grazing. A reduction in wildlife numbers implies a reduction in the welfare of hunters as well as of preservationists, sightseers, and so on. If the range is to be managed in a way that maximizes the total welfare of society, and not just that of one group, it needs to be managed for multiple use.

Finally, there is the problem of setting grazing fees. Efficient fees can be determined by means of auctions or bids. While actual grazing rights may be worth more than is indicated by current charges and may depend on range condition, access distance, and so on, auctions may not be practical as there may be local monopsony that militates against an efficient use of auctions. Appropriate fee setting is a difficult and politically dangerous task, but the best way to move towards economic efficiency is to charge variable fees, depending upon, for example, regional climatic and productivity factors, season of use, distance to access, species of livestock, and, perhaps, breed of animals. However, this requires a level of knowledge that is beyond the reach of the public agencies and is simply too expensive to obtain. So, despite the problems, auctions may be the best option for allocating scarce range resources.

Income Distribution and Multiple Use

Issues of income distribution are often the preoccupation of politicians. Consider, for example, the effect of lobbying by environmental groups in British Columbia to protect old-growth and wilderness areas. Government policies have reduced the annual cut by about 10% province-wide (although effects in some regions are greater than in others). An important cost of preservation is the net value of the lost timber, which, if harvested, would contribute to society's overall welfare. Additional social welfare losses (or real economic costs) show up as job search costs, retraining costs, higher government administration costs, and higher prices to consumers for forest products. It also shows up as negative environmental effects – this being the result of using nonwood substitutes or increasing harvests in areas (such as the tropics) with more fragile ecosystems. On the other hand, there are benefits to preservation, such as those that accrue from maintaining biodiversity, recreational opportunities, existence value, and so on. But it may be the regional development and income distributional impacts that are most important to the politicians.

Major public land issues in the western USA have been associated with attempts by the BLM and the US Forest Service to increase grazing fees or to reduce the numbers of cattle grazed on public lands. The reasons have to do with agency revenues, the fact that grazing fees are below market value (although it remains to be determined by how much), and with carrying capacity. (Biologists have suggested that overgrazing is taking place, but others dispute this, because they feel that public agencies need to invest resources in range improvements.) Either an increase in grazing fees or a reduction in grazing allotments on public lands will result in a welfare loss to ranchers. An increase in fees will reduce ranch values and will result in a transfer of income from private ranchers to public agencies. Such a loss might be considered a violation of ranchers' inalienable property rights to the public range. In addition, there is a loss in economic activity in the regions that are impacted by reduced grazing or higher grazing fees. At the center are questions regarding compensation to ranchers and the viability of resource-dependent communities. It is the reduction in regional economic activity that is usually cited as the main cost of reduced grazing.

Similar issues are raised with respect to logging (timber harvesting) both in Canada and in the United States. A reduction in the allowable annual cut or removal of old-growth from future logging results in an outcry not only from the timber companies but also from individuals and communities whose economic lives are tied to logging and other timber operations. These individuals and communities are concerned about the effects that the use of land for nonlogging purposes (e.g., preservation or recreational use) will have on their ability to earn a living, or, in the case of communities, their long-term viability. In some sense, these individuals and communities have an inalienable property right to continue harvesting trees on public lands.

Historically, the method for analyzing the regional economic development impacts of changes in land use has been via regional impact models, such as input–output models. In a multiple-use context, regional input–output models can be used to determine the impacts on a local community of changes in the allocation of range resources, logging activity, tourism and hunting, which may occur as a result of public decisions concerning the optimal use of public lands. While such models can aid in identifying the income distributional consequences of public planning, it is left to the decision-maker to determine how, or if, these are to be mitigated.

The point is that the cost of reduced exploitation of a natural resource is simply given by the loss in resource rent plus the loss in producer surplus (see Chapter 3). For some resource activities, such as grazing of cattle in arid regions, this loss in surplus might be quite small. To it must be added the costs that people in the local community incur when they have to seek employment elsewhere, perhaps outside the region. The costs of moving and finding employment elsewhere are a real cost of the policy to reduce exploitation of a natural resource. Some people might find employment in the local community, but at a lower wage. The reduction in wages does not, however, constitute an economic cost as defined in Chapter 2. Rather, it amounts to a redistribution of income, and, as such, needs to be dealt with at the political level.

Fairness and Political Acceptability

An important aspect of public land management concerns historical property rights. While historical rights to publicly owned resources, such as rangelands and timber, appear to be well established in the United States, they are less obvious in Canada. However, there is implicit recognition of historical property rights when, for example, federal funds for agricultural programs include contributions to improve public range resources in BC. Further, any subsidy component related to public provision of forage is capitalized in ranch values, and attempts to dramatically depart from previous policies (e.g., by large increases in grazing fees) will result in unanticipated losses to ranchers. Based on criteria of both fairness and political feasibility, it is unlikely that government decision-makers would restrict ranchers' access to public range or even reduce the number of AUMs available to them (either through regulation or substantial increases in grazing fees). However, there may be circumstances in which it is necessary to restrict domestic grazing on public range for reasons of economic efficiency (e.g., grazing by elk has greater social value than grazing by domestic livestock).

Likewise, individuals living in resource-dependent communities perceive that they have a property right to continued harvesting of timber from public lands. The government implicitly recognizes this property right when it makes land-use decisions that favor timber interests; where a large number of jobs depend on logging operations, it may not be politically feasible to restrict harvests.

Whenever public land-use decisions result in a reduction in domestic grazing or timber harvests, it may be necessary to compensate or otherwise help those individuals who lose their jobs and those communities whose tax base is eroded. The question that needs to be addressed is not whether compensation should take place but, rather, how compensation should occur. In some cases, it is possible to use economic incentives to address income distributional issues. In Chapter 8, transferable development rights were suggested as one method of mitigating against the adverse income redistributional effects of zoning. In other situations, it is not possible to use economic incentives. For example, if a reduction in access to timber for logging saves a stand of old-growth timber but causes a sawmill in a remote town to close down, the compensation may simply take the form of payments from a state or provincial government to local government and/or individuals. But even in these circumstances, it may be possible to get environmentalists to help defray some of these costs. Indeed, it is economically efficient to get non-users to pay the costs, because it causes them to place a more realistic value on preservation or the alternative use of the resource.

Difficulties in making transfer payments can be illustrated by the example of ranching and access to public rangeland. An approach that can be used when access to range is restricted is to simply pay ranchers according to the AUMs of grazing that are lost. This poses a difficulty associated with the evaluation of such losses, but this is not an insurmountable measurement problem (although it is a problem that could have political ramifications). The greatest difficulty is that some compensation schemes (e.g., ones that look more like pure subsidy) may not be politically acceptable either to the ranchers or to the public at large (as represented by the government).

One approach to resolving the rangeland conflict between multiple use and historic property rights, and yet obtaining a solution that is economically efficient, is to charge ranchers a higher fee for grazing, while, at the same time, providing compensation based on the amount of forage left behind or not used. This is referred to as an *offsetting grazing fee*. The reason for increasing grazing fees is that they might not reflect the true opportunity cost of grazing. The current system of grazing fees results in inefficient allocation of the range between cattle and other uses (primarily big game). Further, grazing fees do not now take into account differences in range productivity, and that is both inefficient and unfair. An increase in grazing fees and/or a change in the structure of fees will increase efficiency of land use, but it will also take away implicit rights that ranchers currently enjoy. This is the reason that fee increases have been resisted.

An offsetting fee structure (in which producers are paid for unused grazing) can improve land-use efficiency, since it takes into account other uses of the range. For such a system to work, range utilization by cattle and wildlife, and range productivity, will need to be determined and monitored by biologists. Although there are practical difficulties in implementing an offsetting fee system, these problems can be overcome. While such a system is likely to result in a more efficient, effective and fair allocation of range resources among competing users, it will need to be extended to include wildlife. Wherever they can be identified and assessed, fees need to be assessed for nongrazing services received by environmentalists and recreationists. This will help to allocate public lands in an economically efficient manner among multiple users.

The offsetting fee system recognizes issues of economic efficiency, fairness (equity) and political acceptability. It is fair because the grazing fee and payment for unused forage could be set in a way that leaves the welfare of ranchers unchanged; their historical property right is protected, and ranch values remain unaffected. It would seem that an offsetting fee structure is politically acceptable, because ranchers' rights are protected while, from society's standpoint, users of the range pay according to its actual grazing value. Yet, by addressing equity and political feasibility, the offsetting fees system would not necessarily result in an efficient allocation of range resources, and there remains the problem of finding the funds needed to pay ranchers for leaving behind forage. In the end, an offsetting grazing fee system remains a theoretical constraint that has never been attempted in practice.

A mechanism for charging hunters, recreationists and environmentalists according to the value they place on the land in an alternative use needs to be determined. This can be done via increased hunting fees, which are somehow related to the probability of hunter success (i.e., wildlife numbers), hiking tolls, and so on. Where environmental groups, recreationists, hunters, and other users of scarce resources are not charged for their use of the natural resource, distortions in land use occur. These distortions contribute to a lower level of general welfare for all members in society.

NOTES

1. Forestlands beyond the extensive margin (and thus unable to earn rents) were poorly stocked, too distant from water transport or generally inaccessible, while rangeland was often too dry to be profitable for domestic grazing after an initial pass by livestock, especially sheep.

2. Land was divided into sections that were 1 mile (1.6 km) on every side and contained 640 acres, which were then split into quarters. A township consisted of 36 sections, one of which was generally assigned to public purposes (e.g., a school).

3. Recreation subsumes wildlife viewing and hunting, but a distinction is made here because these activities are important in relation to wildlife herbivores and waterfowl. Recreation thus includes such things as swimming, hiking, water activities besides swimming, biking, motorized vehicle use (including off-road), camping and so on, most of which involve nonconsumptive use.

4. Suppose $B = f(x)$ refers to total benefits. The average benefit function lies above marginal benefits if $f(x)/x \geq f'(x)$, $\forall x$, and $f(x)/x > f'(x)$ for at least one x. This condition can be rewritten as $f(x) > xf'(x)$, which is true, e.g., if $f(x) = a+bx+cx^2$ as long as $a>0$. As the reader can verify, it also holds for other functional forms.

5. This is the difference between the area under MC (total costs) and MB (total benefits) between 0 and W^*. It is the net social cost (negative benefit) of providing W^* amount of wetlands.

6. For example, one authoritative reference still used as a text in courses on range management (Holechek et al. 1989) focuses only on biophysical aspects of multiple use management, and relegates economic analysis to a small section in the last chapter entitled "Computer Applications and the Future".

7. The problem can be solved using the "solver" in Excel, for example. A graphical illustration of the problem is found in Figure 10.5, where the curve represents the objective function and the straight line represents the constraint. The optimal solution that the solver would find would be equivalent to point E.

8. It is inappropriate to compare benefits in the scenarios of the last four columns of Table 10.1 with the base case scenario, because the value of hunting or grazing is assumed to differ across scenarios, and these values are used to estimate benefits. For example, reducing grazing fees clearly lowers overall benefits in Table 10.1.

Part IV: Forest Economics

11. Forest Economics I

Forests are one of the most important natural resources on the planet, covering some 4.3 billion ha or one-third of the world's land area. Yet, this is less than the area capable of growing trees, which amounts to some 40% of the earth's landmass. Forests are important as a source of income and employment because of the wood products industry, but they also contribute ecosystem services, such as carbon uptake and storage and weather regulation functions, absorb pollutants, provide recreational and scenic amenities, contribute wildlife habitat, and protect watersheds. Therefore, management of forestlands for both commercial timber production and other amenities is vital to the overall wellbeing of society.

In this chapter, we begin our examination of the economics of forestry with an overview of the globe's forest resources. Then, in section 11.2, we discuss how foresters calculate rotation ages. Rotation ages are generally based on a criterion, such as maximum sustainable yield or maximization of the net present value of returns from planting and harvesting trees (known as maximization of the *soil expectation*). However, since forest operations result in environmental spillovers, it is important to calculate the effect that an accounting for these externalities has on rotation age. Indeed, if the standing value of a forest is sufficiently high, it might turn out that the optimal rotation age is infinity – the forest should never be harvested. In section 11.3, we examine the role of regulation. We consider the role of public ownership of forestlands and the allowable cut effect, because it is the result of regulation. In Chapter 12, a nonstate, market governance market structure for addressing spillovers is examined in more detail, as is trade in forest products. Tropical deforestation is dealt with in Chapter 13. Finally, the role that forestland and forestry play in contributing to or mitigating global warming is discussed in Chapter 14.

11.1 BACKGROUND

Of the globe's forested area, 2,900 million ha or 68% is considered productive forestland, defined as land capable of growing merchantable stands of timber within a reasonable period of time (see Table 11.1). It is estimated that the standing volume of timber on productive forestlands is some 320 billion m³. Canada's forests account for about 10% of the world's forested land and 8% of its productive forestland; the United States accounts for about 7% of the world's total forested land and the same proportion of productive forestland. As a country, only Russia has greater forest resources (Table 11.1).

Table 11.1: World Forest Resources

Country/region	Total forestland (10⁶ ha)	Productive forestland (10⁶ ha)	Timber volume (10⁹ m³)
Canada	418	245	25.0
United States	298	217	29.0
South and Central America	988	739	97.0
Africa	744	236	25.0
Europe (excl. former USSR)	195	141	15.2
Former USSR	957	770	86.7
Asia and Oceania	767	585	44.0
WORLD	4,367	2,933	321.9

Source: FAO (2001).

The USA is the largest producer of softwood lumber and wood products in the world, followed by Canada and Russia (Table 11.2). Some 70% of total roundwood and 90% of all the paper products produced globally come from forests in northern latitudes (Table 11.2). The majority of wood products are produced from coniferous forests in the Northern Hemisphere.

Production of pulp from hardwood species has become increasingly important as a result of technical advances in pulp making and the existence of substantial indigenous (boreal) stands of mixed hard and softwood species, and the use of hardwood species in plantation forests. Principal producers of pulp and softwood lumber are the USA, Canada, Sweden, Finland, Russia and Japan. Among tropical countries, only Brazil produces globally significant amounts of pulp, although the amount is relatively small (less than 5% of world production). Countries such as Chile, New Zealand and Australia are also expected to become important, at least in export markets.

Tropical forests do not contribute large amounts to global industrial wood output. Even for countries such as Brazil that are significant in terms of pulp production, fiber comes from plantation forests. Less than one-third of the world's industrial wood harvest originates with old-growth forests, or forests that have not previously been commercially exploited (Table 11.3).

Table 11.2: World Forest Products Production (2000)

Country/region	Industrial roundw'd 10^6 m^3	Sawn-wood 10^6 m^3	Wood-based panels 10^6 m^3	Pulp 10^6 tonne	Paper products 10^6 tonne
Canada	176.6	69.6	14.5	26.5	20.9
United States	427.7	114.1	45.5	57.2	86.5
South & Cen America	166.0	34.9	8.4	12.0	14.2
Africa	68.8	7.7	2.1	2.3	2.9
Europe (excl. Russia)	372.9	105.8	55.6	41.2	95.1
Russian Federation	105.8	20.0	4.8	5.8	5.3
Asia & Oceania	256.8	72.4	45.8	42.6	98.6
WORLD	1,574.6	424.5	181.6	187.5	323.6

Source: FAO (2003).

Table 11.3: Global Timber Harvests by Management Type

Management Type	Proportion of industrial wood production
Old growth	30%
Second growth, minimal management	14%
Indigenous second growth, managed	22%
Industrial plantation, indigenous species	24%
Industrial plantation, exotic species	10%

Source: Sedjo (1997, p.11).

Commercial timber production from old growth occurs principally in Canada, Russia, Indonesia and Malaysia (Sedjo 1997). Industrial plantations account for more than one-third of industrial wood harvest, with the remainder accounted for by second-growth forests. The continuing trend toward intensively managed plantation forests occurs for both financial reasons and concerns related to security of supply, with increasing investment in the technology of growing trees stimulated by declining global reliance on old growth – the dwindling of the "old growth overhang" (Sedjo 1997). Increasingly trees are considered an agricultural crop, with rapidly growing trees competitive with annual crops as a land use (as is the case with loblolly pine (*Pinus taeda*) plantations in the US South and hybrid cottonwood plantations on irrigated agricultural lands in the US Pacific Northwest).

Canada is the world's foremost exporter of wood products followed by the USA and the countries in Nordic Europe. Compared to other timber-producing regions in the world, Canada and Russia are likely at a disadvantage in timber production because of climate (particularly in the interior regions of these countries); to a lesser degree, the same might be true of the Scandinavian countries. Working forest area, degree of public ownership of forestlands, average annual growth and average annual harvest levels are provided in Table 11.4 for the major timber-producing regions.

Table 11.4: Working Forest Area, Public Ownership, Annual Growth and Harvest, Selected Jurisdictions (Data for Early- to Mid-1990s)

Country/ region	Working forest (10^6 ha)	% Public	Average annual growth (10^6 m^3)	Annual harvest (10^6 m^3)
Finland	20	29	77	63.6
Sweden	23	13	98	68.0
New Zealand	2	4	22[a]	17.0
Chile	2	–	22[b]	20.0
Russia	446	90	617	300+[c]
United States	198	45	612	469.0
– PNW	16	56	82	73.0
– South	37	11	128	117.0
Canada	227	94	233	183.0
– BC	51	96	72	71.0
– Alberta	25	96	22	20.3

Notes:
[a] New Zealand's annual growth is expected to rise to some 25 million m^3 by 2005.
[b] Chile's annual growth is expected to reach 47 million m^3 in 2018.
[c] Russian harvests have fallen to some 232 million m^3, but have exceeded 300 million m^3 previously.
Source: Wilson et al. (1998, p.13).

Timber shortfalls have been forecast for the US Pacific Northwest and South and Canada, particularly British Columbia. In BC, a "fall down" in timber production is predicted because of the time lag between the availability of virgin forests and second growth. This is caused by past delays in plantings and silvicultural investments and the mere fact that old-growth forests contain greater timber volume and are increasingly being set aside as protected areas. Globally these shortfalls will likely be covered by production of radiata pine (*Pinus radiata*) from Chile and New Zealand. Unless adequate investments are made in planting and silviculture, countries such as Canada will decline in importance in terms of world timber production. Unfortunately, reforestation and silvicultural investments on many sites are often uneconomic and it may well be that forests in these regions provide nontimber benefits to society that exceed their commercial timber value.

11.2 ECONOMIC INCENTIVES AND ROTATION AGES

Harvesting timber provides benefits to society equal to the stumpage value of standing trees. The decision of when to harvest trees depends on prices, including importantly the interest rate (or opportunity cost of cash). On the other hand, by using financial incentives as the criterion for determining when to harvest trees, environmental benefits could be foregone. The authority needs to provide economic incentives that cause forestland owners or concessionaires to harvest trees at a time that is optimal from society's point of view rather than solely from a private, commercial point of view. To determine what these incentives might be, various criteria related to the age of harvest can be considered.

Maximizing Sustainable Yield

Biologists use maximum sustainable yield (MSY) as the criterion to determine optimal harvest ages for timber. As implied by its name, the objective is to find the forest rotation age that leads to the maximum possible annual output that can be maintained in perpetuity. The allowable annual cut (AAC) is based on the MSY concept. The AAC is the amount of timber that can be harvested each and every year without diminishing the amount that can be harvested in the future. The AAC is simply the net increase in timber volume in a region or district that results from tree growth – the *mean annual increment* (MAI).

Denote the growth of a stand of timber over time by $v(t)$. In the parlance of production economics, this is the total product function, where the input time or age, t, replaces the usual input labor or capital (Figure 11.1). Then average product/growth is simply the MAI, which is given by $v(t)/t$, and graphically in the figure by the slope of a straight line from the origin to a point on the growth curve, $v(t)$. The current annual increment (CAI) is analogous to marginal product, and is given by the slope of a line tangent to the growth curve; mathematically, CAI $= v'(t) = dv(t)/dt$. It is well known from microeconomic theory that the marginal product curve intersects the average product function (from above) at the point where average product attains its maximum. This occurs in Figure 11.3 where a straight line emanating from the origin is exactly tangent to the cumulative yield (growth) curve. This line has the greatest slope of any such line that still reaches $v(t)$ and thus is the point in time (the age) at which MAI reaches a maximum, at age a_2 in Figure 11.1. Since $v(t)$ is steepest somewhat earlier (at age a_1), CAI = $v'(t)$ achieves a maximum before MAI and, with $v'(t)$ falling beyond this point, CAI intersects MAI from above at the latter's maximum. Finally, CAI = $v'(t) = 0$ when $v(t)$ reaches a maximum, at age a_3. This would imply a reduction in (usable) timber biomass as trees age further, but this is unlikely. Rather, the increase in biomass slows down as biomass approaches some asymptotic maximum (so that the growth function is more like an S curve).

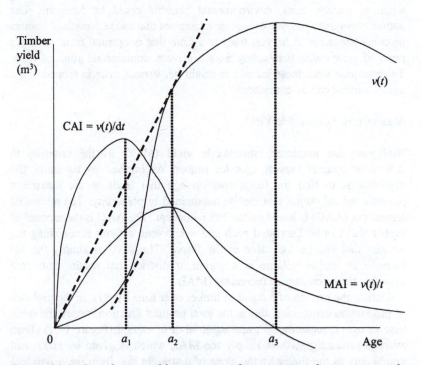

Figure 11.1: Cumulative yield, mean annual increment and current annual increment

The MSY rotation age, t_M, is simply the culmination of mean annual increment, and is found by setting the MAI equal to CAI:

$$(11.1) \qquad \frac{v(t)}{t} = v'(t).$$

Rearranging (11.1) gives the usual relation for finding the MSY rotation age:

$$(11.2) \quad \frac{v'(t_M)}{v(t_M)} = \frac{1}{t_M},$$

where the LHS of this expression is the rate of growth of the timber stand.

As an illustration, consider two functions in Table 11.5 that can be used to describe the growth in the yield of commercial timber for a stand of trees. One function describes the growth of native spruce (*Picea spp*) trees, while the other describes that of fast-growing, hybrid poplar. The maximum sustainable yield rotation ages for slow-growing spruce and hybrid poplar are 50 years and 13 years, respectively. The case of spruce is also illustrated in Figure 11.2.

Table 11.5: Comparison of Various Rotation Ages for Different Functional Forms for Stand Growth

		Functional form[a]	
		Spruce[b]	Hybrid poplar[c]
Rotation	Means to calculate the associated rotation age	$v(t) = kt^a e^{-bt}$ $k = 0.25, a =$ $2.00, b = 0.02$	$v(t) = \gamma(1-e^{-\varepsilon t})^{\phi}$ $\gamma = 300.00, \varepsilon =$ $0.15, \phi = 3.00$
MSY (t_M)	Equation 11.2	50 years	13 years
Fisher (t_S)	Equation 11.4	33 years	17 years
Faustmann (t_F)	Equation 11.13	23 years	11 years

Notes:
[a] Timber volume v is measured in m^3.
[b] This function is easy to estimate and $v'(t)/v(t) = (a - bt)/t$.
[c] This is referred to as the Chapman–Richards growth function. Binkley (1987) demonstrates that, for fast-growing species, the financial rotation age can exceed the MSY age.

For plantation forests of hybrid poplar under an MSY rotation, the AAC is by definition set equal to the MSY. For uneven-aged forests consisting of mature, over-mature and young stands of trees, the AAC and MSY are subject to vagaries of harvesting and planting (see below). If one's desire is to maximize society's wellbeing, the MSY rotation may not be appropriate, however.

The problem with maximum sustainable yield is that it is a knife-edge rule, with harvests exceeding the sustainable level if growth does not for whatever reason achieve its expected level, perhaps due to uncertainty related to weather, fire, wind and disease. This is not a major problem since any mismatch between sustainable and actual yield can be corrected in the future, although doing so requires that the authority be vigilant by investing in measurement and stock assessment.

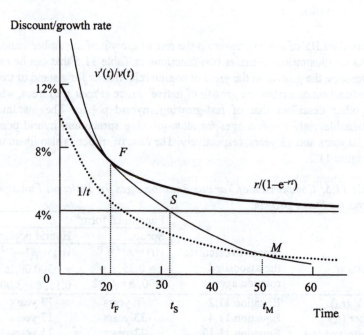

Figure 11.2: Comparison of MSY, single-period and Faustmann rotation ages for spruce (r = 4%)

Maximizing Benefits from a Single Cut: Fisher Rotation Age

Suppose the objective of forest operations is to maximize the net benefit from a one-time harvest of the forest, ignoring the future use of land for timber production. The forestland owner will harvest growing trees when the net discounted return achieves a maximum. Mathematically, the objective is to

(11.3) $\underset{t}{\text{Maximize}}\,(p-c)\,v(t)\,e^{-rt},$

where p is the price of logs at the mill, c is the associated cost of felling, bucking, yarding, loading and hauling the logs to the mill, and e^{-rt} is the continuous-time discount factor. The stumpage value is $(p - c)$. To keep things simple, assume that the cost per m^3 of harvest remains the same regardless of harvest level. Then, the first-order conditions for a maximum give:

$$(11.4) \quad \frac{v'(t_S)}{v(t_S)} = r,$$

where r is the (instantaneous) rate of discount (interest rate). Thus, trees should be left standing as long as the rate of growth of the value of the trees (and with fixed prices the rate of growth of the trees themselves) exceeds the discount rate. As long as the investment in growing trees yields a higher return than can be earned elsewhere in the economy (as determined by r), trees should be left to grow; the moment the alternative investment yields a higher return, the trees should be harvested and the funds invested at rate r. The rotation age found from (11.4) is known as the Fisher rotation age, t_S (where subscript S denotes single harvest).

Assuming a discount rate of 4%, the single rotation age is found to be about 33 years for spruce and 17 years for hybrid poplar (Table 11.5). The single rotation age can be found graphically as illustrated in Figure 11.2.

In results (11.2) and (11.4), the decision to harvest appears to be independent of net stumpage value $(p - c)$. However, net stumpage value remains important for one reason: if $(p - c) < 0$ (that is, $c > p$), the net revenue from harvesting a stand of trees is negative and trees will not be harvested regardless of their rate of growth. If the cost of harvesting c varies with the rate of harvest, size of trees or some other factor, then solving (11.3) yields the following modification of equation (11.4):

$$(11.5) \quad \frac{pv'(t)}{pv(t) - c} = r.$$

Of course, c can also vary with time, but in that case it will not be possible to determine a constant rotation age as rotation ages would possibly vary over time.

Faustmann (Financial) Rotation Age

We begin our investigation of the financial or Faustmann (1849) rotation age by looking at the value of forestland. Assume forestland is to be used only for the purpose of growing and harvesting trees (so we can ignore speculative factors other than those related to timber prices) and that there are no environmental spillovers. Now, let

V = discounted value of returns from all future harvests;

V_n = discounted value of returns over n rotations;

$v(t)$ = volume of commercial timber growing on site at time t;

t = length of a harvesting rotation;

$p - c$ = net stumpage value;

C = cost of planting trees on the site immediately after harvest (as required in most jurisdictions by law); and

r = the discount rate, which may include a risk premium.

The discounted returns from timber harvest over n rotations are given by:

$$(11.6) \quad V_n = \frac{(p-c)v(t)-C}{(1+r)^t} + \frac{(p-c)v(t)-C}{(1+r)^{2t}} + \ldots + \frac{(p-c)v(t)-C}{(1+r)^{nt}}$$

Multiply both sides of (11.6) by $(1+r)^{-t}$:

$$(11.7) \quad \frac{1}{(1+r)^t} V_n = \frac{(p-c)v(t)-C}{(1+r)^{2t}}$$

$$+ \frac{(p-c)v(t)-C}{(1+r)^{3t}} + \ldots + \frac{(p-c)v(t)-C}{(1+r)^{nt}} + \frac{(p-c)v(t)-C}{(1+r)^{(n+1)t}}$$

Subtracting (11.7) from (11.6), and solving the resulting expression for V_n gives:

$$(11.8) \quad V_n = \frac{(p-c)v(t)-C}{(1+r)^t - 1}\left(1 - \frac{1}{(1+r)^{nt}}\right).$$

Then, the value of forestland V is the value of V_n as n approaches infinity. This value is also referred to as the *soil expectation* or land expectation. Since the second term on the RHS of (11.8) approaches zero as $n \to \infty$,

$$(11.9) \quad V = \frac{(p-c)v(t)-C}{(1+r)^t - 1}.$$

This is the discrete-time version. The continuous-time version of (11.9) is found in the same way (but substituting e^{-rt} for $(1+r)^{-t}$):

(11.10) $\quad V = \dfrac{[(p-c)v(t) - C]e^{-rt}}{1-e^{-rt}}$.

In the foregoing expressions, t is assumed to be the rotation age. The optimal financial or Faustmann harvest age, denoted t_F, is found by finding the value of t that maximizes expression (11.9) or (11.10). Further, no up-front planting cost is included. Rather, expressions (11.9) and (11.10) assume that seedlings have already been planted on the site at time $t=0$. If seedlings still need to be planted, then these expressions need to be adjusted as follows:

(11.9') $\quad V = \dfrac{(p-c)v(t) - C}{(1+r)^t - 1} - C$

(11.10') $\quad V = \dfrac{\left[(p-c)v(t) - C\right]e^{-rt}}{1-e^{-rt}} - C.$

If trees are already growing on the site, expression (11.9) also needs to be modified. If the trees are already of harvestable age, then the net return from harvesting the site today must be added on the RHS of (11.9). If the trees are not yet at harvestable age, then again net returns must be added on the RHS of (11.9), but, in addition, the RHS must now be multiplied by $(1+r)^{-k}$, where k is the number of years until the trees currently growing on the site are harvested. Then the formula for determining the value of land when trees are growing on the site is:

(11.11) $\quad V = \dfrac{1}{(1+r)^k}\left(\dfrac{(p-c)v(t) - C}{(1+r)^t - 1} + ((p-c)v(t) - C) \right).$

In the forgoing expressions, t is simply some arbitrary rotation age. Now, let us calculate the optimal financial rotation age, known as the Faustmann rotation age, t_F. Consider expression (11.10). Maximizing (11.10) by setting the first derivative with respect to t equal to zero gives:

$$(11.12) \quad \frac{(p-c)v'(t_F)}{(p-c)v(t_F)-C} = \frac{r}{1-e^{-rt_F}}.$$

If trees regenerate naturally and $C=0$, then expression (11.12) can be rewritten as:

$$(11.13) \quad \frac{v'(t_F)}{v(t_F)} = \frac{r}{1-e^{-rt_F}}.$$

Compared to the cutting rule in equation (11.4), the fact that the denominator on the RHS of (11.13) is less than one but greater than zero has the same effect as that of increasing the discount rate in (11.4). An increase in the discount rate would cause one to harvest sooner (see point F in Figure 11.2).

What is not taken into account in the Fisher (single-harvest) case is the possibility that, once timber is harvested, a new stand of trees can be generated on the land. The second growth can be harvested at a later date. By taking into account the potential of the land to grow another stand of trees, the harvest period is actually shortened. The reason is that, by cutting trees sooner, it also makes available a second and third harvest sooner than would otherwise be the case. Mathematically, the denominator on the RHS of equation (11.13) effectively increases the value of the RHS compared to the case of a one-time harvest – compared to the RHS of (11.5) – because $(1-e^{-rt})<1$.

Regeneration can be hastened through reforestation and silviculture. In the one-period case, initial planting costs do not affect the optimum unless net returns are less than zero, in which case there is no harvest (Samuelson 1976, p.472). The same is true in the multiple-period case.

For spruce, the Faustmann or financial rotation age is just over 20 years of age, while it is about 11 years for hybrid poplar (Table 11.5 and Figure 11.2). The financial rotation age is below that which maximizes sustainable yield. Where institutions permit (e.g., public ownership), biological considerations have led governments to legislate harvest ages that exceed the Faustmann age. While this has resulted in lower timber benefits, it is not clear that it has also resulted in lower overall benefits to society.

The Effect of Forest Tenure on Financial Rotation Ages

Forest legislation and forestland tenure have an important impact on rotation ages. Since property rights are subject to government legislation that often seeks to address environmental spillovers from forestry, private landowners may be constrained in terms of when and how they harvest trees, and in the silvicultural practices employed. For example, due to its small forest area, Denmark does not permit private landowners to cut trees once they are planted. Sweden uses moral suasion backed by forest legislation to get woodlot owners to practice sustainable forestry. The upshot is that timber rotation ages are often extended beyond the financial rotation age by government actions.

As indicated in Table 11.4, in some countries the state is an important, perhaps even the dominant, owner of forestland. A variety of tenure arrangements exist that enable private forest companies to access public timber. In Canada, for example, two main forms of tenure have evolved (see also section 11.3).

One form of tenure grants large forest companies long-term (20–25 year) rights to harvest timber on public forestlands in exchange for the construction and operation of sawmills and/or pulp mills, all under the rubric of regional development. Such "forest management licenses" give the tenure holder sole access to timber, although it requires the holder to harvest a certain amount of timber each year (a constraint meant to ensure community and employment stability), with levels predetermined in periodic (say, five-year) management plans. Each year the sustainable amount that can be harvested from the entire forest management unit equals the timber growth that accrues on the unit. The average of the annual growths (averaged over time and over sites within the unit) is referred to as the mean annual increment (MAI) for the management license. The MAI is the amount that can be harvested each year without jeopardizing future harvests and is used to determine the allowable annual cut (AAC) – the annual harvest. The AAC is usually set equal to the MAI, unless there exists mature (old-growth) forest. In that case, the *Hanzlik formula* is used to calculate AAC: AAC = MAI + Q/t, where Q is the volume of timber in the management unit that exceeds rotation age t (Pearse 1990, pp.153–69). For plantation forests, no sites exceed age t, so that the second term is zero.

A company with public land tenure may decide to include its private lands in the forest management license because, if trees on private land are immature but growing very fast, they enhance the MAI of the entire management unit, thereby increasing AAC and harvests from the entire management unit (public plus private land). In effect, by including private lands, forest companies may be able to harvest more timber from public lands than would otherwise be the case. Within the forest management license you can cut the MAI-equivalent of what is growing on the private land elsewhere in the unit.

The second form of tenure is a harvest license. In this case, forest companies have a right only to cut a predetermined amount of timber from public land within a short period of no more than 10 years but often less. The state is responsible for forest management and perhaps even road construction. Timber is often auctioned to the highest bidder, although other criteria (e.g., high bid plus achievement of a local employment target) can and often are used as well. This system is in place for timber harvested from US National Forests and from some public forestland in Canada.

Tenure has implications for rotation age and determination of land values. If a particular private forest site is part of a larger public forest management license, then the contribution of the site to the public component is required to determine its bare land value, or soil expectation (V). The value that a recently harvested site (i.e., bare land) has to the management unit as a whole is the growth that the new trees (whether planted or naturally regenerated) contributes to the unit's total annual increment. If the recently harvested site is excluded from the management unit, then the contribution of the young trees growing on the site cannot be included in the calculation of the entire unit's AAC.

Suppose the rotation age t is 80 years. Then the management unit can be thought of as being divided into 80 sites, with one site harvested every year. The removal of a single site from the management unit means that each of the remaining sites must be made smaller so that a new site can be made from the remaining 79. What, then, is the value of keeping the site in the management unit? It is the lost benefits that would result by taking a small amount from each of the remaining 79 units; that is, each year the loss would be equal to the amount of timber taken from one of the remaining 79 sites multiplied by its stumpage price ($p - c$). As shown below, the value of the timber lost each year is equal to $mai \times (p - c)$, where mai is the timber that cannot be cut each year.

The soil expectation when it is included in a larger management unit is given by the site's mean annual increment (mai) multiplied by ($p - c$) divided by the discount rate:[1]

$$(11.14) \quad V_L = \frac{mai \times (p - c)}{r},$$

where V_L refers to the soil expectation of a site in management unit, $mai = $ MAI $\times \xi$, with ξ ($0 < \xi < 1$) being the proportion of the management unit's MAI attributable to the specific site (that is, the area proportion adjusted for productivity characteristics of the site), and ($p - c$) is the net stumpage price.

How does (11.14) compare with (11.10) – the value of bare land when it is not part of a larger management unit? First of all, it is important to recognize that (11.14) is simply a variant of the well-known bond formula derived in Chapter 6 (equation 6.4) applied to forestland. It requires a return to be realized every year, rather than when trees reach harvest age. In actuality, a return is realized only when the stand is harvested, with the return at that time given by $(p - c) \times v(t)$, where $v(t) = mai \times t$. It is easy to demonstrate that equation (11.14) leads to a higher soil expectation than does the Faustmann formula by showing that:

$$(11.15) \quad \frac{mai \times (p - c)}{r} - \frac{[mai \times t \times (p - c)]e^{-rt}}{1 - e^{-rt}} \geq 0.$$

The first term on the LHS is simply (11.14), while the second term is the Faustmann formula (11.10) with $C=0$ and $v(t) = mai \times t$. Rearranging (11.15) gives:

$$(11.16) \quad rt \geq \ln(1 + rt),$$

which holds for all $r \geq 0$ (i.e., for all positive discount rates) and $t \geq 0$ (all rotation ages).

As an example of the magnitude of the difference in soil expectation between a site that is part of a larger management unit (where value is dependent on the interdependency) and a stand-alone site, consider an *mai* of 10 m³/ha, a rotation length of 60 years, a net stumpage price of $25/m³, and a discount rate of 10%. Equation (11.14) yields a bare land value of $2,500/ha, while the correct formula (11.10) yields a bare land value of $49.43/ha. It is also clear that, since reforestation costs are in the hundreds of dollars, reforestation might only pay if private land is included in a larger management unit that includes public forest land (but see equation 11.25). Therefore, it pays firms to include private land in a forest management unit, especially if the private land has immature or new forest.

Capitalization Rate versus Interest Rate

Now consider the discrete-time version of land value as given by equation (11.9), but ignore regeneration costs:

$$(11.17) \quad V = \frac{MAI \times (p - c) \times t}{(1 + r)^t - 1},$$

Expression (11.17) can be rewritten as:

(11.18) $V = \dfrac{MAI \times (p - c)}{\delta}$,

where δ is the capitalization rate such that

(11.19) $\delta = \dfrac{(1+r)^t - 1}{t}$.

Determining the appropriate capitalization rate is the crux of the problem, because use of δ rather than r can be misleading. It is clear from (11.19) that δ is not independent of either the discount rate r or the rotation age t. Table 11.6 gives discount (interest) rates (r) associated with various given capitalization rates (δ) that lie in the range of 2% to 14%; this is done by specifying values for δ and t and solving (11.19) for r. Then, Table 11.7 presents capitalization rates that are associated with various realistic interest rates; this is done by specifying values for r and t and using expression (11.19) to calculate δ.

Table 11.6: Calculated Interest (Discount) Rates Associated with Various Capitalization Rates

Capitalization Rate (δ)	Forest rotation age (t)			
	60 years	80 years	100 years	120 years
2%	1.323%	1.202%	1.105%	1.025%
4%	2.061%	1.810%	1.623%	1.476%
6%	2.576%	2.222%	1.965%	1.769%
8%	2.973%	2.533%	2.222%	1.987%
10%	3.296%	2.785%	2.427%	2.161%
12%	3.569%	2.995%	2.598%	2.305%
14%	3.805%	3.176%	2.745%	2.428%

Table 11.7: Calculated Capitalization Rates Associated with Selected Interest Rates

Interest rate (r)	Forest rotation age (t)		
	60 years	80 years	100 years
4%	15.866%	27.562%	49.505%
6%	53.313%	130.995%	338.302%
8%	167.095%	588.694%	2,198.761%
10%	505.803%	2,559.250%	13,779.961%

Based on the 4% capitalization rate, and assuming rotation ages of 80 to 120 years, the implicit interest rate is less than 2%. Likewise, using a discount rate for evaluating projects of 10% implies that one would have to use a capitalization rate exceeding 2,000% if the rotation age is 80 years or greater. Even using low market rates of interest, such as 4–6%, requires that one use capitalization rates that exceed 15% (see Table 11.7). The point is that one cannot separate the capitalization rate and interest rate.

Effect of Taxes on the Financial Rotation Age

Montgomery and Adams (1995) demonstrate the effects on rotation age of three types of timber taxes. Their results are summarized as follows:

1. An *ad valorem* tax constitutes a fixed percentage levy against the market value of the timber stand (land plus timber) each year. The effect of such a tax is similar to that of increasing the rate of interest that the forest manager faces, thereby reducing the optimal rotation length. In the case of uneven-aged stands, the effect of an *ad valorem* tax is to reduce the optimal holdings of timber stocks.
2. Yield taxes have been implemented to counter the adverse effect of *ad valorem* taxes, namely, that the timber is harvested sooner. A yield tax is based on the value of the timber when it is harvested. The effect of such a tax is a percentage reduction in the effective output price, thus extending the rotation age. In the case of uneven-aged stands, the effect of a yield tax is neutral – it does not change the optimal rotation age.
3. Finally, the effect of an annual site or land tax that is based only on the value of the land and not the timber on it, is neutral. This is true both for even and uneven-aged stands.

Environmental Spillovers: Hartman Rotation Age

Where growing forests provide beneficial environmental spillovers, an economic argument can be made for extending rotations beyond the financial age. Standing trees have value to society in addition to commercial timber value; these values are derived from scenic amenities, watershed functions, waste receptor and carbon uptake services, nontimber products such as mushrooms, wildlife habitat functions, and so on. If nonmarket values are related to timber volume, then, if society is to maximize its welfare from managing the forest, the Faustmann rotation age needs to be modified to take into account these values. External benefits need to be correlated with timber (forest) growth before it is possible to determine directly the optimal harvest age that would take external values into account. The difference between commercial timber and nontimber benefits in determining optimal rotation age is that commercial timber benefits accrue only at the end of the rotation, when the trees are harvested. Nontimber benefits, on the other hand, accrue continuously (or annually in the discrete case).

The Hartman (1976) rotation age is based on the maximization of external or amenity values. Suppose that amenity values are given by $A(t)$, $A'(t)>0$ and $A''(t)<0$; amenity value increases over time (marginal amenity value is always positive), but at a decreasing rate. The objective is to choose the rotation age that maximizes the discounted stream of such benefits, recognizing that benefits fall to zero each time the stand is cut. Substituting $A(t)$ for $(p - c)v(t)$ in expression (11.10) gives the following problem (assuming that the cost of planting trees on the site is zero):

$$(11.20) \quad \underset{t}{\text{Max}}\left[\frac{A(t)e^{-rt}}{1-e^{-rt}}\right].$$

Maximizing expression (11.20) with respect to t yields an expression for determining the Hartman rotation age, t_H:

$$(11.21) \quad \frac{A'(t_H)}{A(t_H)} = \frac{r}{1-e^{-rt_H}}.$$

This expression has a similar interpretation to (11.13): As long as the rate of increase in amenity values exceeds the rate of increase in social opportunities (given by the social discount rate r), one delays cutting trees. When that relationship is reversed, it is worthwhile cutting the trees as nontimber benefits to society can be improved by harvesting the trees (perhaps because wildlife benefits of an old stand of trees are small compared to those that could be had by removing the trees). If one solves (11.21) for the Hartman rotation age, t_H, one finds that it is longer than the Faustmann age (and even MSY age), but only if amenity values increase with stand age; if they decline with age, the Hartman rotation is shorter. The challenge for economists is finding $A(t)$, which is much harder than determining $v(t)$.

Hartman–Faustmann Rotation Age

Consider the case where the manager seeks to maximize the combined commercial timber and nontimber (spillover) amenities over an infinite planning horizon. The problem now becomes much more difficult analytically, but not intractable. In the usual formulation, the manager begins with bare land, plants trees and maximizes the present value of total forest benefits (Swallow et al. 1990; Swallow and Wear 1993):

$$(11.22) \quad \max_t \left[\frac{\left[(p-c)v(t) + A(t) - C\right]e^{-rt}}{1 - e^{-rt}} \right],$$

where $(p - c)v(t)$ is the commercial timber benefit, $A(t)$ amenity benefits over rotation t, and C regeneration costs (as before). The necessary conditions for an optimum give:

$$(11.23) \quad \frac{(p-c)v'(t_{HF}) + A'(t_{HF})}{(p-c)v(t_{HF}) + A(t_{HF}) - C} = \frac{r}{1 - e^{-rt_{HF}}}.$$

This expression is similar to earlier ones and is to be interpreted in the same way.

The Hartman–Faustmann rotation age t_{HF} should be chosen so that the marginal present value of delaying harvest, or marginal benefit of delay (MBD), equals the marginal opportunity cost of delay (MOC).[2] This can be seen by rearranging (11.23):

$$(11.24) \quad \left[(p-c)v'(t_{HF}) + A'(t_{HF})\right] \left(\frac{1 - e^{-rt_{HF}}}{r} \right) = (p-c)v(t_{HF}) + A(t_{HF}) - C.$$

The marginal cost of delaying (MOC) is given on the RHS of (11.24), which equals the immediate timber benefits minus regeneration costs if the stand is harvested today, plus the amenity benefits received over the next growing period. The marginal benefit of delaying harvest (MBD) is given by the LHS and is equal to the marginal value of tree growth (the additional timber from delaying multiplied by its value) plus the added amenity value, all discounted to the current time. To maximize society's benefit from forest management, MOC = MBD.

As a policy, the state would need to subsidize the forest manager who is interested in commercial timber production only to take into account nontimber amenity values. The policy would provide a subsidy of $A'(t)$ to those who hold timber of age t, or pay a total of $[r/(1 - e^{-rt})]\, e^{-rt}\, A(t)$ to managers who harvest at age t.

The problem is that there are many nontimber values (e.g., wilderness preservation, provision of forage for wild ungulates, wildlife habitat) that vary in different ways with forest age (see, e.g., Calish et al. 1978; Bowes and Krutilla 1989). Indeed, some amenities are unrelated to forest age. Examples of the relationship between a forest stand's age and nontimber amenities are provided in Figure 11.3. For example, amenity flows might represent the value of wildlife species (e.g., herbivores) adapted to young forests with plentiful forage (I), wildlife values that are independent of forest age (II), and the value of species reliant on more mature forests, such as trout and spotted owls (III). Benefit stream IV represents the sum of these amenity flows (Swallow et al. 1990). When nontimber values are combined with commercial timber benefits to form the objective function in (11.22), solving for a maximum is more complicated because it is not easy to find a global maximum. Often one discovers local minima or local maxima by solving the first-order conditions for a maximum. Looking to find a maximum, but settling (wrongly) at a local minimum (minimizing social benefits!) is a particularly vexing problem in economics – referred to as a *nonconvexity* (Vincent and Binkley 1993; Helfand and Whitney 1994).

A nonconvexity can easily prevent a tax/subsidy policy from achieving the socially desirable rotation age. The reason can be illustrated with the aid of Figure 11.4. From (11.24), the condition for a socially optimal solution occurs where the marginal opportunity cost of delaying harvest equals the discounted marginal benefit of delay, or MBD = MOC.

Suppose that the Faustmann rotation age is given by rotation age t_F. Points x and y, with accompanying rotation ages t_x and t_y, represent cases where (11.24) is satisfied. Because MOC intersects MBD from above, a nonconvexity occurs at x but not at y – the point x is an equilibrium that is not optimal, but y is. Providing the forest manager with a myopic subsidy equal to the value of the nontimber benefits will result in a rotation age, t_x, that is shorter than the financial rotation age t_F. That is, a subsidy to get the manager to take into account environmental spillovers results in a too-soon harvest – one that reduces nonmarket values compared to a later harvest at t_F. However, a policy that rewards the forest owner or manager with an appropriate subsidy only over the period $t_x \le t \le t_F$ will achieve the desired solution at y.

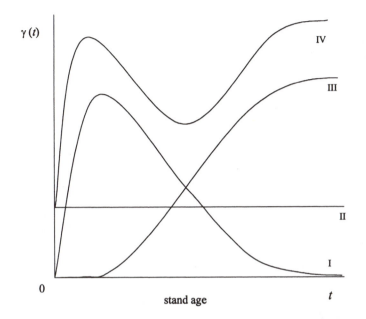

Figure 11.3: Relationship between stand age and various amenity values

For some standing forests the spillover amenity benefits might be so great that it would not be economically feasible to harvest the forest at any time in the future. This would be the case if equilibrium points existed at ages beyond those indicated in Figure 11.4 (e.g., MOC and MBD may intersect again, with MOC upward and MBD downward sloping). If this is the case and society inherits "ancient" forests, it may be worthwhile delaying harvests, perhaps indefinitely.

Finally, Swallow and Wear (1993) and Swallow et al. (1997) extend the notion of convexities and external benefits to multiple use across forest stands. First consider two sites, one publicly owned and the other private. Suppose that harvest of the private forest stand affects the flow of amenity benefits from the public stand, thus shifting both the MOC and MBD functions at the public site. While it may be optimal to harvest the public stand, the public manager may wish to delay harvest in anticipation of felling of the private site, thus extending the public rotation age beyond that which would be socially optimal in the single-stand case. When both sites are managed together for their joint commercial timber and amenity values, the sequence of harvest schedules can take rather odd forms. For example, even though two forest stands may be nearly similar in all respects, it might be socially optimal to permit one site to mature to beyond 100 years before harvesting it, while the other site is harvested several times during this period. This caused Vincent and Binkley (1993) to recommend the use of zoning rather than subsidies as a public policy for increasing social wellbeing.

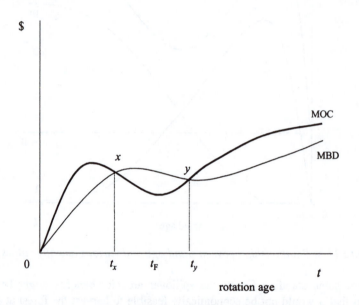

Figure 11.4: Nonconvexities and optimal Hartman–Faustmann rotation age

11.3 REGULATION AND CONTROL IN FORESTRY

In the past several decades, one response to market failure has been to increase emphasis on multiple use management, and even more recently on forest ecosystem management. While managing for multiple use is commonly understood and accepted by foresters (e.g., see Bowes and Krutilla 1989), the same cannot be said about ecosystem management (Sedjo 1996b). The problem is that it is not at all clear what the objectives of ecosystem management might be – they are vague and ill defined – and there is no way of knowing when objectives are achieved. This makes management difficult if not impossible.

In section 11.2, we examined market-based approaches to address multiple use management. Timber, nontimber product and nonmarket values can be taken into account by choosing the appropriate rotation age of various stands.[3] As noted, work is ongoing to determine optimal rotation ages when harvest decisions on one stand affect nonmarket values on other stands, but this is a technical issue that has been solved in practice by a variety of mathematical programming methods (see Hof 1993; Buongionro and Gilless 1987). The point is that, in order to get firms to harvest forest stands at times that confer the greatest benefits to society, it is possible to harness the power of the market, using taxes and subsidies for example. In practice, however, governments have eschewed this approach, preferring instead to rely on control, either direct ownership or regulation, or a combination of these.

In the past decade, many countries have implemented new forest acts that have included forestry regulations of one form or other (see Wilson et al. 1998). Both Finland and Sweden introduced new forest acts in the early 1990s meant to protect nature. However, the most onerous and detailed regulations have been implemented in British Columbia in the form of a detailed Forest Practices Code (analyzed in section 6.4). (Surprisingly, as evident from Table 11.4, BC also has the highest public ownership of forestland of any jurisdiction.) Countries have also put in place harvest restrictions, particularly by setting aside environmentally important ecosystems. This has been most evident in the US Pacific Northwest and BC, where large tracts of old growth have been removed from the working forest and protected in perpetuity. Rather than considering interactions among various forest stands, or even interactions across a much larger landscape, this approach is best described as zoning. The problems with zoning were considered in Chapter 8 and are well known, particularly that it leads to variances that, in the case of forestry, have led to slow erosion of protected areas (Sinclair 2000). Nonetheless, zoning has been promoted for California (Vaux 1973) and British Columbia as appropriate means for conserving nontimber amenities (Sahajananthan et al. 1998), for addressing market failure.

There are several problems with state intervention via regulation. First, as already alluded to in the previous paragraphs, it is likely to be expensive and ineffective in the longer run. Regulations lead to bureaucratic red tape that increases costs above what they need be. This has been the case in BC where the Forest Practices Code is estimated to cost more than society receives in benefits (section 6.4). A regulatory environment also creates opportunities and incentives for corruption: those enforcing regulations can be bribed in various ways (not always monetary) to overlook certain contraventions of the law (perhaps because regulations can be interpreted in more than one way), while politicians might grant variances in order to gain support ("bribes") from industry or to please voters (e.g., local communities, forest-sector workers).

Second, politics enter into decisions and that often leads to inconsistences. Thus, Sinclair (2000) complains that governments have been quick to identify protected ecosystems, but have not made available adequate funds to protect them from encroachment. Pressey (2000) demonstrates that governments have been unwilling to purchase important ecologically-sensitive lands from private owners, a complaint echoed by Sinclair (2000), while putting into reserves only public lands, often lands that are marginal for protection of biodiversity or ones that are targeted by environmental groups.[4] Governments want to be seen as promoting biodiversity, as providing nature, but are unwilling to incur the budgetary costs that are required. They are also unwilling to rely on markets on ideological grounds, even when there are benefits to so doing.

Third, a regulatory environment often leads to a classic principal-agent problem, where the principal and agent do not have the same objectives so that the former must monitor the latter – enforcement is a problem. This is truer for regulations involving harvesting methods and silvicultural investments that are aimed at protecting nature than for the case of zoning or wilderness set-asides. With regulations that involve silvicutlural prescriptions to provide more nature, there remains the problem that the product, nature, is ill-defined or vague in that it is not precisely clear when the outcome has been achieved. Even when outcomes are defined in terms of specific silvicultural tasks, such as reforesting a site to the point where trees are "free to grow" (free from competing vegetation), there remains a certain amount of ambiguity. For instance, what is the state of trees at the time they are "free to grow"? What proportion is likely to survive? How many stems were planted? Are they appropriate species for the site? Are they native or exotic species, or genetically engineered to grow quickly for a short period in order to satisfy other requirements (e.g., green-up and adjacency)? Are nontimber values promoted?

Finally, there has been increasing demand by buyers of wood products for guarantees that such products come from forests that are sustainably managed, or managed in an environmentally preferred way. In response, a variety of certification schemes have been proposed, including ones that are sponsored by the state, industry and environmental NGOs (see Chapter 12). To a large extent, private-sector (including NGO) efforts have mitigated the need for regulations such as those embodied in BC's Forest Practices Code.

While such regulations remain in place, they could serve as an impediment to certification as some certification schemes require that local codes be met in addition to other requirements, even if those codes are onerous and costly. Further, in the case of BC, its forest practices have reduced its flexibility in addressing costs, as any attempt to ease restrictions will be regarded by the United States as a subsidy to the wood products industry (see Chapter 12).

In this section, we examine forestland ownership in more depth as a response to real or perceived market failure. We also examine the allowable cut effect because it is an artifact of regulation, as we demonstrate.

Emergence and Evolution of Forestland Tenures

While many have studied land ownership and tenure (e.g., Powelson 1987, 1988), research specifically focused on forestland is limited. The UN Food and Agriculture Organization (FAO) accorded considerable attention to land tenure and property rights in forestry during the 1980s (de Saussay 1987; Hummel 1989), but its emphasis was mainly on management of forest resources and the policy framework, with particular focus on Europe.

The history of the advancement of human civilization is sometimes described as a history of deforestation – the conversion of forestland to agriculture (Bechmann 1990; Perlin 1989). As cultivation expanded and became more permanent, because of growth in population and advancement in technology, society forged a "more durable relationship of the cultivator to the soil" (Lewinsky 1913, p.16). This led to a more permanent life pattern, with the cultivated land as its center.

The evolution of forestland tenures tended to follow a sequence from open access exploitation to communal ownership, then state property, and finally private (individual and corporate) ownership, primarily as a consequence of the intensification of human activities (Bechmann 1990). Transitions from open access to other ownership forms tended to be gradual, organic processes. In Africa and Asia, communal (tribal) ownership was an ownership characteristic that was skipped in other regions, particularly North America (Jeppe 1980). Bechmann (1990, p.232) cites the "Law of Beaumont" as resulting in communal ownership in Europe as kings granted woodlands to hundreds of communities in the Middle Ages. It was perpetual usage rights that were granted and not freehold title, with such rights revocable by the feudal rulers. State ownership of the forest in Europe in the Middle Ages was the rule rather than the exception.

In North America, governments extensively own forests, although some forestland tends to be marginal. The reason is that high-quality and easy to access forestland was privatized first, but that, as a result of the conservation movement, governments stopped granting forestland to private holders beginning in the latter part of the 1800s. In the USA, this began with the creation of the Yellowstone National Park in 1872, but was followed shortly thereafter by the creation of the National Forest system. However, National Parks were designed as set asides, while the National Forests were originally created as a timber reserve, against the time when timber from private land would run short. Of course, lands that were marginal in the late 1800s and early 1900s are no longer marginal today because of technical advances in harvesting and hauling equipment, road construction and processing.

In other regions, culture and political systems had an impact on forestland ownership. In particular, communism led to state ownership in Russia, China, the Ukraine, and many other countries.

So how did private ownership of forests develop? Three reasons come to mind (Bechmann 1990). First, in Medieval Europe the king and the nobles granted freehold rights to individuals for the services that they rendered, especially during wartime. Second, farmers could become owners of smaller pieces of forestlands by clearing and developing larger areas for the original owner under a labor-for-partial-title deal. Finally, merchants, artisans and lawyers could purchase forestlands with cash payments, but this process was essentially limited to the period before the 1200s.

The extent of private forest ownership is a function of culture, economic and political institutions, personalities (*viz.*, Gifford Pinchot establishing the US Forest Service), historical precedence, the size of the forest resource, the relation of forests to other resources, and a host of other factors. For instance, private ownership of forestland is more common where land was at some time in the past used extensively for agriculture. If the forest has traditionally been a major source of fuel and timber, private ownership is not inevitable; instead, forest tenure involves usufructuary rights for fuelwood and construction timber rather than fee simple title. Corporate holdings of forestland appeared between the 1600s and 1800s, primarily in Sweden and, to a lesser extent, Finland; in Sweden, corporate holding began in order to provide charcoal for the iron industry (Wilson et al. 1998). Today, corporate ownership of forestland remains a tenure characteristic in Nordic Europe. In the United States, all lands west of the Appalachians began as federal lands gained as a result of war and/or land purchases from other countries, but most were transferred to private ownership as a result of the Homesteader Act. Remaining (marginal) lands were transferred into state hands or kept as BLM and Forest Service lands (see also Chapter 10). Forest companies acquired their forest holdings through decades of purchases from government as well as from small, private forest owners.

The extent of private, state and communal ownership of forestland in various jurisdictions is provided in Table 11.8 (see also Table 11.4). Different forms of ownership can and do co-exist within jurisdictions, but private property appears to be the most important and perhaps dominant form of forestland ownership in many parts of the world.

It is difficult, *a priori*, to say that one form of ownership is preferred over another. Indeed, it is argued that public ownership of forest resources enables the state to protect and enhance the values of forestlands that are economically unattractive to private owners, and provides the state with powerful means of shaping the pattern and pace of economic development in a jurisdiction (Pearse 1976, 2001). Nonetheless, theoretical and empirical evidence presented by Hart et al. (1997), Shleifer and Vishny (1998), and La Porta et al. (1999) suggests that the state may not be an efficient manager of public lands for reasons noted in the previous section. Perhaps this helps explain why the governments of Sweden and New Zealand have recently reduced their holdings of productive forestlands in an effort to promote not only efficient timber production but also better environmental performance (see Wilson et al. 1998).

Where there is widespread public ownership, exclusive use rights are generally given to private loggers; these are referred to as concessions in developing countries and contractual or tenure arrangements in developed countries. The usefulness of these arrangements depends on the degree of certainty that the concession or tenure provides, particularly with respect to duration, renewability and replaceability. If the property or usufructuary rights are transferable with few limitations, and contracts are of sufficient duration (e.g., exceeding normal rotation age), then there is very little difference between private property rights and concessionaire rights with public ownership of forestland. However, if a concession or tenure is of short duration (say, shorter than a rotation length), loggers' efforts are oriented only on timber harvesting, and not on preservation of soil fertility and timber growing. There are no incentives for the licensee in this case to maintain and develop the forest resource. Lack of clarity concerning property rights leads to incentive failure (see Pearse 1998).

Recent evidence from Sweden, Australia, New Zealand and other jurisdictions indicates that forestland ownership forms do change (Wilson et al. 1998; White and Martin 2002). Factors that result in a change in forestland ownership include, among others, changes in (1) the relative scarcity of forest resources, (2) relative prices of forest products, (3) technology that results in new investment opportunities, (4) societal values, or perception of the extent of market failure, and (5) the economic circumstances of the state owner.

Table 11.8: Forestland Ownership in Selected Jurisdictions

Country/ region	Forest area 10^6 ha	Forest cover[a] %	Managed forest by ownership (%)[b]				
			Public		Private		
			State	Other[c]	Individual	Industry	Other[d]
North America							
Canada	244.6	26.5	84.3	0.2	11.9	3.6	–
USA[e]	217.3	23.7	34.9	9.9	25.8	23.8	3.5
East Asia							
Japan	24.1	66.0	30.0	11.0	42.7	6.3	10.0
Korea (South)	6.5	65.3	22.0	7.0	71.0	–	–
P.R. China	133.0	14.3	45.0	55.0	–	–	–
Taiwan	1.9	52.1	83.0	7.0	10.0	–	–
Europe							
Austria	3.8	46.5	13.7	2.7	69.1	–	14.5
Belgium	0.6	21.3	10.8	32.4	55.1	0.2	1.6
Denmark	0.4	10.5	26.8	5.0	45.5	–	22.7
Finland	21.9	71.9	29.6	–	55.6	9.2	5.5
France	15.2	28.0	10.1	16.0	62.1	–	11.7
Germany	10.7	31.0	33.4	19.9	46.7	–	–
Greece	3.4	25.7	74.8	8.8	10.7	–	5.7
Ireland	0.6	8.6	69.3	–	30.7	–	–
Italy	9.9	33.5	5.1	94.3	0.6	–	–
Netherlands	0.3	10.0	36.6	14.3	20.7	–	28.3
Norway	8.7	28.4	10.8	3.1	75.4	4.5	6.3
Portugal	3.4	37.2	5.8	40.9	6.5	46.7	–
Spain	13.5	27.0	0.4	20.1	79.5	–	–
Sweden	27.3	66.8	1.9	7.1	51.4	39.6	–
Switzerland	1.2	30.0	1.0	64.9	30.5	–	3.6
UK	2.5	10.2	42.0	3.8	38.0	1.2	15.1
Oceania							
Australia	156.9	20.6	57.3	–	42.7	–	–
New Zealand	7.9	29.3	21.8	2.7	6.3	32.6	36.6

Notes:

[a] "Forest cover" refers to land with at least 10% crown cover.

[b] "Managed forest" refers to forest available for wood supply; total may not add to 100% due to rounding.

[c] "Other public ownership" refers to that by municipal government and local authorities, collectives, church and so on.

[d] "Other private ownership" refers to that owned by private institutions.

[e] Approximately 2% of the managed forest in the United States is owned by indigenous or tribal peoples.

Source: Wang and van Kooten (2001); White and Martin (2002); FAO (2001, 2003).

Although large areas of forest plantations were successfully privatized in some countries, privatization may not be a panacea for addressing policy failure, just as control (regulation, state ownership) may not be appropriate in solving instances of market failure. It is useful to note, however, that privatization itself is a public choice, with attendant, even large, distributional and political consequences. The process of asset transfer may open new opportunities for the pursuit of private agendas by political decision-makers. The effects of privatization in any particular context will, therefore, be highly dependent upon the wider institutional framework, and socio-cultural milieu, in which it is implemented (Putnam 2000).

In some cases, rapid privatization might leave inadequate time for the creation of durable incentive structures for efficiency. For example, without market liberalization, many state-owned enterprises might simply be transformed into private monopolies. As events in a number of Eastern European countries suggest, other institutional changes may be required to permit proper functioning of private markets. Primary among these is a court system that protects property rights and contracts. Such things as honesty, trust and other social capital may also be required (Fukuyama 1995, 1999, 2002; Dasgupta 2000).

Evolution of Forestland Control: A Case Study of British Columbia

In Canada, public management and decisions over land use occur at the provincial level, so it is at that level that land-use management needs to be examined. We consider British Columbia because, while Canada is the largest single exporter of wood products in the world, BC accounts for about half of Canada's forest product exports while providing a significant contribution to global wilderness preservation values (see Wang and van Kooten 2001; Wilson et al. 1998). Forestland covers 60.6 million ha, or 64% of BC, with a standing inventory of some 8,000 million m^3 of mature timber. Productive forestland comprises some 26 million ha. About 93% of the forest is coniferous, giving BC nearly half of Canada's softwood inventory. The Province's forestland is, by and large, publicly owned, except for about 4% that is owned by private individuals and companies. This is the highest degree of public ownership of forestland of any jurisdiction in the industrialized world, with the exception of Russia and China (Wilson et al. 1998). BC also has more diversity of wildlife species than has any other province. British Columbia accounts for 70% of native breeding bird species, 72% of the terrestrial mammal species, 49% of the amphibian species, and 41% of Canada's reptile species. Of the province's bird species, 77% are forest dwelling; for mammals, 81% are forest dwelling. About a quarter of forest-dwelling wildlife species may be dependent on mature (old-growth) forests. BC's forestlands are also important for maintaining forms of biodiversity.

The forest tenure system is, without question, the driver of BC's forest policy and institutions. Early disposals of public lands in BC granted freehold ownership to the buyer, including all timber rights. However, by 1865, land ordinances became popular, introducing the principle that individuals or companies could acquire rights to timber without purchasing land. This arrangement enabled the provincial government to access revenues over a long period of time without losing control over land, while loggers were primarily interested in the timber and not ownership of land. The Land Act of 1884 anticipated the US's Taylor Grazing Act by 50 years, in that it formalized the land ordinances and made additional sales of forestlands difficult.

During the 1800s, the government permitted timber harvests on public lands through a number of timber and pulp lease or license arrangements. Initially, such tenures were not associated with charges, because the government was interested in development; but that changed in 1888, when charges for public timber were implemented. To encourage economic development, a system of export permits was brought into effect in 1901, followed in 1906 by a law that required timber cut on public lands to be processed in BC. This amounted to a ban on log exports from public lands, although the ban was effectively circumvented by exports of "cants" (squared logs).

In 1907, concerned that it had given away too much of the timber resource, the government suspended further issue of cutting rights and placed all unallocated forestlands in reserve. Existing leases at the time subsequently became known as "old temporary tenures". While no such tenures were ever issued again, legally, the old licenses and levies remained until 1978, when they were changed to timber licenses (see below). In 1910, the first royal commission into forestry (chaired by F.J. Fulton) recommended that all unalienated forestlands be placed in a forest reserve (as was done in the USA in 1891) and that a Ministry of Forests be established. The Province approached Gifford Pinchot for advice and consultation, with the result that a provincial Forest Service was established in 1912 (by the Forest Act), along the lines of the US Forest Service. The Forest Act of 1912 defined what was meant by "forest reserves" and introduced the timber sale license (TSL), which was the primary form of forest tenure (except for the old temporary tenures) between 1912 and 1947.

The problem with these timber sale licenses was that they were short term (3–5 years), providing the holder with the right to harvest a certain area. They provided no incentives for management of forestlands, investments in silviculture, or management for more than one use. As an institutional device, timber sale licenses did not (and do not) promote sustainable development in forestry, with this task left to the Forestry Service.

In 1945, the second forestry commission, the Sloan Commission, recommended adoption of a formal sustained yield policy. As a result, the Forest Act was amended in 1947 and two types of management units were established – a private and a public one. In the first case, companies were given Forest Management Licenses – that is, long-term tenures of 21 years – in order to encourage them to invest in basic and intensive silviculture. While the old temporary tenures were renewable annually in most cases until the timber was harvested, the Forest Management Licenses were made perpetual over the period 1947–58, but, in 1958, they were converted into renewable, 21-year tenures and redesignated Tree Farm Licenses (TFLs). Management plans were to be submitted every five years for approval, the tenure holder was required to operate a mill, and the holder was responsible for reforestation. In the second case, Public Sustained Yield Units (PSYUs), later to be renamed Timber Supply Areas (TSAs), were managed by the government and were designed initially to provide timber to smaller operators. The smaller operators do not have the resources to manage the forests and make investments in silviculture. As part of the sustained yield policy, an annual allowable cut was determined for each PSYU based on productivity estimates. In 1967, the Timber Sale Harvesting License (TSHL) was introduced, and TSLs were amalgamated with TSHLs to increase the license term from 3–5 years to 10 years. Further, the TSHLs were volume based rather than area based, but they shifted some timber management responsibilities onto the holder. By 1976, TSHLs accounted for some 30% of BC's annual harvest (Wang and van Kooten 2001, pp.120–5).

In 1956, a third royal commission, also chaired by Gordon Sloan, reiterated the sustained yield policy. However, sustained yield referred only to commercial timber, not to other forest uses.

During the 1960s, pulpwood harvesting area agreements were introduced to encourage pulp production in the interior of BC. The agreements required the user to construct a pulp mill and to purchase residual wood chips from sawmills located in the interior. Professor Peter Pearse was the sole commissioner of the fourth royal commission, which released its report in 1976. While reiterating the concept of public ownership of forestlands, Pearse recommended that the old temporary tenures be eliminated and that the 21-year TFLs be made "evergreen". This meant that TFLs would become 25-year tenures, with renegotiation of a new 25-year term occurring every 10 years; this enabled the tenure holder to have a secure timber supply for 15 years if the license was not renewed. Pearse also recommended that area-based forest licenses replace the volume-based TSHLs and that competition be increased by issuing more timber sale licenses. The commissioner's report was also concerned about integrated resource management (e.g., recommending that the Forest Service be amalgamated with Fish and Wildlife), that economic criteria be incorporated in utilization standards, that greater competition and efficiency be encouraged in the processing sectors, and that more public investment in forests take place. Consequently, in 1978, the Ministry of Forests Act (1978), a new Forest Act, and the Range Act (1978) were passed. These require that public lands be managed for multiple use. Unlike in the USA, the courts have played no role in the interpretation and enforcement of multiple-use legislation.

In response to changing public values and threats in export markets, the government took steps in the early 1990s to protect public lands. It began in 1992 with a Protected Areas Strategy that doubled (from 6% to 12%) the area of public lands set aside for parks and wilderness. This was followed by a timber-supply review process, a Forest Land Reserve (1994) for Vancouver Island that prevents private forestland owners from putting forestland into competing uses,[5] and a Forest Practices Code (1995). While the Protected Areas Strategy, timber-supply reviews and the Forest Practices Code are expected to reduce annual harvests, public investments in the resource base and the Forest Land Reserve were designed to increase future timber availability. Regulations under the Forest Practices Code are perhaps the most onerous to be found in any forest jurisdiction (Wilson et al. 1998), yet they came at a time when forest certification is making such regulations redundant.

The end result of incremental policymaking over the past decades, is that the forest industry in British Columbia has lost its competitiveness in global markets (Pearse 2001). Tenure arrangements require forest companies to process harvested logs locally in their own mills (known as *appurtenancy*), but this has prevented firms from closing inefficient mills. Five-year management plans also require licensees to harvest within 50% of AAC in any given year and within 10% of total approved harvest over the five years of the plan, but this has resulted in excessive harvests when wood prices were low and insufficient harvests when they were high. This not only reduced profits but also reduced available resource rents (see Chapter 3). The Forest Practices Code also added needlessly to costs because they created an additional bureaucratic layer to administer detailed environmental regulations rather than monitor and enforce environmental performance, as private schemes to certify sustainable forest practices have done (see Chapter 12). Finally, because the tenure system is not very transparent, US producers have argued that BC and other Canadian provinces that employ similar forms of tenure effectively subsidize wood products firms by selling timber below market value.

In recognition of these developments, the government of British

Columbia has moved to relax the Forest Practices Code and rely more on private certification schemes, permit companies to close inefficient mills without requiring them to construct new ones, and make more timber available through timber auctions (BC Ministry of Forests 2003). These and other policies are designed to increase efficiency in the industry and mitigate the adverse impacts of the principal-agent problem.

The Allowable Cut Effect and Even Flow Constraints

Governments are interested in sustainable resource use. In forestry, this is pursued through the allowable annual cut, with the AAC set equal to the mean annual increment (or, in the case of mature stands, an adjustment is added according to the Hanzlik formula). For example, BC's Chief Forester sets the AAC, but allows tenure holders to deviate from AAC by as much as 50% in a given year (to take into account market conditions). Companies are not permitted to deviate from total AAC by more than 10% over a five-year period, however. Under this regulatory regime, the AAC will increase if slow-growing, mature trees are harvested and replaced by faster-growing young trees. This is an example of the *allowable cut effect* (ACE). If there is much mature or over-mature timber, harvesting such timber and reforesting the site will increase growth (the MAI), and subsequently the AAC. Similarly, investments in silviculture that lead to an increase in tree growth can result in an ACE. In essence, the ACE is the "immediate increase in today's allowable cut which is attributable to expected future increases in (timber) yields" (Schweitzer et al. 1972).

The ACE can easily be illustrated using a linear production function, as in Figure 11.5 (Binkley 1980, 1984). The production function [the line S to $(1+g)S$] indicates the trade-off between current and future harvests. In the figure, the maximum harvest available in period t is S, but, if no timber is harvested in t, then $(1+g)S$ is available for harvest in period $t+1$, where g is the growth of timber between periods t and $t+1$. Thus, the production function gives the maximum amount that can be harvested in period t (h_t) and period $t+1$ (h_{t+1}). Suppose that a silvicultural investment that costs c leads to an increase in growth from g to g'. (This investment might simply be the harvest and reforestation of a stand of mature timber.) Under the even-flow constraint (shown as a 45° line in Figure 11.5), there is a permissible increase in timber harvest given by $h_t'' - h_t'$, which equals the ACE.

Let r denote the (social) discount rate and c the cost of the silivicultural investment. Then, the objective of maximizing net present value from timber harvests is represented by the parallel lines denoted PV. In terms of these, the ACE effect leads to a benefit of $PV'-PV^0$. If $PV'-PV^0>c$, then the silvicultural investment is worth undertaking. Even though investments in fertilizing and reforestation yield high rates of return via the ACE, these returns are illusory and hold only because of the even-flow constraint (Price 1990). In terms of Figure 11.5 and in the absence of the even-flow constraint, agents would harvest all of the trees in the first period, thereby gaining a discounted net benefit given by PV^*, which is greater than any other possible net discounted gain. For reasons presented in the previous section, it is only if $g'>r$, and the gain in present value exceeds the cost of the investment (r), that the investment is worth undertaking in the absence of a constraint.

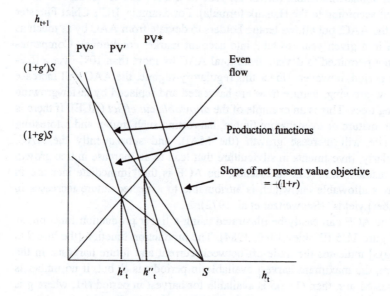

Figure 11.5: Allowable Cut Effect

Decisions about replanting or fertilizing are taken within the regulatory environment. From an economic perspective, the costs of replanting need to be recouped by the timber removed at the end of the rotation. Likewise, the costs of fertilizing need to be recouped when the trees are cut. However, legal constraints require companies to replant cutover sites, so costs of planting get charged to the current rotation rather than to future harvests, but this results in the transfer of resource rents from the current to the future, as noted in Chapter 3. Nonetheless, governments use legal constraints such as sustained yield or even flow as means to implement sustainable development and employment stability.

As Price (1990) points out, sustainable development permits depletion of an old-growth stand of trees "only if an environmentally compensating project is instituted to replace it – in this case by accelerating the growth of another stand" (p.574). The environmentally adverse effect of harvesting old growth is to be balanced by positive environmental effects (replanting, fertilizing) in each time period. This is a sustainability requirement. This obligation makes it possible to escape "the bogey of rotation-long compound interest" (p.577) that works against the viability of silvicultural investments because of the long rotation ages. Nonetheless, the escape relies on the existence of a constraint or some arbitrary necessity that an environmentally compensating project be instituted. It does not address the question of whether replanting or fertilizing is the environmental project that is most efficient in achieving strong sustainability, or whether strong sustainability is even the objective of society.

Many silvicultural investments are not economically viable, particularly in temperate and boreal forests (Benson 1988; Thompson et al. 1992; Wilson et al. 1998). While long rotations and the bogey of compound interest are the main culprit, nature itself works against economic efficiency. Many sites that have been denuded for whatever reason (say clear felling) will regenerate on their own within five or at most ten years. Thus, the benefits of artificial regeneration are not given by the discounted benefits at harvest time, but by a much smaller amount determined by:

$$(11.25) \quad \frac{B}{(1+r)^T} - \frac{B}{(1+r)^{T+\Delta T}},$$

age, and ΔT is the time it takes to regenerate a stand naturally. Suppose that the cost of replanting is $2,000 per ha, but that B is $50,000 per ha after trees grow for $T = 60$ years. Assume a low discount rate of 2% ($r = 0.02$). Then, using the left-hand-side term in (11.25), the present value of B is $15,239. If trees did not regenerate on their own, then replanting yields a net discounted benefit of $13,239 (benefit–cost ratio of 6.6). If trees regenerate naturally, but it takes five years, then the true benefit from replanting is only $1,436 upon applying both terms in (11.25). The investment is no longer viable and the benefit–cost ratio (= 0.7) is less than one.

NOTES

1. We use *mai* to denote the mean annual increment for a single site, and MAI more generally for an entire management unit of forest regime.
2. We employ the term Hartman–Faustmann to distinguish between a rotation age based only on nontimber benefits versus one that includes nontimber plus timber benefits, although the term Hartman rotation is generally used for both.
3. Nontimber products are sold in markets, but some forest amenities are nonmarket in nature.
4. Environmental groups have targeted coastal rain forests for protection, but have neglected interior, arid areas (such as the BC Okanagon and south-central Oregon) that have greater biodiversity.
5. Nearly all of the Province's private forestland is located on Vancouver Island.

12. Forest Economics II

In Chapter 11, we provided an overview of the economics of forest management, with particular focus on rotation age and sustainability. A much more recent economic issue in forestry relates to environmental spillovers, and how these are addressed. As discussed in Chapter 1, state intervention can lead to policy failure. So why not rely on markets to ensure sustainable forest management (SFM) rather than state regulation? In this regard, forest certification has recently emerged as one of the better examples of a nonstate, market-driven governance structure for addressing environmental spillovers. Forest certification emerged primarily out of concern of excessive tropical deforestation (and attendant loss of biodiversity), but it subsequently prevailed to a greater extent in the industrial forest-products producing countries. This chapter begins in section 12.2 with an examination of economic and other issues related to forest certification, leaving the subject of tropical deforestation to a separate chapter (Chapter 13). Another important topic in forest economics concerns trade in wood products, particularly the ongoing softwood lumber trade-dispute between Canada (the world's largest exporter of softwood lumber) and the United States (the largest producer and consumer). A partial equilibrium trade model is introduced in section 12.2 and used to examine the dispute between Canada and the United States.

12.1 FOREST CERTIFICATION

One of the most challenging tasks facing policymakers today is that of developing appropriate policy instruments for addressing environmental spillovers. There exist a number of different instrument choices that governments can use to protect the environment and encourage sustainable development, including market-based incentives, such as taxes/subsidies and cap and trade schemes (see van Kooten 2004). However, whether regulations or incentives are employed, state involvement is required, if only to determine the cap level and enforce and monitor the subsequent trading mechanism. Reliance on private transactions to resolve environmental spillovers, as argued by Coase (1960), is generally eschewed because the transaction costs of reaching agreements are onerous. So some form of state involvement is required. Even where firms have voluntarily agreed to "correct" an environmental externality, the explicit threat of state intervention is generally a prerequisite for such an agreement (Segerson and Miceli 1998). Even so, moral suasion (where the state encourages voluntary compliance) is unlikely to work unless there is a credible threat of penalties or a carrot to get firms or individuals to comply. Thus, van Kooten and Schmitz (1992) found that landowners in southwestern Saskatchewan could not be persuaded to participate voluntarily in protection of waterfowl habitat, and Takahashi et al. (2001) found that few firms participated in Canada's Voluntary Climate Registry that was meant to encourage firms to comply with Kyoto targets.

More recently, there is increasing evidence of the emergence of nonstate, market-based governance structures for addressing environmental spillovers. These governance structures are appearing in a number of sectors (Bernstein 2001), but forest certification is possibly the most comprehensive example of this governance structure. Forest certification seeks to address environmental spillovers related to the "proper" and "sustainable" exploitation of forests – that forest operations do not endanger wildlife and watersheds, and that logging companies and landowners practice sustainable forest management (SFM). Thus, under forest certification, private firms address spillovers voluntarily.

The United Nations Conference on Environment and Development (UNCED) at Rio de Janeiro in 1992, also known as the "Earth Summit", is widely considered to be the harbinger of the most recent wave of discussions about sustainable development and sustainable forestry. Although many of the concerns preceding Rio focused on tropical forests, the Rio Summit's main document, "Agenda 21", contained a Statement of Principles on Forests that set forth nonbinding principles on forest use, management and protection, which applied to temperate as well as tropical countries. UNCED also spawned the UN Commission on Sustainable Development (UNCSD) and its working group, the Intergovernmental Panel on Forests (IPF), which gave way in 1998 to the Intergovernmental Forum on Forests. UNCED also set the stage for international efforts such as the Intergovernmental Working Group on Forests, the Helsinki Process (1993) for European forests, and the Montreal Process (1994, 1995) for non-European northern and temperate forests, among others (see Sedjo et al. 1997). Thus, most of the attention since the Earth Summit has been within northern forested countries. Wang (2001) provides an excellent review of international forestry agreements.

The binding Helsinki intergovernmental ministerial agreements and the nonbinding Montreal agreement represent a key development, because they outline for the first time a common understanding of measures to monitor biological and social conditions at the national level associated with most of the world's temperate forests. Since they are directed specifically at temperate and boreal (northern) forests, the Helsinki and Montreal Processes have influenced moves to protect temperate rain forests in the US Pacific Northwest and British Columbia in Canada. Concern has also been expressed about depletion of old-growth forest in Russia, some of which is being harvested for Finish mills. However, none of these processes dealt with definitions of sustainable forest management. Governments have been reluctant to pursue common, binding standards of forest management, because each country faces unique circumstances regarding forestry that extend down to the local level. Further, certification of forest management practices and products is market driven, so that the role of government is primarily to encourage transparency, the full participation of all stakeholders, nondiscrimination and open access to any voluntary schemes.

Indeed, it was the failure of governments to sign a global forest convention at the Earth Summit that was important for stimulating increased interest in forest certification as an innovative market mechanism to achieve sustainable forest management (Bernstein and Cashore 2000). Environmental nongovernmental organizations (NGOs) felt that they had spent a significant amount of effort and resources on state-sanctioned international efforts with no discernible gains. As a result, following a proposal by the Woodworkers Alliance for Rainforest Protection, and with support from leading environmental groups such as the World Wide Fund for Nature (WWF), the Forest Stewardship Council (FSC) was founded in 1993. This effort was perceived as a logical jump from the existing work of the Rainforest Alliance's Smartwood Program because it facilitated expanding certification from tropical forests to temperate and boreal forests (Ozanne and Smith 1998), reducing consumer confusion resulting from multiple certification programs, and side-stepping national interests that stifled progress among governments in reaching some form of agreement with respect to SFM. Essentially, it expanded the instruments available to environmentalists from the traditional stick of boycotts of wood products to include a carrot related to marketing of "green" products, howsoever such a carrot might be perceived (see discussion below).

The FSC conception of certification envisioned new governance structures where social, economic and environmental interests would all compete in the private decision-making. Concerned that the FSC would produce strict rules administered by nonforestry professionals, domestic forest industry and landowner associations began to create their own "competing" certification programs. Thus, competing programs were established in Canada, the United States, Scandinavia and Europe more broadly. Before we examine competing certification systems, we discuss certification of sustainable forestry practices and eco-labeling more generally. We conclude the section by considering economic and other reasons why firms might wish to certify forest practices.

Certifying Sustainable Forestry and Eco-labeling

Government efforts to address environmental spillovers from forestry activities have primarily focused on the development of criteria and indicators for implementing sustainable forest management (SFM). These have generally been national in scope, with efforts among governments to agree on common standards across similar forest ecosystems and to obtain consensus about what constitutes SFM in various countries. SFM certification deals with how forests are managed, using environmental, economic, social and cultural criteria that vary from region to region. While development of international SFM standards for certification should be straightforward, because it should be possible to agree on what indicators to measure, getting agreement on performance levels for each indicator is more difficult. The other problem with SFM certification is that it deals only with how a particular forest is managed (it is forest specific), not with the forest company logging the stand or the "chain-of-custody" of forest products – it focuses on logging practices and their effects on the ecosystem, while ignoring what happens to the logs themselves as these get processed into final products. Thereby it provides no link between the forest practice and the customer, although it does say something about the forest company, which is why forest companies seek to have as many of their forest operations certified. Determining chain-of-custody is much easier for lumber and similar products than for pulpwood. Wood chips used to produce pulp derive from various sources (pulp logs, sawmill residues) and are mixed together in the production phase, making it difficult to track pulp back to its source logs. The addition of recycled fiber adds to the complexity. Chain-of-custody and labeling of products are not needed to meet sustainable forestry management objectives.

In terms of environmental (or eco-) labeling, there are three forms that environmental labels can take (see Karl and Orwat 2000).

1. Type I eco-labeling involves attaching a symbol, mark or stamp to a product to indicate that it comes from a sustainably managed forest and/or that it meets certain production process standards. The "stamp of approval" is usually provided by an NGO, although governments have been involved in the initial set-up of such programs (e.g., Canada's

Environmental Choice program founded in 1988 and privatized in 1995). Selectivity criteria are such that eco-labels are awarded to only 20–30% of products. Since eco-labeling is aimed at the retail customer, it is not possible to provide the type of detail found with labels that target an intermediary producer.

2. The second form of environmental label (Type II) consists of self-declared environmental claims, with no third-party verification. Such claims are made by a manufacturer, importer, distributor and/or retailer, but buyers must determine the truth or accuracy of the claim.

3. Finally, Type III environmental labeling refers to quantified environmental life-cycle product information provided by a supplier, based on critical reviews by a third party. The product information is presented as a set of categories or parameters, with detail too great to enable its provision on the product at the retail level. The Environmental Profile Data Sheet used by pulp producers in Canada (see below) is an example of a Type III environmental label.

Third-party verification (certification) is a key to any certification or eco-labeling scheme. In the end, success depends upon the credibility of the auditing scheme that leads to certification or the granting of a label.

A number of problems remain. Small, private woodlot owners, principally in Scandinavia, have generally opposed efforts to certify forest management practices. There it has been an obstacle in joint private, government and NGO efforts to certify management practices, mainly because the process of certification costs money and increases management costs. Without compensation many private forest owners are unwilling to spend money in order to become certified. Hence, these owners have banded together through national landowner organizations to develop their own Europe-wide certification scheme in competition with the FSC system.

Further, certification that involves chain-of-custody is easier for vertically integrated forest companies to implement, thereby giving them an advantage. Large companies are also better able to fund the costs associated with the certification process. Hence, certification could lead to mergers and acquisitions and increasing concentration in global wood products markets (Haener and Luckert 1998).

Perhaps the greatest problems associated with forest certification are related to its effect upon trade. Under the rules of the World Trade Organization (WTO), certification cannot explicitly be used as a barrier to trade. Thus, a country cannot require that imported wood be certified without also requiring that all domestically produced wood be likewise certified. Clearly, a country creates a technical barrier to trade (TBT) by imposing certification standards that domestic producers can attain, but which competitors cannot attain. A particular TBT of this nature occurs if a certification scheme requires maintaining natural forests. In this case, Canada and some other timber-producing countries (notably in the tropics) cannot possibly meet (a strict interpretation of) this requirement, because most of the timber that these countries harvest is from natural forests. Even second-growth forests have, for the most part, regenerated naturally. Trade problems can be reduced only if approaches to certification take into account local management conditions in producing countries and if such regional certification standards are developed in an open and transparent manner.

Forest Certification Systems

As of Decemberr 2003, 164 million ha of forests had been certified globally (Figure 12.1), but this constitutes only about 4.2% of the world's forests. Yet, this is one-third more than was certified in June 2002, about 2½ times that certified in 2001, and more than four times as much as was certified in 1999. North America has 16.8% of its forests certified and Europe 7.3%, but other regions have less than one percent of their forests certified. Only 5.2% of all certified forests are in Asia, Africa and Latin America Each of the major certification schemes is briefly described in the following paragraphs, with a summary provided in Table 12.1. Since the FSC scheme was the first to get started, we consider it first.

Forest Stewardship Council certification
The Forest Stewardship Council has developed a worldwide forest certification network, with more than 200 members from 37 countries. It has articulated 10 international principles and criteria, accredited organizations that certify forest operations according to those principles and criteria, and overseen processes that set regional standards. Briefly, the FSC's principles and criteria are as follows:

1. Compliance with local regulations and FSC principles
2. Tenure and use rights and responsibilities
3. Indigenous peoples' rights
4. Community relations and workers' rights
5. Benefits from the forest
6. Environmental impact
7. Management plan
8. Monitoring and assessment
9. Maintenance of natural forests
10. Plantations

The FSC uses chain-of-custody to label products as originating from forests that are managed according to the above principles and criteria.

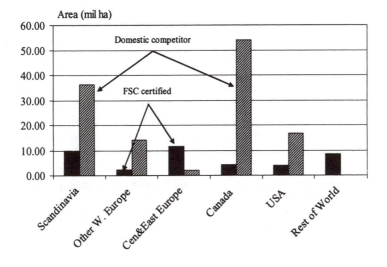

Figure 12.1: FSC Certified Area versus Area Certified under a Competitor Program, January 2004

FSC thus takes an outcome (performance standards) as opposed to means (management systems) approach to forest certification. Because economic, environmental and social considerations are to be treated equally, FSC recognizes the need for regional standards, rather than ones that apply globally.

As already indicated, there is a problem with Principle #9 that requires preserving natural forests. Further, many small woodlot owners are excluded because of the costs of FSC certification. These owners have established a variety of competing certification schemes, as indicated below. Further, governments are excluded from participation in FSC certification, which may create obstacles for countries where the state is the dominant forestland owner, as in Canada. This is less of a problem for certain types of tenures (*viz.*, long-term, company managed tenures such as BC's Tree Farm Licenses) than for short-term cutting licenses on public timberlands. For the latter, it is not possible to expect forest companies to become certified, particularly as these may be small logging outfits.

ISO 14001 certification

At the international level, as early as 1991, the Business Council for Sustainable Development, comprised of business leaders from around the world, suggested that the International Standards Association (ISO) develop standards of environmental management. Consequently, ISO 14001 ("Environmental management systems – specification with guidance for use") was established in 1996. This standard specifies the requirements of an environmental management system for any industry, including forestry. Although designed for all sectors, ISO 14001 is relevant to the forestry sector as it deals with both resource management and the production phase. ISO 14001 seeks to establish environmental management system (EMS) standards that are site and organization specific. A corporate environmental policy must apply to all forest sites, but for each site relevant data must be documented. A forest company may implement ISO 14001 in its pulp mills and sawmills. Hence, the ISO 14001 process is both complementary with and a substitute for national SFM certification. It is complementary with respect to production, but a substitute with respect to resource management. Thus, ISO 14001 certification is a generic, system-based certification scheme that focuses on industrial processes.

Canadian Standards Association (CSA) certification and labeling

In Canada, the Canadian Pulp and Paper Association (now the Canadian Forest Products Association) asked the Canadian Standards Association to develop a forest certification program based on a systems approach to SFM, using criteria and indicators for sustainability developed by the Canadian Council of Forest Ministers. To become certified, companies would have to establish environmental management forestry systems that include auditing requirements. CSA certification has built-in flexibility to encourage ongoing improvements in forest management. Although CSA certification was initiated by industry, its requirements are quite stringent; costs of obtaining and complying with CSA certification are now comparable with those of FSC certification, although it currently lacks the same global recognition as FSC.

The Canadian Pulp and Paper Association (CPPA) also developed the Environmental Profile Data Sheet (EPDS) in response to customer concerns regarding the production and life-cycle environmental attributes of pulp and paper. The EPDS is meant to provide detailed information to bulk purchasers of pulp and paper about resource management and production practices (e.g., recycled fiber content, mechanical vs. chemical pulping process). Buyers can purchase pulp and paper with those attributes that are most desirable, even mixing purchases from various firms to achieve an optimal mix of attributes. Producers are encouraged to improve their environmental performance over time, which makes it a more dynamic approach than simple eco-labeling. The key to this approach is third-party verification (certification).

Sustainable Forestry Initiative (SFI), Tree Farm and Green Tag

In the United States, the international trend toward forest certification resulted in the reorientation of the American Forest and Paper Association's Sustainable Forestry Initiative as a forest certification program. The SFI has taken a different approach to certification as it envisions continual improvement and discretionary, flexible policies. Such an approach is believed to foster innovation and avoid straight-jacketing companies with costly wide-ranging rules that fail to capture specific circumstances. Individual firms retain ultimate authority over the kinds of objectives and goals they pursue (Auld et al. 2001). Participating firms are required to file reports with SFI regarding their SFM plans. Importantly, governance of the SFI certification scheme is dominated by the industry, with other nongovernmental organizations acting only in an advisory capacity, although that role could change in the future. Like CSA certification, no attempt is made to follow wood fiber through its various stages to the final consumer – the chain-of-custody.

Following SFI, small landowners reinvented the "Tree Farm Program" as a competitor to FSC; a mutual recognition agreement with SFI incorporated as well. Another small landowner program, "Green Tag", also emerged as a forest certification policy choice.

Pan-European Forest Certification (PEFC)

In Europe, it was also the landowners who developed their own certification program, because they felt that their needs and opinions were ignored by FSC. In particular, small landowners were concerned with the large costs they would incur in certifying SFM on their lands. The various national forest landowner associations began the Pan-European Forest Certification scheme in 1999. PEFC endorses national schemes that then rely on third-party certification. In addition, there exist smaller certification schemes, most notably the Scandinavian "Natuurland" that offer firms alternatives to the major certification systems.

A summary of the main schemes and their attributes is provided in Table 12.1. Certification schemes differ with respect to: (1) the governance of certification processes (e.g., setting standards and accrediting certifiers); (2) the types of standards employed; (3) the inclusion of labeling (chain of custody); and (4) geographic and sectoral scope. Although all schemes rely on some form of third-party verification, only the FSC scheme has chain-of-custody provisions; SFI, CSA and PEEC are all moving in the direction. Indeed, the latter three schemes are competitor schemes to FSC certification (see Figure 12.1), and, in attempting to emulate the FSC scheme, the schemes appear to be converging somewhat (see below).

Table 12.1: Comparison of Major Competing Forest Certification Schemes

Item	Forest certification scheme				
	FSC	ISO 14001	PEFC	SFI	CSA
Originator	ENGOs, retailers, foresters	Industry	Landowner	Industry	Industry
Territorial focus	Inter-national	Inter-national	Europe, but open to outsiders	National/ binational	National
Verificatio n options	Indepen-dent (acts as 3rd party)	3rd Party	3rd Party	Self, industry or 3rd party	3rd Party

Why do Firms Certify?

In this section, we examine reasons why firms might be interested in certifying forest operations, or certifying that they manage forests in a sustainable fashion, without state coercion. Motives range from economic or market ones to social considerations that range from ethical concern on the part of managers or yielding to pressure from the community in which they operate.

Economic motives

The economic incentives for firms to embark on unilateral environmental initiatives are several. First, eco-certification may resolve problems of information asymmetry and consumer mistrust of firms' "green" claims. Second, unilateral action may be undertaken because it leads to a reduction in production costs; goodwill benefits that accrue to the firm as a result of marketing an environmental program are then a nice side bonus. Segerson and Li (1999) cite 3M Company's "Pollution Prevention Pays" and Dow Corporation's "Waste Reduction Always Pays" programs as having led to a lowering of costs, but such results might not apply in other sectors. Likewise, programs that promote energy efficiency, thus reducing pollution, can lower a firm's energy costs and, if packaged correctly, earn the company public relations' benefits. In the forest sector, forest certification might cause a change in forest management practices that reduces operating costs and enhances resource productivity (see also Porter and van der Linde 1995).

Third, markets might dictate whether firms enter environmental agreements (certify their forest operations) without state involvement. Threats of product boycotts (loss of market share) or lawsuits related to spillovers (e.g., destruction of critical wildlife habitat, polluting of rivers with runoff from forest operations, emission of dangerous pollutants), which increase costs or threaten a firm's survival, can motivate companies to take action voluntarily. Markets for wood products can be delineated according to whether consumers care that (derive higher utility from) products come from sustainably managed forests. SFM appears to be of greater concern to European buyers, for example, than North American or Asian ones (Cashore, Auld and Newsom 2004), so one would expect firms selling into European markets to be more prone to certify their forest operations.

Finally, firms may earn a price premium if it can be demonstrated that their products are from sustainably managed forests. Sedjo and Swallow (1999) examine whether a price premium for certified products will be generated in a competitive market. In some cases, firms simply purchase goodwill by becoming certified, thus enabling them to sell wood products to large retailers while their competitors are shut out of the market. In British Columbia, for example, the large forest company, Weyerhaueser Corporation, has funded research by biologists and, as a result, adopted variable retention forest practices. This action was sufficient to convince Home Depot, a large wood products retailer, to make them a preferred supplier.

The real or perceived benefits of forest certification need to be balanced against its costs. Costs are divided into the direct costs of getting and maintaining certification (filling out application forms, bargaining with the certifier, audit preparation, paying monitoring costs, etc.) and the indirect costs of changing sustainable forest practices to meet certification requirements. One would expect, therefore, that firms that are already incurring the latter costs are more likely to seek certification than other companies. Thus, certification would be higher among Canadian firms, because they are already subject to onerous regulations and have already incurred the costs of changing forestry practices in line with those required for certification. Perhaps this explains why a greater proportion of firms in Canada were certified early on compared with those in the USA or Germany (Table 12.2). Now, however, almost all forest companies in Canada, the United States and Europe are certified but domestic certification schemes dominate FSC certification (see again Figure 12.1). Domestic schemes are seen as a competitor of FSC certification, with companies seeking FSC certification only if management itself is concerned about the environment (Cashore et al. 2004). Otherwise, the domestic schemes (SFI in the USA, CSA and SFI in Canada, PFEC in Europe) are considered adequate for achieving goodwill and other benefits of certification. Furthermore, FSC was developed to address SFM in tropical regions, and many still take the view that this is and should be its main function.

Table 12.2: Forest Certification by Number of Firm and Location, as of 2001

	Firm location			
Item	USA	Canada	Germany	Total
Number of certifications				
Not certified	85.5%	71.3%	93.3%	83.8%
Certified				
– under at least one scheme	14.5%	28.7%	6.7%	16.2%
– under more than one scheme				
	3.2%	9.1%	2.2%	4.5%
Type of certification				
FSC	9.5%	6.3%	3.0%	7.1%
ISO	2.1%	19.2%	0.7%	5.4%
CSA (Canada)	n.a.	2.1%	n.a.	0.5%
SFI (USA)	7.1%	n.a.	5.2%	4.8%
FOREST CARE (Canada)	n.a.	16.3%	n.a.	3.6%

Notes:
n.a. not applicable.

Corporate responsibility and social license
There is the view that firms will voluntarily enter environmental agreements without the threat of the state because it gives them the social license to operate in a manner that permits some environmental harm, since not all spillovers can be mitigated in any event. This is another form of the ethical argument of "corporate responsibility" – managers of firms feel that they have to behave in a socially acceptable manner. Managers may have a social/environmental social conscience that needs to be assuaged. It could also be the case that shareholders demand that forest companies behave in an environmentally friendly manner, and that forest companies certify practices as a consequence. There exist several investment funds that seek out "green investments" only, although they are likely in the minority and have little effect on share prices (although whether that is true can be tested

empirically).

Community pressure

Community pressure may well be an important reason for seeking certification. Because forest management often imposes negative (or positive) externalities at the local level, communities may attempt to influence forest management in their region. Pargal and Wheeler (1996) find, for example, that community pressure may work informally (in the Coasian sense) to regulate pollution, via negotiation between a firm and the local community. A firm's response to community pressure can be viewed as the price it pays for using environmental services that are implicitly "owned" by the community. To the extent that a local community can impose "penalties" on a firm, the firm will choose a level of pollution (or certification scheme) that equates the marginal costs imposed by the community to the marginal costs of abatement (certification), even in the absence of formal regulation.

As for the costs that a community may impose, "penalties" consist of demands for compensation by community groups, social ostracism of the firm's employees, the threat of physical violence, boycotting of the firm's products locally, and monitoring and publicizing the firm's "bad" behavior. Through forest certification, a firm may attempt to "buy" the approval of a local community.

It is likely the case that all of the above factors, plus others that have not been documented or simply not pointed out here, play a role in the decision to certify. There remains a concern, however, if corporate responsibility is the driving factor behind voluntary environmental agreements. This suggests that firms behave contrary to profit motives. While this is likely true in many cases, the concern here is that, while most people would not object to firms going out of their way to behave in an environmentally friendly fashion, there exists the possibility that firms conduct themselves in a manner that opposes the interests and cause of civil society. The managers of corporations can just as well use the excess profits (or rent) that the firm accrues to do good or to foment evil. Likewise, community pressure can prevent forest companies from becoming certified if the community is more interested in preventing the short-term loss of jobs than it is in sustainable development of the resource.

12.2 INTERNATIONAL TRADE IN FOREST PRODUCTS

Some 70% of total roundwood and 90% of all the pulp produced globally come from forests in northern latitudes (Table 12.3; Table 11.2). The majority of wood products are produced from coniferous forests in the Northern Hemisphere. Production of pulp from hardwood species has become increasingly important, however, as a result of technical advances in pulp making and the existence of substantial indigenous (boreal) stands of mixed hard and softwood species, and the use of hardwood species in plantation forests. Principal producers of pulp and softwood lumber are the United States, Canada, Sweden, Finland, Russia and Japan. Among tropical countries, only Brazil produces globally significant amounts of pulp, although the amount is relatively small (less than 5% of global production). Countries such as Chile, New Zealand and Australia are also expected to become important, at least in export markets. Therefore, it is the developed countries that dominate international trade in forest products.

Table 12.3: Global Output and Exports of Industrial Wood Products by Region, 2000

Country/Region	Indust Roundw'd		Sawnwood		Wood Panels		Wood Pulp		Paper Products	
	Output	Exports	Output	Exports	Output	Exports	Output	Exports	Output	Exports
	10^6 m^3						10^6 tonnes			
Developed	1,144.0	92.2	334.5	113.2	129.6	38.3	146.2	29.1	243.3	84.1
	72.7%	80.7%	78.8%	89.3%	71.4%	67.7%	78.0%	79.5%	75.2%	86.8%
North America (excl. Mexico)	604.2	14.9	183.7	55.1	60	13.1	83.7	17.2	107.4	24.8
	38.4%	13.0%	43.3%	43.5%	33.0%	23.1%	44.6%	47.0%	33.2%	25.6%
Europe (excl. Russia)	372.9	39.8	105.8	48.7	55.6	22.7	41.2	9.5	95.1	54.5
	23.7%	34.9%	24.9%	38.4%	30.6%	40.1%	22.0%	26.0%	29.4%	56.2%
Russian Federation	105.8	30.8	20	7.8	4.8	1.4	5.8	1.6	5.3	2.3
	6.7%	27.0%	4.7%	6.2%	2.6%	2.5%	3.1%	4.4%	1.6%	2.4%
Japan	18.0	0.0	17.1	0.0	5.7	0.0	11.3	0.1	31.8	1.6
	1.1%	0.0%	4.0%	0.0%	3.1%	0.0%	6.0%	0.3%	9.8%	1.7%
Oceania	43.1	6.7	7.9	1.6	3.5	1.1	4.2	0.7	3.7	0.9
	2.7%	5.9%	1.9%	1.3%	1.9%	1.9%	2.2%	1.9%	1.1%	0.9%
Developing	431.0	19.7	90.0	8.8	52.1	15.6	41.4	2.5	80.2	11.2
	27.4%	17.3%	21.2%	6.9%	28.7%	27.6%	22.1%	6.8%	24.8%	11.6%
Africa	68.8	6.1	7.7	1.9	2.1	0.7	2.3	0.6	2.9	0.6
	4.4%	5.3%	1.8%	1.5%	1.2%	1.2%	1.2%	1.6%	0.9%	0.6%
Latin America	166.1	0	34.9	0.4	8.4	0.3	12	0	14.2	0.2
	10.5%	0.0%	8.2%	0.3%	4.6%	0.5%	6.4%	0.0%	4.4%	0.2%
China	96.4	0.8	7.2	0.8	18.6	2.1	18	0.0	35.5	3.6
	6.1%	0.7%	1.7%	0.6%	10.2%	3.7%	9.6%	0.0%	11.0%	3.7%
Asia (excl. Japan, China)	95	10.5	39.9	5.7	23	12.5	9.1	1.9	27.6	6.8
	6.0%	9.2%	9.4%	4.5%	12.7%	22.1%	4.9%	5.2%	8.5%	7.0%
Oceania	4.7	2.3	0.3	0.0	0.0	0.0	0.0	0.0	0.0	0.0
	0.3%	2.0%	0.1%	0.0%	0.0%	0.0%	0.0%	0.0%	0.0%	0.0%
WORLD	**1,574.60**	**114.2**	**424.5**	**126.7**	**181.6**	**56.6**	**187.5**	**36.6**	**323.6**	**96.9**

Source: FAO (2003).

Partial Equilibrium Trade Modeling

Trade in any product can be analyzed using a spatial, partial equilibrium model of international trade. Such models require understanding of excess demand (ED) and excess supply functions (ES). How these are constructed is demonstrated with the aid of Figure 12.2. Quantity traded and price in a country that does not trade (referred to as autarky) are determined by the intersection of the domestic demand (D) and supply (S) schedules. In the figure, the no-trade equilibrium quantity and price are $q*$ and $p*$, respectively. A country will generally engage in trade if the world price for the good in question is greater or less than the domestic price (ignoring the transportation cost). If the price is higher than the domestic equilibrium price, the country will export the commodity; if the price is lower, it will import the good. How much will it supply, or how much will be demanded?

Suppose that the world price, or what firms in the country can get by selling abroad (after transportation costs), is p_w (Figure 12.2). The amount the country will supply to the world market is equal to the difference between what domestic producers are willing to supply at p_w (given by q_w^S) and what domestic consumers will buy at that price (q_w^D). The difference between what producers are willing to supply and what domestic consumers are willing to buy at each price above $p*$ constitutes excess supply, with the ES function tracing out this excess supply at various prices. Likewise, if world price is below $p*$, it is the difference between what consumers are willing to buy and what producers are willing to sell that constitutes excess demand and enables one to trace out the ED schedule. Both ES and ED are shown in Figure 12.2.

The results can be addressed mathematically. Suppose the (inverse) demand and supply curves in Figure 12.2 are linear:

(12.1) $P^D = \alpha - \beta q$, $\alpha, \beta \geq 0$, and

(12.2) $P^S = a + bq$, $a, b \geq 0$.

The excess demand and supply curves in the figure are then given by:[1]

(12.3) $ED = \gamma - \delta q$,   with $\gamma = \dfrac{a\beta + b\alpha}{\beta + b} \geq 0$ and $\delta = \dfrac{b\beta}{\beta + b} \geq 0$.

(12.4) $ES = \gamma + mq$,   with $\gamma = \dfrac{a\beta + b\alpha}{\beta + b} \geq 0$ and $m = \dfrac{b\beta}{\beta + b} \geq 0$.

Notice that γ is the equilibrium domestic price, so that, in the absence of transportation costs, the excess supply and demand curves start at the same point on the vertical (price) axis.

Now consider, as an illustration of a partial-equilibrium trade model, trade in softwood lumber between Canada and the United States. Assume that these are the only two trading regions, which serves as a good first approximation since USA imports of lumber from other countries are small compared to annual imports from Canada, while Canadian exports to other countries (mainly Japan) are also relatively small. Indeed, the only problem with our assumption is that Canada–USA trade in softwood lumber is really characterized by trade among a number of distinct Canadian and US regions. (There is market fragmentation so that some regions in Canada may export wood to the USA while others import wood. In that case, a diagram is inadequate for modeling trade and a mathematical programming model is required instead.) Nonetheless, the Canada–USA example offers an excellent way to illustrate how spatial, partial equilibrium trade models can be used to analyze policy.

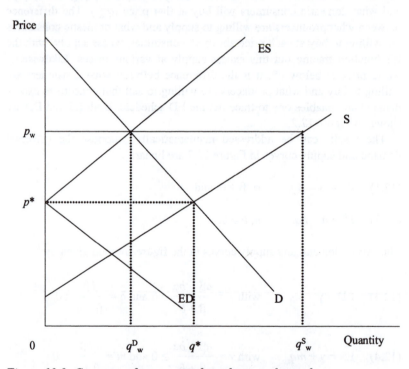

Figure 12.2: Concepts of excess supply and excess demand

The partial-equilibrium trade model for Canada–USA trade is illustrated in Figure 12.3. In the figure, the domestic demand functions for lumber in Canada and the USA are given by D_C and D_U, respectively, while respective supply functions are given by S_C and S_U. Without trade, an amount q^* of lumber will be consumed in Canada at a domestic price of P_C (see panel (a)); in the USA, consumption will be q' at a price P_U (panel (c)). Note that, unless $P_U > P_C$ in autarky, there can be no trade. Indeed, the difference between the domestic, no-trade prices must exceed the cost of transporting the good from one market to another, as we demonstrate below. The wellbeing of citizens in each country is determined by the sum of the benefits they receive as consumers (consumer surplus) and as producers (producer surplus). As shown in Chapter 2, economic wellbeing or welfare is always determined as the sum of surpluses (e.g., net revenues rather than gross sales). In the absence of trade, the consumer surplus associated with softwood lumber production is given by area $a+b+c$ in Figure 12.3(a) for Canada and area α in Figure 12.3(c) for the USA. The producer surplus (or economic rent) is measured, in the absence of trade, by area $e+d$ for Canada and by area $\beta+\gamma$ for the USA. Total economic wellbeing is the sum of producer and consumer surplus, and is simply given by the area between the demand and supply curves. For Canada, total surplus in the absence of trade is given by area $a+b+c+d+e$, while it is area $\alpha+\beta+\gamma$ for the United States.

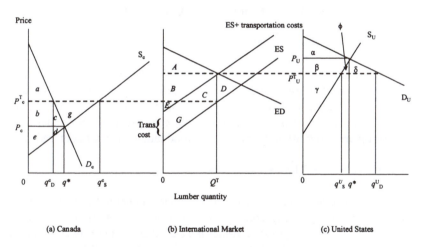

(a) Canada   (b) International Market   (c) United States

Figure 12.3: Model of international trade in softwood lumber

Unrestricted Free Trade

To demonstrate that trade improves the wellbeing of citizens in each of the trading countries, it is necessary to show that total surplus in each country increases. The case of trade can also be analyzed using Figure 12.3. Since in the absence of trade the US domestic price is greater than that in Canada, lumber will flow from Canada to the USA as long as the difference in price between the two regions exceeds the transportation costs.

With trade, the price in Canada rises from P_C to $P_C{}^T$, while US price falls from P_U to $P^T{}_U$. Canadian consumers lose as a result of the price increase, consuming less; consumption in Canada falls from $q*$ to $q^C{}_D$ and consumer surplus falls to area *a*. However, Canadian producers face a higher price ($P^T{}_C > P_C$ in panel (a)), causing them to increase production from $q*$ to $q^C{}_S$. An amount $q^C{}_S - q^C{}_D$ ($=Q^T$) is traded to the US, while producer surplus increases to $b+c+d+e+g$. The wellbeing of Canadians as a whole increases by area *g*, with producers (and those earning a living in the softwood lumber sector) being the main beneficiaries from trade.

The situation in the United States is a mirror image of that in Canada. The fall in US prices causes consumers to purchase more lumber (from q' to $q^U{}_D$) and increase their overall consumer surplus by an amount given by $\beta+\phi+\delta$. US producers now face a lower price and curtail output to $q^U{}_S$, giving up a producer surplus or rent of β in the process. However, the gain to consumers is greater than β, with the net gain to US citizens given by $\phi+\delta$.

The main results can be summarized in the international market, panel (b) of Figure 12.3. The amount traded between Canada and the USA is $Q^T = q^C{}_S - q^C{}_D = q^U{}_D - q^U{}_S$. The net gain to the USA is area A, which is equal to area $\phi+\delta$ in panel (c); this net gain accrues to US consumers and therefore is measured under the excess demand curve ED. The gain to Canada equals the area above the excess supply curve ES below the demand price, or area $B+C+E+G$, but transportation costs of $B+C$ are incurred. Hence, the net gain from trade is $E+G$, which is equal to area g in panel (a). Note that both countries are better off with trade in softwood lumber than without trade.

Restricted Trade: The Case of Quota

Consider the case of an exporter that sets a quota either voluntarily or at the request of the importing country. We consider two quota models using Figures 12.4 and 12.5. First, consider the case that existed between Canada and the USA under the Softwood Lumber Agreement (SLA), which is illustrated in Figure 12.4. Suppose the quota comes about because the importing country charges a duty for sales above the quota amount (i.e., the amount that Canada is allowed to export free of duty). Then, with a quota, the excess supply curve (USA) in Figure 12.4(b) has a vertical segment with a height equal to the charge on sales above quota amount Q'.

The consumer surplus is given by area *a* for Canada (panel (a)) and by area $\alpha+\beta$ for the USA (panel (c)). Canadian producers gain area $b+c+d$, while US producers gain γ. Even with a quota, the two countries are better off than under autarky. The gains over autarky are shown in Figure 12.4(b). In this case, transportation costs are given by area $C+D$, while the net producer surplus as a result of trade is E. The net gain to the USA (to its consumers) is area A. Area B represents an unearned rent attributable to the quota (the *quota rent*), and it accrues to Canadian producers because they receive a price that is higher than the marginal cost of production including transportation.

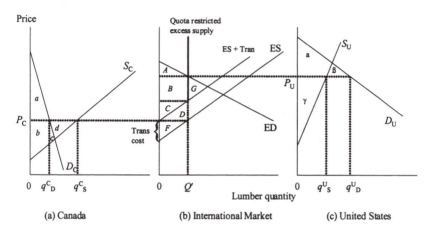

Figure 12.4: Economics of softwood quota in an international trade model

Compared to unrestricted free trade, however, the Canadian price is lower (Canadian consumers are better off) and the US price is higher (US producers are better off, consumers worse off). Overall, the two countries are worse off with the quota by area G.

What is interesting about the quota model is that Canadian producers are better off with a quota in place than they would be under unrestricted free trade. The reason is that the loss of producer surplus caused by the lower price in Canada is more than overcome by the quota rent. Since Canadian consumers are also better off (due to a lower domestic price) as are US producers, the big loser is the US consumer. The extent of any gain to Canadian lumber producers depends on the nature of the price changes, or the extent to which US prices are sensitive to the level of Canadian imports: it depends on elasticities of supply and demand in the two counties. The size of welfare gains and income transfers is an empirical issue. For example, is it possible to show that the quota has created a "significant" wedge between Canadian and US prices? If so, then there will be quota rent.

Let us re-examine the quota situation by considering the case of pure quota with no surcharge. This is illustrated using Figure 12.5. For ease of exposition, the transportation cost component is ignored; thus, the US and Canadian prices are equal under unrestricted trade (alternatively $P_C=P_U$ minus transport cost). The qualitative results are unaffected by this simplification.

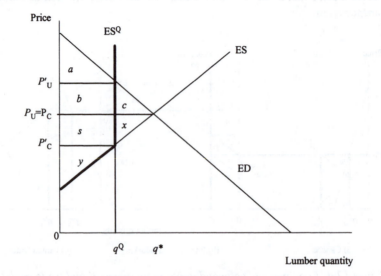

Figure 12.5: Available US market under a quota

The quota is set at q^Q and the excess supply curve shifts to ES^Q (denoted by the dark lines). It is important to note that the US price rises because of the quota, while the Canadian price actually falls. A wedge is created between the Canadian price and the US price that is greater than the transportation cost (otherwise there would be no trade). It can be thought of in the following way. An economic agent can buy an amount q^Q from Canadian producers at a price P'_C and sell it to US consumers at P'_U, thereby collecting a rent equal to area ($b+s$) in Figure 12.5. Of course, it is the Canadian companies that gain from a quota system.[2]

Consider only Canadian producers. Because the domestic Canadian price falls from P_C to P'_C, producers will lose producer surplus in Canada. The US price increases, on the other hand, from P_U to P'_U. Thus, Canadian lumber producers will sell less to the USA, but receive a higher price for what they sell. In terms of Figure 12.5, the loss in producer surplus is measured by area x, while the gain from selling at the higher price, albeit a smaller quantity ($q^Q<q^*$), is area b. Area s was previously earned as

producer surplus, but now constitutes part of what determines the quota rent. The overall gain to Canadian producers is given by area (b–x) in Figure 12.5 minus the loss in producer surplus in the domestic (Canadian) market. Under what conditions are Canadian producers better off with a quota than they would be under free trade or some other trade regime?

For the case of linear US and Canadian demand and supply functions, and thus linear excess demand and excess supply, van Kooten (2002) demonstrates that the quota rent is maximized when quantity is exactly one-half of the free trade quantity q^* (Figure 12.6). However, this is not where lumber producers maximize their gains because it does not take into account the loss in producer surplus associated with lower prices in the domestic market. The darkened curve indicates the correct producer gain from various quota levels. The maximum amount that producers can gain from a quota scheme occurs at q^m, which lies between $\frac{1}{2} q^*$ and q^* in Figure 12.6. Notice that the quota rent here is a form of scarcity rent, except that it is not a result of the scarcity of a natural resource. Rather, it is the consequence of deliberate action to restrict trade and create the rent.

Export and Import Taxes

Import taxes levied by the US (the countervail duty) or export taxes levied by Canada have the same effect on price as a quota if the duty or tax is set to achieve the same quantity reduction. Taxes are discussed with the aid of Figure 12.7. Countervail duties and export levies are *ad valorem* taxes that pivot the ED and ES curves, respectively. Both taxes are shown in Figure 12.7: the import duty shifts excess demand to ED′ while the export tax shifts excess supply to ES′. The taxes result in the same trade quantity as with the quota in Figure 12.5. Again the tax (whether export or import) creates a wedge between the US price and the Canadian price that exceeds the transportation cost. The only difference between the quota and tax cases is the distribution of rents. In the quota case, Canadian lumber producers collect the (quota) rent. With an export tax, it is the Canadian government that collects an amount given by area b+s in Figure 12.7; with a countervail duty (CVD), it is the US government that collects this same area.

An optimal import tax would be set so that $q=\frac{1}{2}q^*$, which is identical to the quota level that would maximize the quota rent (see Figure 12.6). However, as noted above, it would not be the optimal quota level if producer returns are taken into account. Further, with either a CVD or an export tax, Canadian producers are worse off than under either free trade or under a quota (assuming no middleman to collect the quota rent), because they do not collect the rent while they continue to lose surplus due to lower domestic prices.

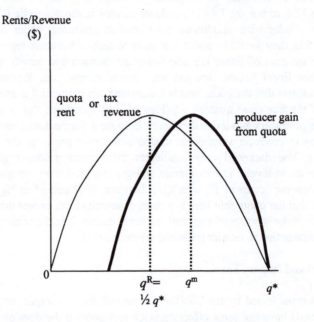

Figure 12.6: Quota rents versus producer gains from quota

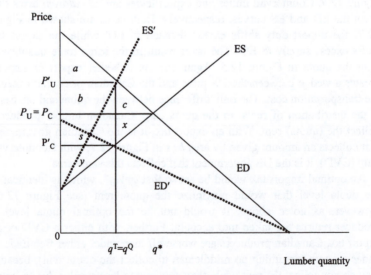

Figure 12.7: Available US market with export and import taxes

Canada–United States Trade Dispute in Softwood Lumber

Canadian exports of softwood lumber have been a source of aggravation to US lumber producers since at least 1962. In 1981, as a result of recession and declining lumber demand, lobbyists in the Congress asked the Commerce Department to investigate whether the Canadian timber licensing system constituted a subsidy that would warrant imposing a countervail duty on Canadian lumber. In 1983, the Commerce Department concluded that there was no evidence that Canadian producers were being subsidized. However, in 1986, as a result of pressure from the US Coalition for Fair Lumber Imports, the US government imposed a 15% CVD in response to the International Trade Commission's (ITC) judgment that Canadian producers were indeed being subsidized. Negotiations between the two governments led to a Memorandum of Understanding (MOU) whereby the Canadian government imposed an export tax of 15% beginning in 1987. In late 1991, the Canadian government announced that it would drop the MOU. In response, the USA imposed a CVD of 6.5% in mid-1992 as a result of an ITC ruling favoring US lumber producers. After an extremely contentious process under the US–Canada Free Trade Agreement binational dispute settlement procedure, the CVD was dropped and the USA refunded US$800 million in duties collected.

This process cost the Canadian industry dearly in legal fees, so, when further threats of duties arose in 1995 and 1996, the two governments concluded the Canada–US Softwood Lumber Agreement (SLA), which employed a quota mechanism. The SLA ran from April 1, 1996 to March 31, 2001, and constrained annual lumber exports to the USA from four provinces (British Columbia, Alberta, Ontario and Quebec), which in 1998 accounted for 87.4% of all softwood lumber exported by Canada to the USA (Canadian Forest Service 2000). By Article 2.2, Canada was bound to collect US$50 per thousand board feet (mbf) for lumber exports exceeding 14.7 billion board feet (bbf) and a fee of $100 for amounts in excess of 15.35 bbf, with fees to be adjusted annually for inflation.[3] The SLA has been the subject of disputes concerning the scope of coverage, particularly as to whether pre-drilled and notched studs and rougher-headed boards were included; high-priced, manufactured products were excluded, however. It has also created distortions as provinces not covered by the SLA increased exports to the US from 1.04 bbf in 1995 to 2.75 bbf in 1999, while US imports from other countries rose from 0.40 bbf to 0.94 bbf over the same period (Canadian Forest Service 2000). While the allocation of the total annual (and quarterly) quota is left up to Canada, it has been the subject of conflicts at both the provincial, regional (e.g., BC coast vs. interior) and individual firm levels. The allocation was on the record of exports to the USA in the years before the SLA, so a lumber producer that focused on Asian markets (as did coastal BC lumber producers) could not simply shift to the US market when Asian markets turned down.

The SLA was not renewed in 2002, but the issue of lower-priced softwood lumber imports from Canada did not disappear, mainly because of Canada's economic institutions (and declining currency), the high degree of public ownership of forestlands and continued Canadian restrictions on log exports (see Chapter 3). Indeed, the province that accounts for nearly 60% of total lumber exports to the USA, British Columbia, also has the highest degree of public ownership of forestlands of any major forest jurisdiction in the world and, arguably, is the most interventionist (see Wilson et al. 1998). Since the underlying factors that led to the softwood lumber dispute remain, efforts to regulate softwood lumber exports from Canada will likely continue in the future. The latest development is that the USA has imposed a CVD of some 27% (consisting partly of a CVD and partly of an anti-dumping duty) on imports of lumber from Canada, so the dispute is not about to be resolved any time soon.

In Table 12.4, we provide some notion of the potential magnitude of income gains and losses as a result of trade restrictions on softwood lumber between Canada and the United States. If one sums each of the columns in the table, the result is a negative number that indicates the total loss from the trade restriction. In all cases, the US consumer is the big loser: The quota increased the cost of a house in the USA by some $8,000. If Canadian producers were to create a cartel to sell lumber to the USA and implement an optimal quota, US consumers would lose nearly $1.8 billion annually. Even under a USA-imposed countervail duty, US consumers would lose more than $780 million per year, and upwards of $2 billion under some scenarios. The only consistent "winners" are Canadian consumers and US producers who stand to gain more than $500 million to more than $1 billion per year. Little wonder that they lobby for trade restrictions.

In practice, it has been difficult to verify the impact of a quota regime, or even countervail duties. The first attempts by the USA to impose a countervail occurred in the late 1980s and early 1990s when US public timber sales, especially in the Pacific Northwest, dropped dramatically, with Canadian sales increasing to fill the gap, at least partly. With the SLA, not all Canadian provinces were covered; in particular, the Maritime provinces and Saskatchewan were exempt. As a result, these provinces, but most importantly, New Brunswick, increased timber harvest and exports, as did some European countries, most notably Austria. Furthermore, lumber with high value added was exempt, so exports of pre-drilled studs and other higher-valued products increased to offset declines in somewhat lower-valued lumber products. At the time the SLA expired, this loophole was rapidly being closed.

Table 12.4: Annual Welfare Gains and Losses from Canada–US Softwood Lumber Trade ($ millions)

Item	Scenarios				
	SLA[a]	Optimal quota	15% CVD	6½% CVD	15% Export tax
Canada					
Δ Consumer surplus	108.76	253.67	241.86	104.67	103.89
Δ Producer surplus[b]	21.56	192.13	–878.65	–407.23	–404.37
Δ Government revenue	n.a.	n.a.	0.00	0.00	534.06
United States					
Δ Consumer surplus	–810.63	–1,796.29	–1,719.42	–781.35	–775.78
Δ Producer surplus	544.36	1,233.34	1,178.52	524.35	520.55
Δ Government revenue	n.a.	n.a.	1,070.42	537.60	0.00

Notes:
[a] SLA refers to Softwood Lumber Agreement. Changes (Δ) are relative to free trade.
[b] Includes a quota rent, where applicable.
Source: Adapted from van Kooten (2002).

Canadian lumber products have countered the most recent (countervail and anti-dumping) duties by increasing output in order to reduce per unit costs. For example, sawmills have gone from two to three shifts. Thus, rather than leading to a reduction in Canadian exports to the USA, the duties have had little effect in practice. However, just as the SLA, duties reduce the value of logs and stumpage, meaning that eventually the public owner of the resource will need to absorb the costs unless the authority wishes to reduce the scope of the Canadian forest sector.

NOTES

1. Equations (12.3) and (12.4) are derived as follows. First solve equations (12.1) and (12.2) for q^D and q^S. Excess demand and excess supply results (12.3) and (12.4) are found, respectively, by solving q^D-q^S and q^S-q^D for demand and supply prices, ED and ES.
2. In the case where a US agent is given exclusive right to import Canadian lumber, a situation of bilateral monopoly emerges and it is uncertain who will benefit. However, quantity traded will fall and US price will rise.
3. It is confusing that lumber is measured in two ways. The USA uses board feet while all other countries use cubic meters. The conversion factor is: 1 mbf = 2.36 m³.

13. Economics of Tropical Deforestation

Forests are and have historically been important natural resources. They have long provided wood for burning and even today fuel wood accounts for about one-half of all wood use. Industrial wood accounts for the remainder, with roundwood logs, sawn timber (lumber) and fiberboard important for construction and decoration, and pulp for paper and paper products. Because forests are a renewable resource, their future commercial use is assured if managed correctly; from an environmental standpoint, an attractive option is to rely more on wood products, through their substitution for nonwood products in construction (replacing concrete and aluminum studs) or burning (replacing fossil fuels). However, as the non-commercial timber values of forests increase with greater environmental awareness, the pressure on forestland owners to take into account such values in their land-use decisions will increase.

Denudation of forests occurs by natural means (fires, disease, windfall) or as a result of human activities (harvest of timber, clearing of land). Human activities to cut trees for commercial wood products, or to clear land for agriculture, are of great concern to environmentalists and the general public. Some see tropical deforestation in particular as a failure of the market system to account for noncommercial timber values of the forest, a failure often linked to inadequate property rights over nontimber resources that forests provide.

As a result of processes deriving from the Earth Summit in Rio de Janeiro in 1992 (see section 12.1), timber harvests from federal lands in the US Pacific Northwest have nearly been halted, while BC has reduced harvest levels and implemented stringent environmental controls, as have Finland and Sweden (Wilson et al. 1998; Sedjo 1997). With the globalization of wood product markets, timber harvests from forests in northern latitudes have important impacts on forestland use in southern and tropical countries (Sedjo 1996a). A reduction in northern harvests increases fiber prices in the short term, increasing the attractiveness of timber mining in tropical regions. However, higher prices also increase the value of forestlands, thereby reducing incentives to convert them to agriculture, and raise the profitability of plantation forests whose outputs reduce pressure on pristine forests. But to speak of deforestation in the context of northern and temperate forests is simply wrong. In most countries (e.g., Finland, Sweden and Canada), forest laws require reforestation of sites after harvest, and evidence indicates that forests in temperate and boreal areas have actually expanded (Korotov and Peck 1993).

Deforestation in developing countries is another matter, and it is mainly in these countries where tropical forests are found. The United Nations Food and Agriculture Organization (FAO) defines tropical forests as ecosystems with a minimum of 10% crown canopy of trees and/or bamboo; they are generally associated with wild flora, fauna and natural soil conditions and not subject to agricultural practices (FAO 1997). Tropical forests cover a large portion of the globe's land surface between the Tropics of Cancer and Capricorn, 23° north and south of the Equator. The largest expanse of tropical forest is found in the South American equatorial region, predominantly in the Amazon Basin, but extending up into Central America and down into northern Argentina. Large tropical forests are also found in the equatorial regions of Africa and West Africa and in Southeast Asia, running from India to Malaysia, north into China, and continuing to the islands of the East Indian Archipelago and extending into northeastern Australia. While the climate of the tropics is uniform in terms of a steady year-round temperature, differences in tropical ecosystems are the result of different soil and slope conditions, and variation in the amount and timing of annual rainfall. For example, annual rainfall may vary from less than 10 millimeters (mm) along the Peruvian coast to more than 10 meters (m) along the Colombian coast only a few hundred kilometers (km) to the north (Terborgh 1992).

Tropical forests range from open savannahs where precipitation is limited, to dense tropical rainforests, where rainfall is most abundant. Large areas of dry tropical forests exist in almost all of the above regions, covering large areas in South and Central America as well as Africa and, to a lesser extent, Southeast Asia. Obviously, the type of tropical forest that occurs in an area depends critically on the availability of precipitation and moisture. The annual cycle of seasonal change is also an important feature of tropical climates, but the seasons are characterized by variation in rainfall rather than temperature. Evergreen forests occur where there is little or no dry season.

One feature of tropical forests is that they contain much, if not most, of the world's biodiversity in the trees and plants that comprise the vegetative system and in the animals, especially anthropoids, which exist in the forest soils, floor and canopy. Tropical forests, especially wet tropical forests, typically contain far more species of trees, plants, birds, butterflies, and so forth than their temperate counterpart. Another feature is that, despite soils that are poor in nutrients and minerals, net primary productivity (NPP) of tropical ecosystems is higher than that of temperate and boreal ecosystems. For example, NPP amounts to 224 grams (g) per m^2 per year in boreal forests, 360 to 590 $g/m^2/yr$ in temperate forests (depending on type – conifer, deciduous or broadleaf evergreen), but nearly 900 $g/m^2/yr$ in tropical forests (FAO 1992).

In this chapter, we examine the complex subject of tropical deforestation, although the experience of developed countries helps shed light on what is happening in tropical countries. There are many misconceptions, and one purpose is to identify some of these. The other purpose is to examine the extent of deforestation, its causes and policies that can protect those attributes (*viz.*, biodiversity and carbon storage) that are really the objective of efforts to reduce or halt deforestation. We also consider the values of various forest products other than commercial timber products (e.g., pharmaceutical values, nontimber products), ecosystem functions and preservation values as these are a major component of economic arguments to prevent deforestation. We begin in the next section by examining tropical forests in a global context. We consider patterns and rates of tropical deforestation, and the role of deforestation in loss of biodiversity and release of carbon dioxide into the atmosphere. Economic values of tropical forests are reviewed in section 13.3, while causes of tropical deforestation are analyzed in section 13.4.

13.1 TROPICAL DEFORESTATION IN A GLOBAL CONTEXT

As noted in Chapter 12 and, especially, Table 12.3, tropical forests do not contribute large amounts to global industrial wood output. Even for countries such as Brazil that are significant in terms of pulp production, fiber comes from plantation forests (ones that are planted in the expectation of earning a profit on future harvests). Less than one-third of the global industrial wood harvest originates with old-growth forests, or forests that have not previously been commercially exploited (Table 12.4). Commercial timber production from old growth occurs principally in Canada, Russia, Indonesia and Malaysia (Sedjo 1997), although commercial harvests of old growth in Papua New Guinea (PNG), the Solomon Islands, Laos, Vietnam, Burma and Cambodia have become an important source of tropical logs (Dauvergne 1997, especially pp.186–7). Of the industrial wood harvest that does not originate with old growth, industrial plantations account for more than one-third, with the remainder accounted for by second-growth forests.

The continuing trend towards intensively managed plantation forests occurs for both financial reasons and concerns related to security of supply, with increasing investment in the technology of growing trees stimulated by declining global reliance on old growth – the dwindling of the "old growth overhang" (Sedjo 1997). Increasingly trees are considered an agricultural crop, with rapid growing trees competitive with annual crops as a land use (as is the case with loblolly pine plantations in the US South and hybrid cottonwood plantations on irrigated agricultural lands in the US Pacific Northwest).

Tropical Deforestation: Patterns and Rates

Confusion and lack of clarity have featured prominently in debates about tropical deforestation. Deforestation occurs when forestland is cleared and converted to another use, principally agriculture. Forest degradation, on the other hand, involves significant degrading of the forest ecosystem without eliminating all of the forest cover outright (Downton 1995, p.23). Degradation is an arbitrary concept, although the term is used interchangeably with deforestation. FAO defines tropical deforestation as occurring when canopy cover is reduced to 10% or less. However, for developed countries, it defines deforestation as taking place when canopy cover is reduced to 20% or less, so that, given different thresholds, direct comparisons between developed and developing countries need to be made with caution. Global patterns of deforestation are indicated in Table 13.1.

Approximately 40% of forest cover is secondary growth, having been reforested naturally or replanted (see Table 13.2). Some 55% of the secondary forest consists of residual forest, which was cutover in the past 60 to 80 years (but never completely felled), and the remainder is referred to as "fallow" forest that invaded after cultivation stopped (Sedjo 1992). Residual secondary forests maintain many of the ecosystem characteristics (physiognomy, systemic processes, tree species and other organisms) of natural forests. Fallow forests, on the other hand, consist of a large number of species that declines rapidly as tree sizes increase; while many of the ecosystem characteristics of natural forests have disappeared, these return as the forest matures.

Throughout North America, Europe, the former USSR and Oceania, forested area has increased since 1990 (Tables 13.1 and 13.2). These regions also account for the bulk of global wood production (Table 12.3).

Table 13.1: Forest Area and Rates of Deforestation, 1981–2000

Region/country	Forest cover, 2000[a] (10⁶ ha)	Average annual change in forest cover					
		1981–90		1990–95		1990–2000	
		Area (10³ ha)	Rate (%)	Area (10³ ha)	Rate (%)	Area (10³ ha)	Rate (%)
Africa	*649.9*	*–4,100*	*–0.7*	*–3,748*	*–0.7*	*–5,264*	*–0.7*
Tropical	634.2	n.a.	–0.7	–3,695	–0.7	–5,295	–0.8
Nontropical	15.7	n.a.	–0.8	–53	–0.3	+31	+0.2
Asia	*524.1*	*n.a.*	*n.a.*	*–3,328*	*–0.7*	*–651*	*–0.1*
Tropical	288.6	–3,791	–1.2	–3,055	–1.1	–2,427	–0.8
– South Asia	76.7	–551	–0.8	–141	–0.2	–98	–0.1
– SE Asia	211.9	–3,240	–1.4	–2,914	–1.3	–2,329	–1.0
Europe	*161.6*	*n.a.*	*n.a.*	*+389*	*+0.3*	*+424*	*+0.3*
– Northern	58.0	n.a.a	n.a.	+8	+0.0	+40	+0.1
– Western	67.8	n.a.	n.a.	+358	+0.6	+311	+0.5
– Eastern	35.8	n.a.	n.a.	+23	+0.1	+73	+0.2
Former USSR	*901.4*	*n.a.*	*n.a.*	*+557*	*+0.1*	*+739*	*+0.1*
Canada	*244.6*	*n.a.*	*n.a.*	*+175*	*+0.1*	*0*	*0.0*
USA.	*226.0*	*n.a.*	*n.a.*	*+589*	*+0.3*	*+388*	*+0.2*
Central Am. & Mexico	*73.0*	*–1,112*	*–1.5*	*–959*	*–1.2*	*–971*	*–1.2*
Caribbean	*5.7*	*–122*	*–0.3*	*–78*	*–1.7*	*+13*	*+0.2*
South America	*885.6*	*n.a.*	*n.a.*	*–4,774*	*–0.5*	*–3,711*	*–0.4*
Tropical	834.1	–6,173	–0.7	–4,655	–0.6	–3,456	–0.4
– Brazil	543.9	–3,671	–0.6	–2,554	–0.5	–2,309	–0.4
Temperate	51.5	n.a.	n.a.	–119	–0.3	–255	–0.5
Oceania	*197.6*	*n.a.*	*n.a.*	*–91*	*–0.1*	*–365*	*–0.2*
Tropical	35.1	–113	–0.3	–151	–0.4	–122	–0.3
Temperate	162.5	n.a.	n.a.	+60	+0.1	–243	–0.1
Global total[a]	**3,869.5**	*n.a.*	*n.a.*	**–11,269**	**–0.3**	**–9,397**	**–0.2**

Notes:

n.a. implies not available or not applicable.

[a] Totals may not tally due to rounding.

Source: FAO (1993, 1997, 2001).

Increasingly, forest practices in the rich countries have taken into account ecological concerns, but, given globalization of the forest products industry, reducing fibre output in (some) rich countries provides incentives for poor countries to develop their forest resources as noted above. This is a reason cited for Venezuela's decision in 1997 to open to logging the country's largest forest reserve – the 37,000 km^2 Sierra Imataca rainforest reserve near the Guyanese border.

In contrast to northern latitudes and with some exceptions (Caribbean), deforestation in developing countries remains at perhaps unacceptably high rates, although, for the most part, it has been declining (Table 13.1). Annual rates of tropical deforestation were greater on average in the latter half of the 1980s than in the first, and have generally fallen during the 1990s. Rates of deforestation for the period 1995–2000 are lower than they were in the 1980s and, with the exception of the Caribbean and tropical Oceania, have shown a steady decline over the past several decades.

Table 13.2: Annual Change in Forest Cover, 1990–2000 (10^6 ha)

	Natural forest					Forest plantations			Total forest Net Δ
	Loss			Gain		Gain			
Domain	Defores-tation	Conversion to forest plantations	Total loss	Natural expansion of forest	Net Δ	Conver-sion from natural forest	Affores-tation	Net Δ	
Tropical areas	−14.2	−1.0	−15.2	+1.0	−14.2	+1.0	+0.9	+1.9	−12.3
Non-tropical areas	−0.4	−0.5	−0.9	+2.6	+1.7	+0.5	+0.7	+1.2	+2.9
Global total	**−14.6**	**−1.5**	**−16.1**	**+3.6**	**−12.5**	**+1.5**	**+1.6**	**+3.1**	**−9.4**

Source: FAO (2001).

In 1995, tropical forests were estimated to cover an area of about 1,733.9 million ha or about 13.4% of the globe's land area, excluding Antarctica and Greenland. This was down from an estimated 1,756.3 million ha in 1990 and 1,910.4 million ha in 1981. Total annual deforestation for the period 1981 to 1995 averaged 11.8 million ha, falling to 11.3 million ha over the period 1990–95 and down to 9.4 million ha over the period 1995–2000. In tropical areas, the loss was greater, with some 14.2 million ha of tropical forest disappearing each year between 1990 and 2000, although this was partially offset by average annual plantings of 1.9 million ha (Table 13.2). However, rates of deforestation have varied substantially throughout the tropics (Table 13.1). Perhaps somewhat surprisingly, the tropical rainforest, which appears to be the forest type of most concern to the international community, experiences relatively slower rates of deforestation than other tropical forests (Table 13.3). Indeed, the highest rates of deforestation in tropical regions appear to occur in the upland forests, whether moist or dry.

Table 13.3: Estimates of Forest Cover and Rate of Deforestation, Tropics

Forest formations	Land area	Population density 1990	Annual population growth (1981–90)	Forest area 1990		deforestation (1981–90)	
	10^6 ha	#/km^2	%	10^6 ha	%	10^6 ha/yr	%
FOREST ZONE	4,186.4	57	2.6	1,748.2	42	15.3	0.8
Lowland formations	3,485.6	57	2.5	1,543.9	44	12.8	0.8
–Tropical rainforest	947.2	41	2.5	718.3	76	4.6	0.6
–Moist deciduous forests	1,289.2	55	2.7	587.3	46	6.1	0.9
–Dry deciduous forests	706.2	106	2.4	178.6	25	1.8	0.9
–Very dry zone	543.0	24	3.2	59.7	11	0.3	0.5
Upland formations	700.9	56	2.9	204.3	29	2.5	1.1
–Moist forests	528.0	52	2.7	178.1	34	2.2	1.1
–Dry forests	172.8	70	3.2	26.2	15	0.3	1.1
NONFOREST ZONE[a]	591.9	15	3.5	8.1	1	0.1	0.9
TOTAL TROPICS[b]	**4,778.3**	**52**	**2.7**	**1,756.3**	**37**	**15.4**	**0.8**

Notes:
[a] Hot and cold deserts.
[b] Totals may not tally due to rounding.
Source: FAO (1993).

According to the FAO, if forest cover declines from 15% to 8%, the area has been deforested; however, if forest cover declines from 90% to 15% no deforestation has taken place. Myers (1991, 1994) argues that the 10% threshold criterion for determining when deforestation has taken place is too strict; instead, he defines deforestation as having occurred when the remnant ecosystem no longer resembles a natural forest in appearance or in terms of the services that it is able to provide. Myers is concerned with forest degradation and, in his view, a planted forest would not be treated as a forest in his statistics. In Myers' words, a forest can be reduced to a "travesty of a natural forest as properly understood" without reducing the tree crown cover to less than 10%. Not surprisingly, Myers' estimates of deforestation exceed those of the FAO by a considerable margin; compared to an FAO estimate of a 10.7 million ha per year decline in tropical moist forest area, Myers (1991) provides an estimate of 14.2 million ha per year (see van Soest 1998, p.32). The advantage of the FAO estimates, however, is that they are likely the most consistent and reliable for international comparisons.

It is estimated that 90% of (modern) tropical deforestation occurred between 1970 and 1990 (Skole et al. 1994). If this estimate is correct, the tropical forest of the world at its apex would have covered about 22 million km^2 (2.2×10^9 ha), or about 16.8% of the earth's land surface. Although reduced in size, the world's tropical forests still constitute an area equal to the whole of South America. Even at the current rate of tropical deforestation, the world's tropical forests would continue to exist through the entire 21st century and well into the 22nd century. Of course, the current rate of tropical deforestation will almost surely change over time.

In many respects, tropical deforestation today is not dramatically different from temperate deforestation that occurred one and two centuries earlier. During that period, pressures for land-use change, primarily demand for new lands for agriculture, resulted in large-scale deforestation of areas of Europe and North America. In the USA much of the forestlands of the eastern seaboard, the south and the Lake States were converted to cropland and pasture. This same phenomenon had begun earlier in Europe, and continued in places well into the early part of the 20th century. The denuding of the forest landscape was often the result of spontaneous actions, but also reflected governmental policies. In the USA, for example, the Homestead Act required land clearing as a prerequisite for obtaining land title. A similar policy existed in Brazil until very recently. For North America and Europe much of the early land clearing has been offset by the renewal of the forest, largely through natural processes. Today, the European forest has reclaimed large areas once deforested (Kuusela 1994; Table 13.1). Similarly, in America the forest has reclaimed much of the area deforested in New England (Barrett 1988), the Lake States and the south as abandoned agricultural lands regenerated naturally into forest and, more recently, planted forests cover many former tobacco, cotton and other crop lands.

It has sometimes been claimed that it is difficult to renew tropical forests, but some evidence suggests otherwise, given a long enough time span. For example, it is believed that large areas of the American tropics had been in terraces, irrigated agriculture and agro-forestry in the pre-European settlement (or pre-Columbian) period, but reverted to forests as disruptions and disease decimated local populations. These areas then returned to tropical forest. Turner and Butzer (1992) argue that "the scale of deforestation, or forest modification, in the American tropics has only recently begun to rival that undertaken prior to the Columbian encounter". Similarly, the great temples of Angkor Watt in Cambodia, Borobodor in

Java and other similar large structures in Southeast Asia, once located in the midst of a high level of human activity, were lost for centuries due to the incursion of tropical forest when human activity declined (Budiansky 1995, pp.113–9).

Deforestation is generally a reversible process, but it appears irreversible because of the length of time that is required to restore forests to some semblance of their original state. Indeed, it is unlikely that the original state will ever be duplicated because the dynamics of ecosystems, and interspecies interactions, militates against this. In some cases, exotic species of flora and fauna may replace the indigenous species (as happened in Hawaii as a result of human influence). However, many of the ecosystem functions and other values associated with the original forest return. It is only in rare circumstances that changes in climate and soil loss are such that forests do not re-establish on their own.

Tropical Deforestation and Loss of Biodiversity

There appears a general consensus that current tropical deforestation is one of the most pressing environmental problems of our time, because it leads to loss of species. Tropical deforestation is claimed to result in an annual loss of 14,000 to 40,000 species, and as many as 16 million populations (geographical entities within species that are ecologically or genetically unique) (Hughes et al. 1997). The basis of claims for high rates of extinction is the species-area curve (Wilson 1988, p.11; Hughes et al. 1997). The species-area curve relates the number of species (S) to land area (A): $S = cA^z$, where c and z are arbitrary constants to be determined empirically (MacArthur and Wilson 1967). This relation is not a law of nature, but an assumed (empirical) relationship. It is accepted by some scientists because it works – it gives "correct" answers – although statistical verification of the species-area curve and estimation of the parameter values are based on sparse evidence from small, uninhabited islands. Major criticisms of the species-area function are that it ignores the patchy distribution of habitats and that it is an *ad hoc* and continuous relation between deforestation and species loss, precluding the possibility of catastrophic or discontinuous effects, which are often a concern of ecologists. Budiansky (1995) provides a popular but critical discussion of the species-area relation.

To illustrate how estimates of species loss are obtained, let S_0 and A_0 be the initial number of species and area of tropical forest, respectively, and S_1 and A_1 the species and area after one year. The species-area relationship can be rewritten to eliminate c as follows (Pimm et al. 1995): $S_1/S_0 = (A_1/A_0)^z$. According to Pimm et al. (1995), the value of z lies between 0.1 and 1.0, and is often taken to be ¼. If there are 14 million species globally, and two-thirds are found in tropical forests, then S_0 is some 9.4 million species (Hughes et al. 1997). Then, assuming an annual rate of tropical deforestation of 0.8%, $S_1 = S_0 (A_1/A_0)^z = 9.40$ million $(1-0.008)^{0.25} = 9.38$ million. The number of species lost annually is thus 20,000, which is approximately 80,000 times higher than the natural, or background rate of extinction (Leakey and Lewin 1995, p.241). For $z=0.2$, 15,000 species are projected to be lost annually, while for $z=1.0$, more than 75,000 species per year are projected to go extinct as a result of tropical deforestation. The problem is that the "species-area curve (in a mainland situation) is nothing more than a self-evident fact: that as one enlarges an area, it comes eventually to encompass the geographical ranges of more species. The danger comes when this is extrapolated backwards, and it is assumed that by reducing the size of a forest, it will lose species according to the same gradient" (Heywood and Stuart 1992, p.102).

Many have commented on extinction and declining animal and plant populations. Many have made crude calculations of the rate at which species are disappearing, but these claims are only guesses based on observed and perceived destruction of habitat and not actual loss of species (Myers 1979; Wilson 1988; Pimm et al. 1995; Hughes et al. 1997). Some have questioned the extent of species extinction (Simon and Wildavsky 1984, 1995; Simon 1996, pp.439–58; Mann 1991). Using the species-area curve, for example, researchers predicted that 50% of the species in the Brazilian state of Sao Paulo should have disappeared as a result of reducing the original natural forests in the state by almost 90%. However, an exhaustive list of extinctions compiled by the Brazilian Society of Zoology indicates that only two birds and four butterflies had gone extinct over the period that deforestation was occurring. One of the birds had recently been seen again, while the song of the other was unknown (making it almost unidentifiable as the lost one should it "re-appear"). The four butterflies had not been observed for decades, but no special effort was made to look for them. While ignorance or lack of data could explain the difference between predicted and actual extinctions, it appears that recorded extinctions in the Amazon are inversely related to effort to tally them – the greater the effort to track species the more species that were thought to be extinct turned out to still survive in the wild (Mann and Plummer 1995, pp.69–70). Further, even with the loss of 90% of total forest area, enough representative samples of all types of microhabitat survive to ensure survival of the great majorities of species and biodiversity (Nee and May 1997; Budiansky 1995).

So how prevalent is actual species extinction? According to data from the International Union for the Conservation of Nature and Natural

Resources (IUCN) (Edwards 1995; World Conservation Monitoring Center 1992), there were 626 documented extinctions between 1600 and 1994, including 83 species of mammals, 20 reptiles, 36 fishes and 368 invertebrates (which is still higher, but more in line with, expected background extinction). Of these, 105 extinctions occurred in Africa and 6 in South America. The documented extinctions in modern times have been few, at least compared to (pre-)historical rates of extinctions (Leakey and Lewin 1996). For example, the fossil record suggests that an extinction event during the late Permian period resulted in the loss of 44% of the families of fish and 58% of those of tetrapods (World Conservation Monitoring Centre 1992, p.197).[1] Most modern extinctions (75% of those recorded) have taken place on islands and are the result of hunting, with habitat destruction playing a significant but lesser role (p.199). "Very few extinctions have been recorded in continental tropical forest habitat, where mass extinction events have been predicted to be underway" (Edwards 1995, p.218). However, since there are many species in rainforest ecosystems that are as yet unknown to science, this does not necessarily imply that actual losses are also modest.

For an economist, it is not the number of extinctions that is important, but, rather, the foregone economic value of the species concerned. Suppose that 10,000 species are projected to go extinct out of a total 50 million species. This might be less important economically (and even biologically) than 1,000 species going extinct out of 3 million. Many species could go extinct in a given year with no (actual or potential) loss of value, but it is also possible that the loss of one or two species is very costly. It all depends on the (marginal) value of the soon-to-be-extinct species.

13.2 ECONOMIC VALUE OF TROPICAL FORESTS

Tropical forests, indeed all forests, provide many values to humans. Human benefits often involve the collection of various forest items for food and fiber, such as various timber and nontimber forest outputs, but they also include non-use values associated with the knowledge that tropical forests exist now (existence value) and in the future (option and bequest value). In addition, tropical forests provide local and regional ecological services in the form of watershed protection, mitigation of soil erosion and reduction of downstream flooding. Tropical ecosystems also provide habitat for much of the world's biodiversity and, together with the rest of the world's forests, provide a sink for carbon (see Chapter 14). How do these various values compare? Do forestland owners take them into account in their decision calculus?

Conservation of tropical forest ecosystems is often more difficult than conservation of marine ecosystems because the opportunity costs of holding on to natural forests are higher. The reason is that land has more alternative uses capable of producing economic surpluses. Absent government, if forest ecosystems are to be protected, the returns from sustained forestry should be competitive with those of alternative land uses, such as agriculture and mining (see Barbier and Burgess 1997). Loosely speaking, government intervention is justified only if it can be shown that the total economic value (market plus nonmarket benefits) of the next hectare left as natural forest is greater than the market returns from a competitive use, with the difference being greater than the (marginal) cost of the government intervention. Since nonmarket values do not accrue to forest owners, governments can intervene to reflect such benefits, either by regulating conversion or by providing payments to landowners to prevent land conversion. Unfortunately, the records of most governments, rich and poor, in representing this constituency are spotty.

One way to compare the social returns to different land uses is to estimate the value of the various functions in monetary terms, where possible, so that straightforward comparisons can be made. For this purpose, we distinguish between production functions (production of timber and nontimber forest products), regulatory functions (e.g., carbon sink, watershed protection) and wildlife habitat/biodiversity functions, where the latter include non-use values associated with preservation.

Production Functions of Tropical Forests

Tropical rainforests produce tangible products such as timber, fuelwood and nontimber forest products (e.g., rattan, oils, fruits, nuts, ornamental flowers, bush meat), plus less tangible assets such as opportunities for eco-tourism. Clear felling is not a common practice in the tropics, but, if clear felling does occur, say to make room for other activities such as agriculture or growing pulpwood for paper, net discounted returns can be high. Tropical stands contain some 200 m^3 to 400 m^3 of timber per ha (Thiele and Wiebelt 1993; Pearce and Warford 1993, p.130), but much of this consists of noncommercial species and unusable wood. If 30% to 40% of the harvest is usable and assuming total rents of US$30/m^3, clear felling yields a rent (or social surplus) of $1,800–$4,800 per ha, not including returns from subsequent land uses. Subsequent use of the land in forestry yields a positive but small return (less than US$1/ha/yr for artificially regenerated stands), while managed plantations frequently yield negative returns and proceed only with government subsidies (Sedjo 1992).

Estimates of the value of sustainable selective logging per hectare vary considerably, with differences due to (among other things) discount rates, stumpage prices, management costs, site conditions and productivity (see, e.g., Vincent 1990; Pearce and Warford 1993; Barbier et al. 1995). Evidence from Costa Rica suggests that sustainable timber extraction from primary forest ranges from 0.5 to 2.0 m³/ha/yr (Carranza et al. 1996; Quiros and Finnegan 1994). For Indonesia, Pearce and Warford (1993) estimate that selective logging yields a discounted net return of US$2,409/ha (assuming a 6% discount rate). Presumably selective logging is synonymous with *sustainable* logging, which is the ability to extract the same physical volume (or value) of commercial timber from a site indefinitely, absent discounting. Other estimates of the value of *sustainable* selective logging per hectare vary considerably. Vincent (1990) provides estimates of present value ranging from +US$850 down to –$130/ha, with the outcome of the most realistic scenario in the vicinity of $250/ha.

Small-scale gathering of nontimber forest products (NTFP) such as rattan, oils, fruits, nuts and bush meat is competitive with commercial logging only in some regions. The value of these products can be large on occasion (de Beer and McDermott 1989; Peters et al. 1989) and, in some cases, large numbers of forest dwellers depend critically on them for survival. However, many authors have cautioned against extrapolating these high figures to large stretches of tropical rainforests due to, for example, downward sloping demand for NTFP, uncertainty concerning sustainable supply, and increasing costs of production and transportation. For the case of Latin America, most researchers produce relatively low estimates of about $10 ha/yr(see Bulte et al. 1997).[2] Hence, reliance on such activities alone may perpetuate poverty (Homma 1994).

Likewise, eco-tourism is only locally important. Although tropical (moist) forests are generally not very attractive to tourists because of the humid climate and their limited scenic value (compared to East African game parks, say), recreation and tourism have the potential to become important sources of foreign exchange. Based on observations for South and Central America (especially Ecuador), de Groot (1992) estimates that eco-tourism may contribute as much as US$26 per hectare per year to the national economy of a country with tropical forests (although this is not a measure of consumer surplus as costs of providing this return are ignored). Ruitenbeek (1989) estimates the present value of tourism in Korup National Park (Cameroon) to be approximately US$13/ha. However, the role of eco-tourism in promotion of forest conservation will likely remain small, and its value will fall on a per hectare basis as more areas are made available for tropical forest recreation.

Regulatory Functions of Tropical Forests

Tropical ecosystem services consist of watershed protection, prevention of soil loss, carbon storage, and other regulatory functions. Although Costanza et al. (1997) have estimated the earth's entire ecosystems' services to be worth some US$33×$10^{12}$, the method they used to obtain their estimate is suspect because it is based on GDP-type components, and global GDP only amounts to $18×$10^{12}$. Nonmarket benefit estimates employ willingness to pay from contingent valuation surveys, expenditures to avoid damages, travel cost expenditures, costs of cleaning up damages, and so on. All of these items are based on an ability to earn income, which cannot exceed global GDP. If it does, the globe's budget constraint is violated. Nonetheless, the globe's ecosystems provide services that undoubtedly have a large value by any standard, and must be considered infinite as life ultimately depends on (some minimal amount of) them, but knowing this is not very helpful for policymaking. As noted in Chapter 6, economic decisions are made at the margin; decisions need to be made about whether to harvest the next elephant, whale or bear, or whether to cut the next hectare of forest. It is necessary, therefore, to determine the value of ecosystem services at the margin, or on a small region basis.

Postel and Heisse (1988) estimate that deforestation in Costa Rica resulted in revenue losses of $133–$274 million from sedimentation behind one dam. Ruitenbeek (1989) computes the benefits of forest conservation by examining fishery protection and agricultural productivity gains from forests in Korup National Park; these amount to some $3/ha/yr, or a present value of about US$60/ha using a discount rate of 5%.

Apart from protection against soil erosion and sedimentation, tropical forests are believed to provide protection against floods and a more balanced supply of water when there are seasonal differences in precipitation because the soil acts as a sponge. Ruitenbeek (1989) estimates the present value of the watershed function to be US$23 per hectare of forest protected in Korup National Park. However, it is important to recognize that tropical forests are not the only ecosystem capable of producing these effects. In fact, there is evidence that it is not deforestation *per se* that is important, but rather the nature of the succeeding land use. Clearcutting followed by agricultural practices that leave soils exposed during the wet season creates erosion problems and nutrient losses, and will be more damaging than land uses that provide crop cover all year long, such as coffee plantations or pasture.

Finally, release of carbon may be the most important nonmarket cost associated with tropical deforestation. The Intergovernmental Panel on

Climate Change (IPCC 1996a) cites estimates of discounted future damage of US$5–$150 per metric ton of CO_2 emitted. Assuming a realistic shadow price of US$10–$25 carbon per metric ton, and that some 50–140 metric tons are released when land use changes as a result of deforestation, the costs amount to $500 to $3,500 per hectare, or $25–$175/ha/yr (using a 5% discount rate). But without knowledge of the shadow damage caused by carbon released to the atmosphere, it is impossible to unambiguously determine the value of tropical forests as a carbon sink, or the damages brought about by tropical deforestation.

Habitat, Biodiversity and Non-use Values

While the problem of valuing regulatory functions is intrinsically related to the diversity of effects and consequences, and the uncertainties that surround them, a major problem in valuing habitat functions of tropical forests is rooted in ethics. Tropical forests are home not only to millions of people for whom forests may be an integrated part of economic, social and religious life, but also to millions of animal and plant species, most of which are endemic to the local forest ecosystem. The various species have both use and non-use (preservation) value. The direct use values of biodiversity have attracted the attention of economists and ecologists alike, not in the least spurred on by the belief that demonstration of high values provides a convincing argument against human intervention in "vulnerable" ecosystems. Thus Leakey and Lewin (1996), for example, describe how lucrative and important the drugs Vincristine and Vinblastine, alkaloids from the rosy periwinkle from Madagascar, have been in curing acute lymphocytic leukemia and Hodgkin's disease. The rainforest may be a valuable source of new medicines, and searching for these uses is referred to as "biodiversity prospecting" (Simpson and Sedjo 1996a).

Consider pharmaceutical uses. There are some 250,000 species of higher plants, and approximately 125,000 of these are found in tropical regions. To date about 47 major drugs have come from tropical plants. Mendelsohn and Balick (1995) estimate that tropical forests might be worth $48 per hectare in prospecting for pharmaceutical drugs, concluding that the "potential value of undiscovered drugs is an additional incentive to conserve species-rich forests throughout the world" (p.227). However, the values they provide are small and cannot, on their own, be used to justify protection of tropical species. This is confirmed by Barbier and Aylward (1996), and by Simpson et al. (1996), who investigate the (potential) industrial, agricultural and pharmaceutical values of biodiversity hotspots. Even under the most optimistic assumptions, the present value of marginal species is small, less than $10,000 at best. As the number of species increases, the value of marginal species falls – from almost $3,000 when there are 250,000 species to a negligible amount when there are more than one million (Simpson and Sedjo 1996b). If the value of marginal species is small, then, by extension, so is the value of a marginal hectare in biodiversity prospecting. This is seen in Table 13.4, where data are provided for selected tropical hotspots. Even the most favorable set of assumptions yields an estimate of pharmaceutical value of approximately US$20 per hectare, and then for the case of an ecological "hotspot" in Ecuador. Estimates for other regions are much lower. Barbier and Aylward (1996) conclude that "the potential economic returns from pharmaceutical prospecting of biodiversity are on their own insufficient justification for the establishment of protected areas in developing countries" (p.174).

Table 13.4: Maximum Willingness to Pay to Preserve a Hectare of Land for Biodiversity Prospecting, Selected Hotspots

Hotspot	Max. WTP	Hotspot	Max. WTP
Western Ecuador	$20.63	Cape Floristic province, S. Africa	$1.66
Southwestern Sri Lanka	$16.84	Peninsular Malaysia	$1.47
New Caledonia	$12.43	Southwestern Australia	$1.22
Madagascar	$6.86	Ivory Coast	$1.14
Western Ghats of India	$4.77	Northern Borneo	$0.99
Philippines	$4.66	Eastern Himalayas	$0.98
Atlantic Coast of Brazil	$4.42	Columbian Choco	$0.75
Uplands of western Amazon	$2.59	Central Chile	$0.74
Tanzania	$2.07	California Floristic province	$0.20

Source: Simpson et al. (1996).

Obviously, limited direct use value does not imply that the economic value of biodiversity is modest. For example, ecosystem stability may be positively linked to diversity.

In addition to direct and indirect use values, non-use values are also important. As a rough indication of the magnitude of these existence values, Pearce and Warford (1993, pp.131–2) guess that the existence value of tropical forests amounts to some US$8 per adult in Australia, Western Europe and North America. This implies that total existence value is no less than $3.2×10^9$ a year, or, dividing by the total tropical forest area (about 1,750 million ha in 1990) approximately $1.80/ha. Dividing instead by the total area of tropical rainforest (about 720 million ha), existence value per hectare rises to $4.50 per year. Using a discount rate of 5%, this gives present values of $36 and $90/ha, respectively. These estimates are much higher than estimates of household willingness to pay obtained by Kramer and Mercer (1997) for the USA. They estimated that preservation of global tropical forests had a one-time value of US$1.9–$2.8×10^9 ($21–$31 per household), or annual value of only $95–$140 million (using a 5% discount rate). Conservatively multiplying by four to take into account Canada, Australia, New Zealand and Western Europe yields an estimate of annual existence value of $0.38–$0.56×10^9, or $0.53–$0.78 per hectare of tropical rainforest, well below that reported above. Whatever value is chosen, they are small compared to those from logging and other land uses (such as agriculture). Further, since non-use values likely decline at the margin as the forest stock increases, the marginal preservation value is lower yet.

Summary

A summary of the values of tropical forests is provided in Table 13.5. For comparison, estimates of the economic values of tropical forests as calculated by Costanza et al. (1997) are also provided in Table 13.5. The problem with the latter estimates is that they are based on a methodology that permits violation of the global budget constraint, and, more important, employs average and not marginal values. It is easy to demonstrate that, even for very large average nontimber values, high rates of deforestation may be economically optimal, depending on what is assumed about the changes in nonmarket values at the margin (van Kooten 1998; Bulte et al. 1997).

In conclusion, while it is true that tropical forests provide a wide range of ecosystem services and other nontimber amenities, their marginal value is small compared to that of logging and land-use conversion (with the possible exception of carbon uptake). Nonetheless, as more of the tropical forest is converted to other land uses, it is likely that the costs of further conversion (the value of foregone ecosystem and other nontimber amenities) will increase as well. At some point, the marginal costs of additional land conversion, including the costs of associated risks, will equal or exceed marginal benefits and no further deforestation of tropical forests should occur. Halting further deforestation should be induced by establishing well-defined and enforced property rights, and by internalizing external effects. However, it does not appear that the discounted net economic benefits of sustainable forest management are higher than those of alternative land uses; in some cases they will, but in others not, depending on the profitability of alternative land-use options (and location) (see Sedjo 1992). It would appear, therefore, that it may not yet be globally optimal to stop all tropical deforestation and land-use conversion. This picture could change if carbon-uptake benefits are taken into account (Chapter 14).

Table 13.5: Summary of the Economic Values of Tropical Forests (US$/ha/yr)

Item	Marginal[a]	Average[c]
Commercial logging		
–Clear felling	72–192	not calculated
–Natural forest management	≈ 1	315 (all raw materials)
Agriculture[b]	120–140	not calculated
Sustainable land use		
–Selective logging	10–145	not calculated
–Nontimber forest products	≈ 10	32
–Tourism	≈ 1	112 (all outdoor recreation, incl. tourism)
Preservation		
–Watershed protection[b]	≈ 2	8
–Prevention of soil loss	≈ 3	245
–Flood preventation	≈ 1	6
–Other	not calculated	1,024
–Global climate change	2–140	223
–Biodiversity prospecting	1–2	41
–Non-use value	1–4	2

Notes:
[a] Unless otherwise indicated, these data are based on discussion in the text. Values are annualized using a 4% discount rate.
[b] Source: van Soest (1998, p.25).
[c] Source: Costanza et al. (1997). Not all categories correspond to those in the marginal column.

13.3 CAUSES OF TROPICAL DEFORESTATION

The causes of tropical deforestation are complex and not well understood. It is complicated by:

1. poor and inadequate data;
2. a failure to define properly terms such as "deforestation" and "shifting cultivation";
3. neglect in distinguishing between "logged" areas converted to another use in the long term and residual forest cutovers and "fallow" forest that retain their natural characteristics or revert back to natural forest over time; and
4. confusion regarding final and proximate causes of deforestation.

Proximate causes refer to the mechanical circumstances of deforestation, while final causes require establishment of a connection between events (deforestation) and the purpose or intent behind the event (Bromley 1999, p.275). While building roads into remote forest may trigger deforestation by peasants, this is a proximate cause as roads do not cause deforestation. Rather, we must look at the reason (purpose) for road building as this constitutes the ultimate or final cause of deforestation. We note that conversion of tropical forest to other uses is the most important fact of deforestation.

Different proximate and final causes of deforestation can be identified depending on the viewpoint of the investigator, the level of analysis (local or small region, country-level or cross-country comparisons), the region considered (Southeast Asia versus Latin America, say) and the type of model (normative, positive, statistical, structural, etc.) employed. Because of these differences, there is often no consensus about the actual causes of deforestation. Nonetheless, we investigate some of the main factors that have been raised – commercial logging, conversion to agriculture, population pressure, poverty, and the role of institutions and social capital (and government).

Commercial Logging

A common but simplistic view, now largely rejected by most analysts familiar with tropical forests, is that tropical deforestation is due to commercial timber logging. Commercial logging in the tropics rarely results in significant direct land conversion, although it does make indirect contributions to the process of deforestation. Unlike much of the commercial logging in the temperate forest, commercial logging in the tropics almost never involves the clear-cutting of the forest. Rather, the usual approach is to select and log only trees that are suitable for commercial uses, leaving large numbers of live trees in the forest. In the past, relatively few trees were removed, and those that were felled were done by hand and commonly transported out of the forest by animals. The forest would be periodically "re-logged" as trees reached desired sizes. With the arrival of modern logging (with chainsaws, roads and equipment), larger areas have been logged, reflecting expanded demand.

Selective cutting continues to be almost universally practiced with only the larger trees of desired species harvested. This reflects the fact that, due to the high diversity of tree species, only a relatively few of the total trees in a tropical forest are commercially suitable (Panayotou and Sungsuwan 1994). Studies of Western Africa, for example, indicate that few trees are harvested per hectare, frequently less than 10 out of a total of more than 350 trees (Grainger 1993; Panayotou and Ashton 1992). For Cameroon, Thiele and Wiebelt (1993) estimate that, from a hectare of primary forest endowed with on average 250 m^3 of timber, only about 8 to 33 m^3 are extracted per round of harvesting. Within the tropical belt there are strong regional differences in logging intensity, with highly selective logging in Africa and Latin America and more intensive timber harvesting in Asia (where sometimes 40% of the trees is extracted, and sometimes clearfelling takes place). There are two main factors that determine logging intensity: (1) the share of marketable trees per hectare (which is typically much lower than in temperate zones) depending on species composition and output demand; and (2) transport costs that depend on the proximity of markets and the mode of transport (river or road) (van Soest 1998).

Selective logging is generally conducive to forest regeneration and regrowth. Although selective logging can be damaging in practice (e.g., because of careless logging induced by perverse incentives, or simply because it is too costly to untangle trees that are linked by lianas and vines), in most cases the forest is able to regenerate (Grainger 1993). During the period immediately following logging, sunlight reaches the forest floor, stimulating growth of seeds and seedlings, especially of the so-called pioneer species, which include many of the more important timber species such as teak, mahogany and many of the dipterocarp (i.e., commercially valuable) species. Typically the stock of seed and seedlings is adequate, but this can be supplemented by human activities if required. The idealized tropical forest management regime following logging varies with forest type. However, in the timber rich forests of Southeast Asia it is common to allow a period of 30–70 years after logging for the forest to recover and grow new trees of the desired size. Additionally, existing saplings and medium size trees will continue and in some cases accelerate their growth now that the dominant trees are gone. When such an approach is followed a viable and sustainable forest system can be achieved. The most damaging aspect of the harvesting process may be the construction of roads, resulting in significant felling of trees, soil compaction and erosion (Myers 1980; Grainger 1993; Panayotou and Ashton 1992). However, the latter effect is most likely to occur for roads that are used frequently, and is in general not important for skidding tracks and feeder roads that usually revert back to forest after they are abandoned (van Soest 1998).

Estimates of the direct contribution of commercial logging to deforestation are therefore modest, typically varying from 2 to 10% (e.g., Amelung and Diehl 1992). According to Myers (1991), the share of commercial logging in deforestation is no less than 20%. Nonetheless, even with this higher estimate, it is clear that the bulk of tropical deforestation should be attributed to other causes, although it likely remains a catalyst for those other causes.

Conversion to Agriculture

Market failure occurs because social benefits from natural tropical forests, such as their value in contributing genetic material that may lead to new pharmaceutical drugs and their existence values, spill over to other countries – citizens in other countries benefit from the preservation of forests (e.g., see Kramer and Mercer 1997). As long as forest owners are not compensated to take into account these benefits, they will choose to ignore them in making decisions about the use of natural forests. This increases the probability that agriculture is preferred to preservation or sustainable tropical forest management.

Deforestation is primarily caused by a desire to convert forests to agriculture, which is particularly true in Africa and Latin America but perhaps less so in Asia. About 80% of the world supply of tropical timber comes from the Asia-Pacific region because tropical forests in the Amazon basin, for example, are characterized by a higher degree of heterogeneity, with a relatively lower proportion of trees having commercial value (Sedjo 1992). Nonetheless, there is an indirect relation between logging and agricultural conversion (Barbier et al. 1994, 1995; Sunderlin and Resosudarmo 1997). To transport the logged wood from isolated rainforest areas to ports or markets, commercial foresters have to construct a road network. This road network facilitates access for cultivation and increases the profitability of producing cash crops by reducing transportation costs. Further, the actual conversion process is easier in selectively logged forests than in pristine rainforests because the biggest trees have been removed and because the microclimate is more favorable for burning (Panayotou and Sungsuwan 1994). Hence, agricultural conversion proceeds at a much higher pace in secondary, or over-logged forests, as compared to pristine, undisturbed primary forests (Amelung and Diehl 1992). This evidence suggests that commercial logging is a catalyst for the deforestation process by providing the necessary infrastructure. This is the indirect damage of selective harvesting.

The general consensus then is that agricultural conversion (shifting cultivation and conversion for "permanent" agriculture) is the most prominent cause of tropical deforestation, although commercial logging may be the catalyst. However, a fundamental distinction needs to be made between "shifting cultivators" and "forest pioneers", with a continuum between these two extremes (Sunderlin and Resosudarmo 1997; also Myers 1994). The former clear the forest, crop the land for one to three years and then leave the land fallow for a period of 20 or more years, during which time it reverts back to natural forest. Traditional shifting cultivation can be sustainable, with products consisting of crops (low yield rice) plus a wide range of timber and nontimber products. The "forest pioneers" clear the forest with the intention of establishing permanent or semi-permanent agricultural production (Sunderlin and Resosudarmo 1997). Slash and burn is used in both cases, but the implications for sustainable resource management differ substantially along the continuum. Myers (1991) attributes a relatively higher share of tropical deforestation (degradation) to shifting cultivation (about 60%), at the cost of the share of permanent agriculture in the FAO statistics; the sum of permanent agriculture, mining, etc, amounts to no more than 18% in his statistics. From the point of view of sustainability, this may be a good thing. Clearly, forest clearing followed by a short cropping period and subsequent reversion back to natural forest is not the same as a permanent change in land use, and would be preferred. However, no distinction is made between these extremes.

Forests are converted to both permanent and shifting agriculture as a result of factors such as high agricultural prices, conversion subsidies, access roads, population pressure, lack of tenure security, and so on, although the significance of these factors varies. Once established, permanent agriculture is clearly, in most cases, less of a factor in deforestation than shifting agriculture, *ceteris paribus* (Kaimowitz and Angelsen 1998). By its very nature, shifting agriculture continues to be a contributing factor to deforestation, and anything that causes farmers to change from sedentary or permanent to shifting cultivation will increase rates of deforestation. While shifting cultivation may be well suited for agricultural production in areas with low and medium levels of population density and sustainable, it is ill-suited to situations where in-migration or high population densities put pressure on land use (Sunderlin and Resosudarmo 1997; Grainger 1993; Southgate et al. 1991). Thus, increasing integration in the (inter)national economy and increasing population pressure (especially brought about by regional migration of landless or otherwise displaced peasants) results in the abandonment of traditional cultivation patterns and their replacement by less sustainable production techniques.

Income and Deforestation

The relation between income and deforestation is complex and ambiguous, having direct and indirect effects (Palo 1994). The Kuznets "inverted-U" hypothesis (see Chapter 7, section 7.5) suggests that deforestation is positively correlated with low income levels, but negatively correlated with high levels of income. One explanation for this relationship is that, as income rises, people demand more wood products as well as more of the amenities associated with natural forests. As a country's citizens become better off, there comes a point where the demand for natural forest amenities exceeds a desire to permit further deforestation. Further, associated with increases in per capita income are higher education levels (and potentially less corruption in resource management), improved land tenure arrangements, fewer individuals engaged in primary production (agriculture and forestry) as a proportion of the population, and general improvements in the economy as a result of "technical" changes. In reference to tropical deforestation, Cropper and Griffiths (1994) argue that economic development and associated higher incomes will:

- reduce the conversion of forests into arable land by stimulating the use of modern agricultural practices (lowering land requirements) and inducing a shift of labor to nonagricultural sectors;
- initially stimulate commercial logging as the ability to process logs improves and demand for agricultural products increases (raising their price), but, at a later stage of development, reliance on logging declines as industrialization provides opportunities for alternative employment; and
- increase the demand for energy, including fuelwood, with more efficient and cleaner-burning energy sources substituting for fuelwood at higher income levels.

As a result, an environmental Kuznets curve, or inverted-U relationship between rates of deforestation and income, is expected.

Empirical evidence for the environmental Kuznets curve in the case of tropical deforestation is mixed, partly due to the way empirical models are specified but also because deforestation itself is defined differently in different studies and because only poor tropical countries are investigated. For studies where an inverted-U relation is found, turning points vary among studies from annual incomes of US$500 to $3,500 to $5,000 (Kaimowitz and Angelsen 1998). If deforestation is narrowly defined to exclude the re-establishment of natural forests, it will be considered irreversible, meaning that the rate of deforestation will decrease in any event as forests disappear. Hence, the relevance of the inverted-U relation in the case of deforestation may also be limited.

In order to investigate if there is a Kuznets relationship between deforestation (as an example of environmental degradation) and income, we regressed country deforestation rates for the period 1990 to 2000 on per capita gross domestic product and a variety of other country-level data. The regression results are presented in Table 13.6. Both variables are statistically significant at 1% or less and have the correct signs, but as indicated by Figure 13.1, they do not provide the expected support for an estimated EKC relation. As GDP increases during early development, the rate of deforestation declines immediately. There is no evidence of an increase in deforestation followed by a fall in deforestation rates.

Table 13.6: Factors Determining 1990–2000 Rates of Deforestation (n=115)

Variable	Estimated coefficients
Intercept	0.018592[**]
	(5.41)
Per capita GDP	–3.50e–06[**]
	(–4.67)
Per capita GDP squared	9.04e–11[**]
	(3.51)
R^2	0.2491

Notes:
[a] Values in parentheses are robust *t*-statistics.
[**] Significant at 1% level or better.

This is different from the Kuznets relationships found by Bhattarai and Hammig (2001) for countries in Africa, Asia and Latin America, and by Ehrhardt-Martinez et al. (2002) for less developed countries. Deforestation rates fall to zero as income rises to about $6,000, and, as it rises further, countries begin to reforest areas previously deforested (Figure 13.1). Thus, forest area increases, but reforestation rates decline beyond about $19,500, with deforestation/reforestation rates reaching equilibrium (no change in forested area) in the richest countries. In this sense, there clearly does exist an environmental Kuznets relation.

The results do not provide direct support for the notion that, as per capita incomes rise, countries initially increase environmental degradation in an effort to enhance growth, but, beyond some income level, the environment improves because citizens demand higher environmental quality (an income effect). Rather, the results suggest that poor countries have higher rates of deforestation because they are poor, and that deforestation is not used as a tool of development. Rates of deforestation decline continuously as income increases from a low of some $500 per person per year (purchasing power parity basis) to about $6,500, after which countries begin to afforest. The rate of afforestation peaks at some $19,500 per capita after which it declines to zero for the richest countries.

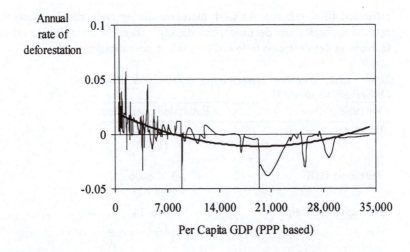

Figure 13.1: Environmental Kuznets curve for deforestation, actual versus estimated (thick curve)

Population and Deforestation

The effect of population growth and population density on rates of deforestation is also ill understood. This is partly because there are two views about the role of population. The neo-Malthusian view is that current trends in population growth will inevitably result in large-scale deforestation with its associated massive species extinctions and loss of agricultural potential; people and trees compete for space, as more people imply greater demand for fuel and food. Those subscribing to this view generally find evidence of a positive relation between population and deforestation (Saxena et al. 1997; Southgate 1994; Repetto and Gillis 1988). The (technological) optimists, on the other hand, argue that more people results in more labor, more skills, changing relative scarcity, potential for greater innovation, and so on (Beisner 1990; Simon 1996). Studies of population change that take a more optimistic view have found evidence that increased population density leads to less erosion and more forests (Tiffen and Mortimore 1994), and that accompanying wood scarcity leads to increased tree planting (Hyde and Seve 1991).

Historical evidence indicates that there have been cases where population and forest have increased together, but most is for temperate countries. For example, the forest resources of France have been expanding since the late 18th century. An estimate of the forested area in 1890 was almost 50% higher than the area estimated in 1790, while the area of forest estimated for

1994 is again some 50% higher than that of 100 years earlier (Ministry of Agriculture and Fisheries 1995). Similarly, as noted earlier, the forest area of New England has been expanding since the 1860s despite increasing population (Barrett 1988). However, studies that look only at the tropics have found that population growth and population density are inversely related to forest cover in almost all cases. Yet, the evidence is not overwhelming, with many studies finding that density or growth, or both, have no effect on deforestation (Palo 1994; Cropper and Griffiths 1994).

Nonetheless, the overall picture for tropical forests remains unclear, primarily because the direction of causality has not been identified (see Sunderlin and Resosudarmo 1997; Brown and Pearce 1994). The matter is much as Kummar and Sham (1994) note:

> It is impossible to draw any firm conclusions regarding the effect of population on deforestation. For example, population per square kilometer in 1990 for five selected countries was as follows: Brazil (18), Indonesia (100), Malaysia (54), Thailand (108), Philippines (220). Absolute rates of deforestation are higher in Indonesia, Malaysia and Thailand than in the Philippines. ... Brazil, which has the most extensive ongoing deforestation in the world, has a population density which is only 8% of that of the Philippines. (p.156).

Kaimowitz and Angelsen (1998) summarize empirical studies of the potential links between population and deforestation. Population growth affects deforestation directly through demand for fuel, other wood products and agricultural outputs, although trade and barriers to trade (e.g., tariffs) need to be taken into account. It affects deforestation indirectly through labour markets (lower wages make forest conversion more profitable), induced technological change and institutions. The latter is discussed in the context of the role of government.

Other Proximate Causes

The complex nature of tropical deforestation implies that, in many instances, economic explanations have to account for the behavior of peasants and small-scale farmers, as well as firms and governments (Binswanger 1989; Brown and Pearce 1994). Poverty, population pressure, regional migration and attitudes towards risk are some of the factors that affect the behavior of peasants and small-scale farmers, although determining their exact role or importance is difficult. We have already identified definitional and data problems as one reason. Other reasons have to do with the scale of models that are used to identify and analyze these factors, with scale varying from the farm to the region to the global levels, and with the types of economic models employed at each scale.

At the farm level, the variables thought to explain deforestation are different for subsistence models than open economy models. The reason is that small-scale farmers are assumed not to be responsive to market prices (households only seek to achieve a consumption target) and labor markets are assumed not to exist in subsistence models, while open economy models permit sale of labor off the farm. Thus, open economy models predict an increase in deforestation as a result of increases in agricultural output prices and agricultural productivity, and lower transportation costs (as the value of the marginal product of forest conversion for agriculture increases); wage increases reduce deforestation rates, while population growth has no direct effect. In contrast, increases in agricultural output prices and agricultural productivity reduce rates of deforestation in subsistence models, as do lower transportation costs; the effect of wage increases is not available from subsistence models (as labor markets do not exist), while population growth increases rates of deforestation (Kaimowitz and Angelsen 1998).

Taken together, therefore, farm-level models provide no definitive conclusions about the role of economic variables in the deforestation process. Increased agricultural input costs could reduce or increase rates of deforestation, while the same has been demonstrated for agricultural output prices. Availability of off-farm employment opportunities reduces pressure on tropical forests, while deforestation increases on sites with good quality soils, as might be expected. Population growth also contributes to deforestation in the farm-level models.

Conclusions from regional spatial (cross-section) and time series regression models are that more access roads, proximity of forest edges to urban areas, nearness to markets, and better and drier soils all contribute to increasing rates of deforestation. Any variables that raise agricultural profitability (higher output prices, easier access to credit, better access to markets, more roads, higher productivity) also increase rates of deforestation. Conclusions with regard to the role of higher population and per capita income as factors in increasing deforestation are mixed. Rather than population growth causing deforestation, it is the underlying source of population in-migration into regions with a low population density (due to road access, available high-quality agricultural lands, and growing demand for agricultural outputs) that results in deforestation. Finally, official forest protection leads to some reduction in rates of deforestation, while increased security of land tenure lowers rates of deforestation.

Models disagree on the impacts that currency devaluation, trade liberalization, changes in tax/subsidy regimes, and other macroeconomic variables might have on deforestation. Currency devaluation leads to an increase in deforestation in most models, but the cause differs between Brazil and the Philippines, for example. In Brazil, the higher agricultural prices that devaluation brings about will cause an expansion of cultivation into forest areas, while in the Philippines, devaluation raises timber prices causing more to be harvested. For African countries, reduced government spending decreases deforestation as demand for agricultural commodities declines (since governments in Africa subsidize food prices), but, in Southeast Asia, it leads to increased deforestation due to the higher export elasticity of demand for agricultural products and timber in those countries. In Southeast Asia, the reduction in domestic demand for agricultural and wood products is more than offset by greater exports. Reduced fertilizer subsidies and elimination of agricultural output price supports affects agricultural productivity, thus reducing deforestation, but it also increases rural unemployment which increases forest encroachment; the net effect is indeterminate and varies among countries (Kaimowitz and Angelsen 1998). In general, trade liberalization and other macroeconomic policies that raise agricultural output prices (e.g., reductions in agricultural export taxes) will affect rates of deforestation in the same way as currency devaluation.

A strong case can be made that explanations of tropical deforestation are situation dependent. That is, the forces that bring about deforestation differ by region and country, and over time. Factors relevant in one time period may not be important in another. Factors influencing one country at some point in time are not relevant at that time for another country, although they may become important at a later date (Dauvergne 1997).

The Role of Government

According to Bromley (1999), the ultimate cause of deforestation is that "governments wish for it to happen … [and] most governments know precisely what they are doing and why they are doing it" (pp.283, 279). It may well be that forest represents an inferior investment and that social welfare is enhanced by converting some part of it to other uses. However, government intentions need not be benevolent. For example, a developing country government may permit or encourage forest conversion by peasants to avoid dealing with land reform, thereby maintaining the *status quo* in which most of the privileges accrue to the ruling elite. Thus, while population growth is a proximate cause of deforestation, the ultimate or final cause is the government's unwillingness to deal with the institutional changes required to alleviate poverty and bring about a more equitable distribution of income.

As long as a particular nation state is driven by a desire to earn rents from harvesting trees, and as long as land hunger (itself often the result of other policy failures) drives governments to open up remote areas, then very little is to be gained by suggesting that nations stop building roads, or that property rights be made more secure, or that population growth be implemented, or that government corruption be rectified, or that the powerful logging interests be reined in. The only way to confront deforestation is to focus on its final cause. (Bromley 1999, p.278)

Policy or government failure may be as important or a more important underlying cause of tropical deforestation than market failure. Repetto and Gillis (1988), Panayotou (1993) and Mendelsohn (1994), among others, demonstrate that government policies, whether deliberate or inadvertent, can result in deforestation at the cost of reducing welfare for society at large. Major forms of public intervention include (Sunderlin and Resosudarmo 1997; Repetto 1997; Repetto and Gillis 1988; Binswanger 1989): (1) direct subsidies to cut down forests; (2) indirect subsidies to forest companies through forest concessions that fail to capture all of the available rents and encourage excessive harvesting and wasteful rent seeking; (3) creation and protection of an inefficient (i.e., "log demanding") domestic forest industry (e.g., in Indonesia); (4) direct subsidies to cattle ranchers (e.g., in Brazil) to generate foreign exchange; (5) generous investment tax credits; (6) exemption of agricultural income from taxation; (7) subsidized credit for agriculture; (8) rules on public land allocation that favor large land holders or require "development" of land to demonstrate ownership; (9) development of public infrastructure (roads for access, hospitals, etc.); and (10) overpopulation and migration policies (sometimes rooted in ethnic politics). In essence, government action distorts incentives, consequently wasting valuable assets and tilting the balance against conservation (Brown and Pearce 1994).

Clearly, governments often deliberately seek to exploit forest resources knowing full well that this leads to deforestation. Some of the reasons why governments may choose to promote deforestation include:

- Governments overstate the value of forests for timber and understate the value of nontimber products, and their regulatory and habitat functions.
- The value of forest soils for agriculture is often overstated, with soils quickly depleted by cropping.
- Forest regions sometimes serve as an outlet for crowded populations, with peasants encouraged to move into forested regions rather than the cities, thereby avoiding social unrest (Reed 1992).
- Investment in the forestry sector may be promoted to secure doubtful employment and other benefits (Osgood 1994).

- The value of minor forest products is systematically ignored because the majority of economic benefits accrue to powerless social groups (de Beer and McDermott 1989).
- Forests are not considered essential for economic development, more or less consistent with experience in the Western world. Forests may even be viewed as an asset to be liquidated in order to diversify the economy. Sometimes resource prices are kept artificially low to encourage industrial and agricultural activity, and economic growth.

We briefly consider public policies concerning land tenures in forestry and agriculture, and restrictions on log exports, as sources of inefficiency and deforestation in tropical countries.

Forest Management and Land Tenure

Tenure plays an important role in deforestation. Markets cannot function properly without some degree of tenure security, be it formal or not. Forest companies are often "awarded" logging concessions of 20 years or (much) less, and are charged low stumpage fees, implying low rent capture (see Chapter 3). The incentive to take care, sustainably and carefully, of logging operations and the incentive to "protect" the forest from agricultural expansion will depend on the subjective probability that the concession will be renewed. Further, concessionaires are often allocated too much land, partly because royalties are volume-based rather than area-based and partly for political reasons. Again, this provides companies little incentive (or ability) to prevent encroachment by agricultural interests (peasants or other).

The result of the short tenures and low rent capture is rent-seeking behavior that encourages concessionaires to exploit the forest resource as quickly as possible in case fees are raised at a future date. It also encourages "premature re-entry", where companies re-enter sites prior to expiry of their concessions, thereby damaging immature timber. Thus, lack of (secure) tenure rights and low rent capture – forms of government failure – promote rapid exploitation and destructive harvesting. The result is poor forest management. In order to improve management practices, therefore, it is recommended that: (1) royalty fees be raised and the degree of rent capture be improved; (2) concession cycles be lengthened and tenure security be enhanced; (3) (market) competition in the allocation of concessions be introduced; and (4) the amount of area-based fees be raised relative to volume-based fees. By increasing area-based fees, companies will hold less area while managing more intensely those areas that are held.

Using subsidies, governments often encourage conversion of natural forests to tree plantations for development purposes. Plantation forests provide more jobs than sustainable logging in natural forests. However, with the exception of some high-quality sites, the discounted net returns of plantation forestry are below those associated with sustainable logging of natural forests. The reason is that establishment costs are high, while returns (harvests) accrue too far in the future (Sedjo 1992).

Finally, the timber in natural forests often has significant value over and above the costs of harvesting the trees and bringing them to market. These resource rents may be captured by national or local governments, timber firms, local "strongmen", and/or others involved in the wood products chain, or they can be squandered through directly unproductive rent-seeking activities that involve any of the players in the chain. The existence of rents results in patronage and patron-client relations in the exploitation of tropical forest resources. According to Dauvergne (1997), Japan has been a catalyst for tropical deforestation in Southeast Asia as a result of its policies that deliberately keep domestic log prices low (Japanese firms do not maximize short-term profits), thereby encouraging wasteful consumption. The Japanese have encouraged patron-client links that "distort state timber management guidelines, weaken state supervision, channel profits to a small elite, encourage logging companies to hide profits overseas, and undermine implementation of logging rules" (p.4). Illegal logging is supported by patrons at the state (region) level. Illegal logs are smuggled overseas or enter "legal" markets via inefficient local mills (that survive partly as a result of the illegal logs). Regional governments receive a low share of the royalties, if any, and this gives them little incentive to implement policies that protect forests.

While Dauvergne (1997) has focused on Southeast Asia and the role of the Japanese, others have examined similar political factors as an explanatory factor in deforestation. Deacon (1994) found deforestation to be positively linked to political instability and lack of accountability, and associated tenure insecurity. Reed (1992) mentions that in Côte d'Ivoire extraction of rents from the forestry sector is a principal tool of patronage and a method for preserving social privileges for the ruling elite.

Agricultural Land Tenure

As noted above, forestland (hinterland) serves to relieve population pressure on urban areas. Some governments actively encourage peasant farmers to locate in forested regions, while others simply do not enforce rules over land use. In Ecuador, for example, nearly all of the tree-covered land is designated as national parks, but the government allows peasants to make claims on forestland, but they must clear their land in order to acquire formal property rights. Indeed, for small landowners, land clearing for agriculture is often a prerequisite to gaining title, as it was with the Homestead Act in the USA. This encourages deforestation and conversion to production of tree crops (rubber, coconut and palm oil), even where it is more profitable to keep land in natural forests.

Using an optimal control model of land use in tropical forests, Mendelsohn (1994) demonstrates that insecure property rights lead a society to wastefully destroy its forests. This is true even if land ownership is not directly tied to forest clearing. Suppose that sustainable forestry yields higher net returns than agriculture, but that returns to forest activities are more evenly spread out over time, while those in agriculture are high initially but decline quickly as land is degraded (a common situation in tropical rainforests). Then, even a low probability that a peasant farmer will be evicted from the land will lead to the choice of the more destructive land use. The conclusion is that full property rights must be secured in an efficient and prompt manner.

Log Export Trade Restrictions

Restrictions on trade in logs were discussed in Chapter 3. Export restrictions reduce domestic prices of fiber, leading processing firms to substitute greater use of fiber for improvements in technology that reduce wood waste. Log export bans reduce the value of growing trees, making forestry a less attractive land use compared to agriculture, say. This is potentially compounded by local inefficiencies in the processing of logs, or the value-added sector. For example, Indonesia's trade restrictions may have resulted in the use of 15% more wood to produce the same plywood as elsewhere in Asia. With respect to deforestation, two forces operate against each other – lower fiber prices reduce supply of fiber and harvest of trees (but wood wastage has offset this effect to some extent), while the lower opportunity cost of converting land to agriculture increases the incentive to cut trees. Overall, restrictions on exports of logs dissipate available resource rents.

Institutions and Social Capital

The problems of economic development and social dilemmas, such as the environmental spillovers caused by excessive deforestation, are not that economic explanations are inappropriate, but rather that they are incomplete. For a democratic market economy to function properly, or for market-oriented economic policies to have effect, three criteria or factors other than markets and private property are required (Fukuyama 2002; see also Chapter 1).

A country must have a set of institutions within which policy change can occur. Institutions consist of formal rules (constitutions, laws and property rights) that constrain political, economic and social interactions, and include such things as commercial and criminal courts. Unlike cultural constraints, they are human-made and are therefore amenable to change, although this might require inertia to overcome vested interests. Economists have often ignored institutions, while existing institutions have not always been the right ones (Bromley 1999, p.3). Recent research in economic development now stresses the need for good institutions, as some institutions retard rather than promote growth (La Porta et al. 1999), or become an obstacle to resolving social dilemmas. Institutions need to evolve over time as a result of changing circumstances, and the rate at which they evolve must not serve as a drag on policy change.

Second, economic policies can only be carried out by the state, but the state must be limited in scope and yet able to enforce the rule of law, competent and sufficiently transparent in formulating policy, and with enough legitimacy to be able to make painful decisions. The role and performance of government is essential to economic development (La Porta et al. 1997; Olson 1996), just as it is to the resolution of social dilemmas in the ranch community. Good governments protect property rights and individual freedoms, keep regulations on businesses to a minimum, provide an adequate (efficient) level of public goods (e.g., infrastructure, schools, health care, police protection, court system), and are run by bureaucrats who are generally competent and not corrupt (La Porta et al. 1999). Unfortunately, regulatory agencies often prevent entry, courts resolve disputes arbitrarily and sometimes dishonestly, and politicians use government property to benefit their supporters rather than the population at large (Shleifer and Vishny 1998, p.8).

The third factor is "the proper cultural predispositions on the part of economic and political actors" (Fukuyama 2002, p.24). The "cultural factor" constitutes informal constraints (sanctions, taboos, customs, traditions, and norms or codes of conduct) that structure political, economic and social interactions. Informal constraints are commonly referred to as "social capital", which is "the shared knowledge, understandings, norms, rules, and expectations about patterns of interactions that groups of individuals bring to a recurrent activity" (Ostrom 2000). It refers to "features of social organizations, such as networks, norms, and trust, that facilitate action and cooperation for mutual benefit" (Putnam 1993, pp.35–6).

In the context of forestry, these factors can result in higher than socially-desired rates of deforestation. Lack of proper institutions and social capital increases the possibility of environmental spillovers, and increases transaction costs of mitigating them. Their lack leads to lower rates of economic growth and an inability to address environmental problems such as those associated with unsustainable forestry practices.

13.4 IS TROPICAL DEFORESTATION EXCESSIVE?

As a result of market and government failures, it is often assumed that current rates of deforestation must be excessive (Barbier and Burgess 1997). But conservation of tropical forests involves considerable opportunity costs – the foregone benefits from log sales and subsequent returns to agriculture (see Table 13.4). What then is the optimal stock of tropical rainforest that the world community (a country) should protect in order to maximize the present value of global (national) welfare?

In one of the few studies, Ehui and Hertel (1989) compute an optimal tropical forest stock for Côte d'Ivoire, which had the highest rate of deforestation of any nation during the 1980s but also achieved the fastest agricultural growth in sub-Saharan Africa. Their empirical analysis does not include all forest services, however, focusing only on the relation between forest preservation and agricultural productivity. The authors assume that society maximizes the discounted utility of net revenues from forest and agricultural output over an infinite time horizon. They found that the optimal forest stock ranged from 5.4 million hectares (for a real discount rate of 3%) to 1.9 million hectares (for a discount rate of 11%). Their estimates of the optimal steady-state forest stock exceed the actual (1990) forest stock of approximately 3.2 million hectares for discount rates lower than about 8%. Thus, the optimal stock of forests in Côte d'Ivoire (and elsewhere) is dependent on the social discount rate, with further deforestation only optimal when social discount rates are higher than, say, about 10% (if one leaves some room for uncertainty). Whether this is the case is an open question. In the short term, real rates of discount exceeding 20% are not uncommon in developing countries, with rates of less than 10% indicative of a much healthier economy.

Ehui and Hertel conclude that their estimates of optimal forest stock size are underestimates of the true optimal stock, since positive externalities like preservation and ecosystem benefits are not taken into account. Also excluded are the values of nontimber forest products, possibilities for eco-tourism and existence values, although some of these values may not be entirely incompatible with some forms of logging, although one would suspect that their inclusion would lead to higher optimal forest stocks.

Empirical research by Bulte et al. (1997) for the Atlantic Zone of Costa Rica, where the opportunity costs of sustainable timber management are likely higher because multinational firms are willing to invest in highly profitable plantations of fruit and vegetables, provides support for the forgoing conclusions for Côte d'Ivoire. The authors conclude that the optimal forest stock is below the current stock: "Since the bulk of Costa Rican forests are located in protected areas, we conclude that the government of Costa Rica has set aside too much (as opposed to not enough, as claimed by some critics) of its forests". This conclusion holds even when non-use values are taken into account and the value of nontimber forest products is increased to a value that is five times the authors' optimistic estimate of its true value.

In another study of Costa Rica, Bulte et al. (2002) examine the role of uncertainty about the future value of humid, tropical forest and agriculture. They find that, although the impact of uncertainty on conservation incentives is substantial, other values are more important. In particular, uncertainty about future benefits of conservation are swamped by two factors. First, if future benefits of forest conservation are assumed to be increasing, more natural forest will be protected. Second, compensation by the international community for beneficial spillovers is perhaps the most important factor determining optimal holdings of forest stocks. Without compensatory payments, the authors show that further deforestation in tropical Costa Rica may well be warranted.

Despite these and similar calculations, the political decision might favor conserving a higher level of tropical forest stocks than is considered economically optimal. Because of the role transboundary spillovers play, the economist needs to consider means for implementing conservation in a global context.

International Forest Conservation Measures

Barbier and Rauscher (1994) demonstrate that trade restrictions by industrial countries (bans on log imports, tariffs on tropical wood products, etc.) constitute a second-best option for controlling tropical deforestation. A preferred approach, at least in theory, is to provide direct subsidies to countries to reduce rates of deforestation, as noted above. International compensation for forest preservation in poor countries raises issues concerning property rights. If the rights to the forest assets are global in nature, then the country depleting its forests at a globally excessive rate must compensate foreigners for such deforestation. However, it is unlikely that such a system of property rights could ever be enforced, nor would it be agreed upon by sovereign nations. The reason is that what applies for externalities related to forest preservation could, in principal, apply to other situations where spillovers occur. For example, foreigners could oppose any country's domestic policy related to biodiversity, environment, and so on on the grounds that it creates a negative spillover, whether real or imagined. Hence, we must adopt the principle that tropical forests (and their assets) are owned by sovereign nations; any other guiding principle could constitute grounds for international intervention in domestic affairs.

Roughly speaking, two types of trade measures are possible – those that reduce the level of logging (demand-reducing measures such as trade bans and import levies) and those that affect the way exploitation takes place (e.g., forest management certification, discussed in Chapter 12). These measures are motivated by the belief that currently a very small percentage of tropical wood production takes place sustainably. In any event, the effects of trade measures on deforestation are probably modest. Barbier et al. (1994, p.8) argue that the share of trade in total tropical roundwood production is small: only 17% of the tropical wood is used for industrial purposes, with the majority of the remainder consumed as fuelwood (see Table 12.4). Of the industrial amount, no more than 31% is subsequently exported (with an increasing share involved in so-called South–South trade), so exports account for only about 5% of total tropical roundwood production. Also recall that commercial logging accounts for only a small proportion of deforestation, and it is evident that the direct effects of trade measures are relatively modest for most countries. Yet trade measures can be expected to have some impact.

Demand-reducing measures are considered because they are expected to reduce the opportunity costs of forest preservation (or nonexploitation), and thereby may reduce logging. This argument may be flawed for two reasons. First, and most obviously, reducing the terms of trade may negatively affect the economically optimal forest stock a country holds. When the returns of sustainable forestry decline, the relative attractiveness of alternative (agricultural) land-use options increases, and forest cover should fall in the long run. Second, timber exports may be considered an important source of foreign exchange for some countries. When the terms of trade fall, this implies that the marginal utility of consuming imported goods increases (depending on demand elasticity), the marginal utility of forest conservation should also increase. According to conventional economic reasoning, this is done by reducing the forest stock (see Chapter 2).

Trade measures aimed at affecting harvesting practices, specifically to promote sustainable harvesting by preferential treatment, may also impact land allocation decisions of governments – the objective of forest certification (see Chapter 12). Certification of tropical forestry management may increase or reduce the competitiveness of forestry as a land-use option. When the costs of certification are more than compensated for by increased revenues, the profitability of applying sustainable practices increases. The scope for a "green premium" for sustainably produced timber may be limited, but it is an open question whether this will have a big impact on land allocation decisions. When selective trade measures reduce the profitability of unsustainable forest management practices, it is possible that conversion of forests for alternative land-use options is accelerated, giving rise to a trade-off between short- and long-run conservation objectives.

Consider next the case of international transfers to compensate for the transboundary externality effects. Transfers to protect tropical forests are currently going on through, for example, the Global Environmental Facility (a joint agency of the United Nations and the World Bank) and the World Heritage Program. They may also increase with efforts to increase carbon storage in terrestrial carbon sinks (see Chapter 14). Such transfers should take the form of lump sum payments to prevent development of a resource, technical assistance and/or loans for environmentally benign projects, or debt relief in return for sustainable resource management. In theory, a direct international transfer should unambiguously increase the long-run equilibrium forest stock. The reason is that imports must be paid for with foreign exchange, earned by selling tropical timber. Transfers will ease the stringency of the foreign exchange constraint, which implies that more imports can be purchased. As a result, the marginal value of these imports falls. The marginal value of owning forests should also fall, and thus the steady-state forest cover should increase. However, it is an open question to what extent this is the case in the real world.

When transfers are directly coupled to the size of the conserved forest stock (i.e., a greater forest stock implies more funding), the expectation is that funding unambiguously increases the forest stock in developing countries. However, Stahler (1996) has demonstrated that this may not be the case, due to strategic behavior by governments in developing countries. As marginal external benefits are probably declining in stock size (so that the demand curve for forest conservation is downward sloping), governments of some recipient countries are in a position to increase the compensation per hectare (and thereby their total revenues) by reducing their forest stock. Thus, it is possible that compensating for external benefits will produce the adverse result of smaller stocks and high compensation per hectare.

Finally, a word of caution is necessary for the debt-relief option. Despite some well-publicized successes in the past, debt relief may not be a very good mechanism for attaining the desired aims of the international community. The reason is that money markets are trading the debt of developing countries at a discount that takes into account expected ability to repay. Bolivia's debt was discounted at $0.06 to the $1 when Bolivia paid $34 million to buy back $308 million in bonds in 1988. The price of remaining bonds rose from $0.06 to $0.11 as a result, with the real value of outstanding debt declining from $40.2 million ($670 million at six cents on the dollar) to $39.8 million ($362 million at 11 cents) (Pearce et al. 1995). In effect, Bolivia paid $34 million to reduce its debt by only $400,000. The problem of debt-for-nature swaps is that, while they protect vulnerable ecosystems in some cases, the large nominal reductions in debt barely touch nations' real burdens, and may even increase expected repayments. The same might also be true for other types of transfers, such as lump sum payments and other compensation.

13.5 DISCUSSION

This chapter raises a number of issues concerning tropical deforestation. First, although rates of tropical deforestation might be considered excessive by some, it may well be that global stocks of tropical forests are too large from an efficiency standpoint. The local discounted benefits of further conversion of tropical forests into agriculture or other uses may exceed the global discounted costs (e.g., foregone potential benefits due to loss of species, lost existence values). Not preventing further deforestation may be an optimal policy choice for some countries. While the most important value of tropical forest preservation might be as a carbon sink, evidence suggests that other values, such as those related to biological prospecting and non-use value, are small, particularly at the margin. The problem with carbon sink benefits is that they are difficult to determine as too much uncertainty surrounds issues of climate change and benefits of preventing global warming.

There is no consensus on what causes tropical deforestation, although change in land use is its identifying characteristic. Reasons probably vary with each particular situation that a region or country finds itself in. Clearly, logging is not a main factor, but is certainly a catalyst as it opens up natural forests to peasants seeking land for growing agricultural crops. Countries with tropical forests might well be reducing their stocks of forests because they are going through development stages similar to that experienced in Europe and North America. If this is the case, we should expect stocks of natural forests to increase at some future date. It does appear, however, that final causes (e.g., government policy to encourage people to live in forest regions), and a country's stock of social capital and its institutions, play a large role in determining whether environmental degradation via excessive rates of deforestation takes place.

It is unlikely that market failure is a primary or even major factor in tropical deforestation. Forestland owners are likely to convert land to other uses even if they are properly compensated for the external benefits of preserving forests, although compensation will undoubtedly reduce rates of deforestation by increasing the optimal size of natural forests that countries desire to hold. However, global transfers to tropical nations to encourage them to preserve forests will likely continue to be modest (no agreements to transfer large sums of money will be agreed to), and, even should large sums be considered, their effectiveness may be limited. Likewise, the effects of trade measures will probably be modest, with little effect on the area of tropical forest protected. When all is said, however, market failure may be less of a factor in deforestation than policy failure. Government policies in many countries encourage deforestation for development and revenue purposes, thereby providing some support for the idea that tropical forest stocks may be excessive.

Finally, in conclusion, deforestation is a concern to noneconomists, but it may be that this concern is unfounded. The evidence that confronts the economist suggests that, while greater effort should be devoted to sustainable management of forest ecosystems, the situation may not be as bad as the doomsayers suggest. Sound economic policy, including much less of the types of intervention by governments that encourage deforestation, may enable humans to protect tropical forest ecosystems and the amenities associated with them. Evidence for this is found in the declining rates of deforestation that occurred in the past 20 years.

NOTES

1. Leakey and Lewin (1996) suggest that some 30 billion species have appeared on earth, but that only 30 million remain. The Big Five of mass extinctions "comprises biotic crises in which at least 65 percent of [marine animal] species became extinct in a brief geological instant. In one of them, which brought the Permian period and the Paleozoic era to a close, it is calculated that more than 95 percent of marine animal species vanished" (p.44). Almost as many terrestrial species also vanished (p.49).
2. This compares with an estimated benefit of US$0.50/ha from harvest of NTFPs in the US Pacific Northwest and Coastal BC, where data are more readily available (van Kooten 1998).

Part V: Land Use and Climate Change

14. Climate Change: Land Use, Land-Use Change and Forestry

Climate change constitutes a long-term threat to the earth's ecosystems and possibly to the way people lead their lives. For island dwellers, for example, global warming constitutes a clear and present danger, and it may also be a threat to agriculture, particularly subsistence farming in developing countries. However, the full extent of the potential damages from global warming remains unknown (IPCC 1996b).

A variety of greenhouse gases (GHGs) cause a greenhouse effect by permitting the sun's rays to pass through them, but preventing dissipative heat from escaping. Although GHGs include methane, chlorofluorocarbons, ozone in the troposphere and nitrogen oxides, the most important driver of global warming (an enhanced greenhouse effect) is atmospheric carbon dioxide (CO_2). In this chapter, the objective is not to examine all aspects of climate change, but to focus on aspects of climate change related to land use, land-use change and forestry (LULUCF). In particular, as we discuss in section 14.2, LULUCF both causes climate change (e.g., because conversion of land from forest to agriculture releases carbon into the atmosphere) and mitigates it (e.g., growing trees take CO_2 out of the atmosphere). We begin in the next section by considering some technical aspects of climate change. Then, in section 14.2, we examine the role of terrestrial carbon sinks.

14.1 BACKGROUND

Technical Aspects

Is the climate changing? Of course, the earth's climate is always in a state of flux. Is a warming trend outside of historical norms actually taking place? This is a more difficult question to answer. There has been a discernible rise of some 0.3 to 0.6°C in the earth's average surface temperature over the past century (Wallace et al. 2000). This is evident from Figures 14.1 and 14.2. However, this does not mean that either the trend or fluctuations are somehow outside historical norms.

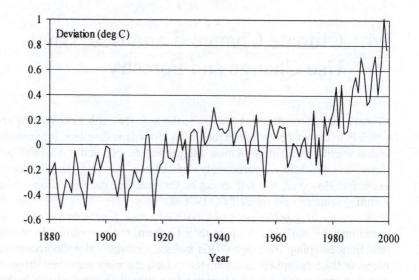

Figure 14.1: Deviation of surface land temperatures from trend (13.1°C)

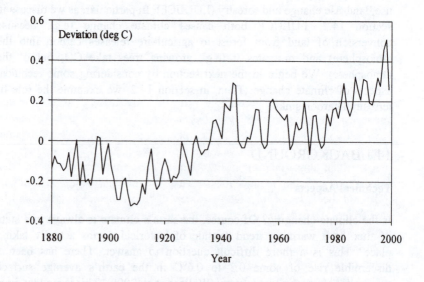

Figure 14.2: Deviation of ocean temperatures from trend (15.2°C)

Ascertaining whether temperature trends or fluctuations are outside historic norms is difficult because temperature data are only available since about the mid-1800s. The mid-1800s also corresponds to the time when the earth completed an unusually cool period, known as the little ice age, so a warming trend is not unexpected. However, based on the observable increase in average global temperatures over the past hundred or more years, and the science of climate change, most scientists are convinced that climate change is occurring. Is the trend in Figures 14.1 and 14.2 human caused? This is an even more difficult question that most scientists have answered in the affirmative, although debate continues (e.g., see Lomborg 2001, pp.258–324). As economists, we begin with the more interesting and economically challenging premise that human activities do indeed cause changes in the climate, and that such changes could have large, negative consequences. Hence, policies to reduce GHGs and, particularly, atmospheric CO_2 are required. Such policies need to be economically sound.

Given that humans continue to spew an increasingly broad array of gases into the atmosphere and that these are bound to have some impact on the atmosphere's chemistry, there could exist critical thresholds in the atmosphere's chemistry that could lead to substantially harmful and irreversible consequences. For example, if the Gulf Stream in the North Atlantic should flip-flop as a result of global warming, this could have a dramatic effect on the climate of Northern Europe, making places like Sweden, Norway and Finland much less livable. Decision-making in this uncertain environment is difficult, with most commentators suggesting that society take some steps to guard against extreme events (Arrow and Hurwicz 1972; Woodward and Bishop 1997). Thus, it is prudent to take some cautious steps to reduce CO_2 and other GHG emissions. Drastic steps that adversely impact economic growth, particularly in developing countries, are unwarranted at this time because these will have known adverse impacts on the growth of their economies, making them more rather than less susceptible to damage from global warming. If there is indeed a link between atmospheric concentrations of CO_2 and climate change, then some global warming is inevitable because of the large accumulation of past CO_2 and because of the long residence times of these gases in the atmosphere. Hence, all countries should be prepared to adapt to a warmer world, with richer countries better able to do so.

Information about anthropogenic contributions to various greenhouse gases is provided in Table 14.1. Not all GHGs have the same radiative impact (power to warm the earth) or atmospheric life. As a result, the effect of each of these GHGs is expressed in CO_2-equivalent units, which requires discounting for atmospheric life and taking into account emissions and atmospheric concentrations. The length of time each gas remains in the atmosphere and the relative instantaneous and total contributions of each of the gases are provided in Table 14.2. Efforts to control warming will, for the most part, need to focus on controlling CO_2 emissions or otherwise remove CO_2 from the atmosphere. Given this focus on carbon dioxide, it also helps to know about the carbon content of various fuels, since these are used for comparison in determining where and how best to reduce CO_2 emissions. This information is provided in Table 14.3. It appears, from these tables, that the CO_2 problem is, primarily, a coal problem. Indeed, burning all of the noncoal fossil fuels that are currently economic to extract will only double atmospheric CO_2.

The focus in this chapter is on policies that rely on terrestrial carbon sinks to remove CO_2 from the atmosphere.

Table 14.1: Summary of Key Greenhouse Gases Affected by Human Activities

	CO_2 ppmv[a]	Methane ppmv[a]	CFC-11 pptv[a]	CFC-12 pptv[a]	Nitrous oxide ppbv[a]
Atmospheric concentration					
Pre-industrial (1750–1800)	280	0.8	0	0	288
Present day (1990)	353	1.72	280	484	310
Current annual rate of change	1.8	0.015	9.5	17	0.8
– % rate of change	0.5	0.9	4	4	0.25
Atmospheric lifetime (years)	50–200[b]	10	65	130	150
Global warming potential[c]	1	21	4,500	7,100	290
Emission reductions to stabilize concentrations at current levels	>60%	15–20%	70–75%	75–85%	70–80%

Notes:
[a]ppmv: parts per million by volume; pptv: parts per trillion by volume; ppbv: parts per billion by volume.
[b]Absorption of CO_2 by oceans and biosphere is not known, so a range of values is provided.
[c]Based on release of 1 kg of gas in 1990 and 100-year horizon.
Source: Grubb (1990, pp.14–7).

Table 14.2: Contribution of Various Greenhouse Gases to Global Warming

Greenhouse gas	Atmospheric lifetime (years)[a]	Relative instantaneous contribution to warming[b]	Relative total contribution to warming[b]
CO_2	50–200[c]	53.2%	80.3%
Methane	10	17.3%	2.2%
CFCs	65, 130[c]	21.4%	8.8%
Nitrous oxides	150	8.1%	8.7%

Notes:
[a] Source: Grubb (1990, pp.14–7).
[b] Source: Nordhaus (1991, p.39).
[c] Absorption of CO_2 by oceans and biosphere is not known so a single value cannot be given. The atmospheric lifetime for CFC-11 is 65 years; for CFC-12 it is 130 years.

Table 14.3: Carbon Content of Different Fossil Fuels[a]

	Tonnes of carbon per million tonnes oil equivalent	Tonnes of carbon per 10^{12} joules
Natural gas	0.61	13.8
Crude oil	0.84	19.0
Bituminous coals	1.09	24.5
Anthracites	1.14	15.5
Oil products		
Gasoline	0.80	18.0
Kerosene	0.82	18.5
Diesel/gas oil	0.84	19.0
Fuel oils	0.88	10.0

Notes:
[a] 1 barrel of oil = 0.136 tonnes; 1 calorie = 4.2 joules (J); 1 British thermal unit (Btu) = 1.05 kJ (kilojoules); 1 kilowatt-hour (kwh) = 3.6 J.
Source: Grubb (1990, p.26).

International Agreements and Terrestrial Carbon Sinks

Concern about anthropogenic emissions of GHGs led the World Meteorological Organization (WMO) and the United Nations Environment Program jointly to establish the Intergovernmental Panel on Climate Change (IPCC) in 1988. The first IPCC report was published in 1990; it led to the signing of the United Nations' Framework Convention on Climate Change (FCCC) in Rio de Janeiro in June 1992 by 174 countries. The Convention committed signatories to stabilize atmospheric CO_2, with developed (Annex I) countries to reduce emissions to the 1990 level by

2000. The Second Conference of the Parties (COP) to the FCCC endorsed the IPCC's second assessment report. At COP3 in Kyoto, December 11, 1997, industrialized countries agreed to reduce CO_2 emissions by an average 5.2% from the 1990 level by the commitment (measurement) period 2008–12, or by a total of some 250 megatons (10^6 metric tons) of carbon, denoted Mt C, per year from 1990. The IPCC's Third Assessment Report was released in 2001, and endorsed at COP7 in Marrakech, Morocco.

The Kyoto Protocol's emissions targets include the following six greenhouse gases: CO_2, methane (CH_4), nitrogen oxide (N_2O), hydrofluoro-carbons (HFCs), perfluorocarbons (PFCs) and sulfur hexafluoride (SF_6). Interestingly, each country chose its own emissions reduction target, with the European Union having picked an overall target to be allocated internally among members (see van Kooten 2004). KP targets for Annex B countries and the EU are provided in Table 14.4. The current focus of governments is on the commitment period 2008–12 and not beyond.

Table 14.4: Countries Included in Annex B to the Kyoto Protocol and Their Emissions Targets

Country/region	Target (2008–12 relative to 1990)
EU-15, Bulgaria, Czech Republic, Estonia, Latvia, Liechtenstein, Lithuania, Monaco, Romania, Slovakia, Slovenia, Switzerland	–8%
United States	–7%
Canada, Hungary, Japan, Poland	–6%
Croatia	–5%
New Zealand, Russian Federation, Ukraine	0
Norway	+1%
Australia	+8%
Iceland	+10%

Notes:
Some economies in transition have a baseline other than 1990.

The Kyoto Protocol (KP) is seen as a necessary first step to get nations to take the threat of global climate change seriously. The reason is that, as early as 1995, at the first COP in Berlin, it was recognized that the 1992 Rio commitments would not be enough. The Berlin Mandate began a process that would lead to a strengthened international accord with legal instruments. The KP was a result of that process. Both developed and developing countries can ratify the KP; it comes into effect 90 days after it is ratified by 55 states, but the industrialized countries that ratify must account for 55% of the CO_2 emitted by industrialized countries in 1990. As of 27 June 2003, 110 countries had ratified, with developed countries' proportion of the 1990 emissions at 43.9% (see http://unfccc.int/resource/kpthermo.html). The pressure is now on Russia to ratify the Protocol, because it accounts for 17.4% of 1990 CO_2 emissions and, with the United States (which accounts for 36.1% of industrial countries' emissions) and Australia (2.1%) having decided not to ratify, Russian ratification is required before the Kyoto Protocol comes into effect.

The KP is not legally binding, while the penalty for noncompliance is ineffectual. Countries that fail to comply with the KP will be "required" to reduce their emissions by an additional 30% in a negotiated future round of emission reductions. This cannot be seen as a true penalty since countries have not declared their intentions concerning future cuts in emissions, and can simply include the impact of the penalty in any future declaration of the emissions control target they set for themselves. Indeed, one purpose of this book is to demonstrate that most countries that have ratified the Kyoto Protocol will not meet their self-imposed targets (see also Stavins and Barrett 2002).

Nonetheless, the United States withdrew its support for the KP after a breakdown of negotiations during COP6 at The Hague in late 2000, citing high costs. Kyoto's flexibility mechanisms – Joint Implementation, the Clean Development Mechanism and International Emissions Trading (see van Kooten 2004) – were not considered flexible enough, and the role for terrestrial carbon sinks under the KP was considered inadequate. The latter was a particularly important factor in US intransigence as a group of countries that initially included Japan, the United States, Canada, Australia and New Zealand, pushed for a greater role for terrestrial carbon sinks in meeting KP targets. At the Hague, the EU proposed a cap on Article 3.4 activities (forest and agricultural management) of 20 Mt of carbon annually, later increased to 40 Mt C, while the USA offered a cap of 221 Mt C, later reduced to 137 Mt C.

Withdrawal by the USA cannot be attributed solely to the issue of sinks, however. Also important is the fact that American institutions (especially the courts) would override a weak, nonbinding international agreement, which is how the KP can best be characterized, forcing a future administration to meet its obligation when other countries can renege. Partly as a result, the USA has a history of refusing to ratify international treaties but then complying with their most important provisions (Bernstein 2002, p.216). Although compliance with the KP is unlikely, the United States has taken steps towards reducing GHG emissions, with large industrial emitters in that country having become involved in various efforts to reduce or offset emissions (e.g., see Richards and Andersson 2001).

COP6 negotiations continued as COP6$_{bis}$ at Bonn in July 2001, with the EU relenting to a much broader definition of and role for carbon sinks, mainly to appease the Umbrella group of countries, and especially the United States in absentia. The Bonn compromise was subsequently approved by COP7 in Marrakech in November 2001, but with an even greater cap on the amount of carbon that could be stored annually in terrestrial sinks. The cap on carbon uptake in sinks for the first commitment period increased from 201 Mt C per year (139 Mt C if the United States is left out) at COP6$_{bis}$ to 219 Mt C at COP7. The COP6$_{bis}$ and COP7 agreements permit countries to substitute carbon uptake from land use, land-use change and forestry (LULUCF) activities in lieu of greenhouse gas emissions in meeting targets during the first commitment period, thereby avoiding expensive controls on the emission of CO_2 and other GHGs – as sinks could conceivably account for more than 80% of the required 250 Mt C annual reduction from 1990 levels (although not from the much higher 2010 business-as-usual emission levels).

Afforestation and reforestation since 1990 provide carbon credits, while deforestation results in a debit. Since most countries have not embarked on large-scale afforestation/reforestation projects in the past decade, harvesting trees during the five-year commitment period (2008–12) will cause them to have a debit on the afforestation, reforestation and deforestation (ARD) account. Therefore, the Marrakech Accords permit countries, in the first commitment period only, to offset up to 9.0 megatons of carbon (Mt C) per year for five years through (verified) forest management activities that enhance carbon uptake. If there is no ARD debit, then a country cannot claim the credit. In addition, some countries are able to claim carbon credits from business-as-usual forest management that need not be offset against ARD debits. Thus, Canada can claim 12 Mt C per year, the Russian Federation 33 Mt C, Japan 13 Mt C, and other countries much lesser amounts – Germany 1.24 Mt C, Ukraine 1.11 Mt C, and remaining countries less than 1.0 Mt C. Japan expects to use forestry activities to meet 65% of its KP obligation, while Canada can use forest management to achieve one-third of its emissions reduction target (but only 6% if projected 2010 emissions are used as the baseline from which to achieve the KP target).

In addition to forest ecosystem sinks, the latest Accords include agricultural activities that enhance carbon stocks. Thus, revegetation (establishment of vegetation that does not meet the definitions of afforestation and reforestation), cropland management (greater use of conservation tillage, reduced summer fallow, more set asides) and grazing management (manipulation of the amount and type of vegetation and livestock produced) are activities that lead to enhanced soil organic carbon (SOC) and/or more carbon stored in biomass. The problem with enhanced agricultural sinks is that they are likely ephemeral, while carbon flux is difficult to measure.

The accounting stance for CO_2 measurement has changed as a result of including terrestrial carbon sinks for meeting KP obligations. In determining 1990 baseline emissions, countries did not count carbon flux in terrestrial sinks. However, for 2008–12, both emissions and terrestrial carbon flux are counted. Thus, we have gone from a gross measure of emissions in 1990 to a net measure for the commitment period. This is rather strange because it implies that a country could potentially change its gross emissions, while leaving net emissions unchanged or at a higher level, and still meet the KP target. However, efforts are being made to reconcile this difference, although ratifying countries will likely be given leeway in employing whatever accounting stance is most beneficial to them (van Kooten 2004).

In any event, terrestrial carbon sinks have been provided a function in international agreements to mitigate climate change. This role is significant enough to warrant further investigation. Are terrestrial sinks an economically important means of achieving meaningful reductions in atmospheric CO_2? Can biological sinks compete with other means for mitigating climate change? How might land use change as a result? These issues are investigated in more detail in this chapter.

14.2 ROLE OF LULUCF ACTIVITIES

A country can obtain carbon credits at home by planting trees where none grew previously, increasing the rates at which trees grow through enhanced forest management, or potentially other land-use activities that increase carbon in soils or growing plants. The KP permits carbon sequestration in trees planted as a result of an afforestation or reforestation program to be counted as a credit, while carbon lost by deforestation is counted as a debit (article 3.3). While only carbon sequestered in wood biomass is currently counted, the Protocol leaves open the possibility for including other components, such as wood product carbon sinks, wetlands and soil carbon sinks (article 3.4). Carbon credits can also be obtained for activities in developing countries and economies in transition. Kyoto's Clean Development Mechanism (CDM) enables industrialized countries to purchase certified offsets from developing countries by sponsoring projects that reduce CO_2 emissions below business-as-usual levels in those countries. Likewise, emission reduction units can be produced through Joint Implementation (JI) projects in other developed countries, but the implication is that it would occur in countries whose economies are in transition. Only LULUCF projects that prevent or delay deforestation and land-use change, or result in the establishment of plantation forests, are eligible under the CDM and JI – no projects to increase SOC are eligible under current agreements.

In principle, a country should get credit only for sequestration above and beyond what occurs in the absence of carbon-uptake incentives, a condition known as "additionality" (Chomitz 2000). Thus, for example, if it can be demonstrated that a forest would be harvested and converted to another use in the absence of specific policy (say, subsidies) to prevent this from happening, the additionality condition is met. Carbon sequestered as a result of incremental forest management activities (e.g., juvenile spacing, commercial thinning, fire control, fertilization) would be eligible for C credits, but only if the activities would not otherwise have been undertaken (say, to provide higher returns or maintain market share). Similarly, afforestation projects are additional if they provide environmental benefits (e.g., regulation of water flow and quality, wildlife habitat) not captured by the landowner and would not be undertaken in the absence of economic incentives, such as subsidy payments or an ability to sell carbon credits (Chomitz 2000). Which LULUCF projects meet the additionality requirement?

Land Use Change

In recent decades probably all of the net carbon releases from forests have come from tropical deforestation (since temperate and boreal forests are in approximate carbon balance[1]) and thus have contributed to the build-up of atmospheric CO_2. Houghton (1993) estimates that tropical deforestation was the cause of between 22 and 26% of all greenhouse gas emissions in the 1980s. This is roughly consistent with findings of Brown et al. (1993), who report that total annual anthropogenic emissions are nearly 6.0 gigatons (10^9 metric tons, Gt) of carbon, with tropical deforestation contributing some 0.6 to 1.7 Gt per year. Tropical forests generally contain anywhere from 100 to 400 m^3 of timber per ha, although much of it may not be commercially useful. This implies that they store some 20–80 tonnes of carbon per ha in wood biomass, but this ignores other biomass and SOC. An indication of total carbon stored in biomass for various tropical forest types and regions is provided in Table 14.5. The carbon sink function of soils in tropical regions is even more variable across tropical ecosystems (Table 14.6). This makes it difficult to make broad statements about carbon loss resulting from tropical deforestation. Certainly, there is a loss in carbon stored in biomass (which varies from 27 to 187 tC/ha). There may or may not be a significant loss in SOC depending on the new land use (agricultural activity) and the tropical zone. While conversion of forests to arable agriculture will lead to a loss of some 20–50% of SOC within 10 years, conversion to pasture may in fact increase soil carbon, at least in the humid tropics (see Table 14.6). One thing is clear, conversion of forestland to agriculture leads to a smaller carbon sink, with a greater proportion of the ecosystem's carbon stored in soils as opposed to biomass (Table 14.7). To address this market failure (release of carbon through deforestation), policies need to focus on protection of tropical forests (see Chapter 13).

Table 14.5: Carbon Content of Biomass, Various Tropical Forests and Regions

Country/forest	Wet tropical	Dry tropical
Africa	187 tC/ha	63 tC/ha
Asia	160 tC/ha	27 tC/ha
Latin America	155 tC/ha	27 tC/ha

Source: Papadopol (2000).

Table 14.6: Depletion of Soil Carbon Following Tropical Forest Conversion to Agriculture

Region	Soil carbon in forest (tC/ha)	New land use	Loss of soil carbon with new land use
Semi-arid	15–25	Shifting cultivation (arable agriculture)	30–50% loss within 6 years
Sub-humid	40–65	Continuous cropping	19–33% loss in 5–10 years
Humid	60–165	Shifting cultivation Pasture	40% loss within 5 years 60–140% of initial soil carbon

Source: Adapted from Paustian et al. (1997).

Consider the role of land-use change more broadly. Conversion of pasture into cropland will release carbon stored in the soil, while draining wetlands releases methane. Changes in management practices will also cause carbon to be released or stored. An indication of the effect on terrestrial carbon sinks of enhanced management of existing land uses and changes in land use is provided in Table 14.8. This table gives estimates of the potential of these activities for mitigating climate change (i.e., the potential of land-use management to achieve KP targets). However, these activities are currently not eligible under KP's CDM. But it also demonstrates how current land uses have resulted in the release of C over time – for example, cultivation alone has resulted in the historical release of 54 Gt C (Paustian et al. 1997). While a strategy to reduce forest degradation (*viz.*, deforestation) is addressed in Table 14.8, reforestation and afforestation programs are ignored. These are considered next.

Table 14.7: Total Carbon in Tropical Ecosystems by Sink, Percent[a]

Land use	Tree	Understorey	Litter	Root	Soil
Original forest	**72**	**1**	**1**	**6**	**21**
Managed & logged over-forest	72	2	1	4	21
Slash & burn croplands	3	7	16	3	71
Bush fallow	11	9	4	9	67
Tree fallow	42	1	2	10	44
Secondary forest	57	1	2	8	32
Pasture	<1	9	2	7	82
Agroforestry & tree plantations	49	6	2	7	36

Notes:
[a] Average of Brazil, Indonesia and Peru.
Source: Woomer et al. (1999).

Enhanced Management of Existing Forests and Afforestation

Contrary to the definitions agreed upon at COP7, the IPCC (2000) interprets reforestation as tree planting on land that had at some time in the past been in forest, but has recently been in agriculture. Other countries and the latest KP agreement interpret this as afforestation. According to the IPCC, afforestation refers to tree planting on lands that have never been and would not naturally be in forest. These disparate views are rooted in Kyoto's failure to take proper account of carbon in wood products.

Canada and other major wood product exporters feel that their definition of reforestation simply recognizes the fact that much of the carbon in harvested timber gets exported and that the debit from logging should therefore be charged to the importing country.

Table 14.8: Effects on Potential Net Carbon Storage of Land-Use Activities, Excluding Afforestation and Reforestation[a]

Activity	Potential area (10⁶ ha)	Rate of C gain (tC/ha/yr)	Potential (Mt C/yr) 2010	2040
1. Improved management within a land use				
Cropland (reduced tillage, improved management of crop rotations, cover crops, etc.)	1,289 (45.7%)	0.34	125 (60%)	258 (51%)
Rice paddies (better irrigation, improved residue management)	153 (2.6%)	0.10	8 (<10%)	13 (<7%)
Agroforestry (better management of trees on cropland)	400 (20.8%)	0.28	26 (46%)	45 (38%)
Grazing land (better management)	3,401 (38.1%)	0.77	261 (36%)	523 (36%)
Forestland (enhanced silviculture, reduced degradation)	4,051 (46.9%)	0.41	170 (59%)	703 (72%)
Urban land (tree planting, improved wood product management & waste management)	100 (50%)	0.30	2 (50%)	4 (50%)
2. Land use change				
Agroforestry (conversion of poor crop/grassland to agroforestry)	630 (0%)	3.1	391 (0%)	586 (0%)
Restoring severely degraded land (to forest, crop or grass land)	277 (4.3%)	0.25	4 (<20%)	8 (13%)
Grassland (converting cropland to grassland)	1,457 (41.3%)	0.80	38 (63%)	82 (59%)
Wetland restoration (converting drained land back to wetland)	230 (91.3%)	0.40	4 (100%)	14 (93%)
GLOBAL TOTAL			**1,027 (39%)**	**2,235 (44%)**

Notes:
[a] Contribution by developed countries provided in parentheses.
Source: IPCC (2000).

Reforestation needs to take into account the carbon debit from harvesting trees, but it also needs to take into account carbon stored in wood product sinks (and exported carbon) and additional carbon sequestered as a result of forest management activities (e.g., juvenile spacing, commercial thinning and fire control). Even when all of the carbon fluxes are appropriately taken into account, it is unlikely that "additional" forest management will be a cost-effective and competitive means for sequestering carbon (Caspersen et al. 2000). Global data on the potential for carbon uptake via forest management is provided in Table 14.9.

Table 14.9: Global Estimates of the Costs and Potential Carbon that can be Removed from the Atmosphere and Stored by Enhanced Forest Management from 1995 to 2050

Region	Practice	Carbon removed & stored (Gt)	Estimated costs ($US $\times 10^9$)
Boreal	Forestation[a]	2.4	17
Temperate	Forestation[a]	11.8	60
	Agroforestry	0.7	3
Tropical	Forestation[a]	16.4	97
	Agroforestry	6.3	27
	Regeneration[b]	11.5–28.7	44–99
	Slowing deforestation[b]	10.8–20.8	
TOTAL		**60 – 87**	

Notes:
[a] Refers primarily to reforestation, but this term is avoided for political reasons.
[b] Includes an additional 25% of above-ground C to account for C in roots, litter and soil (range based on uncertainty in estimates of biomass density).
Source: Adapted from IPCC (1996b, pp.785, 791).

Evidence from Canada, for example, indicates that reforestation does not pay even when carbon uptake benefits are taken into account, mainly because northern forests tend to be marginal (van Kooten et al. 1993). The reason is that such forests generally regenerate naturally, and returns to artificial regeneration accrue in the distant future. Only if short-rotation, hybrid poplar plantations replace logged or otherwise denuded forests might forest management be a competitive alternative to other methods of removing CO_2 from the atmosphere. Hybrid poplar plantations may also be the only cost-effective, competitive alternative when marginal agricultural land is afforested (van Kooten et al. 1999, 2000).

Surprisingly, despite the size of their forests and, in some cases, large areas of marginal agricultural land, there remains only limited room for forest sector policies in the major wood-producing countries (Canada, Finland, Sweden, Russia). We illustrate this using the TECAB model for northeastern British Columbia (Krcmar et al. 2001; Krcmar and van Kooten 2003). The model consists of tree-growth, agricultural activities and land-allocation components, and is used to examine the costs of carbon uptake in the grain belt–boreal forest transition zone of BC. These estimates, extended to similar regions, provide a good indication of the costs of an afforestation-reforestation strategy for carbon uptake for Canada as a whole, and likely for other boreal regions as well. The study region consists of 1.2 million ha, of which nearly 10.5% constitute marginal agricultural land, with the remainder being boreal forest. The boreal forest is composed of spruce, pine and aspen. For environmental reasons and to comply with BC's Forest Practices Code, the area planted to hybrid poplar in the model is limited only to logged stands of aspen and marginal agricultural land. Other harvested stands are replanted to native species or left to regenerate on their own, depending on what is economically optimal. Carbon fluxes associated with forest management, wood product sinks and so on are all taken into account. An infinite time horizon is employed, land conversion is not instantaneous (as assumed in some models), carbon fluxes associated with many forest management activities (but not control of fire, pests and disease) are included, and account is taken of what happens to the wood after harvest, including their decay.

Results indicate that upwards of 1.5 million tonnes of discounted carbon (discounted at 4%) can be sequestered in the region at a cost of about $40/t or less. This amounts to an average of about 1.3 t/ha, or about 52 kg/ha per year over and above normal C uptake. If this result is applied to all of Canada's productive boreal forestland and surrounding marginal farmland, then Canada could potentially sequester some 10–15 Mt of C annually via this option. This amounts to at most 7.5% of Canada's annual KP-targeted reduction, well below the 22% that had been envisioned. This is a rather pessimistic conclusion given that, in general, plantation forests are considered a cost-effective means of sequestering carbon (see above). Again, the reason may be that boreal forests are globally marginal at best and silvicultural investments simply do not pay for the most part, even when carbon uptake is included as a benefit of forest management.

Manley and van Kooten (2003) investigate 49 studies to investigate the average and marginal costs of creating carbon offsets in forest sinks. Estimates of the uptake costs ($US/tC) are derived from three meta-regression analysis models: (1) a linear regression model where reported costs per tC are regressed on a variety of explanatory variables; (2) a model where total project costs are converted to a per ha basis and then regressed on the explanatory variables using a quadratic functional form; and (3) a model where per ha uptake costs are regressed on the explanatory variables using a cubic functional form. Projected costs of carbon sequestration ($US/tC) for various scenarios are provided in Table 14.10.

Baseline estimates of the average costs of sequestering carbon (of creating carbon offset credits) through forest conservation in the tropics are US$11–$40/tC. Sequestering carbon in terrestrial forest ecosystems is (generally) somewhat lower in the Great Plains than elsewhere, including the tropics. Surprisingly, costs are higher in the Corn Belt than in the tropics or Great Plains.

Table 14.10: Projected Costs from Three Models of Creating Carbon Offsets through Forestry Activities, 2002 ($ per tC)

Scenario	$ per tC	Total Cost per ha	
		Quadratic	Cubic
Baseline (Tropics/Conservation)	11.06	30.22	40.44
Tropics			
Planting	17.98	55.79	77.46
Agroforestry	25.39	63.81	87.79
Forest Management	10.57	25.38	33.33
Soil Sink	8.02	14.64	16.29
Fuel Substitution	5.51	18.96	24.45
Product Sink	3.57	10.92	13.35
Opportunity Cost of Land	40.42	109.81	140.58
Great Plains			
Conservation	13.91	23.99	30.91
Planting	22.61	44.29	59.20
Agroforestry	31.93	50.66	67.09
Forest Management	13.30	20.15	25.47
Soil Sink	10.09	11.62	12.45
Fuel Substitution	6.94	15.05	18.68
Product Sink	4.49	8.67	10.20
Opportunity Cost of Land	50.83	87.18	107.44
Corn Belt			
Conservation	17.37	33.92	43.30
Planting	28.24	62.63	82.93
Agroforestry	39.88	71.64	93.99
Forest Management	16.61	28.50	35.68
Soil Sink	12.60	16.43	17.44
Fuel Substitution	8.66	21.29	26.17
Product Sink	5.61	12.26	14.29
Opportunity Cost of Land	63.50	123.27	150.51
Other Regions			
Conservation	18.41	39.92	51.58
Planting	29.94	73.70	98.79
Agroforestry	42.28	84.30	111.96
Forest Management	17.61	33.53	42.50
Soil Sink	13.36	19.34	20.77
Fuel Substitution	9.18	25.05	31.18
Product Sink	5.95	14.42	17.03
Opportunity Cost of Land	67.31	145.07	179.29

Compared to simple conservation of existing forests, tree planting increases costs by nearly double, and agroforestry activities increase costs even more while forest management is the least costly option. Needless to say, if the opportunity cost of land is appropriately taken into account, costs are some 3.5 times higher than the baseline where such costs are assumed negligible or ignored.

When post-harvest storage of carbon in wood products, or substitution of biomass for fossil fuels in energy production, are taken into account, costs are lowest – some \$3.57/tC to \$31.18/tC (\$1 to \$8.50/t CO_2) depending on location and type of project. Accounting for carbon entering the soil also lowers costs. Naturally, although not shown in Table 14.10, discounting carbon increased costs of creating carbon offset credits because this results in "less carbon" from a project, while discounting financial outlays reduces the cost of creating carbon offsets. However, since most outlays occur early on in the life of a forest project, costs of creating carbon offset credits are not as sensitive to the discount rate used.

Finally, while the average costs reported in Table 14.10 are useful to decision-makers, they are not truly indicative of the potential costs of creating carbon offsets because they fail to take into account the fact that costs rise as more carbon is sequestered in terrestrial ecosystems. This is true not only as tree planting activities gobble up agricultural land of increasing productivity, but also as an attempt is made to create more carbon offset credits on the same site.

The only thing neglected in these studies is the issue of "leakages". Leakages occur because, when subsidies are used to encourage ARD activities, the additional timber will eventually lead to increased harvests. In anticipation of lower prices, forestland owners who do not benefit from subsidies (because they already have timber on their lands or do not quality for a particular program or are located in another jurisdiction) will reduce plantings and/or increase harvests. These actions result in less carbon uptake than would otherwise occur, or even release of CO_2 due to sooner harvests. Research indicates that leakages may be as much as 100% or even more of a terrestrial sequestration project (Alig et al. 1998; Richards and Andersson 2001).

Prognosis for Agricultural Sinks

Much the same story can be told about agricultural soil-carbon sinks that are likely to be included in a future climate accord. In order to increase soil organic carbon, farmers need to change their agronomic practices. In drier regions where tillage summer fallow is used to conserve soil moisture, this requires the use of chemical fallow or continuous cropping, or cessation of cropping altogether (i.e., return to grassland). In other agricultural regions, a movement from convention tillage (CT) to reduced tillage (RT) or no tillage (NT) can increase soil organic carbon. Continuous cropping in place of summer fallow, RT and NT increase soil carbon by increasing plant biomass and/or reducing rates of decay of organic matter. Are such practices worth pursuing, and can they result in significant reductions in C flux?

West and Marland (2001) review previous studies comparing CT, RT and NT in terms of their carbon flux, and provide a detailed carbon accounting for each practice using US data. The researchers include not only carbon uptake in soils, but also carbon flux associated with machinery operations, production of agro-chemicals, and so on. They conclude that RT does not differ significantly from CT in terms of carbon uptake benefits, and that NT results in an average relative net carbon flux of –368 kg C/ha/yr. Of this amount, –337 kg C/ha/yr is due to carbon sequestration in soil, –46 kg C/ha/yr due to a reduction in machinery operations and +15 kg C/ha/yr due to higher carbon emissions from an increase in the use of agricultural inputs. While annual savings in carbon emissions of 31 kg C/ha/yr last indefinitely, accumulation of C in soil reaches equilibrium after 40 years. West and Marland (2001) suggest that the rate of uptake is constant at 337 kg C/ha/yr for the first 20 years and then declines linearly over the next 20 years.

Estimates of carbon uptake by soils in the prairie region of Canada as a result of going from CT to NT vary from 100 to 500 kg C/ha/yr (West and Marland 2001). Assume an annual carbon flux of –200 to –400 kg C/ha/yr in SOC, plus another –31 kg C/ha/yr in saved emissions, due to a change from CT to NT in Canada. Then the net discounted carbon prevented from entering the atmosphere as a result of a shift to NT from CT depends on the discount rate as indicated in Table 14.11. Total carbon uptake due to agricultural operations varies from about 4 tC/ha to at most 12.5 tC/ha. Compared to plantation forests, the amount of carbon that can potentially be prevented from entering the atmosphere via a dramatic change in agricultural practices is small compared to forest plantations.

Table 14.11: Expected Annual and Total Carbon Savings from Adopting Zero-Tillage Practices (tonnes of C per ha)

Assumed annual sequestration in soil organic C during first 20 years	2% Discount rate		4% Discount rate	
	Total	Annual	Total	Annual
200	5.94	0.12	4.16	0.17
300	8.13	0.16	5.86	0.23
400	10.33	0.21	7.55	0.30
500	12.52	0.25	9.24	0.37

Neglected in the forgoing analysis are potential carbon leakages, which are similar in origin to those mentioned in connection with plantation forests. NT generally leads to lower yields, causing prices to rise. This will cause an expansion in output as grass or forestland is converted to crops and more inputs are employed, and this will lead to greater release of carbon.

Also neglected in this analysis are the adverse environmental impact of increased chemical use and the potential cost of reduced- or zero-tillage to farmers. With the exception of conversion to grassland, continuous cropping and NT usually increase production costs (because more chemical inputs and/or high investments in specialized equipment are required) and reduce yields (Lerohl and van Kooten 1995). Using data reported by Lerohl and van Kooten (1995), consider the costs of carbon uptake under continuous cropping of wheat versus a two-year, wheat–tillage fallow rotation. Under the best conditions or most productive land, average annual wheat yields are 2.95 t/ha under continuous cropping compared with 1.68 t/ha with the two-year, wheat–fallow rotation, while respective annual net returns are $69.86 and $117.45 per ha. Assuming that organic matter is 50% carbon and that cropping leaves 15–20% crop residue, the cost of carbon uptake amounts to $373–$498/t C! This ignores lower levels of carbon flux with the wheat–fallow rotation since there are fewer machinery operations and less inputs are employed. If the cost difference between CT and NT is just as great as that between continuous cropping and tillage fallow (about $47.5/ha), then, from data in Table 14.11, the cost of carbon uptake via changes in agricultural practices amounts to approximately $130–$400/t C. This is clearly an expensive means for sequestering carbon.

Manley et al. (2004) conducted two meta-regression analyses to determine the costs of sequestering carbon using zero-tillage practices. First, 52 studies comparing the costs of conventional- versus zero-tillage were compared. With the exception of the US Corn Belt and Prairies, the studies indicated that conventional tillage yielded higher net returns. For the Corn Belt and Prairies, no-till yielded net returns that exceeded conventional tillage by about $32/ha for wheat and $63/ha for corn and other crops.

A meta-regression analysis based on 24 studies was then used to determine the carbon-uptake benefits of employing NT. The results were rather surprising: they depended on the depth of measurement of the soil. The evidence suggests (although further research is warranted) that, with no-till, organic matter left on the surface will decay, releasing carbon into the atmosphere. With conventional tillage practices, the organic matter is plowed under. Thus, SOC content is higher under NT than CT if measurement is confined to the plow layer, but it is less under NT than under CT if measurements are made to a greater depth.

Finally, using the data in the available range of measurements, Manley et al. (2004) estimated the costs (if any) of sequestering carbon through changes in agricultural practices. These estimates are provided in Table 14.12 for zero- or no-till agriculture. The results indicate that costs per metric ton of carbon removed from the atmosphere and stored in agricultural soils by a change in tillage practices are unacceptably high, ranging from about $130/tC to over $400/t C.

Table 14.12: Net Costs of Carbon Sequestered under No-till Agriculture[a]

Region	Crop	Cost per tC at 25 cm	Cost per tC at 50 cm
Great Plains	Wheat	$350.11	***
	Other crop	$312.50	$440.55
Corn Belt	Wheat	$132.21	$173.36
	Other crop	$178.21	$183.15

Notes:
[a] Costs in 2001 US dollars for crops harvested in 1986 (the sample mean) after 20 years of NT. *** indicates that under those conditions, NT is not expected to result in net carbon sequestration compared to CT

McCarl and Schneider (2000, pp.150–1) point out that, by reducing the intensity of tillage, soil organic matter will increase, resulting in an increase in carbon storage as well as greater moisture-holding capacity, which could result in a reduced need for irrigation. However, reduced tillage also has negative environmental impacts associated with greater use of pesticides for control of weeds, fungus and insects. This may have negative spillover effects on ecological systems and water quality.

Adaptation to Climate Change by the Primary Sectors

It is unlikely that climate change can be avoided. The major expressed concern related to global warming is associated with crop production, the ability of the world to feed itself. Global warming is expected to have a greater impact on northern latitudes, so Canada and Russia should experience the greatest changes. Given lack of good economic and crop production data for Russia, early studies focused on western Canada. Darwin et al. (1995) provide some indication of the extent to which land use in Canada is likely to be affected by climate change. The model employed by these researchers consists of a geographic information system and a computable general equilibrium economic model of the global economy. Climate projections from four global circulation models (GCMs) are used to determine land-use potentials. Land-use potential in their model is based primarily on climate factors (moisture and temperature) since these also affect soil formation.

Results indicate that, "across scenarios, world wheat production increases, while production of nongrains falls. Output of other grains increases or decreases depending on the scenario. Production of livestock and forest products generally increases" (Darwin et al. 1995, p.23). Output of other food products increases in all scenarios, so that "... climate change's overall impact on world food production is likely to be beneficial" (p.26). Real global GDP is projected to increase slightly. However, this is true only if landowners are free to shift into other activities, by taking advantage of new agricultural lands or changing crop mixes. Ignored in these projections is the effect of higher atmospheric CO_2 concentrations on crop yields – the so-called CO_2–fertilization effect, which will increase crop yields by as much as one-third over those projected (see Fround-Williams et al. 1996), but they also used earlier GCM results that projected higher temperatures.

Of all the regions in the model, Canada stands to gain the most from climate change. Canadian GDP is projected to increase by an average of 2.2% across the four GCM scenarios, which is the largest increase in GDP of any region. Cropland is projected to increase by an average of 125%, while output of wheat is projected to increase by an average of 130%, other grains by 274%, nongrains by 456%, and livestock by 256%. Output of forest products also increases (by 33%), although the forestland base is reduced by an average of 7%. Cropland, pasture and forestland are simply more productive under projected global warming, despite the absence of a CO_2–fertilization effect. Much of the increase in arable crop production in Canada comes from a northward shift in the western grain belt at the expense of boreal forest, and a shifting of the highly productive corn belt in the USA into the eastern portion of the grain belt.

Adaptation of forest management to a changing climate will ensure that forest sector returns are maximized. Examples of management adaptation include salvaging dying trees, vegetation control to help offset drought, replanting with more suitable species, and shifting processing capacity to areas where timber is relatively plentiful. In addition, as the frequency of pest outbreaks and forest fires increases, investment in the management of pests and fire is also expected to rise. As the northern fringe of the boreal forest shifts northward, tree planting will help to maintain forested area as land is lost to agriculture on the southern border.

The conclusion from economic research is that climate change is unlikely to bring about reductions in the global supply of primary commodities (including wood products) (Schimmelpfenning et al. 1996). Rather, if economic markets and institutions are sufficiently flexible, landowners will make decisions to take advantage of changes, whether these be production of different crops or new crop/tree varieties, adoption of new management regimes (e.g., greater use of irrigation, enhanced silviculture), or expansion of activities to new areas. However, market failure and policy failure can be obstacles to attainment of enhanced wellbeing in the face of climate change.

Public ownership of forestlands may be one impediment to adaptation. Policy failure occurs, for example, if the public authority requires forest companies to reforest cutover lands on the boreal-grassland interface, thereby preventing their conversion to a better use (pasture or cropland) (van Kooten 1995c). An example of market failure occurs if no account is taken of climate change impacts on recreation and other nontimber benefits of forests, particularly biodiversity.

Sohngen et al. (1999) address questions related to biodiversity and climate change. They link ecosystem productivity and economic trade models to GCM output to demonstrate that climate change leads not only to greater wood fiber output (as predicted by Darwin et al. 1995), but also greater biodiversity. The reason for the increase in biodiversity is that, although all forests become more productive as a result of CO_2 fertilization, there is also greater investment in plantation forests for the same reason. As plantation harvests increase, wood fiber prices fall and natural forests, those that harbor biodiversity, are less susceptible to logging. The area of natural forests unattractive to logging increases.

14.3 CREATING TERRESTRIAL CARBON CREDITS

An emissions-trading system that includes carbon offsets faces two challenges. The first pertains to the creation and acceptability of carbon trading exchanges, while the second relates to the factor that converts an ephemeral carbon offset to a permanent CO_2-emissions reduction.

Carbon Trading and Market Exchanges

Perhaps the most important market-based initiative with respect to forestry and land use is the establishment of the exchange-traded markets for carbon uptake credits. Through exchange farmers could potentially profit from practices that enhance soil carbon or carbon in vegetation, but studies indicate that this will require a well-functioning design mechanism for implementing carbon trading. Indeed, we have seen emission trading schemes fail not because of a lack of interest, but from a breakdown in necessary economic and market conditions, such as imperfect information and high transactions costs. One example in this regard is the Kefi Exchange which has suspended trading (see below).

The Chicago Climate Exchange (CCX) may soon alleviate concerns about the lack of an exchange, at least in part. The CCX was launched early in 2003 as the first North American central market exchange to allow trading of GHGs between industry and agriculture (Sandor and Skees 1999).[2] The purpose of the CCX is to provide price discovery, which will clarify the debate about the costs of emissions reduction and the role of carbon sinks. Carbon sequestration through no-till farming, grass and tree plantings, and other methods will enable farmers to sell carbon credits on the CCX. However, the prices that are "discovered" may not reflect the true costs to society because the CCX is a credit trading scheme as opposed to an allowance trading scheme (Woerdman 2002).

Trading is also possible through the fledgling UK market for carbon emissions allowances (CO2e.com), which began in April 2002. Many British firms already hold agreements to cut emissions under the UK's climate change levy scheme, for which they receive tax rebates on energy use. Companies failing to meet targets are able to buy allowances to offset their above-target emissions. Companies participating in the exchange are hedging their exposure to losing a tax rebate on energy use. By mid-July 2003, carbon was trading for as much as US$10.50/t CO_2, with transaction sizes in the range of 5,000 to 15,000 tonnes. As of May 2003, 900 companies were registered with the climate exchange and 7 Mt CO_2 had been traded. These trades have not involved forestry or agricultural offsets, however.

A number of traders in carbon credits can be found on the internet, including, among others, eCarbontrade, the Kefi exchange, and CleanAir Canada, which is government backed. The Kefi Exchange is a private exchange begun in Alberta by traders with experience in the trading of various commodities on-line, including electricity. However, a CO_2 emissions trading market appears to present a greater challenge. As pointed out on the Kefi Exchange website (van Kooten 2004):

> The on-going uncertainty of the global endorsement of the Kyoto Protocol
> has left the future of the KEFI Exchange in limbo. ... [T]he actual operation
> of the exchange cannot proceed without some clarity in the regulation of
> emissions. As a result of the current stalemate, the KEFI Exchange has
> opted to move to a 'stand down' mode pending a clearer determination of
> the directions to be taken in Alberta and the rest of Canada in respect to
> emission reductions.

Commodity markets, such as the Winnipeg Commodity Exchange, are
also looking into trading carbon emissions and carbon sink credits. With all
the problems, it is not surprising that trades are few and far between,
especially those that involve carbon offsets. Indeed, Australian solicitors
McKean & Park, who were asked to make a judgment on the proposed
Australian trading system, indicate that any trading in carbon credits is
unlikely to occur before 2005. Tietenberg et al. (1998) also indicate that
there are a significant number of obstacles to overcome before trading can
occur, including most importantly a means of verifying emission reduction
and carbon sequestration claims.

Clearly, a market-based approach to carbon sinks will be effective only
in the presence of certain market conditions. For example, carbon offsets
need to be certified, and a method for making exchanges between emission
reductions and offsets needs to be found (see below); as well, an overseeing
body with well-defined rules and regulations is needed. Carbon rights were
first created in legislation in New South Wales, Australia, but they are
rudimentary at best. In order to buy and sell carbon offset credits, it is
necessary to have legislation that delineates the rights of landowners,
owners of trees and owners of carbon, because what any one of these parties
does affects the amount of carbon that is sequestered and stored. Without
clear legislation, buyers of carbon offsets are not assured that they will get
proper credit – their claims to have met their emission reduction targets with
carbon credits is open to dispute.

The problem for agriculture is similar, especially where the landowner
and farmer are not the same. Further, even if all conditions for trade are
present, there remain concerns about the extent of agriculture's willingness
to participate in GHG trading programs due to other indirect costs or
barriers to entry, such as uncertainty about farm payments and subsidies,
implications for trade, or transactions costs associated with the creation of
carbon sinks on agricultural land (van Kooten et al. 2002).

It is imperative to identify methods by which agricultural landowners are
willing to create carbon credits and their capacity to create and market
carbon offsets. In suggesting the use of sinks as a flexible mechanism for

meeting CO_2 emissions goals, it is important to understand landowners' incentives, motivations and preferences. Farmers' preferences for different carbon sequestration methods are likely influenced by the available information and methods, institutional support and structure, and relative risk and uncertainty with regard to maintaining a profitable enterprise and remaining eligible for government programs.

Recent research by van Kooten et al. (2002) into landowners' willingness to plant trees or otherwise create carbon credits suggests that costs may be higher than is often thought, particularly in regions that had previously been treed and where they or their forbears had incurred substantial sacrifice to carve out farms. Further, based on the results of a 2000 survey of agricultural producers in western Canada, landowners appear reluctant to engage in carbon offset trading, stating that they preferred contracts with governments, NGOs or even large firms to conduct specified LULUCF activities. That is, landowners prefer to enter into a contract to change land use (or take on certain activities) over the sale of carbon credits *per se* (see Tables 14.13 and 14.14). However, the research also indicates that there may be high transaction costs associated with contracting that could significantly increase costs of creating carbon offsets.

Temporary Nature of Terrestrial Carbon Sinks

The other problem of mixed CO_2 emissions–carbon offset credit trading concerns the exchange rate used to convert temporary into permanent removal of CO_2 from the atmosphere. Compared to not emitting CO_2 from a fossil fuel source, terrestrial sequestration of carbon is unlikely to be permanent. Yet, temporary removal of carbon is important because it postpones climate change, buys time for technological progress, may be a lower cost option than simply reducing CO_2 emissions, buys time to replace fuel-inefficient capital equipment, allows time for learning, and some temporary sequestration may become permanent (Marland et al. 2001).

Table 14.13: Western Canadian Farmers' Ranking of Means for Establishing Carbon Sinks

Governance structure	Normalized rank
Tree-planting contracts with government/state agency	1.00
Tree-planting contracts with private firms (large CO_2 emitters)	0.87
Sell carbon credits in markets established to allow trade	0.71
Tree-planting contracts with ENGOs	0.44

Table 14.14: Preferences for Activities that Produce Carbon Offsets for Sale: Western Canadian Farmers Responding "Yes" to Survey Questions

Strategy	%
Reduce tillage operations	60.7
Replace tillage summer fallow with chemical fallow	47.4
Reduce summer fallow by increasing cropping intensity	54.1
Plant fast-growing trees in large blocks	23.7
Plant native trees in large blocks	20.7
Plant shelterbelts and/or individual trees	57.8

The ephemeral nature of terrestrial carbon uptake can be addressed in a variety of different ways. First, instead of full credits, partial credits for stored carbon can be provided according to the perceived risk that carbon will be released from the sink at some future date. The buyer or the seller may be required to take out an insurance policy, where the insurer will substitute credits from another carbon sink at the time of default. Alternatively, the buyer or seller can provide some assurance that the temporary activity will be followed by one that results in a permanent emissions reduction. For example, arrangements can be put in place prior to the exchange that, upon default or after some period of time, the carbon offsets are replaced by purchased emission reduction credits. Again, insurance contracts can be used. Insurance can also be used if there is a chance that the carbon contained in a sink is released prematurely, but it is also possible to discount the number of credits provided by the risk of loss (so that a provider may need to convert more land into forest, say, than needed to sequester the agreed upon amount of carbon). However, the risk that default will occur remains. This is especially true in the case of the KP as there is currently no requirement that countries that count terrestrial carbon uptake credits during the commitment period 2008–12 are penalized for their release after 2012.

Another proposal is to employ a conversion factor that translates years of temporary carbon storage into a permanent equivalent can be specified. The IPCC (2000) uses the notion of ton-years to make the conversion from temporary to permanent storage.

Suppose that one ton of carbon-equivalent GHG emissions are to be compensated for by a ton of permanent carbon uptake. If the conversion rate between ton-years of (temporary) carbon sequestration and permanent tons of carbon emissions reductions is k, a LULUCF project that yields one ton of carbon uptake in the current year generates only $1/k$ tons of emission reduction – to cover the one-ton reduction in emissions requires k tons of carbon to be sequestered for one year. The exchange rate ranges from 42 to 150 ton-years of temporary storage to cover one permanent ton, with central estimates around 50:1.

As Marland et al. (2001) note, the ton-year accounting system is flawed: ton-year credits (convertible to permanent tons) can be accumulated while trees grow, for example, with an additional credit earned if the biomass is subsequently burned in place of an energy-equivalent amount of fossil fuel (p.266). To avoid such double counting and the need to establish a conversion factor, the authors propose a rental system for sequestered carbon. A one-ton emission offset credit is earned when the sequestered carbon is rented from a landowner, but, upon release, a debit occurs. "Credit is leased for a finite term, during which someone else accepts responsibility for emissions, and at the end of that term the renter will incur a debit unless the carbon remains sequestered and the lease is renewed" (p.265, emphasis in original). In addition to avoiding the potential for double counting, the landowner (or host country) would not be responsible for the liability after the (short-term) lease expires. Further, rather than the authority establishing a conversion factor, the market for emission credits and carbon credits can be relied upon to determine the conversion rate between permanent and temporary removals of CO_2 from the atmosphere.

The issue of the impermanence of carbon sinks as they relate to the Clean Development Mechanism was considered by COP8 in New Delhi in October 2002. It was resolved that a "workshop" would examine (1) insurance against the destruction or degradation of forest sinks, and (2) the creation of a "temporary" CER unit, denoted TCER, whereby CERs accruing to sinks would expire at the end of each commitment period but would have to be covered by substitute credits at that time or reissued credits if the original project were continued. This issue was to be on the agenda at COP9 in Italy, December 2003.

The methods for dealing with the question of permanence do not resolve the issue of transaction costs related to contracting. Transaction costs could increase overall costs of creating carbon offset credits by a significant amount. Again, the least cost option appears to be that of taxing emissions when they occur, whether these are emissions from LULUCF activities or fossil fuel burning, and providing a subsidy of the same amount as the tax when carbon is sequestered through some sink activity.

14.4 DISCUSSION

The KP failed to implement the best incentive mechanisms from the outset. These would have been a co-ordinated global carbon tax or an international system of permit trading, whereby each country issued sufficient allowances (permits) to cover its 2008–12 emissions with economic agents (large industrial emitters) allowed to buy permits globally. Instead, the KP process initially rejected the idea that countries could purchase cheap emission reductions abroad and, instead, relied on individual countries to choose their own domestic means for achieving their targets. Belatedly, the KP process instituted a number of flexible instruments – CDM, JI and trading of emission credits – that make some sense from an economic perspective. Yet, there remain huge obstacles to the development of credit trading on a large scale, and these are mainly related to lack of institutions and social capital, and capable governments. Further, countries are prone to rely on command and control, and calls for voluntary action, rather than market instruments, and to the lack of social capital and institutions in many countries to establish markets of any kind, let alone markets for emissions trading. As a result, the costs of implementing comparatively small targets such as those of the KP are likely much higher than they need to be, making it less palatable for countries to embark on a major emissions reduction effort.

The main point here, however, is that terrestrial carbon sinks feature prominently in the KP, but reliance on such sinks is often distracting and an excuse for doing nothing to address global warming. Soil scientists, foresters and conservationists more generally are keen to see more forest area and less intensive agricultural operations (reduced tillage and greater soil conservation) – to reduce environmental spillovers. However, the KP is not the appropriate manner for addressing environmental externalities related to land use. Most terrestrial sink activities are ephemeral, and likely to lose their carbon quite quickly after subsidies or "payments" are removed, and countries have been given sink credits for ongoing activities so that the carbon sequestered is not additional. That is, countries can claim carbon credits even though nothing has been done to mitigate climate change. Further, leakages are a particular problem for carbon sinks and may reduce the true amount sequestered by more than 50%, while the costs of creating carbon sink credits is much higher than generally anticipated, so that biological sinks are uneconomic compared to other means for reducing atmospheric CO_2. It is doubtful, therefore, that terrestrial carbon sinks can compete in a proper and truly integrated emissions trading scheme.

There may, nonetheless, be room for some action, perhaps even action compatible with the creation of carbon forest and agricultural sinks, particularly if these are linked to policies that address other forms of environmental spillovers related to land use. For example, tree planting and reduced/zero tillage practices may provide substantial soil conservation benefits that, when combined with carbon-uptake benefits, are worth pursuing from a societal point of view. In many cases, however, it is not more government intervention that is required, but, rather, a reduction in government interventions. Government subsidies often encourage more energy-intensive agriculture, while implicit and explicit subsidies have encouraged land conversion and/or energy consumption. Lobbying by US lumber producers to restrict Canadian imports of softwood lumber has increased prices, resulting in a shift towards the use of more energy-intensive building products, such as steel, aluminum and cement, and less carbon storage in wood products. Such policies and exercise of market power do much to encourage activities that enhance climate change.

NOTES

1. Some analysts believe that the failure to account fully for the sources of all of the build-up of carbon in the atmosphere, the so-called "missing carbon sink", is explained by the expanding forests of the northern hemisphere.
2. Some 33 companies representing about 20% of emissions in the Chicago areas are involved in the CCX (see Canada's *National Post*, Sep. 24, 2002, p.FP10). Participating companies have agreed to reduce their CO_2 emissions by 5% from 1999 levels over five years, purchasing (selling) permits through the CCX to make up for deficiencies (overshooting targets). The companies involved are doing this only in anticipation of future US regulations to control emissions.

References

Adamowicz, W.L., 1995. 'Alternative Valuation Techniques: A Comparison and Movement to a Synthesis', in K.G. Willis and J.T. Corkindale (eds), *Environmental Valuation. New Perspectives*. Wallingford, UK: CAB International, pp.144–59.

Adamowicz, W.L., J.J. Fletcher and T. Graham-Tomasi, 1989. Functional Form and the Statistical Properties of Welfare Measures, *American Journal of Agricultural Economics* 71: 414–20.

Adamowicz, W.L., P. Boxall, M. Williams and J. Louviere, 1998. Stated Preference Approaches to Measuring Passive Use Values: Choice Experiments versus Contingent Valuation, *American Journal of Agricultural Economics* 80(February): 64–75.

Agriculture Canada, 1991. News Release: Federal Government Announces New Safety Net Program for Farmers. Ottawa: Communications Branch, January 11.

Alig, R., D. Adams and B.A. McCarl, 1998. Economic and Ecological Impacts of Forest Policies: Interactions across Forestry and Agriculture, *Ecological Economics* 27: 63–78.

Amelung, T. and M. Diehl, 1992. *Deforestation of Tropical Rain Forests: Economic Causes and Impact on Development*. Tubingen: J.C.B. Mohr.

Anderson, J.R. and J. Thampapillai, 1990. *Soil Conservation in Developing Countries: Project and Policy Intervention*. Policy & Research Series 8. Washington: World Bank.

Arrow, K.J., 1951. *Social Choice and Individual Values*. New Haven: Yale University Press.

Arrow, K.J. and A.C. Fisher, 1974. Environmental Preservation, Uncertainty, and Irreversibility, *Quarterly Journal of Economics* 88: 312–19.

Arrow, K.J. and L. Hurwicz, 1972. 'An Optimality Criterion for Decision Making under Ignorance', in C.F. Carter and J.L. Ford (eds), *Uncertainty and Expectations in Economics: Essays in Honour of G.L.S. Shackle*. Oxford, UK: Basil Blackwell.

Arrow, K., R. Solow, E. Leamer, P. Portney, R. Randner and H. Schuman, 1993. Appendix I – Report of the NOAA Panel on Contingent Valuation, *Federal Register* Vol. 58, No. 10 (January 15), pp.4602–14.

Arrow, K.J., B. Bolin, R. Constanza, P. Dasgupta, C. Folke, C.S. Holling, B.O. Jansson, S. Levin, K.G. Mäler, C. Perrings, D. Pimental, 1995. Economic Growth, Carrying Capacity and the Environment, *Science* 268: 520–21.

Asheim, G.B., 1986. Hartwick's Rule of Open Economies, *Canadian Journal of Economics* 19: 395–402.

Auld, G., B. Cashore and D. Newsom, 2001. 'A Look at Forest Certification through the Eyes of United States Wood and Paper Producers', in *Global Initiatives and Public Policies: First International Conference on Private Forestry in the 21st Century*. Proceedings of a conference held in Atlanta, GA, 25–27 March. 22pp.

Aylward, B., 1992. 'Appropriating the Value of Wildlife and Wildlands', in T.M. Swanson and E.B. Barbier (eds), *Economics for the Wilds*. London, UK: Earthscan, pp.34–64.

Baland, J. and J.P. Platteau, 1996. *Halting Degradation of Natural Resources*. Oxford, UK: Clarendon Press.

Barbier, E.B. and B. Aylward, 1996. Capturing the Pharmaceutical Value of Biodiversity in a Developing Country, *Environmental and Resource Economics* 8: 157–81.

Barbier, E.B. and J. Burgess, 1997. The Economics of Tropical Forest Land Use Options, *Land Economics* 73: 174–95.

Barbier E. B. and A. Markandya, 1990. The Conditions for Achieving Envrionmentally Sustainable Development, *European Economic Review* 34: 659–69.

Barbier, E.B. and M. Rauscher, 1994. Trade, Tropical Deforestation and Policy Interventions, *Environmental and Resource Economics* 4: 75–90.

Barbier, E.B., A. Markandya and D.W. Pearce, 1990. Sustainable Agricultural Development and Project Appraisal. *European Review of Agricultural Economics* 17: 181–96.

Barbier, E.B., J.C. Burgess and C. Folke, 1994. *Paradise Lost? The Ecological Economics of Biodiversity*. London: Earthscan.

Barbier, E., J.C. Burgess, J.T. Bishop and B.A. Aylward, 1994. *The Economics of the Tropical Timber Trade*. London: Earthscan.

Barbier, E.B., N. Bockstael, J.C. Burgess and I. Strand, 1995. The Linkages between the Timber Trade and Tropical Deforestation—Indonesia, *World Economy* 18(3): 411–42.

Barde, J.-P., 2000. 'Environmental Policy and Policy Instruments', in H. Folmer and H.L. Gabel (eds), *Principles of Environmental and Resource Economics*, 2nd edition. Cheltenham, UK and Northampton, MA, USA: Edward Elgar, pp.157–201.

Barlowe, R., 1986. *Land Resource Economics*, 4th edition. Englewood Cliffs, NJ: Prentice Hall.

Barnett, H.J. and C. Morse, 1963. *Scarcity and Growth*. Baltimore: Johns Hopkins University Press.

Barrett, J.W., 1988. 'The Northeast Region', in J.W. Barrett (ed), *Regional Silviculture of the United States*. New York: John Wiley & Sons, pp.25–66.

Bateman, I.J. and K.G. Willis (eds), 1999. *Valuing Environmental Preferences: Theory and Practice of the Contingent Valuation Method in the US, EU, and Developing Countries*. Oxford, UK: Oxford University Press.

Batie, S.S. and A.G. Sappington, 1986. Cross-Compliance as a Soil Conservation Strategy: A Case Study, *American Journal of Agricultural Economics* 68(November): 880–85.

Baumol, W.J. and W.E. Oates, 1988. *The Theory of Environmental Policy*. Second edition. Cambridge, UK: Cambridge University Press.

BC Ministry of Environment, Lands and Parks, 1996. *British Columbia Land Statistics*. Victoria, BC: Government of British Columbia.

BC Ministry of Forests, 1991. *Outdoor Recreation Survey 1989/90. How British Columbians Use and Value their Public Forest Lands for Recreation*. Recreation Branch Technical Report 1991–1. Victoria, BC: Queen's Printer for British Columbia.

BC Ministry of Forests, 1992a. *An Old Growth Strategy for British Columbia*. Victoria, BC: Queen's Printer for British Columbia.

BC Ministry of Forests, 1992b. *An Inventory of Undeveloped Watersheds in British Columbia*. Recreation Branch Technical Report 1992:2. Victoria, BC: Queen's Printer for British Columbia.

BC Ministry of Forests, 1996. *Forest Practices Code: Timber Supply Analysis*. Victoria, BC: Queen's Printer for British Columbia. 33pp.

Bechmann, R., 1990. *Trees and Man: the Forest in the Middle Ages*. New York: Paragon House.

Beckerman, W., 1992. Economic Growth and the Environment. Whose Growth? Whose Environment? *World Development* 20: 481–96.

Beisner, E.C., 1990. *Prospects for Growth*. Westchester, IL: Crossway Books.

Beisner, E.C., 1997. *Where Garden Meets Wilderness*. Grand Rapids, MI: William B. Eerdmans Publishing.

Benson, C.A., 1988. A Need for Extensive Forest Management, *The Forestry Chronicle* 64: 421–30.

Bentkover, J.D., 1986. 'The Role of Benefits Assessment in Public Policy Development', in J.D. Bentkover, V.T. Covello and J. Mumpower (eds), *Benefits Assessment: The State of the Art*. Dordrecht: D. Reidel Publishing Co., pp.1–12.

Berck, P., 1995. 'Empirical Consequences of the Hotelling Principle', in D.W. Bromley (ed), *The Handbook of Environmental Economics*. Cambridge, MA, USA and Oxford, UK: Blackwell Publishers, pp.202–21.

Berck, P. and M. Roberts, 1996. Natural Resource Prices: Will They Ever Turn Up? *Journal of Environmental Economics and Management* 31: 65–78.

Bernstein, S., 2001. *The Compromise of Liberal Environmentalism*. New York: Columbia University Press.

Bernstein, S., 2002. International Institutions and the Framing of Domestic Policies: The Kyoto Protocol and Canada's Response to Climate Change, *Policy Sciences* 35: 203–36.

Bernstein, S. and B. Cashore, 2000. Globalization, Four Paths of Internationalization and Domestic Policy Change: The Case of Eco-forestry Policy Change in British Columbia, Canada, *Canadian Journal of Political Science* 33(1): 67–99.

Berrens, R.P., D.S. Brookshire, M. McKee and C. Schmidt, 1998. Implementing the Safe Minimum Standard Approach, *Land Economics* 74(May): 147–61.

Bhattarai, M. and M. Hammig, 2001. Institutions and the environmental Kuznets Curve for deforestation: A crosscountry analysis for Latin America, Africa and Asia. *World Development* 29: 995–1010.

Binkley, C.S., 1980. Economic Analysis of the Allowable Cut Effect, *Forest Science* 26(4): 633–42.

Binkley, C.S., 1984. Allowable Cute Effects with Even Flow Constraints, *Canadian Journal of Forest Research* 14(3): 317–20.

Binkley, C.S., 1991. Imperfections in Timber Markets: Theory and Practice. Vancouver: University of British Columbia, Faculty of Forestry, mimeograph.

Binkley, C.S., 1987. When is the Optimal Economic Rotation Longer than the Rotation of Maximum Sustained Yield? *Journal of Environmental Economics and Management* 14: 152–58.

Binswanger, H.P., 1989. Brazilian Policies that Encourage Deforestation in the Amazon. Environment Department Working Paper No. 16. Washington, DC: The World Bank. April. 24pp.

Bishop, R.C., 1978. Endangered Species and Uncertainty: The Economics of a Safe Minimum Standard, *American Journal of Agricultural Economics* 60(February): 10–8.

Bishop, R.C. and T.A. Heberlein, 1979. Measuring Values of Extra–Market Goods: Are Indirect Measures Biased? *American Journal of Agricultural Economics* 61: 926–30.

Bishop, R.C. and T.A. Heberlein 1990. 'The Contingent Valuation Method', in R.L. Johnson and G.V. Johnson (eds), *Economic Valuation of Natural Resources: Issues, Theory and Application*. Boulder, CO: Westview, pp.81–104.

Bishop, R.C., P.A. Champ and D.J. Mullarky, 1995. 'Contingent Valuation', in D.W. Bromley (ed), *The Handbook of Environmental Economics*. Cambridge, MA, USA and Oxford, UK: Blackwell Publishers, pp.629–54.

Boadway, R.W., 1974. The Welfare Foundations of Cost–Benefit Analysis. *Economic Journal* 84: 426–39.

Boadway, R.W. and N. Bruce, 1984. *Welfare Economics*. New York: Basil Blackwell, Chapter 7.

Bockstael, N.E. and K.E. McConnell, 1993. Public Goods as Characteristics of Nonmarket Commodities, *Economic Journal* 103(9): 1244–57.

Bohm, P. and P.-O. Hesselborn, 1999. 'Transportation and Environmental Policy', in H. Folmer and T. Tietenberg (eds), *International Yearbook of Environmental and Resource Economics 1999/2000*. Cheltenham, UK and Northampton, MA, USA: Edward Elgar, pp.1–43.

Boserup, E., 1965. *The Conditions of Agricultural Growth: The Economics of Agrarian Change under Population Pressure*. Chicago: Aldine.

Bovenberg, A.L. and L.H. Goulder, 1996. Optimal Environmental Taxation in the Presence of Other Taxes: General-Equilibrium Analysis, *American Economic Review* 86(4): 985–1000.

Bowes, M.D. and J.V. Krutilla, 1989. *Multiple-Use Management: The Economics of Public Forestlands*. Washington: Resources for the Future.

Boyce, J.K., 1994. Inequality as a Cause of Environmental Degradation, *Ecological Economics* 11: 169–78.

Boyle, K.J., F.R. Johnson, D.W. McCollum, W.H. Desvousges, R.W. Dunford and S.P. Hudson, 1996. Valuing Public Goods: Discrete versus Continuous Contingent-Valuation Responses, *Land Economics* 72(August): 381–96.

Brännlund, R., P.O. Johansson and K.-G. Löfgren, 1985. An Econometric Analysis of Aggregate Sawtimber and Pulpwood Supply in Sweden, *Forest Science* 31: 595–606.

Bratton, S.P., 1992. *Six Billion & More: Human Population Regulation and Christian Ethics*. Louisville, KY: Westminster/John Knox Press.

Bromley, D.W., 1999. *Sustaining Development. Environmental Resources in Developing Countries*. Cheltenham, UK and Northampton, MA, USA: Edward Elgar.

Brown, K. and D.W. Pearce (eds), 1994. *The Causes of Tropical Deforestation*. London: UCL Press.

Brown, S., C. Hall, W. Knabe, J. Raich, M. Trexler and P. Woomer, 1993. 'Tropical Forests: Their Past, Present, and Potential Future Role in the Terrestrial Carbon Budget, in Terrestrial Biospheric Carbon Fluxes', in J. Wisniewski and R.N. Sampson (eds), *Quantification of Sinks and Sources of CO$_2$.* Dordrecht: Kluwer Academic Publishers, pp.71–94.

Buchanan, J.M. and W.C. Stubblebine, 1962. Externality, *Economica* 29(November): 371–84.

Budiansky, S., 1995. *Nature's Keepers*. New York: The Free Press.

Bulte, E.H. and G.C. van Kooten, 1999. Marginal Valuation of Charismatic Species: Implications for Conservation, *Environmental and Resource Economics* 14(1 July): 119–30.

Bulte, E., M. Joenje and H. Jansen, 1997. Socially Optimal Forest Stocks in Developing Countries: Theory and Application to the Atlantic Zone of Costa Rica. Department of Development Economics Working Paper, Wageningen Agricultural University, Wageningen, Netherlands. Mimeo. 18pp.

Bulte, E.H., D.P. van Soest, G.C. van Kooten and R. Schipper, 2002. Forest Conservation in Costa Rica: Optimal Forest Stocks under Uncertainty and Rising Non-use Benefits, *American Journal of Agricultural Economics* 84(February): 150–60.

Buongiorno, J. and J.K. Gilless, 1987. *Forest Management and Economics*. New York: MacMillan.

Calish, S., R.D. Fight and D.E. Teeguarden, 1978. How Do Nontimber Values Affect Douglas-fir Rotations? *Journal of Forestry* 76(April): 217–21.

Canadian Forest Service, 2000. Canada–United States Softwood Lumber Agreement. Quarterly Statistical Monitor No. 14. Ottawa: Natural Resources Canada.

Carranza, C.F., B.A. Aylward, J. Echeverria, J.A. Tosi, and R. Mejias, 1996. *Valoracion de los servicios ambientales de los bosques de Costa Rica*. Document prepared for ODA–MINAE. San Jose, Costa Rica: Centro Cientifico Tropical. 78pp.

Carson, R.T., N.E. Flores and N.F. Meade, 1996. Contingent Valuation: Controversies and Evidence. Discussion paper #96–36, Department of Economics, University of California, San Diego.

Carson, R.T., W.H. Hanemann, R.J. Kopp, J.A. Krosnick, R.C. Mitchell, S. Presser, P.A. Ruud, V.K. Smith, M. Conaway and K. Martin, 1997. Temporal Reliability of Estimates from Contingent Valuation, *Land Economics* 73(2): 151–63.

Cashore, B., G. Auld, D. Newsom, 2004. *Governing Through Markets: Forest Certification and the Emergence of Non-state Authority*. New Haven, CT: Yale University Press.

Cashore, B., G.C. van Kooten, I. Vertinsky, G. Auld and J. Affolderbach, 2004. Private or Self-Regulation: A Comparative Study of Forest Certification Choices in Canada, the United States and Germany, *Forest Policy & Economics*, in press.

Caspersen, J.P., S.W. Pacala, J.C. Jenkins, G.C. Hurtt, P.R. Moorcroft and R.A. Birdsey, 2000. Contributions of Land-Use History to Carbon Accumulation in U.S. Forests, *Science* 290(10 November): 1148–51.

Castle, E.N., R.P. Berrens and R.M. Adams, 1994. Natural Resource Damage Assessment: Speculations About a Missing Perspective, *Land Economics* 70(August): 378–85.

Chant, J.F., D.G. McFetridge and D.A. Smith, 1990. 'The Economics of the Conserver Society', in W. Block (ed), *Economics and the Environment*. Vancouver, BC: The Fraser Institute, pp.1–93.

Chipman, J.S. and J.C. Moore, 1978. The New Welfare Economics 1939–1974, *International Economic Review* 19(October): 547–84.

Chomitz, K.M., 2000. Evaluating Carbon Offsets from Forestry and Energy Projects: How do they Compare? Working Paper. Washington, DC: World Bank, Development Research Group. (As found at www.worldbank.org/research, November).

Ciriacy-Wantrup, S.V., 1968. *Resource Conservation. Economics and Policies*, 3rd edition. Berkeley, CA: University of California, Agricultural Experiment Station (original 1952).

Clark, E.H., J.A. Haverkamp and W. Chapman, 1985. *Eroding Soils: The Off-Farm Impacts*. Washington: The Conservation Foundation.

Clawson, M., 1959. *Measuring the Demand for and Value of Outdoor Recreation*. RFF Reprint #10. Washington: Resources for the Future.

Coase, R., 1960. The Problem of Social Cost. *Journal of Law and Economics* 3(October): 1–44.

COFI, 1994. Review of Government Estimates of the Costs and Benefits of the Proposed Forest Practices Code. Vancouver: Council of Forest Industries of British Columbia. March.

Common, M., 1995. *Sustainability and Policy: Limits to Economics*. Sydney: Cambridge University Press.

Common, M. and C. Perrings, 1992. Towards an Ecological Economics of Sustainability, *Ecological Economics* 6: 7–34.

Common, M.S., I. Reid and R.K. Blamey, 1997. Do Existence Values for Cost Benefit Analysis Exist? *Environmental and Resource Economics* 9: 225–38.

Conrad, J.M., 1999. *Resource Economics*. Cambridge, UK: Cambridge University Press.

Copithorne, L., 1979. *Natural Resources and Regional Disparities*. Report prepared for the Economic Council of Canada. Ottawa: Ministry of Supply and Services.

Corbett, R. (ed), 1990. *Protecting Our Common Future: Conflict Resolution Within the Farming Community*. Ottawa: The Canada Mortgage and Housing Corporation.

Cory, D.C. and W.E. Martin, 1985. Valuing Wildlife for Efficient Multiple Use, *Western Journal of Agricultural Economics* 10: 282–93.

Costanza, R., R. d'Arge, R. de Groot, S. Farber, M. Grasso, B. Hannon, K. Limburg, S. Naeem, R.V. O'Neill, J. Paruelo, R.G. Raskin, P. Sutton and M. van den Belt, 1997. The Value of the World's Ecosystem Services and Natural Capital, *Nature* 387: 253–61.

Cropper, M. and C. Griffiths, 1994. The Interaction of Population Growth and Environmental Quality, *American Economic Review* 84(May): 250–54.

Crosson, P.R. and N.J. Rosenberg, 1989. Strategies for Agriculture, *Scientific American* 261(3 September): 128–35.

Crowards, T., 1997. Non-use Values and the Environment: Economic and Ethical Motivations, *Environmental Values* 6: 143–67.

Cummings, R.G., D.S. Brookshire and W.D. Schulze (eds), 1986. *Valuing Environmental Goods: An Assessment of the Contingent Valuation Method.* Totowa, NJ: Rowman and Allanheld.

Daly, H.E. and J.B. Cobb Jr., 1994. *For the Common Good.* 2nd edition. Boston: Beacon Press.

Darwin, R., M. Tsigas, J. Lewandrowski and A. Raneses, 1995. *World Agriculture and Climate Change. Economic Adaptations.* Agricultural Economic Report No. 703. US Department of Agriculture, Economic Research Service, Washington. June. 86pp.

Dasgupta, P.S., 1993. 'Natural Resources in an Age of Substitutability', in A.V. Kneese and J.L. Sweeney (eds), *Handbook of Natural Resource and Energy Economics,* Vol. 3. Amsterdam: Elsevier, pp.855–80.

Dasgupta, P.S., 1995. The Population Problem: Theory and Evidence, *Journal of Economic Literature* 33: 1879–902.

Dasgupta, P.S., 2000. 'Economic Progress and the Idea of Social Capital', in P. Dasgupta and I. Serageldin (eds), *Social Capital. A Multifaceted Perspective.* Washington, DC: The World Bank, pp.325–424.

Dasgupta, P.S., 2002. Public vs Private and Constant vs Hyperbolic. Keynote speech, 2nd World Congess of Environmental and Resource Economists, Monterey, CA, June 24.

Dasgupta, P.S., S. Marglin and A.K. Sen, 1972. *Guidelines for Project Evaluation.* New York: United Nations International Development Organization.

Dauvergne, P., 1997. *Shadows in the Forest. Japan and the Politics of Timber in Southeast Asia.* Cambridge, MA: The MIT Press.

de Beer, J and M.J. McDermott, 1989. *The Economic Value of Non-Timber Forest Products in Southeast Asia.* Amsterdam: IUCN.

de Groot, R., 1992. *Functions of Nature.* Dordrecht: Wolters–Noordhoff.

de Saussay, C., 1987. Land Tenure Systems and Forest Policy. FAO Legislative Study No. 41. Rome: Food and Agriculture Organization.

Deacon, R., 1994. Deforestation and the Rule of Law in a Cross-Section of Countries, *Land Economics* 70: 414–30.

Diamond, P.A. and J.A. Hausman, 1994. Is Some Number Better than No Number? *Journal of Economic Perspectives* 8(Fall): 45–64.

Downton, M.W., 1995. Measuring Tropical Deforestation: Development of Methods, *Environmental Conservation* 22(Autumn): 229–40.

Drake, L., 1992. The Nonmarket Value of the Swedish Agricultural Landscape, *European Review of Agricultural Economics* 19: 351–64.

Eberstadt, N., 1995. 'Population, Food and Income: Global Trends in the Twentieth Century', in R. Bailey (ed), *The True State of the Planet.* New York, NY: The Free Press, pp.7–47.

Eckstein, O., 1958. *Water Resource Development: The Economics of Project Evaluation.* Cambridge: Harvard University Press.

Edwards, J.A., K.C. Gibbs, L.J. Guedry and H.H. Stoevener, 1976. *The Demand for Non-Unique Outdoor Recreational Services: Methodological Issues*. Corvallis: Oregon Agricultural Experiment Station Technical Bulletin. May.

Edwards, S.R., 1995. 'Conserving Biodiversity. Resource for Our Future', in R. Bailey (ed), *The True State of the Planet*. New York, NY: The Free Press, pp.212–65.

Ehrhardt-Martinez, K., E.M. Crenshaw and J.C. Jenkins, 2002. Deforestation and the environmental Kuznets Curve: A cross-national investigation of intervening mechanisms, *Social Science Quarterly* 83: 226–43.

Ehrlich, P.R. and A.H. Ehrlich, 1972. *Population. Resources. Environment. Issues in Human Ecology*, 2nd edition. San Francisco, CA: W.H. Freeman.

Ehrlich, P.R. and A.H. Ehrlich, 1990. *The Population Explosion*. New York, NY: Random House.

Ehrlich, P.R. and A.H. Ehrlich, 1991. *Healing the Planet*. New York, NY: Addison Wesley.

Ehui, S.K. and T.W. Hertel, 1989. Deforestation and Agricultural Productivity in the Côte d'Ivoire, *American Journal of Agricultural Economics* 70(August): 703–11.

Ehui, S.K., T.W. Hertel and P.V. Preckel, 1990. Forest Resource Depletion, Soil Dynamics and Agricultural Dynamics in the Tropics, *Journal of Environmental Economics and Management* 18: 136–54.

El Serafy, S., 1989. 'The Proper Calculation of Income from Depletable Natural Resources', in Y.J. Ahmad, S. El Serafy and E. Lutz (eds), *Environmental Accounting for Sustainable Development*. Washington: The World Bank.

Epstein, R.A., 1985. *Takings. Private Property and the Power of Eminent Domain*. Cambridge, MA: Harvard University Press.

Ervin, D.E., J.B. Fitch, R.K. Godwin, W.B. Shepard and H.H. Stoevener, 1977. *Land Use Control: Evaluating Economic and Political Effects*. Cambridge, MA: Ballinger.

Eswaran, H., P. Reich and F. Beinroth, 2001. 'Global Desertification Tension Zones', in D.E. Stott, R.H. Mohtar and G.C. Steinhardt (eds), Sustaining the Global Farm. Selected papers from the 10th International Soil Conservation Organization Meeting held at Purdue University, May 24-29. pp.24–28.

FAO (Food and Agriculture Organization), 1992. *FAO Yearbook: Forest Products, 1981–1992*. FAO Forestry Series No. 27. Rome: Food and Agriculture Organization of the United Nations.

FAO, 1993. *Forest Resources Assessment 1990*. Paper 112. Rome: Food and Agriculture Organization of the United Nations.

FAO, 1997. *State of the World's Forests 1997*. Rome: Food and Agriculture Organization of the United Nations.

FAO, 2001. *State of the World's Forests 2001*. Rome: Food and Agriculture Organization.

FAO, 2003. FAOSTAT online statistical database. Found at: http://apps.fao.org/page/collections?subset=forestry (August 9).

Farmer, M.C. and A. Randall, 1998. The Rationality of a Safe Minimum Standard, *Land Economics* 74(August): 287–302.

Farzin, H., 1992. The Time Path of Scarcity Rent in the Theory of Exhaustible Resources, *Economic Journal* 102: 813–30.

Faustmann, M., 1849. On the Determination of the Value which Forest Land and Immature Stands Possess for Forestry. Reprinted in *Journal of Forest Economics* 1(1995/1): 7–44.

Feeney, D., S. Hanna and A.F. McEvoy, 1996. Questioning the Assumptions of the 'Tragedy of the Commons' Model of Fisheries, *Land Economics* 72: 187–205.

Fischhoff, B., S. Lichtenstein, P. Slovic, S.L. Derby and R.L. Keeney, 1981. *Acceptable Risk*. Cambridge, UK: Cambridge University Press.

Fisher, A.C., 1981. *Resource and Environmental Economics*. Cambridge, UK: Cambridge University Press.

Flowerdew, A. D. J., 1972. 'Choosing a Site for the Third London Airport: The Roskill Commission's Approach', in R. Layard (ed), *Cost-Benefit Analysis*. Middlesex, UK: Penguin Books, Chapter 17.

Freeman, A.M. III, 1979. *The Benefits of Environmental Improvement. Theory and Practice*. Baltimore: Johns Hopkins University Press.

Freeman, A.M. III, 1993. *The Measurement of Environmental and Resource Values: Theory and Methods*. Washington, DC: Resources for the Future.

Freeman, A.M. III, 1995. 'Hedonic Pricing Methods', in D.W. Bromley (ed), *The Handbook of Environmental Economics*. Cambridge, MA, USA and Oxford, UK: Blackwell Publishers, pp.672–86.

Froster, L., C.P. Bardos and D.D. Southgate, 1987. Soil Erosion and Water Conservation and Treatment Costs, *Journal of Soil and Water Conservation* 42(5): 340–52.

Fround-Williams, R.J., R. Harrington, T.J. Hocking, H.G. Smith and T.H. Thomas (eds), 1996. *Implications of Global Environmental Change for Crops in Europe*. Special issue of *Aspects of Applied Biology*, Volume 45 (annual).

Fukuyama, F., 1992. *The End of Time and the Last Man*. New York: The Free Press.

Fukuyama, F., 1995. *Trust. The Social Virtues and the Creation of Prosperity*. New York: The Free Press.

Fukuyama, F., 1999. *The Great Disruption. Human Nature and the Reconstitution of Social Order*. New York: The Free Press.

Fukuyama, F., 2002. Social Capital and Development: The Coming Agenda, *SAIS Review* 22(1 Winter–Spring): 23–37.

Furubotn, E.G. and R. Richter, 1997. *Institutions and Economic Theory. The Contribution of the New Institutional Economics*. Ann Arbor, MI: University of Michigan Press.

Gaffney, M.M., 1965. Soil Depletion and Land Rent, *Natural Resources Journal* 4(January): 537–57.

George, H., 1879 (1929). Progress and Poverty: An Inquiry into the Cause of Industrial Depression and of Increase of Want with Increase in Wealth. New York: Modern Library.

Gittinger, J.P., 1982. *Economic Analysis of Agricultural Projects*, 2nd edition. Baltimore: The Johns Hopkins University Press.

Gowdy, J.M., 1997. The Value of Biodiversity: Markets, Society and Ecosystems, *Land Economics* 73: 25–41.

Grafton, R.Q., R.W. Lynch and H.W. Nelson, 1998. British Columbia's Stumpage System: Economic and Trade Policy Implications, *Canadian Public Policy* 24(May): S41–50.

Graham-Tomasi, T., 1995. 'Quasi-Option Value', in D.W. Bromley (ed), *The Handbook of Environmental Economics*. Cambridge, MA, USA and Oxford, UK: Blackwell Publishers, pp.594–614.

Grainger, A., 1993. *Controlling Tropical Deforestation*. London: Earthscan Publications.

Gregory, R., S. Lichtenstein and P. Slovic, 1993. Valuing Environmental Resources: A Constructive Approach, *Journal of Risk and Uncertainty* 7(Oct): 177–97.

Grossman, G.M., 1995. 'Pollution and Growth: What do we Know?' in I. Goldin and L. Winters (eds), *The Economics of Sustainable Development*, OECD Publication. Cambridge, UK: Cambridge University Press, pp.977–87.

Grossman, G.M. and A.B. Krueger, 1995. Economic Growth and the Environment, *Quarterly Journal of Economics* 112: 353–78.

Grubb, M., 1990. *Energy Policies and the Greenhouse Effect, Vol. 1. Policy Appraisal*. Dartmouth: The Royal Institute of International Affairs.

Haener, M.K. and M.K. Luckert, 1998. Forest Certification: Economic Issues and Welfare Implications, *Canadian Public Policy*, 24(S2): 83–94.

Hagen, D.A., J.W. Vincent and P.G. Welle, 1992. Benefits of Preserving Old-Growth Forests and the Spotted Owl, *Contemporary Policy Issues* 10(April): 13–26.

Hall, D. and J. Hall, 1984. Concepts and Measures of Natural Resource Scarcity, *Journal of Environmental Economics and Management* 11: 363–79.

Hall, J.A., 1985. *Powers and Liberties. The Causes and Consequences of the Rise of the West*. London: Penguin Books.

Halvorsen, R. and T. Smith, 1991. A Test of the Theory of Exhaustible Resources, *Quarterly Journal of Economics* 56: 123–46.

Hamilton, G., 1997. Frustrated silviculture contractors get less work, *Vancouver Sun*, Friday, February 7. pp.D1, D19.

Hamilton, J.R., N.K. Whittlesey, M.H. Robison and J. Ellis, 1991. Economic Impacts, Value Added, and Benefits in Regional Project Analysis, *American Journal of Agricultural Economics* 73(May): 334–44.

Hammack, J. and G.L. Brown, Jr., 1974. *Waterfowl and Wetlands: Toward Bioeconomic Analysis*. Baltimore, MD: Johns Hopkins University Press.

Hanemann, W.M., 1984. Welfare Evaluations in Contingent Valuation Experiments with Discrete Responses, *American Journal of Agricultural Economics* 66: 332–41.

Hanemann, W.M., 1991. Willingness to Pay and Willingness to Accept: How Much can they Differ? *American Economic Review* 81(June): 635–47.

Hanemann, W.M., 1994. Valuing the Environment through Contingent Valuation, *Journal of Economic Perspectives* 8(Fall): 19–44.

Hanemann, W.M. and B. Kriström, 1995. 'Preference Uncertainty, Optimal Designs and Spikes', in P.-O. Johansson, B. Kriström and K.-G. Mäler (eds), *Current Issues in Environmental Economics,* Manchester, UK: Manchester University Press, pp.58–77.

Hanley, N., 2000. 'Cost–benefit Analysis', in H. Folmer and H.L. Gabel (eds), *Principles of Environmental and Resource Economics*, 2nd edition. Cheltenham, UK and Northampton, MA, USA: Edward Elgar, pp.104–29.

Hanley, N., R.E. Wright and V. Adamowicz, 1998. Using Choice Experiments to Value the Environment, *Environmental and Resource Economics* 11(Special): 413–28.

Harberger, A.C., 1972. *Project Evaluation. Collected Papers*. Chicago: University of Chicago Press.

Hardie, I.W., P.J. Parks and G.C. van Kooten, 2004. 'The Economics of Land Use at the Intensive and Extensive Margins', in H. Folmer and T. Tietenberg (eds), *International Yearbook of Environmental & Resource Economics, 2003/2004*. Cheltenham, UK and Northampton, MA, USA: Edward Elgar, in press.

Harris, M., 1998. *Lament for an Ocean*. Toronto: McClelland & Stewart.

Harrison, G.W., 1989. Theory and Misbehaviour of First-Price Auctions, *American Economic Review* 79(September): 749–62.

Harrison, G.W. and B. Kriström, 1995. 'On the Interpretation of Responses in Contingent Valuation Surveys', in P.-O. Johansson, B. Kriström and K.-G. Mäler (eds), *Current Issues in Environmental Economics*. Manchester, UK: Manchester University Press, pp.35–7.

Hart, O.D., A. Shleifer and R.W. Vishny, 1997. The Proper Scope of Government: Theory and an Application to Prisons, *Quarterly Journal of Economics* 112(4): 1127–61.

Hartman, R., 1976. The Harvesting Decision when a Standing Forest has Value. *Economic Inquiry* 16: 52–8.

Hartwick, J.M., 1977. Intergenerational Equity and the Investing of Rents from Exhaustible Resources, *American Economic Review* 66: 972–4.

Hartwick, J.M. and N. Olewiler, 1998. *The Economics of Natural Resource Use*, 2nd edition. New York: Harper and Row.

Hausman, J.A. (ed), 1993. *Contingent Valuation: A Critical Assessment*. Amsterdam: North Holland.

Hecht, N., 1965. From Sesin to Sit-in: Evolving Property Concepts, *Boston University Law Review* 45: 435–66.

Helfand, G.E. and M.D. Whitney, 1994. Efficient Multiple-Use Forestry May Require Land-Use Specialization: Comment, *Land Economics* 70(August): 391–5.

Heywood, V.H. and S.N. Stuart, 1992. 'Species extinctions in tropical forests', in T.C. Whitmore and J.A. Sayer (eds), *Tropical Deforestation and Species Extinction*. London, UK: Chapman and Hall, pp.91–117.

Hicks, J.R., 1939. The Foundations of Welfare Economics, *Economic Journal* 49(December): 696–712.

Hodge, I., 1984. Uncertainty, Irreversibility and the Loss of Agricultural Land, *Journal of Agricultural Economics* 35(May): 191–202.

Hof, J., 1993. *Coactive Forest Management*. San Diego, CA: Academic Press.

Holechek, J.L., R.D. Pieper and C.H. Herbel, 1989. *Range Management. Principles and Practices*. Englewood Cliffs, NJ: Regents/Prentice Hall.

Holling, C.S., 1973. Resilience and Stability of Ecological Systems, *Annual Review of Ecological Systems* 4: 1–24.

Holling, C.S., D.W. Schindler, B.W. Walker and J. Roughgarden, 1995. 'Biodiversity in the Functioning of Ecosystems: An Ecological Synthesis', in C. Perrings, K.-G. Mäler, C. Folke, C.S. Holling and B.-O. Jansson (eds), *Biodiversity Loss*. New York, NY: Cambridge University Press, pp.44–83.

Homma, A.K.O., 1994. 'Plant Extractavism in the Amazon: Limitations and Possibilities', in M. Clüsener-Godt and I. Sachs (eds), *Extractavism in the Brazilian Amazon: Perspectives on Regional Development*. Paris: MAB Digest 18, UNESCO, pp.34–57.

Houghton, R.A., 1993. 'The Role of the World's Forests in Global Warming', in K. Ramakrishna and G.M. Woodwell (eds), *The Worlds Forests for the Future: Their Use and Conservation*. New Haven: Yale University Press.

Howarth, R.B. and R.B. Norgaard, 1993. Intergenerational Changes and the Social Discount Rate, *Environmental and Resource Economics* 3(4): 337–58.

Howarth, R.B. and R.B. Norgaard, 1995. 'Intergenerational Choices under Global Environmental Change', in D.W. Bromley (ed), *The Handbook of Environmental Economics*. Cambridge, MA, USA and Oxford, UK: Blackwell Publishers, pp.111–38.

Howe, C.W., 1979. *Natural Resource Economics*. Toronto: John Wiley & Sons.

Hueting, R., 1989. 'Correcting National Income for Environmental Losses: Towards a Practical Solution', in Y. Ahmed, S. El Serafy and E. Lutz (eds), *Environmental Accounting for Sustainable Development*. Washington, DC: The World Bank.

Hughes, J.B., G.C. Daily and P.R. Ehrlich, 1997. Population Diversity: Its Extent and Extinction, *Science* 278: 689–92.

Hummel, F.C., 1989. Forestry Policies in Europe: An Analysis. FAO Forestry Paper No. 92. Rome: Food and Agriculture Organization.

Huszar, P.C. and S.L. Piper, 1986. Estimating the Off-Site Costs of Wind Erosion in New Mexico, *Journal of Soil and Water Conservation* 41: 414–6.

Hyde, W.F. and R.A. Sedjo, 1992. Managing Tropical Forests: Reflections on the Rent Distribution Discussion, *Land Economics* 68(3): 343–50.

Hyde, W.F. and J.E. Seve, 1991. 'Malawi: A Rapid Economic Appraisal of Smallholder Response to Severe Deforestation', in R. Haynes, P. Harou and J. Mirowski (eds), *Pre-proceedings of Working Groups S6.03–03 and S6.10–00; Meetings at the 10th World Congress*. Paris: International Union of Forest Research Organizations.

IBRD, 1992. *World Development Report 1992: Development and the Environment*. New York: Oxford University Press.

IPCC (Intergovernmental Panel on Climate Change), 1996a. *Climate Change 1995: Economic and Social Dimensions of Climate Change*. New York: Cambridge University Press.

IPCC, 1996. *Climate Change 1995b. Impacts, Adaptations and Mitigation of Climate Change: Scientific–Technical Analysis* edited by R.T. Watson, M.C. Zinyowera, R.H. Moss and D.J. Dokken. Cambridge, UK: Cambridge University Press.

IPCC, 2000. *Land Use, Land-use Change, and Forestry*. New York: Cambridge University Press.

Irwin, E.G., 2002. The Effects of Open Space on Residential Property Values, *Land Economics* 78(4): 465–81.

Irwin, J.R., P. Slovic, S. Lichtenstein and G.H. McClelland, 1993. Preference Reversals and the Measurement of Environmental Values, *Journal of Risk and Uncertainty* 6(Jan): 5–18.

Jeppe, W.J.O., 1980. *Bophuthatswana. Land Tenure and Development*. Cape Town: Maskew Miller.

Johansson, P.-O., 1987. *The Economic Theory and Measurement of Environmental Benefits*. Cambridge, UK: Cambridge University Press.

Johansson, P.-O., 1991. *An Introduction to Modern Welfare Economics*. Cambridge, UK: Cambridge University Press.

Johansson, P.-O., 1993. *Cost–Benefit Analysis and Environmental Change*. Cambridge, UK: Cambridge University Press.

Just, R.E., D.L. Hueth and A. Schmitz, 1982. *Applied Welfare Economics and Public Policy*. Englewood Cliffs, NJ: Prentice–Hall.

Kahneman, D. and J.L. Knetsch, 1992a. Valuing Public Goods: The Purchase of Moral Satisfaction, *Journal of Environmental Economics and Management* 22: 57–70.

Kahneman, D. and J.L. Knetsch, 1992b. Contingent Valuation and the Value of Public Goods: Reply, *Journal of Environmental Economics and Management* 22: 90–4.

Kahneman, D. and I. Ritov, 1994. Determinants of Stated Willingness to Pay for Public Goods: A Study in the Headline Method, *Journal of Risk and Uncertainty* 9: 5–38.

Kahneman, D. and A. Tversky, 1979. Prospect Theory: An Analysis of Decisions under Risk, *Econometrica* 47: 263–91.

Kahneman, D., J.L. Knetsch and R.H. Thaler, 1990. Experimental Tests of the Endowment Effect and the Coase Theorem, *Journal of Political Economy* 98(December): 1325–48.

Kaimowitz, D. and A. Angelsen, 1997. *A Guide to Economic Models of Deforestation*. Jakarta, Indonesia: Centre of International Forestry Research. Mimeograph. 96pp.

Kaimowitz, D. and A. Angelsen, 1998. *Economic Models of Tropical Deforestation. A Review*. Bogor, Indonesia: CIFOR.

Kaldor, N., 1939. Welfare Propositions of Economics and Interpersonal Comparisons of Utility, *Economic Journal* 49(September): 549–52.

Kanninen, B.J., 1993. Optimal Experimental Design for Double-Bounded Dichotomous Choice Contingent Valuation, *Land Economics* 69: 138–46.

Karl, H. and C. Orwat, 2000. 'Environmental marketing and public policy', in H. Folmer and H.L. Gabel (eds), *Principles of Environmental and Resource Economics*, 2nd edition. Cheltenham, UK and Northampton, MA, USA: Edward Elgar, pp.363–95.

Kealy, H.J. and R.W. Turner, 1993. Test of the Equality of Close-Ended and Open-Ended Contingent Valuations, *American Jouirnal of Agricultural Economics* 75: 321–31.

Keith, J.E. and K.S. Lyon, 1985. Valuing Wildlife Management: A Utah Deer Herd, *Western Journal of Agricultural Economics* 10: 216–22.

Kelly, A.C., 1988, Economic Consequences of Population Change in the Third World, *Journal of Economic Literature* 26: 1685–728.

Kennedy, J.O.S., 1987. Uncertainty, Irreversibility and the Loss of Agricultural Land: A Reconsideration, *Journal of Agricultural Economics* 38(January): 75–80.

Kline, J. and D. Wilchens, 1996. Public Preferences Regarding the Goals of Farmland Preservation Programs, *Land Economics* 72: 538–49.

Knetsch, J., 1989. The Endowment Effect and Evidence of Nonreversible Indifference Curves, *American Economic Review* 79(December): 1277–84.

Knetsch, J.L., 1993. 'Resource Economics: Persistent Conventions and Contrary Evidence', in W.L Adamowicz, W. White and W.E. Phillips (eds), *Forestry and the Environment: Economic Perspectives*, Wallingford, UK: CAB International, pp.251–61.

Knetsch, J.L., 1995. Asymmetric Valuation of Gains and Losses and Preference Order Assumptions, *Economic Inquiry* 33: 134–41.

Knetsch, J.L., 2000. 'Environmental Valuations and Standard Theory: behavioural findings, context dependence and implications', in H. Folmer and T. Tietenberg (eds), *International Yearbook of Environmental and Resource Economics 2000/2001*. Cheltenham, UK and Northampton, MA, USA: Edward Elgar, pp.267–99.

Korotov, A.V. and T.J. Peck, 1993. Forest Resources of the Industrialized Countries: An ECE/FAO Assessment, *Unasylva* 44(3).

Kramer, R.A. and D.E. Mercer, 1997. Valuing a Global Environmental Good: U.S. Residents' Willingness to Pay to Protect Tropical Rain Forests, *Land Economics* 73(May): 196–210.

Krcmar, E. and G.C. van Kooten, 2003. Timber, Carbon Uptake and Structural Diversity Trade-offs in Forest Management. FEPA Working Paper, University of British Columbia, Vancouver.

Krcmar, E., B. Stennes, G.C. van Kooten and I. Vertinsky, 2001. Carbon Sequestration and Land Management under Uncertainty, *European Journal of Operational Research* 135(December): 616–29.

Kriström, B., 1997. Spike Models in Contingent Valuation, *American Journal of Agricultural Economics* 79(August): 1013–23.

Kriström, B. and T. Laitila, 2003. 'Stated Preference Methods for Environmental Valuation: a Critical Look', in H. Folmer and T. Tietenberg (eds), *The International Yearbook of Environmental and Resource Economics 2003/2004*. Cheltenham, UK and Northampton, MA, USA: Edward Elgar.

Kummar, D. and C.S. Sham, 1994. 'The Causes of Tropical Deforestation: A Quantitative Analysis and Case Study from the Philippines', in D.W. Pearce and K. Brown (eds), *The Causes of Tropical Deforestation*. London, UK: UCL Press.

Kuusela, K., 1994. *Forest Resources in Europe*. European Forest Institute Report. Cambridge, UK: Cambridge University Press.

Kuznets, S., 1955. Economic Growth and Income Inequality, *American Economic Review* 49: 1–28.

La Porta, R., F. Lopez-de-Silanes, A. Shleifer and R.W. Vishny, 1997. Trust in Large Organizations, *American Economic Review* 87: 333–38.

La Porta, R., F. Lopez-de-Silanes, A. Shleifer and R.W. Vishny, 1999. The Quality of the Government, *Journal of Law, Economics & Organization* 15: 222–79.

Landes, D.S., 1998. *The Wealth and Poverty of Nations*. New York: W.W. Norton & Company.

Larmour, P., 1979. The Concept of Rent in 19th Century Economic Thought. Ricardo, Mill, Marx, Walras, and Marshall. Resources Paper No. 36. Vancouver: Department of Economics, Univ. of British Columbia. May. 45pp.

Larson, D.M., 1993. On Measuring Existence Value, *Land Economics* 69(November): 377–88.

Layard, R., 1972. 'Introduction', in R. Layard (ed), *Cost–Benefit Analysis*. Middlesex, UK: Penguin Books, pp.9–70.

Leakey, R. and R. Lewin, 1996. *The Sixth Extinction*. London: Weidenfeld and Nicolson.

Lerohl, M.L. and G.C. van Kooten, 1995. Is Soil Erosion a Problem on the Canadian Prairies? *Prairie Forum* 20(Spring): 107–21.

Lesser, J., D. Dodds and R. Zerbe, 1997. *Environmental Economics and Policy*. New York: Addison–Wesley.

Lévêque, F. and A. Nadaï, 2000. 'A firm's involvement in the policy-making process', in H. Folmer and H.L. Gabel (eds), *Principles of Environmental and Resource Economics*, 2nd edition, Cheltenham, UK and Northampton, MA, USA: Edward Elgar, pp.235–64.

Lewinsky, J., 1913. *The Origin of Property and the Formation of the Village Community*. London: Constable & Company Ltd.

Li, C.-Z., 1996. Semiparametric Estimation of the Binary Choice Model for Contingent Valuation, *Land Economics* 72(November): 462–73.

Li, C.-Z. and L. Mattsson, 1995. Discrete Choice under Preference Uncertainty: an Improved Structural Model for Contingent Valuation, *Journal of Environmental Economics and Management* 28: 256–69.

Lindblom, C.E., 1959. The Science of "Muddling Through", *Public Administration Review* 19: 79–88.

Lipsey, R.G., 1996. *Economic Growth, Technological Change, and Canadian Economic Policy*. Benefactors Lecture, November 6, Vancouver. Toronto: C. D. Howe Institute. 87pp.

Little, I.M.D., 1957. *A Critique of Welfare Economics*. New York: Oxford University Press.

Little, I.M.D. and J.A. Mirrlees, 1974. *Project Appraisal and Planning for Developing Countries*. New York: Basic Books.

Löfgren, K.-G., 2000. 'Markets and Externalities', in H. Folmer and H.L. Gabel (eds), *Principles of Environmental and Resource Economics*, 2nd edition, Cheltenham, UK and Northampton, MA, USA: Edward Elgar, pp.3–33.

Lomborg, B., 2001. *The Skeptical Environmentalist. Measuring the Real State of the World*. Cambridge, UK: Cambridge University Press.

Loomis, J.B. and K. Giraud, 1997. Economic Benefits of Threatened and Endangered Fish and Wildlife Species: Literature Review and Case Study of Values for Preventing Extinction of Fish Species. Fort Collins, CO: Department of Agricultural and Resource Economics, Colorado State University. Mimeograph. 45pp.

Loomis, J.B. and D.S. White, 1996. Economic Benefits of Rare and Endangered Species: Summary and Meta-analysis, *Ecological Economics* 18: 197–206.

Lowe, M.D., 1989. *The Bicycle: Vehicle for a Small Planet*. Worldwatch Paper 90, September. Washington: World Watch Institute.

Lowe, M.D., 1990. *Alternatives to the Automobile: Transport for Livable Cities.* Worldwatch Paper 98, October. Washington: World Watch Institute.

Luckert, M.K. and J.T. Bernard, 1993. What is the Value of Standing Timber?: Difficulties in Merging Theory with Reality, *The Forestry Chronicle* 69: 680–85.

Luckert, M.K. and D. Haley, 1993. Canadian Forest Tenures and the Silvicultural Investment Behavior of Rational Firms, *Canadian Journal of Forest Research* 23: 1060–64.

Lynch, L. and W.N. Musser, 2001. A Relative Efficiency Analysis of Farmland Preservation Programs, *Land Economics* 77(November): 577–94.

MacArthur, R. and E.O. Wilson, 1967. *The Theory of Island Biogeography.* Princeton, NJ: Princeton University Press.

Manley, J. and G.C. van Kooten, 2003. How Costly are Carbon Offsets? A Meta-analysis of Carbon Forest Sinks. Working Paper, Department of Economics, University of Victoria, Victoria, Canada. January. 35pp.

Manley, J., G.C. van Kooten, K. Moeltner and D.W. Johnson, 2003. The Viability of Storing Carbon through No-tillage Cultivation: A Meta-analysis of the Costs and Carbon Benefits of No-till, *Climatic Change* In press.

Mann, C., 1991. Extinction: Are Ecologists Crying Wolf? *Science* 253: 736–38.

Mann, C. and M.L. Plummer, 1995. *Noah's Choice.* New York: Alfred A. Knopf.

Manne, A.S., 1979. 'ETA Macro', in R.S. Pindyck (ed), *Advances in the Economics of Energy and Resources*, Vol. 2. Greenwich, NJ: JAI Press.

Marchak, M.P., 1995. *Logging the Globe.* Montreal and Kingston: McGill–Queen's University Press.

Marglin, S.A., 1963. The Social Rate of Discount and the Optimal Rate of Investment, *Quarterly Journal of Economics* 77: 95–111.

Margolick, M. and R.S. Uhler, 1986. *The Economic Impact of Removing Log Export Restrictions in British Columbia.* FEPA Report 86–2. Vancouver: Forest Economics and Policy Analysis Research Unit.

Marland, G., K. Fruit and R. Sedjo, 2001. Accounting for Sequestered Carbon: The Question of Permanence, *Environmental Science & Policy* 4(6): 259–68.

Martin, W.E. and G.L. Jeffries, 1966. Relating Ranch Prices and Grazing Permit Values to Ranch Productivity, *Journal of Farm Economics* 48: 233–42.

Martin, W.E., J.C. Tinney and R.L. Gum, 1978. A Welfare Economics Analysis of the Potential Competition Between Hunting and Cattle Ranching, *Western Journal of Agricultural Economics* 3(December): 87–97.

Mattey, J.P., 1990. *The Timber Bubble That Burst: Government Policy and the Bailout of 1984.* New York: Oxford University Press.

Maurice, C. and C.W. Smithson, 1984. *The Doomsday Myth.* Stanford, CA: Hoover Institution.

McCarl, B.A. and U.A. Schneider, 2002. U.S. Agriculture's Role in a Greenhouse Gas Emission Mitigation World: An Economic Perspective, *Review of Agricultural Economics* 22: 134–59.

McConnell, K.E., 1997. Does Altruism Undermine Existence Value? *Journal of Environmental Economics and Management* 32: 22–37.

McIntosh, R.A., M.L. Alexander, D.C. Bebb, C. Ridley-Thomas, D. Perrin and T.A. Simons, 1997. *The Financial State of the Forest Industry and Delivered Wood Cost Drivers*. Report prepared for the BC Ministry of Forests. Vancouver: KPMG. 51pp plus App.

McKean, R.N., 1958. *Efficiency in Government Through Systems Analysis*. New York: Wiley.

McKenzie, G.W., 1983. *Measuring Economic Welfare: New Methods*. Cambridge, UK: Cambridge University Press.

McNeill, D. and P. Freiberger, 1993. *Fuzzy Logic*. New York: Touchstone.

Mead, W.J., 1967. *Competition and Oligopsony in the Douglas Fir Lumber Industry*. Los Angeles, CA: University of California Press.

Meadows, D.H., D.L. Meadows, J. Randers and W.W. Behrens III, 1972. *The Limits to Growth*. New York: Universe.

Mendelsohn, R., 1994. Property Rights and Tropical Deforestation, *Oxford Economic Papers* 46: 750–56.

Mendelsohn, R. and M.J. Balick, 1995. The Value Of Undiscovered Pharmaceuticals In Tropical Forests, *Economic Botany* 49: 223–28.

Ministry of Agriculture and Fisheries (France), 1995. *Forestry Policy in France*. Paris: Countryside and Forest Department.

Mishan, E.J., 1971. *Cost–Benefit Analysis*. London: George Allen and Unwin.

Mishan, E.J., 1972 (1970). 'What is Wrong with Roskill?', in R. Layard (ed), *Cost–Benefit Analysis*. Middlesex, UK: Penguin Books, pp.452–72.

Mitchell, R.C. and R.T. Carson, 1989. *Using Surveys to Value Public Goods: The Contingent Valuation Method*. Washington, DC: Resources for the Future.

Mitchell, R.C. and R.T. Carson, 1995. 'Current Issues in the Design, Administration, and Analysis of Contingent Valuation Surveys', in P.-O. Johansson, B. Kriström and K.-G. Mäler (eds), *Current Issues in Environmental Economics*. Manchester, UK: Manchester University Press, pp.10–34.

Mishan, E. J., 1959. Rent as a Measure of Welfare Change, *American Economic Review* 49: 386–95.

Montgomery, C.A. and D.M. Adams, 1995. 'Optimal Timber Management Policies', in D.W. Bromley (ed), *The Handbook of Environmental Economics*. Cambridge, MA, USA and Oxford, UK: Blackwell Publishers, pp.379–404.

Moore, P., 1995. Energy and Power Sources, *The Wall Street Journal Europe*, 20–21 October, p.10.

More, T.A., J.R. Averill and T.H. Stevens, 1996. Values and Economics in Environmental Management: A Perspective and Critique, *Journal of Environmental Management* 48: 397–409.

Murty, M.N., 1994. Management of Common Property Resources: Limits to Voluntary Action, *Environmental and Resource Economics* 4: 581–94.

Myers, N., 1979. *The Sinking Ark*. Oxford, UK: Pergamon Press.

Myers, N., 1980. *Conversion of Tropical Moist Forests*. Washington: National Academy of Sciences.

Myers, N., 1991. Tropical Forests: Present Status and Future Outlook, *Climatic Change* 19: 3–32.

Myers, N., 1994. 'Tropical Deforestation: Rates and Patterns', in D.W. Pearce and K. Brown (eds), *The Causes of Tropical Deforestation*. London: UCL Press.

Nath, S.K., 1969. *A Reappraisal of Welfare Economics*. London: Routledge & Kegan Paul.

Nautiyal, J.C. and D.L. Love, 1971. Some Economic Implications of Methods of Charging Stumpage, *Forestry Chronicle* 47: 25–8.

Nautiyal, J.C. and J.L. Rezenck, 1985. Forestry and Cost Benefit Analysis, *Journal of World Forest Management* 1: 184–98.

Nee, S. and R.M. May, 1997. Extinction and the Loss of Evolutionary History, *Science* 278: 692–94.

Neher, P.A., 1990. *Natural Resource Economics: Conservation and Exploitation*. Cambridge, UK: Cambridge University Press.

Newell, R.G. and W.A. Pizer, 2003. Discounting the Distant Future: How Much do Uncertain Rates Increase Valuations? *Journal of Environmental Economics and Management* 46: 52–71.

Newman, P. and J. Kenworthy, 1989. *Cities and Automobile Dependence: An International Sourcebook*. Aldershot, England: Gower.

Niewijk, R.K., 1992. Ask a Silly Question. . . : Contingent Valuation of Natural Resource Damages, *Harvard Law Review* 105(June): 1981–2000.

Niewijk, R.K., 1994. Misleading Quantification. The Contingent Valuation of Environmental Quality, *Regulation* 1: 60–71.

Nordhaus, W.D., 1991. The Cost of Slowing Climate Change: A Survey, *The Energy Journal* 12: 37–66.

Norgaard, R.B., 1984. Coevolutionary Development Potential, *Land Economics* 60(May): 160–73.

Norgaard, R.B., 1990. Economic Indicators of Resource Scarcity: A Critical Essay, *Journal of Environmental Economics and Management* 19: 19–25.

North, D.C., 1990. *Institutions, Institutional Change and Economic Performance*. Cambridge, UK: Cambridge University Press.

North, D.C., 1994. Economic Performance through Time, *American Economic Review* 84: 359–68.

Norton, B.G. and M.A. Toman, 1997. Sustainability: Ecological and Economic Perspectives, *Land Economics* 73(November): 553–68.

Oldeman, L.R., R.T. Hakkeling and W.G. Sombroek, 1992. World Map of the Status of Human-Induced Soil Degradation: An Explanatory Note. Mimeograph. Wageningen, NL: International Soil Reference Center, Wageningen University.

Olson, M., Jr. 1996. Distinguished Lecture on Economics in Government: Big Bills Left on the Sidewalk: Why Some Nations are Rich, and Others Poor, *Journal of Economic Perspectives* 10: 3–24.

Osgood, D., 1994. 'Government Failure and Deforestation in Indonesia', in D.W. Pearce and K. Brown (eds), *The Causes of Tropical Deforestation*. London, UK: UCL Press.

Ostrom, E., 1998. A Behavioral Approach to the Rational-Choice Theory of Collective Action, *American Political Science Review* 92(March): 1–22.

Ostrom, E., 2000. 'Social Capital: A Fad or a Fundamental Concept?' in P.S. Dasgupta and I. Serageldin (eds), *Social Capital. A Multifaceted Perspective*. Washington, DC: The World Bank, pp.172–214.

Ozanne, L.K. and P.M. Smith, 1998. Segmenting the Market for Environmentally Certified Wood Products, *Forest Science* 44(3): 379–88.

Palo, M., 1994. 'Population and Deforestation', in D.W. Pearce and K. Brown (eds), *The Causes of Tropical Deforestation*. London, UK: UCL Press, pp.42–56.

Panayotou, T., 1993a. *Green Markets*. San Francisco: ICS Press.

Panayotou, T., 1993b. Empirical Tests and Policy Analysis of Environmental Degradation at Different Stages of Economic Development. Working Paper WP238, Technology and Employment Program. Geneva: International Labour Office.

Panayotou, T. and P. Ashton, 1992. *Not by Timber Alone: Economics and Ecology for Sustaining Tropical Forests*. Washington, DC: Island Press.

Panayotou, T. and S. Sungsuwan, 1994. 'An Econometric Analysis of the Causes of Tropical Deforestation', in D.W. Pearce and K. Brown (eds), *The Causes of Tropical Deforestation*. London: UCL Press.

Papadopol, C.S., 2000. Impacts of Climate Warming on Forests in Ontario: Options for Adaptation and Mitigation, *The Forestry Chronicle* 76(January/February): 139–49.

Pargal, S. and D. Wheeler, 1996. Informal Regulation of Industrial Pollution in Developing Countries: Evidence from Indonesia, *Journal of Political Economy* 104: 1014–27.

Parry, I., R.C. Williams III and L.H. Goulder, 1999. When Can Carbon Abatement Policies Increase Welfare? The Fundamental Role of Distorted Factor Markets, *Journal of Environmental Economics and Management* 37: 52–84.

Paustian, K., O. Andren, H.H. Janzen, R. Lal, P. Smith, G. Tian, H. Thiessen, M. van Noordwijk and P.L. Woomer, 1997. Agricultural Soils as a Sink to Mitigate CO_2 Emissions, *Soil Use and Management* 13: 203–44.

Pearce, D.W. and G. Atkinson, 1995. 'Measuring Sustainable Development', in D.W. Bromley (ed), *The Handbook of Environmental Economics*. Cambridge, MA, USA and Oxford, UK: Blackwell Publishers, pp.166–81.

Pearce, D.W. and J.J. Warford, 1993. *World without End*. New York: Oxford University Press.

Pearce, D., N. Adger, D. Maddison and D. Moran, 1995. Debt and the Environment, *Scientific American* June, pp.52–56.

Pearce, D.W., G. Atkinson and K. Hamilton, 1998. 'The Measurement of Sustainable Development', in J.C.J.M. van den Bergh and M.W. Hofkes (eds), *Theory and Implementation of Economic Models for Sustainable Development*. Dordrecht, NL: Kluwer Academic Publishers, pp.175–94.

Pearse, P.H. (Commissioner), 1976. *Timber Rights and Forest Policy*. Report of the Royal Commission on Forest Resources (2 Volumes). Victoria: Queen's Printer.

Pearse, P.H., 1980. Property Rights and Regulation of Commercial Fisheries, *Journal of Business Administration* 11: 185–209.

Pearse, P.H., 1985. Obstacles to Silviculture in Canada, *The Forestry Chronicle* 61(April): 91–6.

Pearse, P.H., 1990. *An Introduction to Forestry Economics*. Vancouver: University of British Columbia Press.

Pearse, P.H., 1993a. It's time to break the log jam, *The Globe and Mail*, June 17.

Pearse, P.H., 1993b. 'Forest Tenure, Management Incentives and the Search for Sustainable Development Policies', in W.L Adamowicz, W. White and W.E. Phillips (eds), *Forestry and the Environment: Economic Perspectives*. Wallingford, UK: CAB International, pp.77–96.

Pearse, P.H., 1998. 'Economic Instruments for Promoting Sustainable Forestry: Opportunities and Constraints', in C. Tollefson (ed), *The Wealth of Forests: Markets, Regulation, and Sustainable Forestry*. Vancouver: UBC Press, pp.19–41.

Pearse, P.H., 2001. Ready for Change. A report to the Minister of Forests on British Columbia's Coastal Forest Industry. Available at: http://www.for.gov.bc.ca/hfd/library/documents/phpreport/ November, 36pp.

Percy, M.B., 1986. *Forest Management and Economic Growth in British Columbia*. Report prepared for the Economic Council of Canada. Ottawa: Ministry of Supply and Services.

Perez-Garcia, J. and B. Lippke, 1991. The Future Supply of Timber from Public Lands: Recent Sales Will Not Support Competitive Processing. Cintrafor Working Paper 32, University of Washington, Seattle.

Perlin, J., 1989. *A Forest Journey: The Role of Wood in the Development of Civilization*. New York: W.W. Norton.

Perman, R., Y. Ma and J. McGilvray, 1996. *Natural Resources and Environmental Economics*. New York: Longman Publishing.

Peters, C., A. Gentry and R. Mendelsohn, 1989. Valuation of an Amazonian Rainforest, *Nature* 339: 655–56.

Pezzey, J.C.V., 1997. Sustainability Constraints versus "Optimality" versus Intertemporal Concern, and Axioms versus Data, *Land Economics* 73(November): 448–66.

Phillips, W.E., W.L. Adamowicz, J. Asafu-Adjaye and P.C. Boxall. 1989. An Economic Assessment of the Value of Wildlife Resources to Alberta. Department of Rural Economy Project Report No. 89–04. Edmonton: University of Alberta. August. 70pp.

Pimm, S.L., G.J. Russell, J.L. Gittleman and T.M. Brooks, 1995. 'The Future of Biodiversity', *Science* 269: 347–50.

Pizer, W.A., 1997. Prices vs. Quantities Revisited: The Case of Climate Change. Resources for the Future Discussion Paper 98–02, Washington. October. 52pp.

Porter, M.E. and C. van der Linde, 1995. Toward a New Conception of the Environment–Competitiveness Relationship, *Journal of Economic Perspectives* 9: 97–118.

Portney, P.R., 1994. The Contingent Valuation Debate: Why Economists Should Care, *Journal of Economic Perspectives* 8(Fall): 3–17.

Postel, S. and L. Heisse, 1988. Reforesting the Earth. Worldwatch Paper No. 83.

Powelson, J.P., 1987. Land Tenure and Land Reform: Past and Present, *Land Use Policy* 4(April): 111–20.

Powelson, J.P., 1988. *The Story of Land: A World History of Land Tenure and Agrarian Reform*. Cambridge, MA: Lincoln Institute of Land Policy.

Pressey, R.L., 2000. 'The End of Conservation on the Cheap, Revisited', in G.C. van Kooten, E.H. Bulte and A.E.R. Sinclair (eds), *Conserving Nature's Diversity: Insights from Biology, Ethics and Economics*. Aldershot, UK: Ashgate, pp.45–67.

Prest, A.R. and R. Turvey, 1974. 'Cost–Benefit Analysis: A Survey', in J.E. Reynolds, J.M. Redfern and R.N. Shulstad (eds), *Readings in Natural Resource Economics*. New York: MSS Information Corporation, pp.145–71.

Price, C., 1990. The Allowable Burn Effect: Does Carbon-fixing Offer a New Escape from the Bogey of Compound Interest? *The Forestry Chronicle* 66: 572–8.

Prins, R., W. Adamowicz and W. Phillips, 1990. *Nontimber Values and Forest Resources. An Annotated Bibliography.* Project Report No. 90–03. Edmonton: Department of Rural Economy. 27pp.

Putnam, R.D., 1993, March 21. The Prosperous Community: Social Capital and Public Life, *The American Prospect* 4(13): 35–42.

Putnam, R.D., 2000. *Bowling Alone: The Collapse and Revival of American Community.* New York: Simon & Schuster.

Quayle, M., 1998. *Stakes in the Ground. Provincial Interest in the Agricultural Land Commission Act.* Report to the Minister of Agriculture and Food, Government of British Columbia, Victoria. September 25. (http://www.agf.gov.bc.ca/polleg/quayle/stakes.htm).

Quiros, D. and B. Finnegan, 1994. Menejo Sustenable de un Bosque Natural Tropical en Costa Rica. Proyecto Silvicultura de Bosques Naturales. Informe Técnico, No. 225. Colección Silvicultura y Manejo de Bosques Naturales. No. 9, CATIE, Turrialba, Costa Rica.

Randall, A., 1994. A Difficulty with the Travel Cost Method, *Land Economics* 70(February): 88–96.

Randall, A. and M.C. Farmer, 1995. 'Benefits, Costs, and the Safe Minimum Standard of Conservation', in D.W. Bromley (ed), *The Handbook of Environmental Economics.* Cambridge, MA, USA and Oxford, UK: Blackwell Publishers, pp.26–44.

Randall, A. and J.R. Stoll, 1980. Consumer's Surplus in Commodity Space, *American Economic Review* 71(June): 449–57.

Rawls, J., 1971. *A Theory of Justice.* Cambridge: Harvard University Press.

Ready, R.C., 1995. 'Environmental Evaluation under Uncertainty', in D.W. Bromley (ed), *The Handbook of Environmental Economics.* Cambridge, MA, USA and Oxford, UK: Blackwell Publishers, pp.568–93.

Ready, R.C., J.C. Buzby and D. Hu, 1996. Difference between Continuous and Discrete Contingent Value Estimates, *Land Economics* 72(August): 397–411.

Reed, D., 1992, *Structural Adjustment and the Environment.* London: Earthscan Publications.

Reisner, M., 1986. *Cadillac Desert.* New York: Penguin.

Reisner, M. and S. Bates, 1990. *Overtapped Oasis: Reform or Revolution for Western Water.* Wahington, DC: Island.

Rennings, K. and H. Wiggering, 1997. Steps Towards Indicators of Sustainable Development: Linking Economic and Ecological Concepts, *Ecological Economics* 20: 25–36.

Repetto, R., 1997. 'Macroeconomic Policies and Deforestation', in P.S. Dasgupta and K.G Mäler (eds), *The Environment and Emerging Development Issues*, Vol. 2., Oxford, UK: Clarendon Press.

Repetto, R. and M. Gillis, 1988. *Public Policies And The Misuse Of Forest Resources.* Cambridge, UK: World Resources Institute/Cambridge University Press.

Ricardo, D., 1977 (1817). *Principles of Political Economy and Taxation.* London: J. M. Dent and Sons Ltd.

Rice, R.E., C.A. Sugal, S.M. Ratay and G.A.B. da Fonseca, 2001. Sustainable Forest Management. A Review of Conventional Wisdom, *Advances in Applied Biodiversity Science* No. 3. Washington, DC: Conservation International. 29pp.

Richards, K.R., 1997. The Time Value of Carbon in Bottom-up Studies, *Critical Reviews in Environmental Science and Technology* 27(Special Issue): S279–92.

Richards, K. and K. Andersson, 2001. The Leaky Sink: Persistent Obstacles to a Forest Carbon Sequestration Program Based on Individual Projects, *Climate Policy* 1: 41–54.

Romer, P.M., 1994. The Origins of Endogenous Growth, *Journal of Economic Perspectives* 8: 3–22.

Romstad, E. and H. Folmer, 2000. 'Green Taxation', in H. Folmer and H.L. Gabel (eds), *Principles of Environmental and Resource Economics*, 2nd edition. Cheltenham, UK and Northampton, MA, USA: Edward Elgar, pp.529–63.

Ruitenbeek, H.J., 1989. Social Cost–Benefit Analysis of the Korup Project. Report prepared for the Worldwide Fund for Nature and the Republic of Cameroon. London: WWF.

Ruzicka, I., 1979. Rent Appropriation in Indonesian Logging: East Kalimantan 1972/3 – 1976/7, *Bulletin of Indonesian Economic Studies* 15(July): 45–74.

Sagoff, M., 1988a. *The Economy of the Earth*. Cambridge, UK: Cambridge University Press.

Sagoff, M., 1988b. Some Problems with Environmental Economics, *Environmental Ethics* 10(Spring): 55–74.

Sagoff, M., 1994. Should Preferences Count? *Land Economics* 70(May): 127–44.

Sahajananthan, S., D. Haley and J. Nelson, 1998. Planning for Sustainable Forests in British Columbia through Land Use Zoning, *Canadian Public Policy* 24: S73–81.

Samuelson, P.A., 1976. Economics of Forestry in an Evolving Society, *Economic Inquiry* 14(December): 466–92.

Sandler, T., 1997. *Global Challenges: An Approach to Environmental, Political and Economic Problems*. Cambridge, UK: Cambridge University Press.

Sandor, R.L. and J.R. Skees, 1999. Creating a Market for Carbon Emissions Opportunities for U.S. Farmers, *Choices*, First Quarter: 13–18.

Sassone, P.G. and W.A. Schaffer, 1978. *Cost–Benefit Analysis: A Handbook*. New York: Academic Press.

Saunders, H., 1993. *The Cost of Implementing a Proposed Forest Practices Code for British Columbia*. Report prepared for the Ministry of Forests. Vancouver: H&W Saunders Associates Ltd. Mimeograph. September. 58pp plus App.

Saxena, A.K., J.C. Nautiyal and D.K. Foote, 1997. Analyzing Deforestation and Exploring Policies for its Amelioration: A Case Study of India, *Journal of Forest Economics* 3(3): 253–89.

Schaeffer, F.A., 1972. *Genesis in Space and Time*. Downers Grove, IL: Intervarsity Press.

Schimmelpfenning, D., J. Lewandrowski, J. Reilly, M. Tsigas and I. Parry, 1996. *Agricultural Adaptation to Climate Change. Issues of Long-run Sustainability*. Agricultural Economic Report No. 740. US Department of Agriculture, Economic Research Service, Washington. June. 57pp.

Schmitz, A. and W.H. Furtan, 2000. *The Canadian Wheat Board. Marketing in the New Millennium*. Regina, SK: Canadian Plains Research Center.

Schweitzer, D.L.R., R.W. Sassaman and C.H. Schallou, 1972. Allowable Cut Effect: Some Physical and Economic Implications, *Journal of Forestry* 70: 415–18.

Schwindt, R., 1992. Report of the Commission of Inquiry into Compensation for the Taking of Resource Interests. Victoria: Government of BC Printing Office.

Scitovsky, T., 1941. A Note on Welfare Propositions in Economics, *Review of Economic Studies* 9(November): 77–88.

Scott, A., 1973. *Natural Resources. The Economics of Conservation.* Toronto: McClelland and Stewart. (Originally published in 1955.)

Scott, A. and P. H. Pearse, 1992. Natural Resources in a High-Tech Economy: Scarcity versus Resourcefulness, *Resources Policy* 18(3): 154–66.

Scruggs, L., 1998. Political and Economic Inequality and the Environment, *Ecological Economics* 26: 259–75.

Sedjo, R.A., 1992. 'Can Tropical Forest Management Systems be Economic?' in P.N. Nemetz (ed), *Emerging Issues in Forest Policy.* Vancouver: UBC Press, pp.505–17.

Sedjo, R.A., 1996a. Environmental Impacts of Forest Protection: Some Complications. Paper presented at the "International Seminar on Forest Industries toward the Third Millennium: Economic and Environmental Challenges", European Forestry Institute and University of Joensuu, Joensuu, Finland, March 18.

Sedjo, R.A., 1996b. Toward an Operational Approach to Public Lands Ecosystem Management, *Journal of Forestry* 94(August): 24–7.

Sedjo, R.A., 1997. *The Forest Sector: Important Innovations.* Discussion Paper 97–42. Washington, DC: Resources for the Future. 50pp.

Sedjo, R.A. and Swallow, S.K., 1999. Eco-labeling and the Price Premium. RFF Discussion Paper 00–04. Washington, DC: Resources for the Future.

Sedjo, R.A., A. Goetzl and S.O. Moffat, 1997. Sustainability in Temperate Forests— Key Developments and Issues. Draft Working Paper. Washington, DC: Resources for the Future. December. 43pp.

Segerson, K., 2000. 'Liability for environmental damages', in H. Folmer and H.L. Gabel (eds), *Principles of Environmental and Resource Economics*, 2nd edition. Cheltenham, UK and Northampton, MA, USA: Edward Elgar, pp.420–44.

Segerson, K. and N. Li, 1999. 'Voluntary Approaches to Environmental Protection', in H. Folmer and T. Tietenberg (eds), *The International Yearbook of Environmental and Resource Economics 1999/2000.* Cheltenham, UK and Northampton, MA, USA: Edward Elgar, pp.273–306.

Segerson, K. and T.J. Miceli, 1998. Voluntary Environmental Agreements: Good or Bad News for Environmental Protection? *Journal of Environmental Economics and Management* 36: 109–30.

Selden, T.M. and D. Song, 1994. Environmental Quality and Development: Is There a Kuznets Curve for Air Pollution? *Journal of Environmental Economics and Management* 27: 147–62.

Self, P., 1972. *Econocrats and the Policy Process.* London: Macmillan.

Sellar, C., J. Chavas and J.R. Stoll, 1986. Specification of the Logit Model: The Case of Valuation of Nonmarket Goods, *Journal of Environmental Economics and Management* 13: 382–90.

Sen, A.K., 1977. Rational Fools: A Critique of the Behavioural Foundations of Economic Theory, *Philosophy and Public Affairs* 6(4): 317–44.

Shafik, N. and S. Bandyopadhyay, 1992. Economic Growth and Environmental Quality: Time Series and Cross-Country Evidence. Background Paper for the World Development Report 1992. Washington, DC: The World Bank.

Shleifer, A., 1998. State versus private ownership. *Journal of Economic Perspectives* 12(4): 133–50.

Shleifer, A. and R.W. Vishny, 1998. *The Grabbing Hand: Government Pathologies and their Cures*. Cambridge, MA: Harvard University Press.

Shogren, J.F., S.Y. Shin, D.J. Hayes and J.B. Kliebenstein, 1994. Resolving Differences in Willingness to Pay and Willingness to Accept, *American Economic Review* 84(March): 255–70.

Simon, J.L., 1996. *The Ultimate Resource 2*. Princeton, NJ: Princeton University Press.

Simon, J.L. and A. Wildavsky, 1984. 'On Species Loss, the Absence of Data, and Risks to Humanity', in J.L. Simon and H. Kahn (eds), *The Resourceful Earth: A Response to "Global 2000"*. New York: Basil Blackwell, pp.171–83.

Simon, J. L. and A. Wildavsky, 1995. Species Loss Revisited. In J.L. Simon (ed) *The State of Humanity*. Oxford UK: Blackwell, pp.346-61.

Simpson, R.D. and R.A. Sedjo, 1996a. Investments in Biodiversity Prospecting and Incentives for Conservation. Discussion Paper 96–14. Washington, DC: Resources for the Future.

Simpson, R.D. and R.A. Sedjo, 1996b. Valuation of Biodiversity for Use in New Product Research in a Model of Sequential Search. Discussion Paper 96–27. Washington, DC: Resources for the Future.

Simpson, R.D., R.A. Sedjo and J.W. Reid, 1996. Valuing Biodiversity for Use in Pharmaceutical Research, *Journal of Political Economy* 104: 163–85.

Sinclair, A.R.E., 2000. 'Is Conservation Achieving its Ends?' in G.C. van Kooten, E.H. Bulte and A.E.R. Sinclair (eds), *Conserving Nature's Diversity: Insights from Biology, Ethics and Economics*. Aldershot, UK: Ashgate, pp.30–44.

Skole, D.L., W.H. Chomentowski, W.A. Salas and A.D. Nobre, 1994. Physical and Human Dimensions of Deforestation in Amazonia, *BioScience* 44(5): 314–22.

Slade, M., 1982. Trends in Natural Resource Commodity Prices: An Analysis of the Time Domain, *Jornal of Environmental Economics and Management* 9: 122–37.

Slade, M., 1991. Market Structure, Marketing Method and Price Instability, *Quarterly Journal of Economics* 106: 1309–40.

Smith, A., 1776. *An Inquiry into the Nature and Causes of the Wealth of Nations*. Books I–IV edited by E. Cannan (1976). Chicago: University of Chicago Press.

Smith, F.D.M., G.C. Daily and P.R. Ehrlich, 1995. 'Human Population Dynamics and Biodiversity Loss', in T.M. Swanson (ed), *The Economics and Ecology of Biodiversity Decline*. Cambridge, UK: Cambridge University Press, pp.124–42.

Smith, V.K., 1986. 'A Conceptual Overview of the Foundations of Benefit–Cost Analysis', in J.D. Bentkover, V.T. Covello and J. Mumpower (eds), *Benefits Assessment: The State of the Art*. Dordrecht: D. Reidel.

Smith, V.K., 1992. Arbitrary Values, Good Causes, and Premature Verdicts. *Journal of Environmental Economics and Management* 22: 71–89.

Smith, V.K., 1997. 'Pricing of what is Priceless: a Status Report on Nonmarket Valuation of Environmental Resources', in H. Folmer and T. Tietenberg (eds) *The International Yearbook of Environmental and Resource Economics* 1997/1998. Cheltenham, UK and Lyme, US: Edward Elgar, pp.156–204.

Snoddon, T. and R. Wigle, 2003. Overview and Evaluation of the Climate Change Plan for Canada. Mimeograph. School of Business and Economics, Wilfred Laurier University, Waterloo, ON. April 24. 21pp.

Sohngen, B., R. Mendelsohn and R. Sedjo, 1999. *American Journal of Agricultural Economics* 81(February): 1–13.

Solow, R.M., 1974. Intergenerational Equity and Exhaustible Resources, *Review of Economic Studies* 41(Symposium): 29–45.

Solow, R.M., 1986. On the Intertemporal Allocation of Natural Resources, *Scandinavian Journal of Economics* 88: 141–9.

Solow, R.M., 1993. An Almost Practical Step Toward Sustainability, *Resources Policy* 19(September): 162–72.

Sorensen, D.M. and H.H. Stoevener (eds), 1977. *Economic Issues in Land Use Planning*. Agricultural Experiment Station Special Report 469. Corvallis, OR: Oregon State University. April.

Southgate, D., 1994. 'Tropical Deforestation and Agricultural Development in Latin America', in K. Brown and D. Pearce (eds), *The Causes of Tropical Deforestation*. London: UCL Press, pp.134–44.

Southgate, D., R. Sierra and L. Brown, 1991. The Causes of Deforestation in Ecuador: A Statistical Analysis, *World Development* 19: 1145–51.

Squire, L. and H.G. van der Tak, 1975. *Economic Analysis of Projects*. Baltimore: Johns Hopkins University Press (A World Bank Research Publication).

Stabler, J.C., G.C. Van Kooten and N. Meyer, 1998. Methodological Issues in Appraisal of Regional Resource Development Projects, *Annals of Regional Science* 22(July): 13–25.

Stahler, F., 1996. On International Compensation for Environmental Stocks, *Environmental and Resource Economics* 8: 1–13.

Standiford, R.B. and R.E. Howitt, 1992. Solving Empirical Bioeconomic Models: A Rangeland Management Application. *American Journal of Agricultural Economics* 74(May): 421–33.

Stavins, R.N., 2002. 'Lessons from the American Experience with Market-Based Environmental Policies', in J.D. Donahue and J.S. Nye Jr. (eds), *Harnessing the Hurricane: The Challenge of Market-Based Governance*. New York: Brookings Institution Press.

Stavins, R.N. and S. Barrett, 2002. Increasing Participation and Compliance in International Climate Change Agreements. FEEM Working Paper No. 94.2002/Kennedy School of Government Working Paper No. RWP02–031. http://www.feem.it/web/activ/ _wp.html 35pp.

Stern, D.I., M.S. Common and E.B. Barbier, 1996. Economic Growth and Environmental Degradation: The Environmental Kuznets Curve and Sustainable Development, *World Development* 24: 1151–60.

Stevens, T., J. Echeverria, R.J. Glass, T. Hager and T. More, 1991. Measuring the Existence Value of Wildlife: What do CVM Estimates Really Show? *Land Economics* 67(4): 390–400.

Stollery, K., 1983. Mineral Depletion with Cost as the Extraction Limit: A Model Applied to the Behavior of Prices in the Nickel Industry, *Journal of Environmental Economics and Management* 10: 151–65.

Sunderlin, W.D. and I.A.P. Resosudarmo, 1997. Rate and Causes of Deforestation in Indonesia: Towards a Resolution of Ambiguities. Occasional Paper No. 9. Jakarta: CIFOR.

Swallow, S.K. and D.N. Wear, 1993. Spatial Interactions in Multiple-Use Forestry and Substitution and Wealth Effects for the Single Stand, *Journal of Environmental Economics and Management* 25: 103–20.

Swallow, S.K., P.J. Parks and D.N. Wear, 1990. Policy-Relevant Nonconvexities in the Production of Multiple Forest Benefits, *Journal of Environmental Economics and Management* 19: 264–80.

Swallow, S.K., P. Talukdar and D.N. Wear, 1997. Spatial and Temporal Specialization in Forest Ecosystem Management under Sole Ownership, *American Journal of Agricultural Economics* 79(May): 311–26.

Tahvonen, O. and J. Kuuluvainen, 2000. 'The economics of natural resource utilization', in H. Folmer and H.L. Gabel (eds), *Principles of Environmental and Resource Economics*, 2nd edition. Cheltenham, UK and Northampton, MA, USA: Edward Elgar, pp.665–99.

Takahashi, T., M. Nakamura, G.C. van Kooten and I. Vertinsky, 2001. Rising to the Kyoto Challenge: Is the Response of Canadian Industry Adequate? *Journal of Environmental Management* 63(2): 149–61.

Terborgh, J., 1992. *Diversity and the Tropical Rain Forest*. New York: Scientific American Library.

Teter, D., 1997. Briefing Paper on Forestry Revenue. Memorandum 256/96/377 to W. Nitisastro in Jakarta, Indonesia, August 15. 12pp.

The Economist, 2001. The Next Global City? The Blob that Ate East Texas, *The Economist* June 23, pp.30–2.

Thiele, R. and M. Wiebelt, 1993. National and International Policies for Tropical Rain Forest Conservation: A Quantitative Analysis for Cameroon, *Environmental and Resource Economics* 3: 501–33.

Thompson, W.A., P.H. Pearse, G.C. van Kooten and I. Vertinsky, 1992. 'Rehabilitating the Backlog of Unstocked Forest Lands in British Columbia: A Preliminary Simulation Analysis of Alternative Strategies', in P.N. Nemetz (ed), *Emerging Issues in Forest Policy*. Vancouver: UBC Press, pp.99–130.

Thrice, A.H. and S.E. Wood, 1958. Measurement of Recreation Benefits. *Land Economics* 34(August): 195–207.

Tietenberg, T., M. Grubb, A. Michaelowa, B. Swift and Z.-X. Zhang, 1998. International Rules for Greenhouse Gas Emissions Trading: Defining the Principles, Modalities, Rules and Guidelines for Verification, Reporting and Accountability. Geneva: United Nations. UNCTAD/GDS/GFSB/Misc.6.

Tiffen, M. and M. Mortimore, 1994. Malthus Converted: The Role of Capital and Technology and Environmental Recovery in Kenya, *World Development* 22: 997–1010.

Toman, M.A., J. Pezzey and J. Krautkraemer, 1995. 'Neoclassical Economic Growth Theory and "Sustainability"', in D.W. Bromley (ed), *The Handbook of Environmental Economics*. Cambridge, MA, USA and Oxford, UK: Blackwell Publishers, pp.139–65.

Treasury Board Secretariat (Planning Branch) 1976. *Benefit–Cost Analysis Guide*. Ottawa: Canadian Government Publishing Centre.

Turner, B.L II and K.I. Butzer, 1992. The Columbian Encounter and Land-Use Change, *Environment* 34(8): 16–20, 37–44.

US Inter-Agency Committee on Water Resources, 1962. *Policies, Standards and Procedures in the Formulation, Evaluation, and Review of Plans for Use and Development of Water and Related Land Resources.* Senate Document No. 97, 87th Congress, Second Session.

US Inter-Agency River Basin Committee (Sub-Committee on Costs and Budgets), 1950. *Proposed Practices for Economic Analysis of River Basin Projects* (The Green Book). Washington, DC.

US National Research Council (Policy Division), 1996. *Linking Science and Technology to Society's Environmental Goals.* National Academy Press.

US Water Resources Council, 1973. Water and Related Land Resources: Establishment of Principles and Standards for Planning. *Federal Register* 38(174, 10 December): 24778–869.

US Water Resources Council, 1979. Principles and Standards for Planning Water and Related Land Resources. *Federal Register* 44(242): 72878–976.

US Water Resources Council. 1983. Economic and Environmental Principles and Guidelines for Water and Related Land Resources Implementation Studies. Washington, DC. Mimeograph. 10 March. 137pp.

van den Bergh, J.C.M.J. and M.W. Hofkes, 1998. 'A Survey of Economic Modelling of Sustainable Development', in J.C.J.M. van den Bergh and M.W. Hofkes (eds), *Theory and Implementation of Economic Models for Sustainable Development.* Dordrecht: Kluwer Academic Publishers, pp.11–38.

van den Bergh, J.C.M.J. and H. Verbruggen, 1999. Spatial Sustainability, Trade and Indicators: An Evaluation of the "Ecological Footprint", *Ecological Economics* 29(1): 63–74.

van Kooten, G.C., 1993a. Bioeconomic Evaluation of Government Programs on Wetlands Conversion, *Land Economics* 69(February): 27–38.

van Kooten, G.C., 1993b. Preservation of Waterfowl Habitat in Western Canada: Is the North American Waterfowl Management Plan a Success? *Natural Resources Journal* 33(Summer): 759–75.

van Kooten, G.C., 1995a. Modeling Public Forest Land Use Trade-offs on Vancouver Island, *Journal of Forest Economics* 1(2): 189–215.

van Kooten, G.C., 1995b. Economics of Protecting Wilderness Areas and Old-Growth Timber in British Columbia, *The Forestry Chronicle* 71(1): 51–8.

van Kooten, G.C., 1995c. Climatic Change and Canada's Boreal Forests: Socioeconomic Issues and Implications for Land Use, *Canadian Journal of Agricultural Economics* 43(March): 133–48.

van Kooten, G.C., 1998. Cost–Benefit Analysis of Adaptive Forest Management Strategies in British Columbia's Coastal Region. Vancouver: FEPA Research Unit, UBC. 26pp.

van Kooten, G.C., 1999. 'Preserving Species without an Endangered Species Act: British Columbia's Forest Practices Code', in M. Boman, R. Brännlund and B. Kriström (eds), *Topics in Environmental Economics*, Dordrecht: Kluwer, pp.63–82.

van Kooten, G.C., 2002. Economic Analysis of the Canada–United States Softwood Lumber Dispute: Playing the Quota Game, *Forest Science* 48(November): 712–21.

van Kooten, G.C., 2004. *Climate Change Economics. Why International Agreements Fail*. Cheltenham, UK and Northampton, MA, USA: Edward Elgar.

van Kooten, G.C. and E.H. Bulte, 1999. How Much Primary Coastal Temperate Rainforest Should Society Retain? Carbon Uptake, Recreation and Other Values, *Canadian Journal of Forest Research* 29(12): 1879–90.

van Kooten, G.C. and M.E. Eiswerth, 2003. When is a Species Endangered? Policy Insights from Bioeconomic Modeling. Working Paper. Victoria: Department of Economics, University of Victoria. January.

van Kooten, G.C. and A. Schmitz, 1992. Preserving Waterfowl Habitat on the Canadian Prairies: Economic Incentives vs. Moral Suasion, *American Journal of Agricultural Economics* 74(February): 79–89.

van Kooten, G.C. and A. Scott, 1995. Constitutional Crisis, the Economics of Environment and Resource Development in Western Canada, *Canadian Public Policy/Analyse de Politique* 21(June): 233–49.

van Kooten, G.C. and S. Thiessen, 1995. Estimating Economic Damages of Wind Erosion from Draw Down of the Arrow Lake Reservoir in Southern British Columbia, *Northwest Journal of Business & Economics* 1995: 1–14.

van Kooten, G.C., W.P. Weisensel and E. de Jong, 1989. The Costs of Soil Erosion in Saskatchewan. *Canadian Journal of Agricultural Economics* 37(March): 63–75.

van Kooten, G.C., W.P. Weisensel and D. Chinthammit, 1990. Valuing Trade-offs between Net Returns and Stewardship Practices: The Case of Soil Conservation in Saskatchewan, *American Journal of Agricultural Economics* 72(February): 104–13.

van Kooten, G.C., W.A. Thompson and I. Vertinsky, 1993. 'Economics of Reforestation in British Columbia When Benefits of CO_2 Reduction are Taken into Account', in W.L. Adamowicz, W. White and W.E. Phillips (eds), *Forestry and the Environment: Economic Perspectives*. Wallingford, UK: CAB International, pp.227–47.

van Kooten, G.C., B. Stennes, E. Krcmar-Nozic and R. van Gorkom, 1999. Economics of Fossil Fuel Substitution and Wood Product Sinks when Trees are Planted to Sequester Carbon on Agricultural Lands in Western Canada, *Canadian Journal of Forest Research* 29(11): 1669–78.

van Kooten, G.C., B. Stennes, E. Krcmar-Nozic and R. van Gorkom, 2000. Economics of Afforestation for Carbon Sequestration in Western Canada, *The Forestry Chronicle* 76(January/February): 165–72.

van Kooten, G.C., B. Stennes and E.H. Bulte, 2001. Cattle and Wildlife Competition for Forage: Budget versus Bioeconomic Analyses of Public Range Improvements in British Columbia, *Canadian Journal of Agricultural Economics* 49(March): 71–86.

van Kooten, G.C., S.L. Shaikh and P. Suchánek, 2002. Mitigating Climate Change by Planting Trees: The Transaction Costs Trap, *Land Economics* 78(November): 559–72.

van Soest, D, 1998. *Tropical Deforestation: An Economic Perspective*. Groningen, NL: Rijksuniversiteit Groningen, Graduate School of Systems, Organisations and Mangement. 268pp.

Vaux, H.J., 1973. How much Land do we Need for Timber Growing? *Journal of Forestry* 71(7): 399–403.

Victor, P.A., 1991. Indicators of Sustainable Development: Some Lessons from Capital Theory, *Ecological Economics* 4: 191–213.

Vincent, J.R., 1990. Rent Capture and the Feasibility of Tropical Forest Management, *Land Economics* 66: 212–23.

Vincent, J.R., 1993. Managing Tropical Forests: Comment, *Land Economics* 69(August): 313–18.

Vincent, J.R. and C.S. Binkley, 1993. Efficient Multiple-Use Forestry May Require Land-Use Specialization, *Land Economics* 69(November): 370–76.

Vold, T., B. Dyck, M. Stone, R. Reid and T. Murray, 1994. Wilderness Issues in British Columbia: Preliminary Results of a 1993 Province-wide Survey of British Columbia Households. Victoria: BC Forest Service, BC Parks and BC Environment, Mimeograph. 30pp plus App.

von Thuenen, J.H., 1966 (1840). *The Isolated State*. New York: Pergamon.

Wackernagel, M. and W. Rees, 1996. *Our Ecological Footprint: Reducing Human Impact on the Earth*. Gabriola Island, BC and Philadelphia, PA: New Society Publishers.

Wackernagel, M. and W. Rees, 1997. Perceptual and Structural Barriers to Investing in Natural Capital: Economics from an Ecological Footprint Perspective, *Ecological Economics* 20: 3–24.

Wackernagel, M., L. Onisto, P. Bello, A.C. Linares, I.S.L. Falfan, J.M. Garcia, A.I.S. Guerrero and M.G.S. Guerrero, 1999. National Natural Capital Accounting With The Ecological Footprint Concept, *Ecological Economics* 29: 375–90.

Walker, D.J. and D.L. Young, 1986. The Effect of Technical Progress on Erosion Damage and Economic Incentives for Soil Conservation, *Land Economics* 62(February): 83–93.

Wallace, J.M., J.R. Christy, D. Gaffen, N.C. Grody, J.E. Hansen, D.E. Parker, T.C. Peterson, B.D. Santer, R.W. Spencer, K.E. Trenberth and F.J. Wentz, 2000. *Reconciling Observations of Global Temperature Change*. Washington, DC: National Research Council.

Wang, S., 2001. Towards an International Convention on Forests: Building Blocks versus Stumbling Blocks, *International Forestry Review* 3(4): 251–64.

Wang, S. and G.C. van Kooten, 1999. Silvicultural Contracting in British Columbia: A Transaction Cost Economics Analysis, *Forest Science* 45(2): 272–9.

Wang, S. and G.C. van Kooten, 2001. *Forestry and the New Institutional Economics*. Aldershot, UK: Ashgate Publishing.

Wang, S., G.C. van Kooten and B. Wilson, 1998. Silvicultural Contracting in British Columbia, *The Forestry Chronicle* 74(6): 899–910.

Weisberg, H.F., J.A. Krosnick and B.D. Bowen, 1989. *An Introduction to Survey Research and Data Analysis*, 2nd edition. Glenview, IL: Scott, Foresman and Company.

Weisensel, W.P., 1988. The Economics of Soil Erosion in Saskatchewan: A Stochastic Dynamic Programming Approach. Unpublished MSc thesis. Saskatoon: Department of Agricultural Economics, University of Saskatchewan.

Weisensel, W.P. and G.C. van Kooten, 1990. Estimation of Soil Erosion Time Paths: The Value of Soil Moisture and Top Soil Depth Information. *Western Journal of Agricultural Economics* 15(July): 63–72.

Weitzman, M., 1974. Free Access versus Private Ownership as Alternative Systems for Managing Common Property, *Journal of Economic Theory* 8: 225–34.

Weitzman, M.L., 1998. Why the Far-Distant Future Should be Discounted at its Lowest Possible Rate, *Journal of Environmental Economics and Management* 36(3): 201–08.

Weitzman, M.L., 1999. *Gamma Discounting*. Cambridge, MA: Harvard University Press.

Weitzman, M.L. 2002. 'Landing fees vs harvest quotas with uncertain fish stocks', *Journal of Environmental Economics and Management* 43: 325–38.

West, T.O. and G. Marland, 2001. A Synthesis of Carbon Sequestration, Carbon Emissions, and Net Carbon Flux in Agriculture: Comparing Tillage Practices in the United States. Environmental Sciences Division Working Paper. Oak Ridge, TN: Oak Ridge National Laboratory. 39pp.

White, A. and A. Martin, 2002. Who Owns the World's Forests? Forest Tenure and Public Forests in Transition. Washington, DC: Forest Trends and Center for International Environmental Law.

White, L. Jr., 1967. The Historic Roots of Our Ecologic Crisis, *Science* 155(March): 1203–07.

Whiteman, A., 1996. Economic Rent and the Appropriate Level of Forest Products Royalties in 1996. Indonesia–UK Tropical Forest Management Program Report SMAT/EC/96/1. Jakarta: UK Overseas Development Administration. 17pp.

Willig, R., 1976. Consumer's Surplus Without Apology, *American Economic Review* 66(September): 589–97.

Wilman, E.A., 1988. 'Modeling Recreation Demands for Public Land Management', in V.K. Smith (ed), *Environmental Resources and Applied Welfare Economics*. Washington, DC: Resources for the Future, pp.165–90.

Wilson, E.O. (ed), 1988. *Biodiversity*. Washington, DC: National Academy Press.

Wilson, B., G.C. van Kooten, W. Hyde and I. Vertinsky, 1998. *Forest Policy: International Comparisons*. Wallingford, UK: CAB International.

Woerdman, E., 2002. Implementing the Kyoto Mechanisms: Political Barriers and Path Dependency. Ph.D. Dissertation, University of Groningen, The Netherlands. 620pp. As viewed on 30 July at: http://www.ub.rug.nl/eldoc/dis/jur/e.woerdman.

Woodward, R.T. and R.C. Bishop, 1997. How to Decide when Experts Disagree: Uncertainty-based Choice Rules in Environmental Policy, *Land Economics* 73(4): 492–507.

Woomer, P.L., C.A. Palm, J. Alegre, C. Castilla, D. Cordeiro, K. Hairiah, J. Kotto-Same, A. Moukam, A. Risce, V. Rodrigues and M. van Noordwijk, 1999. Carbon Dynamics in Slash-and-Burn Systems and Land Use Alternatives: Findings of the Alternative to Slash-and-Burn Programme. Working Paper. Nairobi, Kenya: Tropical Soil Biology and Fertility Program.

Workman, J.P., 1986. *Range Economics*. New York: MacMillan.

World Bank, 1993. Production Forestry: Achieving Sustainability and Competitiveness. Draft of working paper. Jakarta: The World Bank. 160pp.

World Commission On Environment and Development, 1987. *Our Common Future*. New York: Oxford University Press.

World Conservation Monitoring Centre, 1992. Global Biodiversity: Status of the Earth's Living Resources. London: Chapman and Hall.

World Resources Institute, 1995. *World Resources 1994–1995*. Oxford: Oxford University Press.

Zadeh, L.A., 1965. Fuzzy sets, *Information and Control* 8: 338–53.

Zebrowski Jr., E., 1997. *Perils of a Restless Planet. Scientific Perspectives on Natural Disasters*. Cambridge, UK: Cambridge University Press.

Zhang, D. and C.S. Binkley, 1995. The Economic Effect of Forest Policy Changes in British Columbia: An Event Study of Stock-Market Returns, *Canadian Journal of Forest Research* 25(6): 978–86.

Zylicz, T., 1998. 'Environmental Policy in Economics in Transition', in T. Tietenberg and H. Folmer (eds), *The International Yearbook of Environmental and Resource Economics 1998/1999*. Cheltenham, UK and Northampton, MA, USA: Edward Elgar, pp.119–52.

Zylicz, T., 2000. 'Goals, principles and constraints in environmental policies', in H. Folmer and H.L. Gabel (eds), *Principles of Environmental and Resource Economics*, 2nd edition. Cheltenham, UK and Northampton, MA, USA: Edward Elgar, pp.130–56.

Index